# COMPETITION LAW AND POLICY IN THE MIDDLE EAST

Written by a leading authority on the topic, *Competition Law and Policy in the Middle East* examines and critically analyses the development and role of competition law and policy in one of the most interesting regions of the world. This is the first book of its kind – to date this topic has not received sufficient attention, nor has it been adequately explored.

The importance of the Middle East within the global political and economic arenas gives this book huge international significance and interest. The book will prove useful to a variety of audiences around the world: to the competition law specialists, to the students of the subject, to policy-makers and politicians in the Middle East and to those whose work deals with law and economics and who wish to know more about competition law and policy in this special part of the world.

MAHER M. DABBAH is a reader in Competition Law and Director of the Interdisciplinary Centre for Competition Law and Policy (ICC) at Queen Mary, University of London. He is a barrister and acts as a consultant to international bodies, governments, regulatory authorities and firms in the field.

# COMPETITION LAW AND POLICY IN THE MIDDLE EAST

MAHER M. DABBAH

*Barrister; Reader in Competition Law and Policy*

*Director, Interdisciplinary Centre for Competition Law and Policy (ICC), Queen Mary, University of London*

CAMBRIDGE
UNIVERSITY PRESS

CAMBRIDGE UNIVERSITY PRESS
Cambridge, New York, Melbourne, Madrid, Cape Town, Singapore, São Paulo

Cambridge University Press
The Edinburgh Building, Cambridge CB2 8RU, UK

Published in the United States of America by Cambridge University Press, New York

www.cambridge.org
Information on this title: www.cambridge.org/9780521869089



First published 2007

Printed in the United Kingdom at the University Press, Cambridge

*A catalogue record for this publication is available from the British Library*

ISBN 978-0-521-86908-9 hardback

To my parents for making the Middle East
have its special place in my heart

## CONTENTS

# PREFACE

Writing a book on competition law and policy in the Middle East was, many years ago, merely an idea, which later became a dream and eventually turned into a reality. The transition from idea to reality in this case was only possible because of my own personal background and experience. I was born and raised in a small village suffering from illiteracy and swamped with poverty, in an extremely underdeveloped society and in a region where violence, conflict and confrontation were and still are extremely widespread. That region is called the Middle East. What fed many of the thoughts in the book was my experience as a specialist in the field of competition law. Other thoughts, however, could not have materialised without my own background. An example of this is chapter 2. My decision to examine the relationship between Islam and competition law within the context of the present book was not 'pulled out of a hat' but was rather the result of an encounter with this (unusual) relationship which happened at the age of eight. Of course at that very young age there was no awareness on my part of this relationship or competition law at all. The timing of the encounter – which occurred during the summer holidays – was highly interesting. During the preceding academic year, I became aware of some of the fundamental values of Islam through my religious studies lessons at primary school. Among the values that had particular impact on my outlook was Islam's prohibition of exploitation. During the summer holidays a new grocery shop opened in the village and I came to witness clear acts of dishonesty and exploitation on the part of the shop's owner. Considering the situation from a competition law perspective, those acts were nothing short of a clear abuse of dominance directed at a largely impoverished population. Such 'consideration' of course was not possible at the time, though this did not prevent me from viewing the situation as being fundamentally wrong and non-Islamic.

When I began writing the book, I was fully aware that I could be seen to be aiming to produce two books in one: the first a practitioner/textbook type book explaining or 'describing' how it is done in different parts of the Middle East and the second a volume 'analysing' various theoretical (and practical) issues. I decided to proceed nonetheless as my goal was to open the topic on different fronts so that hopefully current and future specialists would then take the issues covered in the book and develop them (when the time is right) in scholarly articles, monographs, practitioner work and (who knows) perhaps even a textbook. In setting out to do this, my aim has not been, however, to write a 'perfect' book; it has been to write an informative one. A perfect book is one which, among other things, *closes* as opposed to *opens* the door(s) to further research and thinking. This is not what I had in mind. As the first volume of its kind, I would like this book to open not just one but hopefully many doors (and windows).

My actual decision to turn to the Middle East on this occasion was not taken lightly. Considerable thinking and rethinking was done. At the end of a very long process, however, it felt it was the 'natural' thing to do. I vividly remember meeting by chance an old colleague several months ago in the beautiful surroundings of Russell Square gardens in central London who asked me what I was writing on at that time. I answered: a monograph on competition law and policy in the Middle East. I recall only one word my colleague said in reply: 'tricky'. It was in fact, and this old colleague was right but for the wrong reasons. Waking up every morning to hear about 'more' violence and loss of innocent lives in the Middle East was not quite the food for thought I was hoping to have as someone engaged in a 'project' on the Middle East. Many times I questioned my decision to write on competition law in particular in this (regrettably) troubled region of the world when the incredible amount of time and energy poured into the project could have been diverted to other Middle Eastern causes. These thoughts at the end did not prove a hindrance but enhanced in fact my desire to complete the project and to do even more on other fronts for the Middle East (and other places in the world). I kept going because of a deep passion to spread competition law around and because I care about the Middle East. Looking back as I am typing these words I have no doubt in my heart that it was the right decision to take.

This book would never have seen the light of day if it was not for the help and support I have received from many friends and colleagues. Many of my colleagues at Queen Mary deserve special thanks for continuous encouragement and support. Many of my friends were also extremely kind and supportive. In particular, I would like to mention

C. Brown, M. Das, T. Gidron, M. Heth, the Lockes, S. Miah, J. Nshf, J. Richardson, G. Rotkopf and D. Tadmor. I would also like to acknowledge the excellent research assistance and huge help received from Z. Awaiz who deserves a big 'thank you'. Valuable assistance was also received from C. Fadous and S. Hanafi in locating some 'hard-to-find' material; they were effective and efficient and I am grateful to them. Special thanks are also due to the professional and always extremely helpful staff at Cambridge University Press. In particular I am grateful to Mrs K. Hughes who is a huge asset at the Press.

Finally, I would like to express my thanks and gratitude to my brothers and sisters for caring and more importantly for remaining strong through difficult days and nights. In particular warm thanks go to my brothers Hassan, Hussein and Hatim who have made their marks in their particular fields of expertise in the Middle East: two truly world-class lawyers and a doctor.

The greatest thanks of all are owed to my parents. I have never known stronger, wiser, more intelligent and more loving people than them. These are quite modest attributes in fact for a lady who can neither read nor write and a gentleman who was fortunate to attend only three years of school in his life. They sacrificed their education to care for their siblings and later sacrificed everything for the happiness and future of their children. Without them it would not have been possible to write this book. I needed an effective ability to communicate in three crucial languages, Arabic, English and Hebrew, to research and write its chapters. They gave me that ability. I also needed an understanding of competition law as both an academic and practitioner. That too, many years ago, they made possible for me to acquire.

I am honoured to be able to dedicate this book to my brothers and sisters who live in the Middle East and to my great and wonderful parents who live in my heart.

Maher M. Dabbah<br>December 2006

# LIST OF ABBREVIATIONS

| | |
|---|---|
| Agadir | Free Trade Zone between the Arabic Mediterranean Nations |
| AMU | Arab Maghreb Union |
| APEC | Asia-Pacific Economic Cooperation |
| ASEAN | Association of South East Asian Nations |
| CAFTA-DR | Central America–Dominican Republic–United States Free Trade Agreement |
| CARICOM | Caribbean Community and Common Market |
| CBI | Central Bank of Iraq |
| CEMAC | Economic and Monetary Community of Central Africa |
| CFI | European Court of First Instance |
| COMESA | Common Market for Eastern and Southern Africa |
| CPA | Coalition Provisional Authority in Iraq |
| CPCM | Conseil Permanent Cunsultatif du Maghreb |
| CUA | Customs Union Agreement between Turkey and the EC |
| DGCEE | Department of Competition and Economic Investigations within the Tunisian Ministry of Trade |
| EAC | East African Community |
| EC | European Community |
| ECJ | European Court of Justice |
| ECOSOC | United Nations Economic and Social Council |
| ECR | European Court Reports |
| EEA | European Economic Area |
| EFTA | European Free Trade Association |
| ENP | European Neighbourhood Policy |
| EU | European Union |
| FTA | Free Trade Agreement |

| | |
|---|---|
| GAFTA | Greater Arab Free Trade Agreement or Area |
| GATT | General Agreement on Tariffs and Trade |
| GCC | Gulf Cooperation Council |
| IAA | Israel Antitrust Authority |
| ICN | International Competition Network |
| IMF | International Monetary Fund |
| MEC | Middle Eastern Country |
| MECs | Middle Eastern Countries |
| MERCUSOR | Southern Common Market |
| MIGA | Arab Investment Guarantee Agency and the Multilateral Investment Guarantee Agency |
| MPO | Iranian Management and Planning Organisation |
| NAFTA | North American Free Trade Agreement |
| NATO | North Atlantic Treaty Organisation |
| NIS | New Israeli Shekel |
| NTC | National Telecommunications Corporation of Sudan |
| OECD | Organisation for Economic Cooperation and Development |
| OFT | UK Office of Fair Trading |
| OJ | Official Journal of the European Community |
| OPEC | Organisation of the Petroleum Exporting Countries |
| OSCE | Organisation for Security and Cooperation in Europe |
| PIEFZA | Palestinian Industrial Estates and Free Zones Authority |
| PFI | Palestinian Federation of Industries |
| QIZ | Qualified Industrial Zones |
| SAARC | South Asian Association for Regional Cooperation |
| SACU | Southern African Customs Union |
| SADC | Southern African Development Community |
| SSAP | Sudan's Structural Adjustment Programme |
| STPC | Sudan Telecommunications Public Corporation |
| TAIEX | Technical Assistance and Information Exchange Instrument of the Institution Building unit of Directorate-General Enlargement of the European Commission |

| | |
|---|---|
| TRA | Telecommunications Regulatory Authority of Bahrain |
| TRL | Turkish Lira |
| UAE | United Arab Emirates |
| UEMOA-WAEMU | West African Economic and Monetary Union |
| UNCTAD | United Nations Conference on Trade and Development |
| UNIDO | United Nations Industrial Development Organisation |
| WTO | World Trade Organisation |

# 1

# Introduction

## 1.1 The Middle East in geographic terms

Very few regions in the world have given rise to uncertainty in terms of geographical definition as has the 'region' known as the Middle East. Whilst everyone agrees that the word 'Middle' is used to refer to the *middle* of other (neighbouring) regions, there has been little consensus – whether within the academic community, within political or diplomatic circles or within any other community or indeed among these communities themselves – in relation to where the outer-boundaries of this 'middle area' lie or exactly how 'East' should one go when attempting a geographical definition in this case. From the various definitions, which have emerged over the years, it would appear that defining the Middle East is an exercise that is 'relative' rather than 'absolute' depending on, among other factors, geographical perspective as well as political, social, cultural and ethnic factors.[1] Thus, if one considers the geographical definition of the Middle East commonly used within the United States of America (USA), one would find that it is a definition that has in large part rested on two important components of US foreign policy, namely the Arab–Israeli or Israeli–Palestinian conflict and the interest in and security of the vast oil resources in the Arabian/Persian Gulf.[2] Hence, the Middle East according to this definition would appear to include Bahrain, Egypt, Iran, Iraq, Israel, Jordan, Kuwait, Lebanon, Oman, Palestine, Qatar, Saudi Arabia, Syria, the United Arab Emirates and Yemen.[3] To this list of countries, however, recently Afghanistan appears to have been a country that many in the USA believe should be added,

[1] This may explain the existence of a few (though not widely used) synonyms for the term Middle East. These include 'Southwest Asia', 'Near East' and 'Western Asia'.

[2] One could add the recent war in Iraq and the occupation of that country as a third component.

[3] Interesting here is the exclusion of Turkey as a Middle Eastern country.

presumably because of the US 'war on terrorism', which is also a component of US foreign policy.

Academically, however, the Middle East appears to have been defined more broadly. Academics often define the area as one that includes: Algeria, Egypt, Libya, Tunisia and Sudan (despite being North African countries), Bahrain, Israel, Iran, Iraq, Jordan, Kuwait, Lebanon, Oman, Palestine, Qatar, Saudi Arabia, Syria, the United Arab Emirates and Yemen. To this list of countries, some would add, Afghanistan, Pakistan and Turkey; and there are those who have advocated a broader definition and would even consider all of the following countries as Middle Eastern: Azerbaijan, Kazakhstan, Tajikistan, Turkmenistan and Uzbekistan.

## 1.2 Geographical coverage of the book

Arguably, a rather influential factor in having such divergence in definition (and thus feeding the uncertainty of the geographical definition of the Middle East) has been the existence of Israel. Indeed, the above-mentioned definitions could be said to come within two broad, competing categories. According to the first category, the Middle East is a geographic area comprising the Arab countries and Israel. The other definition, however, includes the Muslim countries and Israel which would mean that in addition to covering Afghanistan, Iran, Pakistan and Turkey a geographical definition of the Middle East ought to cover the five countries of Muslim Central Asia.

Whilst undoubtedly one would need to include Israel in the group of countries comprising the Middle East, it is questionable whether all of the above-mentioned countries should be taken into account when defining the Middle East geographically. For the purposes of the present book, the Middle East is defined as a geographic area made up of all of the following: Algeria, Bahrain, Egypt, Iran, Iraq, Israel, Jordan, Kuwait, Lebanon, Libya, Morocco, Oman, Palestine, Qatar, Saudi Arabia, Sudan, Syria, Tunisia, Turkey, the United Arab Emirates and Yemen. It is this author's hope that this definition or selection of countries will not be considered as capricious. The aim is to offer a definition that is neutral in geographical terms insofar as is possible. This author is fully aware that in certain quarters these selected countries are referred to geographically as the 'Middle East and North Africa'. However, there are many uniting factors justifying grouping all of these countries together as Middle Eastern ones, most notably in terms of culture, language and religion.

## 1.3 The global significance of the Middle East

It is highly doubtful whether the global significance of the Middle East can be rivalled by that of another geographic region or area in the world. Middle East topics and debates transcend boundaries and reach the most remote places in the world. Whether in the world's most powerful capitals or the world's smallest villages and communities, the Middle East is often the subject of heated discussions and debates.

The huge global significance of the Middle East is extremely unique and rests on the most powerful factors found within the arenas of religion, politics and economics. More often than not the aspects of this significance are *negative* rather than *positive*, especially when one considers the bitter conflicts of the region, the constant potential for dangerous confrontations and the ever-widening circles of vicious violence. From a historical perspective this is a particularly shocking and painful account of a region widely recognised as the birthplace of civilisation and peace-founding religions, including Christianity, Islam and Judaism.

## 1.4 Sharpening the focus

It is a well-known fact these days that competition law has very rapidly and in a relatively short period of time developed into an international phenomenon, with over one hundred jurisdictions – with different types of economies, legal systems and political regimes – having introduced some form of competition law within their domestic systems and with no fewer than thirty countries at present seriously considering following suit. This undoubtedly is an impressive geographical expansion of a highly specialised branch of law which very few other branches of law have seen. In no small part, this expansion has been the direct result of very important developments occurring in the second half of the last century. Notable among these developments are: the clear shift on the part of many countries towards capitalism; the increasing reliance by countries on the market mechanism; and, above all, the growing belief by an increasing number of countries in the value of competition as a reliable tool to benefit local consumers, support the liberalisation of markets and achieve economic efficiency in both domestic and international markets.

Interestingly, however, this development of competition law and policy globally seems to have fallen short of extending adequately to the whole of the Middle East. Indeed, currently only ten of the region's twenty-one countries have a specific competition law and policy in place. Out of these ten countries, fewer than four have fairly adequately developed competition law and policy. Moreover, it is truly the case that in not a single Middle Eastern country (MEC) has competition law developed into a mature branch of law with a sound and strong policy to support it.

## 1.5 The foundations of competition law and policy in the Middle East

The points made in the previous section, among other things, convey the impression that normally one would not associate the origins, development or the topic of competition law and policy more generally with the Middle East. There may be various explanations for this, ranging from the fact that none of the existing competition law regimes in the Middle East is remarkably or particularly advanced whether in terms of having competition law understanding or culture or in terms of enforcement of the law, to the fact that the region has not seen the kind of significance given to competition law and policy as in other parts of the world, such as Western Europe or North America. Added to this 'spectrum' of explanations there is of course the fact that the Middle East is an area that has come to be known in the world more widely as a region of conflict, bloodshed or in the least painstaking way an area of vast oil resources; in light of this perhaps it should be understandable that these matters have come to occupy centre stage in those countries and as a result have pushed debates on competition law and policy to the sidelines. As its central theme, however, the following chapter in particular, will seek to demonstrate – through laying bare the supporting evidence – that the roots of competition law and policy in the region can be traced to the seventh century. In this way, the idea of having a healthy process of competition in the market place, which is worth protecting, and guaranteeing the freedom of market operators to compete is an old and well-established one within the region.

## 1.6 The five issues

Competition law and policy have been developing in different MECs with particular emphasis in the process being placed on five key (and largely interlinked) issues. The efforts of MECs to focus on these issues should be applauded; although, as the discussion in later chapters will reveal, further work is necessary to develop the understanding of the 'link' between these issues and competition law.

### *1.6.1 Foreign direct investment*

Views diverge with regard to the exact relationship between competition law and policy and foreign direct investment (FDI). At one end of the spectrum, there is the view that the existence of the former – with its aim to guarantee competitive markets – would encourage the latter. Therefore, according to this view foreign firms and investors are expected to be attracted to a competitive environment, especially one in which the competition rules are consistent or similar both in letter and application to those prevailing in major jurisdictions, most notably the European Community (EC) and the USA. At the other end of the spectrum, there is the view that foreign firms and investors might be more inclined to invest in countries where the national government maintains a 'protectionist' policy of state control and planning in relation to certain sectors of the economy with an imperfect competition environment. The belief is that they will be able to benefit from such a stance by national governments and be guaranteed the advantages of a quiet life.

It is important to note that these views have been suggested on the assumption that FDI is possible in the relevant jurisdiction(s): it is important to remember that not all countries have maintained a policy of allowing foreign participation in all sectors of the economy, though the position that has come to prevail globally has increasingly been in favour of allowing and encouraging such participation. This position has come to be adopted by most (if not all) MECs in recent years. Currently, heavy emphasis is placed on FDI in MECs and there has been a growing recognition that competition law should be adopted and utilised for the purposes of encouraging FDI in local economies.[4] In some MECs competition law is being used as one of the main tools to attract and foster foreign participation in the local economy. MECs therefore appear to have embraced the former, as opposed to the latter, view on the relationship between competition law and FDI mentioned above.

[4] Notable examples here are Egypt, Jordan, Lebanon, Libya, Syria and the United Arab Emirates. In all of these countries a strong link has been identified between competition law and FDI. The experience of these countries will be discussed in later chapters.

### *1.6.2 Economic growth and poverty*

One of the most serious problems facing all MECs is poverty, which in the case of many MECs is widespread. This problem has grown in recent years with little success being achieved in practice in fighting poverty and reducing it. Of course, the fact that many parts of the region are embroiled in conflict and confrontation does not help at all in this regard; with an increasing number of people becoming displaced and losing their home and income the situation can only deteriorate in the future.

There are several ways in which a government may reduce poverty among the local population. One way is through encouraging economic growth and empowering its poor or disadvantaged citizens. The idea here is not a 'Robin Hood' style of taking away from the rich in order to give to the poor, nor is it 'empowerment' in the current South African context. Rather, it is more about pursuing a sensible economic strategy, which could offer disadvantaged citizens productive employment and access to vital resources, such as land, capital and investment. Of course the success of this depends on various factors. Among these is whether the strategy is based on social responsibility. Equally important, however, the success of the strategy would require establishing crucial links between disadvantaged citizens and markets through ensuring that the latter would function in a way that would generate benefit for the former. Making markets function in this way would demand, among other things, having important economic policies in place. A crucial policy in this regard is competition policy.

The link between efficient markets and the interests of disadvantaged people has been highlighted rather well in the work conducted by the World Bank.[5] A central component of this link is the existence of efficient markets, which in turn requires that activities within those markets be not distorted especially through anti-competitive or abusive behaviour of firms. The desirability and necessity of having a competition law and policy in place in the country concerned is thus apparent. It does not require a great deal of imagination to picture how the disadvantaged would be affected much more adversely than the rich by anti-competitive or abusive behaviour. For a rich person paying a higher price for a product does not usually entail a particular economic

[5] The World Bank has repeatedly pointed out that efficient markets help generate growth and expand opportunities for the disadvantaged. See for example, the *World Development Report 2000/2001*, available at www.worldbank.org.

hardship and the possibility for seeking substitutes or alternative supplies in other places is a real one. For the disadvantaged, however, such a situation can have serious consequences in practice as the higher price would mean that financing important aspects of life such as education becomes much harder and the possibility open to rich citizens is virtually non-existent in their case.

### *1.6.3 Corporate governance*

The topic of corporate governance is one that was neglected for many years in most MECs and has only recently come to receive particular attention and focus in different parts of the region. Many MECs are turning their attention to this topic having realised that corporate governance is a crucial factor in attracting foreign investment and enhancing investor confidence. Additionally, with the strong interest on the part of many MECs for an increased integration into the global community, closer attention has come to be given to the need to improve corporate governance domestically. In doing so, these countries are following the examples furnished by developed countries and taking note of the guidance, general principles and codes of practice which have come to be produced by key international organisations, most notably the World Bank and the International Monetary Fund (IMF).

Competition can play a major role in enhancing corporate governance. It would not be difficult to think of a situation in which a firm that is subject to no competitive pressure whatsoever – whether within or from outside the market – and is the only or one of very few firms in the market – could easily become inefficient and its management becoming lax in their approach, with no real drive for innovation or 'burning desire' for efficiency, especially in cases where such a firm is able to charge for its products whatever price it desires. In such a situation, the management of the firm would feel comfortable and safe in the knowledge that the firm is unlikely to be 'threatened' or its quiet life disrupted, and one adverse consequence that may follow from this situation is a tendency towards or even an engagement in anti-competitive behaviour or abusive conduct. Furthermore, in these situations firms tend to have access to capital through local and international banks. Among other things, such access to capital enhances the economic power of these firms, arms them with a significant business advantage and may even reduce their drive for efficiency further. Hence, the widely held belief is that competition can address this undesirable situation and on the whole it can deliver key benefits in terms of enhancing economic efficiency – notably productive efficiency – in the market and lead to maximisation of consumer welfare.

The focus which has come to be given to corporate governance in different MECs has nonetheless been narrow in its scope, with its focus being devoted almost exclusively to intrinsic factors of corporate governance, namely issues such as the need to protect shareholders' interests, adherence to codes of conduct by senior corporate management and general issues dealing with conflicts of interest among the officers of a firm. However, it is crucial to appreciate that corporate governance is equally concerned with extrinsic factors, most notably the environment in which the firm conducts its business activities and the type of economy prevailing in the relevant country. For this reason, the existence of conditions conducive for competition under the umbrella of such factors can lead to good practices of corporate governance and may in some cases be rather vital to achieve this.

Corporate governance in MECs may be improved significantly through enhancing competition in local markets. To achieve this, however, those countries not only need competition legislation in place but also the necessary mechanism for its effective enforcement. This would necessitate the existence of an independent competition authority with the necessary capabilities and powers to conduct investigations and reach binding conclusions. It would also require a system of checks and balances with an effective judicial branch and the formulation of public policies that do not hinder competition. In relation to the latter, a pro-competitive institutional structure and the function of competition advocacy can play a major role. These two issues will be introduced here with a brief overview; an evaluation of their existence in the region and their application in practice will be conducted in later chapters in relation to different MECs.

### *1.6.4 Institutional structure and design*

Introducing competition laws and designing competition policies in MECs is important and helpful, though seeking to promote competition through these two steps might not be sufficient by itself. MECs are small economies and for this reason their approach to competition law should be suited to the size and type of their domestic economies. The particular geographic location of MECs and their unique political, social and cultural circumstances make this all the more important.

Local institutions – including mainly competition authorities but also other public authorities – within MECs have an important role to play in promoting competition and building an environment in which competition and economic growth, as opposed to anti-competitive situations, will flourish. The approach being suggested here involves creating institutional structures and designs, which are pro-competitive. This approach would entail building institutions, which operate in an efficient and transparent manner, by introducing and implementing suitable, clear and user-friendly rules and guidelines. These rules and guidelines must be suitable to the specifications of the local economy and the legal system in use; they must be clear in order to support legal certainty; and they must be user-friendly in order to ensure they offer the necessary help and comfort to firms and other parties with direct or individual concern under the relevant competition law regime. Above all, to build their pro-competitiveness these institutions will need to design and implement concrete action plans for the purposes of removing artificial barriers to entry in local markets and those facing trade and investment more generally, most notably barriers caused by government rules and regulations. The issue of institutional structure and design has received some recognition in some but by no means the majority of MECs. Some MECs have even introduced rules subjecting competition officials to strict standards in relation to issues such as 'conflict of interest' and 'confidentiality' with serious penalties in case of a breach of these rules by an official; interestingly, in some jurisdictions these penalties may be heavier than those imposed on firms found to have committed a breach of the competition rules.[6]

### *1.6.5 Competition advocacy*

It is generally perceived that damage or harm to the process of competition in the market place is only likely to occur through the anti-competitive behaviour or abusive practices of firms. Whilst this is the most common situation bringing about adverse effect or distortion to competition, it is equally important to appreciate that such harm is also possible without there being any involvement by firms or the occurrence of anti-competitive behaviour or abusive conduct. The most obvious arena where this may arise is that of public policy formulation and

[6] An example here can be found in the case of Egypt and Saudi Arabia. See p 246 and p 205 below respectively.

institutional design. There are many situations where public policies facilitate anti-competitive behaviour or abusive conduct on the part of firms and perhaps equally as many situations where such behaviour is offered protection or cover by the state whether through exemption or through a policy decision not to investigate and punish the behaviour or conduct in question.[7] At one level, the possibility of these situations arising raises the interest in and the necessity for competition law to be adopted. Where such a law is introduced and a competition authority is established it would be relevant to ask whether the mandate of such an authority should extend beyond mere enforcement of competition law towards engaging in competition advocacy.

It is crucial – given how complex economic development and regulation have become – that competition authorities participate in the formulation and design of domestic economic policies and other relevant policies, which impact on the process of competition in the market and its conditions. Such participation by a competition authority is desirable in order to ensure that competition considerations receive adequate recognition and expression in order to facilitate important economic objectives such as lowering of barriers, enhancing deregulation and promoting market liberalisation. In acting in this way, a competition authority would 'advocate' competition law, a task which carries many important advantages. These advantages include facilitating an influential role for the authority to play in the formulation of various public policies. Through this role the competition authority will have the opportunity to ensure that competition concerns arising from new policies are clearly highlighted; where relevant, the competition authority may also be in a position to propose suitable alterations or alternatives to such policies. The competition advocacy role described here essentially provides a 'safety valve' in the mechanism for policy design and formulation. Furthermore, the role has an added advantage of making the future enforcement functions of the competition authority considerably easier, especially when it comes to such authority directing its competition advocacy at the business community and consumers.[8] The latter task of competition advocacy has huge benefits

[7] See Dabbah, 'The development of sound competition law and policy in China: an (im)possible dream?' (2007) *World Competition* 341.

[8] In relation to the business community, competition advocacy could take a variety of forms: publishing enforcement decisions or at least publicising summaries of decisions reached in individual cases in the media and press releases; adopting guidelines on specific areas of competition law and policy which are often appreciated by firms who wish to observe the

in terms of building a competition culture and enhancing awareness of competition law.

The possibility for competition advocacy exists in several MECs, though the utilisation of the mechanism in practice has been extremely limited partly because of inaction on the part of the relevant competition authority and partly due to the difficulty some competition authorities face in convincing legislators and policy-makers to listen to them. In those jurisdictions where a competition advocacy mechanism is found, the grounds for its existence are one of two types: explicit (statutory) or implied (informal). Under the former type the competition authority enjoys the ability to submit its views on specific matters to the relevant ministry, regulatory agency or the legislative or executive branch.[9] Under the latter type, the competition law is usually silent on the role of the competition authority under such circumstances. In such a case, and provided that the competition authority is not prohibited from doing so, it should actively seek opportunities to make the case for competition in the public forum.

Virtually in all MECs the public does not have sufficient experience with competition law and policy let alone an appreciation of the desirability and benefits of competition. In most parts of the region the concept of competition that has been prevailing for many years is not one resting on free market ideology.[10] This state of affairs makes competition advocacy for the purposes of building a robust competition culture and encouraging public awareness particularly necessary in MECs (and countries in similar positions). Most of these countries are slowly moving away from planned economies and are gradually expanding their individual phases of transition with a shift towards the liberalisation of many domestic markets. However, this process is likely to cause disruption, misallocation and inefficient use of resources, unemployment and a high increase in prices of goods, especially in the case of those countries which were formerly controlled economies.

law; and organising competition law and policy workshops, conferences and seminars to explain key aspects of enforcement and changes in substantive law or procedure.

In relation to consumers, the task may include introducing an educational programme designed to equip consumers with valuable knowledge about the values of competition and competition law and policy and how these will benefit them and enhance their interests. This programme may take the form of publishing leaflets prepared in simple, non-technical language or visits by competition officials to shopping centres or markets where they could talk to consumers directly.

9 See below at pp 98–100 in relation to the Turkish regime.

10 See pp 298–9 below for a discussion on the two concepts of competition in the region.

Additionally, markets in most sectors in MECs which are at early stages of development tend to be concentrated and sometimes dominated by one or a few large firms that may engage in anti-competitive behaviour. By engaging in competition advocacy in this case a competition authority would be in a good position to promote competition in these markets without direct intervention on its part or on the part of the government more generally. Among other things, such an approach would save valuable resources and unnecessary intervention in the market place.

Competition advocacy therefore should be recognised as a particularly effective tool. Nevertheless, experience of different jurisdictions in the area of competition law and policy dictates that competition law enforcement has been an effective tool for fostering competition, breaking down barriers to entry, increasing economic efficiency and protecting consumer welfare. Focusing heavily on traditional competition law enforcement should not necessarily mean, however, that competition advocacy needs to be relegated to a marginal role. It is crucial to appreciate that competition advocacy can enlarge the benefits, which may accrue from traditional competition law enforcement. Competition advocacy can be used both for the purposes of complementing competition law enforcement and also where necessary offer a viable alternative to it.

### 1.7 Regional cooperation: past, present and future

The Middle East is perhaps the only region in the world where countries have been timid in forging deep and meaningful regional economic cooperation. Indeed, the prevailing tendency in the Middle East has on the whole been towards division and confrontation with occasionally some form of understanding and informal cooperation – usually bilateral in nature – often materialising behind the scenes at the will of the rulers of the countries concerned. This is particularly interesting given that most MECs enjoy many uniting and common factors. For example, the region does not have the serious language barrier seen in many parts of the world, most notably in the Americas, Europe, Australasia and Africa. In all of these regions, productive forms of regional cooperation have been forged over the years.[11] In the Middle East, such degree of cooperation is nowhere to be found: it has never occurred in the past; it

[11] See p 194 and pp 325–6 below.

does not exist at present; and currently appears to be an impossible dream for the future.

Over the years, only six serious attempts towards cooperation emerged in the Middle East though without any of these reaching full maturity or so far realising its declared objectives. The first is the League of the Arab States established in 1945. Whilst the League aims at the coordination of economic affairs of its members, in practice the League has had little impact and most of the outcomes of its meetings and work are declaratory in nature. Indeed, those familiar with the League's past summits would certainly recall the many collapses of talks before they had even begun, the exchange of strong words between the leaders of the member countries and the incapability of the League to reach binding common positions and implement them in practice. Interestingly, however, the League succeeded in 1997 in adopting a pact aiming at the creation of a Greater Arab Free Trade Area (GAFTA).[12] Among the main objectives of the GAFTA is the creation of a complete economic community in the Arab world – the Pan Arab Market – along the lines of the common market of the EC. It is not clear at present, however, whether the GAFTA will succeed in meeting its objectives given that the results of the League's work in this arena over the past ten years have been anything but impressive. As far as competition law is concerned, a draft of Arab Competition Regulations has been prepared under the auspices of the League's Economic and Social Council. However little progress has come to be made in approving this draft and in relation to the creation of the Pan Arab Market more generally.[13]

The second attempt was the union between Syria and Egypt in 1958 establishing the United Arab Republic. This union, however, did not survive for long and finally collapsed in 1961. The driving forces for the union were not economic but rather political and military. The third attempt was the Maghreb Arab Union created in 1989 under an Agreement between Algeria, Libya, Mauritania, Morocco and Tunisia.[14] The Agreement aims at the creation of economic and political unity among these North African countries. The union, however, has achieved little success since 1989 and no consensus at all has emerged between its members over how to achieve this unity. The fourth attempt is the Agreement for the Establishment of a Free Trade Zone between the Arabic Mediterranean Nations (Agadir). The Agadir was signed in 2004

[12] Referred to occasionally as the Pan Arab Free Trade Area.
[13] See further the discussion in chapter 10. [14] See chapter 5.

by Egypt, Jordan, Morocco and Tunisia, and aims at creating a free trade area among these countries. Although the Agadir has so far led to few achievements in practice, it has attracted the interest of several countries in the region and also that of the EC, as it is considered to be an important step for the purposes of creating a Euro-Mediterranean free trade area and enhancing the GAFTA. The fifth attempt to be mentioned is the Cooperation Council of the Arab States of the Gulf (GCC) created in 1981 and which brings together the Gulf States of Bahrain, Kuwait, Oman, Qatar, Saudi Arabia and the United Arab Emirates. Although containing many economic objectives, the GCC is still far from developing into a mature community and the majority of its economic goals are still far from being achieved, let alone lead to or materialise in supranational competition regulation at the GCC's level.[15] The final form of cooperation that could be mentioned here are the Qualified Industrial Zones (QIZ). These zones – which have been established between Israel, Jordan and the USA *and* Israel, Egypt and the USA – are discussed in later chapters.[16]

There is thus no single regional community or form of economic cooperation bringing together all or most MECs. In light of the current events and circumstances prevailing in the region, there is little, indeed hardly any, evidence that such cooperation is likely to emerge in the future. Furthermore, MECs appear to be notorious in pursuing 'negative' cooperation. By negative cooperation this author means the largely typical attitude of MECs to seek cooperation only where they are forced to, either due to developments at the global level or because of perceived threats to their existence, their regimes or their way of life. For example, recently a suspected American and Israeli military action against Iran and Syria brought these two countries closer together and led them to sign a common defence pact. Similarly, the recent increase in Iranian influence and the surge in the popularity of a group like Hizbollah in the region have forged closer links between countries such as Egypt, Jordan and Saudi Arabia. Thus cooperation appears to be more due to situations of desperation and absolute necessity as opposed to being motivated by a realisation – mainly through economic considerations – of the individual and collective benefits these countries would be able to reap through bilateral and multilateral cooperation.

[15] The GCC is examined in detail in chapter 7.

[16] See in particular the discussion at pp 171–2 and pp 239–40 below.

## 1.8 Relationship with the European Community

The EC takes particular interest in the Middle East for various reasons. Among these are the geographical proximity with the region; the interest in having a stable, peaceful and secure Middle East; the strong desire on the part of the EC to enhance its international standing and global involvement in world affairs; and the rivalry between the EC and the USA where each seeks to strengthen its influence in this key part of the world. The EC–US rivalry has been particularly strong in the field of competition law, not only in the Middle East but also around the world. For many years these two key global powers have been engaged in active advocacy encouraging and, in some cases, even forcing countries to introduce EC and US styles of competition law in their domestic legal systems. In relation to the Middle East, the EC has been much more active than the USA in the field. This may be explained with reference to the fact that the EC has presented the world with a model of an international system of competition law which is highly successful and the fact that many MECs have found EC competition law to be a suitable model; additionally there is the fact that in the case of some MECs at least, a European 'orientation' has come to be developed whether in terms of culture or public administration.[17] Furthermore, the EC has been engaged in 'strategic' EC competition advocacy in the region and has successfully tied competition law to the creation of a free trade zone between it and the different MECs. This has created an incentive for those countries to adopt competition law along the lines of EC competition rules. From the point of view of many MECs, adopting competition rules based on those of the EC helps create a legal and regulatory environment similar to that prevailing in the EC and with which international firms would be familiar. This too is strategic thinking on the part of MECs which is designed to encourage foreign direct investment and foreign participation in domestic economies.[18]

All MECs place special importance on their relations with the EC, whether individually or collectively. Most MECs have concluded general cooperation agreements and/or association agreements (or as more widely known Euro–Mediterranean agreements) with the EC. On its part the EC has adopted a common policy in relation to MECs which began to take shape in the mid-1990s and which has revealed the special

[17] Examples here can be seen in the case of Israel and Turkey and (to a lesser extent) Morocco.

[18] The issue of foreign investment was discussed at p 5 above and is also considered in the case of individual MECs in later chapters of the book.

importance the EC attaches to the region. In 1995 the Euro–Mediterranean Partnership or the Barcelona Process – which represents a unique simultaneous bilateral and regional approach by the EC – was started which led to the Barcelona Declaration by the EC and all of the following: Algeria, Egypt, Israel, Jordan, Lebanon, Morocco, Palestine, Syria, Tunisia and Turkey. The declaration rests on three pillars of partnership: political and security; economic and financial; and social, cultural and human affairs. In relation to the second pillar, a wide range of objectives was set by the parties, in particular the creation of a free trade area by 2010 which falls within the overall objective of the process, namely to create a larger area of peace, security and economic prosperity in the region.[19]

Following the 2004 enlargement of the EC which increased the number of EC Member States from fifteen to twenty-five, the EC adopted the European Neighbourhood Policy (ENP). The creation of this ENP shows the priority the EC has come to give following its expansion to the region, in particular for the purposes of enhancing regional stability and security both in the EC and the Middle East, and to prevent possible undesirable dividing lines, which might appear between an enlarged EC and MECs. It also shows the insufficient progress made (and predicted at that time) within the framework of the Barcelona Process.[20] Work within the ENP is intended to be carried out in practice through jointly agreed *bilateral* action plans between the EC and individual MECs. These action plans have a wide scope and cover areas stretching from political dialogue and justice and home affairs to transport, environment, research and development and social policy. The implementation of the ENP is intended to occur within the framework of the Euro–Mediterranean Partnership and association agreements with different MECs. The EC places high hopes on the ENP for the purposes of realising the goals of the strategic partnership with the Mediterranean and the Middle East. Principally, the strategic partnership aims at the development of a common zone of peace, prosperity and progress in the Mediterranean and the Middle East. In particular, it shows the interest of the EC in seeking partnership and dialogue with countries in the region for the purposes of achieving a variety of goals: political goals

[19] The European Council has adopted a common strategy on the Mediterranean. This strategy builds on the Barcelona Process and aims at achieving a variety of social and political ends. See Council Decision 2000/458/CFSP (Common Foreign and Security Policy), OJ [2000] L183/5.

[20] See further the discussion at pp 317–18 below.

through promoting political reform, democracy and good governance; economic goals by stimulating trade, economic cooperation and liberalisation; and wider goals through preventing conflicts, fighting terrorism and dealing with illegal immigration.

## 1.9 Relationship with EFTA States

Several MECs have also established links and entered into free trade agreements with the European Free Trade Association (EFTA). These countries include: Israel, Jordan, Lebanon, Morocco, Palestine, Tunisia and Turkey. In addition the EFTA has concluded declarations of cooperation with Algeria, Egypt and the GCC.

Competition law features prominently in these free trade agreements although variations in the exact wording of the relevant provisions and their extent and scope exist in relation to all of the agreements. The declarations of cooperation on the other hand contain no specific provisions dealing with competition law, though some brief reference is made to the 'determination' of the parties to liberalise trade between them by, among other things, facilitating the exchange of views on conditions for free and undistorted competition and developing an environment that is conducive to and supportive of free competition and economic activity based on market forces.

## 1.10 A book on competition law and policy in the Middle East

This author is fully aware that for some people the idea of writing a book on competition law and policy in the Middle East appears daunting and extremely challenging. For others (hopefully fewer) possibly the idea is even fanciful. It was hinted above how the Middle East is more generally perceived around the world as a deeply troubled region where (regrettably) on average tens of innocent lives are lost on a daily basis through bitter violence and where poverty, illiteracy, and economic and social underdevelopment are all quite common within different communities and societies in the region. There is no doubt that this is part of the Middle East reality; however, this should not be a reason deterring one from investigating the topic, especially if such an investigation is carried out with the purpose of showing the link between the Middle East and competition law historically, and for shedding light on the attention that has come to be given to competition law in the region and the advantages of developing this branch of law within MECs and possibly regionally.

# 2

# The relationship between Islam and competition law and policy

Twenty of the twenty-one MECs identified in the previous chapter are Muslim countries or countries with a Muslim majority in the population. Indeed, Israel – the only non-Muslim MEC – has a significant Muslim minority, which amounts to over 20 per cent of the population. There is therefore a clear Muslim majority in the Middle East as a whole and a clear, indeed strong association between Islam and MECs especially in light of the fairly strong Islamic culture and tradition prevailing in almost the whole of the region. The fact this is so makes it particularly interesting to consider whether 'links' exist between competition law and Islam, the Middle East's main religion.

This chapter examines the relationship between Islam and competition law and policy. In assessing this relationship, the chapter addresses several issues, which are an integral part of its subject matter. Among these are the role which competition law and policy play in a given system or economy and whether competition law and policy have any expression in Islam either as a past expression through the long history of the religion or as a present one.

## 2.1 The relationship: a myth or reality?

If one were to conduct a search – using a search engine such as Google – of the word 'Islam', over ninety four million results will be generated. Conducting a similar search using the term 'competition law' would generate about 43 million results. However, conducting a search using these two terms together would return a small number of results in comparison. If one were to consult these results randomly it would become clear that none of them shows a direct link between the two terms as such. The absence of such a link may not be surprising to most people with no competition expertise who would naturally look at the situation through non-competition law lenses as well as to most, perhaps all, competition law specialists, who would naturally look at the situation from a competition law perspective. One explanation for this is that people simply *do not* perceive that links exist between Islam and competition law. Another way of explaining the situation would be to accept that for many people there is a divide between competition law and Islam. However, the question that should be asked is whether this divide is a *Chinese wall* or a thin, invisible *veil*. If it is the former, little can be done and the size of the divide perhaps should be accepted as part of reality. If it is the latter, however, perhaps one should appreciate the invisibility and if not then consider either piercing this veil or having it removed. All of these actions should be considered as possible in such a case, given that the veil in this instance should be viewed as nothing but a mere myth.

## 2.2 Setting the scene: competition law and Islamic roots

Perhaps very few competition law scholars would associate the origins, development or the field of competition law and policy with Islam and with the Muslim world more generally. The roots of competition law and policy in Islam, however, can be traced to the seventh century. In this way, the idea of having a healthy process of competition in the market place and guaranteeing the freedom of market operators to compete is well articulated within Islam. To many people, this may come as a surprising finding for various reasons, some of which were mentioned briefly in the previous chapter.[1]

The developments in competition law and policy within the Muslim world in modern times have not quite reflected the existence of a rich or long competition law and policy culture and history. Since the turn of the twentieth century the idea of competition law and policy have been closely associated with Western legal thinking and development, hence the dominance and influence of systems of competition law such as those of the European Community (EC) and the USA. This association (and dominance) appears to have led even the most prominent economics scholars either inadvertently to assume or intentionally to advocate in their writing the non-existence of a hugely important component in the field of economic history and economic regulation, namely Islam's contribution (and that made by Islamic scholars) to the field.[2] However,

[1] See p 4 above.

[2] Perhaps the most prominent scholar in this regard is Schumpeter who inexplicably omitted this contribution when he stated that in relation to economic history and history of thought one 'may safely leap over 500 years to the epoch of St. Thomas Aquinas

strong evidence exists which shows how the work of prominent Muslim scholars and writers was influential in the field of economic development and economic theory from the tenth to the thirteenth centuries.[3]

Examining the relationship between Islam and competition law and policy demands serious consideration of two important matters: the role played by competition law in an economy and identifying the goals of an Islamic economy. These two matters will be highlighted first before examining the different rules, principles and values of Islam which have competition relevance. It is crucial to note, however, that this examination will be conducted by the author for the purposes of considering the place and role of competition law and policy in Islam; it is *not* the author's intention to advocate a religious approach to competition law.

## 2.3 The role of competition law and policy in an economy

Competition law specialists (in particular economists) have a tendency to argue that the development of competition law and policy, including a country's decision to adopt competition legislation, is largely economic in nature. To some extent, such a contention is not implausible especially if one were to consider the goals of competition law and the fact that competition law has been adopted in many countries following the transition from monopolisation to privatisation and liberalisation of markets in order to ensure that former state monopolies do not end up being replaced by private monopolies. However, equally plausible must be the contention that competition law has also served as a tool to help countries make this important transition and that a country's decision to adopt competition law is indeed political in nature and sits at the heart of an agenda drawn up by politicians to embrace the free market economy model, liberalise local markets and support the drive for economic development. There is ample evidence showing that competition law was in origins desired by politicians and policy-makers,[4] and this largely remains the situation until the present day. However, it is

(1225–74), whose *Summa Theologica* is in the history of thought what the south western spire of the Cathedral of Chartres is in the history of architecture'. Schumpeter, *History of Economic Analysis* (Oxford University Press, 1954) at 74. (Footnotes omitted; italics in original.)

3 Among the scholars to be mentioned here are Ibn Nadim, Ibn Nujiam, Al-Farabi, Ibn Sina, Ibn Rushd and Al-Ghazali.

4 See Amato, *Antitrust and the Bounds of Power* (Hart Publishing, 1997).

important to realise that the key issue ultimately is not a country's decision to adopt a competition law or indeed whether a country has such a law in its statutes book; rather the important and crucial question that must be asked is how the law is applied and enforced. For this reason, as competition law practice developed, economists have become its main specialists, given that applying competition law demands in many cases an appreciation of economic concepts and the undertaking of economic analysis often one of a complex nature. Nonetheless, it is crucial to realise that the goals of competition law can only be gleaned from the way the law is applied which in turn depends to a large extent on the role ascribed to the law within an economy and the goals of such an economy in general. There is thus a clear link tying the role of competition law in a particular economy to the broader goals of that economy.

## 2.4 Competition law and policy in an Islamic economy

It is important to appreciate that the broader goals of an economy along with the goals ascribed to competition law to a large extent determine the role competition law and policy are likely to play in the economy. Thus, before determining what role does or should competition law and policy play in an Islamic economy, it is important to become familiar with the goals of such an economy. This in no way is an easy task to accomplish, though it is not an impossible one. Among other things, ascertaining the goals of an Islamic economy requires a consideration of the three important sources of legislation in Islam: Islam's supreme source, namely the *Quran* (including a careful consideration of the teachings of the *Quran* in both theory and practice); the *Sunnah* (i.e. the tradition and teachings of the Prophet Mohammad) and *Ejtihad*.[5] The first and third of these sources are particularly relevant to consider in the present context.

### 2.4.1 *The* Quran

Muslims firmly believe that the *Quran* is the holy book containing the words of *Allah* or God. In various places in the *Quran*, *Allah* commands in unequivocal terms that Muslims must strive to establish justice,

[5] The concept of *Ejtihad* refers to independent thought and interpretation of legal sources. It is in practice a method of interpretation and reasoning used to provide answers for problems regarding which there is no specific express text.

benevolence and equity and to see that these important values are safeguarded and applied fully and fairly in relation to all aspects of life: whether personal, social or economic. In relation to the economic sphere, there is a clear obligation laid down in the *Quran* on the state and its nationals with regard to establishing economic justice and fair play as well as a prohibition on economic exploitation. In very unequivocal terms Islam encourages the pursuit of economic well-being and provides guidance on how this may be achieved. The purpose behind such guidance is to ensure that economic exploitation is prevented and economic power is not abused. Indeed, among the most entrenched and most fundamental goals of an Islamic economy, the establishment of social justice and achieving the maximum desirable use of society's resources must rank very high. This is a clear duty laid on both states and their nationals. In the case of the state the duty must be discharged properly and effectively through the adoption of suitable laws for the purposes of achieving justice and putting an end to all forms of economic exploitation or harm. Thus, the idea is that the state must make proper use of the administrative and legal powers at its disposal in order to prevent or eliminate all types of illegal or harmful transactions and situations. The nationals of such state, on the other hand, must avoid or refrain from behaviour or conduct harmful to the interests of others or the public interest at large.

### *2.4.2 The source of* Ejtihad

The third source of legislation in Islam, *Ejtihad* takes different forms, such as *Istihsan* (bringing comfort and ease to society) and *Istilah* (legislating in the name of public interest), and *Qiyas* (systematic inference or analogy). Among these principles, the principle of *Qiyas* is most noteworthy.[6] This principle operates in a highly interesting way. For example, a simple reading of the *Quran* would reveal the emphasis placed on *Zakah* (donation) to be made by Muslims. Using the principle of *Qiyas* in this case one would be able to infer that Islam encourages and favours good deeds. The same could be said with regard to the *Quran*'s prohibition on illegal economic activities which, using the principle of *Qiyas*, would make it clear that there is a responsibility on the state to

[6] Note that using a literal translation of *Qiyas* in English the concept would mean 'measurement' however it is the technical meaning with which the concept is associated, namely 'systematic inference' or 'analogy'.

prevent and render illegal all harmful economic activities and behaviour and to create and maintain a system which is beneficial and economically enhancing for society and its members.

## 2.5 The role of competition law in Islam: the components

An examination of whether competition law plays or has at any time played a role in Islam can be conducted using three key components, namely the value of trade and competition in Islam; the religion's treatment of pricing policies and practices; and the treatment of abusive conduct and collusion between market operators.

### *2.5.1 The value of trade and competition*

Encouraging and engaging in trade or business activity (which crucially includes the freedom of firms to compete) is a fundamental principle and value in Islam. Indeed, Islam has always facilitated economic activity on the part of individuals. The religion gives individuals the right as well as the freedom to engage in trade and as such to earn an income and make a profit through this.[7] There is a clear duty on the state to respect and protect this right, which arises under *Shariah*.[8] However, the *Quran* recognises a limitation on this right, namely that the right must be safeguarded and where necessary upheld by the state as long as it is not abused; such abuse is prohibited in the *Quran*.

Islam's recognition of the right to trade includes recognition of the special and important relationship that exists between trade and competition in the market place and between trade law and policy on the one hand and competition law and policy on the other. Three important ideas seem to underpin this special relationship: trade is encouraged but competition must not be restricted; the state should take an active role in the sphere of trade; and the freedom to compete is a right that must be safeguarded and upheld so long as it is not abused, which connotes that *normally* there should be no intervention by the state in the market.[9] In relation to the third idea, Islamic thinking on the issue of state intervention appears to conform to one of the very basic modern ideas of

[7] See Abu Hamid Al-Ghazali, *Ihya Ulum Al-Din*.

[8] *Shariah* refers to the body of Islamic law. Note other possible spellings of the concept: *Sharia, Sharee'ah, Shari'ah, Sharii'ah, Šarī'ah* etc.

[9] See the discussion below in relation to pricing practices and policies.

competition law and policy, namely that intervention by public authorities in the market place should be reserved to cases of market failure.[10] Islam recognises that the market should be left to operate on its own and that it should be left to the market to address any problems, which may arise along the way so long as these problems do not develop into a situation of a market failure, in which case intervention would not only be possible but indeed necessary.

Another example demonstrating the important value of competition law and policy in Islam concerns private ownership. Islam allows private ownership without undue limitation, unless limitation becomes necessary for the purposes of protecting the public good or interest. This is, for example, the case where as a result of private ownership a situation of improper exercise of power would materialise. This philosophy stands at the heart of Islam's approach to nationalisation and privatisation. Nationalisation is not totally banned in Islam. In certain cases it may be encouraged, for example where this is necessary for the purposes of achieving or maintaining a social aim or value. This is especially the case in key sectors and industries. Indeed, looking at different Muslim countries one will be able to find examples of this. A notable example here is Iran.[11] In its general approach to this issue, Islam seeks to strike the right balance between society and the individual. One important factor which is given special significance in achieving this balance is the public interest, which is deemed to be of crucial importance in an Islamic system. A major phenomenon widely considered to undermine the public interest is that of the concentration of wealth. Islam strongly disapproves of situations in which the wealth of society is concentrated in the hands of a few. To a large extent, nationalisation can be considered as a policy instrument available to the state for the purposes of removing concentrations of wealth. Different Islamic scholars, however, have come to agree that nationalisation should not be done arbitrarily and must be carried out in a *just* and *fair* way that does not damage the public interest or harm the interests of the nationals of such a state.

### *2.5.2 Pricing practices and policies*

The competition law literature available offers an extremely detailed account on the treatment under competition law and policy of pricing

[10] The concept and situation of market failure are explained below, at p 25.
[11] See pp 303–7 below.

policies and practices of business firms – whether through unilateral behaviour by dominant firms or collusion by two or more firms – in the market place especially where such policies and practices result in harm to consumers and to the process of competition. Whilst interesting and strong arguments may be put forward against competition law intervention in the pricing policies and practices of firms,[12] it is very clear that such intervention is necessary *in certain cases* in order to protect the interests of consumers and the process of competition in the market.[13] A similar approach to this *modern* competition law approach and thinking can be found in Islam. It is not a principle of Islam to control prices or regulate market prices constantly under normal conditions of competition.[14] On the contrary, Islam favours having a free market system and only allows intervention and regulation of prices and market conditions more generally in cases of market failure. In the case of a market failure, Islam lays a duty on public authorities to act for the purposes of putting an end to the 'suffering of the people'. In this case, should prices charged by a dominant market operator rise so as to become excessive or unfair, or should prices become fixed through anti-competitive agreements or other forms of collusion between the market operators, the state should intervene for the purposes of 'fixing' or regulating the price. An important factor behind laying down this duty is the concept of consumer welfare and the need to maximise consumer welfare. This fundamental idea was articulated by several prominent Islamic scholars, who argued that the basis of the state's power of intervention in the market place to regulate the price is a fundamental principle of *Shariah*, namely that such intervention is necessary in *special circumstances* in order to eradicate the suffering of the people. One such scholar is Imam Ibn Taimiyah who commented that in cases where the price in the market 'is not fixed at a reasonable level to fulfil the need of the great public by the operation

[12] Arguments here include claims such as: competition law is not a price-regulatory tool; firms should be entitled to charge whatever price they see fit in order to reward themselves for their investment in developing their products; it is difficult to decide what the right price should be when the particulars of the cost of the product are difficult to establish; the market should be relied on to correct itself and market forces can be expected to provide a constraint on the pricing behaviour of firms to ensure that prices do not become exploitative or excessive.

[13] These certain cases notably include situations of market failure where the market fails to correct itself because there is not sufficient constraint exerted on the firm(s) engaged in an anti-competitive or abusive behaviour.

[14] See Burhan-ud-din Ali ben Abu Bakr al-Marghinani, *Hedaya–Commentary on Islamic Laws*, translated by Charles Hamilton (1994).

of normal principles of marketing, then the price should be fixed for the welfare of the people with justice, neither more nor less'.[15]

An important point of caution needs to be highlighted here in relation to the intervention by the state in the market place under Islam, especially where this is being done for the purposes of setting the prices at a reasonable or fair level. In allowing the 'invisible' hand of the market to be replaced by the 'visible' hand of a public body or authority, it is vital to be aware that this is something that should only happen *in special circumstances*. In other words, situations where the state fixes the price (meaning intervenes in the market place for the purposes of regulating the price) must be considered to be the exception rather than the rule.[16]

### *2.5.3 Abuse of dominance and collusion*

The undesirability and harmful effect of abuse of market power by firms or collusion between firms are well-articulated ideas in Islam. One of the fundamental Islamic ideas of economic nature revolves around the need to fight and unearth such harmful practices. The adverse consequences which may follow from situations in which a market operator may abuse its market power or a group of market operators colluding to fix the price, share markets or limit trading in a certain product have long been recognised in Islam. Indeed, Islam was fairly quick in realising the harmful effect of such practices and for this reason important Islamic principles were developed for the purposes of dealing with such cases.[17] Among these is the principle of *Hijr*[18] which is a power reserved to the state for the purposes of restraining anti-competitive behaviour and practices. It would be important however to note that *Hijr* – despite its importance – is only a principle and for this reason it would be essential for a state to implement this principle as a precondition for the principle to be used in an effective way. Thus, the deployment of the principle in practice would require specific legislative tools for the purposes of implementing it. In a modern law context, these specific tools would include adopting a competition law. This state of affairs would explain the lack or failure of economic regulation in most MECs

[15] Imam Ibn Taimiyah, *Al Hisba Fil Islam*, at p 37. See also Abdul Azim Islahi, *Economic Concepts of Ibn Taimiyah* (1988); Islahi, 'Ibin Taimyiah's concept of market mechanism' 2(2) *Journal of Research in Islamic Economics* 1405 (1985).

[16] See generally, Hazrat Shah Waliullah, *Hujjat al-Balagha*.

[17] See Abu Bakr Yahya bin Umar Al-Kinani, *Kitab Ahkam Al-Suq*.

[18] *Hijr* literally means restraint.

which embrace Islamic tradition and values: despite the existence of a highly important and fundamental principle of *Hijr* in Islam, those countries have failed to implement the principle through creating the necessary legal framework in the form of adequate or suitable laws or regulations. This may explain the 'break' in the chain of competition law and policy development in the majority of those countries.[19]

### 2.6 Enforcement: the principle and institution of *Hisba*

Having a competition law without an effective enforcement of the law would devoid the law of all practical relevance. The above discussion highlighted beyond doubt that within Islam the idea of protecting competition and the need for competition law is well established and well recognised. The specific principles discussed above and the rich Islamic tradition of dealing with competition and competition law show that at its very early inception Islam contained the seeds of competition law. However, the question that we still need to address is whether Islam has developed any tools for 'enforcement' of competition law or whether the religion's contribution has been nothing but a set of ideas, principles and values, albeit attractive and relevant to the field of competition law and policy. In answering this question, it would be essential to turn to an important fundamental Islamic principle, namely the principle of *Hisba*.

The principle of *Hisba* – the meaning of which refers to 'accountability' in a holistic sense – has witnessed a huge and interesting expansion in its scope over the years to an extent that when one discusses the principle nowadays it would be important to note that the meaning of *Hisba* depends on the context in which it is used. The almost universal meaning of *Hisba* in the present day refers to a situation in which a Muslim person volunteers to interfere in the private affairs of other individuals and to commence an action against such individuals where the latter are deemed to have committed apostasy (renunciation of Islam) or any other wrongful act against *Allah* or against society.[20]

19 See further pp 326–7 below.

20 In recent years, *Hisba* (in this context) appears to have been invoked on two occasions in Egypt to demand separation between a husband and wife. In the first case, which arose in 1995, the Supreme Court upheld a decision of the Cairo Court of Appeals ordering the separation of a university professor, a Mr Nasr Hamed Abu Zeid, from his wife on the grounds that she was an apostate and a Muslim cannot be married to one. Following this ruling, in 1996 the Egyptian Parliament enacted Law No. 3/1996 on Ordering of

This is not, however, the principle's original meaning; nor is this the exact role which *Hisba* originally performed in Islam.

Originally, *Hisba* developed as a secular socio-economic institution or agency for the purposes of, among other things, economic regulation and preventing economic exploitation in the market place. The principle of *Hisba* was conceived as a tool for market inspection and as a mechanism for policing market developments and the behaviour of market operators. This was the role that *Hisba* fulfilled for a long time in Islam before it gradually developed into its present role as a pure 'moral censure' in society as explained above.[21]

Conceptually, the vital contribution made by the principle of *Hisba* is that it has reinforced the principles mentioned above as well as those general principles and basic elements of Islam such as social equality and the prohibition of discrimination in all of its forms. Viewed in a wider context, the existence of the principle of *Hisba* shows that as far as the issue of economic regulation of the market is concerned, there is no clash between Islam and Western civilisation and tradition and on that basis the principle appears to help bridge the gap that exists between these civilisations and which regrettably has widened in recent times.[22]

### *2.6.1 The origins of* Hisba

There is some uncertainty with regard to the exact origins of *Hisba* before it was introduced and developed within Islam. Certainly the principle is not Islamic in origins. One claim is that it was borrowed from Jewish sources and indeed the principle features in Judaism, though its use in practice is extremely limited. Another claim is that the principle originated and was taken from Byzantine sources. Putting this question of origins to one side, however, there is sufficient certainty that the principle has existed from the early inception of Islam as a

Procedure for Initiating *Hisba* Cases in Matters of Personal Status allowing only the prosecutor-general to file such cases and preventing *Hisba* actions by private individuals. The second case arose in 2001 and was brought by Nabih El-Wahsh, a lawyer, against a prominent Egyptian feminist writer, Nawal El-Saadawi, alleging that she had insulted and questioned the teachings of Islam. Mr El-Wahsh demanded that Mrs El-Saadawi's husband divorce her because she had deserted Islam. However, the case was dismissed by the Cairo Family Affairs Tribunal on the basis that as a private individual Mr El-Wahsh did not have the right to commence such action.

[21] Note that in its original meaning and role, *Hisba* had a *moral* element, albeit an economic one.

[22] See pp 326–7 below for further discussion of the 'bridge' between these civilisations.

religion, culture, tradition as well as a system for economic development and regulation.

*Hisba* existed between the seventh and seventeenth centuries during which period Islam witnessed a very impressive expansion in both significance and geographical reach. Despite the fact that the relevant terminology existing during that period did not exactly include modern competition law terms such as those of 'anti-competitive' or 'collusion', there is sufficient evidence of an appreciation of such terms given that the concepts formulated and used around that time such as 'fraudulent behaviour', 'monopolisation' and 'dishonesty' on the part of merchants and businesses were intended to convey the same impression.[23] Thus, economic regulation and the ideas associated with it have a long history in Islam. As previous parts of this chapter demonstrated, encouraging economic activity and pursuit, protecting economic freedom and preventing exploitation are among the most fundamental principles on which Islam and Islamic economic law stand. It would be important to note, however, that there is no attempt made by the present author to suggest here that the idea of economic regulation started in Islam: economic regulation of the market place existed through different civilisations preceding Islam. Through those civilisations, economic regulation existed in different forms. For example, Islam's institution of *Hisba* is an equivalent of the position of *Agoranomos* in Ancient Greece, the office of *Prefect* in the Byzantine Empire, and the office of *Aedile* in the Roman Republic.

### *2.6.2 The institutional structure of* Hisba

It was noted above that many centuries ago *Hisba* operated as a socio-economic institution. It would be essential thus to look at the institutional structure of *Hisba* in order to understand further its operation within Islam. Originally, the institution of *Hisba* consisted of one person only, namely the head or director of *Hisba*. This person was widely known as *Amil ala l-suq* meaning the market agent.[24] There is some evidence in the literature that other titles were also used to describe this

[23] As will be seen throughout the discussion in later chapters, these concepts have been incorporated into the modern competition laws of some MECs.

[24] For an individual to be appointed as *Amil ala l-suq* he had to be a person of moral integrity, knowledgeable in Islamic juridical matters and with experience in commerce and familiarity with the way in which markets operated.

position, such as *Sahib al suq* meaning market inspector and *Wali-l suq* meaning market governor. All of these titles essentially referred to the same person and position. For the purposes of the present chapter, however, the term *Amil ala l-suq* (the market agent) will be used.

The duties of the *Amil* were wide ranging and included collecting taxes, ensuring that markets operated well by being well supplied and that the prices charged were not excessive, and the maintenance of public buildings and roads. In some cases the *Amil* acted as an arbitrator or a judge for the purposes of adjudicating in disputes brought to her attention whilst in other cases she was also the head of the police force and service.

The institutional division and structure of *Hisba* became developed over the years with additional positions being created and new departments being set up to support the *Amil* in discharging his duties. For example, a specialist department staffed by a *Muhtasib* (market inspector) and supporting staff was established. The *Muhtasib* was responsible for some of the functions of the *Amil*. Indeed, quite interestingly the position of *Amil* was later replaced by that of *Muhtasib*, with the latter conducting the three main functions of the former, namely performing services to the community, maintaining places of worship and implementation of justice in society including instituting fair-play in the market place and fighting economic exploitation.

The *Amil* (or *Muhtasib*) enjoyed the power to launch investigations into the market on his own initiative as well as to investigate situations brought to his attention by way of complaint from the public. The powers of *Amil* were wide and they included administrating a punishment where he saw relevant, such as imprisonment and issuing injunctions of different types including ordering a particular harmful practice to be brought to an end. For the purposes of ensuring transparency and safeguarding procedural fairness and the rights of those subject to the investigation, it was mandated that the investigations launched by the *Amil* could not be secretive.[25]

### *2.6.3 Expansion and demise of* Hisba

The first person appointed as *Amil* was a woman named Samra bint Nuhayk al Asadiyya who was responsible for Mecca. Not long afterwards

[25] See Imam Ibn Taimiyah, *Public Duties in Islam: The Institution of Hisba* translated by Muhtar Holland (1992).

a second woman was appointed as *Amil* for Medina, namely, Ash Shifa bint Abdullah.[26] Over time there was geographical expansion of the institution of *Hisba* beyond Mecca and Medina,[27] though the head of *Hisba* came to be given different titles in different parts of the Islamic Empire: in Iraq, Iran and Turkey the person was called *Muhtasib*; in India she was called *Kotwal*;[28] and in North Africa he was called *Sahib al-suq*. A turning point in the development of the institution of *Hisba*, however, occurred with the arrival of Western colonialism and the eclipse of Islamic political strength. With that, there was a noticeable and rapid demise of *Hisba* leading to its gradual, virtual disintegration in different parts of the Islamic Empire at the end,[29] though some elements of *Hisba* – despite lack of any form of effectiveness – are still in existence until the present day, mainly in Saudi Arabia.[30]

### *2.6.4* Hisba *Bill in Pakistan*

In 2005 a *Hisba* Bill was introduced in the Provincial Assembly of the North West Frontier Province (NWFP) in Pakistan. The Bill was sponsored by the province's political party, the Muttahida Majlis-e-Amal (MMA), and focused on the appointment of a *Muhtasib* in the province as a public servant who would have complete authority to implement Islamic values and codes and to ensure observance of Islamic teachings. Although this development has no relevance to the subject matter of the present chapter, it is being briefly discussed here for the benefit of the reader, in order to eliminate any possible confusion, which may result in practice from the use in the NWFP Bill of the word *Hisba* and its declared objective to establish the position of a *Muhtasib*.

[26] According to various sources, her real name was Layla bint Abdullah. She was reported to be a highly skilled physician and it appears that she was given this first name, Ash Shifa (healing), because of that.

[27] Mecca and Medina are both cities in Saudi Arabia.

[28] *Kotwal* literally means the keeper of the fort (Kot *Fort* and Wal *Keeper*). To ensure that the *Kotwal's* duties were executed effectively the *Kotwal* acted as the chief of the police force. His main duties included overseeing markets and prices, maintaining public places and keeping the peace, keeping a register of houses and roads, and monitoring the income and expenditure of local people. Interestingly, the *Kotwal's* duties included spying on suspicious state dignitaries.

[29] For example, the position of *Kotwal* in India apparently functioned successfully until around 1800. After that time, however, the position appears to have become largely symbolic until 1843 when it was abolished.

[30] See chapter 7.

The Bill was aimed at ensuring adherence to the tenets of Islam and does not appear to have been intended to revive *Hisba* strictly as a socio-economic institution for the purposes of economic regulation. The Bill gave the *Muhtasib* immense powers to issue directives, with the aid of a police force – the '*Hisba* Police' – to ensure that people live their lives in accordance with the norms and practices of Islam.[31] Furthermore, the Bill vested open-ended authority in the *Muhtasib* to investigate charges of 'maladministration against any agency or its employees',[32] upon receipt of a complaint from any person, higher courts or provincial assembly, and for this purpose the *Muhtasib* would have access to any documents of the agency.[33]

Controversially, the Bill placed the *Muhtasib* above the law with the result that he cannot be reprimanded by any institution or individual and cannot be challenged in court by any person for actions done 'in good faith'.[34] This is highly contentious for it not only creates a one-man system dependent on the interpretations and beliefs of one individual but also places such individual above the law of the land so that his verdicts cannot be overturned. The *Muhtasib* can therefore enjoy vast and vague powers without any accountability.

The Bill was attacked on the basis that it would introduce a process of 'Talibanisation' in the province, by creating a Taliban style moral police as was the case in Afghanistan with the set up of the Department of Vice and Virtue. Subsequently, the Bill, which gained 68 votes in favour and 34 against in the NWFP Assembly, was declared unconstitutional by the Supreme Court of Pakistan on the basis that it would deprive people of their rights and liberties, thus violating fundamental rights guaranteed under the Constitution.

[31] See section 26 of the Bill. [32] See section 10(a) of the Bill.

[33] Section 2(a) of the Bill defines an agency as 'a department, commission or any office of Provincial Government, a corporation or similar other institutions which the Provincial Government may have established or which may be working under its control, the Secretariat of the Provincial Assembly of the North-West Frontier Province, but does not include the High Court and the courts working under its administrative control'.

See also section 13 of the Bill which deals with access to documents and provides that the '*Muhtasib*, any member of his staff or a member of *Hisba* Force, authorised on his behalf, shall have the right to enter into any office of Government for investigation and examine and take copies of documents during such investigation; provided that if any document is taken into possession from the records, he shall give a receipt thereof as a token of such possession'. (Emphasis added)

[34] See section 25(3) of the Bill.

## 2.7 Conclusions

Islam – along with its vision, principles and fundamental values – has suffered and continues to suffer from 'waves' of misconception and misunderstanding as well as 'waves' of internal conflicts and divisions. The existing regimes of many Muslim countries suffer from a high degree of continuous corruption and manipulation of the economy and political process at the hand of very few ruling individuals or families. Whilst perhaps few people would associate Islam with the idea of market regulation or any form of economic regulation, thinking or theory, Islam has a rich tradition and culture in relation to all of these.

This chapter has sought to show the existence of this rich culture and tradition in the particular field of competition law and policy. Using key Islamic concepts and ideas the chapter traced the roots of competition law and policy in Islam to the seventh century. As the following chapters will demonstrate, however, this important culture and tradition have not come to be reflected in the legal systems of the vast majority of MECs in modern times. It is argued that this is a failure on the part of those countries and one that has deprived them of the full benefits of the global wave of liberalisation in trade and development. This position appears to have begun to change in recent years with a process of de-monopolisation and privatisation in many MECs although it remains to be seen *whether* and in *what* way this process will reach full maturity.

# 3

# Israel: the region's oldest competition law

Israel is in many ways a unique country and society. Located at the heart of the Middle East, the country 'officially' shares hardly any commonalities with other MECs, though to a certain extent similarities in culture do actually exist. The population in the country has a very interesting representation of all types of backgrounds and faiths and in this way it is considered to be a multicultural society though special emphasis has been placed on preserving the Jewish character of the state.[1] Diversities in the case of Israel also exist in relation to regional economic development within the country: the differences between certain cities and towns and many villages in the country are extremely vast whether in terms of economic development or cultural patterns. The former are more economically driven and developed whereas the latter – being small local communities – more than anything else are culturally driven and significantly underdeveloped. Such divergences are problematic not necessarily just in political or social terms but also in competition law terms given the huge task in building a competition culture throughout the country which rests on unified, common standards advocated by a central body, the Israel Antitrust Authority. These are serious *intrinsic* factors bound to affect not only the existence of competition law but also its enforcement and the spreading of a competition culture throughout the country.[2]

Internationally, Israel has always attached particular importance to its relations with foreign countries, especially the USA. The motivation for this has been both political and economic. Almost every international political tie or link established by the country has an economic component and vice versa. Strong emphasis over the years has come to

[1] In the Basic Laws on Human Dignity and Liberty and the Freedom of Occupation, Israel is defined as a 'Jewish and Democratic State'.

[2] See the discussion at pp 64–6 below in relation to the competition advocacy function of the Israel Antitrust Authority.

be placed on participating in the global economy and encouraging foreign investment. Several free trade links were set up over the years, most notably with the EC, the European Free Trade Association (EFTA), the USA and Canada.[3] Currently, options are being explored for concluding similar trade and cooperation agreements with a number of other countries.

### 3.1 The origins of competition law in Israel: the 1959 Law

Israel is the land of the oldest twentieth century competition law in the Middle East. Competition law was first introduced in the country in 1959 with the adoption of the Restrictive Business Practices Law 1959 (the '1959 Law'), just over a decade after the State declared its independence in 1948. The 1959 Law was modelled in a large part on the basis of the (old) UK system of competition law; in particular the UK Monopolies and Restrictive Practices Act 1948 and the Restrictive Trade Practices Act 1956 appear to have been influential. The 1959 Law, however, was not effectively enforced in practice nor used as a competition law tool in the proper sense of the word: it brought about little benefit to the economy because of its failure to promote competitive conditions in Israeli markets. The reason for this can be found in the surrounding environment prevailing at the time. When the 1959 Law came into force – and for many years following that – the government regulated all aspects of economic activity and thus the concept of free market competition was given no importance. In fact the concept was not even adequately recognised. The Law therefore was largely *symbolic* and on the whole its enactment could be considered as part of a legal trend, which came to prevail during the early years of the existence of Israel, namely to adopt laws based on those of the UK. This explains the unusual step taken at that time by a young, small country to enact specific competition legislation when very few competition laws existed around the world and competition law was far from becoming a global phenomenon. As competition law came to be developed in its present form in Israel, however, many people appear to trace the concern of the current competition rules about restrictive practices to the 1959 Law itself which for many is regarded as an instrument introduced for the purposes of eradicating cartels and not only as a symbolic measure.

3 See the discussion at pp 68–70 below on the various bilateral agreements concluded by Israel.

The 1959 Law entered into force on 2 August 1960 almost two years before Articles 81 and 82 EC were implemented through the old EC Regulation 17/62.[4] The Law was amended in 1963 and remained in existence until 1988, when it was finally replaced by the current legislation.[5] The 1959 Law was quite a short and benign piece of legislation, which – perhaps understandably so – was not sufficiently comprehensive especially in relation to its treatment of the phenomenon of collusion between firms, something that in fact would dispel the view that it was enacted in response to public concern about cartels. It was also not adequately balanced in several respects. For example, at one end of the spectrum it provided that anti-competitive agreements within the same corporate group would be caught within its scope. At the other end of the spectrum, it provided that an agreement with restrictions related to the use or exercise of intellectual property rights was *not* a restrictive agreement.[6]

Article 13 of the 1959 Law provided for the creation of a Competition Council or Board of five members responsible for 'supervising' restrictive business practices. According to the article, a district court judge would head the council as chairman. At least half of the members could not be civil servants and at least one of them according to the government's view had to be a consumer representative. Additionally, Article 16 provided for the appointment of a director general. In practice the enforcement of the Law was in the hands of the director general and Articles 37 and 38 armed him with fairly wide powers to conduct competition investigations including the power to conduct searches on premises; in the case of private homes Article 38 provided that the director general could only enter such premises if a warrant was issued by the chairman of the council.

The regime ushered in by the 1959 Law was highly administrative in character, with a role reserved for judges in certain cases. The penalties under the regime included a fine, imprisonment or a mixture of both of these. According to Article 45 a prohibited behaviour or conduct, which

4 Regulation 17/62 was the first Council Regulation implementing Articles 81 and 82 EC, OJ [1962] 204/62. The Regulation was replaced, however, by the current EC (Modernisation) Regulation, 1/2003 which entered into force on 1 May 2004, OJ [2003] L1/1.

5 See further below.

6 It would be important to note that this latter provision was incorporated into the current 1988 Law as can be seen from the discussion at p 43 below.

harmed a person would be considered to give rise to an action in tort regardless of whether the harm was caused directly or indirectly.

### 3.2 From the 1959 Law to the 1988 Law and beyond

The 1959 Law was replaced by the current Restrictive Business (Trade) Practices Law 1988.[7] The Restrictive Business Practices Law 1988 (the 1988 Law or Law) is the main competition legislation in Israel sitting at the centre of the competition law regime in the country with additional instruments – mainly regulations – surrounding it and supplementing its provisions and supporting their application.[8] The enactment of the 1988 Law was widely considered as a step which came to further the government's plans in the mid-1980s to build a pro-competitive approach by focusing on free operation of markets, privatisation and the liberalisation of trade. Under normal circumstances, a competition law adopted with this philosophy and such objectives in mind would surely highlight the move in the particular country towards a more competition-oriented economy. The way in which developments in Israel unfolded in practice, however, did not quite reflect this. In the early years of the existence of the Law, the government's favoured approach was to engage in heavy regulation as opposed to promoting free market competition. Under this approach the preference was to have a single monopolist in each market and to subject this monopolist and its behaviour to heavy regulation with scrutiny of the price charged, the quantity produced and supplied, and the trading conditions imposed by the monopolist. Regulation in such manner was considered as a serious viable alternative to free market competition, which many in the government felt had *uncertain* consequences and outcomes. To a large extent this philosophy was shaped by the actual structure of many markets in Israel: highly concentrated markets with strong monopoly and oligopoly tendencies. However, this approach by the government appears to have led to the opposite outcome: harmful conduct became widespread in different sectors in the economy including key ones such

[7] Law No. 5748-1988.

[8] These include the Restrictive Business Practices Regulations (Registration, Publication and Reporting of Transactions) 5754-2004 and the Restrictive Business Practices Rules (the Block Exemption for Restrictions Directly Related and Necessary to Mergers) 2004. Additionally, several block exemption regulations were adopted which are discussed below at pp 50–2.

as: energy;[9] agricultural produce;[10] public transport;[11] construction;[12] telecommunications;[13] and vehicle imports and distribution.[14]

By comparison to the 1959 Law, the 1988 Law is a modern piece of legislation. However, when compared to existing competition laws around the world (and in fact to those existing in some MECs), the Law appears somehow dated and many of its provisions appear problematic.[15] In recent years, there has been a noticeable increase in calls from within many quarters arguing that the Law is not quite adequate as a competition tool in practice and many of its provisions would benefit from clarification. Those calls began with an effort initiated by this author in March 2003, in cooperation with Professor Meir Heth, a leading figure in the banking sector with substantial competition law expertise, and Dr David Tadmor, former director general of the Israel Antitrust Authority (IAA). That initiative resulted in a major conference on the issue which was held in April 2004 in Israel. The conference brought together all of the key actors in the competition law scene in Israel and resulted in the reform question being pushed high up on the government's agenda. With that event, the debate was no longer focused on whether the 1988 Law should be reformed but on how the reform should be achieved and what shape it should take. It was only following that event that the critics of the Law came to outnumber by far those who advocated its preservation. A new proponent in the debate was Ehud Olmert, the current Prime Minister of Israel – who was then the Minister of Industry, Trade and Labour – and who came to agree that the Law should be replaced with more modern and more balanced legislation. For many key persons, however, Mr Olmert's agenda appeared controversial. Nonetheless, a committee, the Review Committee, was set up by him in March 2005 for the purposes of 'recommending' ways in

[9] Hardly any of the main sectors were exempt here, whether electricity, oil refinery, retail petrol market or aviation.

[10] The market here was dominated by Tnuva, Agrexco and production or cooperative associations.

[11] This can be seen in light of how Eged and Dan, local bus operators came to share markets between them.

[12] See for example the position held by Nishr, a large producer of construction material, especially cement.

[13] This sector was dominated by Bezeq.

[14] The market here was dominated by highly restrictive exclusive agreements created by car producers.

[15] See pp 70–7 below on reflections about the Law.

which the Law could be improved. The committee has been fairly slow in conducting its work and has been the subject of some criticism in relation to both its composure and its purpose. As things stand, it remains to be seen whether and when the committee's work will materialise into concrete results. Many people have considered the composure of the committee to be controversial as the selection of its members, according to some people, was handled according to a 'personal-political' agenda of Mr Olmert especially in light of his *alleged* desire to replace the 1988 Law with a new law, which – although it would in effect modernise competition law in Israel – would be 'softer' on firms and one under which the IAA would have more *limited* powers of enforcement. These criticisms and suspicions were fuelled with the government's confirmation in 2005 – of Mr Olmert's decision – to appoint as director general of the IAA a close friend and political ally of the then Minister of Industry, Trade and Labour who enjoyed no previous competition expertise.[16]

### 3.3 The path towards effective enforcement

Although the first competition legislation in Israel was adopted in 1959 – with an attempt to strengthen the regime in 1988 – effective and concrete competition law enforcement did not begin to materialise in the country until around the mid-1990s, almost seven years after the adoption of the 1988 Law and thirty-six years following the adoption of the 1959 Law. This beginning (and later continuation) of a new chapter in the competition law scene in Israel was facilitated by several developments, most notably the amendments to the Law on no fewer than nine occasions, four of which are worth highlighting here: in 1994 to establish the IAA as an independent body;[17] in 1996 to introduce the concept of class actions;[18] in 1998 to give the director general of the IAA

[16] No doubt, however, that Ms Ronit Kan, the current director general is a very capable person with the necessary managerial and administrative skills. Her appointment was defended on the grounds that it came to promote the role of women in public administration and to install into the system someone who was not too narrowly focused on competition law so that future competition decisions of the IAA would benefit from an open-minded business approach and 'non-competition' perspective aimed at taking into account the important implications of competition decisions such as employment considerations and leniency with businesses.

[17] For a discussion on the IAA and its powers see pp 58–60 below.

[18] Articles 46A–46 J of the Law were added in 1996 to enable any person or consumers' association to bring an action on behalf of a group of persons against any defendant.

the power to order monopolists to refrain from abusive conduct that might harm competition;[19] and in 2000 to add the concept of 'aggravating circumstances' to the Law,[20] empower the director general to issue block exemptions,[21] and employ the consent decree procedure[22] and the pre-ruling procedure.[23]

The IAA has been instrumental in pursuing the path towards effective enforcement and major contributions have been made by successive directors general over the years towards converting the IAA into anything but a 'toothless' authority. Although set up in 1994, it would be fair to say that the IAA has in a relatively short period of time established quite an impressive record, mainly due to the important efforts made by the first, second and third directors general, Messrs Yoram Turbovich, David Tadmor and Dror Strum, who succeeded in making the presence of the IAA felt among the business community and ensuring its work is taken seriously. The IAA's achievement, however, has not been that impressive in relation to competition advocacy on the public front: a significant part of the Israeli public still lack sufficient awareness of the existence of the IAA and its role

A class action must be ratified by the court, which will take into account a number of factors when deciding whether to do so. The final judgement in a class action will constitute a *res judicata* for all persons in the group, subject to Article 46C(b) whereby a person notifies the court that he does not wish to be included in the group. However, these provisions have been replaced by the Class Action Act which came into force in March 2006. See note 96 below.

19 See further below at pp 53–5 and pp 74–5.

20 See pp 62–3 below for a definition of the concept.

21 Block exemptions are discussed at pp 50–2 below.

22 Article 50B of the Law empowers any court or the Restrictive Business Practices Tribunal to issue a consent decree (consensual order), upon the request of the director general, rather than initiate criminal, administrative or judicial proceedings. This is a voluntary agreement between the director general and the defendant(s), reached in lieu of proceedings under Articles 26, 43, 47, 48 or 50A, which places an obligation on the latter to pay a sum of money to the State Treasury and undertake or refrain from taking a specific action. A good example of this is provided by the *Elite* case, discussed under the section on Monopolies and Monopolists below.

23 Under Article 43A, a pre-ruling procedure is available whereby the director general may issue preliminary opinions and publish procedures for obtaining a pre-ruling decision. However, the director general is not obliged to provide preliminary opinions and will take into account the IAA's work priorities and the circumstances of each case when deciding whether to do so. The aim behind establishing the pre-ruling procedure is to provide guidance for those who wish to comply with the Law. The IAA published rules relating to the pre-ruling procedure in August 2004 which provide information as to the types of cases in which the IAA will and will not grant a pre-ruling decision. These rules can be found on the IAA's website, www.antitrust.gov.il.

and an awareness of how competition can benefit them and why it would be important to protect it.[24]

## 3.4 The treatment of different business phenomena: scope and limitations

The scope of the 1988 Law is determined by a single term defined in Article 1, namely 'restrictive business practice'. In applying to restrictive business practices, the Law contains a commitment to protecting competition in the Israeli economy. It was this idea that was seized upon by the Supreme Court of Israel when it referred to the 1988 Law as 'the *Magna Carta* of consumer rights and free competition' in the country.[25] The definition given to the term restrictive business practice extends to three types of business phenomena: restrictive arrangements, monopolies and mergers; the Law prohibits all restrictive arrangements, which include cartels but also extend to vertical restraints; imposes a number of conditions on monopolies and prohibits abusive behaviour on the part of monopolists; and provides for a specific mechanism for dealing with merger and acquisition operations.

### *3.4.1 Restrictive arrangements*

#### 3.4.1.1 Definition

One of the key prohibitions of the Law is contained in Article 2, which forbids all restrictive arrangements, providing a rather broad definition of what a restrictive arrangement entails. According to the article, the term is defined as 'an arrangement entered into by persons conducting business, according to which at least one of the parties restricts itself in a manner liable to eliminate or reduce the business competition between it and the other parties to the arrangement, or any of them, or between it and a person not party to the arrangement'. The article specifies four examples of practices, which will be deemed as damaging to competition and therefore prohibited as constituting a behaviour amounting to a restrictive arrangement.[26] The scope of the 'arrangement' extends beyond the 'conventional' cases of agreements, concerted practices and policies set by trade associations which might adversely affect

[24] See below at pp 64–6.
[25] *Director General v. Tnuva Inc.* (1995) 52 *Supreme Court Decisions* 213.
[26] See Article 2(b) of the Law.

competition.[27] For example, the concept appears to catch situations where a firm (or to use the wording of the Law, a person) adapts its actions to an existing restrictive arrangement. This letter and breadth of scope of this definition – which has been the subject of a great deal of criticism – was introduced as a policy instrument within the Law in order to catch as many practices as possible even those that had the most remote *potential* of harming competition.[28] This in effect ushered in a formalistic approach and was preferred to an 'effect-based' approach, which could have meant that scope of the prohibition would have been narrower and its application handled through a consideration of the *actual* effect the relevant situation produces or is likely to produce on competition. It seems that this formalistic approach was taken from the old approach of the European Commission prevailing for many years under Article 81 EC which entailed applying the prohibition contained in Article 81(1) extremely widely and then saving those situations with pro-competitive effect under the exemption contained in Article 81(3) EC. Article 81(1) EC and the case law generated under that provision appear to have been influential in defining the term restrictive arrangement under the Law in such an expansive manner. A notable illustration in this regard can be found in the reference in the definition to a restriction of competition between one of the parties and a third party. This appears to have been taken from the judgment of the European Court of Justice (ECJ) in the landmark case of *Consten and Grundig v. Commission* in which the ECJ stated that distortion of competition under Article 81(1) EC was possible 'not only by agreements which limit it as between the parties, but also by agreements which prevent or restrict the competition which might take place between one of them and third parties'.[29]

It is worth noting that under the Law there are situations which are excluded from the definition of a restrictive arrangement. Article 3(1)–(9) contains a long list of 'exceptions' of such situations,

[27] See Article 5 of the Law.

[28] The breadth in letter and scope can also be seen under Article 6 of the Law which refers to situations where a person managing a business who is aware of the existence of a restrictive arrangement (without being a party to it) *adapts* his action or behaviour to the arrangement. According to the article such person will be 'deemed to be a party to the arrangement'. This is a problematic proposition in many ways and is discussed at pp 72–3 below.

[29] Joined Cases 56/64 and 58/64 *Etablissements Consten SARL and Grundig-Verkaufs-GmbH v. Commission* [1966] ECR 299, paragraph 16.

where an arrangement will not be considered as amounting to a restrictive arrangement. Looking at the list in Article 3 one will be able to notice the broad scope of these exceptions, though some of these exceptions are less controversial than others. For example, exception in Article 3(1) refers to arrangements, the restrictive aspects of which are established by law. Such exception may not be considered to be controversial.[30] On the other hand, the article refers to arrangements with restraints relating to intellectual property rights provided that the arrangement is between the owner of the right and a licensee of the right and that, where relevant, the right is registered by law.[31] It is widely recognised in the field of competition law that it is possible for such situations to contain restraints or restrictions limiting competition.[32] The exclusion of such situations from the scope of the term restrictive arrangement under the Law appears to be somehow misguided, given the harms which may be caused to competition in intellectual property licensing agreements. Apparently, including this specific exception came to create harmony between the rules on competition and those on intellectual property rights.[33]

The expansive definition of the term restrictive arrangement has caused several problems in practice. Israeli courts – notably the Supreme Court

[30] Other exceptions in the same category can be found in Article 3(4) which refers to arrangements the restraints of which relate to the growing or marketing of domestic agricultural produce, including fruits, vegetables, field crops, milk, honey, cattle, sheep, poultry or fish where the parties to the arrangement are growers or wholesalers, in Article 3(5) which deals with arrangements within the same economic group (an agreement between a parent firm and its subsidiary) and in Article 3(6) which concerns exclusive supply and exclusive purchasing between a supplier and a buyer. It would be important to add that some of these products are subject to governmental price regulation. For example, in relation to milk (and dairy products), there is a close eye kept on the price charged by retailers in particular. A recent case illustrates the seriousness of a firm charging excessive prices which arose out of the practices by Super-sol, a supermarket chain. In October 2006 the Magistrates' Court in Rishon Lezion imposed a fine of 450,000 shekels on Super-sol for a 'series of excessive pricing practices'. The firm also undertook – by way of a financial guarantee of 400,000 shekels – not to engage in similar practices for two years from the date of the judgement.

[31] See Article 3(2) of the Law. Among the intellectual property rights listed in the provision are patents, service marks, trademarks, copyrights, performers' rights or developers' rights. There is no mention in the article of know-how.

[32] See for example the experience of the EC in relation to intellectual property licensing agreements and the European Commission's approach to such agreements most notably as embodied in the technology transfer block exemption Regulation, 772/2004, on the application of Article 81(3) of the Treaty to categories of technology transfer agreements, OJ [2004] L123/11.

[33] As noted at p 36 the position under the Law follows that under the 1959 Law.

and the Restrictive Business Practices Tribunal – were fairly quick to realise the problems associated with the broad definition of the term; problems which were originally brought to their attention by firms who expressed major concerns over the 'exact', 'formalistic' and 'automatic' application of the definition. The Restrictive Business Practices Tribunal was quite outspoken in its early case law about the problematic nature of the definition when it held that the difficulty raised by it was its application to 'every arrangement likely to affect or harm competition even when it has no effect on the market and the harm to competition is limited to between the parties only'.[34]

The definition of restrictive arrangements was the first issue the Review Committee[35] turned its attention to and its conclusion that the definition required some amendments was drawn fairly quickly. The committee suggested in particular that the definition should be modified because the present definition carries the risk of rendering illegal behaviour which is not necessarily harmful to competition, and as a result such situation damaged legal certainty, which is vital in legal and economic circles. The committee also questioned the lack of differentiation between horizontal and vertical arrangements in the definition and the fact that it encompasses arrangements which do not have an effect on the market. All of these were considered to be problematic aspects requiring urgent action. In light of this, the committee has proposed an amendment to the definition, which is largely modelled on Article 81(1) EC and one that focuses on those arrangements that restrict competition in the market *as opposed* to those that restrict competition between parties to an arrangement. The proposed definition consists of two parts. In the first part, a restrictive arrangement is defined as an arrangement between persons conducting business which is likely to prevent or lessen competition. In the second part, the definition lists four examples of what will be taken to constitute a restrictive arrangement, covering mainly price fixing, market sharing and limitation of output or supply. According to the committee such amendment should be implemented and take immediate effect even before it has had the chance to complete its review of the Law which may possibly at the end involve a proposal for a new competition law for Israel to replace the 1988 Law as opposed to *another* amendment to it.

[34] Case 2/97 *Amit Mizrahi v. Director General* (1997). [35] See pp 38–9 above.

#### 3.4.1.2 Cartels

The prohibition of cartels is one of the main and most important goals of the 1988 Law and prosecuting these activities is a top priority for the IAA. To further this aim, in May 2005, the IAA adopted a leniency programme to encourage persons involved in restrictive practices to expose such arrangements by providing information to the IAA about these practices. As a result of doing so, full immunity will be granted to these persons from criminal prosecution or fines, relating to the restrictive arrangement offence under the Law. However, this immunity is subject to the fulfilment of certain conditions, such as that the person is the first, among all those involved in the cartel, to 'confess' to the IAA; that such person does so before an investigation has been initiated by the IAA and provides all the information known to such person. As is widely known, the EC, USA, Canada and the UK have all developed leniency programmes under their domestic competition law regimes which have proved to be a highly effective means of detecting and investigating cartels.[36] The experiences of these jurisdictions highly influenced the IAA's decision to introduce its leniency programme.[37]

The IAA has prosecuted cartels in a range of industries over the years with significant results, including imprisonment, being reached in some cases. Five cartel investigations and cases are worth highlighting due to their importance. The first is the *Floor Tiles* cartel. In this case, the harshest prison sentence (nine months' imprisonment) to date was secured. The sentence was imposed on the executives of firms involved in the cartel, which operated for fourteen years, encompassing almost all of the manufacturers in the market. The District Court held that in the case of hard-core cartels such as the one in question, proof of actual damages is not required when determining the sentence, given the 'definite assumption' that harm to consumers and the public has been caused. The (individual) coordinator of this cartel was fined 250,000 shekels and sentenced to eight months' imprisonment by the Supreme Court in 2003 following an appeal by the IAA which considered the sentence

[36] See the US Corporate Leniency Policy 1993, available at, www.usdoj.gov/atr/public/guidelines/lencorp.htm; the European Commission's Leniency Notice, Notice on Immunity from fines and reduction of fines in cartel cases OJ [2002] C45/03 (a revised (new) Leniency Notice was adopted by the Commission in December 2006. See OJ [2006] C298/17); and Canada's Immunity Programme under the Competition Act 1986, available at, www.competitionbureau.gc.ca.

[37] The IAA's *Guidance on Leniency* can be found on its website, www.antitrust.gov.il.

given by the District Court to be 'too lenient'. The second case is the *Electric Pipe* cartel. In November 2003, the appeal of two executives and one firm, that had been sentenced to imprisonment to be served in public service and fined up to 600,000 NIS for being part of a cartel among four electric pipe firms to raise prices and reduce competition, was rejected by the Supreme Court on the basis that the market can be substantially harmed even if the cartel is short-term. Furthermore, the Supreme Court pointed out that for cartels the appropriate sentencing for individuals is imprisonment in jail, not public service. However, in this case the offenders could serve their imprisonment in public service because of the fact that the cartel operated in 1994 – a period in which the Law was not widely enforced; the level of enforcement increased after the IAA was established. In the third case, the *Spare Aircraft Parts* cartel, the Jerusalem District Court found that two firms trading in spare aircraft parts were coordinating, rather than competing for, the purchases of parts from the Ministry of Defence during the 1990s. The firms, along with their owners, were fined and ordered to perform public service in lieu of jail sentences. This decision, delivered in February 2005, has been appealed to the Supreme Court by the defendants and the outcome of this appeal action was pending at the time of writing, December 2006. In the fourth case, the *Frozen Vegetables* cartel, five firms in the frozen vegetables market were the subjects of an indictment filed by the IAA in June 2005. From 1992 to 1998, the firms coordinated the price of their products and the discount that would be given to customers. Their argument that frozen vegetables fell under the agricultural exemption granted by Article 3(4) of the Law was rejected by the District Court of Jerusalem in March 2006; the final judgment had not been delivered by the court at the time of writing. Finally, the fifth case concerned the *Fittings (Installation Accessories)* cartel, which the IAA concluded was formed and operated on a number of restrictive arrangements involving fifteen firms and eleven individuals from 1993 to 1996.

#### 3.4.1.3 Vertical agreements

As noted above, the 1988 Law applies to both horizontal and vertical agreements which restrict competition. Of the six block exemptions enacted in 2001,[38] three relate to vertical agreements: the Block Exemption for Exclusive Dealing; the Block Exemption for Exclusive Distribution; and the Block Exemption for Franchises. These instruments exempt

[38] See p 40 above. The block exemption mechanism is discussed at pp 50–2 below.

those vertical agreements which do not raise concern of foreclosure at any level of the production chain. However, agreements which set a minimum price or profit rate of goods upon their sale to consumers do not fall within the ambit of these block exemptions and are therefore not exempted. A good example of this is provided by the case of *Tambur Ltd.* Tambur, a monopoly in the paints market, was found in 2002 to have fixed prices through vertical agreements with a number of DIY retail chains, whereby its products would be sold to consumers at uniform prices. Tambur was fined 2.25 million shekels with the District Court ascertaining that its monopolistic position constituted an aggravating circumstance.[39] In addition, Tambur's sales manager was fined 20,000 shekels and sentenced to two months' imprisonment to be served in public service. The manager's appeal to the Supreme Court against this decision was rejected on the basis that the penalty imposed was quite lenient in light of the offence committed. In 2001, complaints of vertical agreements between vehicle importers and after-sale service-providers were made to the IAA alleging that these agreements led to an increase in the prices of vehicle servicing and spare parts in Israel. Consequently, the IAA reached an agreement with all motor vehicle importers which stipulated, among other things, that no restriction be imposed on the pricing of vehicle servicing by the importer other than those imposed statutorily. This agreement was validated as a consent decree by the Restrictive Business Practices Tribunal in 2002.[40]

#### 3.4.1.4 Registration, authorisation and individual exemptions

Under the 1988 Law, all restrictive arrangements *must* be registered with the IAA. This in practice results from the submission of a request to the Restrictive Business Practices Tribunal for authorisation by a person intending to enter into a restrictive arrangement. Under the Law restrictive arrangements are prohibited unless they are authorised by the tribunal or exempted by the director general of the IAA.[41] In practice, however, the power to authorise or exempt a restrictive arrangement is

[39] For the meaning of the concept of 'aggravating circumstances', see pp 62–3 below.

[40] The consent decree mechanism is described in note 22 above.

[41] See Article 4 of the Law. The article also refers to the possibility of the arrangement benefiting from a temporary authorisation, which is granted by the president of the Restrictive Business Practices Tribunal in cases where the public interest will be served as a result of the arrangement. The temporary authorisation must have a limited duration of either one year or run until the tribunal delivers its authorisation decision under Article 9 of the Law, whichever is earlier.

not reserved exclusively to the tribunal and the director general: the Law specifically gives such power to the Minister of Industry, Trade and Labour to exempt a restrictive arrangement from the provisions of the Law where doing so is necessary for the purposes of foreign policy or national security.[42] Firms can request an authorisation from the tribunal of a competition-restricting arrangement which may be granted if the authorisation will be in the 'public interest'.[43] There is no exact definition offered as to what may amount to public interest in this case. Article 10 of the Law, however, provides that when the tribunal considers whether an arrangement is in the public interest, it will take into account, among other things, the contribution made by the arrangement to several issues and whether the benefit to the public resulting from the arrangement outweighs in a material way the harm likely to be caused to the public or to anyone who is not party to the arrangement. The tribunal essentially engages in a balancing exercise involving these issues in order to determine the extent and weight of the public interest in a given case. The issues listed in the article include: efficiency in production and distribution and consumer benefits; the existence of sufficient supplies of products to the public; prevention of unfair competition; preventing serious damage to an industry important to the national economy; employment; and improving the balance of payments of the state. Not all of the issues listed in Article 10, however are, strictly speaking, ones constituting public interest considerations or grounds. For example, the article refers to enabling the *parties* to the arrangement to obtain the supply of product(s) on reasonable terms from a person who holds a considerable market share of the supply of such product(s). Clearly, this is not a public interest consideration though it does show the nature and extent of the 'balancing' exercise which the tribunal will engage in when considering a request for authorisation.

A firm intending to enter into a restrictive arrangement, however, does not have to seek authorisation from the tribunal in order to obtain the necessary approval to be able to operate the arrangement. Where possible, such firm may request an exemption from the director general or the IAA effectively exempting the firm from its obligation to seek

[42] Article 52 of the Law. See further below at p 61 for a discussion on the role of the minister.

[43] See Article 9 of the Law. The tribunal's decision to give such authorisation may extend to a part or the whole of the arrangement and may be made subject to one or more conditions, as the tribunal considers necessary in the circumstance of the case for the purposes of protecting or furthering the public interest.

authorisation.[44] If convinced that certain conditions are satisfied, the director general may issue the exemption. According to these conditions – which are cumulative – the relevant arrangement cannot: limit competition in a substantial part of the relevant market; if such limitation is likely, the arrangement does not significantly impede competition; and the objective of the arrangement is not to reduce or prevent competition and all of its restrictions are directly related and necessary in order to fulfil this objective. In practice, the IAA has set quite strict standards for exemption especially given that this option affords firms the opportunity to avoid the need to request authorisation from the tribunal. For this reason, it is very rare that arrangements with a significant effect on competition will be granted exemption. A fairly recent case involving Arad Ltd and Madei Vered, two leading firms in the water management systems market in Israel, which arose in 2005, illustrates this position of the IAA. The firms in question entered into a restrictive arrangement, as part of a litigation settlement, according to which Madei Vered, which was the main competitor of Arad Ltd, would cease its activity in the market in return for a substantial sum of money, leaving Arad as the only competitor. The IAA opposed approval of this arrangement and this decision was upheld by the tribunal on the basis that the arrangement would have a significant effect on competition as its aim was the elimination of existing competition in the market.

In practice the decision of the director general in relation to a request for exemption is reached only after consulting the Advisory Exemptions and Mergers Committee.[45] From 1989 to 2006, the director general received over 450 requests for exemptions, out of which over 300 were granted unconditionally and approximately 110 were granted subject to certain conditions.[46] A refusal to grant exemption was given in about thirty-five cases. It is very interesting to notice the increase in the number of requests for exemption over the years: from a couple of cases per year in 1990 to tens of cases in 2005 and 2006. In more than one way this shows the greater role the director general and the IAA more generally came to play over the years and the concerns of firms over their business arrangements. In light of the increase in the assertion by the director general of the IAA's role as an important public body,

[44] See Article 14 of the Law.

[45] *Ibid*. The role of the committee is discussed at p 61 below.

[46] The director general enjoys the power to issue conditional exemption by virtue of Article 14(b) of the Law.

firms have come to adopt a cautious approach, under which they notify their arrangements to the IAA in order to avoid the serious consequences which may follow from being found to have participated in a prohibited restrictive arrangement.

An exemption by the director general is not necessarily the final say in relation to whether a restrictive arrangement could be implemented or operated. Such exemption can be revoked by the president of the Restrictive Business Practices Tribunal on appeal from any person, industrial and consumers association who may be harmed as a result of the exemption of the restrictive arrangement in question.[47] Before doing so, however, the tribunal does allow the director general and the parties to the restrictive arrangement the opportunity to highlight their arguments for the exemption.

#### 3.4.1.5 The block exemption mechanism

The Law has been influenced by EC competition law and practice in many respects and as a result high similarities have come to exist between the EC and the Israeli competition law regimes. One of these notable similarities was brought about following the decision to introduce within the latter regime a mechanism for block exemptions.[48] The rationale behind this decision was a desire on the part of the IAA to limit the requirement of applying to the IAA or the tribunal for authorisation or exemption of restrictive arrangements: as we noted above, there was a remarkable increase in the number of such applications over the years, many of which revealed no restriction on competition whatsoever but were made nonetheless due to the cautious approach which came to be adopted by an increasing number of firms. The IAA policy here came to be informed by that of many foreign competition authorities, namely that the scarce resources available to it should be directed towards more serious issues, in particular cartel agreements and behaviour.

The thinking underlying the block exemptions introduced within the Israeli competition law regime is that only those agreements or practices which might have the effect of significantly impairing competition will

[47] See Article 15 of the Law.

[48] A block exemption is formulated in practice by the director general of the IAA, though it must be signed into law by the Minister of Industry, Trade and Labour. Article 15(A) contains the power of the director general to issue block exemptions with the approval of the Exemptions and Mergers Committee.

require an authorisation by the tribunal.[49] For other types of agreements or practices where the competition restrictions are either non-existent or can be ignored, a 'collective' approach' may be justified, meaning dealing with such agreements or practices by way of a block exemption. On that basis, six block exemptions were enacted in 2001.[50] These were as follows: Block Exemption for Restrictive Arrangements causing Immaterial Harm to Competition; Block Exemption for Joint Ventures; Block Exemption for Research and Development Agreements; Block Exemption for Exclusive Dealing; Block Exemption for Exclusive Distribution; and Block Exemption for Franchises. In 2004 two new block exemptions were introduced: one for merger ancillary restraints and the other for land agreements. Under the former block exemption instrument – which assumes a more practical significance in the regime – restraints that are ancillary to a merger operation – that is to say those with restrictions directly related and necessary for the merger – will be exempted from the requirement of obtaining the prior authorisation of the tribunal or the director general, provided their term does not exceed five years.[51] Given that such restraints can be necessary for the preservation of the economic value of the merger operation, the IAA has felt that it would be appropriate to follow a collective approach to these restraints.

There is no doubt that the block exemption option offers key advantages, which firms and their legal advisors very much value in practice in light of the obvious benefits this option offers them, namely the legal

[49] Interestingly, Article 15A refers to dissolving firms from the obligation of having to seek *authorisation* from the tribunal without extending this to an *exemption* from having to make an application to the IAA for individual exemption.

[50] The block exemptions were amended in 2006 in light of the practical experience gained by the IAA during the five years in which they were employed. These amendments were intended to make the block exemptions more efficient. In order to ensure the widest possible awareness of the block exemptions and their amendment, the IAA held a workshop – as part of its workshop series – to explain the changes undertaken in order to ensure that firms are able to adapt their agreements and practices swiftly and smoothly. All of the block exemptions can be found on the IAA's website, www.antitrust.gov.il.

[51] The block exemption provides that an ancillary restriction may consist of any of the following: (a) non-competition clause; (b) non-solicitation clause (c) seller's commitment not to transfer any knowledge he acquired due to his holdings in the acquired business; (d) an agreement between the seller and the acquired business regarding the purchase or supply of goods under the same terms as prior to the merger or under beneficial terms, as long as the terms prior to the merger did not infringe the Law; (e) any other restraint that is essential for the preservation of the economic value of the acquired business.

certainty in relation to their business operations and the saving of both time and money. An instrument for block exemption is therefore usually considered to be a much welcomed development. Looking at the case of EC competition law regime, one will be able to see that the various block exemptions adopted over the years have been hugely valuable in practice and have come to play a crucial role especially given the European Commission's decision to abolish the mechanism for notification by firms seeking individual exemptions from the Commission.[52] In Israel, however, the different block exemptions have not afforded business firms and their legal advisors the feeling of legal certainty. On the whole, exactly how the block exemptions operate in practice has remained an obscure matter for the vast majority of the business and legal community. The tendency of firms and their legal advisors has continued to be to favour notification for individual exemption by the director general or authorisation by the tribunal. This in fact can be seen in light of the high number of agreements notified to the IAA since 2001 when the block exemptions were adopted and the high percentage of those cases which are cleared by way of unconditional exemption by the director general.[53]

Among the six block exemptions adopted in 2001, the one for Restrictive Arrangements causing Immaterial Harm to Competition is particularly important to note because it raised the standard for notifying an arrangement to the tribunal for authorisation and to the IAA for exemption from 'any possible reduction of competition' to 'significant harm to competition' thereby reforming competition law enforcement in Israel, albeit indirectly. Accordingly, agreements which do not significantly restrict competition are exempt from obtaining the authorisation of the tribunal or an individual exemption from the director general. This block exemption also applies to joint ventures where there are cooperation agreements between competitors as long as the agreement is 'of minor importance'.[54] In deciding whether a restrictive arrangement is to be considered as causing immaterial harm to competition,[55] the market shares and the number of competitors in the relevant market are taken into account.

[52] This happened with the Commission's decision to 'modernise' EC competition law and with the adoption of Regulation 1/2003. See note 4 above.

[53] See above.

[54] This means a situation in which there is no appreciable restriction on competition.

[55] Immaterial restriction on competition is taken to refer to hindrance or impairment, the probable effect and actual effect of which on competition are slight. In assessing this, several factors are taken into account including the position of the parties in the market,

### 3.4.2 *Monopolies and monopolists*

Under the Israeli system of competition law, a number of obligations are imposed on the existence of monopolies and the behaviour of monopolists. A monopoly under the system is not given the conventional meaning, which has come to be associated with the concept in different parts of the world, namely a situation where a firm controls or enjoys a market share of 100 per cent in the relevant market. Under the Law, the meaning given to the concept is much looser than this: a monopoly is defined as an entity holding more than 50 per cent of sales or purchases in the relevant market.[56] In effect therefore, the Law contains a conclusive *finding* as opposed to a rebuttable *presumption* in such a situation. This has proved to be problematic in practice because in situations where a firm enjoys 50 per cent of the market shares, such firm can still be subject to competitive pressure from different sources, mainly its competitors and customers. It would be an absurdity to label such a firm a 'monopolist' in this case solely on the basis of its market share and without any due consideration of other factors which may usefully indicate the existence of market power or the lack of it in a particular case. Furthermore, such provision of the Law has necessitated a system of registration, with the director general of the IAA maintaining a register containing a list of all the monopolists which is published by the director general every six months. This system of registration thus subjects monopolies to rather intrusive scrutiny under the Law. The concern in relation to this is that over the years the IAA has come to be over-obsessed with the existence of 'monopolies'. A look at the media output in Israel over the years would reveal the particular interest the IAA has come to develop towards declaring as many firms to be monopolists as possible; the IAA has declared a number of big firms to be monopolies in their field.[57] The repercussion this has had in practice is that the Law has come to be used not as an instrument for protecting and furthering

the intended duration of the restriction and the existing degree of competition in the market.

56 See Article 26(a) of the Law.

57 Examples of this include Bezeq (state-owned telecommunications company), Israel Electric and Israel Chemicals. A more recent example is EL AL, the leading airline in Israel in passengers and cargo transports from and to Israel. In October 2005 the director general declared EL AL a monopoly in the transport of passengers to specific destinations.

free competition but rather as a tool for controlling or regulating firms considered by the IAA to be monopolies simply because such firms appear to have a market share of 50 per cent or more. From the IAA's point of view, playing such an active role in regulating monopolies is vital in order to facilitate a more effective policy of dealing with abusive conduct on the part of monopolies in order to ensure that their existence does not harm competition. In other words, the idea underpinning the IAA's point of view is that a monopoly declaration is a vital step in bringing the IAA closer to detecting and addressing actual or possible abuses of economic power by monopolists and allowing private and class actions to be brought against them for abuse of their position. Under this 'doctrine' the IAA sought to fix the framework of competition by acting as an architect in determining the depth and width of its infrastructure. This doctrine has been followed on numerous occasions over the years. A good example of this can be seen from the case of the *Cement* monopoly in Israel, which was ordered by the IAA in 1998 to reduce its prices significantly over a four-year period. Another example arose in 2003 when the IAA undertook an investigation of the firm Elite, which was declared a monopoly in 1988, on the basis that it was abusing its dominant position in the chocolate market. In order to maintain its dominant position, the firm had entered into restrictive practices with a number of distributors and retailers to block Cadbury, a new competitor, from entering the market. Pursuant to its investigation, the IAA reached a consent decree with the firm.[58] Among the conditions stipulated in the decree, Elite undertook not to exclude competitors from the market and to pay 5 million NIS to the State Treasury, which is the largest sum imposed on a firm as part of a consent decree.

Despite the over-zealous approach of the IAA over monopolists, it is important to note that the existence of a monopoly is not prohibited by the 1988 Law. The prohibition of Law – as expressed in Articles 29 and 29A – applies to abuse of market position by monopolists where they behave in a manner that will reduce competition or harm the public. For this purpose, the Law provides a list of what might constitute an abuse of a monopolist's position.[59] This is in line with Article 82 EC, although the concept of 'monopolist' was derived from section 2 of the US Sherman Act 1890. Whilst one would agree that an abuse of dominance or monopoly position

[58] The concept of consent decree was explained in note 22 above.

[59] See Articles 29 and 29A(b)(1)–(4).

should be dealt with by the IAA seriously and harshly especially where there is no objective justification for the behaviour in question, it is interesting to note that the Law appears to empower the director general to go beyond this and to impose restrictions on, regulate and supervise a monopoly in its business activities where its existence is deemed to be harming the public, even if the monopolist is not abusing its position.[60] Such an empowering provision in the Law would confirm the point made above, namely the use of the Law over the years as a tool for the regulation of monopolies.

### *3.4.3 The regulation of mergers*

The 1959 Law did not contain a specific tool for merger regulation; a merger control regime was introduced for the first time in 1988. The inclusion of this highly important competition law tool within the system meant that prior notification of mergers and acquisitions to the IAA was necessary under certain circumstances.

The legal rules applying to mergers in Israel stem from the 1988 Law and the regulations introduced thereunder. In addition, several statutory block exemptions have been enacted that apply to merger transactions.[61] Expanding the scope of the system to include merger control has had huge significance in practice given the ability of the IAA to prevent situations in which damage may occur to the structure of the market.[62] In the field of merger control, the IAA has consulted heavily the experience of the EC, the USA and Canada and came to learn that preserving particular market structure(s) was vital to protecting competition. Additionally, the IAA's expertise in the field came to benefit from its participation as a member in the International Competition Network (ICN) and as an observer in the Organisation for Economic Cooperation and Development (OECD).[63]

The relevant term used in the Law to refer to merger operations or concentrations is that of 'merger of companies', which is defined

[60] See Articles 27 and 30 of the Law. See also the discussion at pp 74–5 below.

[61] See for example the block exemption on ancillary restraints, referred to in note 51 above.

[62] The IAA clearly realises not only the adverse effects mergers may produce but also the need to apply the rules in a manner that promotes legal certainty and ensures consistency and transparency. To this end, the IAA has published important and helpful guidance in the field, most notably the *Mergers Guidelines on Procedural Aspects*, which are available at the IAA's website.

[63] The international outlook and activities of the IAA are discussed further below at pp 66–70.

broadly.[64] Notification of mergers of companies (and following that the approval of the director general of the IAA) is mandated in instances where one of the following thresholds appearing in the Law is met: (i) if the aggregate market share of the merging entities exceeds 50 per cent of production, sale, marketing or purchase of a product or service in the local market;[65] or (ii) if the total domestic turnover of the merging entities exceeds 50 million shekels in the preceding financial year and each entity has a domestic turnover of at least 10 million shekels; or (iii) if one of the merging entities constitutes a monopoly as defined under the Law.[66] With regard to foreign mergers, the Law provides that a merger between an Israeli and a foreign entity is subject to the requirement of notification and approval by the director general, only where the foreign entity has a market share or sales turnover within Israel.[67]

The decision of the IAA, whether (un)conditionally to approve or reject a merger, must be given within thirty days of receiving the merger notification; failure to do so renders the merger as being approved. The director general can block a merger or approve it with conditions if the proposed merger is likely to inflict substantial damage on competition in a market or if the public interest will be significantly harmed.[68] The type of conditions imposed on a merger could include that the merged parties do not abuse their position in the market or restrictions may be placed on the way they conduct business in the future. A good example of this is provided by the recent merger of two large supermarket chains in Israel, namely Super-Sol Ltd and Clubmarket Ltd, in August 2005. Clubmarket had been declared bankrupt at the time and although its merger with Super-Sol would have reduced competition in the retail chains market, the director general found that a conditional approval of the merger would be better than the closure of Clubmarket, especially

[64] The definition in Article 1 of the Law states that merger of companies includes 'the acquisition of most of the assets of a company by another company or the acquisition of shares in a company by another company by which the acquiring company is accorded more than a quarter of the nominal value of the issued share capital, or of the voting power, or the power to appoint more than a quarter of the directors, or participation in more than a quarter of the profits of such company; the acquisition may be direct or indirect or by way of rights accorded by contract'.

[65] The Minister of Industry, Trade and Labour has the authority to declare that a lower market share may constitute a monopoly in a specific sector, for example, in the gas market it has been reduced to 30 per cent.

[66] See Article 17(a)(1)–(3) of the Law. [67] See Article 18 of the Law.

[68] See Article 21(a) of the Law.

given that there was no other offer than that made by Super-Sol. The conditions imposed in this case consisted of the following: (i) competition must be protected in those areas where as a result of the merger the number of competitors is reduced, (ii) small retail chains should be protected from predatory pricing and (iii) the merging firm must not abuse its buying power to the detriment of its competitors.

The decision to reject or subject a merger to the fulfilment of certain conditions can be appealed to the tribunal which can reach one of three conclusions: uphold the director general's decision; revoke it; or amend it. For this reason, the tribunal undertakes its own analysis of the merger from inception. The decision of the tribunal can subsequently be appealed to the Israeli Supreme Court. Where a merged entity was created in violation of the Law, the director general can make an application to the tribunal for its separation.[69] It should be noted that the director general cannot consent to a merger without having consulted the Exemptions and Mergers Committee.[70] Where a merger has been approved, the Law provides a right of appeal to the tribunal, against the director's decision, to any person, industrial association and consumers association that believes its interests will be harmed by the merger.[71] The decisions of the director general in merger cases, whatever they may be, must be published in the *Official Gazette* and two daily newspapers.

In August 2004, the Economic Committee of the Israeli Parliament approved the Restrictive Trade Practices Regulations (Registration, Publication and Reporting of Transactions) regarding the notification of merger transactions.[72] These regulations have changed the form notification of mergers takes, by introducing a long form and a short form, and are thus considered rather revolutionary. The purpose behind this change was to establish a fast-track procedure for the approval of those mergers where the firms hold a market share lower than 30 per cent and which do not raise, *prima facie*, competition concerns, by allowing the parties to such mergers to use a short notification form. The change was motivated and informed by a similar one occurring in different parts of the world, most notably in key merger control regimes and the origins of the change can be found in the work of the ICN. Furthermore, the regulations stipulate that sufficient information be

[69] See Article 25 of the Law. In this case, effectively the director general will be seeking a de-merger.
[70] See Article 24 of the Law. [71] Article 22(b) of the Law. [72] See note 8 above.

provided by the parties in the initial submission to minimise the requests by the IAA for further information, which unnecessarily extends the duration of the whole procedure causing needless delays. This will shorten the process and in turn allow the IAA to focus on those mergers where a more in-depth scrutiny is necessary. The successful implementation of these regulations is reflected in the increase in the number of merger cases in which the IAA reached its decision within the 30-day time limit, which rose from 79 per cent in 2003 to 91 per cent in 2004. To ensure that the public understands the significant changes brought about by these regulations, the IAA held two workshops in 2004 and published a detailed Q&A paper in 2005 to provide guidance on how the new notification forms should be completed.[73]

Dealing with mergers and acquisitions is an important aspect of the work carried out by the IAA. In 2005, over 200 merger notifications were received by the authority of which 8 turned out to be transactions that were not in fact mergers and 5 were withdrawn. Of the rest of the notifications which did involve mergers, 85 per cent resulted in unconditional approval with only one merger being blocked.[74]

## 3.5 Institutional structure

Competition law enforcement in Israel is handled by the IAA with the benefit of recourse to the Restrictive Business Practices Tribunal in certain cases and the opinion of the Exemptions and Monopolies Committee.

### *3.5.1 The Israel Antitrust Authority*

From 1988 and until 1994, the Israel Antitrust Authority (IAA) was under the auspices of the Ministry of Industry, Trade and Labour, which believed in market intervention and *ex ante* regulation and as a result the promotion of free competition in Israel was rather limited. In 1994, the IAA was detached from that Ministry and became an independent government agency. The IAA enjoys similar powers to those of many

[73] See the website of the IAA, www.antitrust.gov.il.

[74] This concerned two major competitors in the fuel market whose merger, according to the director general, would have had a substantial effect on competition.

The year 2005 is used here because it is the most recent full year with the necessary data being available preceding the publication of this book. Within a broader spectrum however, between 1990 and 2006, the director general blocked twenty-one mergers.

competition authorities around the world, most notably the European Commission, the US Federal Trade Commission and the US Department of Justice's Antitrust Division.[75] The IAA is empowered to investigate unlawful business practices, regulate monopolies and mergers, restrain monopolists from abusing their position and preserve competition in the market place. Furthermore, the IAA has the legal power to conduct criminal investigations and prosecute individuals who breach the competition rules; it, thus, administers the civil and criminal enforcement of competition law in Israel. The IAA consists of approximately eighty employees, comprising of lawyers, economists and investigators responsible for conducting the legal, economic, investigative and administrative work of the authority. In practice, however, the power is reserved mainly in the hands of the director general of the IAA with the chief economist and chief legal advisor given some discretion as the director general sees fit. The director general is appointed by the government upon the recommendation of the Minister of Industry, Trade and Labour and enjoys a range of independent powers granted under the Law.[76] The decisions of the director general are subject to judicial review by the tribunal and the Supreme Court.

As we noted above, the enforcement role played by the IAA over the years has come to expand considerably. This has happened mainly due to the influence the position of director general has come to assume, and the increase in the IAA's budget which has meant that the authority has been able to increase its work force and engage in extensive and thorough competition investigations, many of which can be costly in practice. The competition expertise of the IAA, however, remains fairly limited and many of its functions remain largely unexplored, notably in relation to competition advocacy at the public level.[77] This has been a cause of major concern given the need and importance of building a competition culture in Israel. An additional major concern relating to the IAA and its activities revolves around the position of the director general. The current competition law regime in Israel enables a great deal of power and authority to be vested in the hands of the director general. The problems which may arise as a result of this can be seen in

75 Article 45 allows the director general to enter and search any business premises when he believes doing so is necessary to ensure compliance with or prohibit a violation of the Law. For this purpose, the director general may also seize any article which could be used as evidence of an offence.

76 See Article 41 of the Law.

77 The issue of competition advocacy will be revisited at pp 64–6 below.

light of the UK experience where the situation came to be remedied with the enactment of the UK Enterprise Act 2002, which replaced the old position of Director General of Fair Trading within the Office of Fair Trading (OFT) with that of a chairman and chief Executive of a *board* within the OFT. Under the Israeli regime the director general controls both the day-to-day activities of the IAA and its strategic work and agenda. As a result, a great deal of discretion is concentrated in the hands of the director general. The concern over the existence of this discretion is not alleviated by the fact that the possibility of review of the decisions of the director general is available at the level of the tribunal and the Supreme Court. For this possibility to be turned into reality an action for review must be launched against the decision of the director general. In the Israeli system, however, the desire or appetite of persons or associations entitled to bring review actions has not been particularly strong. It would be fitting, especially for the Review Committee, to recommend introducing a system for checks internally within the IAA where the decisions and strategies formulated by the IAA would effectively be the result of a 'collective' vision as opposed to an approach or view adopted by an individual.

### *3.5.2 The Restrictive Business Practices Tribunal*

In addition to the IAA, other specialised bodies also play a role in the enforcement of competition-related matters in Israel. The Restrictive Business Practices Tribunal (or the Antitrust Tribunal as it is referred to occasionally) has jurisdiction over non-criminal anti-competitive practices; the criminal aspects of competition cases are dealt with by the Jerusalem District Court. The tribunal is formed of seventeen members who are appointed by the Minister of Justice and selected from different sectors, including the District Court, consumer associations and economic organisations and the civil service. The purpose behind such diversity is to ensure representation from various backgrounds. The inclusion of two District Court judges as president and vice-president of the tribunal comes to incorporate a 'judicial' character and attribute within the proceedings and decisions of the tribunal. The decisions of the tribunal and the Jerusalem District Court can be appealed to the Supreme Court, which is the highest judicial authority in Israel. The Israeli competition law regime thus establishes a hierarchical system of institutions to deal with competition-related matters.

### 3.5.3 *The Exemptions and Mergers Committee*

The Exemptions and Mergers Committee performs a consultative role within the Israeli competition law regime. Thirteen members form part of this committee, who are drawn from the government and private sectors and are selected for their expertise in economics, accountancy, business administration or law. It is stipulated that among these thirteen members, four members of the Committee must be researchers and teachers in the same fields as the Committee's expertise and another four members must possess academic degrees together with at least seven years of experience in the relevant fields. The director general must consult the committee when ruling on an application for the exemption of a restrictive arrangement and merger of companies. In relation to the latter, a copy of the merger notification must be sent to the chairperson of the committee as soon as it is received.

### 3.5.4 *Minister of Industry, Trade and Labour*

The Minister of Industry, Trade and Labour is given certain important powers under the Law. Most importantly, he is responsible for the implementation of the Law and for this purpose is empowered to issue regulations relating to this. The power to exempt a restrictive arrangement from the provisions of the Law, on grounds of foreign policy or national security, is also vested in the Minister. Block Exemption instruments prepared by the IAA must be signed by the minister, who has the discretion to decide, in exceptional circumstances, that they should not be ratified. Furthermore, regarding the rules on monopolies, the Minister has the authority to declare that a lower market share[78] than 50 per cent may constitute a monopoly and he may also amend the amount specified, regarding the total domestic turnover of the merging entities for notification purposes, with the ratification of the Economic Committee of Parliament, the Knesset. Finally, it is upon the recommendation of the Minister that the director general of the IAA and members of the Advisory Exemptions and Mergers Committee are appointed.

[78] See note 65 above.

### *3.5.5 Other bodies and individuals*

The Law accords limited roles to be played by other bodies and individuals. These include the Magistrates' Court and external investigators. The role played by the Magistrates' Court in the implementation of the Law is limited to Article 45, which deals with 'search and seizure' powers. Article 45(2)(b) provides that the Magistrates' Court will have the jurisdiction to determine to whom an article seized during an investigation should be returned, in cases where there is uncertainty regarding this. Furthermore, it is within the ambit of the court's power to extend the time periods provided under Article 45, in relation to seizure of an article, upon the request of the director general. A right of judicial action before the magistrates' court is also provided to any person whose 'document' has been seized during an investigation. Under Article 46(a) the director general may appoint an investigator to investigate any person related to or who has information relating to a violation of the Law and require such a person to provide all information and documents relevant to the violation committed. Article 45A requires that the investigator be a civil servant and the Israeli police must not have any objections to the appointment of the investigator in question on the basis of reasons relating to public safety. Appropriate training must also be given to the investigator by the director general and the police.

## 3.6 Orders and penalties

Violations of the Law can be a criminal offence and a civil tort, thus having consequences for violators under both categories. Where a breach of the prohibitions contained in the Law has been committed, under a criminal action, those responsible can face imprisonment of up to 3 years as well as a maximum fine of 2,020,000 shekels and an additional fine – in the form of a periodic penalty – of 13,000 shekels for each day that the offence continues.[79] These fines are doubled and the imprisonment sentence rises to five years where the offence is committed under 'aggravating circumstances', defined as circumstances which cause or are likely to cause substantial damage to competition due, among other things, to one or more of several factors, namely the market share and position of the person(s) in question in the relevant

[79] See Article 47 of the Law.

market(s); the duration of the offence; the damage caused or expected to be caused to the public as a result of the offence; and the gains made by the relevant person(s) as a result of the prohibited situation.[80] Where an offence is committed by a corporation, corporate executives and partners will be held responsible for that offence and charged accordingly.[81] In such cases the burden of proof lies with them to show that they ensured compliance with the Law and the offence took place without their knowledge. Employees involved in offences under the Law can defend themselves on the basis that they acted in accordance with the instructions provided by their employer.[82]

In addition to criminal sanctions, civil proceedings can also be initiated against parties who have infringed the Law because actions or omissions contravening the Law are considered tortuous under the Torts Ordinance (New Version).[83] The director general is empowered to order the prohibition of any action that is contrary to the Law and therefore damaging to competition. Furthermore, the director general may request the tribunal to order the separation of a monopoly in circumstances where the public is 'substantially prejudiced' by its existence.[84]

Any competent court in Israel is empowered to adjudicate in civil proceedings but criminal proceedings can only be brought before the Jerusalem District Court.[85] The Israeli courts have been instrumental in ensuring compliance with the Law by ruling on a number of competition cases and on cases with competition relevance.

## 3.7 Role of third parties

The interests of third parties are duly taken into account by the Law in a number of its provisions. Under Article 8(b), any person, industrial association and consumers association that may be injured as a result of a restrictive arrangement is given the right to object to it in writing. The reasons for such an objection must be highlighted to the tribunal within thirty days of the publication of the application for the approval of the restrictive arrangement. Furthermore, where a restrictive arrangement has been approved but there has been a 'substantial change' in the circumstances since its approval, any person, industrial and consumers

[80] See Article 47A of the Law. [81] See Article 48 of the Law.
[82] See Article 49 of the Law. [83] See Article 50 of the Law.
[84] See Article 31 of the Law. [85] See p 60 above.

association, which may be harmed because of this, can file a request before the director general to make an application to the tribunal seeking an order to revoke or amend the approval issued by it.[86] Where the director general rejects such a request, he must notify the parties, outlining the reasons for the decision, within thirty days of the receipt of the application. In some instances, the tribunal may issue a temporary permit or interim authorisation to a restrictive arrangement, which is awaiting approval, if the arrangement appears to be in the public interest. However, once again, the Law allows any person to file an objection against this, asking the tribunal to revoke or amend such permit or authorisation.[87] The tribunal will take into account the arguments of the parties to the restrictive arrangement, those of the director general and the party requesting the revocation before deciding whether to do so. Restrictive arrangements, which have been exempted from the provisions of the Law, can also be contested by the above-mentioned third parties who can seek the revocation of such an exemption by the tribunal on the basis that they may be injured by the arrangement.[88] With regard to mergers, as we noted above, the Law provides a right to seek judicial review by the tribunal against the director's decision to approve a merger – conditionally or unconditionally, to any person, industrial association and consumers association that believes its interests will be harmed by the merger.[89] Finally, where the decision to grant a consent decree has been taken, Article 50B(d)(1) gives third parties the right to raise objections to this to the director general, if they believe they may be injured as a result.

### 3.8 Competition advocacy

In order to promote awareness of competition principles and create a robust competition culture within Israel, the IAA has in recent years increasingly turned its attention to competition advocacy. It would be fair to say that the IAA has been much more active and successful in its competition advocacy work at policy formulation and international levels than in relation to competition advocacy at public level. As we noted above, the IAA's success in linking its work with the public at large has been rather limited and there is certainly scope for an increased and more vigorous competition advocacy programme aimed at educating

[86] See Article 12(b) of the Law. [87] See Article 13(c) of the Law.
[88] See Article 15(a) of the Law. [89] See Article 22(b) of the Law.

the public on the values of competition and the benefits of the Law and building a competition culture in Israel. It would be important to note that a legislative basis for the IAA to engage in such activity is not wholly absent from the Law: Article 42 of the Law clearly shows the importance of having an established relationship between the IAA and the public at large. However, the article is a very general provision and hardly encompasses any active advocacy on the part of the IAA to educate the public on competition law. As things stand, achieving this is still a long way off and it is difficult to claim that a competition culture in the country has materialised. The comments made here should not, however, take away from the IAA the credit it deserves in terms of the significant role it has played in recent years in the enforcement of competition law in Israel, as is demonstrated in its annual reports.[90] These annual reports have become a good source of consultation for anyone who is interested in learning about or evaluating the work of the IAA. For the IAA on the other hand, the annual reports have been utilised as an appropriate tool for building a good reputation for its ability to deal with competition issues. Beyond publishing its annual guidelines, the IAA has published important guidance such as its guidelines on defining the relevant market in 2001.[91] The market definition guidance is a much welcomed development in practice and follows the principles contained in similar guidelines issued in the USA,[92] the EC,[93] and Canada.[94]

As we noted, the IAA has been much more active in its competition advocacy at policy formulation and legislative levels.[95] It routinely takes part in the discussions of the Economic Committee of Parliament (the

[90] The IAA's annual reports can be found on its website, www.antitrust.gov.il.

[91] The guidance can be found on the IAA's website. In addition to publishing the guidance, the IAA has built a 'bank of market definitions', also available at its website, which contains reference to market definition in past cases.

[92] US Department of Justice and the Federal Trade Commission's *Horizontal Merger Guidelines* 1992, available at www.usdoj.gov/atr/public/guidelines.html.

[93] The European Commission, Competition, Commission Notice on the Definition of the Relevant Market for the Purposes of Community Competition Law OJ [1997] C372/3.

[94] Canada Competition Bureau: *The Merger Enforcement Guidelines*. The guidelines can be found on the Bureau's website, www.competitionbureau.gc.ca/internet/index.cfm.

[95] It would be important to note here the following provisions as they have particular significance in relation to the role of the IAA as a competition advocate at this level: Article 26 of the Law, and Rules 14 and 106a of the Rules of Procedure of the Knesset which deal with the relationship between the IAA and the Knesset; Article 20 of the Law which deals with the relationship between the IAA and the government; and Article 1 of the Ordinance of Procedure (the Appearance of the Attorney General) on the relationship of the IAA with the courts.

Knesset) to ensure that competition considerations are recognised as an important part of policy decision-making. Thus, for example, when the new Class Action Act[96] was approved by the Knesset the IAA made sure that the relevant competition aspects were taken into account during the legislative proceedings so that the Act would not have a detrimental effect on claimants in competition cases.

## 3.9 International outlook and activities

For a young competition authority, the IAA has developed quite a broad international outlook in a relatively short period of time. The authority is held in high regard by competition authorities of other jurisdictions with whom the IAA has maintained good cooperation. The IAA's international outlook has been constructed on the basis of three important pillars: participation in the work of important international organisations; association and free trade links with regional blocks and organisations; and a cooperation agreement in the field of competition law with the US competition authorities.

### *3.9.1 Consulting foreign experiences*

Like an increasing number of competition authorities around the world, the IAA has always placed particular emphasis on the need to learn from the experience of foreign competition authorities. In particular, special importance is attached to the experience of the US, the EC and the Canadian systems of competition law. Such consultation has been quite extensive to the extent that there has been heavy 'borrowing' from those systems over the years. The result has been that if one looks at the different rules, regulations and practices within the Israeli competition law regime one will be able to see very clearly how it is influenced by the competition rules of the EC and those of the USA and Canada, relying on concepts and ideas from these models.[97] Whilst the practice of consultation of foreign experiences in competition law, especially those of developed and mature regimes, is beneficial, there is a danger

[96] This Act came into force on 1 March 2006 and replaced the class action chapter in the 1988 Law. Any class action must therefore be handled in accordance with the provisions of this new Class Action Act.

[97] See also the discussion above in relation to the definition of the term 'restrictive arrangement'.

associated with merely 'parachuting' in one country the competition law of another.[98] A good illustration here can be found in the case of the block exemptions introduced in 2001 and 2004. As we noted above, the 2001 block exemptions were modelled on those in existence in the EC competition law regime. However, in practice their application has been extremely difficult and they have not quite achieved their purpose, namely to create legal certainty, ensure effective enforcement and alleviate the administrative burden on the IAA through reducing the number of agreements notified to the IAA for an exemption. It is still the case that many agreements are notified even those that would be considered to fall within the scope of one of the block exemptions: such is the lack of legal certainty firms and their legal advisors feel in practice.

### *3.9.2 Participation in international organisations*

We remarked above that the IAA has been an observer within the Organisation for Economic Cooperation and Development (OECD), and a member of the International Competition Network (ICN) since 2001.[99] These two roles have afforded the IAA the opportunity to establish an international network with key foreign competition authorities but more importantly to learn about how it could develop best practices through its work. Such opportunity has been invaluable to the IAA especially in relation to the improvements it has made to its merger control practice and procedure and also in relation to introducing a leniency programme in its cartel practice.[100] The authority plays an active role in the ICN's proceedings and work. The IAA chairs two important subgroups within the ICN: the Model Advocacy subgroup within the ICN's Advocacy Working Group, which provides guidance on performing an effective advocacy function based on the advocacy practices of the various ICN member countries, and the Merger Investigation Techniques Subgroup, within the ICN's Merger Working Group, the aim of which is to provide guidance for effective merger review processes. It is also a participant in the Cartel Working Group, the purpose of which is to address the best ways of dealing with cartels.

[98] See Dabbah, 'The development of sound competition law and policy in China: an (im)possible dream?' (2007) *World Competition* 341.

[99] The IAA attaches special significance to its international links with one of the director general's staff acting as senior assistant to the director for international affairs.

[100] The IAA's leniency programme was discussed at p 45 above.

### *3.9.3 Links with the EC and the EFTA States*

On the whole, Israel's relations with the EC have been warm although 'disagreements' have materialised between the two, mainly due to the Palestinian issue.[101] Israel and the EC signed an Association Agreement on 20 November 1995 which entered into force on 1 June 2000.[102] The Agreement goes beyond the old 1975 free trade agreement between the parties given its emphasis on various political issues, governance and social goals and objectives.[103] In relation to competition law, the agreement seeks to provide guidance on the implementation of competition rules in Israel and strengthen economic cooperation between the EC and Israel. One of the aims of this agreement is to develop economic relations between the EC and Israel, and – pursuant to this – Articles 36 to 38 of the agreement lay down the rules on competition. All agreements, decisions and concerted practices, which prevent, restrict or distort competition, abuse of a dominant position by an undertaking and state aid which distorts or threatens to distort competition are deemed incompatible with the proper functioning of the agreement because they may affect trade between the EC Member States and Israel. Under the agreement the parties must ensure transparency in the area of state aid by providing annual reports to each other on the total amount of state aid granted. Furthermore, Articles 37 and 38 provide that state monopolies and public undertakings and undertakings to which special or exclusive rights have been granted must be regulated to ensure that trade between the Member States and Israel is not restricted. An Association Council is established by Article 67 to deal with any 'major issues' or other 'bilateral or international issues' and for this purpose it must meet once a year or whenever necessary. The Agreement provided for the Association Council to adopt the necessary rules for the implementation of these provisions within three years of entry into force of the agreement. In addition, an Association Committee is established by Article 70 to oversee the implementation of the agreement.

[101] Despite these disagreements, Israel has slowly come to develop a fairly strong European orientation, especially as far as culture is concerned. See Herman, 'An Action Plan or a plan of action? Israel and the European Neighbourhood Policy' in (2006) *Mediterranean Politics* 371.

[102] Chapters 1 and 10 discuss further the relationship between the EC and MECs within the context of the Barcelona Process and the European Neighbourhood Policy.

[103] The 1975 Agreement was not the first agreement concluded between the parties: Israel entered into a Non-Preferential Trade Agreement with the EC in 1964.

On the other hand, a Free Trade Agreement was signed between the EFTA States and Israel in Geneva on 17 September 1992 and entered into force on 1 January 1993. The aim of this agreement is to liberalise trade and promote economic relations between the EFTA States and Israel. Accordingly, Article 17 of the agreement lays down the rules for fair conditions of competition. For this purpose, it prohibits all agreements, decisions and concerted practices which prevent, restrict or distort competition and abuse of a dominant position by an undertaking. The activities of public undertakings and undertakings to which special or exclusive rights have been granted are also included within this provision. Article 18 further provides that any aid which favours certain undertakings or certain goods and thereby distorts or threatens to distort competition is also incompatible with the agreement and therefore the parties must ensure transparency in this area. Regarding state monopolies, Article 9 of the agreement provides that these must be regulated to ensure that there is no discrimination in the conditions for the marketing and procurement of goods between the EFTA States and Israel. A Joint Committee, in which each party is represented, is established under Article 26 which is responsible for the administration of the agreement and must meet at least once a year or whenever necessary.

### *3.9.4 Cooperation with the USA*

Israel places particular importance on its relationship with the USA, mainly for political and economic reasons. During the last ten years in particular, this relationship came to be strengthened quite remarkably with closer and harmonious cooperation. This cooperation has been extended to the field of competition law and has taken various forms, informal contact, dialogue between the IAA and the US Department of Justice Antitrust Division and the Federal Trade Commission, and a bilateral cooperation agreement which was concluded in 1999 between the US and Israeli governments. The 1999 cooperation agreement is the only bilateral agreement Israel has entered into with another country in the field of competition law.

Principally, the agreement aims at facilitating cooperation and coordination between the competition authorities of Israel and the USA in order to avoid possible conflicts, which may arise from the simultaneous application of Israeli and US competition laws and to minimise the impact of differences between the two competition law regimes on the respective important interests of the parties. The agreement clearly shows the desire of the parties to develop their relationship, including in the economic sphere, and enhance their 'historic' alliance. In this way a strong driving force for the agreement originated outside the field of competition law. This appears to be supported by the fact that notably the agreement is the first bilateral agreement entered into by the USA and a country with a relatively young competition law regime. The agreement acknowledges the existence of the Agreement on the Establishment of a Free Trade Area between Israel and the USA and the close economic relations and cooperation the parties established within the framework of that agreement.

### 3.10 Reflections

It is possible to reflect on the Israeli system of competition law in more ways than one. Several aspects and components of the system are worth drawing on for the purposes of evaluating the strengths and weaknesses in the system and to highlight, where relevant, the scope for improvement within the Middle East's oldest competition law and arguably its most advanced competition law regime.

Technically speaking, Israel can be considered to be a small island located at the heart of the Middle East with no sufficiently strong economic links of trade with its immediate neighbours. Although Israel enjoys relatively peaceful relations with Egypt and Jordan, there are no significant *actual* flows in trade and investment between Israel and its neighbours by land. The trilateral Qualifying Zone Agreements concluded with Jordan in 1997[104] and Egypt in 2004[105] under the guardianship of the USA have constituted an attempt to facilitate and enhance such flows. The impact of these agreements has been quite limited in practice, however, given the prevailing bleak political climate and the strains often placed on the relations between the parties.

In light of this unique situation resulting from an even more unique geographical location, Israel has effectively been forced to turn its attention to trade with countries located beyond Middle Eastern borders. In order to turn this into reality Israel has had to rely on its port facilities, both air and sea, to create the necessary links with the global economy and establish the necessary trade connection in order to promote exports and imports into the country; hence the ports of

[104] See pp 171–2 below. [105] See pp 239–40 below.

Haifa and Ashdod and Ben-Gurion Airport becoming super-essential facilities. These facilities have become breeding grounds for monopolies to exist and flourish.[106] The transport operators to and from these facilities have been allowed to accumulate market power and to engage in anti-competitive behaviour and practices in the form of cartels and abuse of monopoly position. Remarkably, these practices and behaviour were shown the green light under the Law without its net being cast to catch them.[107]

### *3.10.1* Ex ante *regulation v. competition*

In the mid-1980s the government in Israel simply had a choice between two approaches: the *ex ante* approach of regulation and the pro-free competition approach. The government's initial choice was to opt for heavy regulation of the market place. There were suspicions about competition and its implications. It is highly interesting therefore for the government to seek around that time to adopt a 'modern' competition law. As we noted before, the early approach under the 1988 Law was not to favour free competition. Objectively speaking this should not be surprising given that the Law is not an instrument for free competition as such but rather one for regulating powerful firms and their behaviour. Such characteristic is in the very nature of a restrictive business or trade practices law as opposed to a competition law. As the IAA came to be created and with its independence from the Ministry of Industry, Trade and Labour the authority came in the years following 1994 to embrace a competition ideology, which came to be seen in relation to certain aspects of the IAA's practice, most notably, the relatively speaking,

[106] The monopolies have come to be enjoyed by the Israel Sea Portal Authority, Dagon and Masof Mitaneem.

[107] It is worth noting in particular Article 3(7) of the Law which provides that the concept of restrictive arrangement does not cover an arrangement the restrictive aspects of which concern international air or sea transportation (or combined air, sea and ground transportation) where the parties to the arrangement are sea or air carriers or are sea or air carriers and an international association of sea or air carriers which are approved for this purpose by the Minister for Transport.

In December 2006, however, it was decided to repeal the exclusion for international air transportation and to bring the sector within the scope of the Law. This represents a radical change. At the time of writing – December 2006 – the IAA was exploring the possibility of adopting a block exemption for the sector in order to ensure that certain practices containing no competition harm will nonetheless fall outside the scope of the prohibitions on collusion and abusive conduct.

liberal approach to merger control. Such shift by the IAA, however, had limited impact given the government's favoured approach remained tilted towards regulation, though the government came to modify its approach in those years with it removing its 'objections' to opening different markets to competition.

### *3.10.2 The problematic government/business relationship*

Israel suffers from a typical Middle Eastern problem, which also exists in other parts of the world, namely the controversial relationship which exists between government and business. Most powerful firms enjoy enormous political power and influence. Through this (political) power and influence firms usually attempt to curtail the independent (significant) powers of the director general of the IAA by seeking to prevent competition investigations from being launched, continued or concluded. In recent years this placed strains on the relationship between the Ministry of Industry, Trade and Labour and the director general; the government has not been in favour of a powerful competition authority. The powers which the IAA came to enjoy had to be 'wrestled' from the Ministry. As was said earlier in the chapter, the Ministry under Mr Olmert began its review of the Law and, as we noted, whilst this was widely regarded as a much welcomed step many people have come to develop reservations about the exact agenda behind the review. The concern is that such review process may eventually culminate in 'balancing' the situation by limiting the powers of the director general and the scope of the IAA's work through introducing a softer approach to businesses and their market activities.

### *3.10.3 Gaps in the Law*

Many gaps exist within the 1988 Law and the regime created under it more widely. Some of these are minor whilst others are major and in need of urgent attention. Two gaps in particular are worth highlighting here.

#### 3.10.3.1 Adaptation to a restrictive arrangement

As we briefly noted above, Article 6 of the Law provides that in situations where a person managing a business who is aware of the existence of a restrictive arrangement (without being a party to it) *adapts* his action or behaviour to the arrangement, such person will be 'deemed to be a party to the arrangement'. This is a problematic proposition in many ways. First, it is difficult to see how this provision could be applied in practice. Clearly this would require a demonstration that the person in question *knew* about the existence of the restrictive arrangement. It is not clear, however, whether for this to be shown one has to establish that the person actually knew about the arrangement or whether such person could not have not known about its existence. Secondly, it is unclear whether the provision in effect introduces an irrebutable concerted practice presumption through the back door;[108] if this is the case, the position is problematic given that the person adapting his behaviour to the arrangement in this case is not a party to the arrangement. However uncomfortable one would feel in agreeing with this situation, it is difficult to support imposing an obligation under competition law on a person who is not a party to a restrictive arrangement. Thirdly, the provision blurs the line of distinction between a situation of simple alignment and adaptation of behaviour by a firm or person to that of its competitors and that of collusion.

### 3.10.3.2 The block exemptions

Another deficiency in the wording of the Law can be found in Article 15A, which concerns the power of the director general to adopt block exemptions. The article shows that where a restrictive arrangement will come within the scope of a block exemption, the parties will be absolved of the need to apply for authorisation by the tribunal. There is no mention in the article, however, of the parties in this case being additionally relieved from their obligation to seek an individual exemption from the director general. As we noted above, in practice the block exemption instruments have had limited positive effect given that parties to restrictive arrangements still feel quite uncomfortable with the scope and operation of block exemptions. This would in fact support an idea behind the omission of any reference to individual exemptions under Article 15A, namely that the block exemptions should not be considered as having loosened the grip of the director general under the system. The policy of adopting block exemptions and this idea appear to be contradictory: on the one hand, the block exemptions

[108] A concerted practice presumption is also an aspect of competition law in Turkey. See pp 85–7 below for a discussion on this presumption under the Turkish competition law regime.

came to be adopted in order to relieve the IAA, the tribunal and the firms from unnecessary notification of restrictive agreements, which would fall within the scope of one of the block exemptions; on the other hand, the intention behind the block exemption mechanism was to limit the effect of block exemptions to authorisation by the tribunal and not individual exemptions by the director general.

### *3.10.4 The issue of discretion*

The Law places considerable powers in the hands of one individual, the director general of the IAA. Essentially, the director general is found at the heart of the regime. This is regarded as highly undesirable for various reasons, most notably because of the amount of discretion this leaves in the hands of the director general. Many of the powers enjoyed by the IAA are extremely crucial for effective competition law enforcement in Israel. The concern, however, is that these powers are identified with the director general and exercising them in practice depends on how the director general sees fit in the circumstances. Undoubtedly, review of the decisions of the director general at the tribunal level is an important 'safety valve' in the system. However, it is arguable that intervention by the tribunal can be limited.[109] The discretion enjoyed by the director general can translate into heavy intervention in the market place. This can be seen in relation to the powers of the director general to make a variety of orders to monopolists.[110] For example, Article 27 of the Law provides that the director general is empowered to order a monopolist entering or planning to enter into a standard term contract whether with a customer or supplier to seek an authorisation. Article 30 contains even wider powers enabling

[109] For example, by virtue of Article 12 of the Law the tribunal is empowered to cancel a prior authorisation or amend its terms if it is convinced that there has been a material change in the circumstances which existed at the time when the tribunal issued the authorisation. According to the article such action however will be adopted *following* a request by the director general. It is perhaps understandable that this sequence of events is necessary under the regime. Nonetheless, this gives the director general a great deal of discretion especially as paragraph (b) of the article shows that a third party likely to be harmed by an authorised restrictive arrangement due to a change in the circumstances is entitled to approach the director general to request him to exercise his power under the Article (i.e. to make a request to the tribunal for cancellation or amendment), but the director general has *discretion* in relation to whether to accept or reject the third party request. Another example can be found in relation to the fact that an exemption by the director general means that authorisation by the tribunal will be unnecessary as we saw in the discussion at pp 48–9 above.

[110] See for example the powers contained in Article 27 of the Law.

the director general to make any orders even in the case where as a result of the existence of a monopoly either competition or the public interest is harmed. As we emphasised repeatedly throughout the chapter, the rationale behind such policy is to keep strict control on the existence of monopolies and the behaviour of monopolists. Nonetheless, in practice this policy has resulted in an increased burden on the IAA thereby usurping valuable resources which could be better invested in more serious matters. There is no attempt on the part of this author to play down the seriousness of harm which may result from the existence of monopolies and the abusive behaviour of dominant firms. However, under the Israeli competition law regime, the deficiency exists in the fact that the original and to a certain extent the current (modified) policy of the government has been to favour regulation as opposed to encouraging and facilitating competition. The key therefore to unlocking the deficiency should be for the government and the IAA to enhance the recent pro-competitive efforts of the IAA by favouring open markets as opposed to regulating markets with one or a 'few' monopolist(s). In this vein, rethinking the monopoly presumption in Article 26 of the Law would be a sensible step to take in order to promote this policy further. This would enable the market itself to deal with the problems which may exist as a result of a firm having market power and would reserve the power for the IAA to intervene in case of market failure.[111]

### 3.10.5 *Protecting competitors*

Some attention in Israeli competition law and practice is given to the protection of competitors. For example when considering issuing an authorisation to a restrictive arrangement, the tribunal can take into account the interests of competitors and whether and how the arrangement does or is likely to result in harm to competitors.

### 3.10.6 *Non-competition considerations*

Non-competition considerations feature prominently in the Law and are referred to in practice. Among these considerations are: the balance of payments of the state; import and export considerations;[112]

[111] For example where the market *fails* to correct itself because there is insufficient constraint exerted on the firm(s) engaged in an anti-competitive or abusive behaviour.

[112] See Article 10 of the Law, paragraph 7.

employment;[113] damage to important sectors in the economy;[114] and unfair competition.[115] No doubt the existence or recognition of these considerations gives rise to concern over the impact such considerations have on competition-based considerations. In the Israeli competition law regime, however, this concern may be controlled given that their application is handled by the tribunal.

### *3.10.7 Should the 1988 Law be replaced?*

A legitimate, indeed necessary, question that is worth posing is whether the way forward is by replacing the 1988 Law altogether, as opposed to undertaking an additional amendment in the near future. The question is particularly relevant given the current examination of the Law and the regime in operation under it by the Review Committee but more importantly due to the apparent need to address several aspects of the Israeli competition law regime and enhance its effectiveness and workability. In other words, the question is whether a radical competition law reform as opposed to cosmetic treatment is needed in Israel.

It is clear that one of the goals of Israel has always been to secure a role as a leading economy in the Middle East and a vibrant one in an increasingly globalised world. To achieve this goal, however, Israel cannot continue to rely solely on isolated bilateral trade partnerships. Such an ambitious goal would require among other things creating a platform of economic stability with strong and stable growth and employment at its centre. Facilitating such means in turn would demand a comprehensive programme of structural economic reform, including a new system of competition law for Israel. Realistically speaking, there should be no unnecessary delay in working towards achieving this, if Israel is to have an enterprising economy which will enable it to become one of the best places in the Middle East to do business. A radical reform of the 1988 Law would appear to be necessary. Substituting the Law in favour of a world-class system of competition law would be a sensible suggestion to make, especially if one were to recommend making enterprise a central pillar in the system and in the government's economic

[113] *Ibid.*, paragraph 6. [114] See Article 10 of the Law, paragraph 5.

[115] *Ibid.*, paragraph 3. The reference in the paragraph is to unfair competition which is likely to lead to limitation of competition. The language of unfair competition in this instance is nonetheless worth noting given the separate fields to which unfair competition and free competition belong.

policy more generally. Through building a competition law regime based on the pillars of enterprise and free competition, businesses in Israel will be able to realise their skills, boost their business dealings and improve productivity. It is hoped that the Review Committee will conclude with a recommendation for the government to embark on a journey, the purpose behind which would be to conduct a comprehensive reform of the 1988 Law and the regime as whole which would enable it to reach the final destination, namely the agenda of Parliament, the Knesset. A radical reform of the Law will strengthen competition and the powers of consumers. Through this reform, competition and enterprise will be enhanced; consumers and their welfare will be placed at the heart of competition policy in Israel; the powers of the IAA will be strengthened and made more effective, with new and additional ones and more resources and a clearer legal duty on the authority to promote competition in the economy by using active competition advocacy. The result will be increased business and legal certainty for all parties who deal with competition law and greater benefit to both businesses and consumers in Israel – goals which the IAA has clearly sought to further.

## 4

# Turkey: a European dream from the other side of the border

The Republic of Turkey occupies a unique geographical location, which has for long been regarded as the bridge linking East with West. The country's vast territory stretches from its Middle Eastern borders with Iran, Iraq and Syria to its European borders with Greece, Bulgaria and Georgia, making it a Eurasian country of huge significance to both the 'Western' and 'Eastern' worlds. 'Modern' Turkey came into existence in 1923 after the collapse of the Ottoman Empire when the secularisation of the Republic along European models of governance began to take foothold. During the Ottoman Empire, Turkey was unaffected by the various economic and social developments which occurred around Europe at that time. In fact little attention was paid to these developments. However, since the end of the Ottoman dynasty, Turkey has come increasingly to align itself with the West and has deepened its involvement with western affairs and initiatives. Thus, it has become a founding member of several important international organisations and bodies, most notably the United Nations, the North Atlantic Treaty Organisation (NATO), the Organisation for Security and Cooperation in Europe (OSCE), the Council of Europe and the Organisation for Economic Cooperation and Development (OECD). More recently, Turkey has secured the agreement of the European Union (EU) and its Member States to begin accession talks, to which high hopes for eventual membership of the EU are attached.

### 4.1 Arriving at the competition law scene: economic, political and social dynamics

A consideration of Turkey's various economic, social and political developments, which came to unfold in the second half of the twentieth century, together with the Republic's political ambitions and desires is important not only for the purposes of understanding the context in which competition law and policy came to be introduced and developed in this key MEC but also to enable an informed prediction to be made about the possible future directions in the field.

Despite perceptions to the contrary, competition law and policy in Turkey can be considered as being at a relatively early stage of development. In recent years, however, competition law has come to receive particular attention and focus: it has secured high ranking on the government agenda and significant efforts – worthy of praise and recognition – have come to be made for the purposes of developing and strengthening the Turkish competition law regime. In understanding this recent ascendancy in the importance of and attention given to competition law, one must appreciate the nature and shift in Turkish economic policy as well as recognise important developments in the political arena. Competition law in Turkey is driven by an interesting economic ideology founded on strategic political ambitions and desires. These ambitions and desires have been fundamental in shaping this ideology, which would otherwise not have existed.

The origins of the Turkish competition law story date back to the 1960s, during which years the Turkish economy bore no resemblance to the rapidly growing free market economy which the Republic has come to build using its unique and strategic geographic location as an essential tool in the process. During the 1960s, an economic policy of import substitution came to prevail under which growth was sought through large public monopolies controlling key sectors of the industry. As such, competition incentives were sidelined through the concentration of economic power. It soon became clear, however, that import substitution was not sustainable, with it losing favour to liberal theories, such as those encouraging an exploitation of the country's unique 'Eurasian' location through promoting trade flows in both export and foreign direct investment channels. For the first time, thus, competition in domestic markets was regarded not as a *bane* but as a *panacea* for developing key sectors of the local economy. This ideological shift triggered a government initiative to design and implement a provisional structure for safeguarding competitive forces in domestic markets and achieving liberalisation. However, the *actual* liberalisation of Turkey's economy did not begin until the early 1980s with the move away from *étatism*, a government-run regime with state control, planning and intervention in many sectors of the economy, to a more market-based model with increased liberalisation. It is widely considered that this move paved the way for transformation of the economy with a significant shift towards privatisation of many state sectors and market-oriented policies. Liberalisation was promoted in allegiance to Article 167 of the Turkish Constitution imposing a *positive* duty on the government to prevent monopolisation and cartelisation in markets.[1] At the time, the lack of positive regulation of competitive forces prompted the Turkish Parliament to seek methods to regulate the goods and services markets in order to maintain positive competition through which free trading, free access to the markets and functioning of effective competition would be ensured.

By the late 1980s, it became obvious that the process of global commerce was not just the key to growth but indeed to economic survival. This spurred the Turkish Republic to sign various trade agreements with the European Community (EC) and countries within and outside the Middle East. During the 1990s the government began in earnest wide-reaching privatisation of key sectors brought about through the closer links established with the EC and later the EU. These links were conditional upon and necessitated the introduction of a host of key economic laws and policies. One of these was competition law, which rose to the fore as a *positive* legislative mechanism capable of safeguarding against clustering and monopolisation by private forces.[2] From the 1960s' policy of relegating 'competition' to the substitution bench, a new position came to develop in the 1990s with competition becoming the forward player widely seen *per se* as the liberating of economic forces and the pre-requisite for enhancing national welfare.

In political and socio-political terms, Turkey has travelled the furthest in its secularisation amongst MECs, becoming a modern secular Republic due to strategic thinking and planning of the former nationalist leader, Kamal Ataturk. As such and despite its predominantly Muslim population, the country has remained a secularised democracy closely aligning itself with the West. Keeping in line with this secularist tradition, successive administrations in the Republic have, on the whole, expressed a major commitment to guarding its secularist character; though many would argue that this commitment is questionable.

[1] Article 167 requires the state to 'take measures to ensure and promote the sound, orderly functioning of the money, credit, capital, goods and services markets, and . . . prevent the formation, in practice or by agreement, of monopolies and cartels'. Another relevant article in the Constitution worth citing is Article 172 which provides for the need 'to take measures to protect and inform consumers'.

[2] See the discussion at pp 117–18 below in relation to the positive nature of competition law in Turkey.

While its secular character is obvious when compared with other MECs, Turkey's position is less convincing when considered along European or Western lines. For instance, discrimination and the far from adequate protection of human rights make it highly controversial for many people to view Turkey as a secular country or society in European or Western terms. Indeed, many would regard Turkey as only *partially* secular. Despite this, however, successive Turkish administrations and governments have proved remarkably receptive to Western influence, clearly demonstrating a highly diplomatic style of foreign policy compared to most MECs. Unlike most MECs, Turkey has been *pressured* by the West in its path towards maturing democracy. Political and economic conditions attached to possible future EU membership have greatly reinforced internal political reforms, something that other MECs have to a large extent been free from.

## 4.2 The Law on the Protection of Competition

Prior to the enactment of a competition law in Turkey, there was no specific legislation aimed at the protection of free competition in local markets. The Turkish Commercial Code and the Turkish Civil Code provided general provisions to prevent unfair competition. However, these provisions were a mile as opposed to a stone's throw from being used as competition law tools. As we saw in the previous part, the Turkish Constitution provides an explicit order requiring the state to take all necessary measures to protect the functioning of goods and services markets. Furthermore, the Association Agreement between Turkey and the EC, which was signed in Ankara on 12 September 1963 and became effective on 1 December 1964, required Turkey to enact and implement a competition policy and harmonise its competition policy with EC competition rules.[3] For almost thirty years, very little progress was made on this front. Initially, as we saw above, competition was not associated with economic benefits or gains and on the whole was pushed to the sidelines. This was the position prevailing in the 1960s in particular. In the next decade, however – and for some years following the conclusion of the Turkey–EC Association Agreement – a series of attempts to adopt competition legislation in Turkey began to emerge. Most of these attempts did not pass the stage of initial discussion with the rest failing at later stages. On 6 March 1995, the Association Council,

[3] The Agreement is discussed at pp 109–10 below.

created under the Association Agreement, approved the establishment of a Customs Union between Turkey and the EC, to bring the parties closer in economic and trade matters, which commenced on 1 January 1996.[4] Among other things, this crucial development necessitated the adoption of a competition law and policy in Turkey, not only to comply with and implement the provisions of the Turkish Constitution but also to fulfil the obligations placed on Turkey as part of its negotiations of the Customs Union Agreement (CUA)[5] with the EC which required the harmonisation of the Turkish rules in the field of competition with those of the EC.[6] In effect, the prospects of concluding the CUA laid down the foundations of a competition policy within Turkey. Accordingly, on 7 December 1994 the Turkish Parliament enacted the Law on the Protection of Competition, which entered into force on 13 December 1994.[7] In light of the above, it should come as no surprise that this Law is largely aligned with EC competition law, which was in effect its main source. Adopting a specific competition law in Turkey was a step (one of several) in the direction of fulfilling a European dream from the other side of the border.

### *4.2.1 Aims, scope and nature*

The Law on the Protection of Competition is the primary Turkish competition legislation, which is supported by several instruments of secondary legislation (communiqués).[8] The overall objective of the Law

[4] Decision No. 1/95 of the Association Council.

[5] The CUA is discussed further below.

[6] The commitment on the part of Turkey was not limited to the field of competition law. Indeed, it was wider than that extending to free movement of goods, intellectual and industrial property rights and the common external tariff of the EC. The commitment to harmonise in the field of competition law rested on Article 39 of the Association Agreement which provides for approximation of laws. Effectively this required a commitment on the part of Turkey to adopt competition rules based on Articles 81 and 82 EC and to establish an independent competition authority, the Turkish Competition Authority, as an enforcement body.

[7] Law No. 4054. It is understood that a draft competition law to replace the Law has been prepared which aims at further harmonisation of the Turkish competition law regime with that of the EC regime. It is unclear, however, when this draft will be finalised and whether it will be turned into law in the near future.

[8] Several communiqués have been adopted over the years. The main ones are: Communiqué on Mergers and Acquisitions (1997); Communiqué on the Procedures and Principles of Notification of Agreements, Concerted Practices and Decisions of

is 'to ensure the protection of competition'.[9] Competition for the purposes of the Law is defined as 'the contest between undertakings in markets for goods and services, which enables them to take economic decisions freely'.

Although protecting competition is the main goal, it is not the sole goal behind the Law. The Law also contains secondary objectives such as protecting competitors, especially small and medium-size firms. In seeking to protect competitors, the Law aims to facilitate market entry through the removal of barriers to entry erected by firms.[10] Other goals ascribed to the Law include ideas ranging from the need to force firms to become efficient to the need to fight artificial price increases[11] and to introduce a disciplinary mechanism seeking to curtail impediments to foreign investment and enhance the international competitiveness of firms and industries. A notable philosophy behind these specific ideas was the desirability of the Law as a suitable tool for stimulating the development and expansion of the private sector. On a broader level, the legislative intent behind including a variety of goals appears to have come to facilitate wide political and public support, which was considered crucial in highlighting the role of the Law as an effective tool to address some of the major problems constantly haunting Turkey, such as inflation.

The Law and the Turkish competition law regime more generally are based on the EC system of competition law with regard to both substantive and procedural aspects. However, when compared to the equivalent substantive EC competition rules, the relevant provisions of the Law appear to stand out in two notable respects. First, when reading the different provisions of the Law one forms the impression that many of these provisions are highly economics oriented. Economic thinking

Associations of Undertakings (1997); Communiqué on the Conclusion of the Organisation of the Competition Authority (1997); Communiqué on the Rights and Obligations of Undertakings and Association of Undertakings (1997); Communiqué Regarding the Methods and Principles to be Pursued During the Course of Pre-Notifications and Applications for Authorisation Made to the Competition Authority in order for Acquisitions via Privatisation to Judicially be Valid (1998); Block Exemption Communiqué Regarding Vertical Agreements (2002); Block Exemption Communiqué on Research and Development Agreements (2003); Block Exemption Communiqué on Vertical Agreements and Concerted Practices in the Motor Vehicle Sector (2005).

All of these instruments – which largely (and in some cases almost verbum verbatim) follow various tools and instruments contained in the EC chapter on competition – can be found on the website of the Turkish Competition Authority (www.rekabet.gov.tr/eteblig.asp) which also contains an exhaustive list of abolished communiqués.

[9] See Article 1 of the Law. [10] See pp 106–7 below. [11] See further below.

appears to have significantly influenced the formulation of the different concepts and definitions which seem to incorporate concepts such as 'cost' and 'profit'. Secondly, the Law appears to be more 'detailed' in its treatment of those concepts, which also feature in the relevant provisions of EC competition law. This approach comes to give the Law as wide a scope as possible and incorporates within this scope, in addition to the literal interpretation of the relevant EC competition rules, the jurisprudence of the European Court of Justice (ECJ) and the European Court of First Instance (CFI) developed over the years.[12]

To achieve the various goals described above, in particular that of protecting competition, the Law applies to collusion between firms (whether agreements, decisions or practices) which prevents, distorts or restricts competition; prevents the abuse of a dominant position; and regulates mergers and acquisitions which aim to create or strengthen a dominant position.[13] The treatment of these business phenomena by the Law will be discussed in the text that follows.

### *4.2.2 Collusion*

The prohibition on collusion contained in the Law applies to all 'agreements, decisions and concerted practices' between or involving undertakings[14] which restrict or distort competition within a market. It makes no difference whether these forms of behaviour occur at horizontal or vertical levels of the market: collusion at either level will be caught. Article 4 of the Law includes a non-exclusive list of anti-competitive behaviour which includes price-fixing, concerted control of supply and demand and applying dissimilar conditions to equivalent transactions. This provision corresponds to Article 81(1) of the EC Treaty. A notable

[12] Illustration on this will be offered below, especially in relation to collusion and abuse of dominance.

[13] Note that although the primary concern of the Law is with such behaviour, practices and operations engaged in by firms in the private sector, its provisions also extend to the public sector and state-owned enterprises.

[14] The concept of undertaking is defined in Article 3 of the Law as any natural or legal person producing, marketing and selling 'goods or services in the market, and units which can decide independently and do constitute an economic whole'. The implications of the term 'decide independently' are discussed below, but it is appropriate to note here that the term makes it clear that: (a) an entity which is controlled by another (i.e. a subsidiary-parent relationship) will not be considered as an undertaking for the purposes of the Law, and (b) an undertaking will not be found to exist where the decisions of the entity are made by the state.

aspect of the wording and list contained in Article 4 of the Law is the fact that they appear to lower the 'regulatory thresholds' in relation to the prohibition of collusion and appear to do so in a highly ambiguous manner. An example of this is provided by paragraph (d) where there is a reference to cases 'complicating and restricting the activities of competing undertakings'. Whilst the language of restriction of activities of competitors is one that would naturally be considered to fall within the scope of a competition law prohibition on collusion, the term 'complicating'[15] is open to several interpretations and seems to extend the scope of the prohibition to cases falling short of a 'restriction'.

#### 4.2.2.1 The concerted practice presumption

Another example illustrating the lowering of the regulatory thresholds can be found in relation to the concerted practice presumption also featuring in Article 4 of the Law. Given that it may be difficult to prove the existence of an agreement or concerted practice which is harmful to competition, the Law allows their existence to be *presumed* if market conditions are similar to those markets where competition is artificially prevented, distorted or restricted.[16] The presumption was included as an expression of a key idea behind the Law, namely the importance of fighting and eradicating artificial price increases. The use of the presumption in practice means that where it applies the burden of proof shifts to the undertakings, to show, 'on economic and rational facts', that they were not engaged in a concerted practice. This is an important derivation from EC competition law where there is no counterpart to the 'concerted practice presumption' in Article 81(1) EC.[17]

[15] The concept of 'complicating' and its application are discussed at p 105 below.

[16] Article 4 states that 'where the existence of an agreement cannot be proved, that the price changes in the market, or the balance of demand and supply, or the operational areas of undertakings are similar to those markets where competition is prevented, distorted or restricted, constitutes a presumption that the undertakings are engaged in concerted practice'.

[17] Another noteworthy derivation which can be found under Article 4 concerns the reference in the Article to 'likely' effect on competition, after the reference to 'object' or 'effect'. This comes to give the provision a wide reach and to make it clear that the article also applies to *potential* effect, a point which Article 81(1) EC does not say but which was nonetheless confirmed by the ECJ as falling within the scope of the prohibition in that provision. Furthermore, unlike the application of Article 81(1) EC, there is no *de minimis* doctrine under Article 4 of the Law, though the issue has been in the pipeline for quite some time and the understanding is that the board is inclined to introduce this doctrine.

The application of the concerted practice presumption by the Turkish Competition Board[18] raises some concerns given that it relies on certain speculations being made. There has been criticism of the board stretching the limits of the concerted practice presumption to initiate investigations. A brief look at some of the board's decisional practice will certainly assist in understanding the basis for this criticism. In the 2004 *Cement* decision,[19] four cement producers were under investigation for parallel price increases. No agreement between the firms could be found. However, the board employed the concerted practice presumption to analyse the parallel price increases and support its finding of collusion. Furthermore, in a decision against a cartel among ceramics manufacturers,[20] the board held that the presumption could be invoked, even in the *absence* of evidence highlighting deliberate parallel-pricing behaviour, where 'additional factors' such as exchange of commercial data points towards the existence of collusion. In defending its position, the board has maintained that in exchange-of-information cases where it invokes the presumption, the parties could rebut the presumption by establishing that the information exchanged was not for the purposes of price-fixing. This position appears to be controversial given that normal competitive practices could give rise to parallel pricing or other forms of interdependent behaviour, which does not necessarily need to be explained as a concerted practice: many markets may feature oligopolistic interdependence and there may be many situations in which a firm may simply adapt its behaviour to that of its competitors without necessarily communicating with these competitors whether in the form of exchange of information or another form.[21] Given this, it would be prudent for a competition authority relying on presumptions to adopt a cautious approach. For the purposes of legal certainty and clarification, it would be helpful for the board to explain the role which the concerted practice presumption plays in its decisions, highlighting the additional evidence which is relied upon when invoking the presumption. The presumption has given rise to interest from various bodies and organisations. For example, the OECD has recommended that a formal policy

[18] The board and the Competition Authority are discussed further below at pp 95–6.

[19] Decision No. 04-77/1108-277 (2 December 2004).

[20] Decision No. 04-6/123-26 (24 February 2004).

[21] A good illustration of this can in fact be found in some of the key judgments of the ECJ, most notably Joined Cases C–89, 104, 114, 116, 117, 125–129/85 *A. Ahlström Osakeyhtio v. Commission* ('Wood Pulp') [1988] ECR 5193 and Joined Cases 40–48/73, 50, 54–56/73, 111/73, 113/73 and 114/73 *Coöperatieve Vereniging 'Suiker Unie' UA and others v. Commission* [1975] ECR 1663.

statement should be published by the board to explain the role of the presumption, clarify the board's standards for opening investigations and give details of the minimum evidence necessary to justify the launch of an investigation on the basis of a concerted practice presumption.

#### 4.2.2.2 The treatment of vertical agreements

As was noted above, the prohibition in Article 4 of the Law applies also to vertical agreements containing restrictions of competition. Since its inception, the Turkish competition law regime has always followed the EC regime in relation to how vertical agreements should be treated, though certain differences between the two regimes in this regard have also existed. Broadly, however, the regime was modelled on the EC regime and witnessed changes introduced at different stages mirroring changes occurring in the EC regime. For example, the old EC block exemption Regulations on exclusive distribution and exclusive purchasing had Turkish counterparts, though these came to be replaced with a new single block exemption instrument found in the current Block Exemption Communiqué on Vertical Agreements,[22] which follows the current EC Block Exemption Regulation 2790/99.[23] This communiqué, however, is not identical to Regulation 2790/99. For example, a key component in the latter is the market-share threshold.[24] There is no equivalent threshold in the communiqué, however, mainly because the board has taken the view that omitting such threshold allows for greater flexibility in the regime. The board has played down the 'risks' associated with the omission, namely that such an approach may allow anti-competitive effects to filter through the communiqué and its application holding that where this happens or is likely to happen it would be possible for the board to employ suitable means to deal with the situation such as withdrawing the benefit of the block exemption under the communiqué.[25] Objectively speaking however, the omission is problematic and damages legal certainty, which the block exemption

[22] Communiqué No. 2002/2, issued on 30 May 2002.

[23] Regulation 2790/99 OJ [1999] L336/21. Guidelines on vertical agreements, *the Explanation of the Block Exemption Communiqué on Vertical Agreements* (Decision No. 03-46/540-M (2003)) were also issued in 2003 following the EC *Guidelines on Vertical Restraints*, which were produced by the European Commission, OJ [2000] C291/1.

[24] See Article 3 of the Regulation which places this threshold at 30 per cent.

[25] In line with the EC regime, withdrawal is possible in one of two different ways: individual (in relation to a single agreement) and collective (in relation to a group of agreements or a particular sector).

mechanism in essence often aims at providing. The board's more recent thinking on the matter appears to favour introducing market-share threshold, though it is not clear at what level this will be set.

Although it follows EC competition rules and practice on the matter, the communiqué and accompanying guidelines along with the board's practice have been highly formalistic and quite rigid in their application in practice. There is extremely limited evidence of effective utilisation of the rules in practice, and furthermore there appears to be no coherent and consistent economic-based approach being followed when applying the communiqué. For instance, the treatment of resale price maintenance by the board raises several questions. On the one hand, the board's policy appears to convey the impression that resale price maintenance can be objectionable, which no doubt is a correct line of policy for a competition authority to adopt. On the other hand, there is hardly any concern by the board over situations of maximum or recommended resale prices. Looking at competition law practice around the world, most notably the EC competition law regime, would show that these two particular forms of resale pricing are allowed only insofar as they amount to no more than that in practice. Thus, a situation in which maximum or recommended resale pricing amount to minimum or fixed pricing respectively should be considered as objectionable. The Turkish competition law regime, however, does not appear to incorporate such line of policy which undoubtedly amounts to a serious shortcoming. The board's explanation of its approach has been that there is no particular concern over vertical agreements in general and therefore adopting a policy of *strict* approach to the small number of 'black' cases and a flexible approach to the many 'white' cases is both sensible and sufficient as an approach to vertical agreements. Of course, the query this raises concerns the *grey* cases, which can arise frequently in practice including situations of maximum and recommended resale pricing.

#### 4.2.2.3 Exemptions

In accordance with Article 81(3) EC, the Law allows for exemptions to be granted, under certain circumstances, to an agreement, decision or concerted practice from the prohibition contained in Article 4.[26] This

[26] See Article 5(a)–(d) of the Law. It is important to note that the four conditions contained in Article 5 must all exist at the same time and be satisfied in order for the exemption to be granted.

means that such forms of behaviour, which restrict competition, could nonetheless be justified in cases where certain requirements are fulfilled, namely if they have useful effects on production or distribution and if they improve economic progress and allow consumers to share the resulting benefit. Arguably, the last requirement could be said to highlight the social aspect of the Law, though in practice hardly any expression has been given to this aspect. Furthermore, only where the competition restriction is deemed to be essential for achieving the beneficial goals and does not eliminate competition in a significant part of the market will it be eligible for an exemption.

The Competition Board has the power to exempt agreements, practices and decisions individually from the application of Article 4, as well as to issue 'block' exemptions.[27] In addition, case-specific 'negative clearances' can be given where the Law is not violated.[28] This aspect of Turkey's competition law regime differs from that of the EC, where the mechanisms for individual exemptions and negative clearances have been abolished.[29] The only two similarities with the EC regime in this regard are the block exemptions, which the EC has retained and the abolition of the requirement of notification for an individual exemption.[30] Consequently, abolishing the negative clearance procedure would achieve further compliance with EC law, which Turkey appears to be edging closer towards realising.

According to Article 5 of the Law, exemptions may be granted for a definite period and can be renewed subject to re-examination of the specified conditions. This allows the board to monitor changes and developments which emerge after the exemption has been granted. In addition, it should be noted that the Law allows the revocation of individual exemptions and negative clearances in circumstances where

[27] Examples of the block exemptions issued by the board include: the Block Exemption Communiqué on Vertical Agreements (discussed above), the Block Exemption Communiqué on Research and Development Agreements (Communiqué No. 2003/2) and the Block Exemption Communiqué on Vertical Agreements and Concerted Practices in the Motor Vehicle Sector (Communiqué No. 2005/4).

[28] See Article 8 of the Law.

[29] See EC Regulation 1/2003, the Modernisation Regulation, OJ [2003] L1/1.

[30] The requirement of notification to obtain an individual exemption existed under Article 5 of the Law until 2005, when it was finally abolished following the same development in the EC competition law regime. Abolishing the requirement occurred through Law No. 5388 on the Amendment to Certain Provisions of the Law on the Protection of Competition with Communiqué No. 2006/2 abolishing Communiqué No. 1997/2 on the *Notification of Agreements, Concerted Practices and Decisions of the Association of Undertakings.*

there has been a failure to fulfil the obligations or where inaccurate information was provided regarding the agreement in question.[31]

### *4.2.3 Abuse of dominance*

In addition to prohibiting practices which restrict competition, the Law precludes the abuse of a dominant position by one or more undertakings.[32] This aspect of the Law conforms to Article 82 EC, though the relevant provisions of the Law both go further and are more limited than the prohibition set out in that article. In particular, it is worth noting Article 6 of the Law which refers to 'abuse' of dominance by one or more undertakings in a market within the whole part of Turkey whether 'on their own or through *agreements* with others or through *concerted practices*'.[33] It is not entirely clear what the concepts of agreements and concerted practices relate to or aim to achieve in this case. It is fairly clear that the concepts here do not actually concern dominance, meaning that their existence is taken in this case to be indicative of a collective dominant position.[34] Therefore, the reference must be to abuse and the possibility, according to the article, that abuse may occur through agreements or concerted practices entered into by the dominant undertaking(s) and one or more other undertakings. Such reference is problematic in many respects. Apart from the difficulty in defending or justifying a proposition that would effectively detach abuse from dominance, such a reference would confuse the application of the article and Article 4 of the Law which deals with collusion and specifically refers to these concepts as the two main forms of collusion. Article 6 – like provisions dealing with abuse of dominance found in many systems of competition law around the world – is directed at unilateral behaviour and the reference to agreements and concerted practices appears to stretch the scope of the article beyond this scenario to that of collusion.

On the other hand, Article 6 omits a key component in Article 82 EC, namely unfair pricing by dominant firms. This omission is interesting

[31] See Article 13(a)–(c) of the Law. [32] See Article 6 of the Law.

[33] Emphasis added.

[34] Under EC competition law, agreements and concerted practices may constitute links between independent firms and therefore show the existence of a collective dominant position under Article 82 EC. See for example the judgment of the ECJ in Joined Cases C–395/96 P and C–396/96 P *Compagnie Maritime Belge Transports SA, Compagnie Maritime SA and Dafra-Lines A/S v. Commission* [2000] ECR I-1356.

given that the article is based on Article 82 and given that one of the major aims behind the Law is to fight artificial pricing. Apparently this omission conforms to a policy decision behind the Law aimed at ensuring that the Law *will not* be used as a price regulatory tool and the Turkish Competition Authority as a price regulatory authority.[35]

For the purpose of establishing an abuse of a 'dominant position', such position is defined as 'the power of one or more undertakings in a particular market to determine economic parameters such as price, supply, the amount of production and distribution, by acting independently of their competitors and customers'.[36] It should be noted, however, that being in a dominant position itself is not prohibited and nor is the Law concerned with how a dominant position is reached provided that no unlawful means were employed to do so. On the contrary, it is believed that being in a dominant position highlights the competitive power of a firm which is advantageous when competing on an international level. In other words, the Turkish competition law regime recognises the need to resist the temptation of heavy or frequent intervention with dominant positions obtained by firms or the means through which this happened for the purposes of facilitating international competitiveness of local firms which itself is an expression of an idea standing behind the Law as mentioned above,[37] namely facilitating growth in the private sector.

Following EC practice and case law development, the Turkish competition law regime incorporates a concept of collective dominance, to which the board has come to accord particular significance in its decisional practice. There have been a number of cases where such a position was found to exist and abuse of collective dominance established. A notable board decision was that delivered in the *YAYSAT/BBD* case.[38] The firms, YAYSAT and BBD, were newspaper distributors in Turkey.[39]

35 In practice however the board has utilised Article 6 of the Law to deal with cases of excessive pricing by dominant firms. A good illustrative case is the *Belko* decision of the board which is discussed below.

36 See Article 3 of the Law. The definition refers to competitors and consumers with no reference to customers. It is not clear whether 'consumer' is taken also to include 'customer', a connotation which actually goes in the opposite direction of that followed in the world of competition law. In the Turkish language there are separate words for 'consumer' ('tuketici') and customer ('musteri').

37 See p 83 above.

38 *YAYSAT/BBD* (2000).

39 YAYSAT was controlled by the Dogan group (the leading firm in the market for newspaper publishing) and BBD was controlled by the Bilgin group (the second largest firm in the market).

The board found that YAYSAT and BBD occupied a collective dominant position and enjoyed financial, technological and commercial advantage as a result of this position. Another case worth mentioning is the 2002 decision against *Turkcell–Telsim*, in which the board held that Turkcell and Telsim occupied a collective dominant position in the Turkish global system for mobile communications (GSM) market.

There have been a number of cases in which the board has dealt with abuse of a dominant position, whether one held individually or collectively. In the 2001 Belko decision, the board imposed a fine on Belko, the coal sales and distribution firm of the Ankara municipality, for abusing its dominant position by charging excessive prices. It found that the prices charged by Belko were 50–60 per cent above the prices prevailing in similar markets. Furthermore, the board annulled Belko's monopoly in the coal sales market, which had the positive effect of greatly reducing coal prices in Ankara.[40] In 2002, the board imposed a fine of TRL 1.1 trillion on Türk Telekom,[41] the state-owned monopoly in the land-line telephone sector, for abusing its dominant position by excluding competition in the internet service provider market. In the *YAYSAT/BBD* decision mentioned above, the board found that the firms abused their collective dominant position by engaging in harmful practices especially through a systematic exploitation of their financial, technological and commercial advantage.[42]Finally, in its action against Turkcell–Telsim the board imposed the largest fine since its creation in 1997, amounting to TRL 30.4 trillion. In its decision the board invoked the doctrine of 'essential facilities' in holding that Turkcell and Telsim abused their collective dominant position by not giving roaming access to Aria, a third GSM operator. However, the board's decision was later annulled by the Council of State.

### *4.2.4 Control of concentrations*

With regards to mergers and acquisitions, the Law, together with the Merger Communiqué issued in 1997,[43] forbids those mergers and

[40] It is important to note here that a key factor enabling the board to reach its decision was its view that Belko's abusive behaviour was not attributable to the grant of monopoly power by the Ankara municipality to Belko. The issue of attribution of behaviour or decisions of firms to the state is discussed at p 103 below.

[41] Decision No. 02-60/755-305 dated 2 October 2002.

[42] The board also found evidence of practices 'complicating' the activities of competitors. See further below at p 106 in relation to this point.

[43] The Communiqué on Mergers and Acquisitions No. 1997/1.

acquisitions which are aimed at creating or strengthening a dominant position as a result of which competition in a market will be significantly impeded.[44] It is worth highlighting that this aspect of the Law is not in line with the new Merger Regulation 139/2004 of the EC, under which there is a prohibition on mergers or concentrations that 'would significantly impede effective competition, in the common market or in a substantial part of it, in particular as a result of the creation or strengthening of a dominant position'.[45] However, it is understood that this substantive test contained in the Regulation will be adopted for assessing mergers which will in turn further harmonise the Turkish regime with that of the EC.

According to the Merger Communiqué, merger operations, where the combined market share of the firms concerned exceeds 25 per cent of the relevant market in Turkey *or* where their combined turnover exceeds 25 trillion Turkish Lira, require prior notification and authorisation from the board.[46] There is therefore mandatory notification in the regime. In the case of those operations notified (and provided that they fall within the scope of the rules on notification and satisfy the relevant requirements on full and complete information) the board must decide within fifteen days whether it will clear the merger or commence further in-depth investigation and analysis of the operation.[47] If the board does not take any action within the fifteen-days' time limit, the merger will become legally effective after thirty days following the date of notification.

The board's merger control activities have not been particularly extensive. In the period between 1997 and 2006 the board received over 700 merger notifications,[48] out of which the Board blocked only 3 mergers and delivered unconditional clearance in the vast majority of cases.[49] It is worth noting that the board has developed a relaxed approach to merger operations also notified in the EC. This appears to be both a vote of confidence in the practices of the European Commission and its ability to address competition concerns arising from such operations effectively and a policy decision on the part of the board to focus its efforts and attention on fighting cartels and abuses of dominance.

[44] See Article 7 of the Law. [45] See Article 2(3) of Regulation 139/2004, OJ [2004] L24/1.
[46] See Article 4 of the communiqué. [47] Article 10 of the Law.
[48] A considerable number of these notifications were deemed to concern operations falling outside the scope of the rules.
[49] Conditional clearance was given in relatively few cases.

It is important to note that the Law and the Merger Communiqué do not apply in all sectors of the economy: mergers and acquisitions in the banking sector are deemed to fall outside the scope of the regime. The Banking Act contains an express exclusion from the Law by providing that 'under the condition that the market share in terms of total assets of banks to be transferred or merged does not exceed 20 per cent, Articles 7, 10 and 11 of the [Law] . . . shall not apply'. The 2001 amendment to the Banking Act extended this to all mergers in the banking sector; thus bank mergers and acquisitions are subject to control only by the Banking Regulation and Supervision Agency. Such exclusion in the case of merger operations in the banking sector is questionable given that competition problems can arise in that sector as a result of mergers and the need to address such problems adequately and effectively.

On the other hand, the Law has a role to play in privatisation merger operations, which are administered by the Prime Ministry Privatisation Administration.[50] Several communiqués have been issued by the board to deal with competition aspects of such operations.[51] Broadly speaking, prior notification to and authorisation from the Competition Board will be required to ensure that competition is not distorted in the relevant market for goods and services as a result of privatisation.[52] Notification to the board is required where the market share of the undertaking to be privatised exceeds 20 per cent, where the turnover of the undertaking exceeds TRL 20 trillion or the firm enjoys judicial or *de facto* privileges.[53] Where a merger occurring through privatisation is not subject to pre-notification but is covered within the scope of the communiqué, or the acquiring parties' market share exceeds 25 per cent or their turnover exceeds TRL 25 trillion, authorisation from the board *must* be obtained for the merger operation occurring through privatisation to be legally valid.[54] Generally, the board's policy has been to approve such a merger

[50] See www.oib.gov.tr/index_eng.htm.

[51] Communiqué regarding the Methods and Principles to be pursued during the Course of Pre-notifications and Applications for Authorisation made to the Competition Authority in order for Acquisitions via Privatisation to Judicially be Valid No. 1998/4 and the Communiqué concerning the Change to the Communiqué on the Procedures and Principles to be followed in the Pre-notifications and Authorisation Applications to be submitted to the Competition Authority in order for the Acquisitions via Privatisation to gain Validity No. 1998/5

[52] Communiqués Nos 1998/4 and 1998/5 set out the principles and procedures to be followed for the legal validity of transfers made by the Privatisation Administration and any other public institution or organisation.

[53] See Article 3 of Communiqué No. 1998/4

[54] *Ibid.* Article 5.

where it is clear that the merger will lead to efficiency leaving the option of blocking mergers or clearing them subject to conditions where the merger will effectively transfer the monopoly status from the public to the private domain; there is particular anxiety within the authority and board over the creation of monopolies in such cases. A good illustration of this anxiety is provided by the *IGSAS* decision. In this case, the board rejected the privatisation of IGSAS in 2000 because of the possible effects on competition in markets for nitrogenous fertilisers and composite fertilisers, given the prospective purchaser's strong position in the market. However, in 2003 the board allowed the sale of IGSAS to a firm that had no operations in the industry.

### 4.3 The Competition Authority and Competition Board

Under Turkey's Customs Union Agreement with the EC, it is not only necessary for Turkey to adopt a competition law that is compatible with EC law but also to ensure that it is effectively enforced. As we saw above, this meant creating an independent competition authority as a suitable and adequately equipped enforcement body.[55] Prior to the adoption of the Law in 1994, competition policy fell within the competence of the General Directorate of Consumer and Competition Protection, established in 1993 as part of the Ministry of Trade and Industry. Article 20 of the Law, however, provided for establishing the Turkish Competition Authority as the governmental body responsible for the field of competition law. Realising this goal faced significant delay at the end and the deadline set for the creation of the authority expired without the goal being achieved. However, the authority was eventually established in 1997, nearly two years after the adoption of the Law.

The authority has administrative and financial independence and is an autonomous enforcement agency.[56] Its decision-making competence is vested in the Competition Board, which was also established in 1997. The board is formed of seven members,[57] reduced from eleven by the 2005 amendment, who serve for a term of six years[58] and may be removed from office only for cause.[59] The Council of Ministers has the

[55] See note 6 above and accompanying text.

[56] Article 20 highlights that the Competition Authority is 'independent', enjoying the power to reach final decisions with no orders or influence by any body, authority and person. The article also provides that the authority aims to ensure 'the formation and development of markets' and to 'observe the implementation' of the Law.

[57] See Article 22 of the Law. [58] Article 24 of the Law. [59] *Ibid.*

responsibility for appointing board members, from among the nominees put forward by the Ministry of Industry and Trade, the Ministry of State with which the Under Secretariat of State Planning Organisation is affiliated, the Supreme Court of Appeal, the Council of State and the Turkish Union of Chambers and Commodity Exchanges.[60] Board members must be educated in law, economics, engineering, management or finance and possess ten years' experience in the public or private sector.[61]

### *4.3.1 Enforcement and fines*

The board is responsible for ensuring enforcement of and compliance with the Law and accordingly has extensive investigative powers.[62] It is empowered to investigate any violation of the Law, either on its own initiative or following a complaint by any individual or legal entity.[63] Where a violation of the prohibitions in Articles 4 (collusion), 6 (abuse of dominance) and 7 (harmful mergers) has been committed and is established the board can impose a fine[64] of up to 10 per cent of the annual gross revenue of 'natural and legal persons having the nature of punishable undertakings, and of associations of undertakings and/or the members of such associations.[65] In addition, a fine of up to 10 per cent of the corporate fine may be imposed on the managers of the firm,[66] though the Law does not specify under what circumstances the fine will be imposed, for example whether this will happen in cases of dishonesty,

[60] See Article 22 of the Law. [61] See Article 23 of the Law.

[62] Article 27 contains an extensive list of the powers and responsibilities of the board, ranging from conducting investigations and internal administrative functions to engaging in competition advocacy. For a discussion on the latter function, see pp 98–101 below.

[63] See Article 40 of the Law. Article 14 of the Law authorises the board to request any information it considers necessary when conducting investigations, from public institutions, undertakings and associations of undertakings. This information must be provided within the period specified by the board. Furthermore, it has the power to conduct on-the-spot inspections in cases where it is considered necessary to do so. For this purpose, experts of the board carrying out the inspection are entitled to examine and take a copy of the documentation of the undertakings and associations of undertakings and can also request that a written or oral statement be produced. An authorisation certificate must be carried by the experts showing the subject matter and purpose of the inspection and highlighting that where incorrect information is given, an administrative fine will be imposed.

[64] Fines imposed under the Law are administrative in nature; see Article 18 of the Law.

[65] See Article 16 of the Law. The article also provides for a minimum fine of 200 million Turkish Lira.

[66] *Ibid.*

recklessness or knowledge of the infringement or violation in question. Other fixed fines may be possible in the circumstances described in paragraphs (a)–(d) of Article 16 of the Law.[67] Furthermore, periodic fines may also be imposed by the board.[68] Factors such as the seriousness of the infringement, the market power of the undertakings and the severity of the damage may be taken into account as aggravating circumstances when assessing the amount or level of fines.

During the period from 1997 to 2006, the majority of the fines imposed by the board under the Law accounted for violations of Article 4 and the rest for violations of Article 6 of the Law, with a mere fraction of the fines imposed for Article 7 infringements. Currently, the authority and board do not operate a leniency programme, which would treat those firms who cooperated during an investigation more leniently with a view to improving detection of breaches of the Law. It is believed that this matter is under consideration, though it is unclear whether this programme will be finally adopted within the regime.[69]

### 4.3.2 *Appeal and judicial review*

Decisions of the board may be appealed to the Council of State, which can only affirm or reverse the decision.[70] In the majority of cases where

[67] Fines may be imposed on natural and legal persons by the board as follows: 100 million Turkish Lira for supplying misleading or false information in the case of an exemption, negative clearance or merger (paragraph (a)); 100 million Turkish Lira for failure to supply information or incomplete, false or misleading information supplied following a request by a board decision or an 'on-the-spot inspection' (paragraph (b)); 50 million Turkish Lira for consummating a merger which should have been but was not notified to the board (paragraph (c)); and 60 million Turkish Lira for failure to comply with conditions imposed in an exemption decision under Article 5 of the Law (paragraph (d)).

[68] Article 17 of the Law provides that daily fines will be imposed on undertakings and association of undertakings as follows: 50 million Turkish Lira for failure to comply with a decision ordering an infringement to be put to an end and other measures adopted under Article 9 of the Law; 25 million Turkish Lira for failure to comply with a decision or measure adopted by the board concerning a merger consummated in contravention of the Law; 25 million Turkish Lira for behaviour triggering revocation of an exemption or negative clearance as described under Article 13 of the Law; and 25 million Turkish Lira for preventing an on-the-spot inspection under Article 15 of the Law.

[69] The power of the board to impose fines is, however, subject to the rules on limitation as described in Article 19 of the Law. A limitation period of five years starts to run from the day on which the infringement occurs, unless the infringement concerns 'provisions related to the application or notification of undertakings or association of undertakings, provision of information, or on-the-spot inspection' in which case the limitation period is three years.

[70] See Article 55 of the Law. The Council may not replace the board's decision with its own.

the board has imposed significant fines, the decision has been appealed. In this regard, the unfamiliarity of Turkish judges with competition law has posed several problems which is why in 2004 a new chamber was created in the Council of State,[71] to deal with appeals against the board's decisions.

Looking at the Council's intervention over the years, it is quite clear that on some occasions the Council made it clear that its function is not merely to *rubber stamp* the board's decision.[72] Nonetheless, the regime suffers from the length of proceedings with board decisions taking years as opposed to months to review, especially given that the Council does not substitute its decision for that of the board but rather, as we saw above, either affirms or rejects it.

### *4.3.3 Competition advocacy*

As well as carrying out enforcement tasks as described above, the board has responsibility for advocating competition in Turkey. The Law empowers the board to give opinions on government legislation and regulations concerning competition policy.[73] The board may do this on its own initiative or on the government's request; the government agencies are encouraged, under a communiqué issued by the Prime Minister's office in 1998, to consult with the board about proposed regulations and decisions which entail competition policy implications. However, if an agency fails to inform the board of an important regulation, no sanctions are imposed since the communiqué lacks the binding force of the law and in practice carries no legal weight.

The board has been keen on expanding this branch of competition advocacy at legislative and policy formulation level. It has made quite notable contributions on some occasions, although this contribution has not always been made directly. An example would help explain this. In 2002 the board was consulted in relation to the formulation of the

[71] See Article 34(c) of Law No. 5183 (adopted 2 June 2004).

[72] See for example the appeal from the board's 1999 decision in the *Cine 5* case in which the board found that there was abuse of dominance on the basis of the exclusivity clauses entered into between Cine 5 and the Turkish Football League to show football games and the discrimination in prices imposed by Cine 5 on other TV broadcasters. In its decision, delivered in 2003, however, the Council rejected the board's decision on the grounds that discrimination in prices can serve the public interest given the existence of a variety of audiences in the country with different demographics and demand functions.

[73] See Article 27(g) of the Law.

Natural Gas Market Distribution and Customer Services Regulation by the Energy Market Regulatory Authority (EMRA). The board's opinion appears to have counselled against including a particular provision in the Regulation which facilitated acceptance of letters of guarantee of the ten biggest banks in procurements related to the distribution of natural gas. In the end, this provision was included in the Regulation. However, although EMRA did not initially follow the board's opinion, eventually it did so following an investigation by the board triggered by a complaint from the Association of Banks. The conclusion of that investigation showed that the provision adversely affected competition in the banking industry. As a result of the board's investigation and its particular conclusion in the case, the provision was removed from the Regulation. This example demonstrates quite succinctly how the Law and the board have come to play a role in furthering the private sector, which as we noted before is one of the secondary goals behind the Law.

The competition advocacy role at legislative level, which the board has envisaged for itself and has been keen to further, transcends the legislative boundaries and extends to situations of policy formulation in the privatisation and liberalisation of markets and those situations in which such processes are conducted.[74] This role is seen as crucial in ensuring that particular market structures are maintained which would guarantee that competition would flow and anti-competitive behaviour and abusive practices would be harder to devise and implement. A notable contribution made by the board in this regard can be found in the privatisation of Türk Telekom, a former state monopoly in the conventional telephony services, infrastructure and wholesale internet services market. In its pre-privatisation opinion, the board recommended several measures be adopted aimed at ensuring a competitive market structure following the privatisation of the firm. A key measure revolved around creating structural separation between the infrastructure of cable TV and fixed lines, with the privatisation extending to the latter but not the former.[75] Apart from the desire to guarantee the

[74] It is worth mentioning Communiqué 1998/3 which was intended to enhance the role of the board in this process by providing that the Privatisation Authority should seek the opinion of the board *in advance* in order to ensure that privatisation will not lead to restriction of competition.

[75] The board's concern here was to ensure that competition in the infrastructure of broadband internet services would be protected. Other measures sought to prevent acquisition of control, whether directly or indirectly, over Türk Telekom by the dominant GSM operator.

existence of competition following privatisation, these measures were also intended to make it easier for the board and the relevant regulator to monitor and detect anti-competitive practices. Another useful example illustrating the board's contribution can be found in relation to the enactment of the Law on Restructuring of the General Directorate of Tobacco, Tobacco Products, Salt and Alcohol Enterprises and on Manufacturing, Domestic and Foreign Purchase and Sale of Tobacco and Tobacco Products,[76] which came to separate the roles of market operator and market regulator enjoyed by TEKEL, a public monopoly in the alcoholic beverages and tobacco markets. The board saw the need to create a competitive market structure and solve the problem of conflict of interest resulting from *bundling* the roles of operator and regulator which had existed for many years. Additionally, the board was concerned about and wanted to eliminate any hindrances to competition and competitors by transferring the regulatory powers of the firm to a specific regulatory body.

In relation to the public awareness branch of the task of competition advocacy, notable but modest efforts have been made to enhance public awareness of competition principles and to build a competition culture in the country. Among its various efforts, the authority has held one-day conferences on competition law and policy in Turkey's main cities, including Bursa, Antalya, Izmir and Istanbul. The authority's website contains a range of information related to competition law and policy which is accessible to the public and it also publishes a booklet which contains a variety of material ranging from explaining the objectives of the Law to summaries of cases involving various violations of the law. However, the authority has not been successful in fully enhancing the competition culture in Turkey. The OECD has made various recommendations over the years with regard to how the authority could improve its public image and role as a competition advocate.[77] These include a suggestion that the authority encourage the establishment of a competition law committee by the Turkish Bar association to organise interaction between the authority and the legal community; offer more television and radio interviews to media outlets thereby increasing media coverage and exposure of its actions; publish board decisions in competition cases in the press using consumer-friendly language;

[76] Law No. 4733.

[77] See the OECD Peer Review Report on 'Competition Law and Policy in Turkey' (2005), available at www.oecd.org.

expand interaction with the Turkish Industrialists' and Businessmen's Association (TUSIAD); and make more frequent presentations to national and local business groups.

## 4.4 Private enforcement and actions for damages and compensation

The Turkish competition law regime accords important rights on private third parties. A notable role is provided through the possibility for private enforcement under Article 57 of the Law by virtue of which a person harmed by a behaviour or practice caught under the Law is entitled to launch a civil action seeking damages. The Law is silent, however, on whether a prior board's decision finding an infringement of the Law is necessary for such action to be possible. The board's most recent view is that this should be the case.[78]

By virtue of Article 58 of the Law private claimants may seek 'the difference between the cost they *paid* and the cost they *would have* paid if competition had not been limited'.[79] A claim for compensation may be brought by customers as well as competitors,[80] who according to the article may seek compensation from a firm or group of firms for all the damage sustained by them as a result of limitation of competition caused by such firm(s). The article further provides that where a firm suffers damage arising from 'an agreement or decision of the parties, or from cases involving gross negligence by them', it may request the court to award compensation by '*three fold* of the material damage incurred or of the profit gained or likely to be gained by those who caused the damage'.[81]

## 4.5 Regulatory and supervisory aspects of the regime

As was noted above, the Law's primary focus is on the objective in its title. Competition is intended to be protected by performing the 'necessary' regulatory and supervisory tasks.[82] Article 2 provides that

[78] This position was adopted following a ruling by the Supreme Court of Appeals to that effect. At the time of writing it was widely expected that the authority would finalise a draft provision to be inserted into the Law upholding such a position.

[79] Emphasis added.

[80] It is not stated in the article that the right here extends to consumer associations.

[81] Emphasis added. See further below at pp 105–6 for a discussion on the burden and standard of proof which private claimants are subject to.

[82] See Article 1 of the Law.

transactions related to measures, establishments, regulations and supervisions aimed at the protection of competition fall within the scope of the Law. The Law is silent, however, in relation to how these tasks are expected to be carried out in practice, except to provide in Article 20 that the authority is responsible for the formation and development of markets and the implementation of the Law.[83] For example, it does not include provisions dealing with cases of emergency such as natural disasters or depression cartels and regulation of the price of certain commodities. In this regard, the Law differs notably from the competition law in other MECs where such provisions do exist. It is crucial to note, however, that the silence of the Law in this regard does not mean that the authority and the board enjoy competence in relation to these matters. On the contrary, the silence of the Law here – whether intended originally or not – has translated into an *implied* term that the Law is not without prejudice to the right of the government to intervene in certain cases and to regulate prices: the power is reserved to the government to regulate prices in certain sectors, most notably the pharmaceutical sector.[84]

Several sectoral regulators were established over the years in Turkey. The most notable ones are the Energy Markets Regulatory Authority (EMRA), the Telecommunications Authority, the Radio and Television High Council, the Banking Regulation and Supervision Board and the Capital Markets Board. These sectoral regulators, however, do not enjoy expressed powers of enforcement under the Law. Nonetheless, their involvement in competition cases should not be ruled out completely. It should be noted that the Law confers power on the authority to protect free market competition. In particular, regulated sectors' conditions of free market conditions do not normally prevail and the sector is usually controlled by a single firm[85] or by a sectoral regulator. In the former situation, the firm will be afforded protection and granted privileges by the state enabling it not only to operate as market player but also to act as a regulator.[86] Where this is the case, an actual or potential anti-competitive behaviour or abusive practice by such a firm will be deemed to fall outside the competence of the authority for a simple reason: by its wording the Law places such a case

[83] See note 56 above and accompanying text.

[84] According to the 2006 *Index of Economic Freedom*, the Turkish government sets prices for goods 'produced by state-owned firms' and for a range of crops, bread, and drugs. See www.heritage.org/research/features/index/country.cfm.

[85] Often in this case the firm will in turn be controlled or owned by the state.

[86] See as an example of this the position formerly enjoyed by TEKEL in the alcoholic beverages and the tobacco market discussed above at p 100.

outside its scope. As was seen above in relation to the discussion on the meaning of the term 'undertaking' under Article 3 of the Law, a central condition that must be met for a person to be considered as an undertaking is that such a person must enjoy the ability to 'decide *independently*'.[87] Often in the case of firms owned or controlled by the state the requirement will not be met given that the undertaking's decisions in this case will be attributed to the state: the state will be taken to have reached these decisions and not the undertaking itself acting autonomously or independently. The board's conclusion in such cases will be that the Law does not apply.[88] Undoubtedly, the definition of the concept of undertaking in Article 3 has triggered the limitation on the competence of the authority described here. Therefore one may conveniently suggest an alignment of the definition with that featuring in EC competition law.[89] An alternative suggestion would be to expand the scope of the Law to cover situations caught under Article 86 EC.[90] Under this provision, Member States of the EC are prohibited from granting special or exclusive rights to any undertaking, whether public or private, where doing so would contravene the EC Treaty, in particular the provision on discrimination[91] and those featuring in the chapter on competition.[92] The prohibition in Article 86 however is *qualified* and does not have *absolute* application.[93] The suggestion here rests on the view that the focus as far as the concept of undertaking under the Law is concerned should shift from determining the existence of an ability to 'decide independently' to examining whether the undertaking in question

[87] Emphasis added.

[88] Several cases have arisen over the years in which such a conclusion was reached. A notable case is the investigation conducted by the authority into the practices of Türkiye Şeker Fabrikalari A. Ş, the state-owned sugar firm in 2001. The board's conclusion that Türk Sugar's conduct in the case, although abusive, was not determined 'independently' by the firm.

[89] The ECJ has consistently maintained that for the purposes of EC competition law a central component when defining the concept of undertaking is the engagement by a person in an 'economic activity' without a reference to independence in decision-making. See Case C-41/90 *Höfner and Elser v. Macrotron* [1991] ECR I–1979.

[90] It should be noted that there is no uncertainty with regard to whether the Law applies to public firms, rather the issue is whether the scope of the Law should be limited to requiring specifically that an undertaking must have the ability to make decisions independently.

[91] Discrimination is prohibited by virtue of Article 12 EC.

[92] This includes Articles 81–89 EC.

[93] Article 86(2) EC provides that the competition rules apply to undertakings 'entrusted with the operation of services of general economic interest or having the character of a revenue-producing monopoly … in so far as the application of such rules does not obstruct the performance, in law or in fact, of the particular tasks assigned to them'.

falls within a situation covered under paragraph 1 or 2 of Article 86 EC. Essentially, therefore the suggestion is to incorporate into the Law an equivalent provision to Article 86 EC.[94]

With regard to the other side of the 'regulation' coin mentioned above, namely the existence of a sectoral regulator, any involvement by the authority is in effect determined by such regulator.[95] Thus, the authority can only become involved where liberalisation or privatisation is opted for in the relevant sector leading to the creation of free market conditions and forces or where the board is *able* to rely on its competition advocacy role, as happened in the privatisation cases discussed above.[96] As such neither the authority nor the board has the power to intervene directly in special sectors. At an enforcement level, however, the relationship between the authority and sectoral regulators has given rise to major uncertainty where the relevant sector has elements of free market competition. In this case there is the problem caused by the jurisdictional 'overlap' between the authority and sectoral regulators. In cases of such overlap firms are particularly concerned about the prospect of having to deal with two different authorities and having their operations subjected to the review and orders of these authorities. Clearly such a situation maximises legal uncertainty and fuels the likelihood of conflicting decisions.[97]

[94] The CUA contains no obligation on Turkey to adopt Article 86 EC, but rather in the language of Article 41 of the Agreement to 'uphold the principles in EC competition law relating to public undertakings to which special or exclusive rights have been granted'. No concrete effort has been made by Turkey to do so.

[95] In one of the key sectors, telecommunications, the Telecommunications Law has instituted a mechanism for consultation of the authority by the Telecommunication Authority and consultation of the Telecommunications Authority by the authority prior to adopting decisions in competition cases relevant to the sector. There is no reference in this Law nonetheless to the right or power of the authority to intervene directly. Furthermore it should be noted that a similar mechanism for consultation has not been adopted in other sectors, most notably energy, although an interest has been expressed to develop such mechanism in the sector.

[96] See pp 99–100 above. As we saw, however, any opinion produced by the board in its competition advocacy role does not have binding force on the government.

[97] The authority appears to have recognised this problem in relation to certain sectors. With regard to the telecommunications sector, for example the authority, along with the Telecommunications Authority, has attempted to seek harmonisation in the work of the two authorities by concluding a 'Cooperation Protocol' which was entered into on 23 September 2002. The impact of the protocol has been limited in practice, however, and its implementation has not been completed as planned. Among other crucial steps required for an effective application of the protocol, the coordination committee and working group as set up under the protocol need to convene and conduct the tasks assigned to them.

### 4.6 The burden and standard of proof

It would be interesting to consider the burden of proof imposed on the authority, undertakings under investigation and private claimants and the standard of proof which must be discharged by them under the Law. The Law does not appear to be fully harmonious in its treatment of the issues of burden and standard of proof which different parties, including the authority are subjected to. A good illustration of this can be found under Article 4 which, as we saw, applies to collusion between undertakings. On the one hand, Article 4 subjects the Competition Authority to both a light and low burden and standard of proof respectively. This can be seen in the case of the concerted practice presumption, under which a concerted practice does not have to be established but can be *presumed* where the developments in the relevant market in terms of price, demand and supply or operational areas echo those of a market in which competition is restricted. This means that situations of parallel behaviour may be caught under the presumption even though the behaviour is not necessarily the result of concertation.[98] On the other hand, the article affords undertakings the opportunity to escape being caught by the prohibition in cases where they can prove that they did *not* engage in a concerted practice; this is not a light burden of proof. Furthermore the article provides that an assessment in this case will be conducted on the basis of economic and rational facts; this means that an objective test will be applied which conveys the impression that the standard of proof will be quite high.

The light and low standard of proof can also be seen in relation to damages actions brought by private claimants. Article 59 of the Law shows that neither the burden of proof these claimants face is particularly onerous nor is the standard of proof they are subjected to particularly high. The burden on private claimants in this case, according to the article, takes the form of 'proof' of one of several situations which gives 'the *impression* of the existence of an agreement, or the distortion of competition in the market'.[99] These situations include actual market-sharing, lack of change or 'stability' noticed in price in the market for quite a long time or an increase in price at close intervals by firms in the market. Where this is established, the burden of proof will shift on to the defendant firms to establish that no concerted practice has been entered into or is in operation. With regard to the standard of proof, the article

[98] See above at p 86. [99] Emphasis added.

states that the existence of collusion may be proved by 'any kind of evidence', which makes clear that claimants are not subjected to a high standard of proof. The fairly light burden and low standard of proof in Article 59 are intended to further the board's policy in relation to private enforcement, namely to encourage such enforcement and facilitate damages claims by private claimants where possible.

### 4.7 Market entry and barriers to entry

The issues of market entry and barriers to entry are very prominently positioned in the Turkish competition law regime. Practices and conduct are condemned where they restrict or hinder market entry or erect barriers to entry which have the effect of preventing potential competition. The concern over these issues can be seen in particular in relation to the prohibitions on collusion and abuse of dominance. For example, Article 4(d) of the Law which was mentioned above and which contains the concept of 'complicating' activities of competing undertakings makes a specific reference to the prevention of potential new entrants to the market. This is echoed in the prohibition on abuse of dominance with Article 6(a) of the Law making a similar reference in this case to 'preventing, directly or indirectly, another undertaking from entering into the area of commercial activities'. These two ideas come to place the issue of protection of competitors, whether actual or potential at the heart of the application of the prohibitions on collusion and abuse of dominance.[100] The Law therefore is not only concerned with the protection of competition as its title and Article 1 clearly state: it goes further than this and provides for an express protection of competitors as a secondary objective.[101] Competitors are considered to be worthy of protection given the risk of small and medium-size firms being harmed by the anti-competitive behaviour and abusive conduct of bigger firms and given obvious competitive constraints competitors may be able to exert over the behaviour and conduct of colluding or dominant firms. Moreover, as we noted above, one of the aims behind the Law is to

[100] There have been several cases in which the board actually condemned behaviour and practices as 'complicating' the activities of competitors. A notable example can be found in relation to the *YAYSAT/BBD* decision which was discussed at pp 91–2 above. In the case the board found that the firms in question complicated the activities of competing publishers and a distributor, Medya, of a newspaper called *STAR*.

[101] The various secondary goals behind the Law were mentioned above at p 83.

expand the private sector which can be facilitated through protecting firms in local markets.

### 4.8 International links within the Middle East and beyond

Turkey has set up an extensive web of competition-relevant international agreements, all of which are free trade agreements except for two, namely the important Association Agreement and the Customs Union Agreement signed with the EC. Several of the free trade agreements entered into by the Republic have been concluded with other MECs.[102] The authority has not, however, concluded any formal bilateral competition cooperation agreements though the matter has been under active consideration for quite some time. In order to 'fill' the gap created by the lack of such agreements, the board has reverted where possible to *de facto* bilateral cooperation. This effort has, however, met limited success in practice as illustrated by the board's investigation into the seized coal market. This investigation was opened in 2004 by the board following complaints about a significant increase in the retail prices of coal which apparently was caused by an 'artificial' increase in the price of imported coal. The board found that a price-fixing cartel was in operation by two subsidiaries of Glencore International AG, Glencore Istanbul Madencilik Ticaret A.Ş. and Minerkom Mineral ve Kati Yakitlar Tic. A.Ş., Krutrade AG and Mir Trade AG. Whilst the former two firms were established in Turkey the latter two were not: Krutrade AG was established in Austria and Mir Trade AG was established in Switzerland. In its conclusion of the investigation, however, the board was unable to establish a breach of Article 4 of the Law by Mir Trade AG: it needed to obtain the necessary documents to support its investigation and findings which proved impossible in practice. The board attempted to rely on Articles 17 and 23 of the Turkey–EFTA States Free Trade Agreement and made a request to Switzerland seeking cooperation to facilitate access to such documents. This request, however, was rejected by Switzerland citing the impossibility of enforcing Swiss competition rules in this case. With regard to Krutrade AG, the board was able to find a breach by the firm of Article 4 of the Law though the board failed to reach a final decision due to the failure to communicate its finding officially and properly to the firm. Interestingly, the board had sought the cooperation of the Austrian authorities in relation to two

[102] See further below.

aspects: establishing a breach of Article 4 of the Law and communicating its pre-decision finding to Krutrade AG. In relation to the first aspect – which the board aimed to conduct within the framework of the CUA – the request was transferred by the Austrian authorities to the European Commission. On its part the Commission could not answer the board in the positive on the grounds that there were no implementation rules for the competition law provisions within the CUA;[103] restrictions of confidentiality existed;[104] and there was in any case lack of anti-competitive effect in the EC.

Overall, the authority has followed an open and flexible approach to international cooperation.[105] It has paid significant attention to the views of international bodies, notably the OECD, about the development of competition law and policy in Turkey and has sought to improve its practice and work in light of good practices emerging in other jurisdictions and the international level more generally.[106] Two

[103] Apparently the Commission found Article 43 to be *insufficient* as a legal basis for the cooperation sought in the case. The article provides that one party under the agreement may request the other party to initiate enforcement action if the conduct carried out in the territory of the latter adversely affects the interests of the former. Under paragraph 3 of the article, however, the requested party enjoys *complete* discretion in deciding to answer the request in the positive.

[104] Another occasion on which the European Commission rejected a request by the board for cooperation on grounds of confidentiality arose in 2004 following the opening of a cartel investigation by the board into the electrical equipment market. The Commission had collected material to which the board was hoping to gain access but which the Commission felt could not be disclosed due to the prohibition contained in Article 28 of Regulation 1/2003 which provides that 'without prejudice to the exchange and to the use of information foreseen in Articles 11, 12, 14, 15 and 27, the Commission and the competition authorities of the Member States . . . shall not disclose information acquired or exchanged by them pursuant to this Regulation and of the kind covered by the obligation of professional secrecy'. In response to the point raised by the board that exchange of information between the parties was possible under Article 36 of the CUA, the Commission relied on the limitation in the article, namely that such exchange was subject to the requirements of professional and business secrecy.

[105] As far as its relationship with the European Commission is concerned, the authority – as can be gleaned from the *Seized Coal* and *Electrical Equipment* cases – has been prepared to engage in full cooperation even if this would involve exchanging confidential information. On its part, however, the Commission has been reluctant to embrace such an open-ended approach to cooperation and has maintained that confidentiality considerations would always prevail even with full implementation of all of the provisions of the CUA including those dealing with state aid.

[106] Interestingly, there is a legislative expression given to the need to consult foreign experiences. Article 27(h) of the Law specifically lists such consultation through monitoring the 'legislation, practices, policies and measures' of other countries as one of the duties to be performed by the board.

key tools that have been employed here are technical assistance and capacity building.[107] The authority has also engaged quite extensively in the work of the OECD, the proceedings of the United Nations Conference on Trade and Development (UNCTAD), the preparation of the competition agenda of the World Trade Organisation (WTO) and more recently in the work of the International Competition Network (ICN).

The most important agreements concluded by Turkey which have competition relevance are the Association and Customs Union Agreements, the Free Trade Agreement with EFTA States and the Free Trade Agreements concluded with Israel, Morocco, Palestine and Tunisia.[108]

### *4.8.1 The EC–Turkey association*

The Association Agreement between Turkey and the EC was signed in Ankara on 12 September 1963 and became effective on 1 December 1964. The aim of this agreement is to promote and strengthen the trade and economic relations between the EC and Turkey 'while taking full account of the need to ensure an accelerated development of the Turkish economy'[109] and to achieve these objectives the agreement advocates that a customs union be established. In addition, to ensure the proper functioning of the association, Article 4 requires alignment of the economic policies of Turkey and the EC. By virtue of Article 10, matters relating to trade in goods shall be dealt with by the customs union. Regarding competition, the agreement provides that the provisions on competition must be applied by the parties in their relations. According to Article 28, accession of Turkey to the EU is subject to 'full acceptance by

[107] The authority has mainly been the beneficiary but also a provider of technical assistance and capacity-building activities. In the former role, the authority has participated in various programmes and activities organised within the Technical Assistance and Information Exchange Instrument of the Institution Building unit of Directorate-General Enlargement of the European Commission (TAIEX) and the Barcelona Process and those held by national European competition authorities and the Antitrust Division of the US Department of Justice. In the latter role, the authority has offered international technical assistance and organised capacity-building activities for the Balkan States and Mongolia. There has been no effort, however, to engage in similar initiatives with other MECs.

[108] The Turkey–Tunisia Agreement is discussed at pp 151–2 below. Other FTAs concluded by Turkey and MECs are the Turkey–Syria FTA (signed in December 2004) and the Turkey–Egypt FTA (signed in December 2005).

[109] See Article 2 of the agreement.

Turkey of the obligations arising out of the Treaty establishing the Community'. To ensure the proper implementation of the association, a Council of Association is established by Article 6 of the agreement consisting of members representing both parties. The council has the power to settle any disputes relating to the application or interpretation of the agreement, make recommendations to achieve the objectives of the agreement, give decisions in cases and set up committees to assist it in its tasks.

The agreement paved the way for closer relations with the EC. However, its competition law relevance and influence within Turkey does not appear to have emerged in concrete form until the Customs Union Agreement (CUA) began to appear on the horizon.[110] It is arguable therefore that competition law in Turkey was not seriously considered and was not adopted merely as a desire to comply with the agreement but rather as a desire for closer political association with the EC. The relevant competition provisions of the CUA are outlined in Articles 32–34. According to these, all agreements, decisions and concerted practices which prevent, restrict or distort competition are prohibited, especially those which fix prices, limit or control production, markets, technical development or investment, share markets or sources of supply, apply dissimilar conditions to equivalent transactions and make conclusion of contracts conditional upon acceptance of supplementary offers. Article 32(3) exempts from this prohibition those agreements, decisions and concerted practices which contribute to improving the production or distribution of goods or promote technical or economic progress and allow consumers a fair share of the resulting benefit. However, the competition restriction should be essential for achieving the beneficial goals and should not eliminate competition in a significant part of the market. In addition, Articles 33 and 34 proscribe abuse of a dominant position and state aid which distorts or threatens to distort competition on the basis that these practices may affect trade between the Community and Turkey. Article 42 provides that state monopolies must be regulated to ensure that the conditions for the marketing and procurement of goods between Turkey and the EC Member States are not affected. An Association Council was established under the agreement which was given the responsibility of adopting rules for the implementation of the competition law provisions, within two years following the entry into force of the Customs Union.[111]

[110] See further below. [111] See Article 37 of the agreement. See further above at pp 81–2.

### *4.8.2 The Turkey–EFTA States Agreement*

Turkey signed the Free Trade Agreement with EFTA on 10 December 1991 in Geneva, which entered into force on 1 April 1992, to develop economic relations with the EFTA States. For this purpose, the agreement sets out rules for fair conditions of competition within the context of trade between the parties. According to these, all agreements, decisions and concerted practices which prevent, restrict or distort competition and abuse of a dominant position are incompatible with the agreement and thus prohibited.[112] The activities of public undertakings and undertakings to which special or exclusive rights have been granted also fall within the ambit of these provisions. According to Article 18, any state aid which favours certain undertakings or the production of certain goods and thereby distorts or threatens to distort competition is also proscribed. In order to enhance transparency the parties must exchange information regarding state aid. For the purposes of promoting economic development, the agreement did allow Turkey to grant indirect aid to export of goods and aid with higher intensity than would be tolerated for EFTA States until December 1995. Furthermore, Article 9 provides for the regulation of state monopolies to ensure that the conditions for the marketing and procurement of goods between the EFTA States and Turkey are not affected. A Joint Committee is established under Article 25 to oversee the proper implementation of the agreement. Each party is represented at the Joint Committee, which must meet at least once a year or whenever necessary.

### *4.8.3 Free trade agreements with MECs*

#### 4.8.3.1 Turkey–Israel FTA

Turkey signed a Free Trade Agreement with Israel in May 1997 to enhance economic relations between these two countries. The agreement provides the necessary rules for competition to ensure fair trade between Turkey and Israel. According to Article 25 therefore, all agreements, decisions and concerted practices which prevent, restrict or distort competition, abuse of a dominant position and state aid which distorts or threatens to distort competition are prohibited because they may affect trade between Turkey and Israel. Regarding state aid, the agreement further provides that the parties shall submit an annual

[112] See Article 17 of the agreement.

report to each other on the total amount of state aid they have each given. Article 13 provides for the regulation of state monopolies to ensure that the conditions for the marketing and procurement of goods between Turkey and Israel are not affected. A Joint Committee is established under Article 27 as the body responsible for the implementation of the competition law provisions of the agreement.[113]

#### 4.8.3.2 Turkey–Morocco FTA

Turkey and Morocco signed a Free Trade Agreement in April 2004 which entered into force in January 2006. The aim of this agreement is to promote economic cooperation between the parties and for this purpose provide fair conditions of competition. Accordingly, Article 25 lays down the rules relating to competition which prohibit all agreements, decisions and concerted practices which prevent, restrict or distort competition, abuse of a dominant position and state aid which distorts or threatens to distort competition on the basis that they may affect trade between Turkey and Morocco. The parties must annually exchange information about the total amount of state aid given in order to ensure transparency. Regarding state monopolies, Article 21 of the agreement provides that these must be regulated to ensure that there is no discrimination in the conditions for the marketing and procurement of goods between Turkey and Morocco. A Joint Committee, in which each party is represented, is established under Article 30 to ensure the proper implementation of the agreement.

#### 4.8.3.3 Turkey–Palestine FTA

Turkey signed a Free Trade Agreement with Palestine in July 2004, which entered into force in June 2005, to enhance economic cooperation between the parties and create a competition environment. For this purpose, rules relating to competition are provided under Article 24 of the agreement, according to which all agreements, decisions and concerted practices which prevent, restrict or distort competition, abuse of a dominant position and state aid which distorts or threatens to distort competition are prohibited given that they may affect trade between Turkey and Palestine. Transparency must be ensured in relation to state aid and as such the parties must exchange information with each other on individual cases of state aid. Article 26 provides for the regulation of state monopolies to ensure that the conditions for the marketing and

[113] See Article 25(2) of the agreement.

procurement of goods between Turkey and Palestine are not affected. Furthermore, an 'economic cooperation and technical assistance' chapter has been included in the agreement to support economic development in Palestine, since the Turkish economy is more advanced than the Palestinian economy. This will in turn enable Palestine to benefit more from the agreement. Responsibility for the implementation of this agreement is vested in the Joint Committee established under Article 42.

## 4.9 Reflections

### *4.9.1 Social, economic and political issues*

A major observation that should be made about the development of competition law and policy in Turkey concerns the lack of a social dimension.[114] This apparently sets the Republic in a markedly different situation to that of other MECs, where competition law and policy have developed with a strong social and cultural element. The development of the Law and the Turkish competition law regime has adopted a European style of legislating and the various instruments of secondary legislation have reinforced the European orientation of the Law. Competition law in Turkey was developed with a political vision in sight, namely eventual EU membership. Competition law and policy in the Republic should therefore not be viewed in isolation but as part of a larger picture displaying the 'Eur' whilst omitting the 'asian' half of this Eurasian country. The ideology of the Law appears to have been an economic one based on political foundations of strategic ambitions and desires which make the Turkish model of competition law a highly interesting one. In this ideology both the economic[115] and political elements are vital.

### *4.9.2 Following the EC model*

The state of affairs described in the previous section raises many important questions not only about the suitability but also about the

[114] It was said above in the context of the discussion of the requirements for exemption under Article 5 of the Law that arguably the requirement in paragraph (b) of the Article (dealing with benefiting consumers) has a social expression. As we noted, however, this has hardly received any concrete expression in practice.

[115] As was seen at p 80 above the economic dimension in the Turkish competition law regime can be seen as extending to the Constitution of the Republic, in particular Article 167 of the Constitution.

sustainability of a purely European approach not quite within a European environment. The enforcement record of the Competition Authority reveals the need for competition law in Turkey: anti-competitive behaviour and abusive conduct are not non-existent in the country. Therefore the question is not whether competition law is needed in Turkey: but rather whether it should not be shaped and adapted to its geographical setting? Unlike other MECs, the legislative history and intent of the Law does not show any serious uncertainty or legislative indecisiveness with regard to whether the EC should be used as a model for the purposes of enacting a domestic competition law in Turkey. After all, competition law was only considered seriously because of the motivation created by contacts between the Turkish government and the European Commission and the promising links with the EC which began to appear on the horizon in the early 1990s, which seem to be deeper than those initiated in the 1960s with the signing of the 1963 Association Agreement. Policy-makers in Turkey therefore made the assumption that a competition law in the country *must* be based on the EC system. Whilst the EC system is a highly successful one and a reliable model for countries to use as a source for consultation, there has been a failure in the case of Turkey to understand a crucial aspect revolving around competition law and policy, namely that it is highly controversial (indeed wrong) simply to parachute the competition law of one country into the legal system of another. There is a need to appreciate that the adoption and development of competition law and policy in a particular country is very much related to and depends on that country's culture and type of economy as well as on its various socio-economic and socio-political circumstances.[116] Indeed this axiom is all the more important to realise in a country such as Turkey, where a different culture and tradition from those prevailing in all of the twenty-seven Member States of the EC exist. This would have been equally true if we were to look at the situation *retrospectively* as early as 1994 when the Law was adopted. At that time, the EC had twelve Member States and fifteen 'potential' or 'associate' Members, at least eleven of which were Central and Eastern European countries. Even when compared to the latter, which had to adopt competition law based on EC competition rules as part of their future accession to the EC,

[116] Kovacic, 'The competition policy entrepreneur and law reform in formerly communist and socialist countries' (1996) 11 *American University Journal of International Law and Policy* 437.

Turkey had, and still has, a different culture and tradition which must be recognised as influential in the development of competition law and policy. Earlier parts of this chapter succinctly demonstrated the special circumstances of Turkey as a country and as a society. There is no doubt that the EC offers a hugely successful competition law regime which – along with the US regime – is one of the most obvious models to be studied by countries seeking to develop competition law and policy domestically. This does not imply, however, that the regime *must* necessarily be closely followed by such countries, including Turkey, without the necessary adjustments for the purposes of accommodating those countries' particular economic, cultural, political and social circumstances.

### 4.9.3 The Association and Customs Union Agreements

It is not quite clear how the contribution made by the Association Agreement and Customs Union Agreement (CUA) should be judged. From a non-competition law angle, the success in non- but related competition matters has not been particularly impressive. A notable example in this regard can be found in relation to anti-dumping measures and their application within the framework of the CUA. From a competition angle on the other hand, a major observation that is worth making relates to the lack of effective framework for dealing with competition problems and concerns arising under the competition law provisions of the CUA. Currently, the Association Committee and Association Council act as the relevant bodies applying the rules. It is arguable whether the *status quo* should be changed with a specialist body being set up to deal with competition law breaches relating to the territory covered under the CUA. The chances of this happening, however, do not appear to be particularly realistic at the moment, which is likely to limit the effectiveness of the rules.

Beyond the need for an effective framework, the provisions of the CUA have not been implemented. As we saw above, this has given rise to enforcement problems in practice. From the European Commission's perspective, implementation of the rules will not be possible so long as Turkey has not complied with its commitments under the CUA fully and completely, including the adoption of specific rules and suitable mechanism dealing with state aid. The adoption of state aid rules has proved to be a problematic issue. On its part, the Commission has repeatedly 'reminded' Turkey of the need to adopt state aid rules highlighting the absence of such rules from the Turkish chapter on competition and the Law in particular.[117] The fact that Turkey has not adopted state aid rules makes it interesting to enquire whether Turkey is in breach of the CUA which in turn demands an examination of whether it is actually under an obligation to adopt suitable rules and mechanism for dealing with state aid cases. Answering this question requires consideration of three specific provisions of the CUA. Under Article 34 the prohibition on state aid featuring in Article 87 EC is included for the purposes of catching aid granted by the Member States of the EC and Turkey which distorts competition between the EC and Turkey. This corresponds with the treatment of collusion and abuse of dominance. However, whereas Article 37 of the CUA requires Turkey to *adopt* rules dealing with these two business phenomena, Article 39 of the CUA merely lays down an obligation on Turkey to *adapt* its rules and standards in the area of state aid. Therefore, there is no obligation on Turkey to adopt state aid rules compatible with those of the EC despite the fact that interestingly the agreement lays down an obligation on Turkey to implement the prohibition on harmful state aid.[118]

The slow progress made by Turkey in the field of state aid was for a long time caused by daunting bureaucracy and lack of decisiveness over whether a special mechanism with an independent institution should be set up to deal with state aid or whether state aid rules should be added to the Law itself, giving the power of enforcement to the authority and the board. This indecisiveness appears to have been effectively eliminated with the government's decision – contrary to the recommendation and views of the authority and the board –[119] to propose a bill aiming to establish two new specialist authorities: the State Aid Monitoring and Supervising Board,[120] and the Directorate General for State Aid under

[117] With regard to the deeper cooperation the authority has been seeking to establish with the European Commission as outlined above, it appears that the Commission has attempted to use the state aid question as a bargaining chip making it clear that full implementation of the provisions of the CUA can only happen following the adoption of state aid rules and a suitable mechanism for their enforcement by Turkey. The emphasis on implementation here is important given that it is considered by the board to be a key step towards securing such deeper cooperation – a view that is clear to the commission itself and with which the Commission agrees.

[118] See Article 37 of the agreement.

[119] The authority and the board have been particularly concerned about the uncertainty this proposal creates and the controversy it causes. According to the authority's view, it is the better-placed body with the relevant expertise to handle state aid cases.

[120] The proposal is for this State Aid Board to be made up of representatives of the government and to be armed with judicial powers. Its decisions, however, will be subject to review at the level of the Council of State.

the auspices of the State Planning Organisation as the main body responsible for the enforcement of the proposed state aid rules. This proposal to establish an autonomous system for state aid is considered to be problematic given the discretion it leaves in the hands of the government and the real possibility for this discretion to be utilised in a bureaucratic way to further and achieve purely political goals and objectives.[121]

Another aspect of the CUA worth highlighting concerns the obligation of Turkey to apply 'the principles contained in block exemption Regulations in force in the Community'.[122] The various communiqués adopted by the board over the years have incorporated the principles contained in various EC block exemptions Regulations. This legislative exercise, however, has not been exhaustive with none of the communiqués adopted dealing with key block exemptions such as the technology transfer block exemption.[123] Interestingly, the board has not considered its incomplete legislative task to pose any significant problems given that its approach has been to treat all EC block exemption Regulations as *de facto* part of the Turkish competition law regime.[124]

### 4.9.4 Achievement and progress of the authority

The Turkish Competition Authority has secured impressive achievements with quite an effective application of the competition rules. Its style of engagement has been 'positivist', which reflects the nature of the Law. As an instrument, the Law can be considered to be more positive than, for

[121] It should be noted that the European Commission has been in favour of establishing a state aid authority which enjoys operational independence. It is doubtful, however, whether this proposal would fit with the Commission's conception in this case, given the expected lack of independence of the proposed board.

[122] See Article 39(2)(a) of the CUA.

[123] The current technology transfer block exemption Regulation in the EC is Regulation 772/2004 on the application of Article 81(3) of the Treaty to categories of technology transfer agreements, OJ [2004] L123/11 which has replaced the old technology transfer Regulation 240/96. It should be added here that the Law is silent on the treatment of intellectual property rights, especially in relation to licensing of such rights which, as can be seen from the EC experience, can restrict competition especially where exclusivity is granted by the licensor to the licensee. Currently, the only reference to intellectual property rights can be found in Communiqué 2002/2 on vertical agreements, in which it is stated that intellectual property rights would fall within the scope of the communiqué where they are ancillary to a vertical agreement.

[124] The board's view is that situations covered by EC block exemption Regulations are unlikely to be challenged by it and where it becomes involved in such situations it is inclined to adopt a lenient approach.

example the EC rules, on which it is based: it goes beyond mere prohibition of anti-competitive behaviour and abusive practices towards the need to 'establish' competition. This positive nature of the Law could be said to be a reflection of the relevant rules of the Turkish Constitution and the nature of the provisions of the CUA. Both of these important documents lay down *positive* obligations on the government in the field of competition law.[125]

The impressive achievements of the authority have been widely acknowledged by important bodies, most notably the OECD in its 2005 Peer Review Report when it commented that the Turkish Competition Authority has developed 'a reputation as one of Turkey's most effective autonomous agencies, winning respect and support from leaders in the business community, and playing a critical role in moving the Turkish economy forward to greater reliance on competition-based and consumer welfare-orientated market mechanisms'.[126] The authority has played an important role in harmonising Turkey's competition law with EC competition rules. However, in this regard, as we saw throughout the chapter, further improvements remain necessary to achieve the desired alignment with EC competition law and elimination of inconsistencies in the harmonisation of the regime with that of the EC, which are widely considered as crucial in advancing Turkey's goal of achieving full membership of the EU.

The important progress made by the authority has materialised in a relatively short period of time. This has been facilitated by, among other things, the technical assistance and benefits of capacity-building activities it has received from other competition authorities and through its participation in international fora; the increase in recent years in the budget allocated to it; and the recruiting of staff with relevant expertise and qualifications. In relation to the latter the authority's task has not been simple. At various stages it has faced a problem of attracting and keeping such staff with different officials (including potential ones) being attracted to financially more lucrative positions in the private sector. The authority has devised various strategies and programmes to help in its task such as enabling officials to benefit from attending fully-funded postgraduate programmes at European universities and engaging in academic activities.[127]

125 In relation to the Constitution see p 80 above and in relation to the CUA see pp 109–10 also above.
126 Peer Review Report on 'Competition Law and Policy in Turkey' OECD (2005), p 3.
127 The board has placed particular emphasis on academic engagement and input by the authority's staff.

There is scope for further improvement in the work of the authority, however, especially in relation to how the authority relies on and applies the Law in practice. Several provisions of the Law would benefit from improvement and clarification. In addition to those discussed above, such as the concerted practice presumption provision, it is possible to refer to Article 9 of the Law which deals with among other things actions to be taken by the board once it establishes a breach of the provisions of the Law on collusion, abuse of dominance or mergers; the right to complain given to natural and legal persons with legitimate interest; and interim measures which may be issued by the board in exceptional circumstances. Obscurely, the article states that prior to adopting a decision finding a breach of Article 4, 6 or 7 of the Law the board must inform in writing the firms concerned of its view on how the infringement in question should be terminated. A narrow interpretation of this would be to consider this as part of a step by the board equivalent to that taken by many competition authorities around the world by which the authority notifies its findings to the firm(s) concerned and thereby gives such firm(s) the opportunity to submit their views to the authority before the latter adopts its final decision.[128] A wider interpretation of this provision, on the other hand, would be that the purpose behind the provision is to provide a legal basis for competition law settlements to be reached with firms. This interpretation appears to be consistent with the board's conception of the article, namely that settlements, albeit in limited form,[129] are possible under the provision. Nonetheless, the article would benefit from clarification, to make it clear that settlements are possible, outlining the conditions to be met and indicating the stages of the investigation at which settlements may be sought and reached.

### *4.9.5 The strict time frames*

The Law appears to subject the authority and the board to strict time frames in relation to various aspects of competition law practice, not only in the field of merger control where strict time limits on the work of the competition authority are considered to be vital. It is debatable

[128] This would correspond to the 'statement of objections' produced by the European Commission when enforcing Articles 81 and 82 EC.

[129] For a settlement to be possible the firm(s) concerned must enter into a commitment to terminate the infringement in question and to reach the settlement and this must happen at an early stage.

| Situation | Time limit | Article of the Law |
|---|---|---|
| Preliminary investigations (other than mergers) | Thirty days (with ten additional days for the board to decide whether to commence a formal investigation) | Articles 40 and 41 |
| Preliminary investigations (mergers) * | Fifteen days | Article 10 |
| Completion of a formal investigation | Six months (with the possibility for a single extension of an additional Six months) | Article 43 |
| Post investigation communication between the authority and firms | Seventy-five days (one extension of thirty days is possible) | Article 45 |
| Holding an oral hearing | Thirty to sixty days following the end of the investigation | Article 46 |
| Duration of the hearing | Five consecutive days | Article 47 |
| Adoption of final decision by the board | Fifteen days following the hearing | Article 48 |

* The Law here follows in part the German merger control regime, under which if the German Cartel Office intends to block a merger operation it needs to send the merging parties a 'one-month' letter within one month of the start of the investigation.

whether this state of affairs is desirable especially for a developing competition authority facing a challenging task of not only enforcing competition law but also engaging in competition advocacy. The table below illustrates the different provisions of the Law which impose strict time frames on the authority and the board.

### *4.9.6 General deficiencies*

The Law suffers from several problems. Some of these problems call for urgent action whereas others can only realistically be expected to be addressed in light of wider changes in the legal and political arena in

Turkey. Among the former problems are the absence of sufficient public awareness and understanding of competition law and policy and the remarkable absence of a competition culture in the country. The authority and the board have made important inroads into effective enforcement of the Law and advocating competition at the legislative and policy formulation level, ensuring their presence is felt. In relation to the public strand of competition advocacy and the building of a competition culture in the country, however, the authority and the board still lag behind the ambitious goals they have set for themselves whether in light of the desire for full membership of the EU or within the context of participation in the work of the OECD and more recently the ICN. Part of the problem here has been caused by a delay on the part of the authority to engage in a vigorous and comprehensive competition advocacy programme.

Another problem which revolves around competition understanding but at a different level concerns the judiciary. It is difficult to maintain that courts, or the State Council at least, have come to enjoy adequate competence, let alone sufficient independence in terms of their competition thinking and handling of competition matters brought to their attention. The need for judges to enjoy such competence and independence is crucial in light of the fact that the Law facilitates judicial involvement not only at the level of reviewing board decisions but also at that of private enforcement and actions for damages and compensation which the Law clearly encourages and facilitates.[130] It would be useful here to consider the issue of competence of the judiciary to apply competition law and policy in the country within the wider context of the degree of separation of powers in Turkey. The judiciary in Turkey is declared to be independent, but the need for judicial reform and confirmation of its independence are subject to open debate.[131] Nonetheless, it should be noted that only when the judiciary is fully independent from the executive and legislative branches of the state can the courts effectively enforce the competition rules. On the other hand, the second type of problems underlying the Law, which as we noted can only realistically be expected to be addressed as part of wider changes, can be illustrated with reference to the issue of governmental control over the enforcement of the competition rules. Although the Law

130 See p 101 above.

131 A good illustration here can be found outside the field of competition law. Internationally recognised human rights such as freedom of thought, expression, assembly and movement are expressly enshrined in the Constitution. However, judicially these rights have at times been narrowly interpreted.

contains no direct reference to such control, it is important not to be misled by this 'silence' given that such control does actually exist in practice. The control in this case can be seen in relation to legislative activities and policy formulation. As we saw above, the authority and the board have had little influence over the debate and decision-making concerning the proposed state aid rules and mechanism. Another example can be seen in the case of the adoption of the Regulation on Distribution and Customer Services in Natural Gas.[132] A third example can be found in relation to price regulation of certain commodities.[133] All of these examples demonstrate that the government control and the lack of sufficient influence by the authority and the board are problematic and should be addressed. For this to happen, however, it would be realistic to expect a change in the political arena more generally with an effective decision by the government to strengthen and support the authority and the board further by facilitating a greater say and role for them. In fact the failure of the government to offer this greater support is questionable given that – since the EU agreed in principle to commence membership negotiations with Turkey – the goal of EU membership has become an even greater objective and the government has been fully aware that realising this objective rests in no small way on the competition law and policy question.

### *4.9.7 The Law and free market*

In the case of Turkey there is a crucial question that must be asked in relation to the Law, namely whether it should serve as an instrument for the purposes of facilitating and building a free market economy in the country or whether it should be used on the assumption that a free market economy is in existence. It is important to be aware that in the case of countries with developing economies, competition law tends to be used as an instrument to create and maintain competition, whilst in countries with developed economies the law is used for the purposes of promoting competition through protecting it. As will become apparent from the discussion in later chapters this has been the case in several MECs. Therefore the undesirability of the former adopting almost exactly the same competition laws as those found in the latter should be recognised. Looking at the approach of the Turkish Competition Authority over the years – along with the legislative intent behind the Law – it appears that competition law is perceived as a tool used on the

[132] See pp 98–9 above. [133] See note 84 above and accompanying discussion.

assumption that a free market economy is in existence. This assumption is problematic in many respects given that the Turkish economy is still undergoing privatisation in relation to different key sectors[134] and the process of liberalisation – although seeing significant progress – is still quite a way from becoming fully mature.

There may be several explanations for the particular choice made by the authority and the board in relation to their use of the Law in practice. One explanation is that the Law is intended to fit within the country's international economic policy and political agenda and one that would attract foreign investment by firms familiar with the legal environment of the EC.[135] Hence by operating the Law on the basis of this assumption, maturity in thinking and enforcement will be displayed with an EC or Western style. Another explanation is that there is a particular desire and interest on the part of those policy-makers to minimise the potential role judges may play when adjudicating over matters related to the Law,[136] and therefore prevent possible judicial pronouncements, which may derail the Western vision of the Law and the strategic vision underlying its application and enforcement. Such determination nonetheless can be seen as controversial and one that is bound to cause more problems than it seeks to avoid.

### *4.9.8 Future directions*

It would be appropriate to end the reflections on the Law and the Turkish competition law regime with a brief consideration of the future directions of the Turkish competition law scene. It is widely believed that the adoption of the Law has had a positive economic effect both within Turkey as well as in relation to foreign trade, which the Law is

134 These sectors include sugar, tobacco, air transport and airlines, oil refinery, among others; other sectors are expected to be added to this list in the near future which include electricity, petrochemical manufacturing and banking.

135 The need for countries with developing economies to adopt competition rules based on those of countries with developing economies has been advocated by many writers. See Langenfeld and Blitzer, 'Is competition policy the last thing Central and Eastern Europe need' (1991) 6 *American University Journal of International Law and Policy* 347; Feinberg and Meurs, 'Privatization and antitrust in Eastern Europe: the importance of entry' (1994) 39 *Antitrust Bulletin* 797.

136 Interestingly, even if this explanation is accepted as correct it is unlikely this determination will survive in practice given the fact that many provisions in the Law are worded in such a way that the need for guidance, whether judicially or administratively, on their application in the future will be inevitable.

considered to have expanded in addition to attracting increased foreign investment in the country. This is hardly surprising given that one of the aims behind the Law was to expand the private sector and the fact that the Law has encouraged business confidence and created a legal and regulatory environment highly similar to that of the EC, with which many international firms are familiar.

The useful review conducted by the OECD of competition law and development in Turkey over the years has produced several recommendations, which mainly aim at bringing the Turkish competition law regime closer to that of the EC and bringing Turkey to closer compliance with all aspects of the CUA, including those under which *adaptation* as opposed to *adoption* of rules is required. At the present time it is not possible to predict with certainty whether Turkey will accede to the EU. Nonetheless, based on all current indications – whether based on the work and policy of the authority and the board or the position adopted by the European Commission – it appears to be fairly clear that one should expect further and closer alignment of the Turkish competition law regime with that of the EC. To reach this destination, however, several important steps will need to be taken by the authority and the board and the Turkish government more generally. These include: adopting state aid rules and mechanism; clarifying the application of the competition rules in the special sectors and the relationship of the authority with sectoral regulators; abolishing the negative clearance notification mechanism and removing or clarifying the concerted practice presumption; enhancing the authority's merger control practice and refining the merger rules in the regime; engaging in deeper and wider competition advocacy leading to robust competition culture; and remedying the various deficiencies and closing the gaps and loopholes identified in the discussion above. Achieving these will undoubtedly enable Turkey to reach its competition law destination which in turn would enhance the prospects of fulfilling the dream of full EU membership. Until that happens, however, this dream will remain a European dream from the other side of the border.

# 5

# The Arab Maghreb countries

The Maghreb countries – or as more widely known the North African Arab countries of Algeria, Libya, Mauritania, Morocco and Tunisia – have since the early 1990s experienced extremely interesting and important phases of development and transformation. These five countries have strong commonalities and similarities in relation to culture, language, tradition and legal systems which many would argue have been facilitated by their geographic location. Others attribute these commonalities to their link to France and the existence of a French rule in most of them in the early parts of the twentieth century. These commonalities have, among other things, facilitated cooperation between these countries, though they have also been the cause of some frictions and deep disagreements. An important achievement of the Maghreb countries in forging closer economic, social and political ties among themselves has been the Arab Maghreb Union (AMU) which was established in 1989.

The roots of the AMU, however, extend to a fruitless attempt in 1964 by Algeria, Libya, Morocco and Tunisia to coordinate and harmonise their development plans, inter-regional trade and relations with the EC. That attempt took the form of a conference attended by the Economic Ministers of the four countries and the creation of the Permanent Consultation Council of the Maghreb Countries, *Conseil Permanent Cunsultatif du Maghreb* (CPCM) at that conference. The AMU has very ambitious goals and objectives including establishing closer ties and solidarity, common defence and free movement of goods and services. To date, however, these objectives have not all been achieved.

## 5.1 Algeria: replacing draconian legislation with a mechanism for consultation

Algeria has had an interesting experience with competition law and policy. This experience began in 1989 with the Republic adopting the

Law on Prices,[1] which strictly speaking was not a competition tool and suffered from many deficiencies in practice. That Law was repealed in 1995 upon the entry into force of the Competition Ordinance 1995.[2] The Ordinance came to promote competition in Algeria through the introduction of an adequate tool for protecting and organising the patterns of competition forces so that economic efficiency in local markets could be stimulated and the welfare of local consumers could be maximised. Special emphasis was placed on transparency and honesty in commercial relationships. In effect the Ordinance ushered in the beginning of a specific, modern competition law regime in the country but was for many reasons deemed to suffer from shortcomings and in the early years of its existence calls were already heard for replacing it with a more modern competition instrument. Principally, the Ordinance suffered from poor drafting and did not highlight the demarcation between different business phenomena and their treatment, namely collusion between firms, abuse of dominance and harmful concentrations or mergers. Secondly, the Ordinance was largely viewed as having an imposing character and the preference that came to prevail was in favour of replacing such legislative style with an instrument, which could facilitate 'consultation' between the competition authority, the Competition Council, and firms and foster a competition culture and enable the council to engage in competition advocacy. Thirdly, the structure of the Competition Council was considered to require restructuring in order to make it a more 'dynamic' institution able to police markets effectively and help 'upgrade' the level of competition in local markets. A fourth reason was a hybrid intrinsic-extrinsic one and concerned the government's desire to bring the Algerian competition law regime closer to that of the EC and build a strong platform for global integration. Two particular developments appear to have played a major role in this regard. First, Algeria concluded an Association Agreement with the EC which was signed in Valencia on 22 April 2002 and entered into force on 1 September 2005, replacing the Cooperation Agreement between the parties of 1976. Articles 41–43 of this agreement deal with competition issues, setting out rules applying to agreements, decisions and concerted practices which restrict, prevent or distort competition, the abuse of a dominant position, the behaviour of monopolies and public enterprises and enterprises which have been granted special or exclusive rights. The Association Agreement aimed at improving relations between the EC and Algeria in terms of free trade and

[1] Law No. 89–12 of 5 July 1989. [2] Ordinance No. 95–06 of 25 January 1995.

economic liberalisation and for this purpose it obligated Algeria to introduce modern competition legislation. Secondly, in December 2002 a Declaration on Co-operation between Algeria and the EFTA States was issued. The purpose of this is to develop the economic and trade relations between the EFTA States and Algeria which would ultimately lead to the establishment of a free trade area. Accordingly the EFTA States and Algeria must develop their cooperation in a way which will strengthen free competition and liberalise their trade relations. In pursuit of this, the declaration stipulates that views be exchanged between the EFTA States and Algeria to determine the conditions for free and undistorted competition and they must jointly discuss the actions necessary to establish a free trade area. A Joint Committee is created to review the cooperation between the EFTA States and Algeria and to make any recommendations it considers necessary. The possibility of a Free Trade Agreement between the EFTA States and Algeria is currently under discussion.

### *5.1.1 Competition Ordinance 2003*

In light of the above-mentioned developments and to achieve the objectives mentioned above, the government considered modernising its competition legislation a top priority. At the end, Competition Ordinance 2003 (the Ordinance) was adopted and among other things it repealed Ordinance 1995.[3]

#### 5.1.1.1 Aims, objectives and scope

In a similar vein to its predecessor Ordinance 1995, the Ordinance aims at regulating conditions of competition in the market, preventing harms to competition, stimulating economic efficiency and maximising consumer welfare. The Ordinance brings within its scope anti-competitive behaviour, abusive conduct and certain economic concentrations whether those involving private or public firms so long as in the case of the latter, doing so would not interfere with the exercise of prerogatives of public powers or the exercise of public tasks and activities.[4]

#### 5.1.1.2 Pricing activities and policies

Article 4 of the Ordinance shows the importance being attached to the freedom of firms to determine their pricing policies. This is considered to be a cornerstone of the market mechanism and a modern policy

[3] Ordinance No. 03–03 of 19 July 2003. [4] See Article 2 of the Ordinance.

approach which Algeria came to embrace and which the Ordinance came to support. This principle, however, is not without exceptions or limitations: the government regards certain products as being 'strategic', something which in practice may necessitate reverting to special regulation of the pricing of these products.[5] This price regulatory approach is also open to the government in cases where excessive increase in prices occurs as a result of serious disturbances within the market, difficulties in supplying the market or a particular geographical area or due to the existence of natural monopolies. Article 5 of the Ordinance, which provides for this power of the government, requires that the opinion of the Competition Council be sought and that in all cases the measures adopted must be temporary and not exceeding a maximum duration of six months with no possibility for renewal.

#### 5.1.1.3 Influence of EC competition law

The Ordinance shows the great extent to which it is modelled on EC competition rules, in particular Articles 81 and 82 EC and the Merger Regulation,[6] and this confirms the government's intention when considering repealing Ordinance 1995 to bring its competition regime closer to the EC system of competition law. The Ordinance also shows similarities in approach with other European competition law regimes, notably (and perhaps understandably) the French regime and to a lesser extent the German one.[7] The idea for creating an independent competition authority seems to have been informed by the experience of these regimes. Thus, the Algerian regime – as embodied in the Ordinance – has a strong European flavour.

#### 5.1.1.4 Non-competition considerations

Article 9 of the Ordinance contains rather broad criteria making an exemption possible in the case of a behaviour caught under Article 6

[5] See Article 4 of the Ordinance.

[6] Note here that the reference is to the old EC Regulation 4064/89 on the control of concentrations between undertakings, OJ [1990] L257/13 on which the Ordinance is based but which was replaced in May 2004 by a new Regulation 139/2004 (the current EC Merger Regulation), OJ [2004] L24/1.

[7] In relation to the latter this can be seen in the case of the Ordinance's provisions on merger control where a merger operation prohibited by the Competition Council may nonetheless be approved by the government – following receipt of the views of the Minister for Trade and the Minister in charge of the relevant sector – on grounds of general public interest. A common case in practice where such grounds would apply is a situation where the general economic interest of Algeria would justify that and this is measured in terms of improvement in competitiveness, especially internationally.

(collusion between undertakings) or under Article 7 (abuse of dominance). These criteria – whilst embodying key elements featuring in Article 81(3) EC such as ensuring economic or technical progress – contain several non-competition based considerations,[8] namely a consideration of whether the relevant situation: was the result of 'coercion' through the application of a legal provision; facilitates consolidation in the competitive position of small and medium-size firms; and contributes to employment. The existence of such non-competition-based considerations opens a huge scope for discretion to be exercised in practice.

### *5.1.2 The role of the Competition Council*

A major deficiency under the regime set up under Ordinance 1995 was the lack of a sufficiently dynamic competition authority active in promoting competition and building a competition culture in Algeria. The existence of the Competition Council was largely symbolic and its operations were considered to be too rigid, in particular lacking sufficient flexibility to adapt itself to an ever-changing economic climate and fast-evolving economic behaviour and practices. The approach of the council to the application of the competition rules was highly formalistic and this contributed to its 'static' status and lack of dynamism. The enactment of the Ordinance was intended to do away with this deficiency.

According to Article 23 of the Ordinance the council enjoys a legal personality and financial autonomy and is composed of nine members drawn from a variety of backgrounds: two members with judicial background and experience and seven members chosen because of their qualification and expertise in relation to competition, distribution and consumer matters.[9] Without any apparent explanation, the article provides for one of these seven members to be appointed on a proposal from the Minister of the Interior. In addition, the council has a general secretary and rapporteurs to assist in its work. As good practice aimed to enhance transparency in its work and functioning, the council is expected to produce an annual report which is addressed to the Algerian Parliament, the Prime Minister and the Minister for Trade

[8] See Article 9 of the Ordinance.

[9] The appointment is full-time for a term of five years which is renewable.

and which is made public at a later stage following its receipt by these addressees.

The council is a decision-making body with the ability to reach binding decisions, issue final and interim injunctions,[10] and also deliver opinions on any question concerning competition following a request by the government, firms, economic and financial institutions, trade associations and consumer associations. Other key functions of the council include delivering opinions on proposed laws with competition relevance, albeit remote, such as those imposing quantitative restrictions on access to markets or the exercise of different professions or those creating exclusive rights in certain parts of the country or in relation to certain economic activities or those introducing uniform practices with regard to matters such as conditions of sale. Remarkably, Article 37 of the Ordinance provides that in relation to such consultation the council can conduct the necessary investigation into the conditions of application of the proposed law and should such investigation reveal a possible restriction of competition the council will have the power to take the necessary action to eliminate such restriction. This provision is intended to increase the dynamism of the council; however, what is not clear is whether in the case of such a finding the council will be able to *de facto* veto the proposed law or force its amendment. In light of its more general power and the institutional structure – within its legislative, executive and judicial branches – surrounding the Ordinance it appears that the latter course of action is the one that may be open to the council in practice.

The council may launch investigations on its own initiative or upon receipt of a relevant request or a complaint. It has fairly wide powers in this regard and to a certain extent the Ordinance follows the EC competition law regime on the enforcement front.[11]

#### 5.1.2.1 The council's relationship with other regulators

The Ordinance shows the importance which is attached to developing cooperation between the council and sectoral regulators in Algeria and

[10] In the Ordinance, Article 45 deals with final injunctions and Article 46 deals with interim injunctions, which may be ordered to prevent an imminent, irreparable harm or damage to the general economic interest.

[11] It is worth noting the similarities in terms of the internal operations of the council when conducting investigations including the gathering of evidence, arrangements of hearings for firms and the handling of information etc. between the Ordinance and the practices of the European Commission.

the need to build dialogues in relation to the application of the competition rules in individual cases. The Ordinance does not provide for the power of sectoral regulators to apply its provisions in relation to anti-competitive behaviour or abusive conduct in their sectors but instead it offers sectoral regulators the opportunity to deliver their opinion on cases before the council which concern their particular sectors.[12]

#### 5.1.2.2 Penalties and sanctions

The main penalty available under the Ordinance is that of a fine, which may be imposed on firms in a variety of situations: in the case of a collusion or abuse of dominance;[13] the implementation of a merger operation without the council's approval;[14] failure to comply with injunctions issued by the council under Articles 45 and 46 of the Ordinance;[15] the provision of inaccurate or false information or failure to supply complete information if so requested by the rapporteur.[16] The Ordinance also seeks to 'supplement' the provision on fines in the case of firms with the option of fining any individual who participated personally and fraudulently in the planning or implementation of behaviour or conduct caught under the Ordinance.[17]

The Ordinance contains a mechanism for immunity which when used could result in either a reduction in the amount of fine imposed or a

[12] See Article 39 of the Ordinance which also provides that the council must transmit a copy of the file to the relevant regulator for the latter to give its opinion.

[13] The reference here is to the content of Article 6 (horizontal collusion), Article 7 (abuse of dominance), Article 10 (vertical restraints), Article 11 (abuse of dominance) and Article 12 (abuse of dominance) of the Ordinance. The fine in this case cannot exceed 7 per cent of the turnover of the firm concerned. The turnover here is the preceding financial year's generated in Algeria. According to Article 56 of the Ordinance, however, if a turnover figure is not available, a maximum fine not exceeding 3 million Dinars will be imposed.

[14] According to Article 61 the fine in this case will be a maximum of 7 per cent of the turnover of each of the merging firms or the merged entity generated in the preceding financial year in Algeria. A failure to comply with commitments attached to a merger clearance or a breach of those may attract a fine of up to 5 per cent of the turnover of each of the merging firms or the merged entity generated in the preceding financial year in Algeria.

[15] See note 10 above on the difference between the two articles. The fine in this case will be a periodic one with a daily rate of 100,000 Dinars.

[16] According to Article 59 the council having received the opinion of the rapporteur can decide to impose a fixed penalty of 500,000 Dinars with an additional periodic penalty at a daily rate of 50,000 Dinars until the situation is remedied.

[17] Article 57 of the Ordinance provides that the fine is a fixed one totalling 2 million Dinars.

total immunity from such fine. From reading Article 60 of the Ordinance one forms the impression that the conditions are neither sufficiently strict nor mature. Thus, there is no reference to whether as a requirement in the case of total immunity the firm in question must be the first to 'confess' to the council about the infringement under the Ordinance or what the rate of reduction in the amount of fine is in relation to different firms confessing at different stages of the investigation. Having said that, the article is quite developed in providing that no immunity will be possible in case of repeated infringement, regardless of the nature of such an infringement. Whether one agrees or disagrees with the strictness of this approach the inclusion of this provision was motivated more by cultural considerations about the seriousness of recidivism as a highly undesirable phenomenon, which – in light of local norms and customs and which to a large extent also prevails in most countries in the region – deserves to be met with a heavy-handed approach. From a different angle this approach can be considered as being intended to have a 'favourable' deterrent effect.

#### 5.1.2.3 Judicial supervision

The decisions of the council – although binding on the persons to whom they are addressed – are subject to review at the level of the Court of Algiers. This is a very important provision in practice which ensures the existence of a proper system of checks and balances. According to Article 63 of the Ordinance, such actions for review may be brought by the parties concerned or the Minister for Trade within one month from the receipt of the council's decision.[18]

### *5.1.3 International openness and cooperation*

The legislative intent behind the Ordinance of facilitating international openness and cooperation receives particular expression in Articles 40–43, which deal with the council's cooperation with foreign competition authorities. These articles show the willingness of the council to engage in international cooperation and to coordinate enforcement efforts with foreign competition authorities including: entering into formal cooperation agreements; communicating information or documents in the council's possession to those authorities; and gathering

[18] There is a different time-limit for review action in the case of interim measures which according to Article 63 is eight days.

evidence at their request subject to reciprocity and the rule on professional secrecy. The council's cooperation endeavours may even transcend this and include conducting investigations on behalf of foreign competition authorities. Nonetheless, the council's cooperation as described is subject to the strict conditions contained in Article 42 of the Ordinance, namely that such actions may not infringe the national sovereignty of Algeria, undermine the country's economic interests or contravene its internal laws.

### *5.1.4 Comments*

There is no doubt that Ordinance 2003 has brought a significant improvement to the Algerian system of competition law, whether in relation to the substantive law provisions within the system or in relation to the institutional structure and mechanism. Measured in relation to the goals it was intended to achieve, the Ordinance can be said to have facilitated the creation of a consultative dimension within the system and made the competition law mechanism in the country more dynamic. However, the Ordinance suffers from the existence of several gaps in its provisions. For example, its provisions on abuse of dominance are scattered in different articles without any apparent explanation for such an approach: Article 7 addresses abuse of dominance in the case of prohibition of market access, limitation or control of production, investment or technical progress, tying between products, discrimination and abusive pricing practices; Article 11 considers abuse in the case of 'state of dependence' such as situations of refusal to supply without objective justification, imposing obligations of resale price maintenance and exclusive purchasing;[19] Article 12 deals with predatory pricing. Another gap worth highlighting is caused by the rigidity of the rules contained in some provisions of the Ordinance and the lack of clear explanation of the concepts contained in those provisions. For instance, Article 10 lays down a prohibition on exclusive purchasing agreements (in a vertical sense) which give rise to monopoly on the part of suppliers over distribution in the relevant market. Such agreements are considered to prevent, restrict or distort the play of free competition. There is no explanation given with regard to what is considered to amount to 'monopoly' in this case or any appreciation of the fact that

[19] Article 3(d) defines the term state of dependence as a situation where a firm does not have a realistic alternative means to purchase from or sell to another.

such a *per se* rule may cause difficulties in relation to its application in practice or that competition problems may result from vertical agreements even where the supplier does not enjoy a monopoly position. Nonetheless, the explanation for the inclusion of this prohibition is cultural: exclusive purchasing situations are extremely sensitive in Algeria and a great deal of harm has come from them over the years. These situations often involve suppliers with monopoly positions. The choice of a *per se* approach is a reflection of the traditional attitude prevailing in the country, namely that prevention of a harmful situation is the best cure to be sought and applied.

## 5.2 Morocco: a strong desire for modernisation

Competition law was introduced in Morocco as a double-edge sword aiming at providing the government with a political-economic instrument for controlling markets and as a free market economy tool to be used following the liberalisation of domestic markets including that of prices and a process of privatisation aiming at a gradual removal of state monopolies in different sectors of the economy. By adopting a specific competition law, Morocco was considered to have taken a giant leap in its long process of economic and political reform, which was launched several years ago. This reform was based on the Monarch's desire to modernise the economy and the legal and institutional environment within the country in order to enhance creativity, productivity and enterprise on the part of local firms as well as build an environment conducive to foreign investment and foreign participation in the domestic economy.

The regulation of competition in Morocco should not be considered in isolation. Competition law and policy in the country are taken to have supreme 'constitutional' attributes thus making competition infringements offences committed against the fundamental rights of citizens, their liberty and their property. Moreover, competition regulation is part of the general mechanism of economic regulation in the country designed to facilitate a 'dialogue' leading to collaboration between public administration and private firms. Several institutional structures have been set up over the years for this dialogue to begin and progress to be made including: the National Committee of Recovery which aims at identifying and putting into practice measures in order to improve the competitiveness of Moroccan firms; the National Council of Exterior Commerce which aims at promoting a conducive commercial environment and building a suitable strategy to facilitate that; and specific committees and sectoral bodies dedicated to establishing contact-programmes between the private sector and the administration in key sectors such as tourism, textile-clothing and information technology.

### *5.2.1 Western style: linking with the EC and EFTA*

Morocco, whether in name or approach, is focused towards the West and this style came to be reinvigorated in the 1990s with solid links and cooperation mechanism created between the Kingdom and the EC and EFTA. The EC–Morocco Association Agreement was signed in Brussels, on 26 February 1996, and entered into force on 1 March 2000, replacing the Morocco–EC Cooperation Agreement of 1976. The competition provisions are contained in Articles 36–38 of the Agreement. They prohibit agreements, decisions and concerted practices which restrict, prevent or distort competition as well as abuse of a dominant position and aid which distorts or threatens to distort competition. In addition, regulation of monopolies and public enterprises and enterprises which have been granted special or exclusive rights is advocated. These prohibitions are reinforced in Article 17 of the Free Trade Agreement signed between the EFTA States and Morocco on 19 June 1997, which entered into force on 1 December 1999.

### *5.2.2 The Law on the Freedom of Prices and Competition*

The Law on the Freedom of Prices and Competition was adopted against the backdrop of the economic reform mentioned above.[20] The Law has been the result of a calculated decision, seeking to affirm the government's conviction that: protecting the freedom of competition and free pricing and guaranteeing unhindered access to domestic markets are among the tenets of a modern economy. Morocco has always been a society seeking modernity and therefore modernisation of the economy was a highly attractive slogan the government felt comfortable introducing.

The Law is the longest competition legislation in the region with 103 Articles. Its provisions are very detailed though they are overstretched in their number given that the content of the Law could have been covered

[20] Law No. 06–99 of 6 July 2000.

by fewer provisions. The Law is modelled in significant aspects on the competition rules of the EC and is supplemented by a Competition Regulation or Circular, adopted on 6 September 2001 (the Competition Regulation).[21]

#### 5.2.2.1 The scheme of the Law

The aims of the Law, as articulated in broad terms in the preamble, appear to revolve around seeking to guarantee four important objectives: free prices determined according to competitive forces and organising the play of free competition in the market; enhancing economic activities and development; maximising consumer welfare; and achieving transparency and loyalty in commercial relations. Other objectives include guaranteeing unhindered access to markets and ensuring availability of adequate information for consumers.[22] These are highly interesting objectives and appear to encompass an interesting doctrine of competition law which is concerned mainly with structural market issues. Indeed, this is all the more clear from the legislative intent and policy approach behind the Law which sought to introduce a Law to *complement* structural economic reforms already effected and aiming at bringing the Moroccan economy closer to prevailing international economic standards. Morocco places particular importance on the latter and has considered building strategic bilateral and multilateral alliances with key countries and regional economic blocks, such as EC, EFTA, the USA and Arab countries as a key step to achieving its objectives. These reforms concern many arenas and rest on a variety of laws, codes and legal reforms which came to assume fundamental importance in Morocco including: the Law on Unfair Competition and Trade Secrets;[23] the Commercial Code; the Company Law; the tax reforms; reforms of the banking system; the Labour Law; and the Customs Code.

The Law brings within its scope the anti-competitive behaviour, conduct or activities of legal and natural persons, whether established in Morocco or outside (so long as there is an effect on competition in Morocco or part of it) as well as all practices of production and distribution in relation to goods and services. Additionally, export-related agreements are within the scope of the Law insofar as their application

[21] Regulation No. 2–00–854.

[22] See for example Article 6(1) which prohibits collusion hindering market access and Article 47 which deals with price and commercial information.

[23] Law No. 15–2000 of 2 April 2000.

affects competition in domestic markets. The Law does not exclude public entities active in production and distribution from its scope and only insofar as their activities do not concern their exercise of public functions or the provision of public services.[24]

#### 5.2.2.2 Free pricing and price regulation

Despite the articulated goal of the Law to guarantee price competition,[25] the Law contains an element of price regulation which in some cases can translate into deep intervention in the market by the government, albeit this intervention being 'controlled'.[26] This can be seen in Article 3 and Article 83 of the Law. The former article provides for price-fixing by the administration in relation to sectors or geographic areas in which price competition is limited either due to monopolistic activities, enjoyed under law or *de facto*, or due to difficulties related to supply or due to the existence of certain laws or regulations. Article 83 provides for the possibility of price regulation in relation to commodities and services featuring in lists, prepared according to regulations and the price of which is fixed in accordance with the provisions of the Law on Price Regulation and Supervision.[27] According to the article the price regulation in this case may last for a transitional period of five years commencing on the date the Law comes into effect.[28] At the time of writing – December 2006 – the published list contained thirty-one products and services, ranging from drinking water, sugar and wheat flour to transport of people and goods by road, rail and air (within Morocco).[29]

[24] See Article 1 of the Law.

[25] See the discussion above on the price competition goal of the Law and Article 2 of the Law which gives clear expression to this goal.

[26] By 'controlled' this author refers to the fact that such intervention necessitates the administration consulting the Competition Council and establishing guidelines for price regulation beforehand. Note also Article 5 of the Law which provides for the possibility of consultation and agreement between the administration and professional organisations representing different sectors in cases where the administration seeks to regulate the price. Furthermore, in cases of measures taken under Article 4 such measures should be adopted for a period not exceeding six months renewable only once. Article 4 provides that in case of intervention by the administration the latter must take necessary temporary measures to prevent any excessive price increase or decrease which is likely due to exceptional circumstances, public emergency or unusual circumstances.

[27] Law No. 008–71.

[28] 'Comes' here should be taken to mean came as the Law entered into force in May 2001.

[29] The full list can be viewed at the Ministry of Justice's website at www.justice.gov.ma/index_an.aspx.

Additionally, Articles 56–60 of the Law provide for specific rules for products subject to price regulation. The content of these articles appears, on economic grounds, to be questionable given the rules have been set in an economically 'over-simplified' manner, which ignores the complexities of cost and price determinations in practice. For example, Article 56 provides that it is possible to determine prices on the basis of 'total value', profit index applying to a product at the retail level or any other way. The article provides that the profit index – expressed in the difference between the cost and total value – will be applied to the sale price. It is possible for the administration to revert to mandatory declaration of stocking, in any shape or form, in the case of regulated products,[30] and to set the conditions for the stocking of these products and the method for offering them for sale.[31] Article 60 prohibits any price increase in the case of regulated products whether in the sale above the fixed price; the purchase above fixed price; or sharing among agents of profits, which exceed the maximum permitted rate of profit at any level of the distribution chain.

#### 5.2.2.3 Consumer protection

Articles 47–50 of the Law deal with consumer protection and information. Among other things, the provisions mandate that all sellers and service-providers inform consumers through publicising their price lists and the conditions related to sale by way of an announcement, poster or any other suitable means; providing customers with invoices and receipts; refraining from refusing to supply to consumers without justification; tying between different products or making the supply of a product subject to quantitative restrictions; and refraining, in the case of sale of products to consumers, from offering rewards – whether immediate or postponed – in the form of free products, which are not similar nor complementary to the former.[32]

[30] See Article 57 of the Law which also provides for the possibility of the products in question benefiting from compensation from the government budget.

[31] See Article 58 of the Law.

[32] Article 50 provides that the prohibition in this case does not extend to products with low value. The article also provides that reward in this case does not include after-sale services; provision of free services which are not offered under a contract in return for consideration and which lack commercial value; and offering necessary services for the usual use of the product.

#### 5.2.2.4 Conducting investigations

The Law includes a fairly detailed chapter dealing with market investigations and research to be conducted by government officials with the necessary qualification or the members of the Commission for Price Supervision (the inspectors) for the purposes of applying the different provisions of the Law.[33] The inspectors enjoy fairly extensive powers, which in strict competition-enforcement sense translate into the powers many competition authorities have come to enjoy, such as conducting investigations at business premises of firms, inspecting products whether in transit or on business premises and seizing the necessary documents.

#### 5.2.2.5 Transparency between professionals

Another example of deep regulation within the Law can be found in Articles 51–54, which deal with 'transparency in commercial relations between professionals'. The articles detail the steps which professionals must take in conducting business among themselves without, however, defining or explaining the term 'professional'.[34] For example, such steps include producing bills, receipts or invoices in every commercial transaction conducted. Article 51 describes in detail what the exact content of such documents should be: names and addresses of the parties, the quantity of products supplied, price, discount, total amount due and methods of payment. Article 52 states that a producer or service-provider or wholesaler should inform all professional buyers, where the latter so request, of its price list and conditions of sale. Article 53 prohibits setting minimum resale prices. Finally, Article 54 prohibits producers, service-providers, importers or wholesalers from engaging in the following conduct: imposing on a business partner or extracting from the latter prices or payment conditions or other conditions related to sale or purchase which are 'exclusive' without any justification in terms of consideration and which may lead to elimination of competition on the part of such partner; fulfilling a buyer's request of products or services rendered for a professional purpose which does not conform to normal business conditions or was not made in good faith; making the sale of a

[33] See Articles 61–66.

[34] From a general reading of the Law, however, its appears that this term is interpreted quite widely and covers, among other professions, traders active in consumer products such as fish and fruit and vegetables.

product destined for professional activity conditional upon the customers buying other products or a fixed quantity of the product; and selling in towns with wholesale markets fish, fruit and vegetables that have not gone through these markets.

The policy behind Articles 51–54 of the Law is more social and cultural than economic in orientation and comes to ensure that risks of monopolistic or abusive conduct are fully eliminated from key consumer products markets as well as to ensure the smooth running of these markets. However, the policy is problematic in practice given that it contains an element of 'over-regulation', which on the face of things the Law appears to have come to reduce.

#### 5.2.2.6 Limitation of supply

Article 55 of the Law deals with and prohibits situations of 'secretive stocking of products', the purpose of which is to control or limit supply in local markets. The article defines such situations as concealing products through secretive stocking by merchants or associations in the agricultural sector, traditional or modern industries for the purposes of defeating competition;[35] stocking products for the purposes of selling them to persons not appearing on the commercial register;[36] stocking by persons mentioned in the previous point of products which do not fall within the scope of their business or commercial activities for the purposes of sale;[37] and stocking by farmers of products, which have no connection with their activities for the purposes of selling them.[38] The definition of secretive stocking of products – within the meaning of paragraphs (2)–(4) of the article – also extends to situations where the stocking of the products by a person is not justified by professional or business activities or concerns quantities exceeding the domestic needs, in accordance with local customs, of such a person.[39]

### *5.2.3 The relevant authorities*

#### 5.2.3.1 The Competition Council

Article 14 of the Law provides for the creation of a Competition Council, the membership of which according to Article 18 is to be composed of

[35] See Article 55(1). [36] See Article 55(2). [37] See Article 55(3). [38] See Article 55(4).

[39] Other situations caught within the prohibition may be found in Article 59 of the Law which provides that stocking of products without declaring them in accordance with Article 57 (see above) also amounts to secretive stocking.

twelve members, in addition to a chairman of the council appointed on permanent basis by the Prime Minister: six members representing the administration;[40] three members conducting or with past experience in commercial activities involving production or distribution of products;[41] and three members to be selected on the basis of their qualification in law, economics, competition and consumer affairs.[42] There is a strong 'government' presence in the council with the Prime Minister and the administration in general being placed at the heart of the competition law regime of Morocco. As such there is a particular concern over the real prospects of competition 'orientation' in the application of the Law especially in light of the prominence of non-competition factors and considerations featuring in the Law which in practice could override competition factors and considerations. An illustration of this can be seen in light of the exemption provision of Article 8 of the Law which provides that exemptions for collusion or abuse of dominance caught under Articles 6 and 7 respectively are possible in case of proportionate restrictions meeting four conditions.[43] The article, however, empowers the administration,[44] following consultation with the council, to declare certain agreements or types of agreements in particular if these aim to enhance small and medium-size firms or improve the marketing or distribution of farmers' produce as meeting the exemption conditions in the article. Article 6 of the Competition Regulation specifically provides for the possibility for such a situation to prevail over the four specific conditions, which contain important competition considerations.

The functions of the council are mainly consultative. The council may be consulted by the Permanent Parliamentary Committees in relation to bills concerning competition; the government in relation to all competition

40 Article 1 of the Competition Regulation which provides for the administration's representatives to be appointed by the Prime Minister states that the persons must be representatives of the Minister of Justice, the Minister of Interior Affairs, the Minister of Finance, the Secretary General of the Government, the Minister for Government Affairs and the Minister for Planning.

41 Article 1 of the Regulation provides that these should be appointed following a recommendation by the heads of the Chambers of Trade, Industry and Services, the Chamber of Traditional Industries, the Chamber of Fisheries and the Chamber of Farmers.

42 The chairman and members are appointed for a fixed term of five years renewable only once.

43 These are: contribution to economic progress; sufficient compensation for the anti-competitive aspects of the situation; having a fair share of the resulting benefit accruing to consumers; and the absence of the possibility for the elimination of competition.

44 According to Article 6 of the Competition Regulation the decision is taken by the Prime Minister.

issues; the different chambers of commerce and industry and consumer associations in relation to competition issues within their remits; and specialist courts in relation to situations falling within Articles 6 and 7 of the Law arising in cases before them.[45] Article 16 of the Law provides for mandatory consultation of the council by the government in relation to any proposed law, order or regulation introducing a new regime or amending an existing one and which aims at imposing quantitative restrictions on practising a profession or market access; creating monopolies or granting exclusive or special rights to land in Morocco; imposing common or unified practices in relation to prices and terms of sale; and granting declaration by the state or local municipalities.[46] The Moroccan system of competition law therefore provides for no link between firms or customers and the council. The council is able to conduct investigations into matters referred to it and to make recommendations to the Prime Minister, who decides what action should be taken. Such action may include adopting a reasoned decision, ordering a particular behaviour or practice in breach of the Law to be brought to an end and imposing any condition he sees necessary. Additionally or alternatively the case may be transferred to the King's Counsel before the Court of First Instance for prosecution.[47]

#### 5.2.3.2 The Commission for Price Supervision

The Commission for Price Supervision is a cross-ministerial body with limited powers and responsibility under the Law. Most notably, the members of the Commission are responsible for establishing infringements of the provisions of parts 6 and 7 of the Law insofar as products referred to in Article 83 of the Law are concerned, namely commodities and services featuring in lists prepared according to regulations and the price of which is fixed in accordance with the provisions of the Law on Price Regulation and

[45] See Article 15 of the Act.

[46] Under Article 27, the council may, by way of a reasoned decision, given within two months of the date of receipt of a matter referred to it, refuse to accept the matter where it sees that the matter does not fall within the scope of its remit or lacks sufficient supporting evidence or may adopt a reasoned decision (addressed to the referring party and the persons under investigation for alleged infringements of Articles 6 and 7 of the Law) not to continue handling a matter after giving the referring party concerned the opportunity to inspect the file and make its observations.

[47] According to Article 36 this may be done by the Prime Minister as an action of first resort; however, in the case of an order to bring an anti-competitive situation to an end including any conditions imposed not being adhered to, the Prime Minister may, following a recommendation by the council, adopt a reasoned decision referring the case to the King's Counsel for perusal.

Supervision.[48] Cases in which such infringements have been established *must* be referred for enforcement actions in part 6 cases to the King's Counsel and in part 7 cases to the relevant designated authority.[49] Article 25 of the Competition Regulation provides that the membership of the commission brings together the (office of) Prime Minister or a government department authorised to represent him and the Ministries for Interior Affairs; Finance; Farming; Industry and Trade; Employment; Planning; Social Economy and Traditional Industry; and representatives of the relevant government department in charge of the relevant sector under consideration before the commission.

### 5.2.3.3 The Central Committee

Article 96 of the Law provides for the setting up of a Central Committee, composed of representatives of the administration and qualified consultants to be appointed in individual cases where necessary.[50] The purpose behind the committee is to hear petition actions by persons subject to an administrative penalty within the meaning of Article 91 of the Law ordering such a person to pay the total amount of payments received during the breach, namely the difference between the price charged during the period and that which should have been charged and the total amount of payments received during the breach. The action must be in the form of a detailed written submission addressed to the chairman of the committee within thirty days of the date on which the penalty was imposed. The committee will hold an oral hearing for the petitioner or its representative and it may choose to affirm or change the amount of the penalty. The committee's decision must be reached within three months following receipt of the petition.

48 See p 137 above.

49 Article 86 of the Law. According to Article 87, this authority will have the sole power to decide on settlement having received the opinion of the Administration's Foreign Interests Chief for the sector, to which the products in question belong. However, it is possible for the case to be transferred to the Court of First Instance in which case no settlement will be possible.

50 Article 21 of the Competition Regulation provides that the representatives shall be: the Prime Minister or a government department authorised to represent him and the Ministries for Interior Affairs, Finance, Farming, Industry and Trade, Employment, Planning and Social Economy and Traditional Industry. Where relevant and in case of judicial proceedings the committee's membership will include representatives of the relevant government department in charge of the relevant sector under consideration before the committee.

#### 5.2.3.4 The courts

The main courts playing a role under the Law are the Administrative Court and the Court of First Instance. Under Article 46 of the Law, decisions adopted by the Prime Minister in relation to mergers, except those decisions involving a referral of a case to the King's Counsel under the article,[51] may be challenged before the Administrative Court.

#### 5.2.3.5 Sectoral regulators

Two important sectoral regulators are worth mentioning given the role they are able to play in relation to the Law, namely the National Agency for the Regulation of Telecommunications (ANRT) and the High Authority of Audiovisual Communication (HAAC). The ANTR is responsible for protecting fair competition in the telecommunications sector and resolving disputes arising within it as well as dealing with situations with competition relevance, namely those concerning the following provisions of the Law: Article 6 (collusion), Article 7 (abuse of dominance) and Article 10 (regulation of concentrations or mergers).[52] In relation to the HAAC, the Authority/Superior Council of Audiovisual Communication has mainly a referral role, namely its power to refer situations giving rise to competition concerns to the competition authorities.[53]

### *5.2.4 Penalties*

The Law contains a host of possible penalties extending from imprisonment to fines. The system of penalties included in the Law is very complex and caters – in a sophisticated manner – for a variety of situations and offences. The table below sets out and summarises the different penalties and is produced for the benefit of the reader.

[51] This is in the case of failure to notify a merger operation falling within the scope of the Law as stipulated under Article 12 or failure to comply with merger decisions under Article 43 (prohibition or conditional clearance) and Article 45 (effectively ordering de-merger in the case of an abuse of dominance by the merged entity). In such cases, the Prime Minister may, following consultation of the council, refer the case to the King's Counsel. Interestingly, Article 44 provides that in relation to Article 43, decisions cannot be reached until the parties concerned are given the opportunity to make their submission on the report produced by the case-handlers of the council within one month of the receipt of the said report.

[52] See Article 8 A of Law No. 24–96, as amended.

[53] See Article 4 of Decree No. 1–02–212 of 31 August 2002.

Table 1. *Penalties*

| Situation | Type of penalty | |
|---|---|---|
| | Natural persons | Legal persons |
| Participating in planning, whether openly or dishonestly, a breach of Articles 6 or 7 | Imprisonment (2–6 months), a fine (10,000–500,000 Dirhams) or both* | |
| Fabricating or attempting to fabricate a price increase or reduction through publishing false information or making offers for disrupting prices or any other fraudulent means | • Imprisonment (2 months to 2 years), a fine (10,000–500,000 Dirhams) or both.<br>• In the case of consumer products such as food, flour, flour products, drinks, medicines, fuel etc., the penalty is increased to imprisonment (1–3 years) AND a fine (not exceeding 800,000 Dirhams)<br>• The imprisonment may be increased to 5 years and the fine to 1 million Dirhams in case of the products falling outside the offender's normal business activities. | |
| Breach of Articles 6 or 7 or failure to comply with Article 12(1) or the undertakings under Article 36 or the orders and conditions appearing in Article 36(1)** | A fine (200,000–2,000,000 Dirhams)*** | A fine totalling 2–5 per cent of the turnover generated in the preceding financial year in Morocco.*** |

Table 1. (*cont.*)

| Situation | Type of penalty | |
|---|---|---|
| | Natural persons | Legal persons |
| A breach of the provisions in Articles 47–50 (consumer information and protection) | A fine of 1,200–5,000 Dirhams | A fine of 1,200–5,000 Dirhams |
| A breach of Articles 51–54 (transparency between professionals) and Articles 57, 58 and 60 (rules concerning products subject to price regulation)♣ | A fine of 5,000–100,000 Dirhams | A fine of 5,000–100,000 Dirhams |
| Breach of Article 55 and 59 (secretive stocking)♣♣ | A fine (100,000–500,000 Dirhams) and imprisonment (2 months to 2 years) | A fine (100,000–500,000 Dirhams) |
| Concealing products made subject to temporary ceasing order under Article 63 | A fine totalling 10 times the value of the products | A fine totalling 10 times the value of the products |
| Obstructing, cursing or committing acts of violence against inspectors or refusing to allow them access to relevant business documents during the conduct of an investigation, or concealing or falsifying documents or knowingly | Imprisonment (2 months to 2 years), a fine (5,000–200,000 Dirhams) | A fine (5,000–200,000 Dirhams) |

| |
|---|
| providing false information to the relevant authorities or failing to furnish them with explanations and the necessary evidence |

* According to Article 69, it may also be possible for the offender to be deprived of one or more of the rights contained in Chapter 40 of the Criminal Law.

** By virtue of Article 70 of the Law any person found to have committed a breach will be subjected to criminal liability in light of the relevant circumstances; the existence of bad faith; or the seriousness of the breach.

*** A repeated breach within five years will attract double the maximum fine.

♣ Article 86 of the Law provides that in relation to breaches of Articles 56–60 the penalties may be either a settlement or administrative and judicial penalties. Administrative penalties include: a caution; a fine, without exceeding 100,000 Dirhams, 20 times the average weekly turnover (calculated with reference to the preceding financial year) of the relevant person; and, if deemed necessary, the total amount of payments received during the breach, namely the difference between the price charged during the period and that which should have been charged. Note, however, that Article 91 provides that in case of an infringement of Article 58 the fine should be lower and range from 1,000–5,000 Dirhams.

♣♣ It is also possible, according to Article 72, to confiscate the products in question and the means of transport (if relevant). According to Article 74 it is possible for the court to: order the closure of the offices or warehouses of the offender temporarily and for a period not exceeding three months; prevent the offender on a temporary basis from conducting usual business activities or any business for a period not exceeding one year. A breach of any of these orders may attract a fine (1,200–200,000 Dirham), imprisonment (1 month to 2 years) or both. In case of such penalties being imposed, Article 75 provides that an individual will be prevented from working within the firm involved in the breach even if he sells the firm (in case of sole ownership) by will or otherwise, or delegates its running to another individual. Interestingly, the article provides that such an individual cannot be employed in another firm run by his or her spouse.

### 5.2.5 *Reflections*

The Moroccan Law on the Freedom of Prices and Competition lacks an adequate economic flavour in practice and is largely dominated by a social flavour. Many of the Law's provisions are very basic, whether in wording or nature and so lack the 'grounding' for an analytical component, which is normally crucial in the practical application of competition rules. The structure and language of the Law are extremely complicated with excessive cross-references between the different provisions, many of which require very careful and repeated readings in order to understand their meaning. The scheme of the Law is highly bureaucratic and there is huge scope for restructuring and simplifying its provisions. The involvement of different authorities and persons is highly confusing, especially in relation to the administration of penalties where all of the following have a role to play: the Competition Council, the Prime Minister, the Courts of First Instance and the Administrative Court, the Central Committee, the King's Counsel and the General Counsel. In some cases there is a 'springboard' situation with an issue travelling back and forth between these persons and authorities.

As we have seen, the Law contains a fairly strong element of regulation especially in relation to prices and price arrangements. The doctrine underpinning this component of the Law appears to be based on social premise and general considerations, which can conveniently be considered to fall within the realm of the public interest. The purpose and justification behind adding a price regulatory component appear to be policy oriented.

The concerns over the Law and its operations transcend the boundaries of wording and institutional structure and reach the important issue of penalties. There are several points worth making about the mechanism and system of penalties erected under the Law. First, the penalties contained within the system, whether imprisonment or fine, have an extremely wide range. Whilst it is understandable that this might have been done in order to cater for infringements by natural and legal persons in one and the same situation, having such a range affects legal certainty in practice and makes it difficult particularly for legal advisors to deliver accurate advice in individual cases. Furthermore, such a range leaves a great deal of discretion in the hands of the Prime Minister and the courts in individual cases; in a developing system of competition law such as the Moroccan one, minimising (political) discretion is desirable given that a move in this direction would enhance, among other things, consistency in application of the provisions of the Law. Secondly, some of the penalties appear to be draconian, for example those giving the court the power to order effectively a 'shut down' of businesses.[54] Looking at the situation from different angles – including the availability of other penalties – such a measure would be unnecessary to order and to a certain extent highly undesirable in practice: the other penalties may prove to be sufficient in such a case and also there is the risk that jobs may be shed. A third comment related to the one just made is that the system contains a 'social' element given that in cases where a shut down is ordered, the relevant person must continue to pay his/its employees their full salaries, rewards and bonuses and other relevant benefits during the shut-down period, which may be as long as one year. Clearly, this provision was included with the risk of unemployment in mind. However, it is crucial to note that in some cases such a position may not be sustainable due to the size of the relevant person or scarcity of financial resources. Fourthly, it is interesting that in relation to some offences, the same financial penalty is imposed on natural and legal persons without appreciating the major differences existing between them. Finally, in relation to infringement of Articles 56–60 of the Law which deal with products subject to price regulation, the economic basis on which an assessment of whether such infringement has occurred is highly controversial.

## 5.3 Tunisia: a pioneer in the Arab world

Tunisia can be considered as the most promising country of North Africa in terms of economic development. Since the mid-1980s the country has undergone significant economic, political and social reforms, leading to an impressive economic growth through the 1990s. The socialist economic model, initially adopted by Tunisia following its independence from France under which the state-controlled prices, private investment and regulated trade, had limited success primarily because of its failure to advance the economy and on the whole led to a period of stagnation. In 1986, Tunisia adopted a structural adjustment programme in agreement with the World Bank and the International Monetary Fund (IMF) to push Tunisia out of that period of stagnation and to remedy the country's economic difficulties. This involved a

[54] See Article 74 of the Law.

restructuring of the economy and the market mechanism and encouragement towards privatisation; Tunisia's association with the World Bank and the IMF certainly helped in this regard given the significant aid received from these key international bodies. In return, Tunisia was expected to commit itself to liberalising its domestic economy by reducing heavy state intervention in economic affairs, privatising many state-run enterprises, liberalising internal and external trade and attracting foreign investment. The underlying aim of these steps has been to create a competitive environment within Tunisia, which had not previously existed, in order to encourage economic efficiency and strengthen competition at the national level to promote deeper integration into world trade and the global economy.

### *5.3.1 Extensive web of international associations*

Tunisia has established several international links in the economic arena both within and beyond the Middle East. These economic relations – particularly those formed with the EC and the Arab World – have proved beneficial for Tunisia. In 1990 Tunisia acceded to the General Agreement on Tariffs and Trade (GATT) which was a major step towards integration in the global community and Tunisia becoming a founding member of the World Trade Organisation (WTO) five years later. It has entered into free trade agreements with several Arab countries, including the Greater Arab Free Trade Agreement (GAFTA) and was one of the founding fathers of the AMU. In 2004, Tunisia signed the Agadir Agreement to establish a free trade area with Jordan, Morocco and Egypt to enhance economic cooperation. However, as we noted in chapter 1, this Agreement has not yet entered into force.[55]

As far as relations with the EC and the European Free Trade Association (EFTA) are concerned, Tunisia was the first country on the southern coast of the Mediterranean to sign an Association Agreement with the EC on 17 July 1995, which entered into force on 1 March 1998 and is expected to come into full effect in 2008. The main objective of this agreement was the establishment of a free trade zone, to open trade opportunities and attract foreign investment.[56] Competition-related provisions are contained in Articles 36–38 of this

55 See pp 13–14 above.

56 Among other things, the agreement provides for financial cooperation to support Tunisia's reform measures. In this regard, the EC has been assisting Tunisia in its

agreement which prohibit, among other phenomena, concerted practices, abuse of a dominant position and state aid which distorts competition. The agreement aims to create a free trade area between the EC and Tunisia by the year 2010. A Free Trade Agreement between Tunisia and EFTA States was also signed in Switzerland on 17 December 2004, Article 17 of which lays down similar rules on competition to those contained in the Tunisia–EC Association Agreement.

It is interesting to note that Tunisia advanced its integration into European markets by dismantling tariffs in 1996, before the entry into force of the Association Agreement in 1998.[57] This important step demonstrates the desire of Tunisia to forge closer links with the EC. Tunisia has always placed particular importance on these links given the benefit it has actually come to reap from their existence. For example, as a member of the Euro–Mediterranean partnership – which was developed in Barcelona[58] – Tunisia receives substantial financial assistance through the EC's Mediterranean programme, MEDA, as well as significant loans from the European Investment Bank for, among other purposes, the development of economic infrastructure.[59] These benefits have in turn encouraged Tunisia to play a greater role in the European Commission's programmes and strategies on the Mediterranean Region, whether within the framework of the European Neighbourhood Policy (ENP) or the Barcelona Process more widely.

Finally, it is worth noting the Free Trade Agreement (FTA) between Tunisia and Turkey which was signed on 25 November 2004 and entered into force on 1 July 2005. The aim of this agreement is to strengthen trade and economic cooperation between Turkey and Tunisia and accordingly it contains provisions relating to trade, monopolies, state aid and competition. The establishment of a free trade area is envisaged within nine years after the entry into force of the agreement. Chapter IV of this agreement lays down the rules relating to competition, state aid and monopolies in Articles 23, 25 and 26. According to these,

national programme of industrial upgrading, what is known as the '*mise à niveau*', to enhance the productivity of Tunisian businesses. A twinning programme – financed by the EC – has also been established to support Tunisia's efforts to improve its economic competitiveness.

57 Similarly, as the discussion below makes clear, competition law and policy were introduced in Tunisia prior to the conclusion of the agreement, though it would be correct to say that the agreement nonetheless was influential: the prospects at the turn of the 1990s of closer links with the EC enhanced the legislative efforts towards adopting a specific competition law in the country.

58 See p 16 above.

59 European Investment Bank at www.eib.europa.eu/.

agreements, decisions and concerted practices which restrict, prevent or distort competition between the parties and abuse of a dominant position are prohibited on the basis that they may affect trade between the parties. State aid which distorts or threatens to distort competition is also deemed incompatible with the implementation of the FTA and thus the agreement advocates the exchange of information between the parties relating to state aid in order to ensure transparency in this area. With regards to state monopolies, Article 23 stipulates that these be adjusted within four years following the entry into force of the agreement to ensure that trade between the parties is not affected. For the purpose of reviewing the implementation of the FTA, an Association Council and an Association Committee are established.

### *5.3.2 Developing a competition law framework*

In the field of competition law, Tunisia has been a pioneer among Arab MECs. It introduced a specific competition law in its legal system and succeeded in establishing a competition law regime in the early 1990s, well before many Arab MECs thought about directing their attention to economic reform and building a market economy let alone contemplated introducing competition rules domestically. As we noted above, Tunisia sought around that time to adapt to the international environment by building a solid, efficient and competitive economy to prepare for integration into the world economy. Introducing domestic competition rules with an underlying competition policy was an integral part of fulfilling this key purpose. Tunisia adopted a specific competition law in 1991, the Competition and Prices Act (the Act),[60] becoming one of two countries in the Middle East to do so at that time.[61] The need for specific competition legislation was intensified with the way being paved for *future* international commitments of Tunisia under the WTO and the Association Agreement with the EC. This involved opening the Tunisian economy to the outside world thereby increasing competition in the economy through the integration of domestic markets into the global economy. Within this setting, the enactment of a competition law was important to keep pace with economic changes internationally and to protect the interests of local consumers and firms by ensuring that an effective mechanism was in place to deal with practices and situations which harm competition. Moreover, the adoption of the Act

[60] Law No. 91–64 of 29 July 1991. [61] The other country was Israel. See chapter 3.

further developed the whole process of economic reform, liberalisation of trade and the privatisation process undertaken by Tunisia and highlighted the transition from a regulated economy with a strong component of state control and planning to a market economy.

In the years that followed the adoption of specific competition legislation, Tunisia came to play a significant role in developing competition law in other Arab countries and more recently in the work of international organisations.[62] For example, Jordan devoted specific attention to the Tunisian regime when adopting its Competition Act 2004 and made use of the available Tunisian competition law expertise for the purposes of formulating its competition policy.[63] The utilising by some Arab countries of the Tunisian competition law regime as a model shows a degree of comfort those countries feel in leaning more towards the experience of a fellow Arab country as opposed to concentrating *exclusively* on the systems of competition law in existence beyond the boundaries of the Middle East. From a legal and economic point of view, this approach is sensible given that competition law and policy are related to culture, the type and size of the economy and the legal system prevailing in a particular country. Arab MECs share many similarities in relation to all of these and this supports the decision of countries like Jordan to turn to the Tunisian experience with competition law for consultation and in turn enhances the standing Tunisia enjoys in the field of competition law and policy in the region.

### *5.3.3 The Competition and Prices Act: goals, scope and underlying policies*

#### 5.3.3.1 Aims and objectives

The Tunisian Competition and Prices Act regulates competition and prices and seeks to support the process of economic liberalisation in Tunisia, drawing largely on the French Competition Ordinance of 1986. The Act has been amended on several occasions over the years, most

[62] The Tunisian Competition Council has also devoted particular attention to its international outlook; it has been quite active within and outside the Middle East and has offered technical assistance to and organised joint seminars with competition authorities in the region. These seminars have been beneficial to the latter in terms of advancing their case-handling skills and techniques. Internationally, the council has been a keen participant in the work and proceedings of the International Competition Network (ICN) in particular.

[63] See chapter 6.

recently in 2005,[64] in order to ensure compliance with international obligations and to adapt its provisions to new developments within the country and with good international competition practices developing at the international level more generally.[65] Within its framework, a variety of broad (express and underlying) objectives can be identified as being pursued under the Act. For example, Article 1 of the Act specifies its purpose as being that of eradicating anti-competitive and abusive practices including unlawful price increases and protecting the market mechanism for the purposes of guaranteeing price transparency.[66] The overall objective of the Act is therefore to prevent anti-competitive practices, by establishing the principle of 'free play of competition'.[67] Having said this, however, the Act paradoxically allows the government to intervene and fix prices in particular cases where competition is limited as a result of supply difficulties, the effect of legislative or regulatory provisions or because of the existence of a monopoly position.[68] Therefore, although the Act advocates freedom of prices, determined by market forces and the free play of competition, it does not explicitly prevent state intervention in price-setting and state control remains on a number of consumer products. Perhaps this is a result of the influence of the French Competition Ordinance where similar provisions can be found.[69] Regardless of the foundation or origins of this mechanism, however, it is more a part of the wider approach that came to prevail in the vast majority of MECs.

#### 5.3.3.2 Scope of the Act

In order to protect the process of competition, the Act prohibits all concerted practices and agreements which restrict competition, in particular by preventing the free determination of prices by market forces,

[64] The Act has been amended by: Law No. 93–83 of 26 July 1993; Law No. 95–42 of 24 April 1995; Law No. 99–41 of 10 May 1999; Law No. 2003–74 of 11 November 2003; and Law No. 2005–60 of 18 July 2005.

[65] Part of the programme of legislative reform involved working in close cooperation with the United Nations Conference on Trade and Development (UNCTAD). This cooperation involved in-depth consultation and the provision of technical assistance.

[66] See further below in relation to the treatment of price transparency under the Act.

[67] See Article 2 of the Act. [68] See Article 3 of the Act.

[69] The French Ordinance establishes the principle of freedom of prices, except in the case of monopolies or serious crisis. Article 1 of the 1986 Ordinance enables the administration to reinstate price controls in a few sectors in which competition is limited either because there is a monopoly or because specific laws prevent it.

restricting market access by other firms and restricting or controlling production, markets, investments or technical progress or aiming at sharing of markets.[70] This prohibition is in line with the letter and spirit of Article 81(1) EC, though it would be correct to say that the prohibition goes further than the one contained in the latter provision. Originally, the prohibition extended only to horizontal situations: exclusivity clauses and more generally vertical restraints contained in vertical agreements were excluded from the scope of the Act. This aspect of the Act was amended in 1995 to prohibit *all* types of anti-competitive agreements. This position differed from the practice adopted in many systems of competition law around the world where a *rule of reason* is applied to vertical agreements, allowing the competition authority to balance the effect of vertical restraints on competition. To bring the Act more in line with this prevailing practice, the possibility of an exemption was added by the 1999 amendment to the Act, empowering the minister of trade to authorise vertical agreements with exclusivity clauses in certain circumstances. However, it is not clear as to what those circumstances may be and whether in fact a *rule of reason* is employed for the purposes of granting an exemption.

The Act also prohibits abuse of a dominant position 'in the local market or in a substantial part thereof'. Examples of such abuse include the refusal to sell, tied-sales and the imposition of discriminatory commercial conditions; this is parallel to the content of Article 82 EC. According to the Competition Council – the relevant competition authority in Tunisia – being in a dominant position itself is not prohibited unless this position leads to or causes the elimination of competitors or the distortion of the normal functioning of competition and the market mechanism.[71]

Exemption from the prohibition on collusion and abuses of dominance is possible, however, where it could be established that the relevant situation (i.e. that of anti-competitive behaviour or conduct) generates economic or technical progress and provides consumers with a fair share of the resulting benefit or profit. The power to grant exemptions under the Act is placed in the hands of the Minister of Trade who issues these exemptions after seeking the opinion of the Competition Council. The exemption mechanism contained in the Act, although informed by the EC and French systems of competition

[70] See Article 5 of the Act.

[71] Competition Council Decision No. 2135 of 19 December 2002.

law, actually differs from that contained in the latter systems. Among the key differences to be noted here are: the existence of an *express* exemption for abuse of dominance,[72] and the fairly relaxed exemption requirements under the Act. For example, the French and EC competition law regimes allow an exemption only where such agreements do not restrict competition in a manner that is more than necessary for achieving the beneficial objectives and do not eliminate competition in a significant part of the relevant market. In other words, the behaviour or practice in question must be proportionate and cannot lead to the elimination of competition. However, the Tunisian competition law regime does not subject the granting of an exemption to such strict conditions thereby allowing for the possibility of exemption even where competition might be eliminated from a substantial part of the relevant market.

Finally, the 1991 form of the Act did not originally include a special mechanism for the regulation of mergers but this omission was remedied when the 1995 amendment broadened the scope and goals of the Act to include the regulation of such operations.[73] Under the Act, merger operations fall under the heading of 'concentrations', a term defined as any transaction involving a transfer of all or part of the property of a firm allowing another firm or group of firms to exercise, directly or indirectly, a determining influence over the former.[74] Prior to a decree issued in December 2005, mergers, where the joint market share of the firms concerned exceeded 30 per cent and the total sales exceeded 3 million Tunisian Dinars, required the prior approval of the Minister of Trade. The said decree changed these conditions and therefore the total turnover has been set at 20 million Dinars and only one of the two criteria needs to be met for the purposes of merger notification. The Minister of Trade must be notified of mergers within fifteen days of the date of the agreement and must reach a decision within six months of notification; merger operations are assessed on the basis of whether in the relevant situation a dominant position is created or strengthened or is likely to be. Before the amendment to the Act in 2005, the Minister

[72] Note the reference here is to an express exemption. This author therefore does not refer to the doctrines of objective justification and proportionality formulated by the European Court of Justice under Article 82 EC which have the effect – if successfully invoked – of making a particular conduct escape the prohibition on abuse of dominance in the article.

[73] For an account on the Tunisian merger control regime see Dabbah and Lasok, *Merger Control Worldwide* (Cambridge, 2005), pp 1226–30.

[74] See Article 7 of the Act.

could ask for the council's opinion on mergers but had no obligation to do so. The 2005 amendment has made this a mandatory requirement, thus the opinion of the council must be sought.

### *5.3.4 Enforcement: relevant authorities, powers and discretion*

#### 5.3.4.1 The Competition Council

Under the Tunisian regime, responsibility for enforcing the Act and ensuring compliance with its provisions is given to the Competition Council, *Conseil de la Concurrence.*[75] The council was created in 1995 and came to replace the old Competition Commission, *Commission de la Concurrence.* The council is formed of thirteen members who are recommended by the Minister of Trade and appointed by decree by the President of the Republic.[76] The members are selected from diverse backgrounds, including economics, consumer affairs, manufacturing and distribution sectors, so that there is representation from all parties and sectors concerned with the free play of competition. The council is headed by a chairman who must be a judge or a person with a qualification in economics, competition or consumer interests and protection.[77] This particular provision comes to facilitate a judicial attribute on the part of the council. In addition, a permanent secretary, a general rapporteur – along with external recorders[78] – also form part of the council and assist in conducting certain duties.[79] The chairman may also appoint contractual recorders, who are competent and experienced in the field of competition and consumer affairs. The rapporteur is responsible for the registration of petitions, maintaining records and filing,

[75] It is important to note the role played by the Minister of Trade which was noted above and is described further below.

[76] According to Article 10 the members must include: a chairman; a vice-chairman (advisor to the Administrative Court with at least five years of experience in the position); a second vice-chairman (advisor to one of the two chambers in charge of controlling public enterprises); four magistrates of at least second rank; four persons working or having worked in the production or distribution sectors, or the traditional industries and services sectors; and two persons chosen for their expertise in economics, competition or consumer affairs. Article 13A of the Act provides for the appointment of a government representative to the council to represent the Minister of Trade. This representative will be responsible for defending the public interest in competition cases.

[77] See Article 10 of the Act.

[78] The recorders are appointed by the Minister of Trade.

[79] Articles 12 and 13 of the Act. These duties include keeping a register of complaints received, conducting investigations and carrying out other duties as assigned by the chairman.

taking minutes at council hearings and decisions and undertaking any other tasks assigned by the chairman. The rapporteur is appointed to monitor and supervise the work of recorders who initiate the investigation of petitions. In doing so, he may seek and obtain any documents and information considered necessary for the investigation with the permission of the chairman.

The council is an independent authority and is empowered to perform decision-making and advisory functions: it therefore acts as a judicial body and as a consultative body. Accordingly, cases involving anti-competitive practices can be brought before the council and it may also give an opinion on any draft laws and regulations pertaining to competition, when called upon to do so by the minister of trade. The Minister of Trade may consult the council on his own initiative or when requested to do so by the government, professional and consumer organisations, or Chambers of Agriculture, Commerce and Industry regarding competition issues in their sectors.[80] However, it should be noted that the council's opinions are not binding on the parties who request it.

Cases raising competition issues may be referred to the council by any of the following: the Minister of Trade, firms, professional or syndicate organisations, registered consumer organisations and the Chambers of Agriculture, Commerce and Industry.[81] Since the 1999 amendment to the Act, under certain given circumstances the council *may* itself initiate proceedings in a particular situation.[82] Prior to the amendment of 1999, the party who filed a complaint could withdraw it at any stage of litigation and that would have effectively halted the investigation. The change introduced under the 1999 amendment, however, meant the council can continue examining the complaint even where the complainant withdraws it. In addition, the council can initiate an action where it discovers offences in other markets linked to a market which is the subject of the initial investigation.[83]

Where violations of the Act are found, the council has the power to impose financial penalties, order closure of firms and grant injunctions.

[80] See Article 9 of the Act. [81] See Article 11 of the Act.

[82] In practice, however, the majority of cases handled by the council have been the result of a referral from the Minister of Trade.

[83] Paragraph 2 of Article 11 provides that 'the Council may undertake to investigate a complaint on its own accord in case the complainant withdraws the complaint or if the investigation in a case before it indicates practices that harm competition in a market linked directly to the market that is the subject of the case'.

In urgent cases, it can also order interim measures to prevent imminent and irreparable damage to the general economic interest, to the interests of the consumer or one of the parties. The council can impose a maximum fine of up to 5 per cent of the turnover, in the preceding financial year, in the domestic market. Compared with the mechanism of fines available under the competition law regimes of most MECs, this specific provision under the Act has a particular deterrent effect. The council has been immensely in favour of enhancing such effect which is in line with its policy of the need to fight and eradicate harmful breaches of competition law, in particular cartels. During the first eight years of its existence, the council's preferred method of furthering this policy was through 'conventional' investigations. In 2003, however, it came to develop 'modern' tools under this policy, namely a leniency programme encouraging firms which participate in cartel operations to confess to the council about their involvement in return for 'leniency' in treatment by it. The leniency programme was put in place by a 2003 decision of the council providing for total or partial immunity from fines for those offenders who cooperate with the council during the course of the investigation and provide relevant documents and evidence, which support the council's investigation and enable the council swiftly and successfully to bring the investigation to a conclusion.[84] This represents a remarkable policy approach by the council and shows mature thinking on its part.

Beyond the power to impose fines, a closure of firms or their business(es) may be ordered. This is effectively a 'shut-down' power, though it is limited under the Act: the closure cannot exceed a period of three months within which the firm in question must cease the anti-competitive actions of which it has been found guilty. This 'shut-down' power is part of the general powers to grant injunctions. Injunctions are normally ordered by the council for the purposes of putting an end to the anti-competitive practices complained of which must be done within a given period of time; the scope of the injunction may, however, include imposing other conditions on how the business is conducted. In addition, a case can be delegated to the prosecutor and taken to court where criminal charges can be made against the person responsible for the violation of the law. In such a situation punishment can range from

[84] Case No. 2136 of 17 July 2003. The decision was later enshrined, following the 2003 amendment, in Article 19 of the Act.

sixteen days to one-year term of imprisonment and/or a fine from 2,000 to 100,000 Dinar.

The decisions of the Council can be appealed to the Administrative Court's Board of Appeal.[85] The majority of decisions where a fine has been imposed have been appealed by firms, most likely because of the fact that payment is suspended until the appeal is heard which is beneficial to the firm concerned. A right to compensation is also provided for those who have suffered harm as a result of the infringement of competition rules, although this particular branch of enforcement has remained undeveloped in the Tunisian system of competition law.

#### 5.3.4.2 The Minister of Trade

The essential role played by the Ministry and Minister of Trade in the implementation of competition policy in Tunisia is certainly worth highlighting.[86] The Minister of Trade has the power to authorise concentrations and mergers, grant exemptions (in the case of anti-competitive agreements), bring (as we saw above) on his own initiative or upon request from the government cases before the council,[87] and execute the decisions reached by the latter.[88] Furthermore, he is empowered to take any measures he needs, for a maximum of six months, to ensure or reinitiate the conditions necessary for adequate competition in cases involving a crisis or an abnormal situation in a certain sector.[89] Additionally, the possibility for the minister to influence the work of the council is provided by virtue of Article 13A of the Act.[90] Overall, it is clear that the system reserves considerable discretion to the Minister in competition matters.

### *5.3.5 Price transparency*

The issue of pricing is of considerable importance in the Tunisian competition law regime. As we noted above, one of the main objectives of the Act is to ensure price transparency in the market. Part II of the Act deals with price transparency and contains very detailed provisions, the purpose of which is to introduce a mechanism for price regulation.

[85] See Article 21 of the Act.

[86] Within the Ministry, the Department of Competition and Economic Investigations (DGCEE) is responsible for competition enforcement.

[87] See Article 11 of the Act and p 158 above.

[88] See Article 35 of the Act.

[89] See Article 7 A of the Act.

[90] See note 76 above.

These provisions deal with situations ranging from mandating a clear display of price lists by persons active in the retail market for goods or services to prohibiting practices of resale price maintenance.

### 5.3.6 *Reflections*

Broadly speaking, there has been a very low level of competition law enforcement and activity in Tunisia since the instituting of the regime in 1991 and the creation of the Competition Council in 1995. During the first 10 years of the council's existence, the council was presented with a total of 48 cases of which the majority, 60 per cent, were held to be outside the scope of competition law and thus not within the council's jurisdiction.[91] Moreover, not all those assigned the power to bring cases before the council utilised this role despite them being an integral part of the market place. For instance, consumer organisations[92] and chambers of agriculture, industry and commerce filed no petitions in the first ten years of the council's running, which is surprising and disappointing in equal measures given the importance of their position in protecting consumers and ensuring fair play in the market. The main activities of the council have centred around competition advocacy in its advisory role to the government on competition issues. However, even in performing this role, the council is constrained by the Minister of Trade in that it can only give opinions once a matter has been referred to it by the Minister, either on his own accord or upon the request of the government, professional or consumer organisations or the chambers of agriculture or commerce and industry. As was noted above, the Minister of Trade enjoys important powers – with considerable discretion – under the regime, especially those of decision-making in merger cases and in relation to issuing exemptions under the Act.

The council attributed the limited activity to a lack of knowledge on the part of market operators, the absence of a competition culture in the

[91] Thus, on average the council handled four cases per year during the first ten years. In 2004 alone, however, the council opened nineteen investigations which shows a dramatic intensification of its activities. This shows a growing interest and understanding of competition law among firms in particular as well as a more active role on the part of the council. Interestingly, the council came to widen the meaning of the concept of 'undertaking' in order to bring more anti-competitive situations within the scope of the Law.

[92] The Organisation tunisienne de la défense du consommateur (ODC) is the only consumer protection organisation in Tunisia.

country and the fact that the economy is going through a transitional period. Given the high number of cases that were held to be outside the scope of competition law and the council's jurisdiction, it is clear that there is confusion on the part of those who refer cases with regards to the function carried out by the council and the types of disputes it is empowered to deal with. In addition, perhaps there is uncertainty as to the concept of competition itself and the practices which harm the process of competition and its operation in the market place. This is intensified by the apparent confusion over the distinction made between anti-competitive practices and unfair competition.[93] All this certainly provides an explanation for the low number of cases referred to the council and makes it apparent that a more active role needs to be played in defining competition and advocating it, and clarifying the part played by the council in protecting the process of competition in Tunisia. Furthermore, there needs to be greater awareness on the part of the various organisations and institutions, which are authorised to bring cases to the council, as to the vital role they can play in ensuring compliance with the Act by assuring fair competition in the market. For this reason, competition advocacy is extremely crucial in Tunisia and should be part of the council's mandate and activities.

The council has been taking certain steps in order to overcome these hindrances to effective enforcement which appear to be promising. Using the media, it has made itself better known to economic and academic experts and the general public by answering requests for information, explaining the role of the council and highlighting its effectiveness in the annual reports it produces and submits to the President of Tunisia. For this purpose, seminars and Round Tables have also been organised, hosted by the council, to which economic, professional and consumer organisations, as well as judges, lawyers and business advisors are invited. To draw further attention to and to provide a better understanding of the work carried out by the council,

[93] It is important to note that the council differentiates between cases involving anti-competitive actions and unfair competition actions, by considering the latter to be outside the scope of its jurisdiction and falling under Article 92 of the Code of Obligations and Contracts. This was confirmed by the council's decision in Case No. 9/93 of 25 December 2002 where it was held that 'unfair competition cases whose consequences are confined to one or a few enterprises without these cases affecting the market mechanisms and its normal functioning are answerable to before the common law courts'. Over the years, almost half of the petitions or claims brought before the council were held to be cases involving issues of unfair competition and hence not within the council's scope of work.

recent decisions have included an injunction compelling the losing party to publish the council's decision in the case in two national newspapers at their own expense.[94] These efforts by the council have seen an increase in the number of cases handled in the years 2003 and 2004. However, there needs to be a stronger competition culture within Tunisia, which is essential for the successful operation of competition law in the country. This is even more crucial given the long history of state control, which to an extent, continues to influence some economic operators who perceive competition as complementary to state intervention.

## 5.4 Libya: a new policy of unlimited competition

Libya is 'another' Arab country which for many years suffered from considerable international isolation due to painful events and disasters considered linked to its government and old ambitions on the part of the country to develop its non-conventional arsenal. On the other hand, Libya's rigid socialist-oriented ideology and policies have significantly impeded its economic growth and development; these policies and ideology have their roots in the Constitution which provides in Article 7 that 'the state will endeavour to liberate the national economy from dependence and foreign influence, and to turn it into a productive national economy, based on public ownership by the Libyan people and on private ownership by individual citizens'. Article 9 of the Constitution provides further that 'the state will institute a system of national planning covering economic, social, and cultural aspects. Cooperation between the private and public sectors will be necessary for the achievement of the goals of economic development.'

### *5.4.1 The change*

Various events that occurred during the past three years, however, have come to facilitate a u-turn in relation to Libya's international standing and its economic management. In relation to the former, perhaps the most notable developments to mention are the government's decisions to compensate families of the victims of the Lockerbie bombing and more recently to abandon its nuclear ambitions. Both of these events have received warm welcome from many Western governments and

[94] There have been a number of cases in which such an injunction has been granted, most notably in Case No. 2136 of 17 July 2003.

considerable efforts have been made – especially by the UK and the USA – to pull Libya out of its long and damaging international isolation with the relaxing of international sanctions and exploring the prospects for cooperation. The positive results of these developments have been felt quite strongly in the economic sphere and the government has responded with concentrated efforts to build a wide economic platform. With the deterioration of the security situation in Iraq, Libya's efforts have received a particular boost with an increasing demand for oil being diverted from the former to the latter. At no time during its history has Libya appeared to enjoy such promising prospects for economic development and prosperity. In many parts of the capital, Tripoli, there has been serious business congestion caused by the number of foreign investors seeking new and challenging business opportunities in the country. Many of these are returning investors in light of their past involvement in the country, during the 1970s in particular.

### 5.4.2 *Unique style of administration*

Anyone familiar with the policy formulation or public administration in Libya would appreciate the unique style of governance and decision-making in the country which knows no 'middle way' as such. With the developments mentioned above, the government came to appreciate the need for international openness in economic terms, and this has brought it into an encounter with a totally new phenomenon, called competition. The ideology of competition has been fully embraced by the government and an 'open-door' policy in relation to competition especially in the oil sector has been adopted. Currently, the industry is witnessing a very high level of investment activity and Libya's ever-expanding production output has enhanced this investment activity. To some extent this has threatened to cause friction between Libya and other members of the Organisation of the Petroleum Exporting Countries (OPEC). Being interested in avoiding such a situation, Libya has modified its policy and appears to have introduced a capping approach consistent with OPEC's general approach.

### 5.4.3 *Liberalisation, privatisation and WTO accession*

Libya has begun to reform and liberalise its economy by moving away from socialist-orientated policies to an open market economy. In order to achieve this, the government has been cutting subsidies, moving towards privatisation, diversifying the economy to introduce growth in sectors other than oil and encouraging foreign investment. With regards to the latter, the Libyan government's efforts to attract foreign investors into the country came to intensify during the past three years.[95] The origins of these efforts date back to 1997 when the Law Concerning Encouragement of Foreign Capitals Investment was adopted.[96] The aim of this Law, as stipulated in Article 1, is to 'attract investment of foreign capital in investment projects within the framework of the general policy of the State and of the objectives of economical and social development'.[97] Toward this end, the Law provides certain incentives for foreign investors mainly relating to tax exemptions. The Investment Law is considered to be one of the most liberal laws adopted by the Libyan government for attracting foreign investment. It allows foreign investment in a number of sectors which were previously not open to it.[98] Notwithstanding all this, the Law suffers from a number of deficiencies as a result of which the flow of foreign investment in Libya remains low. Foreign investment projects are not afforded 'national treatment'; the licensing procedure is very lengthy; the capital needed is not specified by law; and certain lucrative sectors such as telecommunications, retail

95 The government has also come to place particular emphasis on trade flowing in the 'opposite direction'. In 1999, the Free Trade Act was adopted which provided a legal framework for the establishment of 'offshore free-trade zones' in Libya. The aim behind this was to 'enhance exports, revenue, training, and technology in land, water, energy, telecommunications, and manufacturing facilities'. The movement of goods and services in the free-trade zones can take place free of all taxes, custom duties and trade and monetary restrictions with firms operating in a free zone benefiting from some tax exemptions.

96 Law No. 5 of 1997.

97 To encourage and facilitate foreign investment, the Law established the Libyan Foreign Investment Board which plays an essential role in investment policy. The responsibilities of the board are as follows: to receive and consider the applications for foreign capital investments, supervise foreign investments in the country, gather and publish information for investors, attract and promote investment through various means, deal with complaints, petitions and disputes raised by investors, propose amendments to investment legislations, recommend or renew exemptions, facilities or benefits for investment projects considered important for the development of the economy and undertake other functions assigned to it by the General People's Committee.

98 A list of those sectors appears in Article 8 in which foreign investment is permissible and includes industry, health, tourism, oil-related services and agriculture. However, other sectors can be added to this list by the General People's Committee upon recommendation from the secretary of the General People's Committee for Planning, Economy and Commerce.

and wholesale and the financial sector still remain closed to foreign investors.

Encouragement of the private sector has also been an important part of Libya's economic reform. In September 1992 a Privatisation Law was adopted aiming at increasing private sector involvement in the economy and to permit the sale of state-owned property to 'non-governmental Libyan interests'. In November 2003, an impressive privatisation programme was announced by the government to enhance participation of the private sector in the economy. This programme advocates the privatisation of the country's oil sector amongst other sectors of the economy and will be applied in three phases until 2008. A list of over 380 firms from various sectors was published by the Prime Minister which will be privatised during the 2003–8 period. Since 2003, forty state-owned firms have been transferred by the Privatisation Board. Furthermore, in 2005 the government declared its intention to privatise large enterprises such as TALEF (National Food and Fodder Company), the National Ports Company and Libyan Arab Airlines.

Another important step in Libya's efforts to liberalise its economy is its application for WTO membership. Libya first applied to join the World Trade Organisation (WTO) in 2001 but this was opposed by the USA on the basis of political reasons. In June 2004, Libya once again applied for membership of the WTO and this was approved in July 2004 when the General Council established a working party to analyse Libya's application and assist it in the process. This marks the first step in the accession process and highlights emergence of Libya in the international community. During negotiations, Libya will be given an observer status by the WTO. Membership of the WTO would further strengthen the development and diversification of Libya's economy.

### *5.4.4 A possible competition law for Libya*

With a policy favouring increased competition, the government has turned its attention to drafting a domestic competition law, which is expected to be adopted by the beginning of 2009. The work on the draft, however, has been quite slow; one could say that important external links, such as links with the EC or international organisations – as enjoyed by many other MECs – could have been expected to enhance and speed up the drafting process. Such links, however, are non-existent in the case of Libya. For example, in relation to links with the EC – which are enjoyed by other Maghreb countries – Libya is not a member of the

Euro–Mediterranean Partnership because when it was formed in 1995 Libya was under United Nations sanctions and was therefore not permitted to join. It was instead given the status of observer in the 1999 Stuttgart Conference. As a result, there is no Association Agreement between the EC and Libya and neither have there been any negotiations for such an agreement. However, the council of the EU has stated that such negotiations are subject to the full integration of Libya in the Barcelona Process and its full and unconditional acceptance of the Barcelona Declaration.[99]

[99] The Barcelona Process was discussed in chapter 1.

# 6

# Jordan's 2004 Competition Law

The adoption of a specific competition law in the Hashemite Kingdom of Jordan was a step taken by the Kingdom for the purposes of furthering its economic reform programme, which started in 2000. This programme was in a large part motivated by a desire on the part of the government to attract increased foreign direct investment into the Kingdom. The new Millennium brought new hopes for Jordan within the economic sphere: a new young – many would say Western – Monarch was sworn in; promising peace and harmony, especially between Jordan's neighbours; a serious interest by several key hi-technology international firms in the country looking to create a Middle Eastern silicon valley in the Jordan Valley emerged; and an increasing number of well-educated and wealthy Jordanians returned home bringing with them vast intellectual and financial assets.

Jordan is a small and weak economy, which – along with the Jordanian society and political regime – is incredibly easy to destabilise. The Kingdom enjoys a strong heritage though resources are scarce. Its particular geographic location and the composition of its population – with a Palestinian majority – has been the cause of problems threatening unrest within the country on several occasions. The Kingdom has been, for many years, ruled by the same family and often, according to many people, with an invisible iron fist directed at the country's Palestinian majority. This 'undesirable' reality for many Jordanians, however, has been the driving force behind Jordan's long association with the West, in particular with the USA. Foreign education and experience are highly valued in the country, pushing an increasing number of Jordanians in recent years to seek these 'crown jewels' in European and North American cities. The result has been a transformation towards Westernised legal and economic systems in the country. Nonetheless, governance in Jordan still lacks sufficient duration to enable important policies to be effectively formulated and successfully implemented. If an entry were to be created in the

*Guinness Book of Records* for the shortest-serving governments and ministers, Jordan could be expected to hold this comfortably and without facing any serious challenge from another country.

### 6.1 International outlook and cooperation

Arguably, Jordan's concentrated efforts towards introducing economic reform for the purposes of achieving full economic and trade liberalisation in the country can be said to be motivated in large part by its scarcity of resources. Unlike many Arab countries in the region, Jordan does not enjoy natural wealth and therefore the issue of state control and monopolisation of certain sectors is not relevant. As we noted above, this appears to have turned the country's attention towards the international arena and to seek integration into what has become a fast-developing process of globalisation. In turn, this has pushed the need and desirability for international cooperation high up on the national agenda. Jordan has always been dependent on foreign assistance, support and protection, originally through its association with Britain during the Mandate in different parts of the region and more recently through its special relationship with the USA. The international ties of the country were originally conceived as personal relationships and ties between families: with the British royal family and with former US Presidents, from Harry Truman to Bill Clinton, who served during the reign of the late King Hussein.

This interesting international outlook of a small Middle Eastern economy should be considered as positive and the country's embracing of a free-market economy worthy of the attention of both foreign governments and multinational firms. Since the beginning of the 1990s Jordan secured membership of the World Trade Organisation (WTO), concluded free trade agreements with the USA, the European Free Trade Association (EFTA) and Singapore, and signed an Association Agreement with the EC. However, these remarkable achievements were not to be secured with the country's economic openness alone: crucial and vital political steps had to be taken in parallel, most notably concluding a peace treaty and normalising relations with neighbouring Israel. Indeed, it is the case that the seeds of Jordan's economic development only began to be sewn following this important and much welcomed step, which shows in a way how in the Middle East the competition law question – which in Jordan and other MECs sits at the heart of economic development and reform – is very much tied to the regional and international political arenas and this makes the field more unique and rather unusual in relation to this important region.

### *6.1.1 Jordan–EC Association Agreement*

Although an Association Agreement between Jordan and the EC was only signed in the late 1990s and entered into force as recently as 2002, cooperation between the parties dates back to the 1970s, when they concluded a General Cooperation Agreement in 1977.[1] The main aim of the Association Agreement is the creation of a free trade area between the parties over a twelve-year period, which is a fundamental aspect of the Euro–Mediterranean partnership. The agreement contains provisions relating to competition and state aid worded similarly to Articles 81 and 82 EC, and Article 87 EC respectively. Article 53(1)(a) of the agreement provides that collusion between firms is incompatible with the functioning of the agreement to the extent that it affects trade between Jordan and the EC. Article 53(1)(b) provides a similar rule in relation to abuse of dominance. Article 53(1)(c) provides that state aid affecting trade between Jordan and the EC is also incompatible with the functioning of the agreement.

Article 89 of the Agreement provides for the creation of the Association Council. Article 53(3) allows the council a period of five years from the date the agreement entered into force within which to adopt rules for the implementation of the competition law provisions of the agreement.

### *6.1.2 Jordan–EFTA Free Trade Agreement*

The Jordan–EFTA Free Trade Agreement was concluded in 2001 and entered into force in 2002. Article 1 of the Agreement provides that its objective is to promote harmonious development of economic relations between Jordan and the EFTA countries with the goal of removing by 2014 all customs duties on trade in industrial goods and fish and other marine products. Article 29 provides for the establishment of a joint committee, made of representatives of the parties, in order to supervise and administer the implementation of the agreement.

[1] The Association Agreement was signed on 24 November 1997. It entered into force on 1 May 2002, replacing the General Cooperation Agreement.

Competition law is a prominent feature of the agreement. Article 18 in particular contains the rules on competition under which collusion between firms restricting competition (Article 18(1)(a)) and abuses of dominance (Article 18(1)(b)) which affect trade between Jordan and an EFTA Member State are declared incompatible with the functioning of the agreement. Article 11 provides for the regulation of state monopolies to ensure that the conditions for the marketing and procurement of goods between the EFTA States and Jordan are not affected.

### *6.1.3 Jordan–Israel-US QIZ Agreement*

The Qualified Industrial Zones (QIZ) Agreement between Jordan, Israel and the USA was signed in 1997 and entered into force in March 1998, on the basis of the Jordan–Israel Peace Treaty which was signed in October 1994.[2] The aim of this agreement is to strengthen the Jordanian economy, by attracting foreign investment, and to develop commercial relations between Jordan and Israel. It was considered, especially by the USA, that concluding the agreement and seeking these aims would in turn promote stability in the region, in line with the overall objective of the QIZ initiative which is to support the peace process in the Middle East.

The agreement put in place a highly interesting idea: 'substantial economic cooperation' between Jordan and Israel would be required in order for the goods produced in QIZ to enter the US markets duty-free. There are, at present, thirteen areas in Jordan that have been designated as QIZ by the US Trade Representative. Products manufactured in the QIZ can enjoy quota-free and duty-free entry into the USA – a right which is usually reserved for US free trade partners such as Canada and Mexico – and can thereby enter the US market at a more competitive price than products from other countries than would otherwise be the case. In order for this to take place, however, the relevant conditions set by US law and under the agreement must be satisfied. In particular, the products in question must have been manufactured with an Israeli input. The agreement in general (and this requirement in particular) has significantly developed trade relations between Israel and Jordan. There has been a dramatic increase in Israeli exports to QIZ factories in Jordan and a corresponding noticeable

[2] Another QIZ Agreement was concluded between Israel, Egypt and the USA which is discussed at pp 239–40 below.

increase in Jordan's exports to US markets. Additionally, the existence and operation of the agreement has helped attract considerable foreign investment in Jordan, since investors can reap the benefits of duty-free access to the USA for products manufactured within the qualified industrial zones. Among other things, these significant developments have helped create employment opportunities in Jordan and enhance the Kingdom's regional standing.

## 6.2 The Competition Act

### *6.2.1 The failure of the 1990s and the success of 2002*

Jordan's initiative to enact a specific competition law was shaped in the mid-1990s. There were two specific attempts during the 1990s, namely in 1995 and 1998. Those attempts, however, were not successful and within a short period after their launch were doomed to failure for various reasons. Most notable among these was the heavy-handedness of the government in its approach to parachute into the Kingdom the competition laws of other countries without proper or adequate consideration of the contextual framework and Jordan's own circumstances. A particular failure on the part of the government was the lack of realisation of the need to adopt a *realistic* approach to competition law and policy and to institute a competition law regime suitable for Jordan's small economy and legal system. Instead, the government opted to adopt an *ambitious* competition law regime, the parameters of which went beyond Jordan's economic capability, institutional capacity and national needs. In more than one way, these attempts were quite damaging to the aspirations and hopes of the country to enact specific competition legislation and there was a period of stagnation between 1998 and 2002, when the process was restarted and the legislative work for the purposes of producing a draft competition law resumed. In this third round, the government's approach was much more realistic and in drafting the law, attention was given to the Tunisian system of competition law and help was sought and obtained from Tunisian competition law specialists. This afforded those concerned an appropriate opportunity to consult a benchmark regime of a country with many similarities to Jordan, most notably in terms of culture and economic development. The round was impressive on many fronts, particularly in terms of the speed at which the work developed; the consideration of relevant crucial issues;[3] and the breadth of the consultation with various branches of the government, the private sector and other interested parties. The European Commission also played an important role in this process by providing technical assistance.

At the end of this round, the Competition Act 2002 was adopted on 15 August 2002 and entered into force in the same year.[4] This Act was adopted on a *temporary* basis; it was later readopted in its present form as the Competition Act 2004.[5] The Act is a fairly comprehensive piece of legislation, though many of its provisions have not been drafted carefully and would certainly require clarification in practice. The Act may be considered to be ambitious given that its use in practice is intended to be as a tool for the purposes of achieving many far-reaching goals and objectives, most of which sit at the heart of the Kingdom's declared policy of economic openness. Indeed, its adoption was a step taken by the Kingdom as part of the modernisation of the local economy and economic system for the purposes of building and consolidating a functioning market economy.

### 6.2.2 *The aims of the Act*

There are several goals subscribed to the Act. Among these are: sustainable economic growth; increased foreign direct investment; a healthy economic environment; protection of small and medium-size firms from anti-competitive behaviour and abusive conduct. Additionally, the Act aims at encouraging and creating incentives for firms to improve their competitiveness (especially in international markets) and providing consumers with improved product quality at competitive prices.

Article 3 of the Act contains a fairly broad net insofar as it provides that *all* economic activities are within the scope of the Act, whether conducted or occurring within Jordan or outside it so long as they produce 'an effect inside the Kingdom'. Broadly speaking, these activities fall within the realm of one of three situations, namely anti-competitive practices, abuse of dominance and economic concentrations (mergers) producing negative impact on competition.

[3] Particular attention was given to Jordan's economy, its structure and size, and the number of different market players in different sectors. This enabled the proposed law to be more balanced with a strong 'Jordanian' dimension being added to it.

[4] The Competition Act No. 49. [5] The Competition Act No. 33.

#### 6.2.2.1 Anti-competitive practices

The Act identifies and lists several forms of collusion between enterprises[6] which together are grouped under the prohibition on 'anti-competitive practices'. These include: 'Practices, alliances and agreements, explicit or implicit, that prejudice, contravene, limit or prevent competition'.[7] This wording is clearly very broad, aimed at catching as many harmful situations as possible. A non-closed list of examples caught under the prohibition features in Article 5(A)(1)–(5) which extends to situations aiming at price-fixing, market-sharing, output limitation, hindering market entry or collusive tendering.[8] The prohibition contains three aspects worth noting. First, there is no reference to effect on trade: on the basis of the wording of Article 5 it would appear that the prohibition will apply without the need to demonstrate an effect on trade.[9] Secondly, the article does not contain the words 'object' or 'effect' but appears to have substituted these terms with those of 'explicit' or 'implicit'.[10] It is not clear whether this is a sound substitution. Undoubtedly, a prohibition on collusion should apply to all forms of behaviour or practices whether explicit or implicit; however, the omission of the key terms of object or effect and the apparent reliance on explicit or implicit are only bound to be problematic in practice. Thirdly, it is worth noting the existence of a *de minimis* doctrine under Article 5(B) which is discussed further below.[11]

The prohibition on anti-competitive practices applies in both horizontal and vertical senses. However, such practices may benefit from an exemption under the Act.[12]

[6] The Act uses the term 'enterprise' defined in Article 2 as a natural or legal person carrying out an economic activity and includes a group of such persons.

[7] See Article 5(A) of the Act.

[8] Article 5(A)(5) nonetheless allows the submission of joint bids insofar as such bids are not designed to harm competition and provided that an announcement to that effect is made by the bidding parties in advance.

[9] A similar situation discussed at p 202 below exists under the Saudi Competition Act.

[10] It may be interesting here to contrast this wording of the article with that of Article 19 of the *Instructions on Competition Safeguards in the Telecommunications Sector* produced by the Telecommunications Regulatory Commission in February 2006 which defines collusion as a form of coordination between two or more licensees 'to exert influence on the market with the *objective* or *effect* of fixing prices or otherwise restraining competition' (emphasis added). Article 19 does, however, provide that collusion can be either 'explicit', 'a cartel' or 'tacit'. The *Instructions,* which are also discussed at pp 191–2 below, can be found at the TRC's website, www.trc.gov.jo.

[11] See pp 188–9 below. [12] See the discussion at pp 178–9 below in relation to exemptions.

#### 6.2.2.2 Abuse of dominance

Dominance is defined rather ambiguously and inadequately as the 'condition in which an Enterprise is able to control and affect the activity of the market'.[13] The Act contains no further guidance on how this ability is established and what factors may be used in determining this.[14] The prohibition on abuse of dominance is contained in Article 6 of the Act which also lists seven examples of abuse.[15] During the drafting of the article heavy reliance was placed on Article 82 EC, which deals with abuse of dominance but consultation of section 2 of the US Sherman Act 1890 also took place.[16] However, the article diverges from Article 82 EC in some notable respects. For example, the article does not refer to 'one or more' enterprises, a reference featuring in Article 82 EC. Furthermore, Article 6 makes no reference to effect on trade, though it does – nonetheless – refer to a dominant position 'in the local market or significant part thereof'.[17] The highly expected effect on trade requirement when establishing abuse was in fact at the end replaced with that of preventing, limiting or weakening competition.

[13] See Article 2 of the Act. The reference to 'market' here should be taken as a reference to the relevant market. The term is defined in Article 2 as the 'product or services or all products or services which are, in view of their price, characteristics and uses, interchangeable and mutually replaceable to meet a particular need of the consumer in a particular geographical location wherein exist compatible competition conditions'.

[14] The *Instructions on Competition Safeguards in the Telecommunications Sector*, mentioned in note 10 above, use market-share thresholds when establishing the existence of a dominant position by a licensee in the telecommunications sector. Article 8 of the *Instructions* provides the following: there is a rebuttable presumption of dominance where a licensee holds a market share of 50 per cent or more; a licensee with a market share between 25 per cent and 50 per cent may be found to be dominant if available evidence points in that direction; and there is a rebuttable presumption of non-dominance where a licensee holds a market share of less than 25 per cent.

[15] See paragraphs (A)–(G) which cover situations of pricing abuses and those of refusal to supply and essential facilities, hindrance to market entry, discrimination, tying, and market foreclosure. The *Instructions on Competition Safeguards in the Telecommunications Sector* provide very detailed provisions on the issue of abuse of dominance in the sector. See in particular, Articles 10–18 of the *Instructions*.

[16] In fact this consultation has filtered into the wording of the article which includes the language of 'attempting to monopolize' in a similar vein to section 2 of the Sherman Act 1890.

[17] Article 82 EC includes a similar reference to 'a dominant position within the common market or in a substantial part of it'.

#### 6.2.2.3 Economic concentrations

The Act contains a fairly developed mechanism for merger control; the Competition Directorate has developed this mechanism through, among other things, adopting a merger notification form and establishing the various components of its merger control practice.[18] The Act uses the term 'economic concentration' as opposed to merger or concentration. The term is defined as 'any activity resulting in the full or partial transfer of ownership of or interest in property or rights or shares or obligations of an Enterprise to another, and which may enable an Enterprise or a group of Enterprises to control, directly or indirectly, another Enterprise or group of Enterprises'.[19] The use of the word 'activity' when defining what amounts to a merger or concentration is bound to be considered as not entirely suitable given that it is thought to extend beyond the scope of such business phenomenon. However, the problematic use of the word in this regard is 'watered down' given that the latter part of the definition makes it abundantly clear that the crucial criterion in the definition is the issue of control.[20]

For the purposes of the Act, an economic concentration covers a variety of situations: mergers or amalgamations, acquisitions of control (whether sole or joint) and joint venture operations deemed to be 'concentrative' or more accurately 'full-function' entities. All of these types are subject to mandatory notification under the Act where the enterprises concerned in an economic concentration have a combined market share exceeding 40 per cent of the relevant market.[21] Although the notification in this case must be to the Competition Directorate, the power to approve or block economic concentrations is in the hands of the Ministry of Industry and Trade: the Minister will reach his decision on the basis of whether the operation is likely to impact the level of competition in the market by creating or enforcing a

[18] The form is available electronically (in Arabic) on the directorate's website, at www.mit.gov.jo/competition.

[19] See Article 9(A) of the Act.

[20] The *Instructions on Competition Safeguards in the Telecommunications Sector*, mentioned in note 10 above, may be interesting to consider in relation to the issue of control acquired in operations occurring within the telecommunications sector. Under Article 2 of the *Instructions*, control is defined as 'the ownership of more than 50 per cent of the voting interests in a Person and/or the ability to control in fact the business of a Person, whether by ownership, agreement, or otherwise'.

[21] See Article 9(B) of the Act.

dominant position;[22] there is no indication given about the criteria or factors taken into account when making this assessment.[23] The decision in this case may be unconditional clearance of the operation, conditional clearance[24] or outright prohibition, reached within a strict time-frame of 100 days[25] of the date on which the notification was declared complete by the directorate.[26] Out of these three outcomes, the first one is important to note in light of the considerations listed in Article 11(A)(1) of the Act. This paragraph provides that the Minister will approve a 'concentration operation if it does not negatively impact competition, or has positive economic benefits that outweigh any negative impact on competition, such as leading to a lowering of the price of services or products, or providing employment opportunities, or encouraging exports or attracting investment, or supporting the ability of national Enterprises to compete internationally'. Non-competition based considerations therefore feature very prominently in the operation of the merger control mechanism within the Jordanian competition law regime. Looking at these considerations (in particular those of lower prices, attracting investment and creating national champions), it should be clear that many of them tie in with many of the goals behind the Act.[27]

22 *Ibid.* Although the decision must be that of the Minister himself, it is possible for the Minister, by virtue of Article 11(A) of the Act, to adopt the recommendation of the director of the Competition Directorate on the preferred decision. In any case, the decision of the Minister must be a reasoned one and must be published (or alternatively a summary of it) in at least two daily newspapers (see Article 11(B) of the Act). It may be worth noting here the different test contained in the *Instructions on Competition Safeguards in the Telecommunications Sector* in the case of an acquisition or transfer of interest in control (defined in note 20 above) of a licensee in the telecommunications sector which rests on the concepts of substantial lessening of competition and that of the creation of a monopoly with no reference to 'dominance' or 'impacting' the level of competition.

23 This contrasts with Article 20(b) of the *Instructions on Competition Safeguards in the Telecommunications Sector* which offers a detailed, non-closed list of factors taken into account by the Telecommunications Regulatory Commission when conducting its evaluation of whether an acquisition lessens competition substantially or creates a monopoly.

24 The Act provides for the possibility of having commitments or undertakings submitted by the parties along with their notification for the purposes of – according to Article 10(B) – minimising 'the possible negative impact' of the operation.

25 During the 100-days period, the parties must suspend their operation.

26 The three outcomes are included in Article 11(A) of the Act.

27 See p 173 above for an account of these goals.

As was remarked above, a special notification form has been adopted which must be used when effecting a notification to the Competition Directorate. This notification must take place within thirty days of the date on which the concentration or merger agreement was reached.[28] The type of information required when notifying an economic concentration is listed exhaustively in Article 10(A)(1)–(8) of the Act and the notification form itself.[29] The directorate reserves the power to request additional or missing information for the purposes of completing the notification; however, the Act limits the exercise of this power to only once.[30]

#### 6.2.2.4 Exemptions

Exemptions from the prohibitions on anti-competitive practices and abusive conduct are possible by virtue of Article 7(B) of the Act. To obtain an exemption, firms need to notify their agreement or conduct to

[28] This does not have to be the final agreement and it may in some cases be an informal agreement so long as clear evidence is furnished of the parties' intention to reach a final agreement.

[29] The information required includes, the memoranda and articles of association of the enterprises concerned, a copy of the concentration or merger agreement, an account of the positive (and non-positive) effects and competition implications likely to flow from the operation, a list of the 'most important' products produced by the parties, details about market shares, financial statements covering the preceding two fiscal years, the details of shareholders, partners and officers of the parties and details of the branches of each enterprise concerned. The Competition Directorate has made it clear that as far as information about the competition implications of the operation and market shares is concerned, this must be supplied in a comprehensive manner including a detailed assessment and definition of the relevant market(s).

[30] See Article 10(C)(2) of the Act. Interestingly, the directorate is not given the power to reject a notification on the grounds of incomplete information. The chosen means for curing such deficiencies therefore is a written request by the directorate for additional information. This in effect places the burden on the directorate as opposed to the parties in a concentration and is not the practice followed in the vast majority of merger control regimes around the world. It is important to note, however, that this provision does not deprive the directorate of the power to seek or request further information during its evaluation of the concentration, i.e. following the receipt of complete notification. The directorate must issue a written notice confirming that the notification is complete. According to paragraph (2) of Article 10(C), the particulars of this notice are determined according to instructions issued by the Minister of Industry and Trade. In addition, the directorate must publish the fact of the notification in two daily newspapers at the expense of the parties. The purpose here is to enable third parties to present their views to the directorate provided they do so within fifteen days following the date of publication.

the Competition Directorate using the relevant form.[31] Detailed information is required by the parties when seeking an exemption, in particular highlighting the positive aspects of the behaviour or conduct. The decision on whether to grant an exemption is in the hands of the Minister of Industry and Trade.[32] The exemption criteria contained in the article refer to 'positive results, with a common benefit that cannot be achieved without . . . exemption, including the improvement of the competitive ability of Enterprises, or production or distribution systems, or providing certain benefits to the consumer'. In practice, when considering an exemption, the Minister (and the Competition Directorate) evaluates whether the situation in question operates against the public interest. In addition to the criteria listed in Article 7(B), account is also taken of whether the behaviour or conduct leads to technical or economic progress and whether it contains a risk of elimination of competition. The decision of the Minister must be reached within a period of ninety days from the date on which a complete notification was confirmed by the directorate.[33] The exemption given may be for a limited term or an open one, provided that periodic reviews of the situations are carried out to monitor any material changes.

### *6.2.3 Price regulation*

The Act advocates a broad idea of free pricing regime in accordance with the market mechanism and principles of free competition. However, exceptions to this idea are provided in Article 4 of the Act which concerns situations where prices for basic commodities are regulated by the Industry and Trade Law[34] and any other laws applicable and those where the government may control prices in

[31] The form (which is available only in Arabic) can be downloaded from the directorate's website, at www.mit.gov.jo/competition. Three copies of the form must be submitted; only Arabic can be used, though documents in other languages may be submitted provided they are accompanied with a certified translation into Arabic. Notification may be effected individually (by each relevant firm) or collectively (by all the firms acting together). The directorate welcomes pre-notification consultation where the parties wish to receive the benefit of its views.

[32] According to Article 7(B) of the Act, this must be a reasoned decision on the basis of a recommendation of the director of the Competition Directorate.

[33] See Article 7(D) of the Act. Here too (like the case with merger notifications), the directorate must issue a written notice confirming the notification to be complete.

[34] See the section on market control and supervision below.

exceptional circumstances.[35] In the latter situations the government's intervention or exercise of power is subject to review within six months from the date on which the intervention was mandated.[36] The influence of the Tunisian competition law, which similarly promotes the principle of market forces determining prices but allows the government to intervene and control prices in certain cases, can certainly be seen in this provision of the Jordanian Act. Consequently, although market forces are generally allowed to set prices, government controls remain on a number of consumer products.

### *6.2.4 Fairness of commercial transactions*

Under Article 8 of the Act, the practices of a producer, importer, wholesaler or service-provider are regulated to ensure that these are not detrimental to the fairness of commercial transactions. Accordingly, such persons are prohibited from setting a minimum resale price for a product and from giving or receiving special conditions for sales and purchases which will give a party advantage in the process of competition or cause harm to competition.[37] In addition, under paragraph (B) of the article, the Act prohibits the resale of a product at a price which is lower than the price it was purchased for,[38] if the purpose of doing so is to restrict competition. The Competition Directorate's belief is that the inclusion of these prohibitions will enhance the commercial fairness in the marketplace; the prohibitions are in fact also instrumental in expanding the scope of the application of the Act to harmful vertical agreements and situations of abuse of dominance.

## 6.3 Institutional structure and the different players

The Act creates a rather sophisticated institutional structure with three distinct authorities conducting competition work, namely the

[35] These exceptional circumstances concern cases of emergency or natural disaster. According to Article 7(A) practices adopted by the government in this case will not be considered an anti-competitive practice (under Article 5) or abusive conduct (under Article 6).

[36] According to the provision, price control is effected by way of a resolution adopted by the Council of Ministers.

[37] See Article 8(A) of the Act.

[38] The purchase price is the price set in the invoice after deduction of the discounts specified therein.

Competition Directorate, the Committee for Competition Affairs and the courts.

### 6.3.1 *The Competition Directorate*

The directorate is incorporated within the Ministry of Trade and Industry. Its task force is extremely modest with less than ten officials, who enjoy legal and economic expertise, working in the directorate alongside the director[39] and the chief economist. The directorate operates within a rather limited budget, which is bound in practice to prove insufficient for the purposes of fighting serious anti-competitive practices and abuses and also for regulating merger operations notified to it under the Act. This state of affairs limits the scope of the work of the directorate in practice and it is doubtful whether these conditions will improve given the difficulty in attracting sufficiently qualified persons from private practice, whether within or outside Jordan, to the directorate and the need to conduct training programmes for the purposes of equipping officials and judges with the necessary tools in order to execute their work effectively. Indeed, the picture that has emerged shows a gap has come to exist between the actual aims of the Act and the institutional mechanisms and capabilities available for its application. Interestingly, the directorate itself has come to realise the existence of this gap.[40] It may be necessary at some future point to revise the provisions of the Act in order to minimise or help bridge this gap in practice. The directorate acknowledges that it may become necessary to amend the Act at later stages in light of the experience acquired in future cases. This is a positive and mature approach, which shows understanding on the part of the directorate of the strong link existing between competition law and market developments and those related to the domestic economy more generally.

The directorate is divided into three separate departments, in addition to the offices of the director and assistant director. These are the Competition Policy Department, the Concentrations and Exemption Department and the Consultation and Investigations Department, which receives complaints and conducts research.

[39] As with Egypt and Israel, the person chosen to fill the position of director is a woman, Ms Luna Abbadi.

[40] See Part 3.1 of the directorate's *Annual Report* (2003), available at www.mit.gov.jo/competition/Files/Ar/Annual_Report.pdf.

The Directorate is responsible for enforcing the Act. The enforcement function of the directorate rests on three key pillars: conducting competition investigations and cooperating with foreign competition authorities for the purposes of exchanging information in competition cases with an international dimension, in order to guarantee effective and consistent enforcement; participating in the legislative process where relevant to ensure that competition issues receive adequate attention;[41] and actively engaging in competition advocacy for the purposes of building a competition culture within the Kingdom. This involves conducting training sessions and seminars and publishing important information.

### *6.3.2 The Committee for Competition*

The Committee for Competition Matters or Affairs (CCM) is an advisory and consultative body active in policy formulation surrounding the Act and the general competition strategy in Jordan. Among its specific tasks are those of conducting reviews of the provisions of the Act or those of proposed laws or regulations with competition relevance, as may be delegated to it by the Minister of Industry and Trade, who serves as chairman of the CCM. According to Article 14 of the Act, the membership of the CCM consists of ten individuals, in addition to the chairman. They are: the Undersecretary of the Ministry of Industry and Trade as a vice-chairman, the Director General of the Jordan Insurance Commission, the Chief Executive Officer of the Jordan Telecommunications Regulatory Commission, the Director General of the Jordan Transportation Regulatory Board, the President of the Jordanian Union of Chambers of Commerce, the Presidents of one of the Jordanian Chambers of Industry and one of the Jordanian consumer associations,[42] and three individuals with relevant expertise and specialisation.[43] Meetings of the CCM – which are to take place at least once every six months – may be attended by other individuals

[41] See below.

[42] These two members are named by the Minister of Industry and Trade and are appointed for a two-year term, which may be renewed once.

[43] The Act is silent with regard to the field of work or background of these individuals who are appointed by the Minister of Industry and Trade. The current three individuals who have been named by the Minister are an academic research economist, an engineer and a part-time academic practitioner. The appointment is for two years renewable once.

invited by the Minister of Industry and Trade though they may not participate in voting on decisions of the CCM.[44] The director of the directorate acts as rapporteur for the CCM with responsibility for preparing the agenda for its meetings, keeping a record of the minutes of the meetings and preparing a summary of the CCM's recommendations to appear in the annual report.[45]

It is unclear to what extent this particular composition of the CCM will enable it to engage in deep and serious competition work and thus be in a position to execute its work effectively. The offices of the members of the CCM are not usually held for a long term in Jordan and rotate quite frequently which is likely to impact on the work of the CCM in practice.

### *6.3.3 The courts*

Enforcement of the Act rests in the hands of the courts. Under Article 16 of the Act, the Amman Court of First Instance (the Amman CFI) is the only competent court to enforce the provisions of the Act for a period of two years following the date on which the Act came into force.[46] The aim was to use this two-year period to train judges serving in the Court of First Instance in other regions in the field of competition law and arm them with the necessary tools to handle competition cases. The decision to accord exclusive competence on the Amman CFI was made prior to the adoption of the Act. Two factors appear to have necessitated this decision. First, there is the fact that no specialist competition tribunal was set up in the country as was contemplated early in the legislative debate; some strong views have been expressed in favour of having such a tribunal especially from within the directorate, which considers that the absence of such a tribunal may hinder the process of experience building among judges given the constant change in judicial appointments and the special nature of competition cases. Secondly, there is the risk of possible inconsistencies in the application of the Act which could prove extremely damaging. To avoid this risk, three members of the Amman CFI were nominated to handle competition cases and were offered relevant training in the field.

44 See Article 15(B) of the Act. The first meeting of the CCM was held on 22 May 2003.
45 See Article 15(C) of the Act.
46 See Article 15(B) of the Act.

Competition actions are brought by the office of the Attorney General.[47] However, Article 17(B) of the Act provides that in all cases the Ministry of Industry and Trade shall appear as a party before the court. The judgments of the Amman CFI are not final and may be appealed to the Court of Appeal and the Court of Cassation.[48] In cases of economic concentrations[49] and exemptions,[50] it should be noted that decisions adopted by the Minister of Industry and Trade may be appealed by the parties to the Supreme Court of Justice; there is no role in this regard therefore for the lower courts, including the Amman CFI, to play.

### *6.3.4 The role of the Minister of Industry and Trade*

A particular concern under the Act is the centralised role it affords to the Minister of Industry and Trade. Under the Act the Minister enjoys wide discretion, which is expected to hamper the effective enforcement of the Act. Among other things, the Minister, as opposed to the director of the directorate, is able to submit complaints to the public prosecutor for the purposes of instituting actions by the latter;[51] heads the CCM and in practice controls its work and the appointment of five of its members; is able to reach the final decision in merger cases;[52] and enjoys the power to grant, where appropriate, exemptions for anti-competitive behaviour or abusive conduct.[53]

## 6.4 Powers and responsibilities

### *6.4.1 Investigations*

Article 12 of the Act empowers the Competition Directorate to conduct investigations into violations of the Act, either on its own initiative or on the basis of any complaints it receives. Complaints relating to anti-competitive practices can be brought by the Minister of Industry and Trade, private sector enterprises, licensed consumer protection associations, any group of at least five consumers who have suffered damage, chambers of commerce and industry, professional

[47] See Article 16(E) of the Act which provides that the office of the Attorney General will be represented by a specialised prosecutor general.

[48] See Article 18(E) of the Act. [49] See pp 176–8 above. [50] See pp 178–9 above.

[51] See Article 17(A)(1) of the Act. [52] See Article 11 of the Act.

[53] See the discussion on exemption at pp 178–9 above.

and syndicate organisations and sectoral regulatory authorities.[54] During the course of the investigation, the directorate's officers have, upon the written authorisation of the director, considerable powers to access any information they consider necessary and can conduct inspections and searches during working hours.[55] The Director can also request information and documents relating to the violation committed from any relevant person who holds that knowledge and can ask them to testify.[56] The findings of the investigation carried out by the directorate must be presented in a report to the Minister of Industry and Trade or the court, as is applicable. According to Article 19(D) of the Act, the report must include an analysis of the state of competition and its effect on market balance as a result of the violation of the Law. Cases will then be instituted in court in accordance with the results of the investigation into the complaint. The court must highlight in its decision the extent of the violation committed and can order that an end must be put to the anti-competitive practice within a given period of time.[57] In addition, the court may also impose certain conditions on the violator relating to how the business is conducted, depending on the circumstances of the case, and it can order the publication of its decision in two local newspapers at the violator's expense. Responsibility for executing the decisions reached by the court is vested in the Minister of Industry and Trade, who may take all measures he considers necessary in carrying this out.[58]

### 6.4.2 *Penalties*

The level of fine imposed for a violation of the Jordanian competition rules depends on the provision of the Act which has been violated. Thus, practices, alliances and agreements which contravene, limit or prevent competition and the abuse by an enterprise of its dominant position are subject to a fine of not less than 1 per cent and not exceeding 5 per cent of the total annual value of the sales or revenue from services of the violator. If this value is not specified then the fine imposed must not be less than 1,000 Dinars and not exceeding 50,000 Dinars.[59] Violations of Articles 9 and 10 of the Act, together with the failure to comply with a decision issued by the Minister under Article 11, are punishable by fines

[54] See Article 17 of the Act. [55] See Article 19(A) of the Act.
[56] See Article 19(C) of the Act. [57] See Article 18 of the Act.
[58] See Article 18(D) of the Act. [59] See Article 20 of the Act.

not less than 1,000 Dinars and not exceeding 50,000 Dinars.[60] Those involved in practices which are detrimental to the fairness of commercial transactions,[61] in violation of Article 8, will face a fine not less than 200 Dinars and not exceeding 20,000 Dinars.[62] Furthermore, where confidential information is disclosed by a person, he shall be subject to a fine not less than 1,000 and not exceeding 10,000 Dinars.[63] Finally, anyone who obstructs an officer in the course of his duties or conceals and destroys information necessary in an investigation shall be subject to a fine not less than 500 and not exceeding 5,000 Dinars.[64] When determining the level of a fine, factors such as the harm suffered by others as a result of the violation and the benefit received by the violator will be taken into account. Leniency may be granted by reducing fines where violators provide information to the directorate which exposes anti-competitive practices.[65] In addition to fines being imposed for violations of the Act, violators may also face imprisonment in accordance with the Penal Code or any other law.[66]

### *6.4.3 Competition advocacy*

As we saw in chapter 1, competition advocacy is just as important as competition enforcement, in order to develop a greater awareness of the principles relating to competition. The Competition Directorate has taken a number of steps to promote a competition culture within Jordan. Recently, the directorate published a short and helpful guidance, *A Closer Look at the Competition Law 2004* in which the directorate explains the key objectives of the Act, the benefits which the Act can bring to consumers and firms, the main provisions of the Act and their application, and the institutional structure in the system. The booklet was prepared in simple non-technical language and is available in both Arabic and English at the directorate's website.[67] In addition, the directorate has so far published its first *Annual Report*.[68] The Competition

[60] See Article 21 of the Act.
[61] The issue of fairness of commercial transactions was discussed at p 180 above.
[62] See Article 22 of the Act.
[63] See Article 23 of the Act. Although the provision refers to 'person' in general, the understanding here is that this concerns competition officials.
[64] See Article 24 of the Act. [65] See Article 25 of the Act. [66] See Article 26 of the Act.
[67] The guidance is available at the directorate's website, www.mit.gov.jo/competition/Files/En/English_Brochure.pdf.
[68] See www.mit.gov.jo/competition/Files/Ar/Annual_Report.pdf. The report is published in Arabic.

Directorate's website itself is an effective tool for highlighting the aims of the competition law and the rights, duties and activities of all the parties involved in the enforcement of competition.

### *6.4.4 Assessing the performance of the directorate*

According to the 2003 *Annual Report*, the directorate has in a short period of time become quite active in the field of competition law, whether domestically, regionally or internationally. At an international level, the directorate has formed quite close links with major competition authorities, most notably the European Commission; it is understood that a bilateral agreement is currently being prepared and will be entered into between the EC and Jordan for the purposes of building a network of bilateral cooperation in the enforcement of their competition rules. The Directorate can be expected to benefit enormously from such an agreement, which will, among many benefits, afford it the chance to develop its technical expertise and case-handling function. The directorate has also participated in various workshops and conferences held in Cairo, Barcelona, Beirut and Berlin dealing with competition law, most notably in the context of the United Nations Conference on Trade and Development (UNCTAD) and the WTO. It also played an active role in preparing for and participating in the failed Cancun round of the WTO.

Regionally, the directorate has furthered the cooperation with the Tunisian competition authority through arranging workshops attended by officials of the directorate and judges of the Court of First Instance. It also participated in some of the meetings of the Committee of Competition Experts held under the auspices of the Economic and Social Council of the Arab League out of which a draft of the Pan-Arab Market Competition Regulations has emerged.[69]

Since its creation, the majority of the directorate's work has involved 'consultations', providing advisory opinions in relation to various matters, mainly price rises in different markets. The directorate has initiated a few investigations, received one merger notification and three applications for exemption. This perhaps is a 'big' achievement given the directorate's limited resources and its apparent intention to limit the number of cases at one time in order to conduct thorough investigations

[69] See pp 319–24 below for a discussion on the regulations.

into individual cases.[70] According to the directorate, an analysis of its activities during its first year of operation should lead to five main conclusions: first the diversity of cases opened by the directorate indicates the positive outcomes resulting from the application of the Act and confirms the need for such legislation to guarantee the freedom of competition for the purposes of achieving constant economic growth and protecting the interest of firms and consumers; secondly, complaints brought to the directorate prove the existence of behaviour and conduct hindering the natural operation of the market mechanism; thirdly, turning to the directorate shows a growing general awareness of the Act and a desire to benefit from the protection afforded under it to the freedom of competition and the confidence and hope placed in the directorate; fourthly, the capability demonstrated by the directorate to deal with different cases given their sensitivity and confidentiality proves the importance of training programmes for the future; and fifthly, the volume and type of cases brought before the directorate appears to be 'distinguished' when compared to the experience of authorities in countries similar to Jordan. Perhaps these are particularly positive conclusions; however, they should not lead one to underestimate the enormous task facing the directorate in light of its limited resources in both human and financial terms. Furthermore, the directorate seems to be viewing its role as more of a regulator with a system of continuous checks on the market – a task that is bound to prove impossible to execute in practice.

At the rule-making level, the directorate has pushed for the formulation of the *de minimis Instructions*, which were issued by the Minister for Trade and Industry. The *Instructions* are based on EC practice and the European Commission's *de minimis* Notice (2002).[71] According to the *Instructions* an agreement would be considered to have minor importance or effect where in a situation involving competitors the total shares of all the parties does not exceed 3 per cent of total transactions in the

[70] This intention is apparent from two recent investigations by the directorate into the aluminium sector and one in the vehicle spare parts following the receipt of complaints by competitors. In the three separate investigations conducted by the directorate, however, no infringement of the Act was found. The reactions to the directorate's conclusions in these cases have been mixed. In some quarters the directorate's initiatives were welcomed as an indication of a serious determination to apply the provisions of the Act effectively. In others however, concerns have been raised over the risk of the Act being used as a 'free-riding' tool for firms to undermine and harass their rivals through claims of behaviour by the latter to harm competition.

[71] See Notice on agreements of minor importance OJ [2001] C368/13. As stated in note 36 in chapter 3 above, this notice was replaced in December 2006 by a new (revised) notice.

market and in a situation involving non-competitors the total shares of the parties does not exceed 7 per cent of total transactions in the market. The basis of the *de minimis* doctrine and these thresholds is found in Article 5(B) of the Act. The article states that an agreement will not have an appreciable effect on competition so long as the total share of the parties to the agreement shall not exceed 10 per cent of total transactions in the market and provided that the agreement does not contain any elements of price-fixing and market-sharing.

## 6.5 Market control and supervision

The institutional structure of the Ministry of Trade and Industry includes a Market Control Directorate which is intended to conduct activities other than those carried out by the Competition Directorate. Interestingly, in several Arab countries these activities fall within the scope of the relevant competition law and so are within the competence of the relevant competition authority. Notable among these MECs are the Maghreb countries.[72] In the case of Jordan, however, a different jurisdictional and institutional structure has been opted for.

The Directorate of Quality and Market Control (DQMC) is responsible for ensuring compliance with the Industry and Trade Law of 1998, the aim of which was to develop the economic, commercial and industrial policies in Jordan. In particular the task of the DQMC is to control the basic and essential goods market. According to the articles dealing with market control in the Industry and Trade Law, this involves identifying the basic goods, ensuring that goods are sold in accordance with publicised prices, checking the available stock with wholesalers, monitoring whether basic goods are being concealed or there is a refusal to sell them and monitoring sales, liquidation and promotional prizes. For the execution of these duties, the DQMC relies on receiving complaints from consumers and conducting investigations, field visits covering the entire Kingdom, following up on market observers' performance and holding meetings with businessmen from the private sector. In order to enhance the private sector's role in market control, the DQMC engages in various educational activities to increase the knowledge of different economic sectors about the Industry and Trade Law and highlight the relevant market control articles of the Law on Television and Radio. Furthermore, it aims to publish brochures and

[72] See chapter 5.

advertisements in newspapers to explain the notion of market control and the public's role.

## 6.6 Reflections

Building a competition law regime in Jordan has been a major leap for this small Middle Eastern economy. Apart from the remark made at the beginning of the chapter about the lack of sufficiently water-tight provisions in the Competition Act, several operational aspects of the regime would benefit from some reconsideration. First, the regime does not appear to be fully harmonious in its operation which can be seen in relation to judicial control. Courts have an important role to play in the enforcement of the Act. As we saw, a policy decision was made – when the Act was adopted – to ensure that judges who handle competition cases would enjoy the relevant expertise; hence the Amman Court of First Instance was selected as the relevant court to enforce the Act during an initial period until judges at other Courts of First Instance have been trained in the field of competition law and policy. In relation to merger and exemptions cases (which are bound to form a significant part of competition law enforcement under the regime), the Courts of First Instance have no role to play: decisions adopted by the Minister of Industry and Trade in these cases may be appealed to the Supreme Court of Justice. In a significant way, therefore, the goal of placing the Courts of First Instance at the heart of the regime appears to be defeated as a result of such a provision. Secondly, the powers given to the Minister of Industry and Trade under the regime are very extensive and this raises questions about how effective the enforcement of the Act in practice is likely to be: at one end of the spectrum there is the concern over the short term usually served by governments and ministers in Jordan; at the other end of the spectrum stands the huge scope for lobbying power in the country and the influence which may be exerted on the decisions of the Minister. To be fair, however, it should be accepted that these concerns are partly, though not wholly, alleviated by the fact that decisions of the Minister must be reasoned and are based on recommendations of the director of the Competition Directorate, and may be subjected to review at the level of the Supreme Court of Justice. Nonetheless, the existence of wide powers enjoyed by the Minister usurps the influence which the directorate, as a competition body, would have enjoyed in the absence of these powers. Moreover, within the current institutional structure, there is no independent competition body in Jordan. Whilst one may accept the need for an involvement on the part of the government or the Minister in certain cases, such as those dealing with the public interest, the independence of the Competition Directorate should be ensured.

A third observation to be made about the operation of the regime concerns the relationship between the Competition Directorate and sectoral regulators in the case of competition problems occurring in the special sectors. The Act is silent on how these cases should be handled in practice. The directorate's view is that in such cases, it will seek to coordinate its activities with those of relevant sectoral regulators.[73] This policy of favouring or seeking coordination, however, does not adequately cater for the exact involvement and powers of those regulators. A good illustration can be found in the regulation of the telecommunications sector in Jordan. The relevant authority in charge of regulating the sector is the Telecommunications Regulatory Commission (TRC), established under the Telecommunications Law 1995, as amended.[74] Due to the fact that competition issues assume considerable importance in the work of the TRC, the *Instructions on Competition Safeguards in the Telecommunications Sector* were adopted in February 2006.[75] The *Instructions* provide a binding framework within which competition analysis in the telecommunications sector must be conducted. This covers cases of abuse of dominance, anti-competitive behaviour and harmful acquisitions; the power to conduct this analysis is reserved to the TRC. The adoption of the *Instructions* therefore in effect means that the TRC and the Competition Directorate (and the Ministry of Industry and Trade) will have dual jurisdiction in relation to competition issues arising in the telecommunications sector. This means that firms operating in the sector will have to comply with the Telecommunications Law and the *Instructions* and deal with the TRC on the one hand and comply with the Competition Act and deal with the Competition Directorate on the other. The existence of dual

[73] For example, a draft Memorandum of Understanding between the directorate and the Telecommunications Regulatory Commission has been produced which creates a framework within which the authorities handle the coordination of their work. The directorate has also sought to cooperate quite closely with the Companies Control Department, the Central Bank and the Insurance Commission.

[74] The Telecommunications Law No. 13.

[75] The *Instructions*, which are binding, were mentioned and discussed briefly above under the examination of the issues of anti-competitive practices, abuse of dominance and economic concentrations.

systems should not itself be objectionable especially given that the authorities have made their interest to coordinate their work very clear. What is concerning, however, is the fact that the *Instructions* do not adequately deal with all issues, which may arise in an effort to conduct competitive analysis or seek to protect competition in the sector. In particular, the *Instructions* are silent on procedural issues dealing with submission of complaints about the anti-competitive behaviour or abusive conduct of licensees and the type of actions, which may be taken by the TRC when identifying a competition problem. As a result therefore the exact role of the TRC when dealing with competition problems in the telecommunications sector is not known, given that neither the Telecommunications Law and the *Instructions* nor the Competition Act offer any helpful indication in this regard.

Finally, it is worth noting the existing and intended regulatory approach to competition law enforcement in Jordan. Under the current regulatory approach, a fairly interventionist stance by the directorate and the Ministry of Industry and Trade more generally is adopted. Perhaps this approach has been to a certain extent facilitated by the mechanism for extensive consultation within the regime.[76] The declared goal of the directorate, however, is not to opt for such an approach but rather to rely on the market mechanism and reserve intervention to cases of exceptional nature. The directorate's view is that such an approach would enable it to concentrate more on its competition advocacy and capacity-building activities and focus its attention on serious competition law infringements. For the time being, however, this remains a declared goal.

[76] See pp 187–8 above.

# 7

# The Gulf States: a possible model for regional cooperation

The six Arab states of the Arabian Gulf, namely Bahrain, Kuwait, Oman, Qatar, Saudi Arabia and the United Arab Emirates (UAE), are united by a number of factors.[1] A notable factor among these – in addition to commonality of language and religion and the geographic proximity – is the possession of these countries of vast oil resources which has been a hugely important driving force behind economic development, modernisation of domestic economies and building and expanding infrastructure, and an important source of the vast private wealth of a few families and individuals. An open solidarity between these countries has always existed although many would argue this has been paralleled by quiet rivalry, though not necessarily in a positive economic sense. This solidarity found particular expression in the creation of the Cooperation Council for the Arab States of the Gulf (GCC) in 1981. The GCC is a community offering a form of regional cooperation between these countries and has a wide range of objectives stretching from coordination and integration in all fields to formulating similar regulations in various fields and introducing a single currency within the next four years. Interestingly, the objectives of the GCC appear to have some relevance to natural and legal persons of the Member States insofar as they provide for strengthening ties between their peoples, encouraging cooperation within the private sector and fostering scientific and technical progress. Additionally, the objectives call for setting up joint ventures between the Member States which one could argue offers a golden opportunity for introducing competition law initiatives at supranational level.

[1] Iraq, Iran and Yemen have been excluded from this list. In relation to the former two countries – despite their 'access' to the Gulf – their competition law and policy experience is discussed in chapter 10; the experience of Yemen, however, is discussed in this chapter due to its fairy close links with the Arab Gulf States and its partial membership of the Gulf Cooperation Council.

Table 1. *Free trade agreement and a customs union*

| Name of Community | Existence of free trade agreement | Existence of customs union | Existence of competition law and policy |
|---|---|---|---|
| European Community (EC)* | Yes | Yes | Yes |
| Caribbean Community and Common Market (CARICOM)* | Yes | Yes | Yes |
| Southern Common Market (MERCUSOR) | Yes | Yes | Yes |
| North American Free Trade Agreement (NAFTA) | Yes | No | Yes |
| Association of South East Asian Nations (ASEAN) | Yes | No | Yes |
| Common Market of Eastern and Southern Africa (COMESA) | Yes | No | Yes |
| Southern African Customs Union (SACU) | Yes | Yes | Yes |
| Gulf Cooperation Council (GCC) | Yes | Yes | No |

* Note: a single market is also in existence.

## 7.1 Measuring the success of the GCC

Before considering the development of competition law and policy whether at the GCC level or at national level within the six GCC Member States individually, it would be helpful to assess the achievements and success of the GCC as a regional community in general and as a suitable forum for developing competition law and policy in particular. Two important yardsticks may be used for the purpose of determining how successful the

Table 2. *Population, geographic area, GDP and number of Member States*

| Name of Community | Number of Member States | Geographic area (sq. km) | Population (million) | GDP (USD) millions | GDP (USD) Per capita | Existence of competition law and policy |
|---|---|---|---|---|---|---|
| Economic and Monetary Community of Central Africa (CEMAC) | Six | 3.020 | 35 | | | Yes |
| Southern African Customs Union (SACU) | Five | 2.7 | | 541 | 10,605 | Yes |
| Andean Community | Five | 4.7 | | | | Yes |
| Gulf Cooperation Council (GCC) | Six | 2.3 | 36 | 537 | 14,950 | No |

GCC is as a regional community. The first involves comparing the achievements of the GCC in the field of competition law with those of regional communities around the world. The second concentrates on evaluating the work of the GCC and its activities in the field.

### 7.1.1 *Extrinsic factors: the GCC and other regional communities*

There are at least twenty regional communities in existence around the world.[2] It would be interesting therefore to compare from a competition law angle the GCC with some of those communities. To ensure a fair and

[2] For a list of these communities see p 325 below.

comprehensive account of the situation, the comparison is conducted on the basis of the existence of a free trade agreement and a customs union, population, size of geographic area, gross domestic product and number of Member States.

A brief glance through the tables above would reveal the absence of competition law and policy within the GCC and the markedly different position it occupies in this regard from that of similar regional communities. Undoubtedly, this finding is intriguing and should prompt a consideration of the (possible) reasons for this.

### *7.1.2 Intrinsic factors*

A brief browse through the GCC's documents and output would reveal a highly interesting finding: the absence of any reference to competition law and policy. Remarkably, the word 'competition' appears in only three places in the GCC's various rules, studies and general documents: in relation to economic cooperation in the oil and gas sector among the GCC's members where it is stated that measures are adopted to avoid harmful *competition*; in relation to cooperation in the field of young people, sports and scouts for the purposes of establishing friendly *competitions*; in Article 13 of the Reference Model Regulation Law for the Promotion of Foreign Investment in the GCC States where there is a reference to protection of local industries in the case of unfair *competition* from foreign firms. More remarkably, there is no mention of the term competition at all in the stated foundations and objectives of the GCC.

At one level this state of affairs is highly questionable given that all of the six Member States of the GCC embrace Islamic tradition perhaps more so than the rest of Muslim MECs; the significance which Islam and Islamic principles attach to the concept of competition and competition law and policy was clearly demonstrated in chapter 2. Furthermore, as the tables above clearly show, whereas all the comparable regional communities around the world have opted to engage in competition law and policy the GCC lacks any involvement in the field. The fact that the GCC places economic development and cooperation high on its agenda makes this absence of competition law and policy all the more questionable.

## 7.2 International cooperation

The international cooperation engaged in by the GCC has been quite limited. For example, there has been no interest in building a cooperation network with MECs, whether individually or collectively.[3] The only type of international cooperation with competition relevance entered into by the GCC has taken the form of a cooperation agreement with the EC and a 'declaration' on cooperation with EFTA. In neither of these cases, however, has the purported cooperation resulted in meaningful relations between the parties.

### *7.2.1 Cooperation with the EC*

Relations between the EC and the GCC are governed through a cooperation Agreement signed in 1989. The aim of this Agreement, among others, is to strengthen the economic relations between the parties. A Joint Council, consisting of representatives from both sides, was established to ensure the proper implementation of the agreement and to achieve the objectives set out within it. For this purpose the Joint Council meets once a year and whenever necessary, at the request of the parties. The Cooperation Agreement placed an obligation on the parties to enter into negotiations on a Free Trade Agreement in order to promote further their relations and lead to free trade between the regions.[4] Thus, negotiations for a Free Trade Agreement between the EC and the GCC are currently underway. These negotiations began in 1990 but were halted until the GCC made a decision to move towards a customs union. In 2001, new negotiating directives were adopted by the EC and upon their approval negotiations for a Free Trade Agreement recommenced in 2002 and have been in progress since. The proposed Free Trade Agreement would contain provisions relating to, among other things, the liberalisation of trade and competition.

### *7.2.2 Cooperation with EFTA States*

A Declaration on Cooperation between the EFTA States and the GCC countries was issued in May 2000. This declaration lays down guidelines

[3] Over the years, GCC States have maintained a degree of scepticism about forging close links with other MECs. Politically, they have come to prefer associations with the USA and certain European countries. Economically, they have been concerned over the prospect of having to 'share' their wealth with other MECs as a result of a broader cooperation.

[4] See Article 11(2) of the Co-operation Agreement.

for strengthening the economic and trade relations between the EFTA States and the GCC. To achieve this, the GCC and EFTA States undertake to liberalise their trade relations by extending their cooperation in a range of ways, including exchanging views on the conditions for free and undistorted competition and negotiating a Free Trade Agreement. A Joint Committee makes recommendations and reviews the cooperation between the parties. Representatives of the EFTA States and the GCC met in September 2004 in Geneva to confirm the intention of the parties to establish a 'comprehensive' free trade agreement, pursuant to the declaration, to enhance their economic relations. The 'implementation' of the joint intention, however, was quite slow: negotiations for a free trade agreement between the parties only commenced in June 2006.

## 7.3 The Kingdom of Saudi Arabia

### *7.3.1 Embracing the free-market system*

Saudi Arabia is widely recognised as the birthplace of Islam. The Kingdom has always maintained strong adherence to Islamic tradition and values, though on occasions such adherence appears misguided and unbalanced. Interestingly, however, economic reform and competition law only received attention recently with the Kingdom's timid move towards a free-market system and the focus of the country's economic activity shifting to private market operators. Currently, concentrated efforts are being made by the government to encourage participation by private firms in the economy. This in fact represents an interesting development, though it has not altered the country's declared policy of keeping with Islamic principles and values, for the purposes of ensuring that economic development will take place in a balanced and coordinated fashion. As such, these two developments seem paradoxical, given that the latter has over the years meant that a high degree of state control and planning was in place. This in itself is ironic, given the fact that Islam – as we saw in chapter 2 – does not favour a policy of heavy intervention in the market place or a high degree of planning and control by the state.

The government's policy of encouraging competition and investment in different sectors – mainly developing ones – by private firms, appears to be based on a long-term strategic vision with several components, which include a desire to: improve quality of services and reduce cost through competition leading to economic efficiency; reduce the burden on the government's budget; attract foreign direct investment; build technical expertise and develop modern systems of information technology locally; create new employment opportunities; and keep domestic capital funds at home for the purposes of constructing wider scope for their investment.

To facilitate an effective realisation of these goals, the government has built a modern legal and regulatory framework aimed at facilitating a suitable economic and investment-friendly climate. To this end, the government has come to appreciate the vitality of transparency in its policy on investment with a comprehensive plan for the purposes of laying the foundations for investment [5]

### *7.3.2 Regulation of prices*

Despite the lack of a specific competition law in the Kingdom until 2004, Saudi Arabia has for many years relied on a mechanism of price regulation which is applicable to certain commodities and products, mainly petroleum and gas-based products, wheat flour and pharmaceuticals.[6] The Kingdom's declared goal behind price regulation appears to be socio-economic in nature, in order to ensure continuous stability in the market, protect consumer welfare and safeguard important social interests. It appears that this mechanism is rooted in Islamic principles, most notably the principle of *Hisba*, which we discussed in chapter 2. However, contrary to what these principles mandated, namely intervention by a public authority only where necessary,[7] the Kingdom's mechanism appears to be a tool for continuous intervention, which in practice has translated into excessive regulation.

### *7.3.3 The Competition Act 2004*

Competition law is a new phenomenon in Saudi Arabia. The Competition Act of the Kingdom (the Act) was enacted by Royal Decree No. M/25 on 22 June 2004. The Act was published in the *Official Gazette* of the Kingdom in July 2004 and entered into force on 31 December 2004.[8] Despite this

[5] This includes establishing mechanisms for the provision of flexible loans to the private sector; encouraging private firms to maximise their use of the favourable treatment offered by the government; and providing legal certainty through the formulation of clear and binding rules.

[6] These petroleum- and gas-based products include fuel oil, gasoline, diesel, kerosene, liquefied petroleum gas (cooking gas), natural gas liquids (including propane, butane and natural gasoline), asphalt, natural gas (ethane and methane) and crude oil.

[7] See the discussion on pp 24–6 above.

[8] Article 21 of the Act provides that the Act shall enter into force after 180 days from the date of its publication.

speedy transition through the legislative process, the implementing regulations of the Act – provided for by virtue of Article 20 of the Act[9] – are yet to be adopted. The delay in the adoption of the regulations, which are intended to define the parameters of the Act and its general application, has effectively paralysed the implementation of the Act and thus the commencement of its enforcement.

The adoption of the Act is a step of huge significance in Saudi Arabia though one that would be rendered meaningless should proper enforcement of the Act not materialise. During the past two years, the Kingdom has made its intention to take the Act seriously quite clear. Indeed, some important steps have been taken such as the creation of the Competition Council.[10] Beyond this, however, there has been little evidence of significant progress made in practice.

The Act aims at instituting a system for the protection and encouragement of 'fair' competition.[11] The use of the word fair comes to confirm the strong social objective underlying the Act: efficiency and maximisation of consumer welfare in a strict economic or technical sense are not therefore the sole objectives behind the Act.

The Act follows EC competition law insofar as it provides for the prohibition on collusion between firms, abuse of dominance and harmful mergers.[12] However, the Act excludes from its scope public firms and firms completely owned by the state.

#### 7.3.3.1 Collusion

Article 4 of the Act prohibits all forms of collusion between actual and potential competitors which aims at limiting trade or distorting competition. The prohibition also applies where the collusion leads to such harmful results by way of an effect. The choice of wording in the article is interesting given that Article 4 prohibits collusion restricting trade *or* competition. This makes it arguable that the prohibition will bite in situations where trade itself is restricted without the need to establish distortion of competition. The policy thinking behind the Act supports this and shows the existence of a particular concern with limitation on trade. The choice of

[9] Article 20 provides for the implementing regulations of the Act to be adopted within a period of ninety days following its publication. This would be 5 October 2004.

[10] See p 204 below. [11] See Article 1 of the Act.

[12] The Act uses the term 'undertaking' which is defined in Article 2 as a factory, association or company owned by natural or legal person(s). The definition also includes all associations conducting activities in commerce, agriculture, industry or services or which are active in the sale or purchase of products.

wording reflects the broader context within which the Act was adopted, namely WTO accession. The wording also reflects a cultural aspect in Saudi Arabia, where trade has always received special consideration given that it is viewed as an important component of Islam. Nonetheless, given that Article 1 of the Act makes it abundantly clear that the Act aims at protecting competition and fighting monopolistic practices affecting fair competition, the choice of wording in Article 4 appears somewhat paradoxical. It would be interesting to see how the prohibition on collusion will be applied in practice and whether the choice of wording in the article will survive with the prohibition being applied in cases of restriction on trade only.

Article 4 lists eight examples of situations in which limitation of trade or distortion of competition will be taken to exist. These situations include price-fixing, limitation of output, illegal stocking or hiding of products, refusal to supply hindering market entry or exit by a third party, market-sharing, bid-rigging and freezing or limiting production, development, distribution or marketing or any form of investment activities.

The Act does not contain a separate provision for exemption from the prohibition set out in Article 4 but rather integrates the issue of exemption within the wording of the article giving the impression that a *rule of reason* approach will be adopted in relation to the prohibition. The exemption criteria contained in the article appear to fall short of ensuring that only those situations with extreme minimal harm to competition will be exempted. The article merely refers to improvement in the performance of the relevant firms and realising benefits to consumers which outweigh the limitation of competition. There is no reference therefore to the risk of elimination of competition or whether the relevant restrictions are indispensable. The exemption criteria therefore should be extended in their wording to cover such cases as well. Doing so would broaden the scope of the exemption especially in relation to the first criterion with the emphasis coming as a result on economic performance in general, as opposed to being focused on the firms party to the agreement themselves.[13]

#### 7.3.3.2 Abuse of dominance

The concept of abuse of dominance features in two places in the Act: in Article 4 which as we saw in the previous section deals with collusion

[13] The article provides that the exemption criteria will be clarified in the regulations. However, it is not clear whether the regulations will actually add to the two criteria in the article or explain that they are to be interpreted as covering the requirement of indispensability and non-elimination of competition.

and in Article 5 which prohibits dominant firms from limiting competition. Dominance, however, is defined in Article 2 of the Act as a position through which a firm or *group of firms* are able to influence prices through controlling supply.[14] Among the practices condemned as abuse of dominance in Article 5 are predatory pricing 'aiming at forcing competitors out of the market';[15] limiting supply and creating artificial shortage of supply for the purposes of increasing prices; imposing purchase or trading conditions with other parties which place such parties at a competitive disadvantage *vis-à-vis* their competitors and refusal to supply to hinder the entry of another firm into the market.

Including a reference to abuse of dominance in Article 4 is interesting and was done for two main reasons. First, Article 5 clearly refers to cases of single firm dominance only. However, the Act also deals with collective dominance. A policy decision was therefore made to include a prohibition on abuse of collective dominance in Article 4 as opposed to Article 5.[16] There is no suggestion being made by this author that such a decision is sensible. Indeed, the decision appears to be problematic given the high probability of confusion resulting from 'overlap' between the concepts of collusion and collective dominance. Secondly, the legislative intent behind the Act was to cast the net of the prohibition on abuse of dominance in the Act as wide as possible by expanding the list of abuses and catching as many harmful situations as possible including those where competition will be restricted between *particular* firms (for the benefit of those firms) or where other competitors or conditions of competition in general will be harmed.

One important point to note about the wording of Article 5 (and also Article 4) is the omission of any reference to effect on trade as a result of the abuse of a dominant position. It was noted above that Article 4 contains a specific reference to limitation or effect on trade. However, in relation to its application to abuse of dominance the article refers only to restrictions on competition. In other words, the Act makes particular reference to trade (in addition to competition) under the prohibition on collusion with only reference to competition under the prohibition on abuse of dominance. Apparently, the inclusion and omission of a reference to trade concerning the prohibition on collusion and abuse of

[14] According to the article the regulations will provide the factors to be taken into account in determining this which include among other things the market structure and barriers to entry.

[15] See paragraph 1 of the Article.

[16] Article 4 can also apply to single firm dominance.

dominance respectively resulted from a belief on the part of policy-makers that in the latter situation the concern should be with competition given the existence of a dominant firm or a group of firms, whereas in the former situation given that dominance is non-existent, trade is possible. The logic and rationale behind such thinking are highly questionable especially in the case of the Act, which – as was noted above – was introduced within a broader context of WTO accession by Saudi Arabia and a desire to participate in the global trading order and trade liberalisation.

#### 7.3.3.3 Mergers

The Act's mechanism on merger regulation is extremely underdeveloped and is deficient in many respects. As was noted above, harmful mergers fall within the scope of the Act. Article 6 of the Act includes a brief definition of a merger situation as a situation in which two or more firms merge or a firm is acquired by one or more firms. There is no reference in the definition to what amounts to acquisition in this case or any mention of control having to be acquired or the ways in which this can be done. Article 6, however, indicates that acquisition may be of assets, intellectual property rights, shares and beneficiary rights.

The Act provides for mandatory notification where a merger creates a dominant position. There is no provision, however, for notification thresholds and the Act offers no details on the notification process except to provide that notification must occur at least sixty days prior to the completion of the merger transaction.[17]

The substantive test used by the Competition Council to determine whether a merger should be cleared or blocked rests on the concept of dominance. The Act is silent, however, on whether the substantive test extends beyond the creation of a dominant position to the strengthening of such a position.

Article 7 prohibits merging firms from effecting a notified operation unless a written authorisation clearing the merger has been issued by the Competition Council or where the council fails to block the merger within sixty days of the date of notification or to notify the parties that the operation is under investigation, or ninety days pass from the date of notification without the council delivering its decision whether blocking or clearing the merger.

[17] Article 6(2) of the Act.

### *7.3.4 The Competition Council*

A Royal Decree was issued on 6 September 2006 mandating the creation of a special council (the Competition Council) for the protection of competition, the prevention of monopolisation and achieving fair competition as provided for in Article 8 of the Act. The council is headed by the Minister of Trade and Industry, with eight members serving within its board. The members are made of the Director of the Ministry of Trade and Industry, Director of the Ministry of Finance, the Planning Advisor of the Ministry of Economy, the head of the Investment Authority, and four members from the private sector. One of these members may be designated as Director General of the council.

The council is described as an independent body established under the auspices of the Ministry for Trade and Industry.[18] It is armed with full authority to deal with anti-competitive behaviour and abusive conduct and its creation is widely considered to be an integral part of the continuous economic reform currently being implemented in the Kingdom for the purposes of preparing it for full membership of the WTO. Article 9 lists the council's duties under the Act which include: conducting competition investigations;[19] adopting merger decisions; approving penalty actions; proposing legislation with competition relevance and advising on such legislation as well as proposing changes to the Act in light of market changes; issuing the implementing regulations; and producing annual reports and developing future action plans.

The council began to function in 2006, though its work during that year consisted mainly of four meetings at which various issues where discussed ranging from enforcement to reviewing competition law developments in different parts of the world. Particular attention is being given to competition law enforcement in the EC for the purposes of learning from that rich experience and to the work of the United Nations Conference on Trade and Development (UNCTAD); the council has been designing a programme with UNCTAD aimed at the provision of technical assistance to the former to enable it to build its institutional capacity and the necessary infrastructure.

[18] See Article 8(1) of the Act.

[19] Article 11 of the Law provides for the council with the power to investigate complaints and to inspect all evidence and documents related to the complaint without any obstruction on the part of the natural and legal persons concerned.

### 7.3.5 *Orders, penalties, appeal and private enforcement*

The main penalty provided for under the Act is a fine. Article 12 states that any person found in breach of the Act is liable to a fine not exceeding 5 million Riyals, which is doubled in the case of repeated infringement.[20] Additionally it is possible for measures to be adopted ordering an amendment of a behaviour or practice infringing the Act, the disposal of share, assets or intellectual property rights or taking any other action in order to eliminate the breach,[21] or the payment of a daily fine ranging from a minimum of 1,000 Riyals to a maximum of 10,000 Riyals.

Penalties under the Act also extend to members of the council and officials found to have unjustly or illegally benefited directly or indirectly or infringed the prohibition on breach of confidentiality as provided for under Article 11(5) of the Act.[22] Any such person will be liable to a fine not exceeding 5 million Riyals, a term of imprisonment not exceeding 2 years or both.[23] The Saudi competition law regime therefore treats unlawful conduct by officials very seriously and allows for the possibility of such conduct to be punished as harshly as a breach by a firm or firms of one of the key prohibitions in the Act.

Article 15 of the Act provides that decisions on penalties shall be taken by a committee of five members formed within the council. Decisions adopted by the committee may be contested before the Royal Court Appeals Chambers within sixty days of the notification of the decision. Where the committee considers that the breach merits imprisonment it will transfer the case to the Appeals Chambers for consideration by the latter.

Finally, it is worth noting that the Act provides for a small window for private enforcement actions to be brought before the courts for compensation in situations where a natural or legal person sustains harm in a situation prohibited under the Act. The Act, however, is silent on whether a breach in such situations needs to have been established by the council for such actions to be possible.

[20] The penalty provided for under the article is without prejudice to more serious penalties, which may be available under another law. The article does not specify the type of breach, which will trigger a fine. However, the reference here surely is to breach of Articles 4 (collusion), 5 (abuse of dominance) and 6 (mergers).

[21] Such actions are intended to be used especially in the case of abuse of dominance and harmful mergers for the purposes of issuing approval of those mergers effected in contravention of the Act.

[22] Article 13 of the Act. [23] *Ibid.*

### 7.3.6 *Facilitating competition in the sectors*

The commitment of the Saudi government to liberalisation of different sectors and encouraging private participation in economic activities was discussed above.[24] Two sectors in particular have come to witness and experience this commitment, namely the telecommunications and electricity sectors.

#### 7.3.6.1 The telecommunications sector

The size and significance of the telecommunications sector in Saudi Arabia – along with the government's desire to facilitate competitiveness and enterprise – are worth noting. The Kingdom has taken important steps towards creating an open and competitive environment, encouraging investment (both local and foreign) and protecting local consumers. Among these are the partial privatisation of the sector, the adoption of the Telecommunication Regulations (2002) and the creation in 2001 of an independent Communications and Information Technology Commission as a body responsible for regulating the sector. Since its creation the commission has been active in opening up the sector to greater competition and moving closer to its declared objective of ultimately achieving full market liberalisation.[25]

The Kingdom has been favouring competition in the telecommunications sector. The desire of the government to take such crucial steps appears to be motivated by the quest to join the WTO, to meet the legitimate expectations of firms and consumers and the general drive within the country for economic prosperity.

Competition appears to have begun to develop in the past two years, especially in relation to the provision of mobile phone services with beneficial results; the commission has noted an improved product quality and the availability of more choice for consumers in the market. These important developments, however, have helped highlight various new strategic matters related to market liberalisation and protection of competition. As a response, the commission has begun a review of its regulatory tools for the purposes of adapting these to the changing nature of practices of firms active in the sector and the prevention of possible anti-competitive practices and abusive conduct.

[24] See pp 198–9 above.

[25] Notable in this regard is the issuing of four licences for the provision of telecommunication services via satellite (VAST) and the issuing of three licences in the mobile phones sector to enable new operators to provide cellular services.

#### 7.3.6.2 The electricity sector

The government's long-term strategic vision of market liberalisation and privatisation focuses on the electricity sector as one of the unique services sectors which is considered to be suitable for being opened up to private investment. The government believes this suitability is enhanced by the fact that most of the infrastructure in the sector has been completed; a high increase in the demand for electricity; the need for the government to stop funding the sector following its privatisation; and the need for extensive funding for the generation and transmission of electricity.

The government's prediction for the future of the sector shows that key benefits are expected to flow from introducing competition to the generation and transmission of electricity. In relation to the former, the government believes that competition will guarantee a better service quality at a lower cost; facilitate an expansion in the use of power stations with high sufficiency; ensure optimal operation of power stations and maximisation in the use of resources; and facilitate the use of sophisticated, hi-technology modern machinery. In relation to the latter, the government sees the key benefits of competition as follows: optimal choice of the components for transmission networks and the carrying of electricity; continuous development and modernisation of transmission mechanisms and networks; contributing to decreasing the amount of lost energy; and implementing plans and carrying out projects aimed at connecting different internal electricity networks together and with those in neighbouring countries.

It is worth noting that the government's desire for increased competition in the sector does not extend to the level of distribution, which is the most important among the three levels of generation, transmission and distribution of electricity given it concerns the direct supply of energy to consumers. For this reason, the government decided that this level of the sector should remain a state monopoly.

## 7.4 Qatar: the Law on Protection of Competition 2006

### *7.4.1 Building a competitive environment*

Qatar enjoys considerable significance within and outside the Middle East. The country – which opted for a civil law system with certain elements of Islamic law – benefits from the abundance of oil reserves. The outlook of Qatar has been remarkably Westernised and international. Over the years it has formed close links with the USA in particular, and is viewed as a country of huge strategic significance for US foreign policy.

Qatar's hydrocarbon resources have served as the backbone of its flourishing economy, though in recent years the move has been away from oil towards developing other sectors, ranging from gas to telecommunications. An increasing emphasis has also come to be placed on technology and indeed Qatar is widely regarded as the Arab country with the strongest technological base.[26] To support this move, the government has engaged in quite an extensive privatisation programme,[27] aimed at 'modernising' the local economy and enhancing its participation and standing globally, especially within the WTO to which Qatar attaches particular significance.

### *7.4.2 The Law on the Protection of Competition*

Competition law has been given special attention in Qatar not only domestically but also at a regional level for the purposes of supporting the efforts of Arab countries to adopt a common Arab competition law, the proposed Arab Competition Regulations as part of the Pan Arab market,[28] which is currently under construction. Qatar adopted a specific competition law, the Law on Protection of Competition and Prohibition of Monopolistic Practices, in June 2006. The Law has been welcomed by business viewing it as a crucial aspect of the government's economic policy aimed at stabilising domestic markets and achieving justice – in a social sense[29] – through preventing hurdles which would restrict firms from reaching local consumers.

The Law, however, suffers from numerous shortcomings and many of its provisions will require clarification in practice. For example, the Law is silent on the issue of territorial reach. Its provisions are very general in their wording, which makes it crucial to adopt secondary legislation[30] and provide administrative or judicial interpretation of these provisions. There is an anxiety over this, however, given that it is not possible

[26] Recently however, this position appears to have been shared by other Gulf States. See below.

[27] The privatisation programme has covered the telecommunications sector (in part) and other sectors as well.

[28] See further chapter 10.

[29] An important link is made between the Law and the Constitution of Qatar with the former considered to be a reflection of the principles of the latter, most notably those appearing in Article 28 of the Constitution which provides that the state guarantees the freedom of trade and economic activities on *social justice* grounds.

[30] Article 19 of the Law provides for the adoption of implementing regulations. These, however, have not been adopted but are expected to emerge by the beginning of 2008.

to predict whether such secondary legislation will materialise. Additionally, in light of the virtually non-existent competition expertise in the country it is quite unrealistic to expect competition officials and judges to be able to provide the necessary interpretation in practice.

#### 7.4.2.1 The context of the Law and legislative intent

The adoption of the Law is seen as part of the fulfilment by the government of international commitments within the WTO framework, seeking to facilitate open markets, removing hindrances to market access and ensuring non-discrimination between firms on the basis of nationality. It is considered to be a key tool for attracting foreign direct investment in the country through building a secure competitive environment with a healthy economic climate in which investment and enterprise will flourish. In drafting the Law significant attention was given to the Set of Multilaterally Agreed Principles and Rules for the Control of Restrictive Business Practices produced by the United Nations Conference on Trade and Development (UNCTAD) in 1981 for the purposes of making the Law consistent with the Set.[31] Attention was also given to the EC system of competition law.

Interestingly, the legislative intent behind the Law appears to have dismissed the need to protect competitors, accepting that in some situations firms may be forced out of markets due to their inability to cope with the pressures of competition. The policy behind the Law appears to emphasise the freedom to compete as the best choice for achieving economic growth and development even if some firms might struggle as a result of competition, so long as this is not caused by anti-competitive means.[32]

#### 7.4.2.2 Scope of the Law

The Law applies to all forms of collusion[33] and abusive conduct[34] and mergers leading to the creation or strengthening of a dominant position.[35] However, the Law is declared inapplicable to actions taken by the government or those of entities under government control or

[31] The Set can be found at the website of UNCTAD, www.unctad.org.

[32] It would be important to note that the policy behind the Law does not show an intention to seek cut-throat competition, which is considered to be damaging in the long term. During the legislative process emphasis was given to the need to achieve 'balanced' as opposed to 'absolute' competition.

[33] Article 3 of the Law. [34] Article 4 of the Law. [35] Article 10 of the Law.

supervision. The provisions of the Law also appear to be without prejudice to current international agreements and treaties.[36]

Article 3 of the Law prohibits all agreements, contracts or practices distorting competition in particular those listed in the article itself. The list is quite extensive, stretching from conventional practices harming competition (such as price-fixing and market-sharing) to others introduced for the purposes of giving the prohibition an extensive reach.[37] Exemption from the prohibition is possible. However, Article 5 of the Law which deals with exemption does not provide sufficient details with regard to the exact requirements that need to be met for an exemption to be possible.[38]

Abuse of a dominant position is prohibited under Article 4 of the Law. In parallel with Article 3, the article contains a long list of examples of abuse of dominance. The Law applies to both abuse by a single firm and collective dominance. Dominance, whether by a single firm or collective, is defined in Article 1 of the Law as 'the ability of a person or group of persons together to control the market and to cause a direct effect on prices and quantity independently without competitors being able to limit this ability'.[39] As in the case with the prohibition on collusion, an exemption is possible in the case of abuse of dominance.[40]

Article 10 of the Law provides for mandatory notification of mergers creating or likely to create a dominant position.[41] A merger is understood in light of the article to mean an acquisition of rights, assets or shares,[42] creating joint ventures or amalgamation between two or more firms. The article is silent on when notification needs to made, though it provides that the Committee for the Protection of Competition (to which notification of the merger needs to be sent) must reach its decision within ninety days from the date of notification.[43] Article 11 excludes from the scope of Article 10 merger operations which contribute to economic progress in a manner which compensates for any

36 See Article 2 of the Law.

37 Examples of the latter practices include knowingly publishing false or misleading information related to products or prices.

38 The article merely provides in general language that the Minister for Economy and Trade may grant an exemption where this would serve the interest of consumers.

39 A person for the purposes of Article 1 of the Law includes both natural and legal persons.

40 See note 38 above and accompanying text.

41 Similar to the Saudi Competition Act, there is no reference in the article to mergers *strengthening* a dominant position.

42 There is no reference, however, to what kind of acquisition is required.

43 Failure to adhere to this time limit will amount to clearance of the operation.

adverse effect on competition resulting from the operation. It is not clear, however, how this provision will apply in practice: whether in such a case notification will not be required or whether notified mergers satisfying the requirement will be cleared.

### 7.4.3 *Enforcement*

Article 7 of the Law provides for the creation of a Committee for the Protection of Competition and Prohibition of Monopolistic Practices. The Committee is affiliated to the Office of the Minister for Economy and Trade. The Law does not specify the number of members who will be chosen to serve within the Committee.[44] The Committee is intended to act as the main enforcement authority with powers to conduct investigations,[45] receive complaints about anti-competitive behaviour or abusive conduct,[46] adopt decisions,[47] cooperate with foreign competition authorities, conduct surveys and engage in competition advocacy in the form of delivering opinions on proposed laws with competition relevance.[48] It appears that in deciding to equip the Committee with these extensive powers, the government was keen to follow the example of enforcement furnished by the EC system of competition law. Despite these extensive powers, however, the Law leaves a great deal of discretion in the hands of the Minister for Economy and Trade which can be seen in the power reserved to the Minister to grant exemptions,[49] and decide on the actions to be taken in relation to infringement(s) of the provisions of the Law.[50]

[44] Article 7 provides that the composition of the committee shall be in accordance with a Prime Ministerial order following a recommendation by the Minister for Economy and Trade. It further provides that the members shall enjoy economic, financial and legal expertise and include representatives of relevant ministries and bodies. It is not clear, however, whether the latter include bodies from the public and private sectors: presumably this will be decided in the Prime Ministerial order itself. One or more officials of the Ministry will be appointed by the Minister as rapporteur to serve on the committee.

[45] Article 9 of the Law. [46] See Article 14 of the Law.

[47] The committee is able to adopt merger decisions (and also to cancel such decisions under Article 12 in cases where the information submitted to it turns out to be false or misleading) and order an amendment or termination under Article 15 of behaviour, conduct or activity caught within the prohibitions in the Law.

[48] Article 8 of the Law.

[49] See Article 5 of the Law. The issue of exemption was discussed above in note 38 and accompanying text.

[50] See Article 16 of the Law which provides that no action regarding infringement of the Law may be taken without written authorisation of the Minister or a person representing him

Though the provisions of the Law are not sufficiently detailed to make this absolutely clear, it appears that the decisions of the committee may be appealed before the courts.[51]

### *7.4.4 Orders and penalties*

The committee enjoys the power to order the firm(s) concerned to put an immediate end to a situation contravening Article 3 (collusion), Article 4 (abuse of dominance) or Article 10 (harmful mergers).

In relation to penalties, Article 17 provides for the possibility of a fine in the case of infringement of Articles 3, 4 and 10 which may range between 100,000 Riyals and 5 million Riyals. The article also provides for the power of the court (without specifying which) to decide all cases regarding 'confiscating' the profits made through behaviour, conduct or situations prohibited under the Law. Under Article 18 a penalty may be imposed on any person responsible for the management of an entity found to have committed an infringement under the Law who has knowledge of this and contributed to the infringement through abuse of his position. Interestingly, according to the article an entity will be deemed to be a guarantor of any fine and damages to be paid by such a person who commits an infringement of the Law whether on his own behalf, on behalf of the entity or in his furthering of its interest. It is important to note, however, the power conferred by virtue of Article 16 of the Law upon the Minister for Economy and Trade to choose a settlement in relation to any of the infringements under the Law as an alternative to a final decision being reached, provided that the settlement contains a payment of a sum between 100,000 Riyals and 5 million Riyals.

## 7.5 The Republic of Yemen

Yemen is considered to be a poor country compared to its rich Gulf neighbours. The Republic's legal system is a fascinating combination of Islamic law, Turkish law, English common law and tribal customary law. This combination of 'modern' and 'traditional' law or perhaps more accurately modern law with a traditional approach – along with its

following recommendations by the committee. The article also provides for the power of the Minister or person representing him to reach a settlement in relation to infringements before a final decision is reached. A settlement must take the form of a payment of a sum ranging from the minimum to the maximum level of the fine.

51 This can be seen from the general language of Article 17 of the Law.

definition as a republic – makes it particularly difficult to classify Yemen in terms of its system of political ideology and economic regulation. In recent years, the Republic has come to embrace the ideology of international openness and particular emphasis has come to be placed on the necessity for close links with international organisations, most notably the International Monetary Fund (IMF) and the World Bank. Additionally, Yemen has forged close links with the EC for the purposes of developing a vision to enhance its national directions towards accession to the GCC.[52] These efforts have been rewarded with positive responses, which have helped Yemen engage in an extensive economic reform. This has enhanced the Republic's ambitions to pursue regional integration with full membership within the GCC.[53] To date, however, this has not been achieved, though promising signals have been given by the permanent GCC members.

### *7.5.1 The Competition Law 1999*

Currently, competition law appears at the forefront of Yemen's drive for economic reform and regional integration within the GCC. This is due to the attention the Republic has come to give to anti-competitive and abusive conduct and the realisation that such situations are extremely damaging to consumers and the economy more generally. Fresh beliefs have been strengthened during the past seven years because of the need for competition to fight monopolistic practices. The government's economic slogan has transformed to monopoly is *evil* and competition is a *virtue.*

Yemen adopted its competition law in 1999 becoming the first Gulf state to do so. The Law on Encouraging Competition, and Prevention of Monopolisation and Commercial Dishonesty (the Act) aims at guaranteeing the freedom to compete without the process of competition and consumer welfare being damaged or situations of monopolisation

[52] Relations between the EC and Yemen are governed by the Cooperation Agreement of 25 November 1997, which came into force on 1 July 1998, replacing the 1984 Development Cooperation Agreement. This agreement is much more comprehensive than the agreement concluded in 1984 and is aimed at enhancing cooperation between the EC and Yemen in a range of areas including trade and economic relations. Furthermore, in order to develop a competitive economic environment in Yemen, the agreement advocates 'access to Community know-how and technology'. A Joint Cooperation Committee is established, which meets annually, to oversee the proper implementation of the agreement and make the necessary recommendations.

[53] Yemen has had part membership of the GCC since 2002.

created. The Act emphasises the importance of price determination in accordance with the parameters of free competition as created by the market mechanism.[54] The Act is fairly brief, however, and many of its provisions suffer from obvious shortcomings, most notably the lack of sufficient details in relation to the Competition Authority.[55] It was hoped that most of these shortcomings would be addressed within the implementation regulations.[56] However, these regulations have not been produced to date and there is no indication on whether and when this is likely to occur in the near future.

#### 7.5.1.1 Scope of the Law

The Act excludes from its scope of application all of the following: behaviour or conduct by firms associated with the government through exclusive agreements; arrangements made by the government in exceptional circumstances in relation to a particular sector of the economy, or cases of emergency.[57] According to Article 4(b) the Act does not apply to agency agreements covered under the Agencies Law; undertakings which are government monopolies or ones with agency or exclusive contracts for the purposes of producing foreign products in Yemen.[58] Article 4(c) on the other hand provides that the application of the Act may not limit intellectual property rights insofar as the use of these rights does not amount to an improper exercise leading to competitive harm. This provision, however brief, is one of the most advanced provisions dealing with intellectual property rights contained in the competition laws of all MECs.

#### 7.5.1.2 Collusion, abuse of dominance and harmful concentrations

In broad terms, the Act prohibits collusion between undertakings;[59] abuse of dominance;[60] and concentrations (mergers) leading to the restriction or weakening of competition.[61]

[54] Article 5 of the Act. [55] See below.

[56] Article 24 of the Act provides for the regulations to be adopted by way of a Prime Ministerial Decree following a recommendation by the Minister of Industry and Trade.

[57] Article 4(A)(2) of the Act provides that such arrangements cannot be permanent in duration and must be reviewed within six months of their adoption, though a renewal or extension of the duration may be possible in accordance with orders made by the Minister for Industry and Trade.

[58] The Act, following EC competition rules, uses the concept of 'undertaking', which is defined in Article 2 as any legal or natural person engaged in an economic activity.

[59] See Articles 6 and 7 of the Act. [60] See Article 8 of the Act.

[61] See Article 9 of the Act.

First, Article 6 of the Act contains a prohibition on any situation in which undertakings seek to monopolise[62] the import, production, distribution or purchase or sale of a product in a manner restricting free competition. The wording of the article extends to written contracts or agreements and establishing 'cooperation'. Although on its face this wording appears to exclude an application of the article in the case of an oral or informal agreement, the intention is that in practice these types of agreement,[63] as well as any type of arrangement restricting competition, should be caught within the scope of the prohibition. Article 7 lists various examples of situations considered to prevent, limit or distort competition which extend from situations of price-fixing and market-sharing to those in which the undertakings concerned prevent entry into the market by other undertakings, refuse to deal with particular buyers or engage in collusive tendering.

The Act does not provide for an exempting provision in relation to the prohibition on collusion. It is not entirely clear why such a provision was omitted. The lack of an exemption provision is particularly problematic given that the Act clearly provides for notification to the Competition Authority of any activity by undertaking(s) for the purposes of a determination by the council of the compatibility of the practice or conduct with the Act.[64] Indeed, the requirement of notification is itself also problematic: the requirement appears to extend to *any* as opposed to a *certain* practice or conduct.

It may be interesting to compare the prohibition on collusion in Articles 6 and 7 of the Law with that featuring in Article 4 of the Saudi Competition Act.[65] Neither Article 6 nor Article 7 of the Act contains any reference to effect on trade: the prohibition applies solely on the basis of restriction of competition without an additional requirement that the behaviour must produce an effect on trade, something that Article 4 of the Saudi Competition Act – as we saw – clearly includes and in fact places in a particularly prominent position.

[62] Monopolisation is defined in Article 2 of the Act as any dealing in product in a manner which prevents competition.

[63] Indeed Article 7 of the Act makes this clear with its reference to restriction of competition by way of a written agreement *or* in practice.

[64] See Article 13 of the Act. The article provides for the particulars of the notification to be determined according to the implementing regulations.
The Act also provides for notification in the case of exclusive purchasing (Article 14) and exclusive import (Article 15). Here too, the Act provides for the particulars of notification to be determined in the regulations.

[65] See p 200 above.

Secondly, abuse of a dominant position is prohibited under the Act. In addition to expressly condemning conduct which limits or weakens competition, or one hindering the market entry of potential competitors, or forcing competitors out of the market or preventing their market expansion, the article lists eleven examples of abuse of dominance. These examples concern tying between different products, refusal to supply, predatory pricing, price-fixing, exclusivity, monopolisation of essential facilities and illegal stocking of a product for the purposes of effecting an artificial price increase. There is no definition in the Act, however, of what is meant by a dominant position; nor is there any indication of the criteria or factors to be used in establishing the existence of such a position.

Finally, in relation to merger control the Act's treatment of concentrations or mergers is extremely under-developed. The only provisions in the Act dealing with concentrations are Articles 9 and 2.[66] The former provides for a prohibition on concentrations causing or likely to cause restriction or weakening of competition and the latter inadequately defines concentrations as 'concentration of purchases from a single source, agency or firm'.

### *7.5.2 The Competition Authority*

The Act provides for the creation of an 'Authority for the Protection of Competition and Prevention of Monopolisation' (the Competition Authority). According to Article 10 of the Act, the authority will investigate and unearth all forms of abuse of dominance, collusion, and harmful concentrations whether horizontal or vertical. In addition, the authority will be in charge of formulating the necessary policies for the purposes of protecting and supporting competition in Yemen. The Minister for Industry and Trade serves as the chairman of the authority and is assisted by an unspecified number of members.

The Act does not provide sufficient details of the exact functions of the authority as a competition agency, though its main function appears to be that of making recommendations to the Minister in individual cases. The Minister, however, is not bound by these recommendations.

[66] The understanding is that notification of mergers was intended to be made mandatory. The Act is silent, however, on the relevant requirements in this regard except insofar as it provides in Article 13 for a notification of any activity to the Competition Authority. It is also worth mentioning Article 10 of the Act which deals with the creation of the Competition Authority and appears to provide for the regulation of horizontal and vertical mergers as one of the activities of the authority.

### 7.5.3 *Penalties*

The Act provides for fines as the main penalty. Fines range from 10,000 to 100,000 Riyals or the equivalent amount of profit made by the undertaking(s) through the anti-competitive or abusive behaviour. Interestingly, the Act provides for criminal penalty in the form of an imprisonment in the case of a *repeated* infringement. The decision to impose a criminal penalty lies in the hands of the courts which may also order the name of the offender to be struck out from the Commercial Register, the Importers Register or the Register for Commercial Agents and Brokers.[67]

Prosecution under the Act can only be brought following a decision by the Minister for Industry and Trade to that effect and following a transfer of the file to the Office of the General Prosecutor.[68] Thus, the Act leaves considerable discretion in the hands of a politician, the Minister, when deciding on enforcement and whether or what type of orders to be made in individual cases. According to Article 21 of the Act, the Minister may decide any of the following: informal settlement and accepting undertakings in lieu; adopting interim measures or permanent orders prohibiting a particular behaviour or conduct; and making orders for the purposes of 'remedying' a particular situation within a specified time period.

### 7.5.4 *An added dimension of regulation*

The Act contains an added dimension of regulation beyond its provision for the protection of free competition and the regulation of behaviour, conduct or activities which interfere with the patterns of free competition. This dimension can be seen in light of three articles of the Act. Article 18 provides for a clear prohibition on owners or managers of factories from limiting the distribution of output in a manner that leads to monopolisation or congestion in distribution or engineered and fabricated price increases. Article 20 states that associations of undertakings or cooperative associations active in production or import must adhere to their declared objectives and must not deviate from these objectives for the purposes of fixing prices or engaging in deceitful practices relating to product description. Finally Article 19 shows that the remit of the officials of the authority extends beyond the traditional

[67] Article 22 of the Act. [68] Article 23 of the Act.

role of protection of competition to cover activities of commercial dishonesty. The article provides for cooperation by these officials with the officials of the General Commission for the purposes of determining cases of commercial dishonesty and fabricated or defective products.

## 7.6 Gulf States with no specific competition law

As we noted above, four Gulf States have not adopted specific competition law and policy. These states are Bahrain, Kuwait, Oman and United Arab Emirates (UAE). In all of these countries, most notably the UAE, competition law and policy currently occupy a high ranking on the government agenda and concentrated efforts are being made for the purposes of instituting a domestic competition law regime. In others, however, no particular effort has been made to consider competition law and policy with some of these countries relying on provisions in other laws as their competition law tools.

### *7.6.1 Bahrain*

#### 7.6.1.1 Overview

Bahrain is 'another' example of a Gulf State seeking to create a brand image for itself on the global stage. Considerable efforts have been made by the government in this regard and these efforts have come to intensify during the past seven years with particular focus and importance being placed on foreign direct investment; a special body, the Economic Development Board has been created for the purpose of attracting such investment into Bahrain.[69]

Currently, Bahrain lacks a specific competition law. However, the Constitution of Bahrain, the Law of Commerce and the new Company Law all contain provisions which deal with certain issues relating to competition. With regards to monopolies, Article 117 of the Constitution provides that 'any monopoly shall only be awarded by law and for a limited time'. Indeed, save for this situation, monopolies have for a long time been considered to be undesirable under law and should be eliminated.[70] The Law of Commerce[71] applies to traders and commercial practices of any

[69] The board was established by an Amiri (Royal) Decree in 2000.

[70] See for example Amiri Decree No. 18 of 1975.

[71] Law No. 7 of 1987 available (in Arabic) at the website of the Ministry of Industry and Commerce, www.commerce.gov.bh.

person. This legislation does not deal specifically with monopolies or mergers but it does contain a section dealing with unfair competition. Articles 59 to 64 prohibit those activities which would have damaging effects on competitors. According to these, traders are forbidden to undertake practices which will be detrimental to their competitors or will attract the custom of their competitors. Such practices include resorting to fraud or cheating when marketing goods, providing misleading or false information and utilising methods which emphasise the importance of their trade and goods over that of their competitors. Furthermore, it is illegal for traders to induce those working for their competitors to leave their employment and assist them in learning the trade secrets of their rivals and attracting their custom. Finally, persons who supply information to commercial houses, regarding conditions of traders, are prohibited from supplying a false account of the behaviour or financial standing of a trader.

#### 7.6.1.2 Mergers

The business phenomenon of mergers between firms falls under the Commercial Companies Law of 2001.[72] Articles 312 to 319 of this Law specifically deal with mergers. Some of these provisions are worth mentioning. According to Article 312, mergers must be effected in one of two ways, namely: by acquisition or consolidation, and must not lead to the monopolisation of 'an economic activity, a commodity or a certain product'. Articles 313 and 314 provide rules which apply when the merger is by way of acquisition and when it is by way of consolidation. Mergers must be recorded in the Commercial Registry and published in the *Official Gazette* and in one daily newspaper. Objections by 'holders of rights established before the publication of merger' must be raised by registered letter within sixty days from the date of publication; if no objection is raised within this period then the merger shall be deemed to be effective.

#### 7.6.1.3 The telecommunications sector

The WTO, of which Bahrain has been a member since 1995, obliged Bahrain to open up its telecommunications sector and end monopolies by 2005. Accordingly, Bahrain adopted the Telecommunications Law, which entered into force in 2003.[73] The aim of this Law is to liberalise the

[72] The Law, which repealed the Commercial Companies Law 1975, can be found at the website of the Ministry of Industry and Commerce.

[73] The Law was adopted under Legislative Decree No. 48 of 2002 and is available at the website of the Telecommunications Regulatory Authority, www.tra.org.bh.

telecommunications market and it set up the Telecommunications Regulatory Authority (TRA) to regulate this process. Among the various duties of the TRA listed in Chapter III of this Law, is the duty to 'promote effective and fair competition among new and existing licensed operators'; thus the authority is empowered to make such regulations, orders and determinations as it considers necessary for the promotion of competition. Chapters IX and XVI of the Law are dedicated to issues relating to competition, which are considered to be rather progressive and new to the Gulf region. Chapter IX provides the timetable for introducing competition in the telecommunications sector by issuing licenses to other firms, thereby ending the monopoly of Batelco which had been the sole telecommunications service-provider in Bahrain since 1981. Article 65 of the Law details the anti-competitive behaviour which is prohibited. Any act or omission of a licensed operator, which will have the effect of materially preventing, restricting or distorting competition in the Bahraini telecommunications sector, is prohibited. This includes any agreement, arrangement, understanding or concerted practice which prevents, restricts or distorts competition in the market, abuse of a dominant position by a licensed operator and anti-competitive changes in the structure of the market, especially anti-competitive mergers and acquisitions. For this purpose, dominant position is defined as 'the Licensee's position of economic power that enables it to prevent the existence and continuation of effective competition in the relevant market through the ability of the Licensee to act independently, to a material extent, of competitors, subscribers and users'. However, the Law exempts from the prohibition on anti-competitive practices those agreements which promote economic or technical progress and improve the provision of goods or services provided that such agreements do not restrict competition in a manner that is more than essential for achieving the beneficial objectives and do not eliminate competition in a significant part of the relevant market. It is interesting to note that where this provision is included in the competition laws of other countries, it provides that the exempt agreement must also provide consumers with a fair share of the resulting profits but in the Law it is stated that the agreement will be exempt 'even if' consumers – subscribers and users – have a reasonable share of the resulting benefit.[74] Before deciding whether an act or omission constitutes anti-competitive conduct, the TRA must do all of the following: notify the licensed

[74] See Article 65(c) of the Law.

operator that it is conducting an investigation; provide reasons on the basis of which it believes that a breach has occurred or is about to occur; detail any information which it requires from the operator in order to complete its investigation; explain, where necessary, how the operator could remedy the alleged breach; and give the operator a reasonable period within which to make representations in response. Where a violation of the prohibitions contained in Article 65 of the Law is found, the authority can direct the licensed operator to do or refrain from doing certain things in order to remedy, reverse or prevent the breach and can impose a fine not exceeding 10 per cent of the annual revenues of the licensed operator. Finally, the article authorises the TRA to issue regulations for the purposes of maintaining efficient competition in the telecommunications market and may also issue guidelines explaining what anti-competitive conduct entails.

In September 2004 the Regulation on Mergers and Acquisitions was issued and came into effect in October of the same year. A number of consultations were conducted prior to issuing the regulation for the purposes of making sure that it was fair and in line with international practices. The aim of this regulation is to protect the interests of consumers and competitors when mergers, acquisitions and joint ventures take place. The TRA has the power to analyse these transactions before they occur to ensure that they do not have an adverse effect on competition in the telecommunications market, which will in turn disadvantage consumers. Where this is found to be the case, the authority can prohibit the transaction or impose conditions to remove the anti-competitive aspects. It should be noted that this regulation does not affect the operation of the Commercial Companies Law, discussed above.

### *7.6.2 Kuwait*

#### 7.6.2.1 The Investment Law

The State of Kuwait occupies a rather unique geographical location with it being *squeezed* between much larger neighbours: Iraq and Saudi Arabia. For many years, Kuwait relied heavily on its oil resources as the sole engine for economic growth and development. This reliance has come to be significantly minimised since the turn of the twenty-first century, with the focus of the main economic development plan of the country shifting to diversification and privatisation in the local economy. Realising that foreign investment plays an important role in achieving these goals and making the economy more competitive, the

Investment Law was adopted.[75] The overall objective of the Investment Law is to promote the private sector, liberalise trade and reduce the government's involvement in the economy by encouraging foreign investments in Kuwait. Striving to achieve this objective represents a remarkable policy-change on foreign investment. In the years preceding the adoption of the Law, the door for foreign investment was only partially opened: during those years foreign persons were only allowed to own up to 49 per cent in local firms and this ownership was excluded from certain sectors of the economy including banking and insurance.[76] With the enactment of the Law, this percentage was increased to 100 per cent in certain sectors and a new institutional structure was established to facilitate foreign investment and safeguard the interests and rights of foreign investors;[77] taxation and corporate rules were also relaxed.[78] This more 'welcoming' policy on foreign investment was however made conditional upon compliance with various policy directives and requirements including mandating employing a number of Kuwaitis in the investment project.[79]

#### 7.6.2.2 The privatisation programme

Along with the Investment Law, the government adopted a five-year privatisation programme in July 2001.[80] The Programme outlined a

[75] Law No. 8/2001, Regarding the Organisation of Direct Investment of Foreign Capital in the State of Kuwait.

[76] It may be worth noting here Article 21 of the Constitution of Kuwait which prohibits foreign ownership of Kuwait's natural resources by providing that 'natural resources and all revenues therefrom are the property of the State'.

[77] A Foreign Investment Committee – chaired by the Minister of Industry and Commerce with its membership consisting of representatives of the private and public sectors – was established to authorise investment applications, promote and attract foreign investment in Kuwait, facilitate the investment procedure, deal with complaints by foreign investors and impose penalties for violations of the Law. A Foreign Investment Office was also established, which is responsible for receiving the applications and getting them completed by the relevant authorities, conducting studies and presenting proposals to the committee. Other tasks of the office include notifying the international market of the projects and privileges offered for investment, providing information required by foreign investors, following up projects which were licensed and overcoming any obstacles encountered and assisting foreign investors to enter and reside in the country by coordinating with the relevant authorities.

[78] Among the notable changes were: the reduction in corporate tax rates for foreign firms, the creation of various tax-exemption provisions and the elimination of the requirement to have a Kuwaiti agent when establishing companies.

[79] See Article 13 of the Law.

[80] In fact, privatisation ranked high on the legislative agenda in 1997 when the Kuwaiti National Assembly considered passing a privatisation law to provide legal authority and establish the procedure for privatisation of state-owned enterprises. For the past ten

wide range of activities with the aim of facilitating a transition from a state economy to a market economy. Among other benefits, privatisation was widely considered to be an effective driving force towards making the local economy more competitive and attractive to foreign investors. Privatisation was planned to occur in different sectors over a five year period through the implementation of many proposals, most of which however have yet to materialise into concrete actions.[81]

#### 7.6.2.3 Competition law and policy developments

A specific competition law has not been developed in Kuwait. However, the policies of diversification and privatisation (and their goal of enhancing foreign investment) have produced positive effects on how competition should be viewed and have as a result pushed competition law and policy upwards on the government's economic agenda. A 'highly confidential' draft competition law has been produced which aims at promoting competition and preventing monopolisation.[82] In preparing this draft, particular focus was given to the competition law regimes of the EC, the USA, Germany and Egypt. It is understood that this draft – which contains twenty-six articles – provides for the regulation of monopolies and illegal competition. It is also understood that the draft proposed the creation of an administrative agency and an executive council to deal with matters relating to monopolies and 'tampering with prices'. Significant hopes are attached to the adoption of a specific competition law by Kuwaiti politicians, and policy-makers in particular, who appear to believe firmly that a specific competition law will have a positive impact on the domestic market and economy as well as turning the proposed privatisation law into reality.

In the absence of a specific competition law in the country, several laws have been utilised as competition tools in practice. The most important of these are the Commercial Law and the Law of Commercial Companies.[83] Provisions dealing with issues relating to

years, however, this legislation has been the subject of political debate and it is not certain at present as to when (if) it will be adopted.

[81] For example, Kuwait Airways still remains a state-owned airline and a number of communication services and ports and transport sector have yet to be privatised despite proposals to that effect.

[82] This draft was the subject of discussion within the Committee on Financial and Economic Affairs of the Kuwaiti National Assembly in December 2006 at the end of which the committee decided to approve the draft. The Ministry of Commerce and Industry and the Kuwait Chamber of Commerce and Industry played an influential role in preparing the draft.

[83] Law No. 15 of 1960.

competition can also be found in the Constitution of Kuwait, most importantly Article 153 which stipulates that 'no monopoly may be granted except by a law and for a limited period'.

The Commercial Law[84] provides rules for a range of commercial activities including unfair competition. According to Article 60 of the Law 'unlawful competition' is prohibited which includes, among other things, 'any deliberate act ... that tends to ... impede the freedom of commerce, or to circumvent competition in the field of production or distribution of goods or services'. The specific acts which will constitute unfair competition include the following: fixing the price of goods or services through explicit or implicit agreements, impeding a competitor's entry into the market for no lawful reason, damaging the reputation of competitors or their goods and acts, causing disturbance in the market with the aim of harming competitors. Furthermore, abuse by a party of its 'monopolistic position' is prohibited. For this purpose, 'monopolistic position' is defined as 'the ability to control the prices of goods and services in the market' and abuse of this is said to include obstructing the entry of competitors into the market, reducing the prices of goods and services or obtaining excessive prices or benefits that could not have been obtained in a competitive market.

The Law on Commercial Companies deals with merger situations, or mergers between companies. However, the merger control instrument contained in the Law is not, strictly speaking, a competition law tool and in appraising mergers no competition-based test or considerations are employed or taken into account. According to Article 222 of the Law a merger operation may be effected in one of the following two ways: through winding up one or more companies and transferring their assets and liabilities to an existing company *or* winding up two or more companies and creating a new company to which the assets and liabilities of the companies concerned will be transferred. The Law contains a mandatory pre-merger notification, which must be effected immediately after the passing of the resolution; failure to do so would render the merger null and void. A standard notification form has been designed by the Ministry of Commerce and Industry which must be completed and submitted to the Commercial Registration Department at the Ministry, together with the relevant corporate resolutions and other documents required by the Law. If incorrect or incomplete information is supplied, the

84 Law No. 68 of 1980. The Law is also referred to on occasions as the Commercial Code of Kuwait.

documents would be returned to the parties for correction or completion; the Ministry will clear the merger where the information submitted is complete and valid. This procedure would usually take between one and three months and once clearance has been granted the merger and consolidation resolutions must be registered in the Commercial Register and published in the *Official Gazette* and two daily newspapers. The merger will only come into effect three months from the date of registration and publication, during which period an objection to the merger by third parties or other government bodies may be raised.

### *7.6.3 Oman*

The Sultanate of Oman has achieved considerable economic development and progress through the adoption of consecutive Five-Year Development Plans covering 1976–2010. These plans have been aimed at developing the private sector, attracting foreign investment and achieving diversification in the local economy.

According to the Basic Law of the Sultanate of Oman, promulgated by Royal Decree No. 101, 1996, the economy of Oman is based on the 'principles of a free economy', the chief pillar of which is constructive, fruitful cooperation between public and private activity. The aim behind the Basic Law is to achieve economic and social development that will lead to increased production and a higher standard of living for citizens. Furthermore, the Law guarantees the freedom of economic activity 'in a manner that will ensure the well-being of the national economy'.

#### 7.6.3.1 The privatisation law and programme

Development of the private sector in Oman has always been encouraged, hence the importance attached to privatisation in the Five-Year Development Plans. Oman's Privatisation Programme commenced in 1988 when the government sold some of its shares in Oman Flour Mills Company. Since the Fifth Five-Year Plan (1996–2000), a comprehensive privatisation framework has been in place and is considered to be one of the most advanced in the Gulf region. In this context, a new Privatisation Law was issued by Royal Decree No. 77/2004.[85] The objectives of this Law include providing opportunities to the private sector to enable it to contribute to the development of the economy, creating

[85] The Privatisation Law is available at the Ministry of National Economy website, www.moneoman.gov.om/privatization_law.asp.

competition and attracting foreign investment. According to Article 11 of this Law, the creation of monopolies is to be avoided by establishing more than one firm to provide the service which is to be privatised.

#### 7.6.3.2 Competition law tools

In Oman several laws have been used as competition law tools for the purposes of dealing with harmful situations. Some of these laws have vague competition law relevance; others have no relevance at all but have nonetheless in a misguided manner been treated as so. An example of these can be found in Articles 33 and 34 of the Law of Trademarks, Trade Data, Undisclosed Trade Information and Protection from Unfair Competition.[86] These provisions contain rules for protection against unfair competition.[87] According to the articles, there is a prohibition on 'natural and juridical persons' undertaking any competitive activities which contravene the fair practices of industry and commerce. This includes practices which create confusion, false allegations which harm the reputation, goodwill or trust in a product and statements which mislead the public with regards to the characteristics of goods or services. Furthermore, a prohibition is placed on the disclosure of commercial secrets in a manner which is contrary to the fair conduct of trade. An activity will amount to a secret if 'its nature is unknown, if its commercial value stems from being a secret, if reasonable measures were taken to keep it a secret or if it is not easy for a person with ordinary knowledge in this field to achieve this knowledge'.[88] An intentional violation of these rules is punishable by imprisonment for a period not exceeding two years and/or a fine not exceeding 2,000 Omani Riyals.[89]

The issue of merger operations falls under the Commercial Companies Law.[90] Chapter two of this Law contains the provisions relating to mergers between firms. According to Article 13(4) a merger may take the form of 'incorporation' or 'consolidation' and Article 13(5) and (6) detail how the merger should take place in relation to each of these methods. The merger must be registered in the Commercial Register and published in two consecutive issues of two daily newspapers. It will not take effect until three months from the date of registration, during which period the

[86] Law No. 38/2000.

[87] Unfair competition is also dealt with under Articles 47–50 of Oman Commercial Law 1990, which was issued under Royal Decree No. 55/90.

[88] See Article 35 of the Law. [89] Article 35 of the Law.

[90] Law No. 4/1974. The Law was amended in March 2006.

creditors of the company will have the right to object to the merger by registered letter. Where an objection is raised, the merger will be suspended until the objection is withdrawn, or the Authority for the Settlement of Commercial Disputes overrules the objection. If no objection is raised during this period the merger will be final.[91] Banks and investment companies must obtain the approval of the Central Bank of Oman on the merger resolution before the merger can take effect. Determining the procedures and conditions of mergers and how the assets of the companies merging are to be evaluated is the responsibility of the Minister of Commerce and Industry.

#### 7.6.3.3 The telecommunications sector

Oman had to open up its telecommunications sector to the private sector to satisfy the obligation placed upon it by the WTO, of which it has been a member since 2000, and to allow foreign telecommunications companies to enter the Omani market. For this purpose, the Telecommunications Regulatory Act was promulgated by Royal Decree No. 30/2002 and established the Telecommunications Regulatory Authority[92] for the purpose of regulating the telecommunications sector and introducing competition therein. According to the Act, the duties of the authority include, among others, creating a competitive environment among licensees to ensure the provision of 'world-standard telecommunications services', taking the necessary steps to enable service-providers to compete internationally and taking the necessary measures to examine the activities which prevent competition in the telecommunications sector. Articles 40 and 41 stipulate the rules of competition. According to these, any act or omission of a licensee that prevents or restricts competition in the telecommunications sector is prohibited. These actions or omissions include abuse of a dominant position and the conclusion of agreements excluding or limiting competition in the market as well as merger operations leading to changes in the structure of the market as a result of which competition will be prevented or restricted. With the approval of the Minister of Transport and Communications, the authority may issue further rules relating to the acts or omissions that prevent or restrict competition and it also has the task of deciding whether an act or omission does lead to the prevention of

[91] These provisions are in fact identical to those provided in the Commercial Companies Law of Bahrain, mentioned at p 219 above.

[92] See www.tra.gov.om.

competition. Before reaching a decision on this, the authority must carry out the necessary investigations.

The Executive Telecommunications Regulations produced by the authority further elaborate upon the behaviour which is prohibited pursuant to Articles 40 and 41 of the Act. Clause 14.1 of the regulations provides a whole list of activities which players within the sector must refrain from, including, entering into a contract which is in restraint of trade, monopolisation of any service, practices which reduce competition in the market, discrimination in pricing and other similar practices harmful to competition. Clause 14.2 of the regulations prohibits three types of arrangements between two or more service-providers, namely arrangements, which fix prices or other terms or conditions of services in the telecommunications sector, which determine the result of a contract or business opportunity and which divide, share or allocate telecommunications markets among themselves or other service-providers. Clauses 14.3 and 14.4 of the regulations deal with abuse of dominance. According to the former provision, a licensed operator will be declared dominant by the authority if he enjoys 'significant market power'. In deciding this, the authority will take into account market shares and other 'appropriate factors'. A comprehensive list is contained in Clause 14.4 of the activities which will constitute abuse of a dominant position. These include, among others, inducing a supplier not to sell to a competitor, failing to supply facilities to a competitor within a reasonable time or on reasonable terms, bundling of services and supplying competitive services at a price below the average costs. The authority is empowered to investigate, on its own initiative or on application from any person, whether the activities of a dominant service-provider amount to an abuse of its position within the meaning of Clause 14.4 of the regulations and whether they amount to an anti-competitive practice according to Article 40 of the Act. Under certain circumstances, it may be held that an activity does not constitute abuse of a dominant position or an anti-competitive practice and where this is done reasons for such a decision must be given and be consistent with 'evolution of a competitive market-based telecommunications sector'. Where abuse of a dominant position or anti-competitive practices are found, whether under the Act or the regulations, the authority may impose such fines as it considers appropriate and require the offender to take one or more of the following actions: cease the anti-competitive activities immediately or within a specified time in line with certain conditions; make specific changes to eliminate or reduce the impact of the anti-competitive conduct; meet with those affected by the offenders' actions to determine remedies to prevent the continuation of such actions and resolve any disputes pursuant to Chapter Twelve of the regulations (on dispute resolution); publish an apology of their actions in one or more newspapers as specified by the authority and provide periodic reports to the authority to enable it to examine whether the anti-competitive actions are continuing and their impact on the telecommunications market, competitors and users. Where there has been a repeated breach of a decision issued by the authority, the authority may order the offender to divest itself of ownership of some lines of business or carry out that business in a separate entity with a separate account, after it has given the offender specific notice that such a decision will be made, providing it with the opportunity to put across its arguments and if the authority considers that such a decision is an effective means of deterring the continuation of anti-competitive practices.

### *7.6.4 United Arab Emirates*

#### 7.6.4.1 General

The United Arab Emirates (UAE) is a complex country made from a union of several regions. The country has always promoted its vision and concept of luxury, whether in the social, economic or political arenas. The small geographic size of the country – along with its small population and the extensive wealth its rulers enjoy – have made the pursuit for luxuries extremely possible. Considerable efforts have been made towards creating a modern, developed country at the heart of the Middle East marked by 'dwarfing' remarkable achievements anywhere in the world, whether with constructing impressive skyscrapers or skiing resorts in the heart of the desert with a temperature above forty degrees Celsius. These efforts have been part of a vision for creating global reach for the UAE by attracting extensive foreign participation in the local economy and local life and conducting extensive investment abroad. Despite its economic strengths, however, the UAE still suffers from major domestic problems, most notably the lagging education of its citizens behind the country's impressive economic development.[93]

[93] This indeed is highly surprising given that the majority of the government's budget (over 35 per cent) is dedicated to education and the fact that the country enjoys one of the lowest student:teacher ratios in the world (12:1).

The UAE like many countries in the region is currently in a state of economic transition, though in the case of the UAE this has been much more intensive and radical. The traditional economic approach with heavy reliance on a low-skilled work force is increasingly giving way to a new economic approach based on knowledge and hi-technology. The UAE has come to develop an interesting socio-economic and socio-political model. Economic growth has come to rank extremely high on the agenda with greater emphasis on building a market economy. However, the ideology which appears to underpin this approach places the government at the very centre of economic growth. The government's leadership is seen as crucial for the purposes of creating such growth. The rulers of the UAE strongly believe in the need for the government to act as a 'bulldozer' in opening up the path for growth and prosperity. To this end, political reform has been considered vital for the purposes of reducing bureaucracy by removing unnecessary ministerial committees, creating a new ministerial portfolio for the purposes of improving the functioning of the government, increasing the monetary and administrative powers of ministries and reducing the administrative burden.

The existence of government control over certain economic activities in the country is considered to be controversial. Embracing a free market system entails a *decrease* as opposed to an *increase* in government intervention. A particular concern that has been raised in relation to government control in the UAE revolves around the likelihood of the government separating the regulatory functions of state enterprises from their commercial activities as part of the on-going economic reform.[94] This concern is particularly important in light of the absence of a specific UAE competition law, which may encourage the creation of systems of exclusive agents for imported products with the result that competition may be limited as a result of anti-competitive arrangements implemented by those agents.[95] Furthermore, a heavy degree of state intervention is considered to provide a shield for incumbent firms from competition. This is particularly so in the telecommunications sector, where the government has maintained a policy of limiting competition thus making entry by foreign firms into the market virtually impossible.

[94] A similar situation was discussed above in relation to Turkey which highlighted the role competition law and a competition authority play when a government engages in such a process. See the discussion on p 100 above.

[95] As we note in chapter 9 below in relation to Lebanon, the problem with national exclusive agents can have serious competitive implications in practice.

The WTO has been actively advocating a change of policy in the country from that of *limiting* competition to *facilitating* competition. In this way, the enactment of specific competition legislation has been seen as desirable, if not necessary. The government's response has been favourable, acknowledging that there was evidence pointing to the existence of anti-competitive practices, most notably unreasonable price increases, which appear to be harmful to local consumers.[96] However, such response in itself is problematic given that the government's preferred action appears to be to opt for 'price regulation' as opposed to facilitation of competition.[97]

Another major criticism directed at the government's global vision is that the desire for global reach has compromised the need for ensuring equal economic growth and development in the different regions of the country. A simple look at the UAE would reveal the existence of a highly *developed* entity within a larger *developing* entity. Thus, huge concentration of wealth came to exist in places such as Dubai and Abu Dhabi with other parts of the country being largely neglected. This is seen as failure in economic management and unfair political 'prioritisation' which should be addressed through redistribution of wealth.

#### 7.6.4.2 Price regulation

The UAE maintains quite an interventionist approach on the part of government in relation to prices, most notably in sectors such as food, clothing, furniture, drugs and medical equipment and construction materials. The Ministry of Economy and Planning – the government department in charge of price regulation[98] – publishes on a regular basis price lists for various consumer products. This practice has come to be quite intensive recently.[99] According to the Ministry, its policy on price regulation and publishing lists of prices aims at enhancing consumer awareness and striking a balance between supply and demand. Clearly,

96 See the views submitted to the WTO as part of the government's 'Trade Policy Review: Report by the United Arab Emirates' (2006), available at: www.wto.org.

97 It is arguable that price increases in the country are not necessarily caused by anti-competitive behaviour but rather they are due to, among other factors, a surge in consumer demand, economic growth within the country and sharp increases in the price of oil. Thus, the government's action should not be that of price-regulation but opening up certain markets to competition.

98 Within the Ministry, a Price Control Committee is in existence which is chaired by the Minister.

99 On 20 June 2006 the Ministry of Economy introduced a new policy of publishing price lists for various consumer products on a weekly basis consistent with Ministerial Council Decision for Service No. 35/2/2006.

this shows a social objective being sought in the process which is reflective of an approach followed in many MECs.

#### 7.6.4.3 Turning to competition law

The government's decision to consider the need for a competition law and policy appears to have been largely motivated by calls from different quarters advocating the adoption of specific competition legislation in the UAE to facilitate a removal of the country's problematic barriers to entry in local markets and enable it to reap the full benefits of a liberal economy.

At present, a proposal for introducing specific competition legislation and creating a Consumer Protection Authority in the country is under active consideration within the Ministry of Economy and Planning. It is expected that a final draft of a new competition law will be ready for adoption towards the end of 2007.

There is a particular concern over the government's proposal, however, in light of the likelihood that the new law – when adopted – might institute a regime which would operate as a pure 'price-regulatory' mechanism as opposed to one aiming at facilitating and protecting competition in the market place through emphasis on economic efficiency and maximisation of consumer welfare. This concern does not appear to be alleviated by the recent government declarations that the purpose behind the proposed law is to facilitate an open, competitive environment in local markets. In practice, there appears to be more work for the government to accomplish in terms of facilitating greater privatisation and 'removing' itself from the market place.

#### 7.6.4.4 Car retail market

One particular sector in the UAE has demonstrated both strong competition and the need for competition law, namely the car retail market. During the past two years, there has been a noticeable decrease in the interest on car loans due to sharp competition within the banking sector. In order to attract as many customers as possible, some banks have entered into cooperation and partnership agreements with car-dealers aimed at offering new services with low interest rates to customers. Apparently, these agreements put the onus on car-dealers to bear the reduction in the rates offered.[100] This increased competition in the sector demonstrates that it is possible for competition to exist without

[100] Such condition appears to be acceptable given the interest on the part of dealers to reduce their large stocks of cars.

competition law.[101] However, the manner in which this competition has come to increase, with some players being able to 'abuse' the process and drive prices to below cost level in order to push smaller players out of the market, clearly demonstrates the need for a competition law.

## 7.7 Reflections

The Gulf States are at both a hugely fascinating and hugely frustrating stage of development at present. These countries clearly have a great potential for deep and far-reaching economic development. Currently, they are in a state of economic transition and to a very limited extent political transformation. Six of the Gulf States have formed the GCC, a community of huge potential for meaningful regional cooperation. Together these developments form a positive force. Competition law has been introduced in three Gulf States and is being considered in others as the backdrop of these developments and the liberalisation in trade worldwide and an expansion of the global economy.

An assessment of competition law and policy in the Gulf States cannot be conducted with only *positive* developments in mind; equally important are other developments and additional factors which, although *negative* in nature and their impact, are vital for such an assessment. Among these developments and factors are: the lack of sufficient progress made at the GCC level in terms of bringing the six GCC Member States closer together in economic and political terms; the timid move towards comprehensive economic liberalisation; and the paradoxical approach in embracing the free-market system with privatisation to a certain extent being accompanied with heavy governmental control and regulation. Additionally, there is a crucial 'non-development' concerning the fact that Gulf States are still a long way from completing their political transformation, which is essential for the development of competition law and policy.

The above-mentioned positive and negative developments raise more than one question as far as competition law and policy are concerned. At the GCC level, perhaps the most important question to be asked is what hopes does the existence of the GCC offer for building a competition-law forum and a model of regional approach to competition law more generally. At the national level, the 'equivalent' question concerns what effect

[101] Over the years, some countries have been highly competitive internationally without adopting a competition law. A good example here is Singapore, which came to adopt specific competition legislation in 2005.

does the absence of competition law and policy from the majority of Gulf States have on the prospects for competition law and policy materialising at the GCC level. The questions that may arise therefore (and not necessarily only the two questions mentioned here) are interlinked. As such, the all too familiar options to internationalists or regionalists readily present themselves: competition law and policy in the Gulf may be built and promoted in one of two ways, through a top-down approach or a bottom-up approach. The crucial question, however, is which of these approaches should be followed in practice. Realistically speaking the former approach is unlikely to prove successful for several reasons, most notably the absence of the necessary infrastructure for competition law and policy to get a foothold at the GCC level. This infrastructure *does not* – as might be perceived – include a requirement of competition law and policy being developed domestically. Indeed, there is strong evidence supporting this view.[102] The missing infrastructure referred to here concerns the existence of close economic links between the GCC States and competence to be enjoyed by the GCC institutions over economic matters. Only with the existence of a proper GCC institutional structure and the vesting of powers in bodies within this structure can there be realistic prospects of competition law and policy developing at the GCC level. Judged in light of past and present evidence surrounding the GCC, the future in this regard does not appear to be particularly bright: if anything there is in fact little evidence indicating that this infrastructure is likely to be built. Moreover, even if one were to assume that GCC competition law and policy is possible, there will still be the difficulty existing at the heart of the fact that countries like Bahrain, Kuwait and Oman lack competition law and policy and are unlikely simply to incorporate GCC competition rules and standards within their domestic systems.

The lack of real prospects for a top-down approach makes it necessary to concentrate on the bottom-up approach, which appears to be more suitable in the case of Gulf States. Competition law and policy in this part of the Middle East *must* grow at domestic level. So far this has been the case in Yemen, Saudi Arabia and Qatar and is also soon likely to be the case as far as Bahrain, Kuwait, Oman and the UAE are concerned. The lenses in the competition law and policy assessment referred to above should therefore

[102] This evidence is furnished by the experience of the EC. It is widely known that at the time the Treaty of Rome was signed in 1957 – thus introducing what became later one of the world's most successful competition law regimes – not all of the founding Member States had domestic competition laws and policy.

be adjusted in order to focus on Gulf States individually. As we saw in this chapter, the competition laws of Saudi Arabia, Yemen and Qatar at present fall short of capturing situations of harmful competition effectively. These (new) laws suffer from major shortcomings. Among other things, the provisions contained in these laws would benefit from (in fact require) important clarification.[103] The institutional frameworks or structures within the regimes incorporating these laws are far from developed and the legislative work is far from complete. Introducing competition law in these three Gulf countries probably would have been unthinkable as recently as the mid-1990s and in the case of Saudi Arabia and Qatar was indeed so even as recently as five years ago. Therefore, the fact that competition law has been introduced in these countries is a development of huge significance. Nonetheless, the task of building effective competition law regimes in these countries is still far from being accomplished. To achieve this, first and foremost the competition authorities in the regimes must be made independent and armed with the necessary powers to reach binding decisions. This would necessitate distancing the government, in most cases,[104] from competition law enforcement.[105] As things stand, only the Qatari Committee for the Protection of Competition is given some form of independence. Having an independent competition authority is crucial for the purposes of securing an effective enforcement of competition law. Secondly, special attention must be given to building a robust competition culture and the important task of competition advocacy. The concept of competition within the GCC has featured as one associated with either sporting or harmful rivalry. Neither of these associations, however, is relevant when dealing with competition law, which aims to protect 'free-market' competition. Only in Yemen, the non-full member of the GCC, has competition consistently developed as a free-market concept and on the whole been valued. In the other Gulf States, for many years great reservations were attached to competition and only recently has this attitude

[103] Several examples can be found on this in the discussion in previous parts of the chapter in relation to the three laws. Also, it should be noted that some of the provisions contained in these laws are not really practicable. A good illustration can be found in the merger provision in the Saudi Competition Act mandating pre-merger notification at least sixty days prior to the completion of the merger operation.

[104] It would be appropriate to add this qualification given that in some cases intervention by the government may be appropriate, such as those of public interest or cases of national emergency.

[105] As we saw in earlier parts of the chapter, considerable powers are placed in the hands of ministers and the government in general. One particular power that should be transferred to an independent competition authority is ministerial settlements.

begun to change with an increasing number of Gulf States moving towards the market mechanism and slowly favouring liberalisation. Such change is important and must be welcomed. However, it must be supported by extensive competition advocacy.

The task of competition advocacy – repeatedly highlighted throughout this book as one of major significance especially in a region such as the Middle East[106] – has a huge scope in the case of the Gulf States. Three dates in particular have great significance in the national calendar of these countries. These are the start of the holy month of *Ramadan*, and the two *Eid* festivals: *Eid ul-Fitr* and *Eid ul-Adha*. In the days leading to these three occasions, vast consumer activity takes place in these countries especially in the food, (non-alcoholic) drink, and cosmetic and toiletries sectors. During 2006, remarkable competition came to be witnessed in all of these sectors, in particular the latter two. The increase in competition has been the result of the creation of alternative distribution channels and publicising those in a concentrated and regular manner. For example, in relation to cosmetic and toiletry products the creation of cooperative associations[107] and their work have made a significant contribution in this regard. These associations have been active in organising campaigns and 'festivals' for the purposes of demonstrating that it is possible for consumers to enjoy a choice of different products handled by the same outlet which is virtually absent from the case of exclusive or selected agents, who handle only one brand. Under different circumstances, this would have amounted to competition advocacy undertaken by a competition authority in order to highlight the importance of competition and the key benefits consumers can expect to enjoy from an increased and unhindered process of competition.

[106] See in particular the discussion in chapter 10.
[107] These are associations made of representatives of different firms.

8

# The Arab Republic of Egypt: the chase after globalisation

In recent years, the Arab Republic of Egypt has witnessed dramatic political and economic developments, which have placed the country on its course towards transformation. At times the Republic – which embraced socialist thinking and ideology following the revolution in 1952 – appears uncomfortable with these changes, however, mainly due to the fact that many of them have been *imposed* from the outside, quite often without the necessary preliminary preparatory steps being taken by the government, rather than ones that have come to grow *gradually* from domestic roots. Among these changes are the increasing pressure applied by the US government as part of its agenda of 'democratising' the Middle East; the conflicts in Iraq and neighbouring Israel and Palestine; and the Darfur crisis in Sudan. However, internal factors have stirred this state of play as well, notably the agenda for changing the political system in the Republic and the way in which the President is elected; inadequate protection of human rights; and the apparent growing influence of Islamists and the Muslim Brotherhood.

Economically, the government's agenda during the last two years has been dominated to a large extent by a strong drive towards implementing its privatisation programme. This drive dates back to the 1991 Economic Reform and Structural Adjustment Programme created with the help and support of the International Monetary Fund (IMF) and the World Bank. The drive accelerated with the increase in pace of the process of globalisation; globalisation has had a profound impact on Egypt and so it was considered highly necessary to liberalise domestic markets, attract greater foreign direct investment and 'connect' better with the benefits of the liberalisation of trade globally. A new fifth gear was found by the government and it came to turn its attention to designing and implementing policies for the purposes of intensifying the process of economic reform; lowering trade tariffs; fighting bureaucracy; stabilising the currency, the Egyptian Pound; expanding the export of Egyptian produce; and enhancing tourism in the country. Much of this agenda, however, was yet to materialise into concrete plans or steps. Nonetheless, the manner in which the process of globalisation came to unfold eventually made Egypt realise the need to 'chase' after the process of globalisation and to catch up with its fast-developing dynamics.

## 8.1 Creating European links

The foundations of the government's economic agenda as described above have come to receive significant support with the creation of 'European' links aimed at bringing Egypt closer to Europe in order to facilitate economic growth and enhance the flow of trade and investment to and from European countries. To this end, considerable attention has been devoted in recent years by the government to the Republic's relationship with the EC and the European Free Trade Association (EFTA), in particular, given their significance as major trading blocks. Building a cooperation framework with EFTA, however, appears to have been more quickly sought and achieved than with the EC. Several explanations may be found for this which range from historical reasons to developments occurring as recently as the 1990s, when Egypt's preferred trading partner and political ally was the USA as opposed to the EC. A Declaration on Cooperation between the EFTA States and Egypt was issued in December 1995, which addresses the strengthening of economic cooperation and trade relations between Egypt and the EFTA States. The underlying aim of seeking this closer cooperation was to encourage free competition and economic activity based on market forces and for this purpose the Declaration advocates the exchange of views between the EFTA States and Egypt on conditions for free and undistorted competition, which is expected to play a leading role in achieving liberalisation in the trade arena. Furthermore, in order to establish a free trade area, the EFTA States and Egypt undertook jointly to examine the measures to be taken to meet the necessary economic preconditions for this. To ensure that such goals will be achieved, a joint committee was created which reviews the cooperation undertaken between the parties and makes recommendations as appropriate.[1] On 31 October 2006, Egypt concluded its negotiations of a Free Trade Agreement with the EFTA States and this is expected to enter into force during 2007.

In relation to the Republic's closer cooperation with the EC, although this emerged only recently as we noted above, it appears to have been intended to be deeper than the cooperation created with EFTA. As a

[1] The committee was established under Part V of the Declaration.

matter of fact, this closer cooperation was also intended to be more influential – in terms of having an impact on domestic economic developments in the Republic – and was indeed so. The closer cooperation came to centre around an Association Agreement between Egypt and the EC which was signed in Luxembourg on 25 June 2001 and entered into force on 1 June 2004, replacing the Cooperation Agreement of 1977 between the parties. The aim of the agreement is liberalisation of trade and development of economic relations between the parties, with a view to creating a free trade area during a 12-year transitional period, from the entry into force of the Agreement. The agreement was considered by the government to offer Egypt a golden opportunity and was very much desired. The agreement deals with different aspects of cooperation between the parties and includes provisions relating to, among other things, competition rules and the strengthening of economic cooperation. The rules governing competition are contained in Articles 34–36 of the agreement. For the purposes of ensuring that trade between the EC and Egypt is not affected, the agreement prohibits the following: agreements, decisions and practices which prevent, restrict or distort competition; abuse of a dominant position; and public aid which distorts, or threatens to distort, competition. Furthermore, the agreement provides for the regulation of monopolies and public enterprises and enterprises to which special or exclusive rights have been granted to ensure that there is no discrimination in the conditions for the marketing and procurement of goods between the Member States and Egypt. An Association Council is established under Article 74, which must adopt rules for the implementation of the competition law provisions within five years from the entry into force of the agreement. The Association Agreement therefore has clear and strong competition relevance and its conclusion and existence have played a key role in the development of competition law and policy in Egypt.

## 8.2 Cooperation with the USA: the qualifying industrial zones

In December 2004, Egypt, Israel and the USA signed a Qualifying Industrial Zones (QIZ) Agreement, modelled on an agreement Jordan concluded with Israel and the USA,[2] to advance their economic and trade relations. This agreement stems from the efforts of the USA to promote stronger relations between Israel and the Arab world. The QIZ

[2] See pp 171–2 above.

programme was established by the USA in 1996 for the purpose of encouraging regional economic integration in the Middle East, in particular between Israel and its neighbours to assist Israel in breaking its economic isolation and converting its economic and political status from that of an 'island' into a regionally integrated country. Regional economic integration under the QIZ is achieved by offering preferential treatment to goods manufactured with Israeli inputs when entering the USA. The programme therefore is a hybrid one with strong political and economic flavours.

The QIZ Agreement is the first agreement to be signed by Israel and Egypt since their Peace Treaty of 1979. According to this agreement, goods manufactured in 'qualifying industrial zones' in Egypt containing inputs from Israel will enter the US market tariff-free. A qualified industrial zone is an area designated by Egyptian and US governments as a location from which Egyptian products containing the agreed Israeli content can be exported to the USA without payment of duty or excise taxes. Under the agreement, industrial zones have been created in Cairo, Alexandria and Port Said. In order for Egyptian products to be exported to the USA duty-free, they must contain about 12 per cent Israeli content. Although such provision was considered to be controversial by many people in Egypt, the provision has transformed and enhanced trade between Egypt and Israel dramatically. According to the Israeli Export Institute,[3] trade between the countries rose from 58 million US Dollars in 2004 to 134 million US Dollars in 2005. In addition, the agreement has helped Egypt strengthen its trade relations with the USA and has raised expectations that it will also enhance Egypt's global economic standing and profile by strengthening its competitive position among countries that already maintain strong commercial relations with the USA.

## 8.3 The competition law dilemma

A declared key objective of the government has for long been to streamline market regulation and increase transparency in institutional operations. In striving to achieve this objective, particular emphasis has been placed on the need to accomplish economic efficiency and to stimulate growth in relation to different markets. Realising that this would require structural changes in the local economy, the government came to

[3] Available at www.export.gov.il.

appreciate and strongly believe in the value of competition in helping bring about – indeed mobilise – these changes. Within the boundaries of such a state of affairs therefore, one would have expected that the idea of introducing a competition law in the Republic would be shaped within a framework of desirability to achieve these economic goals. However, in practice the idea came to be shaped within a different framework, namely the closer cooperation with the EC as described above. During the 1990s, and prior to the emergence of the Egypt–EC Association Agreement, a dilemma – relating to the *implementation* of the idea in practice – existed and this appears to have delayed the adoption of specific competition legislation considerably. Key questions were raised especially with regards to whether such implementation should take place, how it should be done and with what considerations.

Interestingly, there appear never to have been any reservations during those years about the 'virtues' of competition. Remarkably, competition was considered to be a good, positive force. However, the question with regard to whether a specific law should be introduced to protect it had two competing answers, one in the positive and the other in the negative. During the relevant period, scholars and some policy-makers in Egypt came to identify the need for specific competition legislation in the country. In particular, many people felt that Egypt was lagging behind the world especially with domestic markets being 'crippled' by widespread monopolistic practices, which undermined competitiveness and enterprise in the domestic economy. The government was not of course unaware of this situation, though its chosen method to deal with the situation was to opt for heavy intervention in the market place. To this end, several measures and policies were adopted to deal with these problems which included *removing* trade barriers in order to encourage foreign competition in relation to key sectors such as cement and steel; *negotiating* with the relevant firms for the purposes of *diluting* the harmful effect of their practices; and *removing* tariffs and duties on anti-dumping. The effect of these measures and policies, however, was extremely limited in practice. The competition law question, although avoided, was now actually more pressing in light of this unsuccessful outcome and appeared to necessitate a fully fledged debate.

This debate was eventually opened with the Egypt–EC Association Agreement effectively mandating this. At an early stage of the debate there was a strong desire on the part of many parties, including the European Commission in particular, for the debate not to rest on pure political considerations and this desire translated into real pressure that could not be ignored. As a result, an opening for socio-economic considerations to filter through was created. Initially, the government attempted to control the situation and determine its outcome unilaterally according to parameters, which suited its various policies. In this way, the government advocated the freedom of firms to decide their economic activities almost unhindered. In certain quarters, however, reservations were expressed over this as this attempt was considered to be the result of strong lobbying on the part of business firms who were the architects behind such political design. It was felt that anti-competitive behaviour and abusive practices resulting from the concentration of wealth and power in the hands of a few persons had been particularly detrimental to consumers and the public interest and therefore it was crucial to address them effectively. With these two opposing considerations gaining strength, policy- and decision-makers were faced with a dilemma, which took the form of a single question: where should one draw the battle lines? Eventually the decision appears to have been made to tilt the balance in favour of the 'duty' to fight and eradicate harmful anti-competitive behaviour and abusive conduct. This appears to have enhanced the 'ultimate' and almost invisible goal behind the proposed competition law, namely to maximise consumer welfare through ensuring lower prices, better product quality and more choice and thus building a more dynamic and efficient economy in the Republic.

## 8.4 The Law on the Protection of the Freedom of Competition

The Republic of Egypt is one of the latest MECs to adopt specific competition legislation.[4] The Law on the Protection of Competition and the Prevention of Monopolistic Practices (the Competition Act) was adopted in February 2005 and entered into force in May the same year.[5] It is supported by the Executive Regulations on the Protection of Competition and Prohibition of Monopolistic Practices.[6] The Act was the result of a heated debate over the form, scope and nature of the legislation and only emerged in its final form after having been driven through an extremely daunting legislative process. A consultation of this

[4] Note that general provisions dealing with competition existed prior to the Act, most notably Articles 345 and 346 of the Egyptian Criminal Law dealing with anti-competitive behaviour and monopolistic practices.

[5] Law No. 3/2005.

[6] Executive Regulations No. 1316/2006 issued under a Prime Ministerial Decree dated 16 August 2005.

process would reveal several key findings such as the inconsistency in the government's approach in terms of the exact role the Act was intended to perform once enacted; the type of sanctions and remedies to be adopted as part of the enforcement mechanism under the Act;[7] and an interesting desire on the part of the government to continue to work on the draft law until 'perfection' was achieved, though eventually the opposite outcome materialised.[8]

### *8.4.1 The ambitious role of the Act*

There appear to be high expectations attached to the Competition Act, mainly given that it is expected to perform a non-traditional role of dealing – through the removal of anti-competitive behaviour and abusive conduct – with the stagnation of Egyptian markets and encouraging business initiatives. Additionally, and as is the case with other MECs, the Act is intended to be utilised for the purposes of helping Egypt make the transition from state control and planning to a market economy. These are ambitious goals and ones which, realistically speaking, are unlikely to be fulfilled in practice for various reasons, the most important of which is the huge ambiguity surrounding the wording and scope of the Act and the major uncertainty with regard to whether effective competition enforcement will emerge.

### *8.4.2 The scope of the Act*

The Act's declaration of the need to protect competition is an interesting one in the sense that it provides that economic activities be undertaken in a manner that does not harm the 'freedom of competition'. Such declaration makes the scope of the Act open to more than one interpretation: first, it can be taken that the Act guarantees the freedom of firms to compete so long as doing so does not cause an injury to competition which is an almost universal competition law idea; secondly, the declaration can be construed as intended to cover situations where firms limit their freedom of competition, meaning competition

7 Several debates took place about whether the penalties under the Act should go beyond fines to perhaps those of injunctions. Indeed, some of these debates were very excessive in length and showed, among other things, a great deal of uncertainty on the part of the government in particular.

8 See the discussion at pp 255–60 below in relation to the deficiencies of the Act.

between them or between one of them and a third party through anti-competitive behaviour on their part, which is also an idea featuring in many competition laws around the world.[9] A third explanation may be that the declaration is meant to bring within the scope of the Act situations in which the freedom of third-party firms is restricted due to the anti-competitive behaviour of firms. The fact that all such interpretations are possible shows an ambiguity and indicates the weakness in the drafting of the Act.[10]

As far as the types of business phenomena falling within the scope of the Act are concerned, the Act applies to collusion, abuse of dominance and harmful mergers whether occurring within or outside Egypt, provided that in the case of the latter acts committed abroad result in the prevention, restriction or harm to the freedom of competition in Egypt.[11] The behaviour and practices of public firms controlled by the state, however, are not within the scope of the Act: it specifically provides that its provisions are inapplicable in the case of public utilities managed by the state. The Act also provides that the Competition Authority[12] may, following receipt of a request from a party concerned,[13] exempt the behaviour of public utilities which are managed by firms subject to the Private Law,[14] where this would serve the public interest or help attain benefits to consumers that outweigh adverse effects on competition. Whilst this is a clear exclusion, it is questionable.

[9] As we saw in chapter 3 above, examples of this can be found in the case of the EC and Israel.

[10] These interpretations are possible whether one reads the original Arabic version or the English translation of that version.

[11] Article 5 of the Act provides for a clear extraterritorial reach of its provisions without any indication, however, of the basis for an exercise of jurisdiction, namely whether this would be possible on the basis of an 'effects', 'implementation' or any other basis.

[12] The composition and powers of the authority are discussed below at pp 246–9.

[13] In practice this refers to the firm in charge of managing a public utility which plans to conclude an agreement for carrying out work related to the activities of the utility in question and which appears to fall within the scope of the prohibitions in the Act on anti-competitive behaviour or abusive conduct.

[14] Article 16 of the Executive Regulations explains the procedure to be followed in this case, namely notification to be made to the chairperson of the authority, review of the notification by the board, possible referral of the notification to the competent department within the authority for investigation and the adoption of a decision by the board within thirty days of receipt of the notification by it. The exemption will be valid for two years, though this period is renewable with the same procedure in Article 16 in this case being followed.

Interestingly, the Act contains no provisions dealing with intellectual property rights (IPRs). In light of the wealth of IPRs in Egypt, most notably the impressive contribution of Egyptians to artistic and literary works and the existence of a huge amount of copyrighted work, this omission amounts to a serious shortcoming and one that is likely to affect the effectiveness of the Act in fighting all types of anti-competitive behaviour.

### *8.4.3 Penalties and fines*

The main penalty available under the Act is fines. According to Article 22 of the Act, a breach of Articles, 6, 7 or 8 (i.e. in case of an anti-competitive behaviour or abusive conduct) will be punished by a fine ranging from a minimum of 30,000 and a maximum of 10 million Egyptian Pounds, although the article leaves open the possibility for a more serious penalty to be imposed under any other law.[15] The same article provides, in very ambiguous terms, that the court 'may, instead of ordering confiscation, order an alternative fine equivalent to the value of the *Product* which is the subject matter of the breach'.[16] There is no further explanation of what is meant by, or in what circumstances, 'confiscation' may be ordered or what is meant by a fine equivalent to the 'value of a product'. Looking at the legislative intention behind the Act it appears that the purpose is to make it possible to impose a penalty amounting to 100 per cent of the sales of the firm(s) concerned in relation to the particular or relevant product during the period of the anti-competitive or abusive practices. Article 25 of the Act provides for the possibility of a fine to be imposed on individuals responsible for the actual management of a firm found in breach of the Act. Whist the Act does not clarify what amounts to 'actual management' and whether this could concern more than one individual, the article states that such an individual will be subject to the *same penalties* stipulated for firms under the Act where he or she had actual knowledge of a breach of the Act, and through a default on his or her part in executing their duties in office contributed to the breach.

[15] Under Article 25 of the Act a firm will also be jointly liable for the payment of fines or damages ordered where the breach of the Act was committed by one of its employees acting in its name or on its behalf.

[16] Emphasis added.

On the other hand, Article 23 of the Act further provides that a breach of Article 16 – which concerns breach of confidentiality on the part of employees of the authority and situations where such employees during a period of two years from the end of their employment at the authority engage in employment with a person who was or is subject to an investigation by the authority – will be punished by a fine ranging from 10,000 to 50,000 Egyptian Pounds. Theoretically, therefore, a firm found in breach of the Act may be subjected to a *lower* fine than that imposed on an employee of the authority where such a person is found to have committed a breach of Article 16. This possibility lacks any logical justification and reveals an absurdity.

## 8.5 Institutional structure and capacity

An Authority for the Protection of Competition and the Prevention of Monopolistic Practices (the Competition Authority) was created under the Act which is responsible for the application of the Act along with relevant Regulations.[17] The Competition Authority is an administrative body established under the auspices of the Ministry for Trade and Industry.[18] It is headed by a chairperson and has a fairly large board of fifteen members (including the chairperson) recruited from diverse backgrounds,[19] including academics and representatives of relevant government ministries, the private sector and trade and other associations.[20] This board is responsible for 'managing' the affairs of the authority. According to Article 11 of the Act, the authority has a variety of powers ranging from receiving complaints, merger notifications and conducting investigations to engaging in competition advocacy and making orders for firms to readjust their behaviour and practices and redress breaches under Articles 6, 7 and 8 of the Act.[21]

[17] This includes the Executive Regulations. See note 6 above and accompanying text.

[18] See Article 11 of the Act. The authority, however, enjoys its own independent budget, following the model of Public Service Authorities (Article 14 of the Act).

[19] See Article 12 of the Act.

[20] It may be of interest to note that as with the current Director General of the Israel Antitrust Authority and the current head of Jordan's Competition Directorate, Egypt too has opted for appointing a woman, Ms Mona Yassine as chairperson who has no competition expertise but who is a Harvard graduate with a wealth of expertise in banking matters.

[21] Article 20 of the Act establishes the power of the board to make such adjustment orders, which if not complied with in practice will render the behaviour in question void. Additionally, the board may make an order bringing a harmful behaviour to an end.

Although the enforcement of the Act is intended to be judicial in character, in practice the decision with regard to whether to proceed to judicial enforcement rests in the hands of the Minister for Trade and Industry or a person acting on his behalf.[22] As far as the authority is concerned, it is able to conduct investigations – whether on its own initiative or following a complaint – and to present its findings to the board with the relevant recommendations and the latter will decide on how to proceed. The board has the power either to rule in favour or against the firm(s) under investigation. In the latter case, however, the board is unable to reach a binding decision on the firms forcing them to comply and so in this case the decision to proceed to enforcement by the courts can only be taken by the Minister for Trade and Industry. This in effect – and indeed according to Article 21 of the Act – enables the Minister to reach a settlement with the firms or individuals concerned. Such power is controversial given that it creates ample room for political manoeuvring and discretion to be exercised. The settlement power reserved to the Minister is a wide one and may be exercised at any time before a final judgment by the court has been delivered, which in practice means that settlements may be reached whilst judicial proceedings are in progress.[23] Such provision clearly enables the Minister's decision to prevail over judicial proceedings. The widening of the scope of the Minister's power in this manner can be explained with reference to an intention on the part of the legislature and government to avoid, where possible, having competition cases becoming entangled in the judicial workload, which is extremely daunting in Egypt and therefore to facilitate 'fast-track' enforcement under the Act.

The Competition Authority currently has a modest task force consisting of ten officials with relevant expertise. For a country like Egypt, however, it would be necessary for this manpower to grow in order to be able to cope with the volume of work expected to emerge in practice.[24] At the time of writing, the Competition Authority was beginning to conduct various enforcement and international activities, though it is still not fully

[22] See Article 21 of the Act.

[23] Article 21 of the Act provides that settlements may be reached in return for the payment of an amount double or more of the minimum level of the fine but not exceeding double of its maximum level. See further above on penalties and fines.

[24] In light of its present capacity, the authority is not expected to be capable of handling horizontal and vertical agreements work, abuse of dominance cases and merger regulation especially given that the Act provides for the possibility of complaints to the authority as opposed to 'referral' of cases to it from the Minister for Trade and Industry, the Prime Minister or another person or body.

functional. Intensive efforts are being made to identify 'talent' and recruit individuals with the necessary expertise as well as the more general efforts of offering competition law training to judges in particular. It is understood that within the first year of its existence the authority received five complaints about anti-competitive and abusive conduct though initially it did not disclose any details about the markets concerned, the identity of the firms involved or the nature or type of the alleged conduct. This raised some concerns, as many came to regard this as a policy that went in the opposite direction of the declared objective of the government to ensure transparency in the market place. It also reignited suspicion about possible lobbying of the government by firms for the purposes of loosening the grip of the authority in individual cases.

## 8.6 Competition advocacy and international outlook

Some of the powers reserved to the Competition Authority revolve around competition advocacy and creating international links. It appears that the authority is enabled under the Act to engage in competition advocacy at both a legislative level and an educational level as far as different groups of audience are concerned. Article 11(5) of the Act specifically provides for the authority's power to give its opinion on draft laws and regulations with competition relevance. Clearly this is quite a crucial provision under the Act given that it arms the authority with the *power* as opposed to a mere *opportunity* conferred upon it by others to be consulted. Therefore, this power should be utilised by the authority effectively in order to ensure that damage to competition does not occur as a result of the formulation of public policies or the enactment of different legislative instruments in Egypt, which in practice is not a remote possibility in the country. Additionally, paragraphs (7), (8) and (9) of the article show that it is within the authority's mandate to enhance public awareness of competition law and its enforcement in Egypt and to spread a competition culture in the Republic.

The Act's treatment of international links, on the other hand, is more limited however.[25] It merely provides for the power of the authority to *coordinate* rather than to *cooperate* with foreign competition authorities in matters of common interest. Presumably, the choice of words in this case was carefully made and appears to signal a limitation on the remit of the authority in furthering its international outlook. So far, coordination has

[25] See Article 11(6) of the Act.

involved organising and attending seminars and conferences, visiting foreign competition authorities and conducting study visits at events organised by international organisations.[26] This may be regarded as a fairly active programme of international activities in the case of a *young* competition authority. In particular, these activities have been especially fruitful in enhancing the international standing of the authority and affording it an opportunity to receive technical assistance.

## 8.7 A mechanism for price regulation

The Act entails an element of price regulation,[27] albeit one that appears both *limited* and *unlimited* in scope in comparison to those contained in the competition laws of other Arab countries. Article 10 of the Act simply provides that the government may, after receiving the opinion of the authority,[28] issue a decree determining the price at which one or more 'essential products' should be sold for a specified period. This price regulation mechanism is limited in scope in the sense that with the authority's involvement the government's intervention could be expected, theoretically at least, to occur on strict competition grounds. On the other hand, the scope of the mechanism is unlimited given that neither the Act nor the Executive Regulations provide any indication of what amounts to essential products or the actual length of the specified period.[29]

## 8.8 Cement, steel and telecommunications: from state control to liberalisation

Three particular sectors of the Egyptian economy, namely cement, steel and telecommunications, offer interesting case studies, which highlight

[26] A full description of the various international activities of the authority can be found on the authority's website, www.eca.org.eg/EgyptianCompetitionAuthority.

[27] The price regulation mechanism can be said to contradict one of the major guarantees for foreign investment stipulated in Law No. 8/1997 on the Privileges and Guarantees of Foreign Investments, which expressly provides that any firm established for the purpose of engaging in an activity under Article 1 of the Law shall *not* be subjected to any kind of price regulation.

[28] Article 19 of the Executive Regulations provides that the authority will conduct the necessary studies in order to enable the government to exercise its power under Article 10 of the Act.

[29] The Act and the Regulations are also silent on whether this information is meant to be provided by other instruments whether executive or otherwise such as the case for example with Saudi Arabia. See p 199 above.

the seriousness of competition problems in the economy and the need for an effective and harmonious application of the competition rules. These sectors also illustrate how intoxicating a cocktail of business and politics can be and demonstrate that privatisation and liberalisation, although desirable and in some cases vital, are not sufficient in themselves for ensuring openness and workability of the market mechanism.

### *8.8.1 The cement industry: a double-edge sword*

The cement industry in Egypt has witnessed some interesting transformations and serious developments within the past seven years. The sector was privatised in 1999, following a government's decision, through the sale of major stakes in former state-owned firms to foreign and domestic investors. That decision was highly influenced by the major difficulties facing the industry, namely the low output and inefficiency in production. The flow within the industry was further damaged due to the existence of a strong distribution network controlled by a few firms which meant that all direct links between cement producers and leading customers, mainly construction firms, were severed and the 'connection' between the two could only have been established through distributors. Distributors enjoyed a strong position approaching a monopoly through which they were able to control output and raise prices. With the privatisation programme of the government, this monopoly was terminated and new windows of opportunity were opened for increased competition given that customers were now able to purchase directly from cement producers. This – along with the potential foreign competition which began to appear possible – led to dramatic reductions in prices in the market, a process that continued until the end of 2002, when there was a quite sharp increase in the prices *apparently* following a meeting and an agreement by all Egyptian cement producers to fix prices. Interestingly, the government appeared to turn a blind eye to this situation, which many would argue could not be controlled in any case given the lack of a competition law in the country at that time.

Only as recently as July 2006, the government decided to launch a competition investigation, which many in Egypt considered to be well overdue. This delay apparently was caused in part by the absence of competition legislation but mainly due to the fact that the cement sector appears to be controlled by influential persons with strong political ties. Despite the decision to launch the investigation, the practices of the cement producers have to a certain extent been defended on the ground that foreign competition and import of cement products into Egypt were nonetheless possible. However, such competition does not appear to have emerged – despite the relatively high prices – mainly due to what many consider to be 'logistical' barriers and the extremely high cost involved in initial investment for the purposes of setting up the necessary local infrastructure and facilities. Although the authority's investigation is still at an early stage, it is quite uncertain to what extent it will succeed in conducting the investigation effectively, given the lack of necessary tools in terms of resources, the strong lobbying power of cement producers and the difficulties the authority will face in imposing its will.

The launch of the investigation has been followed by a Ministerial Decree which was issued by the Minister for Trade and Industry on 23 August 2006 aimed at dealing with the problems related to the high prices in the sector.[30] The Decree is remarkable in three main respects. First, the Decree imposes an obligation on cement producers, dealers and distributors to publicise their selling prices. Secondly, it orders all firms active in the cement market, whether as producers, dealers, or distributors, to submit to the Ministry for Trade and Industry every Thursday full details relating to all of the following: in the case of producers the quantity produced, the quantity exported and the price charged, the details of customers, the quantity destined for local markets and that supplied to all dealers and distributors and the price and the stock level, and in the case of dealers or distributors the quantities acquired and received from each supplier, the name of the suppliers, the quantity sold to every agent and the price and the stock level. Thirdly, the Decree provides that an infringement of any of its provisions will attract a penalty in the form of imprisonment between six months and two years, a fine between 300 and 1,000 Egyptian Pounds or both.[31]

In parallel, the Minister for Trade and Industry, quite remarkably, held a meeting with cement producers and reached an 'unofficial agreement' to fix a maximum cap for the prices of cement to an acceptable level of 300 Egyptian Pounds per tonne. This agreement, which many have come to view as a legitimisation of price-fixing practices by the government, appears to have been implemented by nine out of the major twelve cement producers in Egypt leading to a decrease in prices in the Egyptian market.

[30] See Ministerial Decree No. 615/2006.

[31] See Article 4 of the Decree. The article provides that in case of repeated infringement the penalty will be doubled.

For consumers and firms active in the construction sector perhaps this agreement presents an 'improvement' in the circumstances. However, it remains to be seen what long-term impact the agreement will have on the investigation undertaken by the authority. At the time of writing – December 2006 – the authority's investigation was being suspended which makes one curious as to whether the suspension in this case was brought about in part by the agreement itself.

### *8.8.2 The steel industry: abuse of dominance or freedom of competition*

The steel industry in Egypt has for quite some time experienced competition problems. These problems, which extend to those years preceding the adoption of the Competition Act, have given rise to major concerns in certain quarters in the country. In particular, building and construction contractors have been placed in an uncomfortable position due to the sharp increase in the price of Egyptian steel and they felt that action had to be taken by the government to deal with the situation. The contractors' concerns were shared by others, in particular several Members of Parliament who thought that there was insufficient competition in the sector which in effect caused the price increase. On that basis, a first official inquiry was ordered in January 2003 – some two years prior to the enactment of the Act – by the Egyptian Parliament into the sharp price increases in the sector. There was a lack of consensus, however, on the direction which the inquiry should take: some Members of Parliament felt that the problem with the sector lay with steel importers whilst other Members – indeed the majority – viewed the steel producer, Ezz El Dekheila, as the source of the problem.[32] The latter's view rested on a claim that the government had enabled this firm to increase the prices of steel by 70 per cent over one year from 2002 to 2003 as well as engage – almost unhindered – in monopolistic practices, which virtually stifled competition in this sector.

In order to appreciate the seriousness of such a claim one must take a look at the sector, its players and whether Ezz El Dekheila is a dominant firm. Moreover, it is important to consider whether the developments

[32] Ezz El Dekheila is partially owned by Mr Ahmed Ezz, an influential Egyptian businessman and politician, who controls the strong local firm El-Ezz Steel Rebars. Mr Ezz appears to enjoy strong ties with the President's son, Mr Jamal Mubarak. He is a senior member of the ruling National Democratic Party, headed by Mr Mubarak.

which came to unfold in the sector reveal abusive practices or show a firm merely relying on its freedom to compete.

The steel industry in Egypt is dominated by three firms, which together hold market shares amounting to about 80 per cent; 16 other firms hold the remaining 20 per cent of market shares. The Ezz family have been active in the steel business for more than forty years. The Ezz Group first entered into steel manufacturing in 1994 when it acquired Albaraka Steel Mills. This acquisition was followed by another in October 1999 when El Ezz Steel Rebars acquired a controlling interest in Alexandria National Iron and Steel Company (ANSDK), the largest steel producer in Egypt; the acquisition by the El Ezz Steel Rebars has enabled it to enlarge its share in the Egyptian steel market to approximately 69 per cent enabling Mr Ahmed Ezz to enjoy effective control over the steel industry in Egypt.[33] As a result, Mr Ezz was able to implement a reduction in the production of rebar steel.[34] This policy of limitation of output of rebar steel did not extend, however, to the production of 'bilit', a substance used in the manufacturing of rubber steel with the result that the market became over-supplied with bilit. ANSDK refused to sell any of its excess production of bilit to other local competitors, however, a decision that denied local steel producers access to a vital substance that would allow them to produce rebar steel. This refusal to supply left local producers dependent for a period of time on imported Russian and Ukrainian bilit. Nevertheless, in 2000, the Suez Iron Company and the Steel and Iron Company, two steel producers not linked to Mr Ezz or ANSDK, filed a dumping complaint with the Egyptian government against the importation of Russian and Ukrainian bilit. The complaint was based on the grounds that importing the final product, the rebar steel, was only 10 US Dollars more expensive than importing the bilit raw substance; and, therefore, imposing dumping fees on this intermediate substance would only strengthen the local industry. This complaint was accepted despite the objection to it by most market players, who also highlighted the existence of heavy custom duties imposed on the import of rebar steel.[35]

This chain of events shows how a dominant firm (or indeed an individual) is able to control a single sector and bring about harmful

[33] In November 1999, and following the above-mentioned acquisition, Mr Ezz was appointed as joint chairman and managing director of both El Ezz Steel Rebar and ANSDK.

[34] ANSDK's production capacity was reduced to 1.2 million tonnes per year as opposed to ensuring that the firm operated with its maximum capacity of 1.8 million tonnes per year.

[35] After a period of nearly four years, however, the dumping duties were finally lifted and custom duties lowered to 5 per cent.

results. At the time of writing, the steel sector was also under investigation by the Competition Authority.[36] Among other things, the authority was looking into a possible abuse of dominance by El Ezz Steel Rebar and ANSDK by fixing the prices of bilit and rebar steel.

### *8.8.3 The telecommunications sector: the consequences of liberalisation*

Egypt's former belief in the desirability and necessity of state control in the telecommunications sector was neither exceptional nor short-lived; indeed, this belief dates back to 1854 with the initiation of the telegraph service between Cairo and Alexandria. However, with the new policy of liberalisation and structural reform introduced in the 1990s, the government embarked in 1998 on reform in the telecommunications sector. The government's aim was twofold: to restructure the sector and to open it to private investment. An important step taken in this regard was the creation of the National Telecommunications Regulatory Authority (NTRA), which was armed with the power to grant licences to entities aiming to provide different telecommunications services and which occurred following the enactment of Law No. 19, a hugely important instrument which effectively instituted a new regime in the telecommunications sector. The Law, among other things, brought about a structural separation in relation to the entities carrying out the regulatory and operational functions.[37] Pursuant to Presidential Decree No. 101 issued two months later, in May 1998, the NTRA assumed responsibility with independent status, having a ten members' board of directors headed by the Minister of Communications. The creation of NTRA was followed by that of the Ministry of Communications and Information Technology (MCIT) according to Decree No. 387 in October 1999. On 4 February 2003, the Egyptian Parliament passed the Law on the Organisation of the Telecommunications Sector.[38] The Law sets fundamental principles such as transparency, non-discrimination, neutrality of public operators towards competitive services, provision of universal service and unity of the network from a functional point of view to ensure equality of

[36] The investigation was opened in July 2006 following a request made by the Minister for Trade and Industry.

[37] It may be interesting here to recall the similarity in developments in the telecommunications sector between Egypt and Turkey. See pp 99–100 above for a discussion on the Turkish experience.

[38] Law No. 10/2003.

access. The Law also gives NTRA a more autonomous status, the power to impose sanctions, to establish a universal service fund, the freedom to set rules and regulations properly to manage and administer the organisational structure necessary to carry out all regulatory functions entrusted to the regulatory authority. Also lawful acts related to telecommunication sector activities are incriminated and are liable to a court sentence of imprisonment or a fine according to the severity of the violation.

Article 24 of the new Law requires the NTRA to determine the necessary rules that would prohibit monopolistic practices; accordingly NTRA developed a 'Competition Policy Framework', which was implemented even prior to the adoption of the Competition Act. Through this framework, NTRA sets out the practices that should not be exercised by the licensee entities in their conduct of business. These include restrictions on abusing a dominant position, refusal to supply issues and restrictive vertical agreements. However, it is not clear, now that the Competition Act has been adopted and the Competition Authority established whether or not the work of both entities will overlap. The telecommunications sector is still widely considered as featuring price-fixing practices exercised by the existing two mobile operators and the lack of competition in the fixed-line and international calls market.

## 8.9 Deficiencies, criticisms and concerns

The initiative of the Egyptian government to adopt the Act on the Protection of Competition is a much welcomed development. However the 'end product' suffers from many deficiencies, most of which are fundamental with serious implications in practice. Little attention appears to have been given to detail during the legislative process when the final draft of the Act was rushed through without careful consideration of major aspects of the legislation. This was a failure on the part of the government and Parliament, which many would claim was a calculated one. A more plausible and well-founded explanation, however, is that the true purpose behind the Act was simply to comply with the obligations within the framework of Egypt's Association Agreement with the EC, to catch up with the process of globalisation and to seek to demonstrate the existence of international openness in the country. The Act therefore did not grow from Egyptian roots and in no way – whether small or big – can it be considered as an expression of Egypt's local economic needs and its special cultural, social and political circumstances.

The Act clearly suffers from extremely poor drafting. Its main provisions are ambiguous and lack justification. Furthermore, it contains major loopholes and there are many inexplicable omissions within its provisions. This part of the chapter will highlight these claims in relation to different aspects and components of the Act.

### *8.9.1 The prohibition on horizontal and vertical agreements*

The Act's prohibition of harmful horizontal and vertical agreements contains a requirement of intention: such agreements are prohibited if they are *intended* to restrict competition or, in the case of horizontal agreements, cause the specified results listed in paragraphs (a)–(d) in Article 6 of the Act. The requirement of proving intention is bound to make the task of the authority extremely difficult in practice and, in light of the extremely young experience of the authority, virtually cause the hope for effective enforcement of the Act quickly to evaporate. Whilst it may be an acceptable practice to expect a competition authority to prove that firms found to have participated in an anti-competitive agreement *could not have been unaware* that their agreement was in breach of the relevant competition rule(s), it would be unnecessarily restrictive to go further and require a competition authority to prove intention on the part of such firms. The object of an agreement which restricts competition should be readily established from available evidence such as that furnished by the clauses of such an agreement with its effect considered – using the necessary economic analysis and evaluation – in the absence of such object or evidence of it. It is not fully clear why such a requirement to show intention was stipulated in the Act.

Another deficiency related to the one just mentioned concerns the fact that the prohibitions in Articles 6 and 7 of the Act only mention 'agreements' or 'contracts' without a reference to other possible forms of collusion such as concerted practices. This omission is bound to be problematic in practice and one that is likely to undermine the enforcement of the Act. The omission is not remedied by the Executive Regulations which also only refer to agreements or contracts.

### *8.9.2 The issue of exemption*

The Act does not provide for exemption in the case of behaviour or conduct caught within the net of its prohibitions except in the case of public utilities as explained above.[39] Such an omission is highly surprising. Article 12 of the Executive Regulations, however, appears to provide for the possibility of exemption in relation to vertical agreements though the article gives the impression that such an exemption is to be conducted in a *rule of reason* style in determining whether a vertical agreement restricts competition in the first place. Among other things, the article refers to existence of consumer benefits, considerations relating to protecting the quality of the product and safety and security requirements, and compliance of the agreement with established commercial customs in the relevant sector. The authority's approach, however, appears to signal that exemptions under the Act – whether for horizontal or vertical agreements – are possible and would be granted in exceptional circumstances, namely where the situation yields specific benefits for consumers and the public interest. The fact that this is not specifically reflected in the wording of the Act is bound to be a major contributing factor to the lack of legal certainty under the Act. There is no indication of the exact kind of benefits that must be established for an anti-competitive situation to be exempted and as a result considerable discretion will be left to the government given its power to decide on the issuing of an exemption. Such a state of affairs is further muddied with the lack of a provision on whether notification of agreements to the authority for the purposes of obtaining exemption is possible.

### *8.9.3 The treatment of abuse of dominance*

The Act's application to abuse of dominance is highly curious in two major respects. First, the Act (and the Executive Regulations) deals with dominance and abuse in separate provisions.[40] Secondly, Article 4 of the Act defines dominance as 'the ability of a person, holding a market share exceeding 25 per cent [in the relevant market], to have an effective impact on prices or on the volume of supply on it' without any constraint on this ability by the competitors of such person. It is not readily understandable whether the article establishes an *irrebutable* presumption of dominance where a firm is found to hold a market share of more than 25 per cent; whether this presumption is rebuttable; or whether this

[39] See p 244 above.

[40] Dominance is dealt with under Article 4 of the Act, and Articles 7 and 8 of the Executive Regulations. Abuse, on the other hand, is covered under Article 8 of the Act, and Article 13 of the Executive Regulations.

is not a presumption but rather a fixed requirement, the satisfaction of which would mean that an *automatic* finding of dominance would be made. The Executive Regulations shed hardly any useful light on the situation and merely provide that dominance is established where three elements are found to exist: a market share exceeding 25 per cent; the ability to exercise effective impact on prices or quantity of a particular product in the relevant market; and the inability of competitors to limit such effective impact. Article 8 of the Regulations in effect states that the second element will be taken to exist in situations where the third element is established. This language somehow appears to be circular, an aspect likely to emerge in relation to establishing abuse of dominance under the Act. For example, Article 8 provides that in establishing that a person is able to exercise 'effective impact', several factors will need to be taken into account including such a person's market share, past conduct of the person, number of competitors and the existence of barriers to entry. There is a real concern that the authority may end up misapplying the prohibition on abuse in cases where the conduct of a person will be taken into account in establishing dominance and then the same conduct is used to establish abuse of a dominant position.

### *8.9.4 Lack of adequate mechanism for merger control*

The Act applies to harmful mergers though it is virtually silent on what type of merger operations fall within its scope, what the jurisdictional thresholds are and how mergers should be assessed. This clear omission is very interesting given that in earlier drafts of the Bill, which became the Act, there was a specific chapter devoted to mergers. It is not readily understandable why a decision was made to exclude this chapter from the final draft. The Executive Regulations do not remedy this omission in a significant manner except insofar as Article 44 of the regulations provides for notification to the authority 'by persons within 30 days from the acquisition of assets, proprietary rights, usufruct, shares, the setting up of unions, mergers or amalgamations or joint management or two or more persons'. Article 45 of the regulations merely details in a highly ambiguous manner the kind of information required to be submitted in writing as part of the notification to the authority.[41]

[41] The article requires the provision of the following: the name of the notifying person and other persons concerned, their nationalities, administration centres and the headquarters of their activities; the notified legal disposition, its date and the legal position

### 8.9.5 *Fines and settlements*

As we saw above, fines may be imposed on both firms and individuals found guilty under the Act. It is not clear how effective such a provision will be in practice, especially in light of the ability of such a firm or an individual found to have committed a breach of the provisions of the Act to lobby the Ministry for Trade and Industry (or another person or body with power of influence over the Minister for Trade and Industry) to avoid criminal prosecution or reach a settlement, which may be ordered by the Minister for Trade and Industry under the Act. The effectiveness of the provision on fines may be considered even more questionable given the small magnitude of fines, especially in the case of firms.[42]

### 8.9.6 *The Executive Regulations*

As was noted above, Executive Regulations have been adopted under a Prime Ministerial Decree which are meant to complement many provisions of the Act. Looking at the regulations, however, they too appear to suffer from certain deficiencies. Most notably, many provisions of the regulations constitute no more than mere repetition, *verbum verbatim*, of several provisions of the Act.

### 8.9.7 *The sectoral application of the Act*

There is a clear absence in the Act of any indication with regard to its applicability to special sectors such as the energy and telecommunications sectors.[43] These two sectors have vastly expanded especially following the creation of the Electric Utility and Consumer Protection Regulatory Agency, NTRA and MCIT. From the provisions of the Act it is clear that other than the Minister for Trade and Industry, the government and courts, the authority is the only public body with powers under the legislation. These sectoral regulators therefore have

arising from it; and the licences and approvals obtained. Clearly, this requirement falls short of that in usual merger practice around the world where additional crucial information is required, such as market definition and market shares.

[42] At the time of writing, the authority was conducting a review of the provisions on fines under the Act which is expected to lead to a proposal to amend those provisions in order to render them more effective.

[43] The telecommunications sector in Egypt is discussed further at pp 254–5 above.

no powers under the Act. This makes it particularly important to consider how the application of the Act will be handled in the case of anti-competitive behaviour, abusive conduct or a harmful merger occurring in the special sectors and whether the close cooperation the authority has proposed to establish with sectoral regulators will materialise in practice.

### *8.9.8 The frustrating influence of bureaucracy*

One of the underlying policies of the Act is to reduce bureaucracy which is considered to be one of the factors discouraging investment in Egypt, especially by foreign firms. However, the application of the Act appears to lead to exactly this undesirable outcome particularly in relation to investigations and enforcement under the Act. A case commences with the authority conducting an investigation upon receipt of a complaint or on its own initiative. The findings are then presented to the board which decides on how to proceed with the case and may require the authority to carry out further inquiries. The decision of whether to proceed to court is made by the Minister for Trade and Industry. The bureaucratic level of this process can therefore be quite lengthy given the various parties involved in the execution of a case and this can be further enhanced by the complexity of the case and the information available.

# 9

# Lebanon and Syria: a tale of two states

The Republic of Lebanon and the Arab Republic of Syria have always enjoyed a close association. This closeness in relations between the two countries was facilitated by several factors. Notable among these factors is the influence which Syria came to enjoy over Lebanon and its internal affairs. For many years, there was significant Syrian presence in Lebanon which came to be reduced, however, following the assassination of Lebanon's former Prime Minister, Rafiq Hariri, and the adoption of a specific United Nations Resolution demanding respect for the sovereignty of Lebanon. Syrian presence and political influence in Lebanon has not totally disappeared nonetheless and in many ways the two countries remain two independent states with one tale. In the field of competition law and policy though, the Republics have not shared the same platform and have in fact taken different routes towards achieving their goals of instituting domestic competition law regimes.

## 9.1 Lebanon: the walk to the region's most comprehensive competition law

Lebanon is at present on its way to enacting the most comprehensive competition legislation in the Middle East as a whole. The journey to this destination, however, may prove to be very long. To understand Lebanon's reasons for embarking upon such a journey and to assess the real prospects for success in completing it, including the challenges likely to arise on the way, it is necessary to consider some issues of crucial importance first which sit at the heart of the government's decision to turn to competition law and policy.

### *9.1.1 International openness and economic growth*

The weakness of Lebanon militarily, the composition of its population and the size and nature of its economy have perhaps been the main factors for its dependence on other countries, especially France, the Gulf States and Syria. France has always been keen to maintain its special relationship with its former colony and a significant number of Lebanese have over the years identified with the French lifestyle and the Western approach it represents. The Gulf States have always maintained an interest in Lebanon, not only for business investment purposes but also for the 'different' culture the country offers from theirs. Finally, Lebanon's neighbour, Syria, saw in the country's military and political weakness an opportunity to control Lebanese affairs and in doing so enhance Damascus' regional standing. In light of this and the many common factors uniting the two countries, many similarities came to exist between their domestic systems and style of governance and public administration. In the economic sphere, however, the Lebanese economy and the country's economic approach have been much more open and much more receptive, perhaps more accurately attractive, to foreign investment than the Syrian one.[1] Over the years, significant efforts have been made by successive Lebanese governments aimed at global integration and economic growth and prosperity among the population, and encouraging business and enterprise on the part of Lebanese citizens.[2] The good fortunes of the Republic, however, have been considerably undermined by wars and conflicts, most notably the long Civil War between 1975 and 1991 and the recent Second Lebanon War 2006, which provided a painful reminder of how fragile the Lebanese economy is and how 'easy' it is to inflict serious damage on its modest infrastructure. These bitter conflicts, at different stages, damaged the economic progress of Lebanon and the opportunities for foreign investment. A stable and progressive Lebanon economy was always dependant on peace and security. In 1993 the government launched the 'Horizon 2000' initiative aimed at extensive restructuring of the domestic economy. The initiative was only possible because of the promising prospects the end of the Civil War brought to the country. The achievements made in relation to the initiative during a period of twelve years were very impressive and received a considerable boost with the end of Israeli occupation in South Lebanon in 2000 and the withdrawal of Syrian forces from

[1] As will become apparent from the discussion at pp 278–9 below, however, Syria has come to focus on international openness during the past two years using this as a strategy for addressing its damaging international isolation.

[2] Indeed, Lebanese businessmen have always been encouraged to penetrate foreign markets and seek economic opportunities abroad. Many of them have achieved remarkable success seeing themselves as economic 'ambassadors' of Lebanon in different capitals around the world.

Lebanese territories five years later. However, these achievements were seriously undermined by the recent conflict. As things stand at present, it is not quite clear how the government will be able to 'jump-start' the economy for a second time in a short period of fifteen years (between 1991 and 2006) and resume its economic reform especially given the serious political and diplomatic issues that have recently come to dominate the scene and the need to re-build bridges connecting the reality facing the Lebanese population to their hopes and aspirations for peace and security.

Very few countries in the world share Lebanon's unique position and circumstances as an open democracy with a small economy sharing limited interests in common with its neighbours. As we noted above, links with the Western world have always been valued by Lebanon and its citizens. In this context, Lebanon's relationship with the EC, as the closest major regional economic block, has come to assume particular significance. Lebanon signed an Association Agreement with the EC on 17 June 2002 which entered into force on 1 April 2006. However, the trade-related contents of the agreement have been in force since 1 March 2003 pursuant to the Interim Agreement on trade and trade-related matters concluded between the parties in September 2002. The objective of the Association Agreement is the liberalisation of trade and development of economic relations between the EC and Lebanon. Competition law features prominently in both the Interim Agreement and the Association Agreement.[3] The inclusion of competition law came *literally* to create a mechanism for prohibiting all agreements, decisions and concerted practices which prevent, restrict or distort competition and abusive conduct, on the basis that they may restrict trade between the Member States of the EC and Lebanon.[4] At a different level, however, the inclusion of the provisions has come to serve as a tool for facilitating the enactment of a specific competition law and policy in Lebanon. As is the case with other Association Agreements concluded by the EC and different MECs, an Association Council and an Association

[3] Indeed, the competition provisions of the Interim Agreement have been incorporated into Articles 35–37 of the Association Agreement.

[4] Note, however, that the competition law provisions in the Association Agreement also extend to state monopolies and public undertakings and undertakings to which special or exclusive rights have been granted. The agreement advocates that monopolies be adjusted to ensure that there is no discrimination in the conditions for the procurement and marketing of goods between Lebanon and the EC.

Committee are established under the agreement to ensure its proper implementation in practice.[5]

In addition to the Association Agreement with the EC, Lebanon has also welcomed the opportunity to forge links with the European Free Trade Association (EFTA). A Free Trade Agreement between the EFTA States and Lebanon was signed in Switzerland on 24 June 2004 for the purposes of liberalising trade, with a view to establishing a free trade area between the parties, and developing economic relations. The parties have realised the importance of protecting competition for this purpose and therefore Article 17 of the agreement prohibits all agreements, decisions and concerted practices which prevent, restrict or distort competition and abuse of a dominant position as they may affect trade between the EFTA States and Lebanon. In addition, state monopolies and public undertakings and undertakings to which special or exclusive rights have been granted must also be regulated to ensure that they do not restrict trade between the parties. Article 30 establishes a Joint Committee, consisting of representation from each party, to supervise the implementation of the agreement. For this purpose, the committee must meet at least once every two years or as may be deemed necessary, upon request of any party.

### *9.1.2 The drive for privatisation*

In the five years preceding the recent conflict, privatisation was among the highest-ranking issues on the government's agenda. The issue received particular boosting following some notable developments and events, including the Paris II meeting;[6] the formulation of new proposed laws as part of the government's economic modernisation package;[7] and

[5] See Article 74 of the agreement. The meeting of the council and committee will take place as may be required in the circumstances; the council is established by Article 74 and the committee is established by Article 77.

[6] The Paris II meeting was held in November 2002 to seek support from the international community for the economic reform programme of the Lebanese government, in particular to alleviate the public debt burden. Top officials from several countries and a number of international financial institutions attended the meeting, which resulted in almost four and a half billion US Dollars being pledged by donors. A report entitled 'Beyond reconstruction and recovery – towards sustainable growth' was prepared for this meeting, outlining the government's economic and financial goals and its commitment to privatisation. A second report was produced in December 2003 to highlight the progress made since the Paris II meeting. These reports can be found at the website of Lebanon's Ministry of Finance, www.finance.gov.lb.

[7] See p 269 below.

the adoption of Privatisation Law 2000.[8] The latter development in particular has received significant attention given its aim to enhance the competitiveness of the Lebanese economy and protect the interests of Lebanese consumers. The process of privatisation has been directed especially at the electricity and telecommunications sectors. To support the process and further it, two important pieces of legislation were introduced,[9] namely the Law on Telecommunications 2002[10] and the Law on the Regulation of the Electricity Sector 2002.[11]

### 9.1.3 *The process of emerging competition in Lebanese markets*

#### 9.1.3.1 Overview

Lebanon is a small economy with very limited resources, except perhaps for the availability of talent and a cheap labour force in the population. In relation to the latter, there is no shortage of a strong and willing work force in Lebanon. Under normal circumstances, the abundance of a cheap labour force can be expected to promote productivity and enterprise in a given economy, though this has not actually been the case in Lebanon; the strong labour force in Lebanon is to a large extent dominated by 'sub-optimal-education' and this does not appear to have particularly encouraged or proved attractive for investment especially from abroad. As we noted above, Lebanon has always relied on foreign investment and foreign economic involvement in order to achieve economic growth and progress. In fact, this would explain the impact hi-technology has come to have during the last six years or so in the country: technology has promoted international ties between the Lebanese business community and the international community more generally. In the years following the Civil War limited competition began to emerge in the country, though market forces have not been particularly strong. Being aware of this, interestingly the government developed a model for improving competition through institutional development, namely building strong, efficient and pro-competition institutions in order to facilitate long-term competition in domestic markets. This economic model – which arguably is suitable for small

8 Law No. 228, adopted in May 2000.

9 Note also the adoption of the Investment Promotion Law 2002, Law No. 360 adopted in August of the same year, which created the Lebanon Investment Development Authority (IDLA).

10 Law No. 431, adopted in July 2002.

11 Law No. 462, adopted in September 2002.

economies – focuses as a starting point on encouraging firms to increase their size and to build local initiatives. In a country like Lebanon this is particularly important given that the vast majority of firms or businesses are remarkably small in size.

#### 9.1.3.2 The challenges

Any effort to increase competition and its influence in domestic markets faces two major challenges in Lebanon, in addition to the risk of potential conflicts and the problem of security as highlighted in the first part of the chapter. The first concerns the high level of concentration in domestic markets. In small markets with high rates of concentration, the tendency of firms to engage in monopolistic, collusive or oligopolisitc behaviour is a real one or at least is higher than in the case of markets with normal competition conditions.[12] The issue of concentration has translated into a serious issue in a small economy like Lebanon: Lebanese markets feature high levels of concentration, which appear to be caused by the small size of the economy and the small size of different local markets. The second major challenge facing the effort to increase competition concerns the structure of Lebanese markets, which have been dominated by influential exclusive agents. Due to the effective protection these agents enjoy under law, they are able to control the flow of trade especially since in relation to products that are covered under exclusive agency rules these may only be brought into the country via exclusive agents.[13] Effectively therefore, the system of exclusive agency creates significant barriers to entry, which are artificial and problematic. This challenge presented by exclusive agency has prompted some politicians and policy-makers in Lebanon to take action for the purposes of withdrawing the protection enjoyed by exclusive agents. A proposed law for this purpose is currently under discussion in Parliament. There are high hopes hanging on the proposed law for the purposes of stimulating competition and making markets more dynamic.

The existence of these two particular challenges, as well as other ones, have for many years seriously undermined competition and limited its

[12] See the table below in relation to cellular operations.

[13] The main argument of having a system of exclusive agents is to ensure high product quality and offer consumers full maintenance and after-sales services. However, based on the evidence available from around the world, such an argument does not appear convincing given that it would be possible to guarantee, in relation to relevant branded or technical products at least, such benefits through the creation of 'selective' distribution systems as opposed to a rigid system of exclusive agents.

Table. *Cellular operations market*

| Name of operator | Cost per minute (local) Land Line | Mobile | Cost per minute (int'l) | Fee or connection charge | Twin card monthly subscription | Dial 114 (per call) |
|---|---|---|---|---|---|---|
| Alpha (formerly Cellis) | 0.1303 (USD) | 0.1303 (USD) | 0.1303 (USD) | 25 (USD) | 15 (USD) | 0.40 (USD) |
| MTC Touch (formerly LibanCell) | 0.1303 (USD) | 0.1303 (USD) | 0.1303 (USD) | 25 (USD) | 15 (USD) | 0.40 (USD) |

*Source:* See Alpha's website (www.alfa.com.lb) and MTC Touch's website (www.mtctouch.com.lb).

scope and reach, and have adversely affected economic performance. In particular the challenges appear to have heightened oligopolistic behaviour and the risk of collusion on the part of firms operating in local markets. A good illustration in this regard is the cellular operations market in the Republic which clearly demonstrates the existence of high similarities in the behaviour adopted by the firms active in the market. These high similarities appear to have resulted in serious limitation of competition, though it is not clear whether this has been the result of collusion between the firms in question or merely that of parallel behaviour on their part. As may be gleaned from the table below, the market features a duopoly making it all the more difficult to classify the source of high similarities in this case. Nonetheless, it is abundantly clear that the market features a high level of concentration presenting a major challenge as described above.

### 9.1.4 *Existing legal framework for protecting competition*

At present, competition is afforded protection in Lebanon through general legal provisions, which on the whole are limited in their scope and lack the necessary effectiveness. The main instrument to be mentioned here is Law No. 73 of 1983 which applies to monopolistic practices and acts of unlawful competition. Article 14 of this Law is directed at behaviour and conduct limiting competition and which lead to an artificial price increase or prevent lower prices. The main difficulty which has effectively rendered this prohibition unenforceable is the fact that establishing a breach requires proving artificiality in price and undertaking analysis of a complex nature requiring, among other things, a consideration of two situations: the situation without the artificial price increase (the counter-factual situation) and that with the increase (the factual situation). An effective application of the Law is further hindered by the requirement to establish *intention* to limit competition and to show fraudulent behaviour and intent.[14] Additionally, the Law lacks a supporting framework of effective penalties for it to have a real deterrent effect. According to Article 26 of the Law, the maximum imprisonment term that may be imposed in case of an established breach of the Law ranges between ten and ninety days. Such term may not be considered to be sufficiently long for it to be deemed to serve a meaningful purpose. The same is true with regard to the penalty under Article 34 of the Law, namely a fine which cannot exceed 100 million Lebanese Pounds (equivalent to approximately 70,000 US Dollar). Finally, it is worth noting the lack of competition expertise among judges which is crucial for an effective application of provisions, such as those of Law No. 73.

The difficulties identified above concerning Law No. 73 of 1983 are made even more serious in light of the fact that currently, the powers to eradicate monopolistic and anti-competitive practices and seek punishment of firms engaging in such harmful practices rests in the hands of the Ministry of Economy and Trade. These powers have not been deployed effectively, however, even though the underlying objectives in granting these powers are the protection and promotion of competition, maintaining a good economy and protecting consumers.

Contrary to what one might expect from MECs – in light of the prevailing approach in the vast majority of those countries – Lebanon has not opted for a mechanism of heavy regulation in the market place. Pricing in particular – which is the most sensitive aspect of economic regulation in all MECs – has been subjected to a fairly low degree of regulation, with intervention on the part of the Ministry of Economy and Trade – through its Council for Price Policy – for the purposes of fixing the price being limited to a few products. Interestingly, however,

[14] The difficulty associated with the requirement of proving intention under competition law was discussed in chapter 8 above in relation to the Egyptian Law on the Protection of the Freedom of Competition. See p 256.

Law No. 73 of 1983 provides for a 'ceiling' to be fixed in cases of non-intervention at a level, which represents twice the actual cost of the product.[15]

### *9.1.5 A modern competition law for Lebanon*

During the 1990s, the years of relative peace, Lebanon became particularly interested in global integration. As was noted above, to achieve this, the government set the country on a course of economic modernisation through building and implementing a reform agenda. A strong belief that came to gain ground within government circles was the need for a network of adequate and modern laws to support these efforts. To this end, a legislative reform framework was built which included proposals for new specific laws dealing with intellectual property rights, exclusive agents, anti-dumping and consumer protection. A proposal for a specific competition law was also added to the package following a strong recognition of the need for a modern competition law in Lebanon.

The decision to introduce competition law in Lebanon appears to have been based on the belief in the value of competition and the need to protect it; the process of globalisation and the huge geographical expansion of competition law worldwide; and the recognition of the widespread harmful effect of anti-competitive behaviour and abusive conduct in local Lebanese markets. Determined to achieve economic efficiency and maximise consumer welfare, the government, through the Ministry of Economy and Trade, prepared an action plan. This action plan had a comprehensive set of goals and objectives aimed at: enacting a modern competition law in Lebanon; building an effective enforcement mechanism with a specialist competition authority; promoting competition; and prohibiting all forms of discrimination damaging to competition. A crucial step taken by the Ministry of Economy and Trade was conducting a study of the economy for the purposes of determining the appropriate type and nature of the proposed law. In parallel, the Ministry engaged in consultation with competition officials and experts from the EC, the USA and France. Special emphasis was placed on

[15] See Articles 6 and 7. Economists and competition lawyers with the relevant expertise would be familiar with the difficulty with such a proposition especially given the challenging task of establishing the actual cost of a product in certain cases. This difficulty would perhaps explain the inoperability of this mechanism in the country in practice.

consultation with the latter given the similarity between the legal systems of the countries and the special relationship existing between them. Additionally, some consultation was conducted involving several business firms, local academics and practitioners and various government departments. This important work led to a draft of the proposed Lebanese Competition Act (LCA), which was very much underdeveloped in its original form but was improved significantly leading to an eleventh draft by 15 October 2004. It is understood that this latest draft remains unchanged and further work on it was put on hold at the time of writing.

### *9.1.6 The scope of the LCA*

The LCA is very much derived from both EC and French competition law.[16] Unlike the majority of competition laws of Arab countries, the LCA is intended to apply to all firms, whether public or private.[17] Thus, the LCA does not provide exclusion for state-owned firms; nor does it exempt any sector, whether regulated or general, from its scope. The LCA does, however, exclude from its scope activities undertaken by associations of workers, trade unions or labour syndicates for the purposes of protecting the rights of their members concerning facilitating collective bargaining in relation to matters such as conditions of employment as well as relations falling within the scope of the law on protection of industrial property, copyright and related matters insofar as these do not result in restrictions on competition.[18]

The economic and legal thinking behind the LCA appears to be very mature and one that favours a type of law which is dynamic, mandates competition advocacy and is policy-oriented. If enacted in its current draft, the LCA would be the most comprehensive legislation in the whole of the Middle East, though by no means the least demanding or costly in terms of enforcement in the region.[19] It brings within its scope

[16] Note, however, that in relation to extra-territorial reach, the LCA adopts the effects doctrine in order to bring within its ambit all forms of anti-competitive behaviour and abusive conduct occurring outside Lebanon but which produce 'restrictive effects' within the Lebanese market(s) or part of it.

[17] The LCA uses the term 'person' which is defined in Article 2 as any natural or legal person and entities, incorporated in Lebanon or a foreign country, such as partnerships, associations, corporations, or other business outfits, however constituted, engaged directly or indirectly in economic activity; the term also covers all public sector entities engaged in commercial activity.

[18] See Article 3 of the LCA.

[19] See below at pp 272–4.

horizontal and vertical agreements,[20] abuse of dominance,[21] economic concentrations (mergers),[22] and public aid.[23] It would be important to be aware, however, that further work is still necessary for the purposes of filling existing gaps within the latest draft and for the purposes of tightening various elements within the LCA.[24] One notable absence within the LCA is a specific reference to territorial link. It was said above that the LCA includes an 'effects' doctrine as a basis for asserting jurisdiction in situations with 'foreign' elements.[25] This inclusion – however questionable – is an improvement on the position adopted in early drafts which contained no reference to territorial reach at all. Nonetheless, a careful reading of the provisions of the LCA would reveal a missing element tying the various business phenomena within the scope of its provisions to Lebanon. For example, Article 15 of the LCA prohibits abuse of dominance without supplying the necessary nexus between dominance and Lebanon. The definition of dominance in the LCA follows the one in existence under Article 82 EC, albeit differences between the two pertain. Thus, unlike Article 82 EC – which requires that the dominant position must be held in 'the common market or a substantial part of it' – Article 2 of the LCA contains no such reference and therefore it appears to convey the impression that its application in practice would be necessary regardless of the place where the dominant position is held or the 'appreciability' of such a position.[26] There is therefore a clear absence of geographical link. A similar shortcoming exists in relation to the treatment of anti-competitive agreements and harmful merger operations. In the case of the former, neither Article 11 – which prohibits horizontal collusion[27] – nor Article 12 – which prohibits anti-competitive vertical agreements – contains any reference of a

[20] The prohibitions on harmful horizontal agreements and vertical agreements are contained in Articles 11 and 12 respectively. Article 13 deals with the exemption in relation to prohibited vertical agreements.

[21] See Article 15 of the LCA. [22] See Chapter II (Articles 5–10) of the LCA.

[23] See Articles 16 and 17 of the LCA.

[24] For example, the merger notification thresholds – both in terms of market share and turnover – in Article 5 of the LCA have yet to be determined. Similarly, the drafting of Article 44 (General Provisions) would require completion by providing a list of all laws, regulations, decrees, decisions, memoranda or orders to be repealed – due to contradictions – upon the proposed law coming into effect.

[25] See note 16 above.

[26] It is worth noting that the reference in the definition of dominance under Article 2 to 'relevant market' does not solve this issue given that the issue of appreciability of dominance is not a question of geographic market definition with which the concept of relevant market is concerned.

[27] Article 11 merely lists the types of anti-competitive agreements caught under the LCA.

link to Lebanon; and the same is true in the case of appraisal of concentrations under Article 6.

### *9.1.7 Institutional structure*

The LCA aims to create a strong enforcement mechanism with an independent competition authority enjoying sufficient financial and human resources. Influenced by the French and the EC systems of competition law, the LCA provides for administrative enforcement. It further provides for the creation of a Competition Council and a rapporteur of competition affairs.

#### 9.1.7.1 The Competition Council

The council is intended to be an independent administrative body composed of five members, one of whom will serve as the chairman of the council.[28] Article 20 of the LCA provides that the members must be experts in law, economics, business or consumer affairs;[29] they are to be appointed by the Council of Ministers following a recommendation by the Minister of Economy and Trade for a five-year term which may be renewed once.[30] According to Article 18 of the LCA, the council will exist under the auspices of the Ministry of Economy and Trade with full autonomy however, in relation to finance and administration.[31]

Among the proposed key functions of the council are conducting investigations;[32] producing guidance to firms and their legal advisors,[33]

[28] Articles 26 and 27 of the LCA deal with the appointment and role and duties of the chairman.

[29] The article prevents certain individuals from serving as member(s). These include any person who has been declared bankrupt or insolvent, deprived from civil capacity or has been at any time removed from a public or private position due to misconduct on his part. Interestingly, the prohibition extends to any person who has not been a Lebanese citizen for more than fifteen years.

[30] Article 21 of the LCA which states that the initial term of appointments of members will be as follows: chairman to be appointed for five years and the other four members for (staggered) descending terms between four and one years.

[31] The article provides, however, that the council will be subject to *ex post* control by the *Diwan al Mouhassaba* (a public body with some judicial attributes), but it will not be under the control of the Civil Service Council or the Central Investigation Body. Article 19 of the LCA deals with the council's budget.

[32] By virtue of Article 31, the council can receive complaints from the Minister of Economy and Trade; professional associations, consumer organisations and syndicates; municipalities and other local government departments; and any person harmed or deemed to be directly concerned within the scope of the LCA.

[33] Article 42 of the LCA.

adopting by-laws, regulations, procedures, and enforcement guidelines for the purposes of, among other things, facilitating compliance with the provisions of the LCA; engaging in competition advocacy at government level;[34] taking appropriate enforcement actions; conducting merger review functions; promoting a culture of competition in Lebanon; conducting market studies; and establishing links with foreign competition authorities.

The creation of the council is likely to raise questions about the division of competence between it and sectoral regulators. For this reason, Article 4 of the LCA provides for this division of competence to be addressed and clarified through regulations and memoranda of understanding to be entered into between the council and relevant sectoral regulators. The article further provides that the council will engage in a surveillance duty in the case of public undertakings and ones to which special or exclusive rights have been granted, including services of general interest in order to ensure that the operation of such undertakings does not undermine competition.[35] By-laws, formal and informal rules, administrative guidance, procedural rules, guidelines and subordinate rules in general issued by any government department as well as by non-governmental or professional self-regulatory bodies entrusted with delegated regulatory powers, will be subject to the LCA.

#### 9.1.7.2 The rapporteur of competition affairs

In addition to the council, the LCA provides for the creation of a rapporteur of competition affairs. The office of the rapporteur is intended to be an independent body,[36] hearing or investigating cases either *ex-officio* or ones resulting from complaints transferred from the council. The rapporteur is appointed by the Council of Ministers

[34] According to Article 24 of the LCA the government is required to seek the opinion of the Council prior to taking decisions affecting the competitive environment, such as those giving exclusive rights in certain geographic areas or introducing practices (*pratiques uniformes*) affecting prices and conditions of sale or imposing quantitative restrictions in terms of impeding market access or the function of a profession.

[35] The concept of services of general interest is defined in Article 2 of the LCA as services of an economic nature provided by public or private operators subject to specific obligations, rules or constraints by the government or a public authority which is entrusted with ensuring quality control, consumer interest and welfare, universality of service, or any other general interest. One may note here the similarity between Article 2 and Article 86(2) of the EC Treaty. Article 86(2) EC was discussed above at p 103.

[36] See Article 28 of the LCA.

following a recommendation by the Minister of Justice.[37] The main powers and duties of the rapporteur – in addition to launching and conducting investigations and exercising other powers and conducting other duties as provided in the LCA – include defending and representing the public interest in the economic arena before the council or the courts; defending or contesting decisions delivered by the council before the Court of Appeals; and issuing reports as may be requested by the council. This provides the rapporteur with a wide spectrum of powers and duties affording him the ability to play a key role in competition enforcement in Lebanon. Article 33 of the LCA empowers the rapporteur to appoint a case-designated rapporteur to preside over proceedings in individual cases.

### *9.1.8 Orders and penalties*

Article 36 of the LCA arms the council and rapporteur with the 'widest powers' in carrying out their enforcement functions. According to the article the council may seek the assistance of law enforcement agencies in helping it discharge its functions effectively. According to Article 38 the council is able to issue temporary injunctions; order any anti-competitive behaviour or abusive conduct to be brought to an end; order restructuring of holdings, activities or operations of firms found in breach of the provisions of the LCA; recover damages; impose fines;[38] and impose administrative sanctions on natural persons whose conduct leads to or incites anti-competitive behaviour or abusive conduct.

### *9.1.9 The public dimension of the LCA*

The LCA contains four important public dimensions. First, as noted above, it is intended to apply to public firms, insofar as this will not obstruct the performance of the particular task assigned to and carried out by those firms.[39] Secondly, the LCA advocates the elimination of barriers to entry

[37] *Ibid*. The term of appointment is five years. The main requirement for the appointment is a minimum fifteen years' experience in the legal profession.

[38] The article provides for double-fines where its decision would not be adhered to in due time. It may also impose periodic penalties (daily fines). In the case of legal persons, in addition to the fine imposed on such persons, the council may also impose a fine on any senior executive who was directly involved in the illegal conduct. The maximum fine imposed on a natural person cannot exceed 150 million Lebanese Pounds.

[39] Note also that Article 3 of the LCA brings within its scope situations where competition is restricted or distorted, expressly or tacitly, actually or potentially, by the authorities of

and trade and investment barriers, most notably those caused by public involvement such as through the adoption of certain rules and regulatory requirements. Thirdly, the LCA favours and advocates institutional designs, which are pro-competitive.[40] Fourthly, it applies to different types of aid, whether public, regional or sectoral which distort competition.[41]

The LCA can be considered to be sitting at the heart of the government's agenda of economic reform and comes to enhance its liberalisation policies aimed at promoting competition in local markets, including regulated sectors. A notable effort by the government in relation to the latter has been the 'Open-Skies' policy introduced in 2000 for the purposes of abolishing what have been widely referred to as the 'Fifth Freedom Rights' of Middle East Airlines, Lebanon's national carrier. Similar important steps have recently initiated legislative reform in relation to other sectors, most notably imported pharmaceutical products, energy, oil and telecommunications.

### *9.1.10 Reflections*

The institutional structure of a country's competition regime cannot be viewed in isolation from the country's general institutional pillars, whether judicial, political or economic. In relation to the first of these pillars, Lebanon's judicial structure suffers from being inefficient, a shortcoming that has over the years proved to be costly to the business community in particular. In relation to investment and trade, this state of affairs presents a serious barrier discouraging foreign participation in the economy as it impedes the presence of foreign firms in domestic markets. The LCA appears to attempt to remedy this situation by enhancing legal certainty in the institutional structure and providing for judicial supervision at the level of the Court of Appeals to vet the administrative enforcement within the system.[42] Additionally, Article 41

the executive branch of the central government and of local governments, including those responsible for service of general interest.

40 See pp 8–9 above for a discussion on the issue of pro-competitive institutional designs.

41 These types of aid are prohibited under Chapter IV (Articles 16–17) of the LCA. Note, however, that Article 16 provides for exceptions giving the council the power to authorise any of the following: non-discriminatory public aid of social purpose granted to individual customers; aid aimed at promoting the execution of important projects of national interest or remedying serious disturbances in the national economy; and aid intended to address damage caused in cases of emergency such as natural disasters.

42 Article 39 gives the right to appeal to a 'party' without making it clear whether this extends to third parties, such as competitors. The provision of judicial review in the

of the LCA mandates transparency in the work of the council which can be expected to be extremely crucial in the council's striving for competition advocacy.[43]

Different provisions of the LCA demonstrate a clear lack of balance in terms of its intended regulatory framework and *modus operandi*. Several articles can be cited in support of this view which represent two extremes in this regard: the first extreme (represented by Articles 10(b), 34 and 35) shows *strict* limitations whilst the other (represented under Article 14) reveals a case of *loose* limitations. Article 10(b), which sets out a limitation period, states that a concentration (i.e. a merger operation) subject to prior notification (under Article 5) which was implemented without prior notification to the council *cannot* be challenged after one year from the date of implementation. Whilst such a provision is favourable from a legal certainty point of view, it increases the pressure on the council in its merger review work; the fact that the article provides that the council retains the right at any time to examine any abuse of dominance by a merged entity formed in contravention of the requirement of notification does not necessarily alleviate this burden. It is quite likely that this paragraph may not survive in the final draft of the LCA. Article 34 provides that within ten days following the day on which the council received a complaint it *must* deliver a decision ordering one of the following: opening an investigation and submitting the matter to the rapporteur;[44] rejecting the complaint;[45] or notifying the complainant of any deficiencies in the claim (such as lack of clarity) and inviting the complainant to remedy the situation.[46] In relation to the latter situation the article provides that the council shall set the complainant a time limit of fifteen days extendable in 'justified cases' for a further fifteen days only once. Quite strictly, the article provides that where the situation was remedied, the council must reach its decision within five days. Interestingly, the article provides that a failure on the part of the council to reach a decision under paragraphs (a)–(c) would be deemed as amounting to an investigation being commenced. Finally, Article 35 of the LCA sets a clear time limit on the council to complete its investigation

system is a positive component though it appears to be limited given that Article 40 of the LCA does not allow for further appeal from the decisions of the Court of Appeals.

[43] Among other things, the article provides for the council to conduct its work in public as much as possible and to provide adequate opportunity for interested parties to submit their views on any rules the council proposes to adopt through its rule-making function.

[44] Article 34(a) of the LCA. [45] Article 34(b) of the LCA. [46] Article 34(c) of the LCA.

and reach a reasoned decision within sixty days following the thirty-day period within which a party summoned by the council must submit its affidavit or defence and the thirty-day period within which a party must submit its oral or written pleas.[47]

Article 14 of the LCA on the other hand states that in establishing that a vertical agreement caught under Article 12 should be declared illegal, a claimant must provide 'solid evidence' that the agreement fails to meet the efficiency standards listed in Article 13. This is quite a problematic provision given that establishing that a vertical agreement satisfies the criteria for exemption contained in a provision such as Article 13 must be done by the parties to the agreement; whereas establishing the reverse, namely that these criteria are not satisfied must be the responsibility of the competition authority. In a country like Lebanon, such a provision is particularly problematic given that with vertical agreements having harmful competitive effects being quite widespread in local markets potential claimants might be discouraged from complaining or launching an action because of the heavy burden of proof and high standard of proof of 'solid evidence' imposed under the provision.

At another level, it is quite difficult to ascertain the exact limitation on the council's discretion in certain cases, most notably those arising under Article 31 of the LCA which provides that the council *may* refuse to investigate a request or complaint; however, it must support its decision with reasons and notify the decision to the party making the request or complaint and also publish its decision. However, it is not clear whether such a decision entitles the party concerned to challenge the council's decision before the Court of Appeals. Article 39(a) merely provides for the right of appeal against a decision *if* the council violates the provisions of the LCA or its own procedures in a non-trivial manner in the conduct of the proceedings. The picture is rendered less clear given that the LCA is silent on whether any course of action would be open to the Minister of Economy and Trade as a requested party under Article 31 of the LCA where the council refuses to conduct an investigation and the Minister nonetheless considers that action in the case is necessary.

[47] Note, however, that this does not mean that a decision must be reached within 120 (30 + 30 + 60) days following the launch of an investigation because Article 35(a) does not set a time limit for the council to summon a party nor does paragraph (c) of the article set a time limit on the council to review evidence submitted to it by a summoned party.

## 9.2 Syria: resisting international isolation with international openness

Syria is a country with a rich tradition though little is known about it beyond the borders of the Middle East. The country suffers from many difficulties, namely lack of economic progress, political problems and continuous tension with its neighbour, Israel. During the last eight years the Republic came to endure isolation at the international level, mainly due to the tough stance adopted by the USA towards Syria and the various accusations directed towards it from several capitals around the world. Such isolation has proved to be damaging to Syria's already weak economy.

Within the economic arena, imports into the country as well as the production and distribution of certain domestic products were for many years monopolised at the hands of the state. This system of state control and planning was complemented with the creation of systems of exclusive agencies within the private sector. Syria has a long tradition and a strong belief in state control and planning. The country's current process of economic reform and the government's 'modern' economic thinking and approach appear to have been not to move towards increased privatisation but rather to enhance state control by creating a dynamic public sector through improved public governance and administration of financial institutions and the economy and through reducing bureaucracy.[48] Whist such ends are commendable, the emphasis appears to be on increased rivalry between the public and private sectors as opposed to the creation of harmony between them and to facilitating competition between private forces in the market place.[49] Major forces of the public sector have come to embrace a desire for bitter rivalry with the private sector which appears to be aimed at undermining the latter.

Internationally, Syria's economic cooperation and relations have not been as advanced as those built by many MECs, especially when the latter's relationship with the EC is considered. In the case of Syria, the negotiations of an Association Agreement with the EC were finalised on

[48] For example, the Commercial Bank of Syria has introduced key reforms for the purposes of increasing the number of working hours so they are brought within international standards and shortening the time frame for approving commercial loans.

[49] This increased competition can be seen in the banking sector between the Commercial Bank of Syria and private banks.

19 October 2004. Remarkably, however, the parties have not succeeded in signing this agreement and therefore the agreement continues to await final approval and signature.[50]

### 9.2.1 *Competition law: paradox, contradictions and conflicts*

Considered carefully, the developments referred to above might perhaps be expected to delay rather than speed up an enactment of specific competition legislation in Syria. As we observed, there has been no particular desire to facilitate competition in local markets or any indication on the part of the government to pursue privatisation as has been the case with other MECs. Competition law aims to protect the process of competition and may be used for the purposes of building a market economy. If neither of these goals is desired and instead a government favours public control and undermining private forces through strengthening the competitive advantage of public ones, it would be open to question whether a specific competition law should be adopted under such circumstances or the purpose which the law can be expected to fulfil in practice.

Interestingly, in the case of Syria such considerations and questions do not appear to have received any serious attention. Notwithstanding any reservations one may have about the situation, a draft for a proposed Law on Competition and Prevention of Monopolistic Practices, the Syrian Competition Law (SCL) was prepared by the Ministry of Economy and Trade[51] in April 2005 and was sent to Parliament for discussion. It is expected that the SCL will be adopted and will enter into force by the end of 2007. To a large extent, the decision to turn to competition law has not been the result of a gradual internal realisation within the country, but rather that of a *need* to meet the conditions set for a possible accession to the World Trade Organisation (WTO), and as a *necessity* under the proposed EC–Syria Association Agreement.[52]

The picture that has emerged in light of the government's general economic policy and its decision to enact specific competition legislation shows some paradox: on the one hand the government is seeking to

[50] Until this is done, relations between the EC and Syria continue to be governed by the Cooperation Agreement of 1977.

[51] The Ministry is also referred to sometimes as the Ministry for Economy and Foreign Trade.

[52] This in fact is acknowledged in the preamble to the SCL.

enact a specific law to protect competition which is associated with and requires the existence of a market economy, whereas on the other hand, the general economic approach of the government is to tighten public control and opt for protectionism. This paradoxical situation has been inflated with several contradictions, which are likely to result in either serious conflicts, in law and policy, or in rendering the SCL virtually ineffective and irrelevant. Such a claim can be illustrated with reference to the *additional* government initiative to adopt a specific law aimed at the *protection* of domestic products in light of the increased global flow of trade and competition. This proposed law, which is under active consideration within the Ministry of Economy and Trade at present, has been criticised as contradicting the government's declared intention to integrate into the global economy and to the new model of socialist market economy in the country.[53]

The initial general impression one forms from the legislative developments relating to the SCL for most of 2005 (when the legislative work on the SCL began) is that its enactment was being rushed through the legislative process without proper or adequate consideration of its implications in practice or the competitive context of the economy. For example, for most of 2005 consultation in relation to the SCL was extremely limited, and hardly any adequate research or analysis was conducted. Moreover, there was no meaningful attempt to consult the experience of countries in a similar position to Syria. It appears that the situation came to change slightly during 2006 presumably due to the government realising that its previous approach contained a risk that the application of the SCL – when enacted – will in practice be fraught with difficulties.[54] In light of its modified approach, it appears that the government has formed the opinion that it would be sensible to address several issues related to its general approach to competition, such as those mentioned above, before the enactment of the SCL. There is no doubt that consulting the experience of other MECs is highly desirable for the purposes of understanding the context within which competition legislation should be developed. For this reason, the latest draft of the SCL acknowledged the benefits which could

[53] The government has defended the SCL on the ground that it would enable first an improved quality of domestic products in order to be able to compete more effectively in both local and foreign markets, and secondly an effective mechanism for fighting anti-dumping.

[54] Consultation was sought on the draft from both local and European economic and competition law specialists, though this was quite limited. Additionally, the SCL was debated within the Damascus Chamber of Commerce.

be gained from consulting the experiences of other countries in the region in particular those of Tunisia, Jordan, Algeria, Morocco and Egypt among others and confirms that such consultation did in fact take place.[55]

### 9.2.2 *The thesis of the SCL*

The SCL appears to be based on a highly interesting thesis. In broad terms, it is intended to complement other economic laws adopted by Syria in recent years as well as ones expected to emerge in the near future, which are part of the process of the ongoing economic and legal reform and the recent move within the Republic towards a socialist market economy. According to the government, under the previous economic regime there was no urgent need to enact a competition law given that there was no threat to prices in local markets: under that regime the state had direct control of the market and prices were determined and supervised by the state. In fact the state had a virtual monopoly over different sectors of the economy and therefore there were no prospects for competition being harmed as a result of the behaviour of the private sector given that the latter were non-existent. The government therefore has explained that a move towards market economy and the gradual liberalisation of prices, along with a growing role for the private sector, mandate the enactment of a specific competition law in order to deal with the problems, which are likely to arise in the new economic climate and which may harm consumers and the economy. In this way, the SCL comes to prevent a transition on the part of consumers from a situation of state control and planning through which the state provides social services for consumers to a situation of private monopolies aimed at maximising personal benefits at the expense of the national economy and consumers.

### 9.2.3 *The scope and goals of the SCL*

The SCL appears to have been influenced by the Set of the United Nations Conference on Trade and Development (UNCTAD), the competition rules of the EC and, as we noted above, the competition laws of several MECs.[56] Consequently, in a similar tone it aims at the

[55] It appears that the experience of Saudi Arabia was also consulted and certain provisions of the SCL have been informed by that experience. See further p 294 below.

[56] The preamble to the SCL makes specific reference to all of these sources. In particular, it states that it takes into account the need to *harmonise* the SCL with the kind of competition rules meeting the requirement of developing countries and the

elimination of all forms of restrictive behaviour and abusive conduct and the control of mergers which harm competition and affect domestic and international trade or the economic development of the country.[57] The reference to harm to international trade is interesting though the SCL does not explain whether the reference here is to restrictions of exports, limitation on imports or hindrance to market access by Syrian firms or products to foreign markets. Given that the SCL is being developed within the context of accession to the WTO it may be possible that the idea is for the SCL to be compatible with or complementary to trade policy objectives. It is arguable that such language comes to support the Syrian strategy of international openness.

The SCL applies to both legal and natural persons. These terms are defined widely.[58] In relation to natural persons, Article 39(b) of the SCL provides that it applies in relation to all such persons who personally – in their capacity as the owner, manager or officer of an undertaking – authorise, participate or help commit an act prohibited under the SCL. The SCL has extra-territorial reach embodied in an effects doctrine.[59] Nonetheless, Article 3(d) and (e) declare the SCL inapplicable to the sovereign acts of Syria and undertakings owned or managed by the state which aim at ensuring the availability of drinking water, gas, electricity and petrol as well as public transport activities and telecommunications. In relation to these sectors, special sectoral rules, produced by the relevant authorities,[60] apply which aim at regulating competition.

#### 9.2.3.1 Collusion

Article 5 of the SCL prohibits all forms of collusion between firms whether occurring at horizontal or vertical levels of the economy. The article lists the different types of collusion within the scope of the prohibition such as concerted practices, alliances or agreements, whether written, oral, formal or informal. In this way, the SCL contains a clear advantage over equivalent provisions in MECs, most notably Egypt where, as we saw in chapter 8, there is no reference to the

competition rules of the EC, and to *bring* its provisions *closer* to the competition rules of other Arab countries.

57 See Article 1 of the SCL.

58 Article 2 of the SCL defines the term ‘legal person or undertaking’ as a person carrying out an economic activity.

59 See Article 3(c) of the SCL.

60 These include the Ministry of Electricity, the Ministry of Communications and Technology and the Ministry of Transportation.

collusion taking any other form than an agreement or a contract.[61] Article 5 gives examples of collusion which are prohibited, in particular ones aimed at disturbing the process of price determination according to the natural flow of competition in the market place through fixing, decreasing or increasing prices or other trading conditions including those occurring within *international* trade; bid-rigging; market-sharing on a geographic basis, quantities or customers or any other basis producing negative effect on competition; limitation of output, sale, investment or technical progress; boycotting agreements, whether in relation to purchase from or supply to a particular party; impeding market access or entry to limit or eliminate competition; collective refusal to permit joining any association or organisation which has significant competition importance and relevance. The prohibition contained in Article 5, however, is not absolute in the sense that the article contains in paragraph (c) a *de minimis* doctrine providing that the prohibition will not apply in situations where the aggregate market share of the parties does not exceed 10 per cent in the relevant market, in which case the situation would be considered to have minor importance in competition terms.[62] The applicability of the doctrine in a given situation, however, is further conditioned on three important grounds, the last two of which are alternatives: the absence of a price-fixing or market-sharing element in the situation; the restriction(s) in question is indispensable to ensure technical or economic progress; and the existence of a clear public benefit in the situation. Attaching the latter two grounds to the applicability of the *de minimis* doctrine is a highly interesting step, given that they appear grounds which normally feature in relation to an exemption from a prohibition on collusion which is in fact the case in the SCL itself as will become apparent below.[63]

### 9.2.3.2 Abuse of dominance

The SCL contains a specific prohibition on abuse of dominance, whether achieved individually by a single firm or collectively by two or more firms.[64] The language of the prohibition is highly specific and aims to catch situations where the abuse is directed at limiting market entry, or

[61] See p 256 above.

[62] In would be important to note the 10 per cent in this case is a ceiling figure and that the Minister of Economy and Trade is given the power to set a different percentage under Regulations provided that it does not exceed this ceiling of 10 per cent.

[63] See the discussion on exemptions in the next part.

[64] See Article 6 of the SCL.

preventing, restricting or distorting competition resulting in either case in adverse effects on trade or economic growth. There are several examples contained in the prohibition of what may amount to such abuse, such as: fixing or imposing prices or conditions relating to the resale of products; impeding market access by other firms or subjecting them to serious loss as may happen in the case of predatory pricing; discrimination between customers; compelling customers not to deal with a competitor of the dominant firm(s); seeking to monopolise an essential facility, access to which is required by a competitor to conduct its activities or engaging in purchasing of quantities leading to price increases; refusal to supply; and tying or bundling between different products and services. Although the prohibition on abuse is highly specific, the definition given to dominance in the SCL is very general referring to a position enabling a firm or firms to control or influence market activities. Such a general definition contrasts with the definition in existence in different competition law regimes around the Middle East which, as we saw in previous chapters, are fairly detailed with many of them making specific reference to particular market-share thresholds.[65]

#### 9.2.3.3 Merger control

The SCL assigns the treatment of concentrations or mergers to Article 14 and Chapter 5, which is made up of two Articles: Article 9 which defines the term 'concentration' and contains the substantive and jurisdictional threshold tests and Article 10 which deals with notification and the review by the Competition Council. The brief meaning given to the term 'concentration' appears to centre on situations of acquisition of control, whether sole or joint. In such situations where the concentration is likely to affect the level of competition as a result of creating or strengthening a dominant position notification to the council is mandated, provided that the aggregate market share of the undertakings concerned exceeds 30 per cent of the relevant market. A special notification form will be devised which must be used by merging parties for the purpose of making *prior* notification of the concentration within thirty days from the date of the reaching of the merger agreement.[66] The

[65] See for example chapter 3 regarding the Israeli Restrictive Business Practices Law, which includes a market-share threshold of 50 per cent.

[66] The SCL provides that the council will have the power to take any action it sees fit to deal with concentration which, although falling within the scope of Article 9, was not notified.

information which would (appear to) be required to be submitted as part of the notification is very extensive. In addition to basic information and details about the parties and their plan, there is a requirement for supplying a report on the economic implications of the concentration, in particular its likely positive effects on the market.[67] Remarkably, Article 10(c)(1) of the SCL limits the power of the council to request further information in writing to only once.

By virtue of Article 14 of the SCL, the council will have to complete its review of the notified concentration and reach its decision within 100 days of the date of (complete) notification during which the concentration must be suspended by the parties. Such a decision may be unconditional clearance of the concentration, clearance subject to conditions or outright prohibition.[68] Interestingly, Article 14(a)(1) is highly specific and provides that the unconditional clearance is conditioned on the concentration improving conditions of competition or producing positive economic effects, such as those leading to lower prices, creating employment, encouraging export, attracting investment or enhancing the competitiveness of Syrian firms internationally, or where the concentration is indispensable to achieving desired technical progress.

### 9.2.4 *Exemptions*

The mechanism of exemption under the SCL applies at two different levels. First, exemption applies in relation to intervention by the government in exceptional cases of emergency or natural disaster provided that the measures adopted in this case are reviewed within six months of the date on which they are implemented. Secondly, exemption is possible in the case of situations falling within Article 5 (collusion between undertakings) and Article 6 (abuse of dominance) of the SCL where the relevant situation leads to results yielding benefit to the public interest which are not attainable without an exemption including producing positive effect in terms of improving competition, production and distribution, achieving certain consumer benefits or guaranteeing a particular desired technical progress. Article 7, which contains the

[67] It appears that the intention is to adopt a strict approach on submission of correct and not misleading information by the parties given the proposal to arm the council with the power to cancel a previous clearance decision where it transpires at a later date that such information was misleading.

[68] It is proposed that failure to comply with any conditions which may be imposed by the council empowers it to cancel its previous clearance decision.

exemption provision, does not provide that these are cumulative conditions and therefore appears to convey the impression that an exemption will be possible where any of these results is relevant.

### 9.2.5 *The treatment of pricing policies and practices in special cases*

The SCL provides for the determination of market prices according to the parameters of free market competition. However, in three specified cases this principle will not apply.[69] These cases include: the price of basic commodities and services which is determined by law; the price of goods and services belonging to sectors or geographic areas in which price competition is limited due to monopolistic practices, difficulty of supply or laws and regulations which are determined by a Prime Ministerial decision adopted following consultation of the Competition Council; and prices determined according to a decision by the government taken as a temporary measure in order to deal with exceptional circumstances, in cases of emergency or natural disaster, provided that the situation is reviewed within six months of the date on which the decision was effected. Clearly, therefore, price regulation by the government is possible in certain cases mandating such intervention on public interest grounds. Furthermore, the position of the government on the matter appears to be similar to that adopted by some Arab governments, such as Yemen.[70]

The preamble to the SCL confirms the government's declared intention behind such intervention, namely to enable it to achieve socio-economic goals and objectives for the benefit of the greater good of the people. Clearly therefore the mechanism comes to support the social market model, which the SCL is widely considered to facilitate.

### 9.2.6 *Improper exercise of intellectual property rights*

Remarkably, the SCL contains a specific prohibition on improper exercise of intellectual property rights.[71] The inclusion of such a prohibition is an advancement on the existing competition laws in most MECs and was done due to the influence of EC competition law and also as an

[69] See Article 4 of the SCL. [70] See p 214 above.

[71] Article 5(b)(2) of the SCL provides that intellectual property rights include copyright and neighbouring rights, trade marks, patents, plant breeders' rights, know-how, industrial property rights and designs, geographic indication and trade secrets.

effort by the government to demonstrate an understanding of the balance needed between competition law and intellectual property rights.[72] Article 5(b) of the SCL clearly demonstrates that the SCL does not come to undermine the existence of intellectual property rights though any improper exercise of such rights through licensing of the right leading to an adverse effect on competition or hindering the transfer of technology is prohibited. Interestingly, though not exhaustively, the article lists examples of such improper exercise, namely where the licensee is obliged not to transfer improvements made by him to the technology under a licence agreement except to the licensor, where the licensee is prohibited from challenging, whether administratively or judicially, the validity of the licensed technology or where the licensee is obliged to accept a licence in relation to a group of rights as opposed to a single right.[73]

### *9.2.7 Fairness of commercial transactions*

The SCL emphasises the need to protect the fairness of commercial transactions. In particular, there is a prohibition on situations where minimum resale pricing is imposed by a producer, importer, wholesaler or service-provider. This prohibition also extends to situations where such a person imposes on another party or obtains from such a party prices, purchase or selling terms which are not justified in circumstances giving such a party a competitive advantage or undermining such a party. This is an interesting provision which shows the particular interest the government has in preventing exploitation and discrimination. The provision appears to operate in two opposite directions: where a trading party is placed at a competitive advantage *presumably vis-à-vis* other firms and where such a party is exploited. In this way the provision is a double-edged sword.

The government's interest in preventing discrimination and exploitation can be seen in relation to similar prohibitions on practices harming the fairness of commercial transactions. For example, the SCL specifically prohibits any firm from resale of a product at a price below the product's *actual* purchase price, with taxes and transportation costs

[72] The existence of provisions on intellectual property rights within the WTO was also influential in this regard.

[73] Note that the prohibition here is subject to the *de minimis* doctrine as explained at p 283 above.

being deducted, where the purpose behind the practice is to distort competition.[74] This prohibition is useful and problematic in equal measures. On the one hand, the prohibition could prove useful in practice to deal with situations of predatory pricing which pose a particular problem in local markets in Syria. On the other hand, the provision is problematic because of its use of the term 'actual' and how this would be established in practice. According to Article 8(b)(2) of the SCL, actual price means the price appearing on an invoice. Such definition may, however, enable firms to avoid the application of the provision in practice by ensuring that the price appearing on an invoice is other than the 'actual' price. Furthermore – aside from the concern that it may in effect convert the Competition Council into a price regulatory authority – the prohibition is excessively wide in its scope and its future use as an effective mechanism for controlling predatory pricing is questionable. Whilst Article 8(b)(2) renders the prohibition inapplicable in cases where the 'lower price' is adopted for the purposes of facilitating a quick sale of products with short-life duration, to exit a market or to bring in new stock,[75] the criterion for determining the lower price should be that of cost. In other words, determining actual price for the purposes of the prohibition should be based on actual cost. This in fact would be consistent with competition law practice around the world according to which predatory pricing is established on the basis of several factors, including cost.

### *9.2.8 Institutional structure and enforcement*

The SCL provides for the creation of an independent Commission on Competition and Prevention of Monopolistic Practices (the Competition Commission), which includes a Competition Council.

#### 9.2.8.1 The Competition Commission

The Competition Commission is proposed to be a fully independent authority without any affiliation to a particular ministry, though it is intended to be subject to the Office of Prime Minister.[76] The commission

[74] See Article 8(b)(1) of the SCL.

[75] It would be important also to appreciate that the prohibition does not refer to 'dominant' undertaking but rather merely to 'any undertaking'. In systems of competition law, predatory pricing is prohibited where this is practised by a dominant undertaking.

[76] See Article 11 of the SCL.

is intended to be armed with effective and wide powers to enable it to conduct different functions of administrative and judicial nature in practice. Among these functions are: contributing to the formulation of a general competition plan for Syria and relevant legislation; protecting and encouraging competition, engaging in competition advocacy; conducting competition investigations;[77] and cooperating with foreign competition authorities, where possible,[78] for the purposes of exchanging information relating to competition enforcement.[79]

### 9.2.8.2 The Competition Council

The Competition Council is intended to be the main player in the enforcement of the SCL. It is intended to be composed of eleven members appointed by the Prime Minister following a suggestion by the Minister of Economy and Trade.[80] According to Article 12 of the SCL, the council will function in panels, which will handle cases delegated to them by the president of the council. The council will be responsible for adopting decisions in merger cases,[81] and launching

[77] The powers of investigations to be enjoyed by commission officials are listed in Article 15 of the SCL and include entering business premises in order to conduct searches. Premises for this purpose extend beyond buildings to vehicles.

[78] Note for example, that handing over confidential information to foreign competition authorities is prohibited by virtue of Article 16 of the SCL. Paragraph (b) of the article provides that where a breach of Article 16 occurs the president of the council may hand over to the relevant person(s) the necessary information establishing such a breach or allow them access to this information in order to enable such person(s) to seek judicial or other means of enforcement.

[79] See Article 13 of the SCL. Other proposed functions include submitting an annual report to the President and Parliament and delivering opinions on consultations received from sectoral regulators on merger operations within such sectors. According to Article 13(c) such consultation is *mandatory* given that these merger operations are not regulated by the commission.

[80] According to Article 11(b) of the SCL, three members must be from the judiciary (from an appeal level and above); three members with expertise in economic matters, competition and consumer affairs; three members with current or past experience in the production, distribution or services sector or the independent professions; and two civil servants. In addition Article 18 of the SCL provides for the appointment of a government representative appearing on behalf of the Minister of Economy and Trade to the council responsible for protecting the public interest in competition cases and to present the Ministry of Economy and Trade's views before the council. In this way, the SCL appears to distinguish between competition considerations and public interest considerations and ensures that the latter will not arbitrarily prevail over the former as may likely be the case where the two groups' considerations are handled by the same person.

[81] See Article 14 of the SCL.

investigations *ex officio* or following the receipt of a complaint by the Minister of Economy and Trade, the government, undertakings, professional associations, consumer associations or the Chambers of Industry and Agriculture.[82] Strict requirements appear to be imposed on the council on several fronts. For example, in relation to complaints received the council must provide the necessary details where it rejects a complaint either because the matter falls beyond its jurisdiction or because the complaint is not supported by the necessary facts or evidence. In case of an acceptance of a complaint the council must publish – along with its decision accepting the complaint – an indication of whether the complaint merits punishment. This requirement appears to be unnecessarily strict given that the council can only be expected to reach such a conclusion where it has carried out the necessary investigation and certainly not at the stage of deciding to accept the complaint.[83]

The powers of the council are fairly wide and include both administrative and judicial characters. In relation to the latter,[84] the council will be able to order the termination of a situation restricting competition or to impose conditions on how certain practices or behaviour may be conducted; declare situations within the scope of the SCL null and void; refer the matter to the Public Prosecutor for enforcement actions to be taken and penalties to be imposed; and in the case of abuse of dominance by one or more undertakings following a merger to order such undertaking(s) to amend, complete or terminate all agreements or contracts which effected the merger. In addition, quite drastically the SCL arms the council with the power to 'shut down' temporarily the business activities of the undertaking(s) found in breach of the SCL for a period not exceeding three months, without such activities being allowed to resume until such undertaking(s) put an end to the condemned behaviour. The idea behind including this power to the list was taken from the Moroccan experience. As we saw in chapter 5, a shut-down order is available to the courts under the Moroccan competition

[82] See Article 17 of the SCL. The council's deliberation of the complaints received will be behind closed doors. However, it is possible for other sessions of the council to be public, for example in the case of Article 22 situations where a case is remitted by the Damascus Civil Court of Appeal to the council. See the discussion at p 291 below in relation to judicial action.

[83] This requirement compares less favourably with the *more reasonable* requirement contained in Article 14 of the SCL in relation to merger notification and investigations, where the council will have up to 100 days to complete its investigation and reach its decision.

[84] See Article 21 of the SCL.

law regime, though it appears wider than that included in the SCL. The Syrian model – if adopted – would be a limited version of that found in the Moroccan competition law regime given that the council will not be able to make use of the power as an action of first resort but rather to revert to it in cases where the undertaking(s) in question fail to comply with an order to terminate a problematic or harmful situation. Nevertheless, the power appears to be draconian and arguably is unnecessary given the adverse consequences, which – as we saw in chapter 5 – may follow from its exercise.

#### 9.2.8.3 The courts

Decisions of the council must be notified to the relevant parties in order to afford them an opportunity to challenge such decisions. The council's decisions may be appealed to the Damascus Civil Court of Appeal with expertise in intellectual property rights cases. The court has the power to confirm, amend, cancel and remit the decision to the council.

### *9.2.9 Penalties, remedies and damages*

A host of different types of penalties and remedies are contained in Chapter 7 of the SCL in addition to the possibility of settlements and private actions for damages, which the proposed law encourages and facilitates.

#### 9.2.9.1 Financial sanctions and penalties

Under the SCL, the council has the power, subject to other penalties which may be imposed by the courts, to impose fines on any person who: initiates or conducts activities prohibited under the SCL; contravenes a decision of the council ordering the termination of a prohibited activity; effects or contributes to effecting a merger within the scope of the SCL: without it being notified to the council, or if notified does so prior to the council delivering its decision, or in contravention of a council's decision prohibiting the merger, or in contravention of one or more of the conditions attached by the council to the clearance of the merger; and who supplies false information to the council or refused to supply information or intentionally obstructed the council's work.[85] The fine in this case may be one of two different types depending on the circumstances of the case. First, there is a possibility of a fine ranging from a

[85] See Article 24 of the SCL.

minimum of 1 per cent to a maximum of 10 per cent of the turnover of the undertaking(s) concerned generated in the relevant market. The fact that the reference is to turnover generated in the *relevant market* as opposed to turnover generated *globally* or *nationally* clearly gives the council a great deal of discretion in fixing the level of the final fine. Moreover, this reference to the relevant market may be considered to be a cause for undermining legal certainty given that establishing the relevant market involves a considerable level of uncertainty and subjectivity and may in practice mean that the undertakings concerned will find it difficult to predict the kind of fine which will be imposed in their case.

The second type of fine, on the other hand, will be used in cases where it is not possible to calculate the turnover of the undertaking(s) concerned. In this case a fixed fine will be imposed ranging from a minimum amount of 100,000 to 1 million Syrian Pounds.

#### 9.2.9.2 Penalties imposed on natural persons

The SCL does not exempt a natural person who contributed in 'bad faith' to the planning, organisation or execution of the offences mentioned in Article 24 of the SCL. Such a person may be subjected to a term of imprisonment between one and three years, a fine ranging from half a million to 15 million Syrian Pounds or both of these penalties. The courts may also order the penalty to be published in one or more daily newspapers at the expense of such a person. The SCL therefore contains fairly serious penalties in the case of breaches of its provisions by a natural person. In a remarkable fashion, however, the SCL opens the possibility for a natural person to face a more serious penalty than a legal person.[86]

#### 9.2.9.3 Settlements

Article 25 of the SCL provides the Prime Minister or a person acting on his behalf with the power to reach a decision ordering a settlement in the case of any breach listed in Article 24 before a final decision is delivered by the court in return for a payment of an amount not less than double the minimum fine and not exceeding double the maximum fine stipulated in Article 24. This provision was taken from the Egyptian Act on

[86] Apart from the possibility of a fine, as we noted above in cases where it is not possible to calculate the turnover, a fixed fine will be imposed which does not exceed 1 million Syrian Pounds.

the Protection of the Freedom of Competition, Article 21 of which contains a similar provision.[87] As we noted in relation to our discussion of this article, such a power given to a politician to order or reach settlements is considered to be controversial.

#### 9.2.9.4 Penalties designed for Commission officials

The SCL contains another close similarity to the Egyptian Act in addition to the one just discussed. This concerns the possibility of a penalty being imposed on officials of the commission found to have committed a breach of confidential information obtained through an application of the provisions of the SCL. Such a person will be subject to imprisonment ranging from three months to three years, a fine ranging from 100,000 to 1 million Syrian Pounds or both. In the previous chapter, we discussed the rationale and controversy surrounding such provision under the Egyptian competition law regime and the same comments made there would apply here.[88]

#### 9.2.9.5 Injunctions

By virtue of Article 28 of the SCL the council will have the power to impose an injunction on an undertaking(s) found to have breached Articles 5 or 6 of the SCL, as an alternative to the penalties open to it.[89] In such circumstances the council will be able to prevent such undertaking(s) from conducting any commercial activity with public authorities for a period of not less than a year but not exceeding three years.

#### 9.2.9.6 Damages

The SCL contains an important feature also found in the competition laws in other MECs,[90] namely its encouragement and facilitation of private enforcement. Article 29 paves the way for such actions and

[87] See p 247 above for a relevant discussion. It would be important to note, however, that it is not entirely clear from the wording of Article 25 of the SCL whether settlements in this case apply to both firms and individuals, although the legislative intent appears to indicate that settlements should apply to both.

[88] See p 246 above for an account on Article 23 of the Egyptian Act on the Protection of the Freedom of Competition.

[89] Articles 5 and 6 respectively deal with collusion between undertakings and abuse of dominance.

[90] See in particular the right to compensation provided under Tunisian and Turkish competition law regimes to parties who have suffered harm as a result of competition law infringement.

confirms the right of a person harmed by a situation prohibited under the SCL to bring an action for damages against the undertaking(s) concerned. In this case, the action will be brought before the Civil Court of First Instance specialising in intellectual property cases.

### *9.2.10 Reflections*

Looking at the SCL, it becomes clear that it brings together a variety of elements and ideas taken from different sources: the Set of UNCTAD, the competition rules of the EC, the competition laws of several MECs and the competition policy element of the agenda of the WTO. This policy choice and approach appear to have been facilitated by the government's modified policy towards greater consultation of the experience of other nations in the field of competition law and enhanced awareness of the direct link between the formulation of competition law in the Republic and international obligations, particularly those tied to the Association Agreement with the EC and to the expected WTO accession. It is in fact the case that in relation to the latter, Syria has been forced to adopt a competition law domestically. In this way, EC competition law regime has been influential, though one should perhaps accept that this was due not only to the obligations under the Association Agreement but also to the fact that the EC regime is a highly successful one, which as we have noted before has come to be the preferred model for many countries around the world seeking to adopt or modify domestic competition rules. Equally important to accept, however, is the fact that Syria has come to demonstrate a fairly mature understanding in relation to the SCL and has not simply engaged in a mere 'cut-and-paste' exercise when consulting the EC regime. On the contrary, attention has been given to the fact that Syria is a developing country and it would be prudent if not necessary to adopt a competition law which is harmonised with the type of competition rules meeting the special circumstances and growth needs of developing countries. Hence the government's decision to turn to the Set of UNCTAD, which – although an international code – was initiated by developing countries. Syria appears to have gone further, however, in seeking to bring the SCL closer to the competition laws of other Arab countries. Therefore, one is able to identify the Tunisian, Egyptian, Moroccan, Yemeni and even the Saudi element within the SCL. This is a novel approach and sets Syria apart as the only MEC to consider including a 'regional' dimension within its domestic rules. This is a positive step which if matched by other MECs will make the realisation of a regional approach to competition law and the development of a regional agreement, such as the proposed Pan-Arab Competition Regulations much more likely.[91]

As we saw above the SCL contains socio-economic goals, which receive particular expression in relation to the state intervention mechanism contained in Article 4 of the SCL. These goals are compatible with the broader goal of the SCL to further the social market model which has been emerging in Syria as an alternative to the model of state control and planning.

It would be interesting to reflect not only on the specific provisions of the SCL but also on the type of competition policy, which appears to be emerging slowly in Syria. This type of competition policy appears highly interesting and seems to transcend the 'traditional' boundaries of competition policy as known from the experience of many countries around the world. Under the Syrian model, protecting the process of competition is important and for this reason the SCL prohibits different types of business phenomena which are likely to harm this process. However, the model goes further and advocates the use of competition law in non-competition-based situations, most notably in its prohibition of artificial barriers to entry which may limit or damage conditions of competition, encouragement of economic growth and development and utilisation as a mechanism to enable Syria to make the transition from a controlled economy to a free market economy. The latter two elements are apparent from the competition law regimes of other MECs. In relation to the first, however, the Syrian model appears to stretch competition policy towards the trade policy arena; hence the concern of the SCL with hindrance to international trade which we discussed above. This is a highly non-traditional use of competition law and policy which in the case of Syria can be explained with reference to the impending WTO accession of the country. Issues of market access and hindrance to flows of trade and development have always been considered to belong to the realm of trade policy as opposed to competition policy though overlap between the policies in relation to these issues is possible in practice.[92] Adding these additional components to competition policy has been a purely policy choice by Syria, which should be

[91] See pp 319–24 below for a discussion on these regulations.

[92] See generally Dabbah, *The Internalisation of Antitrust Policy* (Cambridge, 2003), chapter 8.

viewed from a political angle. Syria has for long suffered from international isolation, which the Republic has come to address with international openness. Such openness is considered to be vital for several reasons. International economic developments have therefore come to be regarded as ones that cannot be ignored and Syria has identified that in adopting a specific competition law its policy should be to demonstrate openness and an appreciation of international economic affairs. This in turn has translated into the Syrian competition policy embodying trade policy elements.

# 10

# Conclusions

The Middle East is a region with unlimited economic opportunities. Regrettably, however, these opportunities have always been overshadowed by serious challenges facing almost all MECs and their citizens posed by poverty, illiteracy and conflict, to name but a few. There is perhaps no other 'man-' or 'government-made' reality more bitter and frustrating than the one prevailing in the Middle East. In light of this, it is all the more important to appreciate the remarkable skills enjoyed by many citizens in the region to achieve economic prosperity and to seek innovative ways of promoting enterprise and improving the productivity of MECs and the Middle East as a whole. Equally important here is an appreciation of the considerable efforts made by MECs themselves to advance their economic causes and interests. For many years, Middle Eastern economies were largely underdeveloped, a situation that has come to change in recent times with the noticeable – albeit in the case of some MECs slow – economic transformation throughout the region. Serious attention has come to be given by almost all MECs to achieving highly important economic objectives such as: privatisation within different sectors of domestic economies; trade liberalisation; attracting foreign investment; and establishing technologically advanced and services-based economies. Engaging in these initiatives by different MECs has created fresh hopes for building a generally enabling, transparent and non-discriminatory environment – resting on the idea of having a process of competition – within which domestic and foreign investment can flourish. These hopes have been strengthened with the economic and structural reform programmes set up by different MECs and the enactment of crucial laws and the formulation of key economic policies as part of these programmes. Among these laws and policies, competition law and policy have received particular emphasis. As we saw in previous chapters, competition law and policy currently rank high on the national (political and economic) agenda of most MECs.

## 10.1 Competition in Middle Eastern style

Despite the enormous efforts made over the years to analyse, understand and question competition – whether as a concept or as a phenomenon – a degree of uncertainty remains over whether competition should be considered as a means to an end or an end in itself.[1] This uncertainty can be seen in the case of MECs. The experience of different MECs shows that competition has been considered as both a means to an end *and* as an end in itself. On the one hand, a declared goal within the competition law regimes of these countries is to have competition in the domestic economy. On the other hand, in practice competition has been treated as a tool to achieve a variety of objectives, ranging from economic efficiency and the maximisation of consumer welfare to ensuring economic development and sustainable growth.

Putting the means/end issue to one side, a question that is certainly worth asking concerns the extent to which competition is *desired* in the Middle East and how it is viewed. There are many situations one could identify in which the mentality in the region is driven by competition though in a negative sense. On the whole, Middle Eastern competition has been more of *Modarabah* as opposed to *Monafasah*.[2] The former is a type of competition which has a connection to both competition law and the law on unfair competition. Under competition law, *Modarabah* is a form of 'rivalry' aimed at 'getting-rid' of a rival – mainly through practices of predatory pricing and rebates – for the purposes of capturing the market in order to enjoy a quiet life. Under the law on unfair competition, *Modarabah* involves discrediting a competitor, making allegations against such competitor and engaging in fraudulent behaviour and dishonest practices. *Monafasah*, on the other hand, is a form of competition which is concerned with 'winning' on merit, by striving for the custom of people through legitimate means. In other words, *Monafasah* is a form of competition which competition law aims to protect and one to which the law on unfair competition does not apply.

Over the years, different MECs have come to pay attention to *Modarabah* by enacting rules – mainly unfair competition laws – aimed at eliminating such practices; some MECs did so as early as the first quarter

[1] See Dabbah, *The Internationalisation of Antitrust Policy* (Cambridge, 2003), pp 27–28.

[2] *Modarabah* and *Monafasah* are Arabic terms. Their equivalents in other Middle Eastern languages are *Taharot bilti-Hogainit* and *Taharot* (in Hebrew); *Haksiz Rekabet* and *Rekabet* (in Turkish); and *Reghabateh Monsefaneh* and *Reghabat* (in Farsi).

of the twentieth century.[3] As a result, *Monafasah* was pushed to the sidelines. To a certain degree it is possible to say that this has been caused by a misconception within many parts of the region over the application of the rules on unfair competition with many believing that these rules could be used as an instrument to fight *all* harmful competition practices and that by fighting such practices competition will simply exist. It can be argued that this misconception remains in a *limited* form until the present day: noticeable confusion continues to cloud the difference between *Modarabah* and *Monafasah* and how these two forms of competition should be treated. Such a state of affairs is problematic and would certainly require careful attention and consideration, particularly to facilitate a cultural transformation from the mentality and ideology of *Modarabah* to that of *Monafasah*. This is where competition advocacy becomes a highly crucial and desirable tool for competition authorities and for public authorities in MECs to revert to in order to achieve a change of thinking and to build a robust competition culture, i.e. a culture of *Monafasah*.

## 10.2 Recognising the value of competition and competition law

The discussion in the previous section on the prominence of *Modarabah* and its overshadowing of *Monafasah* should not lead to an oversight of the rich history of protecting competition which can be found in the Middle East: the concept of competition is a very old one as far as the region is concerned and the value of competition was recognised over fourteen centuries ago. This rich history has not come to be reflected in modern times, however: as MECs began their journey through those times insufficient and inadequate recognition was given to the concept and idea of competition and the need to protect it. This 'negative' development unfolded in remarkable contrast to the way in which competition came to be viewed within the rest of the world. Whereas, during a large part of the twentieth century many countries around the world made concentrated and important efforts to recognise the value of competition and the need to protect it by developing and strengthening systems of competition law (as well as other efforts which took shape on the international level),[4] most MECs moved towards more

[3] Lebanon, for example, adopted rules on unfair competition in 1924.

[4] See for example the draft Havana Charter proposing the creation of an International Trade Organisation (1948), the 1953 recommendation of United Nations Economic and

monopolisation and state control and planning in different sectors of their domestic economy. This often took place through strengthening the economic control of a few powerful families and individuals; thus, in almost every MEC the key sectors of the economy ended up being controlled by fewer than ten families. This has led to strong 'concentration of wealth' in the hands of a few and appears to have minimised the prospects for a fair and equitable distribution of wealth within society.

The insufficient and inadequate recognition given to the value of competition within different MECs resulted in a remarkable absence of specific competition laws and policy in the region. This is highly interesting given that, among other things, twenty of the twenty-one countries concerned do maintain a fairly strong Islamic culture and tradition. Those countries have clearly failed to appreciate the importance Islam attaches to the need to protect competition and eradicate practices undermining it. The situation, however, began to change at the beginning of the 1990s in particular, with considerable attention being given by an increasing number of MECs to the value of competition and the need to develop competition law and policy domestically. This development, however, can be seen more as a response to international pressure both within and outside the field of competition law rather than a gradual internal or national awareness within those countries. A close examination – as the one offered in previous chapters of the book – of how competition law came to be developed in different MECs reveals that this has mainly happened due to international obligations;[5] encouragement by third countries and international organisations;[6] a desire by some of those countries to join regional blocks and communities;[7] and the process of globalisation.[8] MECs have come to adopt competition laws with modern elements borrowed from competition law regimes in the developed world and the competition rules and standards developed by international organisations; by looking at the experience of other nations with competition law and policy MECs have come to associate having a competition law and policy with economic progress, sustained

Social Council (ECOSOC) and the work of UNCTAD, the OECD and more recently the WTO and the International Competition Network (ICN).

5 See for example how Syria's accession to the WTO has been conditioned upon the country meeting several requirements. One of these requirements concerns changes to Syria's economic laws and introducing a specific competition law.

6 Notable in this regard are the efforts of the European Commission, the OECD, the World Bank and UNCTAD.

7 This is demonstrated by Turkey's efforts to join the EU.

8 A good example is furnished by Egypt's enactment of its Law on the Protection of Competition and the Prevention of Monopolistic Practices.

growth, modernisation of domestic economies and building a market economy. A good example here is furnished by the current concentrated efforts of Kuwait, Lebanon, Sudan and the United Arab Emirates to adopt a competition law. This important development has occurred in parallel to the wave of deregulation which came to cover many sectors in MECs in recent years. Among other things, this has pushed the competition law 'question' high on the agenda of national governments. However, the risk attached to this shift in approach is that modern competition laws have come to be introduced and developed in MECs without sufficient understanding on the part of MECs of what competition entails or what its role in the economy is. Thus, the legislative developments in the field appear to out-step the maturing and developing of competition as a concept, as free-market ideology and as a culture.

## 10.3 Different forms of competition law but the same competition policy

Competition law within the Middle East has developed in different forms. In those countries in which some form of competition law has been introduced, the law even bears different names. In Israel – the first MEC to adopt specific competition legislation – it is called the Restrictive Business Practices Law. In Tunisia it is called the Law on Competition and Prices. In Turkey it is called the Law on the Protection of Competition. In Jordan and Saudi Arabia the law is called Competition Law. In Qatar – the latest MEC to follow suit – it is called the Law on Protection of Competition and Prohibition of Monopolistic Practices. However, as the discussion and evaluation conducted in relation to these different laws in previous chapters showed, differences between MECs in the field of competition law exist not only in relation to the name and wording of the laws, but also in relation to how these laws are actually enforced. Despite these differences, MECs can be said to have an interesting form of competition policy which, when placed under a magnifying glass, appears to be a policy that includes all policies aiming to achieve trade liberalisation, prevent barriers to entry to the market and facilitate markets which are contestable.[9] All of these issues

[9] A contestable market is one in relation to which there is a realistic likeliness that firms located outside the market (potential competitors) can easily enter the market and begin to compete when market conditions, including market imperfections, provide the opportunity to do so. See Bailey, 'Contestability and the design of regulatory and antitrust policy' 71 *American Economic Review* 178 (1981); Baumol, Panzar and Willig, *Contestable Markets and the Theory of Industry Structure* (1988).

have come to receive expression in the formulation and implementation of competition policy in different MECs; in fact these factors also feature among the goals expressed in the laws of some of these countries. Thus, competition policy seems to have been given a wider framework, which is additionally defined by issues of market access and removal of barriers hindering trade and investment. In this way, governments in MECs have come to use competition law for the purposes of enabling them to achieve a change of outlook: from a situation of state control and planning with the state acting as a 'controller' to the situation of a free market economy with the state acting as a 'regulator' of behaviour and practices of private firms.

An additional similarity of policy approach among different MECs revolves around a high degree of intervention in the market place and giving domestic competition rules a social 'orientation'. There appears to be a particular interest in regulating prices of certain commodities in particular[10] as well as the behaviour of powerful firms in the market.[11] This particular regulatory approach – which differs from the *laissez-faire* approach seen in many Western countries – shows competition law as being a tool for not merely protecting competition but also helping create and promote competition with a mechanism of extra-regulatory function available to the government. The model of competition regulation that has come to be used in those countries therefore appears to be unique and interesting given that apparently an increasing number of MECs have come to embrace the belief in the market mechanism and the desirability of competition in the market place as a tool for the purposes of economic development. However, these countries have been reluctant to relinquish their control of the market totally and as a result they seem interested in reaping the benefits of competition without a readiness to accept the risks that may flow from it, such as a possible increase in price to reward additional innovation and investment on the part of firms and difficulties created for inefficient firms which might struggle in a climate of heated rivalry. Indeed, this shows that competition has not been fully accepted by all MECs, many of which have shown little interest in abandoning their heavy price-regulation mechanism. Perhaps this is understandable given the lack of market stability and the questionable maturity and responsibility of private firms to seek economic efficiency

[10] See for example the discussion in chapters 6 and 7 in relation to Jordan and Saudi Arabia respectively.

[11] See chapter 3 which discusses enforcement by the Israel Antitrust Authority.

and refrain from behaviour or conduct harmful to consumers, competition and the public interest at large. To be fair, it is perhaps necessary to have some price regulation in the case of certain commodities such as milk and wheat. In the Middle East these are considered to be hugely essential as basic products and leaving them to free market forces may lead to an *increase* as opposed to a *decrease* in prices and to *exploitation* as opposed to *welfare maximisation*, not only due to the risks of anti-competitive behaviour or abuse of dominance but also because the price of these products is susceptible to a change upwards even in the absence of harmful practices. A change of this nature would prove extremely damaging to consumers throughout the Middle East.[12] The possibility for intervention by the government to regulate prices *in exceptional cases* should not therefore be considered as objectionable. It is important to note the emphasis in this proposition, however: intervention should be an exception rather than the rule, and the issue of price regulation may certainly be considered as controversial and problematic in relation to other sectors or commodities.

## 10.4 MECs without a specific competition law and policy

Despite the fundamental shift in position made by almost all MECs in recent years, several MECs have not adopted specific competition legislation. Some of these countries were discussed in previous chapters;[13] four MECs which have not been discussed however are Iran, Iraq, Palestine and Sudan.

### *10.4.1 The Islamic Republic of Iran*

Iran or the Islamic Republic of Iran has a highly interesting 'face', which is markedly different from that currently portrayed in the international political arena. Despite the adverse impressions self- and non-self-inflicted on Iran, the country has a rich tradition and its citizens enjoy a strong desire to advance knowledge and a particular interest to contribute in a meaningful way. In the economic arena, mixed impressions are often

12 It is possible to see the seriousness of such an outcome in light of the recent changes in the market for wheat and the 'sharp' increase in the price of bread seen in Europe. See for example 'Bakers set to raise price of a loaf', *Financial Times* (15 August 2006), available at www.ft.com.

13 See pp 163–7 above for a discussion on Libya and chapter 7 for a discussion on Bahrain, Kuwait, Oman and United Arab Emirates.

formed when considering the Republic's economic development and agenda: a declared aim to seek liberalisation and embrace the market mechanism and the free economy model has existed within the country for almost two decades, though in practice little interest has been shown in 'implementing' this aim. A good example here can be found in its 1991 experience when Iran imposed a Structural Adjustment Programme on itself similar to the kind normally imposed by the International Monetary Fund (IMF) on developing countries. The programme sought to set the Republic on a course towards a more market-oriented and liberal economy. The programme had the hugely ambitious (and yet to be realised) goal of introducing many structural adjustments to promote privatisation, foreign investment and deregulation. In practice, however, the Republic is still a long way from achieving this goal.

#### 10.4.1.1 The Constitution

The Constitution of the Islamic Republic of Iran, which entered into force in December 1979, divides the economy into three spheres: public, private and cooperative. The Constitution shows a clear and strong tendency towards nationalisation and the exclusion of foreign participation in the local economy which blatantly contradicts the drive towards liberalisation and privatisation as outlined above. Two articles of the Constitution are particularly worth noting in this context, namely Articles 44 and 81. According to the former 'all large-scale and *mother* industries, foreign trade, major minerals, banking, insurance, power generation, dams and large-scale irrigation networks, radio and television, post, telegraph and telephone services, aviation, shipping, roads, railroads and the like' are to be governed by the state.[14] Article 81 forbids 'concessions to foreigners for the formation of companies or institutions dealing with commerce, industry, agriculture, services or mineral extraction' a provision which effectively prevents multinational or foreign firms from doing business in Iran. Article 43 of the Constitution outlines the criteria on which the economy is based: 'the prohibition of infliction of harm and loss upon others, monopoly, hoarding, usury, and other illegitimate and evil practices' and the prohibition of 'foreign economic domination over the country's economy'.[15]

[14] Emphasis added.

[15] It is worth noting Article 153 which also forbids 'any form of agreement resulting in foreign control over the natural resources, economy, army or culture of the country as well as other aspects of the national life'.

#### 10.4.1.2 The development plans

A series of development plans have been adopted by the Iranian government to improve and strengthen the economy.[16] These development plans – which were launched in 1989 – have sought to rehabilitate the economy following the long Iraq/Iran conflict during the 1980s; facilitate privatisation by reducing government involvement in the economy and transferring state-owned enterprises to the private sector; and liberalise trade. Some of the development plans have also placed special emphasis on competitiveness,[17] boosting productivity and eliminating monopolistic behaviour and practices.

#### 10.4.1.3 Foreign participation and investment

A special Law on Encouragement and Protection of Foreign Investment was approved by the State Expediency Council in 2002, abolishing the 1955 Law on Attraction and Protection of Foreign Investment. According to the Law, foreign investment in Iran must lead to 'economic growth, technological development, improvement in the quality of goods, increase in employment opportunities, boost in exports and the country's entry into world markets'. Furthermore, according to Article 2(c) it should not entail any undertaking for the government to grant special rights to foreign investors as a result of which foreign investors will enjoy a monopolistic position.

#### 10.4.1.4 The competition law scene

Iran has not yet enacted a specific competition law or policy, though the official position adopted by the Republic at the international stage during the past five years or so conveys the impression that Iran does realise the importance and need for such a law.[18] A draft competition law has been prepared with access to this draft being limited to relevant public authorities in the Republic and their officials and very few outsiders. It is unclear when this draft will be turned into law; a realistic

[16] The Management and Planning Organisation (MPO) approves and sets guidelines for the five-year economic, social and cultural development plans in Iran. The MPO's website is available at www.mporg.ir.

[17] See for example Article 37 of the Fourth Development Plan which requires the government to encourage higher economic competitiveness.

[18] See for example the written communication submitted by Iran in July 2002 at the fourth session of Intergovernmental Group of Experts on Competition Law and Policy within the United Nations Conference on Trade and Development (UNCTAD), www.unctad.org.

prediction would point to the second half of 2008 and even possibly the first half of 2009.

At present, matters relating to competition are dealt with under the provisions contained in the Third Development Plan (2000–2004). Rules for state-owned enterprises, privatisation, monopolies and the promotion of competition in economic activities are provided in Chapters 2–4 of this plan. Articles 4–8 of Chapter 2 deal with 'reorganisation of state-owned enterprises'. According to these articles the government has the power to take a number of measures, including divestiture, dissolving or merging, for the purposes of reorganising state-owned enterprises to ensure that their resources and potential are effectively utilised. These measures may also be taken by the government to enhance the productivity and efficiency of those enterprises considered necessary to keep within the public sector and to facilitate the transfer of those enterprises, which no longer wish to operate in the public sector, to the non-public sector. Formation of state-owned enterprises is subject to the approval of the Islamic Consultative Assembly. The relevant ministry is vested with the power of managing state-owned enterprises but their governance will be autonomous and independent of the policy-making function of the ministry concerned. State-owned enterprises must only carry out those business activities provided for in their articles of association, since any other type of transaction is prohibited. It is not permissible to increase prices of goods and services provided by state-owned enterprises beyond 10 per cent annually and the prices shall be set in line with the framework provided by the government. Where the government considers it necessary to fix prices at a level below this rate, the relevant firm will be paid the difference between the imposed and the calculated price through the government's general budget.

Chapter 3 of the plan is devoted to the issue of privatisation, which is dealt with comprehensively in Articles 9–27, highlighting the importance which Iran attaches to this issue for the purposes of having a successful competition policy. It is believed that an enhancement of the private sector will enable Iran to enhance in turn its competitiveness both domestically and internationally.[19]

Finally, Chapter 4 of the plan lays down rules for the regulation of monopolies and promotion of competition in economic activities. According to Article 35, the government must abolish all monopolies and monopolistic practices. Articles 28–34 deal with how competition is

[19] See Article 116 of Chapter 14 which highlights the importance of strengthening the competitive potential of the country in international markets.

to be promoted in specific sectors, namely, post and telecommunications, transportation, tobacco, sugar, petroleum and insurance. The government is authorised to privatise the provision of postal and telecommunication services and to ensure that no monopoly is created in the non-governmental sector.

#### 10.4.1.5 Unfair competition

There has been some confusion arising sometimes – both within and outside Iran – over the competition relevance of provisions on unfair competition. In relation to unfair competition, Iran has incorporated the unfair competition rules in relation to trade mark infringements of the Paris Convention for the Protection of Industrial Property 1833 as amended over the years. Two particular provisions have come to be utilised by Iranian courts over the years contained in Article 10 A of the Convention. The first, Article 10A(2) of the Convention defines unfair competition as 'any act of competition contrary to honest practices in industrial or commercial matters'. The second, Article 10A(3) establishes three categories of cases that have to be prohibited in particular, namely 'acts of such a nature as to create confusion, false allegations of such nature as to discredit a competitor and indications which are liable to mislead the public'. Neither of these provisions, however, is a competition law tool.

### *10.4.2 Iraq*

Perhaps (sadly) the only statement about Iraq with which almost everyone agrees these days is that the country has been freed from a brutal regime to be haunted by an even more brutal force. So much is a very disturbing story for a land that 'once upon a time' flourished with its contribution to science, literature and knowledge. At present, a legal system is not *stricto senso* fully functional in Iraq and perhaps this should hardly be surprising in light of the invasion, occupation and destruction of the 'fabrics' of public institutions and society in the country. Laws pre-dating the US–British invasion in 2003 have not been erased from the statute book in their entirety, though many of them have come to be amended during the past four years.

#### 10.4.2.1 The economy and foreign investment

Prior to the recent occupation, Iraq's economy had been fully controlled by the state. Under that model of state control and planning, foreign investment was virtually prohibited. Most industries were declared to be state-owned enterprises. A change in this regard only emerged with the adoption in October 2005 of the new Constitution of Iraq. Article 25 of the Constitution provides that the state must reform the economy 'in accordance with modern economic principles to ensure the full investment of its resources, diversification of its sources, and the encouragement and development of the private sector'. Article 26 of the Constitution further requires the state to 'guarantee the encouragement of investment in the various sectors'. These two provisions are consistent with the Orders issued by the Coalition Provisional Authority (CPA), in particular Order No. 39, as amended by Order No. 46, which aims to attract foreign investment to Iraq and accordingly sets out the rules for making foreign investments in the country. These rules guarantee that foreign investors will be treated in the same way as local investors and allow unlimited degree of foreign participation in the local economy, unless otherwise specified by law; total foreign ownership of businesses in Iraq is therefore permissible. In October 2006 a new Foreign Investment Law was adopted aimed at attracting foreign investment and thereby improving the economy. This marks an effective move away from a centrally planned economy to a market economy. The aims of this Law include, among others, promoting investment and encouraging the Iraqi and foreign private sector to invest in Iraq and enhance its 'competitive capacities in local and foreign markets'. To achieve these goals a National Commission for Investment was established. According to Article 29, the provisions of the Investment Law apply to investments in all economic sectors in Iraq, except the oil and gas extraction and production and the banking and insurance sectors.

#### 10.4.2.2 WTO membership and privatisation

In September 2004 Iraq applied for membership of the WTO, which had granted it observer status in February 2004. Membership of the WTO would oblige Iraq to open up its markets and economy to competition and enable Iraqi firms to gain access to world markets. According to the government's National Development Strategy 2005–2007 the principal development goal is to 'transform Iraq into a peaceful, unified federal democracy and a prosperous, market-oriented regional economic powerhouse that is fully integrated into the global economy'. It is thus essential for Iraq to develop competitive industries if it is to compete at the global level. This it aims to do by strengthening economic growth and revitalising the private sector. For this purpose, in June 2005, a

Legislative Committee on Privatisation was established by an Executive Order.[20] The task of this committee was to prepare a draft privatisation law with the assistance of the staff of the Private Sector Development Programme of the US Agency for International Development (USAID). The draft law was intended to be developed as 'best practices' legislation which would serve as the basis of privatisation in Iraq. It is understood that the draft law has been prepared which takes into account the practices and experiences of other countries with privatisation. If adopted, the draft law would provide legal authority for the privatisation of state-owned enterprises and would explain the process through which enterprises from the public sector could be transferred to the private sector.

#### 10.4.2.3 Competition law and policy

Iraq has always lacked a specific competition law. Like some of its neighbours, several laws in Iraq have been used as competition policy tools; these, however, have been limited to the field of merger control. The most important of these tools is the Company Law,[21] which contains provisions dealing with merger and acquisition operations. Article 148 of the Law simply states that mergers are permissible. According to Article 149, in order for a merger to be valid it must not lead to 'the joint stock company losing its corporate status in favour of a limited liability company or joint liability company, the limited liability company losing its corporate status to a joint liability company and the joint stock company, the limited liability company, the joint liability company or the sole owner enterprise losing its corporate status in favour of a simple company'. The decision to merge must be made by the general assembly of each firm separately and sent to the Company Registrar within ten days, which must permit the merger within fifteen days if it is not found to be inconsistent with the Law. The firms concerned must then publish the merger in the *Bulletin* and one daily newspaper. Within sixty days of

[20] Privatisation has been considered even in the oil sector. The Iraq Study Group, established by the United States Congress in March 2006 recommended privatisation of the oil sector in Iraq and drafting a national oil law to allow foreign firms to invest in the oil sector. A draft hydrocarbon law has been prepared which allows oil exploration to be carried out in Iraq by local and international firms for the first time and proposes that the government sign production-sharing agreements with foreign firms to upgrade Iraq's oil industry. The draft law has, however, faced fierce opposition by many groups within Iraq who have expressed their concern about the possible foreign control of the industry.

[21] Law No. 21 of 1997.

this the firms must amend the 'contracts'[22] of the existing companies or draft a new one for the merged firm and send it to the Company Registrar for endorsement. The merger will be effective from the last publication date of the contract.

The Banking Law 2004 also deals with mergers in the banking sector.[23] According to Article 23 of this Law, no merger, consolidation, acquisition or assumption of liability can take place without the prior approval of the Central Bank of Iraq (CBI). The CBI must be notified ninety days in advance by any bank intending to undertake the above transactions and be given such information as it requires. The CBI will not approve a request for a merger, consolidation, acquisition or assumption of liability which would 'substantially lessen competition' unless the anti-competitive effects outweigh the positive effects resulting from the transaction. Furthermore, those proposals will also not be approved where the bank resulting from the transaction would not satisfy the criteria set for those seeking to be licensed as a new bank. In making these decisions, the financial and managerial resources as well as future prospects of the existing and proposed bank will be assessed by the CBI. Acquisition of a qualifying holding in a bank will also not be approved by the CBI if it would substantially lessen competition.[24]

The third instrument to be mentioned, which deals with merger operations, is Order No. 76 issued by the CPA. This Order authorises the consolidation and reorganisation of certain state-owned enterprises into government ministries or agencies. The Order has amended the State Companies Law[25] by allowing the merger of two or more state-owned enterprises into a single state-owned enterprise if they engage in a similar activity. All ministries involved in the running of the state-owned enterprises to be merged must agree to the merger in writing and decide as to which ministry shall be responsible for the management of the new enterprise resulting from the merger. The merger must be approved by the Administrator of the CPA in consultation with the Governing Council and will be effective from the date on which approval was granted, unless otherwise specified.

[22] A contract under the Law is equivalent to a Memorandum and Articles of Association.

[23] The Banking Law was promulgated by Coalition Provisional Authority Order No. 94, which aims at establishing 'a sound, competitive and accessible banking system for the purposes of providing a foundation for economic growth and the development of a stable Iraqi economy'.

[24] See Article 22(3) of the Law.

[25] Law No. 22 of 1997.

### 10.4.3 *Palestine*

#### 10.4.3.1 Aspiring to free-market economy

The aspirations of the Palestinian people appear to have extended beyond achieving full statehood to building a free market economy in Palestine. This extension has its foundations in the Basic Law, which was approved by the Palestinian Legislative Council as an interim constitutional document for the Palestinian Authority in February 1996.[26] Article 21 of this Basic Law provides that the 'economic system in Palestine shall be based on the principle of free market economy' and guarantees the 'freedom of economic activity'. A draft Constitution was prepared by the Palestinian Authority in March 2003, pursuant to the 'roadmap' for peace in the Middle East launched by the USA, the United Nations, Russia and the EU in 2003.[27] Article 16 of the draft Constitution provides more detailed rules relating to the economic system of Palestine than those encompassed in the Basic Law and makes a specific reference to the principle of competition. It stipulates that 'the economic system in Palestine shall be based on the principles of a free market economy, and the protection of free economic activity within the context of legitimate competition.' The draft Constitution further provides that the state 'may establish public companies legally, without prejudice to the system of free market economy'. The purpose behind this provision is to prevent public companies from operating outside a legal framework, a practice which was previously allowed in Palestine.

#### 10.4.3.2 Foreign investment

As in the case with several Arab MECs, the Palestinian Authority has adopted a series of development plans, which set out the various short and medium-term goals for the development of the Palestinian economy. These plans emphasise that the Palestinian economy is 'private-sector-driven and market based' and call for limiting the role of the public sector, enhancing the regional and global role of the Palestinian economy and its competitiveness 'to integrate it into the multilateral trading system'.[28] To achieve this, two important steps had to be taken.

[26] The draft was ratified by the late President Arafat in May 2002 and amended in March 2003.

[27] Among other things, the roadmap required the Palestinian Authority to implement a democratic constitution.

[28] To develop globally competitive industries, the Palestinian Federation of Industries (PFI) was established in 1999.

The first was to devise measures in order to support the development of the private sector.[29] The second step revolved around attracting foreign investment, which has always been considered as an influential tool in developing the local economy and supporting the aspirations of the Palestinian people. The Law on the Encouragement of Investment was adopted to provide an 'appropriate environment for encouraging investment in Palestine'.[30] The Law authorises investment in all sectors of the Palestinian economy (with 100 per cent foreign ownership of local firms being possible) and provides a number of incentives to attract foreign investment.[31] To attract and approve foreign investments, the Law established the Palestinian Investment Promotion Agency.[32]

In addition to the Investment Law, the Law on Industrial Estates and Industrial Free Zones was adopted to attract further foreign direct investment in the industrial free zones.[33] These are designated areas which enjoy customs and duty-free movement of goods and services.[34] A number of incentives are provided for local and foreign firms operating in the free zones ranging from tax and custom duties exemptions to easing restrictions on currency transfer.[35]

#### 10.4.3.3 The competition law scene

At present there is no competition legislation in existence in Palestine. However, a competition law has been drafted and is currently in the final stages at the Legislative Council. This draft competition law has been based on the competition rules of the EC. Since the national policy of the

[29] For this purpose, the Centre for Private Sector Development was created as a subsidiary of the Palestine Businessmen Association – the main private sector business association in Palestine. The role of the centre is to support the private sector through seminars, training, publications and advocacy on issues relating to specific economic sectors.

[30] Law No. 1 of 1998.

[31] These are mainly tax incentives in the form of exemptions.

[32] The agency's board of directors is chaired by the Minister of Economy and Trade and consists of members from various ministries and authorities and the private sector.

[33] Law No. 10 of 1998.

[34] The Gaza Industrial Free Zone Estate was the first operational industrial estate in Palestine.

[35] The body in charge of implementing the Law is the Palestinian Industrial Estates and Free Zones Authority (PIEFZA) which is responsible for a wide range of matters including: establishing and developing industrial free zones in Palestine; reviewing applications for the establishment of industrial free zones; analysing applications for licences to work in the industrial free zones and granting Industrial Free Zone Certificates to qualifying investors; and preparing plans and programmes for the development of industrial free zones.

Palestinian Authority is that the principles of free competition should be guaranteed in the market, the draft competition law is aimed at the prevention of anti-competitive practices. The draft has not been made public, though it is expected to surface by the beginning of 2008.

### *10.4.4 The Republic of Sudan*

In recent years, Sudan has come to enjoy huge economic potential, due in large part to the strong links the country has established with global economic powers, most notably China. This significant development has, however, been overshadowed with the Darfur crisis, which has caused considerable damage to Sudan at international level.

Currently there is no specific competition law in force in Sudan, nor is there any competition tool provided under general laws. Perhaps the only provision with competition relevance is found in Article 8 of the Constitution of Sudan 1998 which provides that 'the state shall promote the development of national economy and guide it by planning on the basis of work, production and free market, in a manner fending off monopoly, usury and fraud, and strive for national self-sufficiency for the achievement of affluence and bounty and endeavour towards justice among states and regions'. It is understood, however, that a draft competition law has been prepared which is likely to emerge sometime in 2008. The government's decision to adopt competition legislation was motivated by a desire to attract an increased foreign investment and to undertake several economic and structural reforms seeking, among other things, to comply with the rules and standards of international bodies, especially the World Bank and the IMF.

#### 10.4.4.1 Foreign investment

Attracting foreign investment into Sudan is highly important for the Sudanese government and thus it has made a number of efforts to create an environment conducive to investment. The most prominent of these was the adoption of the Investment Encouragement Act 1999. The aim of this Act is to promote and encourage investment and hence it authorises investment in the majority of economic sectors and empowers the Council of Ministers to add to the list of authorised sectors provided in section 7 of the Act. The Act also provides a number of incentives to investors, which include exemption from tax and custom duties on imports. To oversee the implementation of the Act and to develop and promote local and foreign investments, the Ministry of Investment has been established. Its responsibilities include, among others, improving the investment environment in Sudan, facilitating the investment procedures, executing strategies and policies of investment, issuing licences to investment projects, providing relevant information to investors, organising workshops, forums and conferences to highlight the advantages of investing in Sudan and developing relations with international organisations to facilitate exchange of information.[36]

In addition to adopting the Act, the government has established free zones which are governed by the Free Zones and Free Markets Law 1994. This Law provides the framework for establishing and managing free zones in Sudan.[37] A number of benefits (mainly tax exemptions) are provided to investors investing in the free zones.

#### 10.4.4.2 Economic and structural reform

In early 1990, the Sudanese government launched Sudan's Structural Adjustment Programme (SSAP), similar to those in operation by the World Bank and the IMF. The SSAP was part of the policies of the Three-Year Economic Salvation Programme (1990–1993) aimed at reforming the economy. The policies of the Three-Year Programme were reiterated in the Ten-Year National Comprehensive Plan (1992–2002). The objectives of this programme were to reduce the budget deficit, enhance the role of the private sector, privatise public enterprises, encourage local and foreign investment and deregulate controls on prices, profits and exports. Thus, in 1992 price controls were removed and prices in all sectors were determined by the market forces of supply and demand in order to liberalise the economy. Privatisation was an important feature of the Three-Year Programme and to facilitate the privatisation of public enterprises, the Revolutionary Command Council for National Salvation – the highest decision-making authority of the state at the time – implemented the Disposal of Public Enterprises Act 1990 followed by the Public Enterprise Liquidation Regulations in 1992. The High Committee for the Disposal of Public Enterprises was established by the Act, chaired by the Minister of Finance and Economy, to implement the privatisation process. Approximately 80 per cent of public enterprises

[36] The Ministry of Investment has forged close relations with the United Nations Industrial Development Organisation (UNIDO), the Arab Investment Guarantee Agency and the Multilateral Investment Guarantee Agency (MIGA) amongst a number of other regional and international organisations.

[37] Established free zones include Khartoum Free Zone, Suakin Free Zone and Aljaily Free Zone.

were identified for privatisation but less than half of these have actually been privatised. It is reported that overall the SSAP had a negative impact on the economy, as liberalisation of prices led to a dramatic increase in the price of goods and services and in turn aggravated the living conditions of people. In addition, it resulted in serious developments such as loss of employment; a number of workers were laid off due to the privatisation of public enterprises because Article 4(f) of the 1990 Act arms the High Committee for the Disposal of Public Enterprises with the power to terminate the service of the employees of the Privatisation candidates.

The Three-Year Programme advocated opening the telecommunications market to the private sector to end its monopolistic environment. Accordingly in 1993 the government undertook to reform the telecommunications sector. The state-owned Sudan Telecommunications Public Corporation (STPC) was turned into Sudan Telecommunications Company (Sudatel). In addition, in 2001 the Telecommunications Act was issued, which established the National Telecommunications Corporation (NTC) as the regulatory authority for the information and telecommunications sector. The objectives of the NTC are to regulate and promote the telecommunications sector to conform to 'development and globalisation', encourage investment in the telecommunications sector and to 'ensure and diffuse free and constructive competition … in the field of telecommunications'. Article 41 of the Act provides that 'public telecommunications services shall be provided through free competition'. As a result of the transformation it has undergone, Sudan's telecommunications sector is held to be the most modern in Africa.

## 10.5 The chances for sound cooperation

The chances for sound competition law and policy in the Middle East depend not only on factors which are unique to individual MECs, but also on the prospects for cooperation between those countries. Such cooperation can take a variety of forms in the Middle East including: bilateral cooperation, trilateral cooperation, Gulf States cooperation, Maghreb countries cooperation, Arab MECs cooperation, Muslim MECs cooperation or full regional cooperation bringing all MECs together. One interesting way of looking at these forms of cooperation could be to view them in terms of their 'ambitious' or, on the other hand, 'realistic' nature; obviously some of these forms of cooperation are more ambitious than others and conversely some are more realistic than others.

### *10.5.1 Bilateral cooperation*

A noticeable absence from the Middle East competition law scene is specific bilateral cooperation agreements. This is interesting given the strong ties enjoyed between countries in the region. One explanation for this may be that systems of competition law came to be instituted only recently in different MECs and therefore competition enforcement has not matured to an extent to make the conclusion of such agreements possible. However, there is quite a strong 'cross-border' or inter-regional trade within the Middle East and there are international firms operating in different MECs. The likelihood of anti-competitive behaviour or abusive conduct with a cross-border element is realistic.

As we saw in previous chapters bilateral free trade agreements (FTAs) have been concluded between different MECs. Some of these agreements contain competition relevance. However, FTAs are not the most suitable medium for bilateral cooperation in the field of competition law to be established. The lack of formal or specific competition bilateral cooperation agreements between different MECs does not mean, however, that cooperation is virtually non-existent in the field: as we noted in previous chapters, different forms of bilateral cooperation can be found, such as those involving joint meetings between competition officials and training seminars and workshops.

### *10.5.2 Regional cooperation: myth or reality?*

At present, the chances for a *comprehensive* regional (Middle East-wide) cooperation in the Middle East appear to be slim and perhaps even non-existent, whether with or without such cooperation including competition law and policy. It does not seem realistic for an effort, which aims at bringing the twenty-one MECs together in the field of competition law to be successful. Moreover, even if the enormous political hurdles were to be removed, it is probably premature to embrace this option given that the focus in the first place should be to reach a stage where competition law is incorporated domestically in those countries. Such comprehensive form of cooperation would have little relevance in practice if only some of those countries have domestic competition laws while in others competition law and policy are remarkably absent. The fact that this form of cooperation appears unrealistic prompts the question of what alternatives may be pursued for the purposes of enhancing cooperation in the region generally and for strengthening competition law and policy particularly. There are several possibilities here worthy of being discussed.

#### 10.5.2.1 Cooperation through the European Commission

One possibility would be to engage the Barcelona Process and the more recent European Neighbourhood Policy (ENP).[38] The idea here would be to offer a 'neutral' platform on which regional cooperation could be forged in a meaningful way. A major incentive behind such an idea is the wealth of competition law expertise available within the European Commission and its impressive 'know-how' in technical assistance and capacity-building activities. However, realising such an idea requires a strong commitment by the Commission and an even stronger commitment by individual MECs. It is unclear to what extent this is realistic especially when one consults previous experience with cooperation within the Barcelona Process and the ENP. Looking at the Barcelona Process (and its regional approach), achievements under the process appear to have been modest. To a large extent, the regional approach embodied in the process has fallen short of achieving the declared goals of the process. The causes for this appear to be the significant differences in the stages of developments of MECs, the lack of common interest uniting them and the difficulty in achieving convergence in their individual interests. The 'one size fits all' approach of the process has triggered reservation on the part of the more developed MECs over the real benefits they can reasonably expect to reap from the process. These reservations have reduced the political will of those MECs to further or deepen their involvement within the process.[39]

In more ways than one, the move on the part of the European Commission towards the ENP (with its *differential* bilateral approach) should be seen as an action taken for the purposes of filling the gaps in the Barcelona Process. Comparing the two ideas together, the ENP has a clear advantage in light of the fact that its standards and principles are

[38] See pp 15–17 above for a discussion on the idea behind and objectives of the Barcelona Process and the ENP.

[39] Examples here can be found in the case of Israel and Turkey. The Turkish Competition Authority in particular has adopted a policy of bringing itself closer to Western competition authorities and has sought to distance itself from engaging with competition authorities in other MECs.

intended to apply with a consideration of the individual circumstances of MECs. Nonetheless, the ENP itself suffers from several shortcomings as a suitable tool to further regional cooperation in the field of competition law within the Middle East. First, the ENP has as its legal basis the Association Agreements concluded by the Commission with individual MECs over the years. These Association Agreements have contributed very little towards enhancing regional cooperation. Many of the provisions contained in these agreements are vague with the competition provisions having not been implemented. Secondly, the action plans introduced within the framework of the ENP (and the Association Agreements) cover a wide range of areas, extending far beyond competition law and policy. These areas include justice and home affairs matters, science and technology issues and contact between peoples. With all of these areas being given particular importance, it is not clear what impact the action plans will have on the field of competition law or indeed how they are likely to contribute to furthering cooperation in the field. Thirdly, the ENP framework is not purely bilateral in nature or scope: a regional dimension is identifiable in light of the Commission's intention to apply the rules and standards within the framework regionally. Apart from the fact that this is bound to lead to a situation in which the lowest common denominator will be used, the Commission's approach could be said to be not entirely clear with regard to how the ENP fits with the Barcelona Process. All of these points show that the terrain facing an effort to implement this option of regional cooperation is of an extremely difficult nature.

#### 10.5.2.2 Sub-regional cooperation

Another way in which regional cooperation may be reached is through taking a longer route than the one covered under the previous option, namely by building sub-regional cooperation or introducing competition law and policy through the formation of a sub-regional block. To a large extent this form of cooperation already exists throughout the Middle East. Sub-regional cooperation can be found in the case of the Gulf Cooperation Council;[40] the Arab Maghreb Union[41] and the Agreement for the Establishment of a Free Trade Zone between the Arabic Mediterranean Nations (Agadir).[42] It is doubtful, however, to what extent this type of cooperation will be beneficial in the field of competition law and policy. On the one hand, competition law is lacking from the rules of these

[40] See chapter 7. [41] See p 13 above and chapter 5. [42] See pp 13–14 above.

communities and on the other hand, several MECs are not participants in any sub-regional form of cooperation (whether those mentioned here or others). These include Iran, Iraq, Israel, Lebanon, Sudan, Syria and Turkey.

#### 10.5.2.3 Emerging cooperation within the Arab League

The Arab League has been in existence for over sixty years. Its contribution within the economic arena, however, has been rather limited. In 1997, the idea of creating an Arab Common Market took shape and an ambitious deadline for completing this was set for 2010; it is doubtful that this deadline will be met. Furthermore, the ambit and foundations of the idea are quite ambiguous: there does not appear to be a sufficiently developed and concrete action plan for the purposes of realising this important goal. Broadly speaking the consensus appears to be that the starting point for building a common market in the Arab world should begin with comprehensive structural reform within domestic markets for the purposes of introducing free-market principles and ensuring efficiency in the operation of these markets. Structural reforms in this case should extend to defining the relationship between the public sector and the private sector and the role of the state in the functioning of markets and in relation to the business operations of firms. Structural reforms should be complemented with liberalisation of trade and facilitating the flows of trade and investment in external trade and investment in local economies.

Cooperation in the field of competition law within the framework of the Arab League should not stand alone but should be included within a wider framework of a free trade agreement or a customs union. This would provide essential support given the usefulness of such a framework for the purposes of connecting between the domestic economies of member countries. Indeed, the idea of a common market must be seen as based on this framework.

As noted in chapter 1,[43] a draft of Arab Common Competition Regulations (the Regulations) has been prepared within the Arab League's drive towards building Pan Arab capabilities in the field of competition law as part of the proposed Arab Common Market. Fairly quick progress was made with regard to producing the Regulations. However, extremely limited progress has been made in relation to their implementation: a purported final draft was produced in summer 2002 following receipt of comments by all Arab countries and the

[43] See p 13 above.

intention at that time was to submit that draft to the Economic and Social Council of the Arab League.[44] This draft would benefit from further thinking and work however, and it would be fitting to describe the draft as no more than a good first attempt.

Although bearing the word 'Regulations', the Regulations are not intended to have the binding force of the Law and therefore their role is to serve as a set of guidelines. The fact that this is so can be expected to *limit* the influence the Regulations can have in practice. The Regulations contain twenty-six articles. It could be said that the Regulations essentially take the form of a 'competition law', the provisions of which have been informed by three sources: EC competition rules, the competition laws of Arab MECs and UNCTAD's Set. The declared aim of the Regulations is to protect and encourage competition and to supervise monopolistic practices for the purposes of increasing economic activity. The Regulations apply to collusion between persons,[45] abuse of dominance and harmful mergers, though acts involving the sovereign or the exercise of prerogatives of public powers or the exercise of public tasks and activities fall outside the scope of the Regulations.[46]

**10.5.2.3.1 The prohibitions** Article 4 of the Regulations prohibits any agreement,[47] which has an object or effect of distorting free competition. The article lists as examples of such agreements those which involve: price-fixing; market or customer sharing; refusal to deal with particular suppliers or customers; collusive-tendering; hindering the entry or exit of products from markets and illegal stocking; and limitation of output, production and distribution activities.

Article 5 of the Regulations deals with abuse of dominance[48] and prohibits conduct on the part of a dominant firm with an object or effect

[44] It is understood that a detailed set of explanatory notes is being drafted and will also be submitted to the council for approval. This set of explanatory notes is intended to serve as an accompanying document to the Regulations for the purposes of explaining the different provisions in the Regulations and their application.

[45] A person is defined in Article 2 as a 'natural or legal person, or any other legal entity regardless of its form'.

[46] See Article 3 of the Regulations.

[47] An agreement is defined in Article 2 of the Regulations to include a contract or arrangement whether written or oral, express or implied between two or more persons. The Regulations do not provide whether the prohibition applies to both horizontal and vertical agreements, though the intention of the draftsmen was that this is the case.

[48] Dominance for the purposes of the Regulations can be of two types: single firm dominance and collective dominance. According to Article 2 a dominant position is a position enabling a person or group of persons to control or affect market activities.

harming competition, in particular conduct involving discrimination; refusal to supply without objective justification; predatory pricing; tying between products; complicating the activities of competitors;[49] and engaging in acts leading to unfair or artificial pricing.

Neither of the prohibitions above, however, would bite in the circumstances covered under Article 6, under which the possibility for exemption is provided. According to the article an exemption is possible in three situations. First, where the behaviour or conduct furthers the public interest and leads or is likely to lead to reduction in costs or improvement in production and distribution or technical progress. Secondly, where the conduct or behaviour is required by law or is necessary for the purposes of implementing or applying a provision within any law. The third situation concerns practices of selling below cost. The article provides that selling below cost is caught within the net of the prohibitions, except where the practice is carried out in a situation in which one of the following prevails: the relevant products have short expiry dates; such sale is ordered by court; the purpose behind the sale is to 'get rid' of old stock in order to make way for new products; or the products have 'special characteristics' and are subject to supervision and control by the state.

Finally, it is worth noting that the scope of the Regulations also extends to concentrations[50] creating a dominant position. Chapter 3 (Articles 8–10) of the Regulations deals with concentrations in a rather brief manner. Article 8 provides for prior notification by any person intending to merge with or acquire another where the operation leads to the creation of a dominant position. The article is silent on when this prior-mandatory notification must be effected. It does state, however, that concentrations must be reviewed within a strict (apparently non-extendable) ninety days. According to Article 9 a decision to clear a concentration may be revoked at a later date where it turns out that the information supplied was false. Article 10 makes it clear that a concentration giving rise to competition concerns may be cleared if it is shown

[49] As we saw in chapter 8, the idea of 'complicating' the activities of competitors features in the Egyptian competition law regime.

[50] A concentration is defined in Article 2 as an operation involving a merger or acquisition. An acquisition, according to the article, occurs where there is a transfer of total or partial ownership from one or more persons to another whether through shares, assets or any other means giving such person the ability to influence the strategic decision-making of the former. Although the article does not mention 'control' specifically, the understanding is that the 'transfer' and 'influence' referred to therein concern control.

that the concentration contributes to economic progress in a way that would compensate for the competition harm.

**10.5.2.3.2 Enforcement and penalties** The Regulations are not intended to create a supranational enforcement mechanism. Rather, they provide for the rules referred to in the previous section to be enforced by competition authorities[51] at domestic level. To achieve this, however, Chapter 4 (Articles 12–23) of the Regulations provides for the creation within each Arab country of a competition authority to be armed with a wide range of powers and responsibilities enabling such an authority effectively to enforce the competition rules domestically. Among the powers listed in Article 12 are conducting investigations (including searches);[52] reviewing notified concentrations; engaging in competition advocacy and building a culture of competition; cooperation with foreign competition authorities; preparing annual reports to be submitted to the relevant bodies or persons in the country; and making decisions.[53] The other provisions in Chapter 4 simply deal with issues such as the expertise and qualifications of individuals to be appointed as competition officials;[54] the obligation on officials to observe confidentiality in proceedings within the authority and to avoid conflict of interest;[55] and the way in which decisions should be notified to the persons concerned.[56]

[51] Under Article 2 of the Regulations, an authority is defined as the competent body with responsibility to implement and enforce the Regulations in accordance with the internal rules in operation within each Member State, i.e. each Arab country.

[52] This power is also dealt with under Article 17, which provides for the rights of the officials of the authority to have access to all files and documents and to make copies of these as they see fit.

[53] According to Article 18 the authority will have the power to order a harmful situation to be brought to an end.

[54] See Article 13. [55] See Articles 22 and 21 respectively.

[56] Article 20 is quite detailed on how decisions reached by the competition authority should be notified to the persons concerned. It provides that such decisions must be notified in writing (with confirmation of receipt) to such person(s) with a copy of the decisions being sent to the relevant Minister. According to Article 2 the relevant Minister is the Minister with responsibility for the implementation of the Regulations. This in practice is likely to be the Minister for Trade, Industry or the Economy, depending on the title accorded to this ministerial position in the relevant country. Article 20 also provides that decisions of the authority may be appealed to the competent court in the country concerned. It may be worth noting here Article 18, which provides for the opportunity for the relevant persons to be heard and to express their views on the findings of the authority before the final decision is reached.

Considering the competition law regimes in existence within Arab countries at present (examined in previous chapters of the book), it should be clear that the provisions of the Regulations on enforcement are markedly different from some of those regimes. The Regulations acknowledge the differences in this regard and therefore provide that the provisions in Chapter 4 are without prejudice to the right of individual countries to determine the nature of the authority created under the relevant competition law regime, its composition and its operation.[57]

In relation to penalties, although the Regulations purportedly devote an entire chapter to this issue, this chapter in fact consists of a single provision merely providing for penalties to be determined by individual countries and for these penalties to be doubled in the case of repeated competition law infringements.[58]

**10.5.2.3.3 Commentary** Prior to commencing the drafting process of the Regulations, there was a debate on whether they should serve as a blueprint for a regional competition law to be enforced at a supranational level within the Arab League or as guiding principles for members of the Arab League to follow for the purposes of adopting competition law in their domestic legal systems or modifying their existing rules according to the wording and spirit of the Regulations. Of course at the time this debate emerged a dissimilar position to the present one had existed throughout the Arab world, namely that competition law and policy were absent from the vast majority of Arab countries.[59] In the end the *sensible* decision was made to follow the latter option.[60] It would have been futile and controversial to opt for a regional model that could have resulted in a 'top-down' as opposed to a 'bottom-up' approach to competition law and policy. Those in favour of the top-down model had one good argument, however: the idea was to avoid a situation where some countries would unnecessarily or unavoidably delay the enactment of domestic competition rules and the creation of a regional system of competition law, which would have been beneficial for the purposes of addressing 'cross-border' competition problems. Additionally, through following this model it would have been possible to guarantee that the

[57] See Article 23. [58] See Article 24.

[59] At that time, Jordan, Saudi Arabia, Egypt and Qatar had not adopted their competition laws and so only Algeria, Morocco and Tunisia had domestic competition legislation.

[60] In fact the decision was reached because of political objection to the regional approach. From a competition law perspective, however, the correct outcome was reached.

same standards, rules and policy and the same competition culture and approach would flourish as opposed to a situation where the rules would have to be 'adjusted' to a common approach at a later stage. Nonetheless, opting for this model would have been problematic. Apart from the fact that the model represents an ambitious attempt which requires political approval at the level of heads of states, in the Arab world the domestic competition problems outnumber those with a cross-border element, thus the regional model would have had limited impact on such problems. Furthermore, as we saw throughout this book, there is a lack of a sufficiently robust and widespread competition culture in all the MECs and Arab countries in particular and to a large degree insufficient recognition of competition or understanding of it. A regional model would have contributed very little to building such a culture given the daunting task that the regional competition authority would have had to deal with and the differences that exist between the countries concerned. It should be clear therefore that the regional system of competition law would not have offered a good substitute for domestic systems of competition law in the different countries.

There is no doubt the Regulations can be expected to make an important contribution on several fronts, starting from the fact that they provide a centre of gravity to which all domestic competition law regimes of Arab countries would be linked, to the fact that they would open a new chapter in the regional development of competition law and policy in the Arab world and the Middle East more generally. The drafting of the Regulations has placed competition law and policy on the regional map. Whether the contribution made by this important document will translate into concrete steps depends to a large extent on the political support individual countries are willing to offer in this regard. There is no doubt that the fact that recently competition law has come to be introduced in Saudi Arabia, Egypt, Jordan and Qatar, the fact that Lebanon and Syria[61] are at an advance stage in their competition law projects and the fact that competition law is being considered seriously in other Arab countries, most notably Kuwait and the UAE, offer hope for this to occur; competition law would have been unthinkable in all of these countries even as recently as six years ago – something that makes these important developments of huge significance.

[61] It is important to note here that Syria has in fact given important attention to the draft Regulations in preparing its draft competition law. See pp 294–5 above.

### 10.5.3 *Comparison with other regions*

The discussion above makes clear how unrealistic it is to expect meaningful cooperation to emerge in the field of competition law under current circumstances in the Middle East. What make this unrealistic is not the political hurdles, which are part of everyday life in the region; rather it is the fact that despite the existence of many similarities and commonalities between most if not all MECs, little progress has been made over the past fifty years to achieve even the most basic forms of economic cooperation, let alone serious progress in the field of competition law. This contrasts unfavourably with other key regions in the world, namely Africa, South-East Asia, the Caribbean and North and Latin America, and Europe. All of these regions have significant differences, whether in terms of language or culture, yet meaningful cooperation has materialised in these regions including even in the field of competition law and policy. Thus competition provisions have been concluded in regional communities in Africa with the creation of the Economic and Monetary Community of Central Africa (CEMAC), Common Market for Eastern and Southern Africa (COMESA), West African Economic and Monetary Union (UEMOA WAEMU), Southern African Customs Union (SACU), East African Community (EAC) and Southern African Development Community (SADC); in Asia with the creation of the Association of South East Asian Nations (ASEAN), South Asian Association for Regional Cooperation (SAARC) and Asia-Pacific Economic Cooperation (APEC); in the Americas and the Caribbean with the creation of Southern Common Market (MERCUSOR), the Andean Community, Caribbean Community and Common Market (CARICOM), North American Free Trade Agreement (NAFTA), the Central America–Dominican Republic–United States Free Trade Agreement (CAFTA-DR) and the various Latin American Free Trade Agreements; and in Europe with the creation of the European Community (EC), European Free trade Association (EFTA) and the European Economic Area (EEA).

The experience with these communities has been that building regional cooperation in the field of competition law has several key benefits including: addressing market access problems; harmonisation in national rules and standards which is desirable especially from the perspective of firms who are interested in reducing their costs, having greater legal certainty and operating in similar regulatory environments; adequately addressing competition problems with a cross-border dimension; facilitating the provision of technical assistance between the different (participating) competition authorities and enhancing capacity-building; and creating economically enhancing tools enabling firms to improve their enterprise and to achieve diversification in products and placing consumers in a position to enjoy lower prices and improved product quality.

## 10.6 Competition law: a bridge between civilisations

Islamic principles and values have found their way into the legal systems of all twenty-one MECs.[62] As far as competition law and policy are concerned, however, there has been a limited incorporation of Islamic ideas, concepts and values; principally this incorporation has occurred in relation to one aspect only, namely price regulation and nationalisation. As we saw in chapter 2 Islam does not prohibit nationalisation, nor does it prohibit price regulation by the state in *exceptional circumstances*. In modern legal systems of MECs a very expansive vision of nationalisation has been favoured; hence the fact that public sectors have come to be huge in size. As we saw in the case of some MECs this approach appears to be based on the philosophy that the state undertakes the role of protecting and promoting the interest and welfare of its citizens and aims to conduct vital social functions. The state therefore carries out its various tasks with a social objective and responsibility. Private firms do not enjoy any understanding of this social objective and responsibility, nor are they formed and operated to further such objective or adhere to such responsibility. It was on the basis of this thinking and ideology that those countries came to have little inclination towards privatisation. With many MECs (especially the Arab world) lagging behind and with their influence diminishing over the years, MECs have come to realise the gap that has come to exist between them and the Western world, indeed with the rest of the world; and the gap as they came to perceive it between them and economic development and progress. In a concentrated effort towards dealing with this gap, privatisation and liberalisation came to be considered. Among the laws and policies used to further the process, competition law and policy came to rank very high.

[62] It is important to note that in Israel, the only non-Muslim MECs, Islamic principles are recognised within the legal system. For example, Islamic courts and tribunals exist within the judicial branch.

MECs seem to have turned to Western models of competition as opposed to Islamic tradition, principles and values with the exception of the issue of price regulation and to a limited extent the issue of market control. There may be several ways in which this development may be explained. First, there is a lack of sufficient awareness of links between Islam and competition law. This is understandable given that awareness in this case would demand sufficient or mature understanding of competition law itself, a field in which there is not adequate expertise in many MECs. Another explanation is that these MECs wanted to turn to modern laws to suit modern times. A third explanation may be that these countries thought it would be desirable to distance themselves from an Islamic approach in the field because of the concern that such an approach may prove less attractive to foreign investment and participation in local markets by foreign firms, who would naturally be familiar with legal and regulatory environment prevailing elsewhere; perhaps following Islamic tradition and values would convey the impression that *stricto senso* economic theories with legal standards will not be used and that a religious approach is being adopted instead.

* * *

Competition law and policy has an important role to play in developed as well as developing economies, both in creating and promoting a competitive environment and in building and ensuring public support for a general pro-competitive policy stance by different countries. MECs are no exception in this regard. Furthering and supporting competition law and policy must be placed among the individual governments' main economic objectives and must be made a central item on their economic agenda. By ensuring that there are effective competition law and policy and building strong systems of competition law, MECs governments can narrow the enterprise and productivity gap in existence between them and their major competitors. This view applies to all MECs with no exception: whether those with fairly established competition law and policy; those with quite young experience in the field; those with nascent competition laws; and those currently at the stage of legislating competition law.

Strong competitive forces in the domestic economies are a key driver for productivity and growth. Competition stimulates innovation by firms, economic efficiency, with better quality of products and services, greater choice and lower prices for the consumer. Competition law in

MECs needs to be placed within stronger systems, which incorporate: strong, independent and proactive competition authorities; effective tools to fight all forms of anti-competitive behaviour; a strong deterrent to firms and individuals not to engage in anti-competitive behaviour; legal certainty for all concerned with clear procedures; an increasingly international outlook based on the ideas of consistency and cooperation; and a high profile for competition policy domestically through competition advocacy. At present, it is unclear how far MECs will go towards embracing these principles. This depends on many factors found within and outside the field of competition law. Among those factors found within the field is the extent to which MECs will make an effort to understand competition and show readiness to accept both its benefits and risks.

# INDEX

# Stem Cell Bioengineering and Tissue Engineering Microenvironment

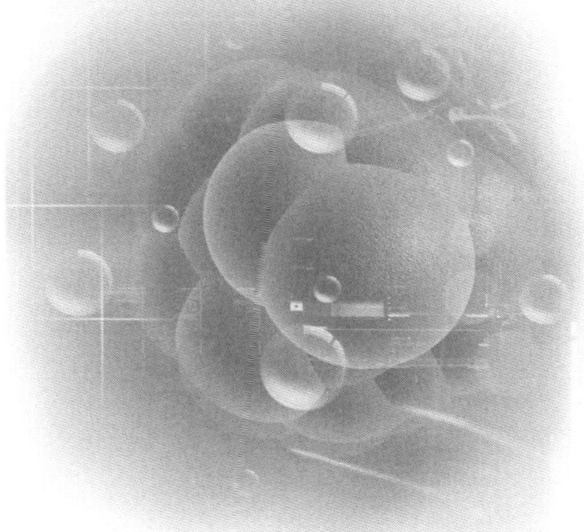

# Stem Cell Bioengineering and Tissue Engineering Microenvironment

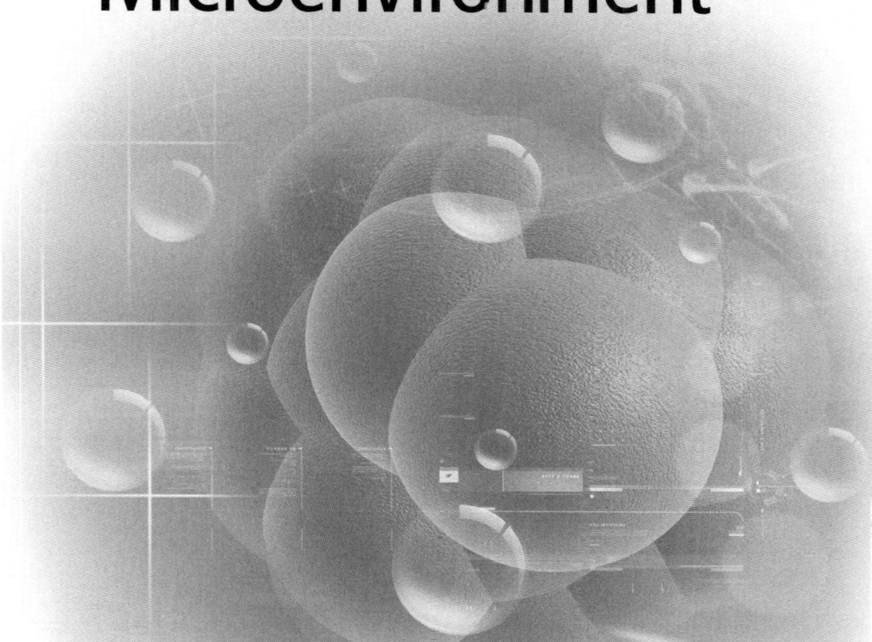

Editors

Satya Prakash & Dominique Shum-Tim

McGill University, Canada

World Scientific

NEW JERSEY • LONDON • SINGAPORE • BEIJING • SHANGHAI • HONG KONG • TAIPEI • CHENNAI

*Published by*

World Scientific Publishing Co. Pte. Ltd.
5 Toh Tuck Link, Singapore 596224
*USA office:* 27 Warren Street, Suite 401-402, Hackensack, NJ 07601
*UK office:* 57 Shelton Street, Covent Garden, London WC2H 9HE

**British Library Cataloguing-in-Publication Data**
A catalogue record for this book is available from the British Library.

**STEM CELL BIOENGINEERING AND TISSUE ENGINEERING MICROENVIRONMENT**



ISBN-13 978-981-283-788-2
ISBN-10 981-283-788-4

Typeset by Stallion Press
Email: enquiries@stallionpress.com

Printed by FuIsland Offset Printing (S) Pte Ltd Singapore

# CONTENTS

# CONTRIBUTORS

**Adil Al-Kindi,** MD, MSc
Cardiac Surgery Resident
Department of Surgery
McGill University Health Centre
Canada

**Kitipan V. Arom,** MD, PhD, FACS, FACC, FACCP, FRCST (Hon)
Director of Bangkok Heart Hospital and Cardiothoracic Surgeon
Bangkok Heart Hospital, Bangkok Hospital Medical Center
Bangkok Dusit Medical Services PLC
Bangkok, Thailand

**Rony Atoui,** MD CM, MSc
Department of Cardiothoracic Surgery
St. Vincent Health Center
Erie, Pennsylvania
USA

**Jasmine Bhathena**, PhD
Biomedical Engineering
Faculty of Medicine
McGill University
Canada

**Jean-François Cailhier,** MD, PhD
Assistant Professor
Department of Medicine, Faculty of Medicine
Institut du Cancer de Montréal and CRCHUM
Université de Montréal
Canada

**Juan C. Chachques,** MD, PhD
Director of Cardiac Research
Pompidou Hospital, Paris
Professor of Surgical Sciences
University of Paris
France

**Yijiang Chen**, MD
Professor and Chair
Department of Cardiothoracic Surgery
Jiangsu Province Hospital
The First Affiliated Hospital of Nanjing University
China

**Herman S. Cheung,** PhD
James L. Knight Professor of Biomedical Engineering
Senior Veteran Affairs Research Career Scientist
Research Service and Geriatrics Research
Education and Clinical Centre
Miami Medical Centre
USA

**Ing-Ming Chiu,** PhD
Distinguished Investigator and Acting Deputy Director
Division of Regenerative Medicine, Institute of Cellular and System Medicine
National Health Research Institutes
Taiwan, ROC

**Ray C.-J. Chiu,** MD, PhD
Professor
Department of Surgery
McGill University
McGill University Health Centre
Canada

**Wendy S. Chiu,** MDCM
Assistant Professor
Division of Geriatric Medicine, Department of Medicine
McGill University
Medical Director, Geriatric Day Hospital
McGill University Health Centre
Canada

**Alice Mira Chung,** BSc
Centre for Biomedical Engineering
Department of Medicine
Brigham and Women's Hospital
Harvard Medical School
Harvard-MIT Division of Health Sciences and Technology
Massachusetts Institute of Technology
USA
Department of Bioengineering,
University of California San Diego
USA

**Bong Geun Chung,** PhD
Centre for Biomedical Engineering
Department of Medicine
Brigham and Women's Hospital
Harvard Medical School
Harvard-MIT Division of Health Sciences and Technology
Massachusetts Institute of Technology
USA

Assistant Professor
Department of Bionano Engineering
Hanyang University
Korea

**David W. Courtman,** PhD
Department of Medicine
Ottawa Hospital Research Institute
University of Ottawa
Canada

**Xiang Gao,** PhD
Director
Model Animal Research Center
Nanjing University
China

**Yin Ge,** MD
Department of Surgery
McGill University Health Centre
Canada

**Tuanzhu Ha,** MD, PhD
Department of Surgery
East Tennessee State University
Johnson City, TN
USA

**Joshua M. Hare,** MD
Louis Lemberg Professor of Medicine
Director of the Interdisciplinary Stem Cell Institute
University of Miami Leonard M. Miller of Medicine
USA

**Pai-Jiun Ho,** PhD
Postdoctoral Fellow
Regenerative Medicine Research Group
Institute of Cellular and System Medicine
National Institutes of Health Research
Taiwan, ROC

**Yi-Chao Hsu,** PhD
Postdoctoral Fellowship
Division of Regenerative Medicine, Institute of Cellular and System Medicine
National Health Research Institutes
Taiwan, ROC

**Yu-Shik Hwang,** PhD
Centre for Biomedical Engineering
Department of Medicine
Brigham and Women's Hospital
Harvard Medical School
Harvard-MIT Division of Health Sciences and Technology
Massachusetts Institute of Technology
USA
Assistant Professor
Department of Maxillofacial Biomedical Engineering
Institute of Oral Biology, School of Medicine
Kyung Hee University
Seoul, Korea

**Race L. Kao,** PhD
Professor and Chair of Excellence
Department of Surgery
East Tennessee State University
Johnson City, TN
USA

**Ali Khademhosseini,** PhD
Associate Professor
Centre for Biomedical Engineering
Department of Medicine
Brigham and Women's Hospital
Harvard Medical School
Harvard-MIT Division of Health Sciences and Technology
Massachusetts Institute of Technology
USA

**Chang Hun Lee,** PhD
Associate Research Scientist
Columbia University Medical Centre
Tissue Engineering and Regenerative Medicine Laboratory
USA

**Paul S. Lee,** BSc
Department of Surgery
Toronto General Hospital
University of Toronto
Canada

**Chuanfu Li,** MD
Professor
Department of Surgery
East Tennessee State University
Johnson City, TN
USA

**Peter X. Ma,** PhD
Richard H. Kingery Endowed Collegiate Professor
Department of Biologic and Materials Sciences
Department of Biomedical Engineering
Macromolecular Science and Engineering
University of Michigan
USA

**Wenzhu Ma,** MD
Professor
Department of Cardiology
Jiangsu Province Hospital
The First Affiliated Hospital of Nanjing University
China

**Samer Mansour,** MD
Cardiologist
Department of Medicine, Faculty of Medicine
CHUM Research Center
Université de Montréal
Canada

**Jeremy J. Mao,** DDS, PhD
Edward V Zegarelli Professor
Director, Tissue Engineering and Regenerative Medicine Laboratory
Columbia University Medical Centre
USA

**Avital Mendelson,** MSc
Department of Biomedical Engineering
Columbia University Medical Centre
Tissue Engineering and Regenerative Medicine Laboratory (TERML)
USA

**Madhur Nayan**
Faculty of Medicine
McGill University
Canada

**Nicolas Noiseux,** MD, MSc
Associate Professor of Surgery
Cardiac Surgeon
Director of Research, Division of Cardiac Surgery
Department of Surgery, Faculty of Medicine
CHUM Research Centre
Université de Montréal
Canada

**Nina Nouraeyan**
Faculty of Medicine
McGill University
Canada

**Arghya Paul,** BTech, MSc
Biomedical Engineering
Faculty of Medicine
McGill University
Canada

**Daniel Pelaez,** MSBE
Department of Biomedical Engineering
College of Engineering
University of Miami
USA

**Satya Prakash,** PhD
Professor
Biomedical Engineering
Professor, BRA Centre for Biomedical Research
Faculty of Medicine
McGill University
Canada

**Katherine M. Ruby,** BSc, MSc
Biomedical Sciences Graduate Program
University of California San Diego
USA

**Permyos Ruengsakulrach,** MD, PhD, FRCST, FCCP
Cardiothoracic and Vascular Surgeon
Division of Cardiovascular and Thoracic Surgery
Cardiac Surgeon, Division of Cardiac Surgery
Bangkok Heart Hospital, Bangkok Hospital Medical Center
Bangkok Dusit Medical Services PLC
Bangkok, Thailand

**Dominique Shum-Tim,** MD CM, MSc
Associate Professor
Department of Surgery
McGill University
McGill University Health Centre
Canada

**Laura A. Smith,** PhD
Department of Biomedical Engineering
University of Michigan
USA

**Terrence M. Yau,** MD, MSc
Associate Professor
Department of Surgery,
Angelo and Lorenza DeGasperis Chair in Cardiovascular Surgery Research
Director of Research, Division of Cardiovascular Surgery, Toronto General Hospital
University of Toronto
Canada

CHAPTER 1

# MICROENGINEERING THE EMBRYONIC STEM CELL ENVIRONMENT

*Yu-Shik Hwang, Bong Geun Chung, Alice Mira Chung and Ali Khademhosseini*

## Abstract

Despite the enormous advances in the biology of embryonic stem cells (ESCs), several challenges still prevent their application to regenerative medicine. These include challenges such as how to control ESC fate decisions as well as how to fabricate complex tissues that mimic the complexity of native tissue architecture and function. Microfabrication technologies and biomaterials offer new opportunities to overcome these challenges to direct ESC differentiation and to fabricate tissue engineered constructs. In this chapter, the use of microengineering approaches and biomaterials to influence ESC self-renewal and differentiation is discussed, and various applications of these technologies are illustrated in controlling the cellular microenvironment.

## 1. Embryonic Stem Cells and Tissue Engineering

### 1.1 *Embryonic stem cells*

The derivation of pluripotent ESCs from mouse embryos was first reported in 1981.[1] In these studies, ESCs were derived from the inner cell mass (ICM) of blastocysts by plating an embyro at the expanded blastocyst stage, either intact or following immunosurgical isolation of ICM, onto a feeder cell layer. After several days of *in vitro* culture, the epiblast-derived cell mass was dissected and disaggregated and then replated onto fresh feeders to generate an ESC line. Upon differentiation, various types of differentiated cell colonies were formed containing cells that make up the organism.[2] During embryogenesis, undifferentiated ESCs from the ICM initiate lineage differentiation through gastrulation, which is the process by which the embryo at an early stage of development generates all its different tissues, namely the mesoderm, endoderm, and ectoderm.[3] Embryogenesis consists of four major stages: a) fertilized egg division (cleavage), b) formation of a ball of cells (morula), c) development of a cavity (blastocyst stage), and d) formation of the three primary germ layers that will give rise to all the cell types of the body (gastrula stage) and ultimately generate all the specialized tissues and organs of a mature organism.[4] Prior to gastrulation, the majority of cells in the pre-implantation blastocyst are composed of the trophectoderm and the primitive endoderm. The pre-implantation embryo consists of the inner cell mass or epiblast cells. Subsequently, three differentiated cell types arrange: the trophoblast, the epiblast (also called the embryonic ectoderm or primitive ectoderm at this stage), and the primitive endoderm. During the developmental step, namely gastrulation, the primitive endoderm differentiates into two different types of endoderm, parietal and visceral endoderm, in the anterior region, which is essential in regulating development during gastrulation. In the next phase, the forward migration of the posterior epiblast cells occurs into the space between the epiblast and the visceral endoderm resulting in formation of primitive streak in a specific region of the epiblast along the posterior axis of the embryo.[5] Mesendoderm, the precursor of mesoderm and endoderm, is derived from primitive streak, as is ectoderm. At this stage, the three primary germ layers that will generate the body of the embryo are finally formed.[6] In culture, ESCs can differentiate into various tissues including gut epithelium (endoderm); cartilage, bone, smooth muscle and striated muscle (mesoderm); and neural epithelium, embryonic ganglia, and stratified squamous epithelium (ectoderm).[7] In contrast to adult stem and differentiated cells, ESCs can continuously divide in culture, while maintaining their ability to

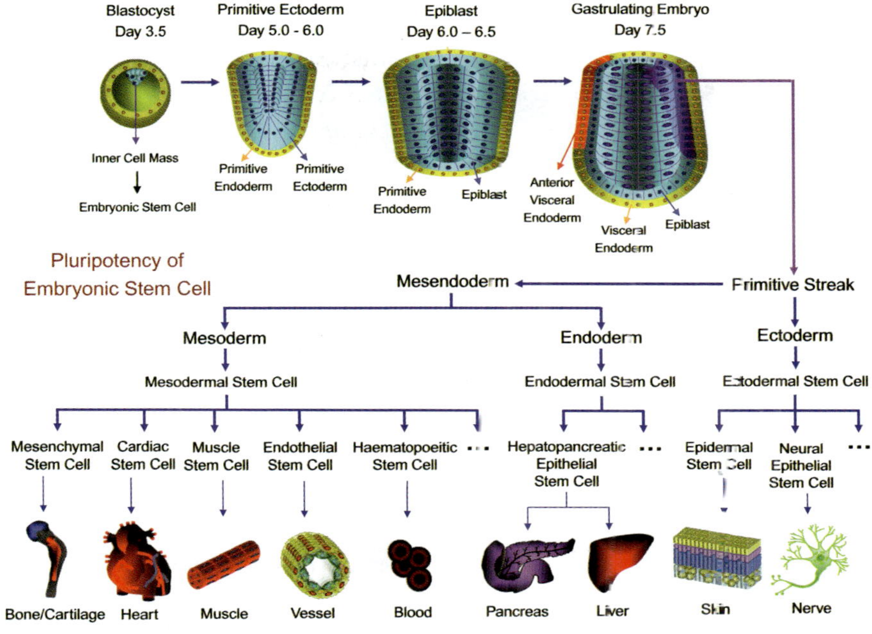


**Fig. 1.** Embryogenesis and differentiation strategy of ESCs (adapted from Tam PP *et al.*[4]).

generate any cell type provided they are placed in the appropriate culture environment (Fig. 1).

In addition to pluripotency, ESCs are also characterized by their "unlimited self-renewal capacity", which allows limitless expansion *in vitro*. These properties make ESCs, potentially, an invaluable cell source for diverse, "off-the-shelf" tissue-engineering and clinical applications. Hence, recently, the use of ESCs as a potential cell source in the field of tissue engineering and regenerative medicine has generated a great deal of interest.

### 1.2 *Tissue engineering*

Tissue engineering is an interdisciplinary field at the intersection of engineering, and biology and medicine that aims to develop biological

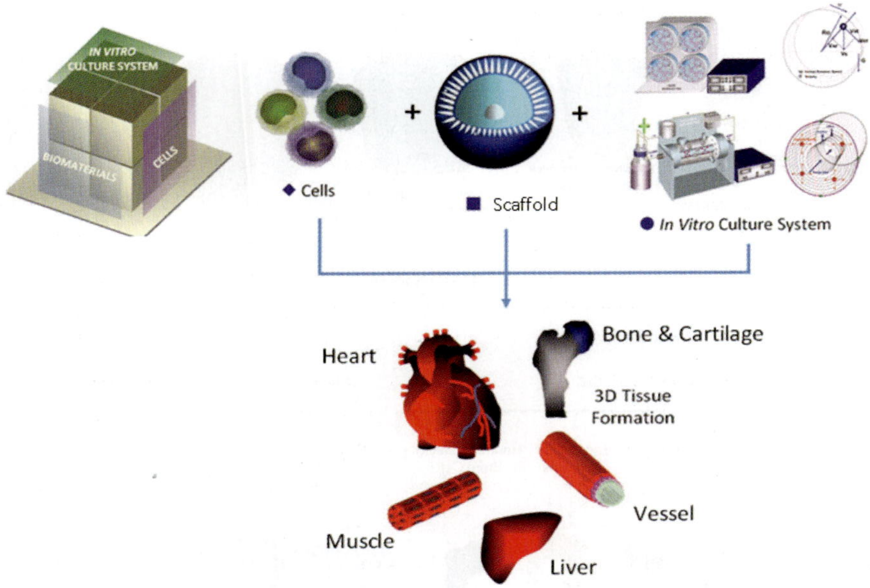


**Fig. 2.** Tissue engineering applications combine cells, microscale carriers, biodegradable materials, and *in vitro* culture system.

substitutes that restore, maintain, or improve tissue function or a whole organ.[8] For the *in vitro* fabrication of tissue engineered constructs, one or more of each of the following three components may be used: 1) cells; 2) a biocompatible scaffold; and 3) *in vitro* culture systems that provide proper environment for 3D tissue growth (Fig. 2).

Research and clinical therapies have explored the use of cells alone, cells in combination with biodegradable scaffolds, and biomaterials that induce host regeneration.[9–11] Transplanted cells are important for the production of new tissue through extracellular matrix (ECM) synthesis as well as restoring the metabolic and mechanical function of the tissues. The scaffold material provides mechanical strength and a template for 3D growth. Also, the addition of cells to the scaffold may aid in repairing tissues at a faster rate as well as in repairing larger defects. Thus, cell adhesion on the matrix surface, cell maturation, ECM production, and cell proliferation are all important for the success of a tissue engineered construct.

To date, there has been significant progress in developing tissue engineered constructs using various scaffolds and cells.[12] For instance, in bone tissue engineering, many suitable materials have been generated, including synthetic hydroxyapatite/tricalcium phosphates and polyglycolic and polylactic acids.[13–14] Other commonly used materials, such as synthetic polylactic acid or poly-L-lactic acid hybridized with natural collagen, have been used as porous scaffolds to provide suitable environment for osteogenic cells growth and function,[15–17] and various polymers could be combined with hydrogels, bioglass, or ceramics.[18–20] In addition, hydrogels, which are cross-linked networks of hydrophilic polymers, provide attractive scaffolds for engineering tissues with high water content, such as cartilage.[21] For instance, alginate, a seaweed-derived polysaccharide approved by the FDA for medical use,[22] has been used to culture annular chondrocytes in hydrostatic loading experiments.[23,24] Recently, researchers have designed various biomaterials to provide more complex and biomimetic environments for ESC expansion and differentiation. For instance, Lammers and colleagues tested biocompatibility of various biomaterials for ESC proliferation and differentiation, and reported that scaffolds made of insoluble collagenous bone matrix in combination with β-tricalciumphosphate were most suitable for ESC differentiation into osteogenic lineage and for the application of ESC-based bone tissue engineering.[25] In addition, Langer and colleagues demonstrated that a rigid polymeric scaffold with proper structure supported ESC differentiation. When ESCs were surrounded by a soft biomaterial such as Matrigel, no tissue was formed. In contrast, when the Matrigel was combined with rigid fibrous scaffolds, tissues were formed.[26] This suggested that the mechanical property of polymeric scaffolds could be a parameter to direct ESC differentiation and induce tissue formation.

Accompanied with suitable cell carriers, efficient culture systems are required to fabricate 3D tissue-like constructs *in vitro*. There are several kinds of *in vitro* culture systems, such as 2D culture flasks and 3D bioreactors (Fig. 3). Conventionally, 2D culture systems have been used to expand and culture cells on a surface. However, such culture processes in static culture system have a number of drawbacks, such as mass transfer limitations that result in limited cell growth.[27,28]

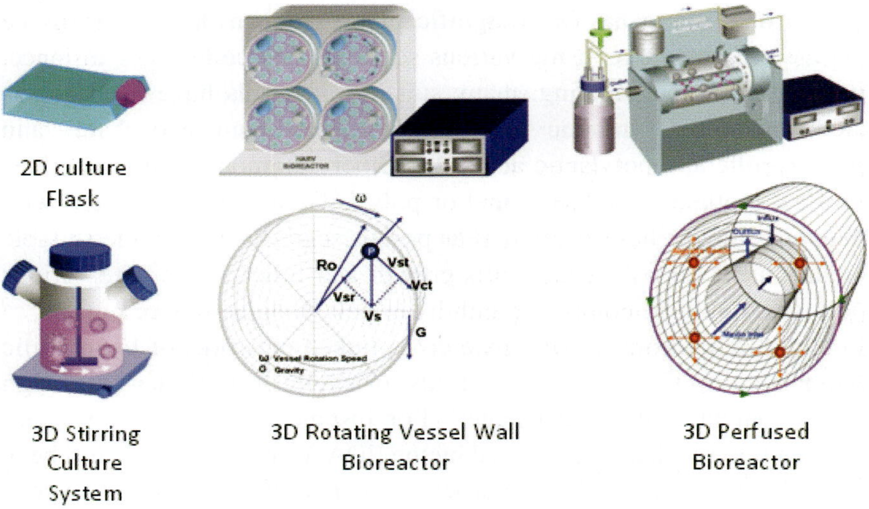


**Fig. 3.** Example of *in vitro* culture systems (2D culture flasks for expansion of mammalian cells, 3D stirring culture system for stirring cells in suspension culture, 3D rotating vessel wall culture system for cell suspension culture by balancing centrifugal force and gravity, 3D perfused bioreactor for cell suspension culture with constant supply of medium *via* perfusion system).

Alternatively, stirred culture systems have been used to simulate 3D tissue formation and enhance mass transport of nutrients and oxygen. However, these cultures cannot control the mechanical stress induced by stirring. Hence, recently, several 3D bioreactor culture systems have been developed to solve the limitations in controlling mass transfer of nutrients and oxygen as well as mechanical stress. Among various types of bioreactors, rotating wall vessel (RWV) bioreactors, such as high aspect ratio vessel (HARV) bioreactors, have been used to culture cells seeded either alone or in combination with scaffolds or microcarriers, in cartilage,[29] and bone[30,31] tissue formation. The RWV bioreactor is designed to generate laminar flow and to minimize the mechanical stress on cell aggregates by minimizing shear and turbulence. It creates a unique environment that provides adequate nutrition and oxygenation, ideal for mammalian cell culture, and supports 3D tissue growth.[32]

The free falling of the microcarrier inside the bioreactor as a result of gravity can be balanced by the centrifugal forces due to the rotation of the outer-cylinder, thus establishing suspension culture environment for microcarrier.[32,33] Recently, such bioreactors have been applied in ESC-based tissue engineering to expand cells and to fabricate 3D tissue-like structures. For example, ESC-derived cardiomyocytes were expanded in bioreactors, and then seeded on porous polymeric scaffolds to make 3D cardiac tissue-like structure.[34] In another study, 3D bone-like structures were generated by culturing encapsulated murine ESCs within alginate hydrogels that were subsequently cultured in a bioreactor.[35]

## 2. Microenvironment

Microenvironment regulation is emerging as a key concept for controlling cell survival, growth, function and differentiation. In microenvironment, the interactions between cells, cells and ECM, as well as cells and soluble factors, play a critical role in regulating ESC behavior (Fig. 4). In the following sections, various components of the cellular microenvironment will be introduced.

### 2.1 *Cell-cell contact*

Cell-cell contact is a major regulatory mechanism that controls cell behaviour.[36] For instance, the differentiation of skeletal myogenic cells has been reported to depend on cell-cell contact which influences cell cycle arrest and gene expression.[37] One representative factor participating and controlling cell-cell adhesion is cadherin. Cadherins are calcium-dependent adhesion molecules that mainly interact in a homophilic manner to bind cells together. There are several classes of cadherin molecules based on different cell types. Cadherins in one class bind only to cadherins of the same class. For instance, E-cadherins are generally found in epithelial tissues, and can bind only to E-cadherin molecules. In addition to E-cadherin, other cell types and tissues express other classes of cadherins. P-cadherin is expressed in placenta, N-cadherin in neural cells, R-cadherin

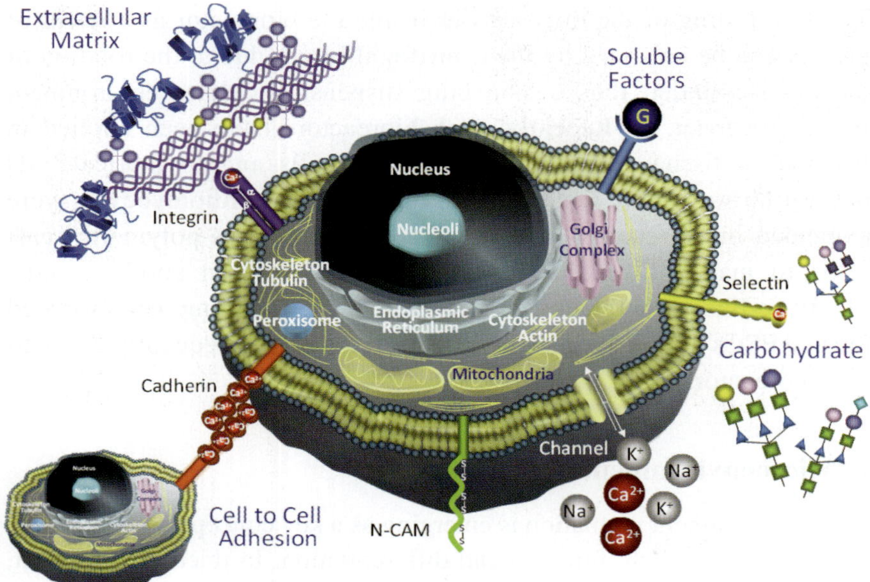


**Fig. 4.** Microenvironment surrounding an individual cell (cell-cell adhesion, cell-ECM interactions, cell-soluble factor interactions).

in renal tissues, VE-cadherin in vascular endothelial cells, M-cadherin in myotubules, OB-cadherin in osteoblasts, and K-cadherin in the kidney cells.[38,39] Cell-cell contacts through binding between cadherins influence cell function *via* signaling pathways. Upon binding of the extracellular domain of cadherins, the intra-cellular domain binds to p120-catenin and beta-catenin containing highly phosphorylated regions, which then bind to alpha-catenin, resulting in regulation of acting-containing cytoskeletal filaments, and control of gene expression.[38,40] Cell-cell contact *via* cadherins plays a key role in ESC differentiation and growth. In ESCs, cadherin in different classes can be expressed according to ESC differentiation stage. For example, E-cadherin investigates cell-cell adhesion for the formation of embryoid bodies (EBs), which are 3D spherical aggregates containing differentiated cells of all three germ layers. Although E-cadherin is constitutively expressed in an early stage embryo, it is downregulated as the cells differentiate[41,42] (Fig. 5).

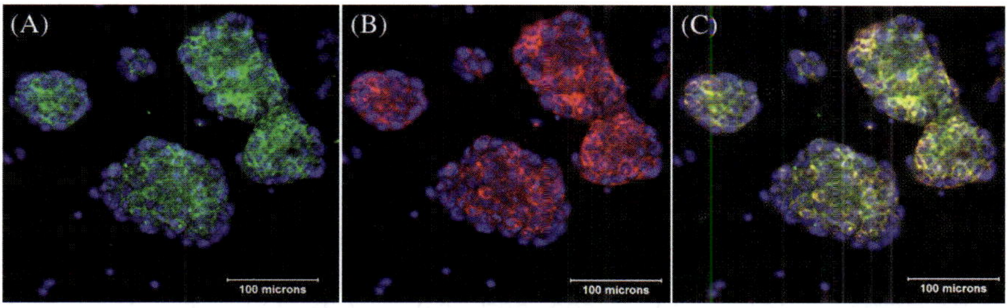


**Fig. 5.** Cell-cell adhesion *via* E-cadherin in ESCs. (**A**) SSEA-1 (stage specific embryonic antigen 1) expression (green fluorescence); for characterizing undifferentiated ESCs. (**B**) E-cadherin expression (red fluorescence): E-cadherin is expressed in undifferentiated ESCs. (**C**) Merged image of (A) and (B), cell nucleus was counter-stained with DAPI to visualize cells.

## 2.2 *Cell — ECM*

ECM is an important component of many mammalian tissues that is made from various protein and polysaccharide molecules. Cellular interactions with ECM play a critical role in their function and physiology. Cells interact with ECM components *via* cell surface receptors, such as integrins. ECM components provide a template for cell adhesion, proliferation, migration, differentiation and for tissue formation, and a reservoir for growth factors.

The ECM is composed of three classes of biomolecules. One class is structural proteins such as collagens. Collagen molecules are structural macromolecules of the ECM that include in their structure one or several domains that have a characteristic triple helical conformation. Collagens form the large fibers of connective tissues and networks in basement membranes. The fibril-forming collagens have a long, continuous triple helix that gives the molecule a rigid, rod-like structure. These collagens form large fibrils that give structural integrity and tensile-strength to the tissues. Type I collagen is the most abundant protein in the human body forming ECM in bone, tendons, and dermis, etc. Type II collagen has a similar function in cartilage. The network-forming collagens have interruptions in the triple helix. Type IV collagen belongs to this subfamily and is an important structural component of basement membranes (BM).[43,44]

lubricating fluid in the joints.[53,54] On the other hand, their rigidity provides structural integrity to the cells.[55] In addition, aggrecan is one of the most important extracellular proteoglycans. Aggrecan molecules are non-covalently bound to the long molecule of hyaluronan, forming bristles to the backbone in a bottlebrush by the linking proteins. To each aggrecan core protein, multiple chains of chondroitin sulfate and keratan sulfate are covalently attached through the trisaccharide linker.[53] Hyaluronan is bound to the surface receptors such as CD44 of many migrating cells. It is also very important during differentiation.[56] For example myoblasts, which are undifferentiated muscle cell precursors, produce hyaluronan-rich ECM to prevent premature cell fusion. Because of its loose and hydrated porous structure, the hyaluronan-rich ECM keeps cells apart from each other such that they are free to move around and proliferate.[57]

During embryonic development and ESC differentiation, ECM plays a critical role in regulating ESC differentiation into specific cell lineages, as well as in cell proliferation. Undifferentiated murine ESCs can be induced to differentiate *in vitro* by removal of the feeder-cell layer and leukemia inhibitory factor (LIF), and subsequent transfer into suspension culture to form 3D spherical aggregates.[58] Much of our current understanding on ESC differentiation is dependent on EBs recapitulating several aspects of early development, displaying regional-specific differentiation processes to generate cells of all three embryonic germ layers.[58] Within the first two to four days of EB formation, ESC aggregates give rise to an outer layer of endodermal cells that begin to synthesize ECM molecules, such as laminin, and a complete basement membrane between the primitive endoderm cells and the remaining cells in the aggregates. Shortly afterwards, the ESCs within the cell aggregate start to differentiate to epiblast cells and, subsequently, around day four some of the epiblast cells that are aligned against the BM polarize to form a columnar epithelium. It has been reported that the deposition of BM beneath the primitive endoderm prevents differentiation of primitive ectoderm towards mesoderm by suppressing the Epithelial-Mesenchymal Transition (EMT) in EBs.[59] In addition, it was also found that FN stimulates endothelial cell differentiation and vascularisation from ESCs, and laminin induces the ability of ESCs to differentiate into cardiomyocytes,[60] although the precise mechanisms have not yet been determined.

## 2.3 *Cell-soluble factor interactions*

One family of soluble factors that influences cell growth and differentiation is growth factors. Growth factors are proteins that bind to receptors on the cell surface to activate cellular proliferation and/or differentiation pathways. Many growth factors are quite versatile, stimulating cellular response in numerous different cell types; while others are specific to a particular cell-type. There are several kinds of growth factors: epidermal growth factor (EGF), platelet derived growth factor (PDGF), fibroblast growth factors (FGFs), transforming growth factors-beta (TGFs-β), transforming growth factor-alpha (TGF-α), nerve growth factor (NGF), erythropoietin (EPO), and insulin-like growth factor-I (IGF-I). Each type of growth factor has specialized biological functions. For example, PDGF promotes proliferation of connective tissue, glial and smooth muscle cells; EGF promotes proliferation of mesenchymal, glial and epithelial cells; FGF promotes proliferation of various cell types and induces mesoderm formation in early embryogenesis; NGF promotes neuritis outgrowth and neural cell survival; and IGF-I promotes proliferation of many cell types.[61,62] Cells express growth factor dependent receptors that activate upon interaction with appropriate ligands to induce intracellular signaling to induce cell proliferation, survival and differentiation.

The use of growth factors has been extensively investigated for directing the lineage specific differentiation of ESCs. For example, Activin A was shown to mediate dorso-anterior mesoderm differentiation, and bone morphogenetic protein 4 (BMP-4) was shown to mediate mesoderm formation of a more ventral character, including hematopoietic cells.[63–65] In addition to the TGF-β superfamily, it has been demonstrated that binding of IGF-II, a member of IGF family, increased mesoderm formation.[66] Moreover, it was demonstrated that Activin-A and TGF-β1 induced mesodermal differentiation, while EGF, BMP-4, and FGF induced ectodermal and mesodermal differentiation of human ESCs.[67]

Although several growth factors have been identified to influence human ESC differentiation, there have been other reports that such growth factors might also participate in sustaining ESC self-renewal. For instance, the self-renewal activity of ESCs was sustained by the addition BMP-4 to the ESC maintenance medium by inhibiting both the extracellular receptor kinase (ERK) and p38 mitogen-activated protein kinase (MAPK) pathways.[68] Furthermore, Johansson *et al.* demonstrated that members of both the TGF-β and the FGF families, such as TGF-β1, -β2, and -β3, acidic FGF, and basic FGF, when applied individually, did not produce any marked increase in the expression of the mesoderm markers, suggesting that these factors normally operate in conjunction with others.[64] These observations are consistent with the fact that ESC differentiation involves multiple dynamic, overlapping signals that progressively give rise to pattern formation.[69,70] Thus, the self-renewal and differentiation pathway of ESCs seems to be controlled by several interactions interactively *via* cell-cell, cell-ECM, and cell-soluble factor interactions.

## 3. Microengineering to Control ESC Microenvironment

Microengineering techniques are emerging biological tools that make it possible to regulate the cell-microenvironment interactions, such as cell-cell, cell-ECM, cell-soluble factor, and cell-mechanical stimuli.[71] To enable the control of ESC niche in a tempo-spatially regulated manner, a number of microengineering approaches, such as microfluidics, surface patterning, high-throughput microarrays, and 3D scaffolds have been recently used (Fig. 6). In the following sections, we have reviewed various microengineering tools for directing ESC fates.

### 3.1 *Microfluidic platforms for controlling cell-soluble factor interactions*

Microfluidic devices are enabling tools for controlling cell-soluble factor interactions, because they can control the spatial and temporal presentation of soluble factors to cells.[72,73] In general, microfluidic devices have been fabricated by photo- and soft lithography techniques. The soft lithographic method utilizes elastomeric materials, such as poly(dimethylsiloxane) (PDMS), to fabricate microstructures. The low Reynold's number regions in microfluidic devices can be used to limit convective mixing to form laminar flows in which multiple fluid streams can flow side-by-side without mixing. In one application of such flow, cells were

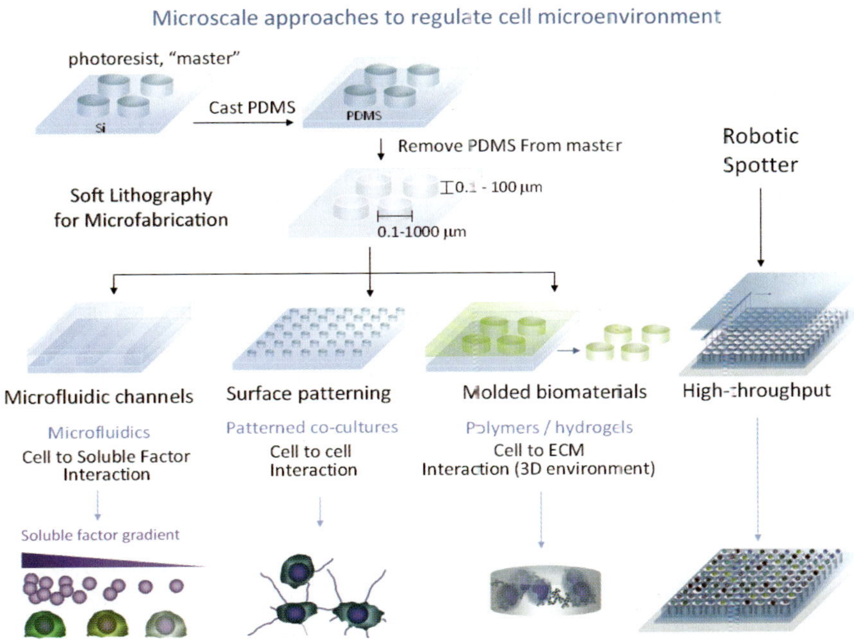


**Fig. 6.** Microengineering techniques (i.e. microfluidics, surface patterning, and high-throughput microarray) to control cell-microenvironment interactions (i.e. cell-cell, cell-ECM, and cell-soluble factor interactions).

locally stimulated by using multiple laminar flow streams to deliver membrane-permeable molecules to cells.[74] Similar microfluidic channels can be useful for studying developmental biology and embryogenesis. For example, nuclear dynamics and the bicoid gradients were studied by using laminar flows of different temperature fluids in a microfluidic device.[75] In this study, temperature gradients on different sides of the embryo enabled a synchronized embryonic patterning.

Microfluidic cell culture systems have been used to control cell docking[76] and direct ESC fates.[77–79] For example, a multiphenotype cell array of microfluidic channels was fabricated by using soft lithographic techniques.[76] In this approach, PDMS molds were reversibly sealed to a microwell substrate. After sealing, cells and fluids could be selectively delivered to the microwells through microfluidic channels. This platform

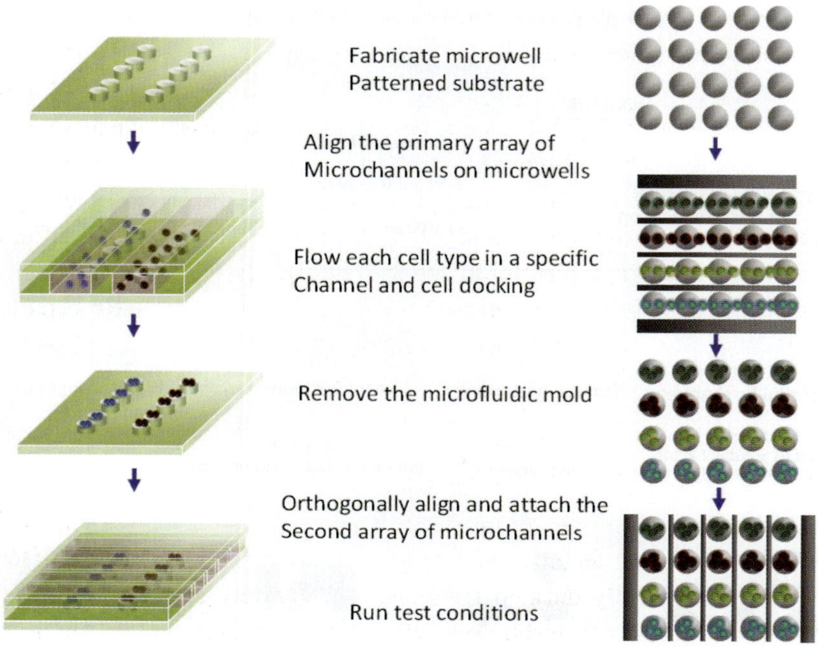


**Fig. 7.** Reversible sealing of microfluidic channels onto microwell patterned substrates to generate multiphenotype cellular arrays (Adapted from Khademhosseini *et al.*[76]).

of sequentially aligned orthogonal microchannels is a potentially useful approach for enabling high-throughput experimentation (Fig. 7). To control EB size and shape, a microfluidic device consisting of two microchannels separated by a semi-porous membrane was used.[80] The upper microchannels enabled cell capture to form cell aggregates and medium was perfused through the lower microchannels. Using this microfluidic device, homogeneous EBs, harvested from the microchannel, differentiated into neurons. To culture murine ESCs within well-defined microenvironments, the microfluidic device was also designed with logarithmic ranges of flow rates.[77] In this application, a logarithmic flow rate-derived concentration gradient was created to study the effect of the medium flow rate for culturing murine ESCs.

The gene expression of human ESCs is a critical aspect for regulating the differentiation.[81] Microfluidic systems that utilize fluids in a nanoliter scale provide an environment to monitor single cell gene expression. It has been difficult to use existing methods for bulk gene expression by using RNA from these heterogeneous samples. To focus on studying the regulatory relationship of genes in the earliest phases of ESC differentiation, a microfluidic system has been used to extract mRNA from single cells for gene expression studies. It is expected that more efficient gene expression processing of single cells can be performed in microfluidic systems. Therefore, microfluidics that control cell-soluble factor interactions and generate concentration gradients could be useful for directing ESC fates and studying developmental biology within well-defined microenvironments.

### 3.2 *Surface micropatterning for controlling cell-cell contacts*

ESC differentiation can be influenced by cell-cell contacts. Microscale surface patterning techniques enable the control of cell-cell contacts within geometrically defined surfaces.[71,72] A variety of microscale technologies including microtopography,[82–87] microfabricated stencil,[88–90] microcontact printing,[91] and layer-by-layer deposition[92] have been used to pattern ESCs on substrates. For example, hyaluronan modified with photoreactive methacrylates was used to make microstructures as functional components of microfabricated devices.[83] These hydrogel microwell arrays generated low shear stress regions that enabled the stable docking of ESCs. Similar microwell arrays were used to generate spatially and temporally synchronised human EBs.[87] The microwell arrays can be directly utilized to screen and characterize ESCs, as well as homogeneous EBs obtained from this microfabricated microwell can direct human EB-mediated differentiation. Furthermore, Poly(ethylene glycol) (PEG) hydrogel microwells have been used to generate homogeneous EBs (Fig. 8).[82,84] It was demonstrated that cells cultured within PEG hydrogel microwell arrays remained highly viable, resulting in directed ESC differentiation.

Cell-cell communication in cell aggregates plays a significant role in controlling ESC proliferation and differentiation. A microfabricated PDMS stencil can be used to regulate the initial size of ESC aggregates.[88] Using this system, it was demonstrated that larger aggregates enhanced

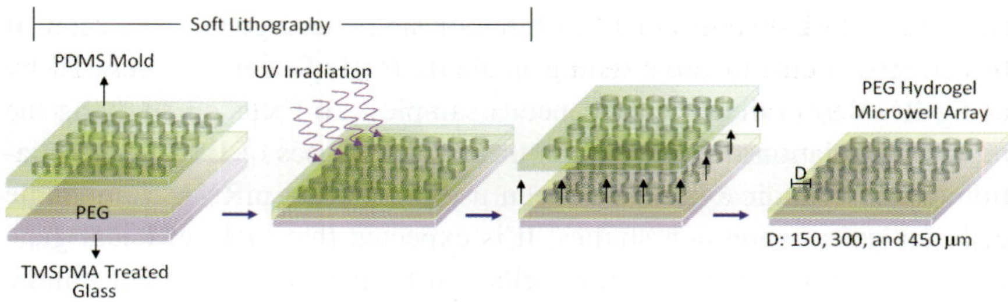


**Fig. 8.** Hydrogel microwell array systems fabricated by using micromolding techniques to form cell aggregates with controlled sizes and shapes.

mesoderm and endoderm differentiation in comparison to small aggregates that enhanced ectoderm differentiation. Also, microfabricated parylene-C stencils can be fabricated to reversely seal on a hydrophobic surface to enable surface patterning.[89,90] Using this inexpensive re-usable stencil, microscale co-patterns of proteins and cells were generated on various substrates. These microfabricated parylene-C stencils were used to pattern co-cultures of ESCs with other developmentally relevant systems in both static and dynamic conditions by sequentially removing several stencils that were placed on top of each other.

In addition to microfabricated stencils, microcontact printing has been used to study the differentiation of micropatterned human ESCs.[91] This method was used to generate homogeneous EBs with controlled sizes. The gene and protein expression analysis of micropatterned human ESCs demonstrated that the endodermal and neuronal expression increased with decreasing colony size. Moreover, higher mesoderm and cardiac induction was observed at larger EB sizes. This analysis demonstrated that heterogeneity in human ESC colony and aggregate size generated subsets of appropriate conditions for differentiation.

To study cell-cell interactions, patterned co-cultures have been fabricated by using layer-by-layer deposition of ionic biopolymers.[92] In this approach, non-biofouling hyaluronan biopolymer was used for micropatterning cells and proteins onto glass substrates. The adhesion of a second cell type was accomplished by switching the cell repulsive property of the hyaluronan surface by ionic adsorption of positively charged poly-L-lysine (PLL). After the PLL adsorption, the surface turned from cell repulsive to cell adhesive. Using this approach, ESCs and fibroblasts were co-cultured to study cell-cell contacts. These microfabrication-based patterning techniques provide a potentially useful approach to manipulate cell-cell interactions for regulating ESC differentiation.

### 3.3 *High-throughput microarray for screening microenvironments*

High-throughput screening enables the analysis of toxic properties and biological activities of large scale compound libraries in a fast and efficient manner.[93] In addition, the complex microenvironment associated with directed stem cell differentiation can be potentially screened by using high-throughput techniques.[93] Synthesizing large numbers of biomaterials and characterizing their interactions with stem cells are cumbersome tasks. To address this limitation, Langer and his colleagues developed a high-throughput microarray system to screen large numbers of biomaterials using a robotic spotter.[94] To study human ESC proliferation and differentiation, different combinations of 25 different monomers with a radical initiator were deposited on substrates, resulting in 1,728 individual polymer microarray spots that were subsequently seeded with ESCs to analyze their response. High-throughput system was also used to study the effects of natural ECM combinations on ESC differentiation.[95] Only 1/1000 of protein used in conventional combinatorial mixtures was required for this microarray system. High-throughput ECM microarray was also used to explore the interactions of different combinations of ECM molecules (i.e., collagen I, III, IV, FN, and laminin) on murine ESCs. It was demonstrated that FN and collagen I stimulated the differentiation of ESCs into the hepatic fate. Therefore, these micro-arrays enable the precise control of cell-biomaterials and cell-matrix interactions in a high-throughput and reproducible manner.

### 3.4 *3D scaffolds for culturing stem cells*

*In vivo*, ESCs are located within a 3D environment that provides the cells with optimal oxygen levels and soluble nutrients. Thus, the merger of

ESCs and 3D scaffolds can be beneficial in recreating this aspect of the ESC environment. There are two main concerns in maintaining cell viability and functions of scaffolds seeded with ESCs: immune reaction from the body, as well as diffusion limitation of oxygen and nutrients.[96] The lack of vascularized structures within tissue scaffolds results in poor oxygen and nutrition diffusivity. Microfabrication technologies can be used to create tissues containing vascular networks. Vascularized tissue construction made by using the microfabricated scaffolds was pioneered by Borenstein, Vacanti, and Langer.[97] Replica molding made from silicon wafers was used to create biocompatible polymer scaffolds with 1 μm high resolution. Dynamic seeding of endothelial cells on these scaffolds was successfully performed without occlusion or contamination for four weeks.[97] Despite the potential of this microfabrication-based application, no study so far has been performed to study ESC proliferation and differentiation on these scaffolds. Therefore, in this chapter, we review the conventional engineering of 3D scaffolds for ESC applications.

Biocompatible and biodegradable polymer scaffolds can be used to control growth and differentiation of human ESCs.[26] Scaffolds provide structural support and physical cues for cell orientation and spreading. Along with chemical cues, the physical cues of scaffolds have impact on the differentiation of ESCs. ESCs cultured within 3D scaffolds can be differentiated into specific tissue lineages, such as bone[98] and brain.[99] The number of neural-like structures identified by neuronal marker (i.e., βIII-tubulin) has been shown to increase within 3D tissue constructs.[99] Moreover, physical structures and chemical compositions of polymer matrices enable the control of hematopoietic differentiation from ESCs.[100,101] For example, the study on hematopoietic differentiation within scaffolds found that smaller scaffold pores and higher polymer concentrations, which resulted in a higher compression modulus of scaffolds, significantly enhanced hematopoietic differentiation from ESCs.[101] High cell seeding densities and co-cultures with stromal cells also enhanced hematopoietic differentiation. Although further studies are required to clarify the effects of physical and chemical parameters on stem cell fate decisions, this area of research is promising for generating 3D tissue constructs. Therefore, engineered 3D scaffolds containing proper pore sizes and microvascularized structures have the potential for addressing main challenges in creating 3D tissue constructs (i.e., the lack of sufficient vascularization for the transport of oxygen and nutrients).

## 4. Conclusions

Although ESCs have been considered as a potent cell source for tissue engineering, significant challenges still remain. Specifically, there is a need to control the ESC microenvironment to direct differentiation. Microfabrication techniques enable more control of cell-cell, cell-ECM, and cell-soluble factor interactions by providing controllable microenvironments and enabling high-throughput screening. It is believed that microengineering will lead to more precise understanding of cell biology, and contribute to the therapeutic potential of stem cells in regenerative medicine.

## Acknowledgments

This paper was partly supported by the National Institutes of Health (NIH), US Army Core of Engineers, and the Charles Stark Draper Laboratory.

## References

1. Evans MJ, Kaufman MH. Establishment in culture of pluripotential cells from mouse embryos. *Nature* 1981;292(5819):154–156.
2. Robertson EJ. Derivation and maintenance of embryonic stem cell cultures. *Methods Mol Biol* 1997;75:173–184.
3. Lu CC, Brennan J, Robertson EJ. From fertilization to gastrulation: axis formation in the mouse embryo. *Cur Opin Gene Dev* 2001;11:384–392.
4. Tam PP, Williams EA, Chan WY. Gastrulation in the mouse embryo: Ultrastructural and molecular aspects of germ layer morphogenesis. *Microsc Res Tech* 1993;26(4):301–328.
5. Lawson A, Schoenwolf GC. Epiblast and primitive-streak origins of the endoderm in the gastrulating chick embryo. *Development* 2003;130(15): 3491–3501.
6. Niederlander C, Walsh JJ, Episkopou V, Jones CM. Arkadia enhances nodal-related signalling to induce mesendoderm. *Nature* 2001;410:830–834.

33. Pollack SR, Meany DF, Levine EM, *et al.* Numerical model and experimental validation of microcarrier motion in a rotating bioreactor. *Tissue Eng* 2000;6(5):519–530.
34. Fromstein JD, Zandstra PW, Alperin C, *et al.* Seeding bioreactor-produced embryonic stem cell-derived cardiomyocytes on different porous, degradable, polyurethane scaffolds reveals the effect of scaffold architecture on cell morphology. *Tissue Engineering Part A* 2008;14(3):369–378.
35. Hwang YS, Cho J, Tay F, *et al.* The use of murine embryonic stem cells, alginate encapsulation, and rotary microgravity bioreactor in bone tissue engineering. *Biomaterials* 2009;30(4):499–507.
36. Robert Y, Tsai L, Ronald D, McKay G. Cell contact regulates fate choice by cortical stem cells. *J Neuroscience* 2000;20(10):3725–3735.
37. Gavard J, Marthiens V, Monnet C, *et al.* N-cadherin activation substitutes for the cell contact control in cell cycle arrest and myogenic differentiation. *J. Biol. Chem* 2004;279(35):36795–36802.
38. Halbleib JM, Nelson WJ. Cadherins in development: cell adhesion, sorting, and tissue morphogenesis. *Genes Dev* 2006;20(23):3199–3214.
39. Takeichi M. The cadherins: cell-cell adhesion molecules controlling animal morphogenesis. *Development* 1988;102:639–655.
40. Aberle H, Schwartz H, Kemler R. Cadherin-catenin complex: protein interactions and their implications for cadherin function. *J Cell Biochem* 1996;61(4):514–523.
41. Bloor DJ, Metcalfe AD, Rutherford A, *et al.* Expression of cell adhesion molecules during human preimplantation embryo development. *Mol Hum Reprod* 2002;8:237–245.
42. Dang SM, Gerecht-Nir S, Chen J, *et al.* Controlled, scalable embryonic stem cell differentiation culture. *Stem Cells* 2004;22:275–282.
43. van der Rest M, Dublet B, Champliaud MF. Fibril-associated collagens. *Biomaterials* 1990;11:28–31.
44. van der Rest M, Garrone R. Collagen family of proteins. *FASEB J* 1991; 5(13):2814–2823.
45. Heino J. The collagen receptor integrins have distinct ligand recognition and signaling functions. *Matrix Biol* 2000;19:319–323.
46. Kadler KE, Hill A, Canty-Laird EG. Collagen fibrillogenesis: fibronectin, integrins, and minor collagens as organizers and nucleators. *Curr Opin Cell Biol* 2008;20(5):495–501.

47. Davis GE. Affinity of integrins for damaged extracellular matrix: avb3 binds to denatured collagen type I through RGD sites. *Biochem Biophys Res Commun* 1992;182:1025–1031.
48. Ruggiero F, Commte J, Cabanas C, Carrone R. Structural requirements for a1b1 and a2b1 integrins mediated cell adhesion to collagen V. *J Cell Sci* 1996;109:1865–1874.
49. Mosher DF, Furcht LT. Fibronectin: review of its structure and possible functions. *J Invest Dermatol* 1981;77(2):175–180.
50. Mao Y, Schwarzbauer JE. Accessibility to the fibronectin synergy site in a 3D matrix regulates engagement of alpha5beta1 versus alphavbeta3 integrin receptors. *Cell Commun Adhes* 2006;13(5–6):267–277.
51. Miner JH. Laminins and their roles in mammals. *Microsc Res Tech* 2008; 71(5):349–356.
52. Belkin AM, Stepp MA. Integrins as receptors for laminins. *Microsc Res Tech* 2000;51(3):280–301.
53. Hardingham TE, Fosang AJ. Proteoglycans: many forms and many functions. *FASEB J* 1992;6(3):861–870.
54. Yanagishita M. Function of proteoglycans in the extracellular matrix. *Acta Pathol Jpn* 1993;43(6):283–293.
55. Kresse H, Schönherr E. Proteoglycans of the extracellular matrix and growth control. *J Cell Physiol* 2001;189(3):266–724.
56. Zhu H, Mitsuhashi N, Klein A, *et al*. The role of the hyaluronan receptor CD44 in mesenchymal stem cell migration in the extracellular matrix. *Stem Cells* 2006;24(4):928–935.
57. Krenn V, Brand-Saberi B, Wachtler F. Hyaluronic acid influences the migration of myoblasts within the avian embryonic wing bud. *Am J Anat* 1991; 192(4):400–406.
58. Itskovitz-Eldor J, Schuldier M, Karsenti D, *et al*. Differentiation of human embryonic stem cells into embryoid bodies comprising the three embryonic germ layers. *Mol Med* 2000;61:88–95.
59. Fuziwara H, Hayashi Y, Sanzen N, *et al*. Regulation of medosdermal differentiation of mouse embryonic stem cells by basement membranes. *J Biol Chem* 2007;282(40):29701–29711.
60. Barttista S, Guarnieri D, Borselli C, *et al*. The effect of matrix composition of 3D construct on embryonic stem cell differentiation. *Biomaterials* 2005; 26(31):6194–6207.

61. Antoniades HN, Owen AJ. Growth factors and regulation of cell growth. *Annu Rev Med* 1982;33:445–463.
62. Gospodarowicz D. Growth factors and their action *in vivo* and *in vitro*. *J Pathol* 1983;141(3):201–233.
63. Huber BTL, Zhou Y, Mead PE, Zon LI. Cooperative effects of growth factors involved in the induction of hematopoietic mesoderm. *Blood* 1998; 92(11):4128–4137.
64. Johansson BM, Wiles MV. Evidence for involvement of activin A and bone morphogenetic protein 4 in mammalian mesoderm and hematopoietic development. *Mol Cell Biol* 1995;15(1):141–151.
65. Valdimarsdotter G, Mummery C. Functions of the TGF-b superfamily in human embryonic stem cells. *APMIS* 2005;113:773–789.
66. Morali OG, Jouneau A, McLaughlin KJ, *et al.* IGF-II promotes mesoderm formation. *Dev Biol* 2000;227:133–145.
67. Schuldiner M, Yanuka O, Itskovitz-Eldor J, *et al.* Effect of eight growth factors on the differentiation of cells derived from human embryonic stem cells. *Proc Natl Acad Sci USA* 2000;97(21):11307–11312.
68. Qi X, Li TG, Hao J, *et al.* BMP4 supports self-renewal of embryonic stem cells by inhibiting mitogen-activated protein kinase pathways. *Proc Natl Acad Sci USA* 2004;101:6027–6032.
69. Kimelman D, Christian JL, Moon RT. Synergistic principles of development: overlapping patterning systems in Xenopus mesoderm induction. *Development* 1992;116:1–9.
70. Wolpert L. Positional information and the spatial pattern of cellular differentiation. *J Theor Biol* 1969;25:1–47.
71. Khademhosseini A, Langer R, Borenstein J, Vacanti JP. Microscale technologies for tissue engineering and biology. *Proc Natl Acad Sci USA* 2006; 103(8):2480–2487.
72. Chung BG, Kang L, Khademhosseini A. Micro- and nanoscale approaches for tissue engineering and drug discovery. *Expt Opin Drug Dis* 2007;2(12): 1653–1668.
73. Underhill GH, Bhatia SN. High-throughput analysis of signals regulating stem cell fate and function. *Cur Opin Chem Biol* 2007;11(4): 357–366.
74. Takayama S, Ostuni E, LeDuc P, *et al.* Laminar flows — Subcellular positioning of small molecules. *Nature* 2001;411(6841):1016.

75. Lucchetta EM, Lee JH, Fu LA, *et al*. Dynamics of Drosophila embryonic patterning network perturbed in space and time using microfluidics. *Nature* 2005;434(7037):1134–1138.
76. Khademhosseini A, Yeh J, Eng G, *et al*. Cell docking inside microwells within reversibly sealed microfluidic channels for fabricating multiphenotype cell arrays. *Lab Chip* 2005;5(12):1380–1386.
77. Kim L, Vahey MD, Lee HY, Voldman J. Microfluidic arrays for logarithmically perfused embryonic stem cell culture. *Lab Chip* 2006;6(3): 394–406.
78. Torisawa YS, Chueh BH, Huh D, *et al*. Efficient formation of uniform-sized embryoid bodies using a compartmentalized microchannel device. *Lab Chip* 2007;7(6):770–776.
79. Song X, Kong B, Li D. A new tool for probing of cell-cell communication: human embryonic germ cells inducing apoptosis of SKOV3 ovarian cancer cells on a microfluidic chip. *Biotechnol Lett* 2008;30(9):1537–1543.
80. Torisawa YS, Chueh BH, Huh D, *et al*. Efficient formation of uniform-sized embryoid bodies using a compartmentalized microchannel device. *Lab Chip* 2007;7(6):770–776.
81. Zhong JF, Chen Y, Marcus JS, *et al* A microfluidic processor for gene expression profiling of single human embryonic stem cells. *Lab Chip* 2008;8(1):68–74.
82. Karp JM, Yeh J, Eng G, *et al*. Controlling size, shape and homogeneity of embryoid bodies using poly(ethylene glycol) microwells. *Lab Chip* 2007; 7(6):786–794.
83. Khademhosseini A, Eng G, Yeh J, *et al*. Micromolding of photocrosslinkable hyaluronic acid for cell encapsulation and entrapment. *J Biomed Mater Res A* 2006;79(3):522–532.
84. Moeller HC, Mian MK, Shrivastava S, *et al*. A microwell array system for stem cell culture. *Biomaterials* 2008;29(6):752–763.
85. Mohr JC, de Pablo JJ, Palecek SP. 3-D microwell culture of human embryonic stem cells. *Biomaterials* 2006;27(36):6032–6042.
86. Rosenthal A, Macdonald A, Voldman J. Cell patterning chip for controlling the stem cell microenvironment. *Biomaterials* 2007; 28(21): 3208–3216.
87. Ungrin MD, Joshi C, Nica A, *et al*. Reproducible, ultra high-throughput formation of multicellular organization from single cell suspension-derived human embryonic stem cell aggregates. *PLoS ONE* 2008;3(2):e1565.

88. Park J, Cho CH, Parashurama N, *et al.* Microfabrication-based modulation of embryonic stem cell differentiation. *Lab Chip* 2007;7(8): 1018–1028.

89. Wright D, Rajalingam B, Karp JM, *et al.* Reusable, reversibly sealable parylene membranes for cell and protein patterning. *J Biomed Mater Res A* 2008;85(2):530–538.

90. Wright D, Rajalingam B, Selvarasah S, *et al.* Generation of static and dynamic patterned co-cultures using microfabricated parylene-C stencils. *Lab Chip* 2007;7(10):1272–1279.

91. Bauwens CL, Peerani R, Niebruegge S, *et al.* Control of human embryonic stem cell colony and aggregate size heterogeneity influences differentiation trajectories. *Stem Cells* 2008;26(9):2300–2310.

92. Khademhosseini A, Suh KY, Yang JM, *et al.* Layer-by-layer deposition of hyaluronic acid and poly-L-lysine for patterned cell co-cultures. *Biomaterials* 2004;25(17):3583–3592.

93. Fico A, Manganelli G, Simeone M, *et al.* High-throughput screening-compatible single-step protocol to differentiate embryonic stem cells in neurons. *Stem Cells Dev* 2008;17(3):573–584.

94. Anderson DG, Levenberg S, Langer R. Nanoliter-scale synthesis of arrayed biomaterials and application to human embryonic stem cells. *Nature biotechno* 2004;22(7):863–866.

95. Flaim CJ, Chien S, Bhatia SN. An extracellular matrix microarray for probing cellular differentiation. *Nature Methods* 2005;2(2):119–125.

96. Colton CK. Implantable biohybrid artificial organs. *Cell transplantation* 1995;4(4):415–436.

97. Borenstein JT, Terai H, King KR, Weinberg EJ, Kaazempur-Mofrad MR, Vacanti JP. Microfabrication technology for vascularized tissue engineering. *Biomed Microdev* 2002;4(3):167–175.

98. Chaudhry GR, Yao D, Smith A, Hussain A. Osteogenic cells derived from embryonic stem cells produced bone nodules in three-dimensional scaffolds. *Journal of biomedicine & biotechnology* 2004;4: 203–210.

99. Levenberg S, Burdick JA, Kraehenbuehl T, Langer R. Neurotrophin-induced differentiation of human embryonic stem cells on three-dimensional polymeric scaffolds. *Tissue Eng* 2005;11(3–4):506–512.

100. Liu H, Roy K. Biomimetic three-dimensional cultures significantly increase hematopoietic differentiation efficacy of embryonic stem cells. *Tissue Eng* 2005;11(1–2):319–330.
101. Taqvi S, Roy K. Influence of scaffold physical properties and stromal cell coculture on hematopoietic differentiation of mouse embryonic stem cells. *Biomaterials* 2006;27(36):6024–6031.

# CHAPTER 2

## STEM CELLS THERAPY FOR ISCHEMIC CARDIOVASCULAR DISEASES: NEW INSIGHTS ON MECHANISMS AND FATE OF THE IMPLANTED CELLS

*Nicolas Noiseux, Jean-François Cailhier and Samer Mansour*

### List of Abbreviations

| | |
|---|---|
| BM | bone marrow |
| BMSC | bone marrow-derived stem cells |
| CABG | coronary artery bypass grafting |
| CSC | cardiac resident stem cells |
| EPC | endothelial progenitor cells |
| ESC | embryonic stem cells |
| GFP | green fluorescent protein |
| HSC | hematopoietic stem cells |
| LV | left ventricle |
| MAPC | multipotent adult progenitor cells |
| MI | myocardial infarction |
| MSC | bone marrow-derived mesenchymal stem cells |
| MSC-CM | mesenchymal stem cells culture-conditioned medium |
| PCI | percutaneous coronary intervention |
| SP | side population cells |

### Abstract

Advances in the treatment of myocardial infarct have led to increased survival, but also to increase number of patients suffering from heart failure. Endogenous repair mechanisms of the human heart are insufficient for meaningful tissue regeneration, so muscle lost is replaced by non-contractile scar tissue, initiating progressive heart failure. Although surgical and catheter-based revascularization of ischemic myocardium can treat angina, reduce the risk of subsequent myocardial infarction (MI), and improve cardiac function, the viability of severely ischemic myocardium, necrotic myocardium, or both cannot be restored. Current pharmacologic and interventional strategies are unsuccessful to regenerate dead myocardium and failed to address clinical challenge caused by the early loss of cardiomyocytes. Moreover, none of the current therapies addresses the underlying cause of the remodeling process, namely the damage to the cardiomyocytes and the vasculature in the ischemic tissue. Therefore, new cardiovascular therapies must be elaborated to promote myocardium repair and regeneration. This "Holy Grail" represents a major challenge in the treatment of ischemic cardiovascular diseases. Cellular transplantation is now emerging as a valuable therapeutic approach to improve healing of the ischemic heart. Promising results from animal studies have prompted several clinical trials to ascertain the safety and feasibility of cell therapy. The exact mechanisms of stem cell therapy have not been yet elucidated and are still intensely debated, cell therapy has already been introduced into the clinical setting. Cell transplantation strategies are faced with many technical issues and are limited to autologous cells, which require bone marrow aspirations, muscle biopsies or blood sampling with cells sorting and/or culture; moreover, they are unable to deliver large cell numbers that would survive the peri-transplantation period. Over the last decade, a plethora of experimental data from pre-clinical and clinical studies has emerged providing both a proof of concept and therapeutic promises for post-MI cardiac repair cell therapies. A major obstacle to the identification of the optimal cell population is that the fate of the implanted cells and the nature of their beneficial effects are ill defined. Moreover, a clear characterization of the cellular effects after transplantation is critical to avoid potentially adverse consequences and to improve outcome. Therefore, better understanding of these new therapies is crucial to identify optimal stem cell applications for the treatment of ischemic cardiovascular diseases.

# 1. Background: Ischemic Cardiovascular Diseases

Despite improvements in survival rate after myocardial infarction (MI) with recent medical and surgical advances,[1] the reduced heart function attributed to irreversible loss of viable cardiomyocytes remains a major clinical problem.[2] Cardiovascular disease represents the leading cause of morbidity and mortality in North America,[3] and remains a significant economic burden for the public health care system. With improving economic conditions and changes in lifestyle in previously third world nations, cardiovascular disease is now threatening to become the leading cause of mortality worldwide.[4] In the current clinical setting, early reperfusion by percutaneous coronary intervention (PCI) including intra-coronary stenting, is the treatment of choice in the situation of acute MI.[5] In patients with diffused coronary artery disease associated with severe ischemic cardiomyopathy, coronary artery bypass grafting (CABG) remains the optimal way of coronary revascularization, and is associated with improved survival and reduction of angina.[6,7] Myocardial dysfunction secondary to ischemic heart disease results from either myocardial ischemia or infarction, with consequent myocyte dysfunction, maladaptation, and ultimately in myocyte death with reduction of effective contractile elements.[4] Following MI, the loss of cardiomyocytes results in the formation of scar tissue, and subsequently, left ventricular (LV) remodeling, aneurysm formation, and progression to congestive heart failure.

The loss of myocardial cell mass and the inability of remaining cells to adequately compensate through hypertrophic or hyperplastic responses result in the development of heart failure due to ventricular dysfunction.[3] Endogenous repair mechanisms of the adult human heart are not sufficient for meaningful tissue regeneration, so muscle lost is replaced by non-contractile fibrotic scar tissue, initiating progressive heart failure.[8] Current treatments for ischemic cardiomyopathy (left ventricular dysfunction secondary to the combined effects of ischemia and infarction) can moderately improve quality of life and increase life expectancy, but cannot cure the disease.[4] Available cardiovascular therapies are largely aimed at counteracting the actions of neurohumoral factors, however mortality remains unacceptably high[9–11] with >50% of patients succumbing within 5 years of the initial diagnosis of heart failure.[3]

Advances in the treatment of acute MI have led to increased survival, but also to an increase in those patients suffering from heart failure.[12] In some patients, cardiac transplantation remains the only therapeutic modality to replace the lost muscle with 5-years survival rates of around 65%. However, due to the current profound shortage of donor organs, its practical use is limited to a minority of end-stage heart failure cases. Although surgical and catheter-based revascularization of ischemic myocardium can treat angina, reduce the risk of subsequent MI, and improve cardiac function, the viability of severely ischemic myocardium, necrotic myocardium, or both cannot be restored.[13] Current pharmacologic and interventional strategies are unsuccessful to regenerate dead myocardium and failed to address the clinical challenge caused by the early loss of cardiomyocytes.[14] Moreover, none of our current therapies addresses the underlying cause of the remodeling process, namely the damage to the cardiomyocytes and the vasculature in the ischemic tissue.[15] Therefore, new cardiovascular therapies must be elaborated to promote myocardial repair and regeneration, this "Holy Grail" represents a major challenge in the treatment of ischemic cardiovascular diseases.

One approach to counteract the effects of myocardial dysfunction could be replacement of damaged contractile cells by healthy myocytes or progenitor cells with the potential of becoming cardiomyocytes.[4] There is growing evidence suggesting that heart muscle has the ability to regenerate through activation of cardiac resident stem cells (CSC), or through recruitment of progenitor stem cells population from other tissues, such as the bone marrow (BM).[14] Cellular transplantation is now emerging as a valuable therapeutical approach to improve healing of the ischemic heart. Experimental studies have shown that adult bone marrow stem cells (BMSC) are capable of differentiation,[16–19] regeneration of infarcted myocardium, induction of myogenesis, as well as promotion of angiogenesis, ultimately leading to a better cardiac contractile performance.[20–29] A variety of embryonic and adult-derived cell types have been investigated for their capacity to mediate cardiac and vascular repair.[30] Positive results from animal studies have prompted several clinical trials to ascertain the safety and feasibility of cell therapy. Despite the fact that the exact mechanisms underpinning stem cell therapy have not been yet elucidated and are still intensely debated, cell therapy has already been introduced into the clinical setting.[24,31,32]

Cell transplantation strategies are faced with many technical issues and are limited to autologous cells, which require bone marrow aspirations, muscle biopsies or blood sampling with cells sorting and/or culture. Moreover, they are unable to deliver large cell numbers that would survive the peri-transplantation period.[29,31,33,34] Over the past several years, a surge of experimental data from pre-clinical and clinical studies has emerged providing both a proof of concept and therapeutic promises for post-MI cardiac repair and regeneration using these cell therapies.[3] However, despite all the excitement in stem cell research resulting from initial experimental data and preliminary clinical trials, many crucial questions regarding stem cells therapy still remain to be answered. A major obstacle to the identification of the optimal cell therapy is that the fate of the implanted cells and the nature of their beneficial effects are ill defined.[4] Moreover, a clear characterization of the cellular effects of stem cell transplantation is critical to avoid potentially adverse consequences and to improve the outcome.[4] Therefore, a better understanding of these new therapies is crucial to the identification of the optimal stem cell applications for the treatment of ischemic cardiovascular diseases.

## 2. Myocardial Infarct: Pathophysiology

Following coronary thrombosis, both infarcted and unaffected myocardial regions undergo progressive changes over the following hours, days and weeks. Ischemia causes an immediate loss of contractility in the affected myocardium, a condition termed hypokinesis. Necrosis starts to develop in the subendocardium about 15–30 minutes after coronary occlusion. The necrotic region grows outward towards the epicardium over the next 3–6 hours, eventually spanning the entire ventricular wall. In the edges of the infarct, the myocardium is stunned and will eventually recover if blood flow is restored. Contractility in the remaining viable myocardium increases, a process termed hyperkinesis.

A progression of cellular, histological and gross changes develops within the infarct. Although alterations in the gross appearance of infarcted tissue are not apparent for at least 6 hours after the onset of cell death, cell biochemistry and ultrastructure begin to show abnormalities within 20 minutes. Cell damage is progressive, becoming increasingly irreversible over about 12 hours. Between 4 and 12 hours after cell death starts, the infracted myocardium begins to undergo coagulation necrosis, a process characterized by cell swelling, organelle breakdown and protein denaturation. After about 18 hours, polymorphonuclear leukocytes (neutrophils) enter the infarct. Their numbers reach a peak after about 5 days, and then decline. After 3–4 days, granulation tissue appears at the edges of the infarct zone, consisting of macrophages, fibroblasts, which lay down scar tissue, and new capillaries. As the granulation tissue migrates inward toward the centre of the infarct over several weeks, the necrotic and apoptotic tissue is engulfed and digested by the macrophages. The granulation tissue then progressively matures with an increase in connective tissue and loss of capillaries. After 2–3 months, the infarct heals, leaving a non-contracting region of the ventricular wall that is thinned, firm and pale grey. This process of ventricular remodelling is caused by an increase in end-diastolic wall stress. Infarct expansion puts patients at a substantial risk for the development of congestive heart failure, ventricular arrhythmias, and free wall rupture. For more details in the physiopathology of MI, refer to Pepine,[35] Reimer[36] and Falk.[37]

The dogma stating that the heart was a post-mitotic organ that was terminally differentiated with approximately 5 billion cells at birth, decreasing only with age, was established in the 1970s and survived for almost three decades.[38] Indeed, until recently, the heart muscle was considered as such without any regenerative capacity, and continuous cell renewal in the adult myocardium was thought to be impossible. No medication or procedure used clinically has shown efficacy in replacing myocardial scar with functioning contractile tissue.[39] The only response to myocardial damage was thought to be cell death followed by hypertrophy of remaining and still viable cardiomyocytes.[40] This simplistic view has been challenged recently by Anversa *et al.* with evidence of cycling myocytes undergoing mitosis and cytokinesis under both physiological and pathological conditions.[41] Furthermore, multipotent cardiac stem cells may be able to renew the myocardium and, under certain circumstances, repair the infarcted heart. The identification of resident cardiac stem/progenitor cells evokes a new understanding of the mechanisms by which the adult heart may maintain cellular homeostasis.[42]

It is still a matter of debate whether cardiac cellular homeostasis is maintained solely by endogenous stem/progenitor cells or *via* extra-cardiac source, notably bone marrow derived stem cells.[42] Studies with transplanted human hearts have shown that adults have extra-cardiac progenitor cells capable of repopulating damaged myocardium, a process occurring at very low levels.[43] Cases have been described in which a male patient received a heart from a female donor (mix-gender donor hearts), and histological analysis revealed that some myocytes, coronary arterioles, and capillaries had a Y chromosome, and showed evidence of cellular proliferation.[44] The observation of Y chromosome-positive resident cardiac cells in female hearts transplanted into male recipients demonstrated the existence of an extra-cardiac source of cells that were either pre-differentiated or with the potential to differentiate into cardiac tissue.[12] Indeed, extra-cardiac circulating progenitor cells may support the regenerative capacity and turnover of the cardiac cells in the transplanted heart.

## 3. Stem Cells for Myocardial Repair

Stem cell therapy is a promising approach to repopulate the injured myocardium,[24] to treat heart failure[24,45] and restore cardiac function.[39,46] Stem cells hold a great potential for regenerative medicine, especially in replacing cells in tissues or organs that hardly have any intrinsic renewal capacity like the heart.[40] The regeneration of functional myocardial tissue will involve the participation/generation of numerous cell types to promote increased contractility with significant functional improvement.[4] Cellular therapy is more likely to be helpful if it can (a) provide a renewable source of proliferating, functional cardiomyocytes; and (b) contribute to the development of a network of blood vessels to maintain and nourish these newly formed cardiomyocytes and the contiguous ischemic myocardium.[30] Ideally, transplanted cells would replace the lost myocytes morphologically and functionally, with the ability to contract and to establish electrical connectivity with the native myocardial cells.[38] Various progenitor stem cells and mature cell types have exhibited an ability to influence positively these mechanisms *in vivo*. Recent observations of the beneficial effects of stem cells on experimental ischemic heart animal models have generated tremendous excitement and stimulated clinical studies, suggesting that this approach is feasible, safe, and potentially effective in human.[38]

Stem cells are undifferentiated tissue progenitor cells that can proliferate and are defined by their ability to self-renew and to form one or more differentiated cell types.[47] They can be categorized anatomically, functionally and by selected cell surface marker, transcription factor, and proteins expression.[38] Of note, to date, there are no specific markers to identify stem cells. In general, two types of stem cells should be discussed separately: embryonic stem cells and adult stem cells found in adult somatic tissue.[48] Whereas embryonic stem cells clearly have the capacity to differentiate into a variety of cell types from the 3 embryonic germ layers and give rise to tissues and organs, most adult stem cells are more differentiated and lineage committed so that their potential for use in regenerative medicine appears to be limited. Adult stem cells comprise at least 3 different groups: bone marrow-derived stem cells (BMSC), circulating progenitor cells and tissue-resident stem cells.[48]

Traditionally, adult stem cells were believed to differentiate only within tissue lineage boundaries, but the recent concept of stem cell plasticity implies that stem cells can transdifferentiate into cell types outside their original lineage.[15,49] The interest in stem cells for cardiac regeneration started in 2001 with the observation of Orlic *et al.* who injected $Lin^-$ $ckit^+$ bone marrow-derived hematopoietic stem cells (HSC) that were able to repair acute MI in mice by transdifferentiating into cardiomyocytes and vascular cells.[25] Nowadays, several cell candidates have been recently investigated for the treatment of ischemic cardiomyopathy such as fetal[50] and neonatal[51] cardiomyocytes, embryonic stem cells,[52,53] cardiac resident stem cells, skeletal myoblasts[54–58] and endothelial progenitor cells.[20,59,60] The bone marrow is known to be an excellent reservoir for many adult stem cells and BMSC have been used to treat hematologic disorders for decades.[42] Bone marrow, which is easily accessible, is presently the most frequent source of cells used for clinical cardiac repair.[38,61] Bone marrow-derived cells contain a complex assortment of progenitor cells, including hematopoietic stem cells (HSC), side population (SP) cells, mesenchymal or stromal, stem cells (MSC), and multipotent adult progenitor cells (MAPC), a subset of MSC.[1,26,27,62–68] Other progenitor/stem cell populations investigated include[38]: fat tissue-derived multipotent stem cells,[69] multipotential cells from bone marrow,[70] skeletal muscle, somatic stem cells from placental cord blood,[71] amniotic fluid-derived stem cells,[72] circulating endothelial progenitor cells (EPC), and cardiac resident progenitor cells (CPC) are already predisposed to adopt a cardiomyocyte phenotype.[62,73]

## 4. What is the Best Donor Cell Source for Cellular Therapy?

Theoretically, many stem and progenitor cell populations are potential candidates to be used for cardiac repair and to treat ischemic cardiomyopathy. Each cell type possesses its own profile of advantages, limitations and practicability issues.[15] There is still uncertainty as to which of the stem cell population is most potent in stimulating cardiac repair. Unfortunately, literature comparing the respective regenerative capacity of each cell population is scant. To circumvent this problem, some investigators have used unfractionated nucleated bone marrow cells, which contain a mixture of cell populations. Herein are some characteristics of the most commonly used adult stem cells for cardiac repair.

### 4.1 *Hematopoietic stem cells (HSC) and endothelial progenitor stem cells (EPC)*

HSC constitute a small cell population of the bone marrow, perhaps as few as 1:10,000 bone marrow mononuclear cells[74,75] and can be enriched to high purity on the basis of surface markers.[39] These cells have been used for stem cell transplantation for more than 25 years in hematology, and are characterized by the marker protein CD34, or the more immature marker protein CD133.[76] They can self-renew and were shown to transdifferentiate into multiple lineages, including endothelial cells,[39,77,78] and can contribute to the regeneration of a variety of non-hematopoietic lineages in multiple organs, including myocardium.[1,18,21,22,25,28,39,63,73,79] To date, the HSC appear to be the most versatile stem cells across all lineages, since adult somatic HSC may share a similar developmental plasticity commonly seen in embryonic stem cells.[74] HSC can be used to repair infarcted hearts by regenerating new cardiomyocytes and vascular endothelium in response to ischemic injury.[1,20,25,78]

Bone marrow-derived endothelial progenitor cells (EPC) are a subtype of circulating cells with the potential to proliferate and to differentiate into mature endothelial cells.[80] EPC are considered to originate from hematopoietic stem cells, and have been defined by their cell surface expression of the hematopoietic markers CD34, CD133,[80–82] and the endothelial marker vascular endothelial growth factor receptor-2 (Flk-1). EPC can be isolated directly from the bone marrow or from the peripheral circulation and expanded *in vitro*.[42] Recent studies suggested that circulating EPC can home to site of tissue ischemia and injury, express endothelial antigens and play a significant role in new blood vessels formation and re-endothelialization.[80,83–85] Normal adults have a small amount of circulating EPC in the peripheral blood.[86] In response to cytokine stimulation, ischemic insult, drugs, and under the influence of other pathological conditions, these cells are mobilized from the bone marrow.[80,86,87] For example, numbers and angiogenic functions of EPC have been reported to be reduced in patients with risk factors for coronary artery disease,[10,83] chronic renal failure,[86] older age[88] and type II diabetics.[89] In contrast, limb ischemia,[80] acute myocardial infarction[90] and HMG-CoA reductase inhibitors (statins)[87] were associated with increased EPC in the circulation and better angiogenic potential. EPC accelerate re-endothelialization and improve vascular healing.[14] A reduction of their numbers and impaired function have been correlated with inflammatory states, adverse vascular events and death.[91–93] EPC are easily isolated from peripheral blood and separated from mononuclear cells using density-gradient centrifugation with Ficoll and they can be expanded *ex vivo* for cellular therapy. After a few days in culture in endothelial cell medium supplemented with growth factors, EPC phenotype can be confirmed by direct fluorescent staining with 1,1′-dioctadecyl-3-3-3,3′-tetramethylindocarbocyanine (DiI)-labeled acetylated low-density lipoprotein (DiLDL) and fluorescein isocyanate (FITC)-labeled Ulex europaeus agglutinin-I (lectin). Dual stained cells positive for both DiLDL and lectin are considered EPC, see Fig. 1.

### 4.2 *Bone marrow-derived mesenchymal stem cells (MSC)*

Adult MSC are a population of stromal cells isolated from bone marrow-derived stem cells (BMSC).[1,26,27,62–68] MSC have been isolated from many species including humans, and are present at a concentration several fold

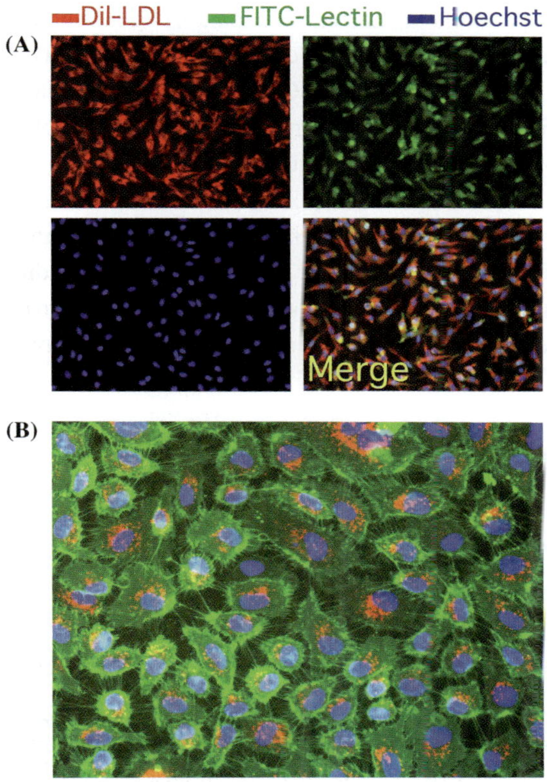


**Fig. 1.** Characterization of cultured EPC by direct fluorescent staining. (**A**) After a few days in culture, adherent cells are stained with 1,1′-dioctadecyl-3-3-3′,3′-tetramethylindocarbocyanine (Dil)-labeled acetylated low-density lipoprotein (DiLDL, red). Stained cells are fixed with 2% paraformaldehyde (PFA) and Lectin staining is performed by incubation with fluorescein isocyanate (FITC, green)-labeled Ulex europaeus agglutinin-I. Nuclei are stained with Hoechst (blue). After staining, samples are viewed with an inverted fluorescent microscope. Dual stained cells positive for both DiLDL and lectin are considered EPC[87] (10× original magnification). (**B**) After many days in culture (second passage, 35 days in this example) in culture medium supplemented with growth factors, some EPC cells can adopt new phenotype from small spindle-like to large, round and flat cells characteristic of mature endothelial cells (10× original magnification).

lower than their hematopoietic counterparts. Their frequency in the bone marrow is estimated to be 1 per 10,000 to 30,000 nucleated cells.[94] MSC are separated from other cells in culture by their preferential attachment to plastic surfaces.[94–96] In their undifferentiated state, MSC do not express hematopoietic or endothelial cell surface markers[94,96–100] such as CD31, CD34, CD45, but may express CD-117 (c-kit) and the majority express CD29, CD44, CD90, and Sca-1.[94,96–101] MSC are easily expandable in culture without losing their differentiation potential,[94] and they constitute an unlimited pool of transplantable cells. MSC fulfilled the stem cells criteria including self-renewing cell division and potential for differentiation.[102] MSC are multipotent,[103] and can differentiate into multiple lineages,[94,101,103–107] including fibroblasts, osteoblasts,[108] chondroblasts and adipocytes, Fig. 2. Differentiation of MSC to cardiomyocyte-like cells has been observed *in vitro* under specific conditions,[27,109,110] and *in vivo* after injection into the myocardium.[27,29,64,66,111,112]

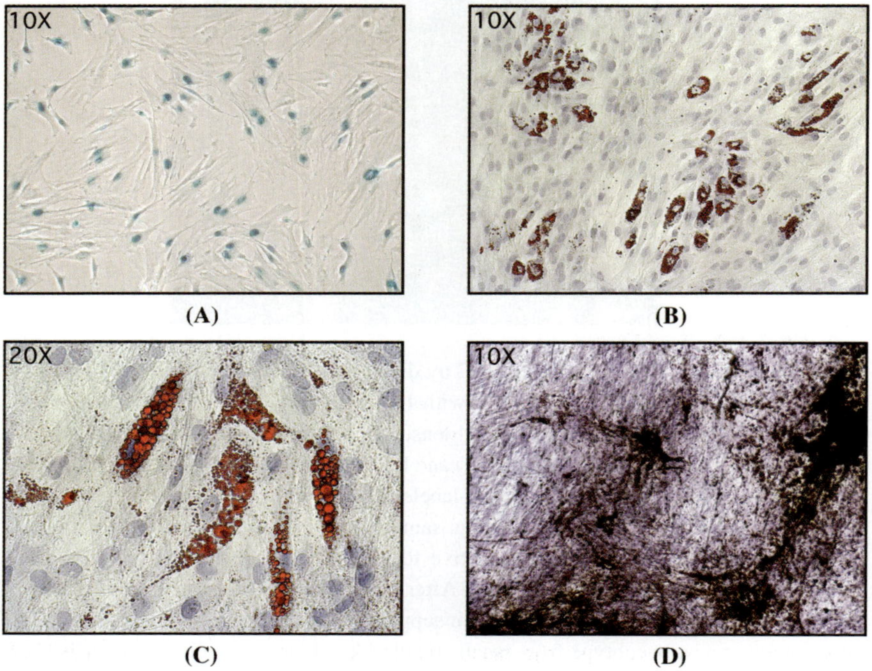


**Fig. 2.** *In vitro* differentiation of human MSC. (**A**) Cultured human MSC as seen under inverted microscope with visible light and phase contrast, nuclei stained with hematoxylin (10X original magnification). (**B**) and (**C**) MSC can differentiate into adipocytes when cultured in specific media, as seen with lipids accumulation revealed by red oil staining. (**D**) Osteogenic differentiation is revealed by silver nitrate staining.

MSC are known to secrete a wide spectrum of biologically active factors and angiogenic/arteriogenic cytokines[113–117] that can be found in the culture-conditioned medium (MSC-CM).[113–117] Under hypoxic culture conditions, the expression of several factors is significantly upregulated.[114,118–121] MSC implantation into the injured heart has been associated with improvement of cardiac performance and repair in animal studies and clinical trials.

Because myocardial infarction leads to permanent loss of tissue with subsequent impaired function, the reports highlighting the capacity of MSC to differentiate into new cardiomyocytes have prompted new perspectives in the treatment of cardiovascular diseases using stem cell transplantation. Among adult stem cells, MSC possess unique properties that make them eligible for convenient and highly effective cell therapy.[3] MSC are particularly suitable for cellular therapy because of their multipotency, low immunogenicity, amenability to *ex vivo* expansion, and genetic modification. However, a recent study by Vulliet *et al.* raised concerns with the use of MSC, and their findings showed acute myocardial ischemia and sub-acute myocardial micro-infarction following intracoronary injection of MSC into ischemic dog hearts due to the formation of small capillary emboli.[122]

### 4.3 *Skeletal myoblasts*

Skeletal myoblasts (satellite cells) are muscle progenitor cells which normally lie in a quiescent state beneath the basal membrane of mature muscular fibers.[15] They can be easily isolated and expanded *in vitro* from a simple skeletal muscle biopsy. When transplanted into an ischemic heart, myoblasts can differentiate into myotubes, but remain committed to a skeletal muscle fate.[123] Therefore, grafted myotubes may contract in response to electrical stimulation but they are not integrated and coupled electromechanically with the host cardiomyocytes.[15] Certainly, an important issue is the possible arrhythmogenicity generated by the transplanted skeletal myoblasts. Their apparent inability to transdifferentiate into cardiomyocytes and to form cardiac-like syncytia with neighboring cells may create a new substrate for ventricular re-entrant arrhythmias.[46] Nevertheless, because of their intrinsic characteristics (autologous origin, *in vitro* scalability, high resistance to ischemia), skeletal myoblasts have undergone extensive pre-clinical testing that has consistently demonstrated their ability to preserve post-infarct left ventricular function and to limit remodeling.[124] Clinical experiences have shown that myoblast transplantation into an infarcted heart could improve systolic and diastolic performance, but with increased risk of malignant ventricular arrhythmias warranting the need for an internal defibrillator implantation.[56] As this therapeutical efficacy occurs despite a poor long-term engraftment rate and the inability of cardiomyocyte conversion, it has been suggested that the predominant mechanism of action could involve paracrine signaling rather than a direct contractile effect of the graft.[24,124]

### 4.4 *Cardiac resident stem cells*

Recently identified by Hierlihy and colleagues in the adult heart, these cardiac stem cell-like populations were identified based on their specific ability to efflux Hoechst dye.[125] These progenitor cells, expressing c-kit, are capable of differentiation into cardiomyocytes and/or vascular tissue. They are self-renewing, clonogenic, and multipotent.[126] Recent studies have suggested that the heart has an inherent ability to replace its parenchymal cells continuously by these resident stem cells.[127] These observations suggest the capacity of adult myocardium to maintain physiological homeostasis, at least partially, through resident cardiac stem cells.[42] The origin of these cardiac stem cells is unclear. These cells could either constitute the remaining endogeneous cardiac stem cells dormant in the myocardium or alternatively, cells that have homed to the heart from another organ (maybe the bone marrow) or in response from injury.[128] These cells can be clonally expanded *in vitro* from an endomyocardial biopsy and be used for cardiac repair.

## 5. Suspected Mechanisms of Stem Cell Repair

Stem cell implantation can prevent deleterious remodeling, improve recovery of infarcted myocardium by cytoprotective effects and promote myogenesis and angiogenesis.[20–29,31,39,98,101,112,129–131] The ultimate goal for cell therapy is the stem cell engraftment into the damaged heart and, ultimately, differentiation into new functional cardiomyocytes, vascular smooth muscle and endothelial cells. Interestingly, while only few groups have observed differentiation of BMSC into cardiomyocytes, most groups have reported a beneficial effect on post-MI remodeling and cardiac functional recovery.[42] As such, these data are certainly encouraging, given the improvement in objective measures such as infarct size and contractility. However, they are also disappointing, since they fail to demonstrate cardiac differentiation. Therefore, it remains unclear whether the beneficial effects resulted from a direct consequence of the transplanted cells integrated into a functional syncytium with the host myocardium, or alternatively from an enhanced cardiac function without direct contribution from the transplanted cell to cardiac contraction.[24] This indirect effect varies and may be attributed to the secretion of biologically active factors that could enhance the angiogenesis,[2,24] the protection of myocytes from apoptosis, the induction of cell proliferation, the improvement of heart function and remodeling, or *via* the recruitment of resident cardiac stem cells.[31] Stem cells may also fuse with the native dysfunctional myocytes to augment function,[78,132,133], see Section 5.2.

The mechanisms by which stem cells can repair damaged myocardium or lead to improved cardiac function are still largely unknown. However, the two most interesting or studied potential pathways are: (a) the use of cell therapy to directly or indirectly improve neovascularization, i.e., vasculogenesis, angiogenesis and arteriogenesis; and (b) differentiation/fusion into cardiomyocytes and formation of myocardial tissue.[38] To which extent these different mechanisms of action are involved may critically depend on the cell type and the clinical setting, such as acute or chronic ischemic injury.[38] For example, in patients presenting acute MI, stem cell transplantation is thought to significantly improve post-MI ventricular remodeling and function through enhanced neovascularization and reduced cardiomyocytes apoptosis, irrespective of long-term engraftment and transdifferentiation. On the other hand, these later mechanisms may have little or no benefit in patients with long established scars, apart from the functional rescue of hibernating cardiomyocytes. Virtually all currently available mechanistic insights have come from pre-clinical studies in animal models, whereas the human experience is rather limited.[8]

## 5.1 *Cardiac regeneration by cell therapy and evidence for transdifferentiation*

When considering the potential mechanisms by which cellular therapy could benefit the ischemic heart, one obvious explanation would be by direct regeneration, or replacement of the necrotic myocardium by viable new cardiomyocytes. Crucial proof-of-principle data in support of this contention were provided by early animal studies where committed cardiomyocytes from fetal and neonatal sources were transplanted following acute MI in the rat.[8] Implanted myocytes formed stable intra-cardiac grafts and resulted in improved left ventricular function.[50,134–137] As expected for terminally differentiated cardiomyocytes, the implanted cells retained their contractile phenotype and expressed the necessary elements for inter-cellular electrical communication (including gap junction proteins).[8,138] Skeletal muscle satellite cells (referred commonly as myoblasts) are another myogenic cell type and have been exhaustively examined as candidate cells for cardiac repair. Skeletal myoblasts are the progenitor cells mediating normal regeneration of skeletal muscle, and have a number of attractive properties for cardiac cell therapy, including relative resistance to ischemia, potentially autologous derivation from readily accessible muscle biopsies, and the capacity for *in vitro* expansion.[138] However, the primary disadvantage of skeletal myoblasts is simply that they differentiate into the wrong form of striated muscle, i.e., skeletal rather than cardiac. Unlike native cardiomyocytes which form an electrical syncytium *via* gap junction coupling, implanted myoblasts are isolated and do not contract in synchrony with the host myocardium.[139] Embryonic stem cells (ESC) are unambiguously cardiogenic cell type, capable of differentiating into cells with ventricular, atrial and pacemaker/conduction system phenotypes.[140,141] Cardiomyocytes derived from ESC are able to form stable intracardiac implant, and provide functional benefit in murine experimental infarct models.[142,143]

Orlic *et al.* were among the first to demonstrate in a mice model of acute MI that bone marrow could provide an extra-cardiac source of progenitor cells with the ability to differentiate into cardiomyocytes and restore cardiac function.[22,25,28] Studies in several species demonstrated that BMSC are stem cells found in various mesenchymal tissues, and precursors of peripheral tissue such as the heart muscle.[144] Cardiogenic potential has also been demonstrated for a surprisingly high number of adult progenitor cell types, including HSC, MSC, circulating EPC, resident cardiac progenitor cells, adipose-derived stem cells and others.[8,25,52,66,69,73,123,145,146] When BMSC are transplanted into an ischemic heart, they can express the cardiac specific markers troponin I and cardiac myosin, suggesting transformation into functional cardiomyocytes.[12,147,148]

Using genetic markers (e.g., Y chromosome) and/or labeled fluorescent dyes (e.g., Green fluorescent protein GFP), many groups reported the transdifferentiation of bone marrow-derived HSC into cardiomyocytes following implantation into ischemic heart.[1,22,25,42] However, these early observations have been called into question by others, who failed to identify similar cardiomyocytes derived from implanted stem cells.[149,150] Further experimental studies addressing the capacity of transplanted BMSC to differentiate into the cardiomyogenic lineage yielded conflicting results.[48,150,151] Indeed, despite the initially positive data reported for HSC, multiple groups have subsequently shown that these cells do not form a significant number of new cardiomyocytes in the infarcted heart.[8,123,150] Using state-of-the-art techniques and genetic markers, it has been suggested that rarely cardiomyocytes would display lineage markers of the transplanted stem cells, but that myocardial cells were derived from the fusion of implanted stem cells with damaged host cardiomyocytes.[8,78,150,152]

Although great enthusiasm was created by the possibility of reconstituting the damaged heart by cell therapy, the exact mechanism is still unclear, and it is possible that findings supporting myocardial regeneration by stem cells differentiation possibly result form technical artifacts. Controversy exists surrounding the ability of BMSC to undergo transdifferentiation, as some techniques that have been used to demonstrate this phenomenon have been questioned.[12] Current failure to label the donor cells adequately and to follow them *in vivo* makes it very difficult to distinguish them from background tissue and could lead to misinterpretation.[46] Indeed, the use of GFP reporter gene is attractive because it is compatible with a variety of imaging techniques, but dead and dying cardiomyocytes have an autofluorescent spectrum that partially overlaps with that of GFP. After injury, autofluorescence increases due to accumulated lipofuscin, blood-derived pigments, and

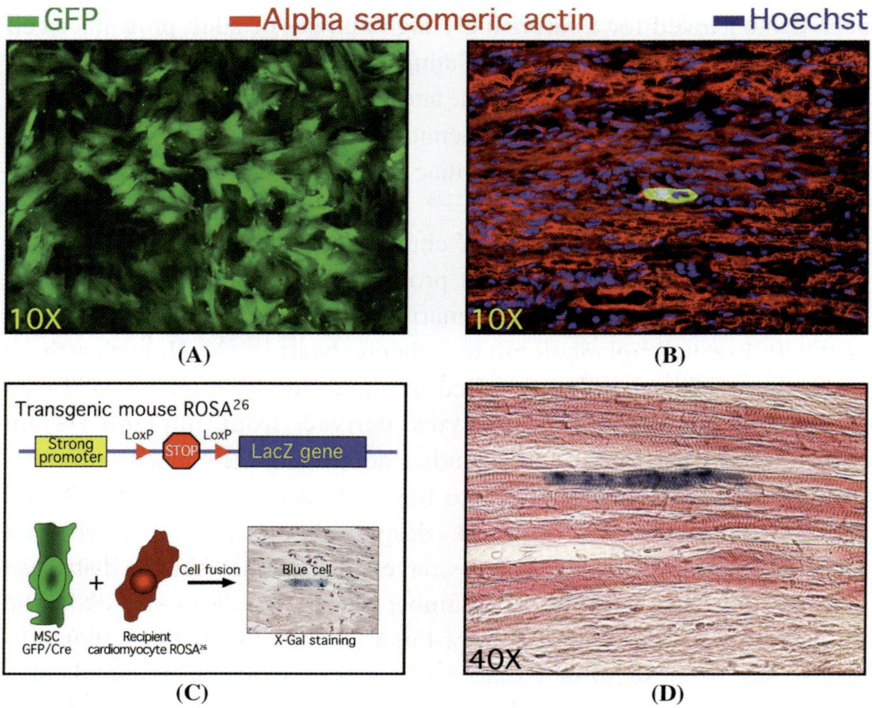


**Fig. 3.** MSC can fuse with recipient cardiomyocytes in ischemic myocardium. (**A**) Mouse MSC were retrovirally transduced to express GFP, image under inverted fluorescent microscope (10X original magnification). (**B**) MSC were injected into ischemic heart in a mouse model of acute MI. We identified MSC-derived GFP$^+$ cardiomyocyte expressing both GFP and cardiac alpha-sarcomeric actin. Such MSC-derived cardiomyocyte could be generated through differentiation of the GFP$^+$ MSC into cardiomyocyte, or by fusion of the transplanted MSC-GFP$^+$ with recipient cardiomyocyte. (**C**) We used a model of Cre/LoxP reporter transgenic ROSA26 mice in which a loxP-flanked stop sequence is present 5′ of the LacZ expression cassette to prevent transcriptional readthrough until selective excision by Cre-mediated recombination from implanted MSC expressing GFP and Cre recombinase.[132] Consequently, X-gal staining is used to detect cellular fusion events. (**D**) Heart sections of recipient R26R stained with Xgal and eosin to detect cellular fusion. We observed cellular fusion with individual blue cells having typical cardiomyocyte morphology.

other intrinsic fluors such as flavins and reduced nicotinamide adenine dinucleotide (NADH).[123] Evidence for regeneration includes colocalization of GFP fluorescence from donor cells, with immunostaining for cardiomyocytes markers, including sarcomeric actin, Figs. 3A and 3B.

Thus, it is possible to misidentify a GFP positive cardiomyocyte as the result from a donor GFP positive cell. For a good review on stem cells in myocardial regeneration and methodological artifacts, please refer to Anversa *et al.*[151]

## 5.2 *Cellular fusion*

Adding to skepticism about the differentiation capacity of transplanted cells have been confounding issues of traditional immunofluorescent and immunohistochemical analysis, including tissue artifacts (see section above).[30] Recently, cellular fusion has been proposed as another possible explanation for stem cell effects. While the main hypothesis for cardiac repair by stem cells was believed to be solely tissue regeneration by stem cell differentiation,[147] fusion of transplanted stem cells with resident cardiomyocytes has been offered as an alternative for the previous claims of transdifferentiation.[15,78,132,149,150,152] Fused donor cells may adopt phenotype of recipient cells, and without detailed genetic analysis, might be interpreted as differentiation.[153] Fusion events can result in cell fusion with 2 nuclei (2n + 2n), or alternatively nuclear fusion will result in cells with larger nuclei (4n chromosomes). Fusion of bone marrow-derived cells with purkinje neurons, hepatocytes and cardiomyocytes has been reported for the first time by Alvarez-Dolado *et al.* in 2003.[152] In their experimental transgenic mouse model, spontaneous fusion was demonstrated *in vivo*, resulting in multinucleated cells, whereas no evidence of transdifferentiation without fusion was observed. Using different genetic markers to track the fate of transplanted cells, fusion with recipient cardiomyocytes has been also reported for peripheral blood $CD34^+$ cells,[154] hematopoietic stem cells,[78,155] cardiac progenitor cells,[62] and skeletal muscle cells.[156]

It is possible that many examples of putative stem cell plasticity are actually due to transplanted cells fusing with a different tissue type, followed by reprogramming of the donor and recipient cell genome.[157] Indeed, some previously reported transdifferentiation of implanted cells into cardiomyocytes could in fact represent a fusion between these two cells, resulting in cardiomyocytes sharing both phenotypes of donor and recipient cells (Fig. 3). To address the issue of cellular fusion, it is imperative to use a method that allows the tracking of the implanted cells, but also a genetic marker that can be triggered exclusively by fusion event. A well-validated technique suitable for this purpose relies on the use of Cre/LoxP system.

Using a model of acute MI in transgenic mice, we recently demonstrated that transplanted MSC could fuse with recipient cardiomyocytes in the infarcted area.[132] MSC from wild type C57BL/6 mice were retro-virally transduced to express GFP (reporter gene) and Cre recombinase (with nuclear localizating sequence). These MSC were transplanted into infarcted hearts of histocompatible R26R mice (similar C57BL/6 genetic background). In these transgenic mice, a loxP-flanked stop sequence is present 5′ of the LacZ expression cassette to prevent transcriptional read-through until selective excision by Cre mediated recombination from implanted MSC.[158] Thus, the LacZ gene is expressed exclusively after a donor MSC expressing Cre fuses with a recipient cell from the R26R mice (Fig. 3C). Consequently, X-gal staining is used to detect cellular fusion events.[78,152] This useful method based on Cre/lox recombination that conditionally turns on the LacZ gene only in the fused cells allowed us to screen rapidly many tissue sections covering a large area of the infarcted and MSC injected heart. Transplanted cells were found within the infarcted myocardium (detection of MSC by GFP immunoreactivity). Early massive engraftment was observed at three days, but the number of implanted MSC decreased significantly over time, and by 28 days post-MI very few cells remained. As early as three days following MSC injection into the ischemic heart, we observed cellular fusion with individual blue cells having typical cardiomyocyte morphology (Fig. 3D). Interestingly, the majority of the fusion events with $LacZ^+$ cells were detected within the infarct border zone, in areas with viable cardiomyocytes.

## 5.3 *Indirect and paracrine effects*

Despite the lack of significant myocardial regeneration by implanted stem cells through cardiomyocyte differentiation, numerous studies reported that cardiac function can be improved by cell therapy, suggesting further evidence for a nonmyogenic pathway of cardiac repair.[8] Regardless of the mechanism responsible for the beneficial effect of cell therapy, fusion *vs* differentiation, it is generally accepted that the number of reported cardiomyocytes derived from exogenously delivered stem cells remains relatively low and cannot account for the impressive observed functional improvement.[42,132] Indeed, the variable observations relating to cell transdifferentiation and fusion, as well as transient cell retention and survival in the ischemic heart,[132] have prompted a rethinking of the mechanisms that account for the functional benefits of cell therapy in cardiac repair.[30] It has been proposed that stem cell transplantation may improve myocardial function recovery predominantly by facilitating endogenous repair mechanisms, rather than through direct regeneration of lost cardiomyocytes and vascular cells. Thus, it is possible that implanted cells could secrete bio-active factors which may stimulate angiogenesis, suppress apoptosis of cardiomyocytes, increase efficiency of cardiomyocyte metabolism, improve inotropy of survival myocytes, modulate interstitial matrix composition and remodeling, and maybe even recruit cardiac resident stem cells.[15,113,114,120,132] The fact that it is possible to improve the heart's function without remuscularizing the infarct is already known from numerous pharmacological studies, e.g., with beta–adrenergic blocker or angiotensin-converting enzyme inhibitors, and this has resulted in a search for other potential mechanisms of action.[8] Furthermore, evidence suggests that stem cells could improve myocardial repair through attenuated remodeling with an increased wall thickness and by preventing subsequent ventricular dilatation. This would represent a significant clinical benefit that is independent of systolic activation of the implanted cells.[8]

MSC are known to secrete a wide spectrum of biologically active factors,[113–117] and under hypoxic culture conditions and serum starvation, conditions that mimic myocardial infarct, the expression of several factors is significantly upregulated.[114,118–121] These growth factors and cytokines are released in the culture medium (MSC-conditioned medium, MSC-CM), and can be concentrated and used therapeutically. In a murine hindlimb ischemia model, Kinnaird *et al.* demonstrated that intra-muscular injection of MSC-CM improved collateral blood flow recovery and limb function, and reduced muscle atrophy.[114] In the MSC-CM, the presence of many cytokines has been confirmed including: VEGF, FGF-2, IL-6, PIGF, MCP-1, etc.[114,116] Therefore, they concluded that it was not direct cell incorporation, but paracrine signaling that may be responsible of the beneficial effects of bone marrow cell therapy in ischemic injury.[116]

We previously reported that transplantation of MSC into ischemic myocardium improved cardiac function recovery and repair as early as 72 hours, which is too early to be explained solely by myocardial regeneration from MSC.[119,120,132] Since such an early recovery cannot be explained entirely by *de novo* myogenesis, we proposed that MSC could achieve cardio-protection by indirect effects, through paracrine mediators, rather than cardiac regeneration. Furthermore, to investigate how MSC could achieve protection of the ischemic myocardium by paracrine mediators and indirect effects, we demonstrated that MSC-CM reduced hypoxia-induced apoptosis, and also triggered vigorous spontaneous contraction of isolated hypoxic adult rat cardiomyocytes *in vitro*, suggesting the presence of - antiapoptotic and inotropic factors.[120] Moreover, when injected directly into infarcted rat hearts, the MSC-CM limited infarct size as early as 72 hours and improved ventricular function[119,120] at levels comparable to those observed following MSC transplantation. These remarkable data strongly support the concept that the effects observed after intra-myocardial injection of MSC into infarcted hearts are to a great extent attributable to paracrine protection and indirect effects on ischemic myocardium. Recently, we investigated the effects of MSC-secreted growth factors on extent of early recovery from MI in a large animal pre-clinical model.[159] Swine subjected to acute MI by temporary balloon occlusion of the left anterior descending coronary artery using percutaneous techniques received intra-coronary injection of either concentrated MSC-derived growth factors or control medium. Treatment with MSC-derived factors significantly reduced cardiac tropinin-T elevation, and improved echocardiographic parameters, including fractional area shortening, stroke volume, and cardiac output. Quantitative evaluation of fibrosis by Verhoff staining revealed a reduction of the fibrotic area in the infracted zone at seven days. Similarly, Masson's trichrome staining revealed reduced myocardial damage as demonstrated by areas of relatively preserved myocardium in the infracted area. TUNEL assay demonstrated less cardiomyocyte apoptosis. Protein array detected the presence of angiogenic (VEGF, endothelin, epiregulin), antiapoptic (Galectin-3, Smad-5, sRFP-1), and anti-remodeling factors (TIMP). RT-PCR confirmed the expression of these factors. In summary, a single intra-coronary injection of concentrated biologically active factors secreted by MSC could achieve early protection of ischemic myocardium, improve cardiac repair, and partially preserve contractility. MSC-derived growth factors injection (rather than MSC themselves) should be evaluated as a novel therapy to treat ischemic heart disease, many practical and technical issues of cell therapy.

## 5.4 *Inflammation and neovascularization*

Myocardial infarction can also be viewed as an inflammatory conditioned characterized by the production of various cytokines such as tumor necrosis factor, IL-1, IL-6, transforming growth factor families and others, that can regulate myocyte survival, apoptosis and can also trigger additional cellular response, contributing to the healing and remodeling of the injured tissue, ultimately influencing the outcome.[160] The immune system plays a crucial role during the acute phase of MI and this constitutes a most appropriate timing where any immunomodulatory effects following stem cell implantation could exert their effects.[8] An adequate microenvironment supporting nutrient delivery and waste removal is necessary to sustain survival, growth and possibly differentiation of the transplanted cells.[2] Normal growth and ultimate stem cell fate depend on engraftment in an appropriate "niche". Thus, it appears that the fate of BMSC is determined by the environment in which they are engrafted rather than by an intrinsically programmed fate, but the mechanisms explaining how the local milieu influences stem cell differentiation are yet to be characterized.[144] Importantly, an angiogenic response has been observed in many studies following cell transplantation.[24] Transplanted cells may act in an indirect supportive role, optimizing the milieu for host vasculature and cells to respond to ischemia and healing.[112,114,115,117–119] Therefore, concurrent revascularization must keep pace with cell repopulation of the infarcted tissue and this could be of importance to allow adequate recuperation.[161]

Much attention has been focused on the direct consequence of cell-based therapy by the renewal of lost parenchymal cells, but restoration of the extracellular matrix and vascular supply are also important issues since both components are essential for structural and functional support of the surviving cardiomyocytes[2] in the ischemic myocardium. It is also important to consider other potential mechanisms by which transplanted cells could benefit cardiac function without directly contributing to systolic contraction.

After birth, blood vessel formation proceeds mainly through 2 mechanisms: angiogenesis and arteriogenesis. **Angiogenesis** consists of several distinct processes which include sprouting and proliferation of pre-existing capillaries to form a new network and is tightly regulated by hypoxia through a number of pro-angiogenic factors, including vascular endothelial growth factor (VEGF), fibroblast growth factors (FGFs), angiopoietins, placental growth factor (PlGF) and hepatocyte growth factor (HGF).[162–168] **Arteriogenesis** is the rapid proliferation of pre-existing collateral arteries[162] that involves remodeling of small arterioles into larger vessels, and is triggered in part by an increase in shear stress in arterioles parallel with the occluded artery.[164,165,167–169] The recruitment of monocytes that differentiate into macrophages and produce abundant angiogenic growth factors such as VEGF, NO, monocyte chemoatractant protein-1 (MCP-1) and other cytokines, is also essential and ultimately leads to endothelial and smooth muscle cell proliferation, migration, vessel remodeling and extracellular matrix synthesis.[117,164] Arteriogenesis is by far the most efficient adaptative mechanism for survival of ischemic organs because of its ability to conduct relatively large blood flow.[162] Angiogenesis and arteriogenesis are complex processes sharing several common mechanisms of action, growth factors and cytokines dependency.[162] Many of these cytokines act not only in a co-ordinated time- and concentration-dependent manner, but one cytokine may potentiate (or inhibit) the effect of another,[117] and the complexity of the process of collateral formation has led to speculate that multiple factor strategies could be used therapeutically to modulate vessel formation.[164]

The observation that BMSC contain a subpopulation of endothelial progenitor cells with the potential for angiogenesis suggests that these cells may contribute to cardiac repair by enhancing the local blood supply in ischemic myocardium.[12] Some reports have suggested that MSC implantation into ischemic tissue promote collaterals development through paracrine mechanisms, but not through direct cell incorporation into growing vasculature.[24,26,98,113–116,164,170–174] MSC express genes encoding a broad spectrum of cytokines with angiogenic properties including VEGF, HGF, FGF, MCP-1, PGF, IL-1 and IL-6, SDF-1, MMP-9.[2,114,117] These cytokines can be found in the media of cultured cells, and have all individually been shown to have positive effects on experimental blood flow recovery.[2,114–117,163] Moreover, media collected from MSC cultures (MSC-derived conditioned medium, MSC-CM) promote *in vitro* proliferation and migration of endothelial cells (EC) and vascular smooth muscle cells (VSMC), and enhance *in vivo* collateral blood flow recovery when injected into ischemic hindlimb.[2,114,117] It is possible that neovascularization by stem cell is leading to enhanced blood supply in the peri-infarct region and thereby promoting salvage of stunned, hibernating, or otherwise susceptible cardiomyocytes.[8] However, controversy persists regarding the exact mechanisms through which MSC transplantation may enhance repair and collateral development in ischemic tissue.[117]

## 6. Delivery and Homing of Stem Cells

The identification of the appropriate route for cell administration to the damaged heart is an essential prerequisite for successful tissue repair.[144] The goal of any cell delivery strategy is to transplant sufficient number of cells into the myocardial region of interest and to achieve maximum retention of cells within that area.[38] Furthermore, the success of cell delivery is determined by the local milieu since it will influence short-term cell survival, cell properties in regard to cell adhesion, transmigration through the vascular wall, and tissue invasion. High cell concentrations within the area of interest and prevention of homing of transplanted cells into other organs are required, therefore targeted and regional administration of cells are preferred.[144] Cell homing, adhesion, transmigration through the vascular wall, and tissue invasion involves many complex steps. Stromal-derived factor-1 (SDF-1) is expressed in the ischemic myocardium and plays an important role in endogenous stem cell migration, adhesion, homing and recruitment from bone marrow. SDF-1 therefore is an important chemotactic factor for progenitor cells and thus plays a crucial role in the migration of these cells into areas of infarcted myocardium.[12]

The most frequently used routes of cell delivery for ischemic cardiomyopathy are percutaneous intra-coronary injection, percutaneous endomyocardial using 3D-guiding systems, and direct intra-myocardial injection during open chest cardiac surgery procedure. Intra-coronary sinus or intravenous systemic deliveries have also been described, as well as stem cell mobilization following G-CSF treatment as described in the FIRSTLINE-AMI trial.[175] Intra-coronary infusion requires migration through the vessel wall into the ischemic heart tissue, which is helped by damaged and permeabilized endothelium as found after acute myocardial infarct. Cells like bone marrow-derived and blood-derived progenitor cells are known to extravasate and migrate efficiently into ischemic areas, whereas skeletal myoblasts do not.[38] The intravenous route is the easiest, but the main disadvantage is that approximately only 3% of normal cardiac output will flow through the left ventricle *via* the coronary arteries, and is limited because of transpulmonary first-pass captation and sequestration.[144]

The intra-coronary route has been used safely and effectively to achieve selective administration and higher first-pass delivery to the heart than systemic therapy.[30] However, there have been reports of microcirculation obstruction following intra-coronary infusion of satellite cells and MSC, resulting in embolic myocardial damage and sub-acute microinfarction.[122] Unlike intra-vascular infusion, direct intra-myocardial injection targets specific regions of myocardium without relying on the up-regulation of inflammatory signals to assist transvascular cell migration and tissue invasion.[30] Pre-clinical and clinical results suggest that direct MSC injection may result in less non-cardiac cell entrapment than intra-coronary or systemic intravenous infusion, along with better retention culminating in greater benefit for cardiac function recovery.[176–178] An intra-myocardial injection delivery approach appears specially well-suited for transplantation of larger and adherent cells (e.g., MSC) and particularly relevant to chronic myocardial diseases such as chronic ischemic cardiomyopathy or dilated failing heart.[30] After more than a decade since the beginning of cell therapy, no one has identified the technique for optimal administration of stem cell into the heart. As a result, more than 90% of the cells delivered to the heart through a needle are lost to the circulation or leak out of the injection site.[123] Indeed, mechanical leakage and washout may account for a major proportion of cell loss after cell implantation.[38] Experiments by Teng *et al.* with microspheres revealed a retention rate of only 11% following direct intra-myocardial injection in the beating porcine heart *versus* 67% in the non-beating heart illustrate the complexity of the approach.[179]

## 7. Optimizing the Reparative Biology of Stem Cells

A promising area of investigation has been the *in vitro* manipulation of the cells prior to transplantation, in an attempt to maximize their biologic and functional properties.[30] Intervention aimed at enhancing donor cell survival, homing, retention, and proliferation may improve regenerative capacity. Investigators have suggested the use of special bio-scaffolds to support growth and differentiation of the cells or various cell preconditionings before transplantation, such as heat shock treatment, exposure to hypoxia, specific growth factors (e.g., FGF-2, IGF-1, BMP-2)[180] or low dose chemical agents (e.g., cyclosporine A, hydrogen peroxide).[30] Others have reported the use retroviral systems for overexpression of therapeutical genes like VEGF, angiopoietin, and hypoxia-regulated hem oxygenase-1 (HO-1).[34,98,132,180]

An important issue limiting cell therapy is the extensive cell death following transplantation into the ischemic heart. The survival of implanted cells is often limited in the infarcted tissue[34,181] and cell death is worsened by the hostile environment caused by the reduced blood flow, hypoxemia, inflammation and scarring in the ischemic myocardium. Regardless of cell type, multiple studies suggest that more than 90% of cells successfully delivered to the heart will die within one week.[34,123,132] Our group investigated the overexpression of antiapoptotic proteins such as Akt, to improve the cell survival, but also the reparative effects of MSC therapy in an animal model of acute MI.[98,119,120,132] We genetically engineered rat MSC to overexpress the prosurvival gene Akt1[182–184] (Akt-MSC). Akt overexpression resulted in better protective and antiapoptotic effects against ischemia *in vitro*, but also *in vivo* as shown by the reduction of the proportion of apoptotic cells following implantation into the infarcted myocardium and increased cell retention. Moreover, intra-cardiac injection of $5 \times 10^6$ Akt-MSC inhibited the process of cardiac remodeling and resulted in normalization of cardiac function at 2 weeks, to a level indistinguishable from sham-operated animals.[98] Although improvements in cardiac function were also observed in other studies, complete recovery of LV function occurred only following transplantation of MSC overexpressing Akt, and these results represent a new threshold in cardiac regeneration using cell therapy.[181] This cell-based therapy, combined with a gene-therapy approach, has the potential to address multiple issues in cell availability and scalability.

The mechanisms underlying the beneficial effects of Akt-MSC are still unclear as protection may result from differentiation of MSC into cardiomyocytes, fusion of MSC with recipient cardiomyocytes, modulation of cardiomyocyte survival/function through paracrine effects or by a combination of these processes. We have evidence that the therapeutic effects of MSC transplantation occur in less than 72 hours. Since early recovery cannot be explained by *de novo* myogenesis, fusion nor differentiation, we postulated that Akt-MSC could achieve better protection of the ischemic myocardium by paracrine mediators rather than cardiac regeneration. We tested this hypothesis *in vitro* by assessing the effects of conditioned medium from cultured MSC on rat cardiomyocytes subjected to hypoxia. Conditioned medium (CM) was collected from normoxic or hypoxic MSC (12 hours culture) and used to replace the normal culture medium of cardiomyocytes exposed to 24 hours of hypoxia. We observed significant cytoprotective effects when the hypoxic cardiomyocytes were maintained in CM from hypoxic cultured Akt-MSC compared to control MSC. *In vivo*, Akt overexpression in transplanted Akt-MSC significantly enhanced cell engraftment within the infarct and improved cardiac function and repair as early as 3 days post-MI in the murine ischemic heart compared to control MSC.[132] Moreover, injection of concentrated CM from hypoxic cultured Akt-MSC markedly reduced the infracted size and the apoptotic index.[119]

To determine how hypoxic culture conditions and Akt overexpression may alter gene expression in MSC and improve cardioprotective effects, we used a genomic approach for large scale identification and functional screening of candidate genes.[118] Using Affymetrix GeneChip, we performed a micro-array analysis of control-MSC and Akt-MSC under normoxic and hypoxic culture conditions. We found 650 transcripts differentially regulated. Our analysis, targeted on angiogenic and secreted factors, revealed that genes significantly upregulated in hypoxic Akt-MSC included VEGF, HGF, laminin$\alpha$4, angiopoietin4, pleiotrophin, early growth response1 (Egr1) and procollagen type VIII and XVIII. Moreover, we showed *in vitro* and *in vivo* that secreted frizzled related protein 2 (Sfrp2), an antiapoptotic gene, is one of the key stem cell paracrine factors mediating myocardial survival and repair by Akt-MSC.[185]

We strongly believe that early paracrine signaling through the release of various cytokines and bio-active factors is important in the beneficial effects of stem cell-based therapy. Conditioned medium injection brings important chemokines on site of the injury without new cell engraftment or immunogenic reaction or rejection. It is therefore interesting to speculate that MSC-CM injection could be used as a novel pharmacological therapy to treat ischemic heart diseases, rather than MSC themselves, thus avoiding all the practical and technical issues regarding cell therapy. This MSC-CM could be produced by an established cell line and be readily available for any patient presenting with an acute myocardial infarct in the emergency room and undergoing acute PCI treatment for myocardial reperfusion (allo-recognition is an issue for cell lines). Moreover, combining stem cell and gene therapies, MSC could be cultured and genetically modified *ex vivo* to alter cytokine expression, making these cells ideal to be used as "minipumps" to produce and release factors required to greatly improved tissue repair, viability and blood vessel formation.

## 8. Examples of Stem Cells Clinical Applications in Acute MI

Following acute MI, the observation that mobilization of BMSC occurs naturally to heal the myocardium, as evidenced by their extravasation from coronary capillaries into the damaged myocardium, led several groups to investigate the potential benefit of these stem cells for cardiac repair.[20,25,39,90] All clinical studies on acute MI included patients, who had undergone primary angioplasty and stent implantation to re-open the infarct-related artery and who received optimal medical treatment during the acute phase and follow-up, and cells were infused intra-coronarily by using the stop-flow balloon-catheter approach. Current trials may be categorized into studies using unselected bone marrow cells or selected stem cell populations.

### 8.1 *Unselected bone marrow cells*

In patients with recent myocardial infarction, Strauer *et al.* demonstrated that intra-coronary (IC) administration of unselected BMSC was safe and was associated with improved cardiac performance.[26] In the same way, the Zeiher group reported that IC administration of purified bone marrow progenitors as early as six days after the MI improved cardiac performance, expressed by a rise of 9% in the left ventricular ejection fraction (LVEF) in the treated group compared to 3% in controls, and enhanced the myocardial perfusion of the infarcted myocardium at 4 months and 1 year of follow-up.[186–188] Following initial safety and feasibility studies, four larger randomized trials of bone marrow cell therapy after AMI have now been completed.[186–188]

The combined experience from these trials indicates that intra-coronary delivery of unselected bone marrow cells is feasible and safe in the short- and mid-term (up to 18 months). Bone marrow harvest and intra-coronary cell delivery are not associated with bleeding complications or ischemic damage to the myocardium. No increased rate of in-stent restenosis have been observed. Clinical surveillance, Holter monitoring, and data from an electrophysiological study indicate that bone marrow cell transfer is not associated with an increased propensity to ventricular arrhythmias. Moreover, intra-myocardial calcifications or tumor formation were not observed after intra-coronary bone marrow cell delivery. The beneficial effects of intra-coronary bone marrow cell transfer were confirmed in the re-infusion of enriched progenitor cells and infarct remodeling in acute myocardial infarction (REPAIR-AMI trial). In this study, mononucleated bone marrow cell transfer promoted an increase in left ventricular ejection fraction of 2.5% after 4 months as compared to a control group that also underwent bone marrow aspiration but received an intra-coronary infusion of a placebo.[189] In addition, the randomized trial “BOOST” showed an improvement in the cardiac function (6.7% increase of the LVEF in the treated group at 6 months of follow-up *vs* 0.7% in controls) following IC injection of autologous BMSC without any adverse effect such as in-stent restenosis or arrhythmia. Furthermore, this beneficial effect was sustained at 6 months[190] and 1 year of follow-up,[191] but not at 18 months.[192]

In contrast to BOOST and REPAIR-AMI, two other randomized studies did not report significant improvements of left ventricular ejection fraction after intra-coronary cell transfer.[193,194] While the exact reasons for the differing results remain elusive, it is worthwhile to mention that in these trials the design was different: timing of cell injection after MI, cell type and control groups. In the randomized and controlled ASTAMI trial, the use of unselected BMSC for PCI treatment following acute MI failed to demonstrate at 6 months any improvement in LVEF.[194] Whilst the cells were delivered late after reperfusion in ASTAMI (after 4–6 days), a particular cell preparation method that leads to an enrichment of lymphocytic bone marrow cells was employed. It is not clear whether this method actually recovers the bone marrow cell populations that are required to achieve functional improvements after AMI. Similarly, Janssens *et al.* reported no significant difference in overall LVEF at 4 months, but showed a decreased infarct size and better regional function in stem cells treated patients.[193] However, cells were delivered 24 hours after coronary reperfusion. In BOOST and REPAIR-AMI, cells were transplanted several days later. Sub-group analyses in REPAIR-AMI indicated that the timing of cell delivery may be important, and that the beneficial effects on ejection fraction are lost when the cells are delivered too early.[195]

Despite the use of various experimental protocols with mixed cells showing mixed results,[195] a recent meta-analysis systematically reviewed all available clinical trials and studied 12 randomized controlled trials plus 6 cohort studies, which altogether combined included nearly one thousand patients. The report compared the outcome data from treated patients to that of controls showing a slight but positive improved LVEF of 3.66%, a reduced infarct scar size of –5.49% and a reduced LV end-systolic volume of –4.80 ml.[196] Thus, available evidence suggests that BMSC transplantation is associated with modest improvement in physiologic and anatomic parameters in patients with both acute MI and chronic ischemic cardiomyopathy, but above and beyond conventional therapy.[196] Therefore, therapy with stem cells appears to be safe, but well-designed double-blind and randomized clinical studies are clearly needed to confirm the promising findings from earlier studies.

## 8.2 *Selected bone marrow cell populations: Are they the optimal stem cell source?*

There is currently uncertainty as to which of the stem cell population is most potent in stimulating angiogenesis and cardiac repair. Nevertheless, the use of hematopoietic progenitor stem cells appears to uniformly induce neovascularization that seems to be a prerequisite of the successful functional repair. The hematopoietic stem cells are characterized by the presence of the surface marker CD34. In addition, CD133 has been identified as a marker that is present on the stem cells that co-express not only CD34, but also other markers such as c-kit. It may be hypothesized that use of these $CD133^+$ cells may involve a larger or more primitive group of stem cells than selection based only on the use of $CD34^+$ marker. Bone marrow-derived endothelial progenitor cells (EPC) are a sub-type of circulating cells with the potential to proliferate and to differentiate into mature endothelial cells.[80] EPC share many surface marker antigens with hematopoietic stem cells, such as CD34, CD133, and Flk-1.[80–82] Recent studies suggested that circulating EPC could home to site of tissue ischemia and injury, to express endothelial markers and to play a significant role in new blood vessel formation.[80,83–85] Early clinical trials of EPC transplantation for ischemic cardiomyopathy indicate the safety and feasibility of this cell-based therapy.[197]

## 8.3 *The use of $CD133^+$ stem cells for acute and chronic ischemic cardiomyopathy*

The use of non-homogenous or non-selected stem cell precursors may contribute to the regeneration of necrotic myocardium and blood vessels, but does not allow the characterization of optimal cell type for cardiac repair. Moreover, different cell types may compete for the engraftment in the injured myocardium.[195] Drexler's group showed that selected BMSC displayed a 7-fold higher retention in the infarcted myocardium, when compared to unfractionated and unselected BMSC.[198] Furthermore, Stamm *et al.* used CD133$^+$ cells, a more specified sub-population of bone marrow-derived cells, for intra-myocardial injections performed during an open-chest procedure, and observed increased LVEF and improved tissue perfusion during follow-up.[199] Experimental studies demonstrated that selected, well-defined hematopoeitic stem cells contribute to cardiac repair of the acutely infarcted myocardium by inducing neovascularization, inhibition of apoptosis and cardiomyogenesis. Indeed, the hematopoietic CD133$^+$ cells possess high engraftment, pluripotent and angiogenic capacity, and appear to be valuable for cardiac repair in experimental myocardial infarction.[200–203] Menasche's team showed that in the situation of post-infarction scars, the transplantation of bone marrow-derived CD133$^+$ progenitors improves cardiac function, and this benefit was similar to that afforded by myogenic cells.[204] In addition, in a phase I pilot study, Bartunek *et al.* tested the feasibility, safety and functional effects of intra-coronary administration of selected autologous CD133$^+$ bone marrow progenitors in patients with recent myocardial infarction. Compared to a matched non-randomized control group, they noted a significant increase of 7% in the LVEF of the treated group as compared to 3% in controls at 4 months of follow-up. They also showed that in patients treated with intra-coronary CD133$^+$ cells the improvement of the global and regional LV function was paralleled with increased myocardial perfusion and viability.[205]

## 8.4 *First ongoing clinical Canadian experience in selected bone marrow stem cell therapy: Comparison of intracoronary injection of CD133$^+$ bone marrow stem cells to placebo in patients after acute myocardial infarction and left ventricular dysfunction: COMPARE-AMI trial*[206,207]

In this randomized, double blind, placebo controlled phase I-II trial, we are investigating the feasibility, safety and efficacy of intra-coronary administration of selected bone marrow stem cells compared to placebo in patients with left ventricular dysfunction following successful stented acute MI.

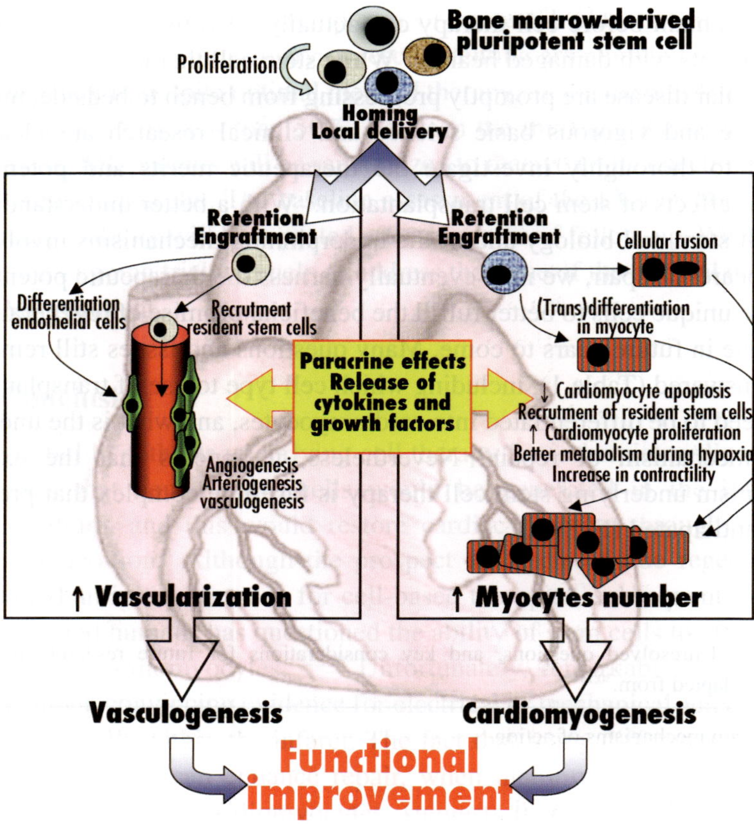


**Fig. 4.** Working hypothesis for mechanism of stem cell transplantation for the treatment of ischemic cardiomyopathy. Stem and progenitor cell transplantation can have a favorable impact on tissue perfusion and contractile performance by promoting vascularization and myocyte formation. Improved vascularization may facilitate beneficial effects in the myocyte compartment. Depending on the stem cell type and local milieu, the relative contribution of cell incorporation (transdifferentiation and/or fusion) vs paracrine effects may vary. Adapted from Dimmeler[48] and Woller.[31]

## References

1. Jackson KA, Majka SM, Wang H, *et al.* Regeneration of ischemic cardiac muscle and vascular endothelium by adult stem cells. *J Clin Invest* 2001;107(11):1395–1402.

2. Timmermans F, De Sutter J, Gillebert TC. Stem cells for the heart, are we there yet? *Cardiology* 2003;100(4):176–185.
3. Jain M, Pfister O, Hajjar RJ, Liao R. Mesenchymal stem cells in the infarcted heart. *Coron Artery Dis* 2005;16(2):93–97.
4. Evans SM, Mummery C, Doevendans PA. Progenitor cells for cardiac repair. *Semin Cell Dev Biol* 2007;18(1):153–160.
5. Topol EJ. Current status and future prospects for acute myocardial infarction therapy. *Circulation* 2003;108(16 Suppl 1):III6–13.
6. Detre KM, Rosen AD, Bost JE, *et al.* Contemporary practice of coronary revascularization in U.S. hospitals and hospitals participating in the bypass angioplasty revascularization investigation (BARI). *J Am Coll Cardiol* 1996;28(3):609–615.
7. Pell JP, Pell AC, Jeffrey RR, *et al.* Comparison of survival following coronary artery bypass grafting vs. percutaneous coronary intervention in diabetic and non-diabetic patients: retrospective cohort study of 6320 procedures. *Diabet Med* 2004;21(7):790–792.
8. Laflamme MA, Zbinden S, Epstein SE, Murry CE. Cell-based therapy for myocardial ischemia and infarction: pathophysiological mechanisms. *Annu Rev Pathol* 2007;2:307–339.
9. Ertl G, Gaudron P, Hu K. Ventricular remodeling after myocardial infarction. Experimental and clinical studies. *Basic Res Cardiol* 1993;88(Suppl 1): 125–137.
10. Pfeffer MA, Braunwald E. Ventricular remodeling after myocardial infarction. Experimental observations and clinical implications. *Circulation* 1990;81(4):1161–1172.
11. Towbin JA, Bowles NE. The failing heart. *Nature* 2002;415(6868):227–233.
12. Grigoropoulos NF, Mathur A. Stem cells in cardiac repair. *Curr Opin Pharmacol* 2006;6(2):169–175.
13. Patel AN, Geffner L, Vina RF, *et al.* Surgical treatment for congestive heart failure with autologous adult stem cell transplantation: a prospective randomized study. *J Thorac Cardiovasc Surg* 2005;130(6):1631–1638.
14. Charwat S, Gyongyosi M, Lang I, *et al.* Role of adult bone marrow stem cells in the repair of ischemic myocardium: current state of the art. *Exp Hematol* 2008;36(6):672–680.
15. Wollert KC. Cell therapy for acute myocardial infarction. *Curr Opin Pharmacol* 2008;8(2):202–210.

16. Blau HM, Brazelton TR, Weimann JM. The evolving concept of a stem cell: entity or function? *Cell* 2001;105(7):829–841.
17. Krause DS, Theise ND, Collector MI, *et al.* Multi-organ, multi-lineage engraftment by a single bone marrow-derived stem cell. *Cell* 2001;105(3): 369–377.
18. Jackson KA, Majka SM, Wulf GG, Goodell MA. Stem cells: a minireview. *J Cell Biochem Suppl* 2002;38: 1–6.
19. Goodell MA, Jackson KA, Majka SM, *et al.* Stem cell plasticity in muscle and bone marrow. *Ann NY Acad Sci* 2001;938:208–218;discussion 218–220.
20. Kocher AA, Schuster MD, Szabolcs MJ, *et al.* Neovascularization of ischemic myocardium by human bone-marrow-derived angioblasts prevents cardiomyocyte apoptosis, reduces remodeling and improves cardiac function. *Nat Med* 2001;7(4):430–436.
21. Orlic D, Kajstura J, Chimenti S, *et al.* Bone marrow stem cells regenerate infarcted myocardium. *Pediatr Transplant* 2003;7(Suppl 3):86–88.
22. Orlic D, Kajstura J, Chimenti S, *et al.* Mobilized bone marrow cells repair the infarcted heart, improving function and survival. *Proc Natl Acad Sci USA* 2001;98(18):10344–10349.
23. Tomita S, Mickle DA, Weisel RD, *et al.* Improved heart function with myogenesis and angiogenesis after autologous porcine bone marrow stromal cell transplantation. *J Thorac Cardiovasc Surg* 2002;123(6):1132–1140.
24. Dowell JD, Rubart M, Pasumarthi KB, *et al.* Myocyte and myogenic stem cell transplantation in the heart. *Cardiovasc Res* 2003;58(2):336–350.
25. Orlic D, Kajstura J, Chimenti S, *et al.* Bone marrow cells regenerate infarcted myocardium. *Nature* 2001;410(6829):701–705.
26. Strauer BE, Brehm M, Zeus T, *et al.* Repair of infarcted myocardium by autologous intracoronary mononuclear bone marrow cell transplantation in humans. *Circulation* 2002;106(15):1913–1918.
27. Tomita S, Li RK, Weisel RD, *et al.* Autologous transplantation of bone marrow cells improves damaged heart function. *Circulation* 1999;100(19 Suppl): II247–256.
28. Orlic D, Kajstura J, Chimenti S, *et al.* Transplanted adult bone marrow cells repair myocardial infarcts in mice. *Ann N Y Acad Sci* 2001;938:221–229; discussion 229–230.
29. Shake JG, Gruber PJ, Baumgartner WA, *et al.* Mesenchymal stem cell implantation in a swine myocardial infarct model: engraftment and functional effects. *Ann Thorac Surg* 2002;73(6):1919–1925; discussion 1926.

30. Psaltis PJ, Zannettino AC, Worthley SG, Gronthos S. Concise review: mesenchymal stromal cells: potential for cardiovascular repair. *Stem Cells* 2008;26(9):2201–2210.
31. Wollert KC, Drexler H. Clinical applications of stem cells for the heart. *Circ Res* 2005;96(2):151–163.
32. Weisel RD, Fazel S, Fedak PW, Li RK. Cardiac restoration by cell transplantation. *Int J Cardiol* 2004;95(Suppl. 1):S5–7.
33. Reinecke H, Zhang M, Bartosek T, Murry CE. Survival, integration, and differentiation of cardiomyocyte grafts: a study in normal and injured rat hearts. *Circulation* 1999;100(2):193–202.
34. Zhang M, Methot D, Poppa V, *et al.* Cardiomyocyte grafting for cardiac repair: graft cell death and anti-death strategies. *J Mol Cell Cardiol* 2001; 33(5):907–921.
35. Pepine CJ. New concepts in the pathophysiology of acute myocardial infarction. *Am J Cardiol* 1989;64(4):2B–8B.
36. Reimer KA, Jennings RB. The "wavefront phenomenon" of myocardial ischemic cell death. II. Transmural progression of necrosis within the framework of ischemic bed size (myocardium at risk) and collateral flow. *Lab Invest* 1979;40(6):633–644.
37. Falk E. Coronary thrombosis: pathogenesis and clinical manifestations. *Am J Cardiol* 1991;68(7):28B–35B.
38. Kocher AA, Schlechta B, Gasparovicova A, *et al.* Stem cells and cardiac regeneration. *Transpl Int* 2007;20(9):731–746.
39. Orlic D, Hill JM, Arai AE. Stem cells for myocardial regeneration. *Circ Res* 2002;91(12):1092–1102.
40. Smits AM, van Vliet P, Hassink RJ, *et al.* The role of stem cells in cardiac regeneration. *J Cell Mol Med* 2005;9(1):25–36.
41. Anversa P, Nadal-Ginard B. Myocyte renewal and ventricular remodelling. *Nature* 2002;415(6868):240–243.
42. Liao R, Pfister O, Jain M, Mouquet F. The bone marrow — cardiac axis of myocardial regeneration. *Prog Cardiovasc Dis* 2007;50(1):18–30.
43. Laflamme MA, Myerson D, Saffitz JE, Murry CE. Evidence for cardiomyocyte repopulation by extracardiac progenitors in transplanted human hearts. *Circ Res* 2002;90(6):634–640.
44. Beltrami AP, Urbanek K, Kajstura J, *et al.* Evidence that human cardiac myocytes divide after myocardial infarction. *N Engl J Med* 2001;344(23): 1750–1757.

45. Raeburn CD, Zimmerman MA, Arya J, *et al.* Stem cells and myocardial repair. *J Am Coll Surg* 2002;195(5):686–693.
46. Hassink RJ, Brutel de la Riviere A, Mummery CL, Doevendans PA. Transplantation of cells for cardiac repair. *J Am Coll Cardiol* 2003;41(5): 711–717.
47. Verfaillie CM. Adult stem cells: assessing the case for pluripotency. *Trends Cell Biol* 2002;12(11):502–508.
48. Dimmeler S, Burchfield J, Zeiher AM. Cell-based therapy of myocardial infarction. *Arterioscler Thromb Vasc Biol* 2008;28(2):208–216.
49. Holden C, Vogel G. Stem cells. Plasticity: time for a reappraisal? *Science* 2002;296(5576):2126–2129.
50. Li RK, Mickle DA, Weisel RD, *et al.* Natural history of fetal rat cardiomyocytes transplanted into adult rat myocardial scar tissue. *Circulation* 1997; 96(9 Suppl):II-179–186;discussion 186–177.
51. Watanabe E, Smith DM, Jr., Delcarpio JB, *et al.* Cardiomyocyte transplantation in a porcine myocardial infarction model. *Cell Transplant* 1998;7(3):239–246.
52. Min JY, Yang Y, Converso KL, *et al.* Transplantation of embryonic stem cells improves cardiac function in postinfarcted rats. *J Appl Physiol* 2002; 92(1):288–296.
53. Min JY, Yang Y, Sullivan MF, *et al.* Long-term improvement of cardiac function in rats after infarction by transplantation of embryonic stem cells. *J Thorac Cardiovasc Surg* 2003;125(2):361–369.
54. Leor J, Patterson M, Quinones MJ, *et al.* Transplantation of fetal myocardial tissue into the infarcted myocardium of rat. A potential method for repair of infarcted myocardium? *Circulation* 1996;94(9 Suppl):II332–336.
55. Menasche P, Hagege AA, Scorsin M, *et al.* Myoblast transplantation for heart failure. *Lancet* 2001;357(9252):279–280.
56. Menasche P, Hagege AA, Vilquin JT, *et al.* Autologous skeletal myoblast transplantation for severe postinfarction left ventricular dysfunction. *J Am Coll Cardiol* 2003;41(7):1078–1083.
57. Murry CE, Wiseman RW, Schwartz SM, Hauschka SD. Skeletal myoblast transplantation for repair of myocardial necrosis. *J Clin Invest* 1996;98(11): 2512–2523.
58. Taylor DA, Atkins BZ, Hungspreugs P, *et al.* Regenerating functional myocardium: improved performance after skeletal myoblast transplantation. *Nat Med* 1998;4(8):929–933.

59. Kawamoto A, Losordo DW. Endothelial progenitor cells for cardiovascular regeneration. *Trends Cardiovasc Med* 2008;18(1):33–37.
60. Kawamoto A, Tkebuchava T, Yamaguchi J, *et al.* Intramyocardial transplantation of auto-logous endothelial progenitor cells for therapeutic neovascularization of myocardial ischemia. *Circulation* 2003;107(3): 461–468.
61. Dimmeler S, Zeiher AM, Schneider MD. Unchain my heart: the scientific foundations of cardiac repair. *J Clin Invest* 2005;115(3):572–583.
62. Oh H, Bradfute SB, Gallardo TD, *et al.* Cardiac progenitor cells from adult myocardium: homing, differentiation, and fusion after infarction. *Proc Natl Acad Sci USA* 2003;100(21):12313–12318.
63. Orlic D. Adult bone marrow stem cells regenerate myocardium in ischemic heart disease. *Ann N Y Acad Sci* 2003;996:152–157.
64. Saito T, Kuang JQ, Bittira B, *et al.* Xenotransplant cardiac chimera: immune tolerance of adult stem cells. *Ann Thorac Surg* 2002;74(1):19–24; discussion 24.
65. Barbash IM, Chouraqui P, Baron J, *et al.* Systemic delivery of bone marrow-derived mesenchymal stem cells to the infarcted myocardium: feasibility, cell migration, and body distribution. *Circulation* 2003;108(7):863–868.
66. Toma C, Pittenger MF, Cahill KS, *et al.* Human mesenchymal stem cells differentiate to a cardiomyocyte phenotype in the adult murine heart. *Circulation* 2002;105(1):93–98.
67. Perin EC, Geng YJ, Willerson JT. Adult stem cell therapy in perspective. *Circulation* 2003;107(7):935–938.
68. Siminiak T, Kurpisz M. Myocardial replacement therapy. *Circulation* 2003;108(10):1167–1171.
69. Planat-Benard V, Menard C, Andre M, *et al.* Spontaneous cardiomyocyte differentiation from adipose tissue stroma cells. *Circ Res* 2004;94(2): 223–229.
70. Jiang Y, Jahagirdar BN, Reinhardt RL, *et al.* Pluripotency of mesenchymal stem cells derived from adult marrow. *Nature* 2002;418(6893):41–49.
71. Kogler G, Sensken S, Airey JA, *et al.* A new human somatic stem cell from placental cord blood with intrinsic pluripotent differentiation potential. *J Exp Med* 2004;200(2):123–135.
72. De Coppi P, Bartsch G, Jr., Siddiqui MM, *et al.* Isolation of amniotic stem cell lines with potential for therapy. *Nat Biotechnol* 2007;25(1):100–106.

73. Beltrami AP, Barlucchi L, Torella D, *et al.* Adult cardiac stem cells are multipotent and support myocardial regeneration. *Cell* 2003;114(6):763–776.
74. Anversa P, Sussman MA, Bolli R. Molecular genetic advances in cardiovascular medicine: focus on the myocyte. *Circulation* 2004;109(23):2832–2838.
75. Harrison DE, Astle CM, Lerner C. Number and continuous proliferative pattern of transplanted primitive immunohematopoietic stem cells. *Proc Natl Acad Sci USA* 1988;85(3):822–826.
76. Dimmeler S, Zeiher AM. Wanted! The best cell for cardiac regeneration. *J Am Coll Cardiol* 2004;44(2):464–466.
77. Urbich C, Dimmeler S. Endothelial progenitor cells functional characterization. *Trends Cardiovasc Med* 2004;14(8):318–322.
78. Nygren JM, Jovinge S, Breitbach M, *et al.* Bone marrow-derived hematopoietic cells generate cardiomyocytes at a low frequency through cell fusion, but not transdifferentiation. *Nat Med* 2004;10(5):494–501.
79. Orlic D. The strength of plasticity: stem cells for cardiac repair. *Int J Cardiol* 2004;95(Suppl 1): S16–19.
80. Asahara T, Masuda H, Takahashi T, *et al.* Bone marrow origin of endothelial progenitor cells responsible for postnatal vasculogenesis in physiological and pathological neovascularization. *Circ Res* 1999;85(3):221–228.
81. Shi Q, Rafii S, Wu MH, *et al.* Evidence for circulating bone marrow-derived endothelial cells. *Blood* 1998;92(2):362–367.
82. Gehling UM, Ergun S, Schumacher U, *et al. In vitro* differentiation of endothelial cells from AC133-positive progenitor cells. *Blood* 2000;95(10):3106–3112.
83. Vasa M, Fichtlscherer S, Aicher A, *et al.* Number and migratory activity of circulating endothelial progenitor cells inversely correlate with risk factors for coronary artery disease. *Circ Res* 2001;89(1):E1–7.
84. Fujiyama S, Amano K, Uehira K, *et al.* Bone marrow monocyte lineage cells adhere on injured endothelium in a monocyte chemoattractant protein-1-dependent manner and accelerate reendothelialization as endothelial progenitor cells. *Circ Res* 2003;93(10):980–989.
85. Crosby JR, Kaminski WE, Schatteman G, *et al.* Endothelial cells of hematopoietic origin make a significant contribution to adult blood vessel formation. *Circ Res* 2000;87(9):728–730.
86. Choi JH, Kim KL, Huh W, *et al.* Decreased number and impaired angiogenic function of endothelial progenitor cells in patients with chronic renal failure. *Arterioscler Thromb Vasc Biol* 2004;24(7):1246–1252.

87. Dimmeler S, Aicher A, Vasa M, *et al.* HMG-CoA reductase inhibitors (statins) increase endothelial progenitor cells via the PI 3-kinase/Akt pathway. *J Clin Invest* 2001;108(3):391–397.
88. Scheubel RJ, Zorn H, Silber RE, *et al.* Age-dependent depression in circulating endothelial progenitor cells in patients undergoing coronary artery bypass grafting. *J Am Coll Cardiol* 2003;42(12):2073–2080.
89. Tepper OM, Galiano RD, Capla JM, *et al.* Human endothelial progenitor cells from type II diabetics exhibit impaired proliferation, adhesion, and incorporation into vascular structures. *Circulation* 2002;106(22):2781–2786.
90. Shintani S, Murohara T, Ikeda H, *et al.* Mobilization of endothelial progenitor cells in patients with acute myocardial infarction. *Circulation* 2001;103(23):2776–2779.
91. George J, Herz I, Goldstein E, *et al.* Number and adhesive properties of circulating endothelial progenitor cells in patients with in-stent restenosis. *Arterioscler Thromb Vasc Biol* 2003;23(12):e57–60.
92. Lambiase PD, Edwards RJ, Anthopoulos P, *et al.* Circulating humoral factors and endothelial progenitor cells in patients with differing coronary collateral support. *Circulation* 2004;109(24):2986–2992.
93. Ruel M, Suuronen EJ, Song J, *et al.* Effects of off-pump versus on-pump coronary artery bypass grafting on function and viability of circulating endothelial progenitor cells. *J Thorac Cardiovasc Surg* 2005;130(3):633–639.
94. Meirelles Lda S, Nardi NB. Murine marrow-derived mesenchymal stem cell: isolation, *in vitro* expansion, and characterization. *Br J Haematol* 2003;123(4):702–711.
95. Colter DC, Sekiya I, Prockop DJ. Identification of a subpopulation of rapidly self-renewing and multipotential adult stem cells in colonies of human marrow stromal cells. *Proc Natl Acad Sci USA* 2001;98(14):7841–7845.
96. Colter DC, Class R, DiGirolamo CM, Prockop DJ. Rapid expansion of recycling stem cells in cultures of plastic-adherent cells from human bone marrow. *Proc Natl Acad Sci USA* 2000;97(7):3213–3218.
97. Annabi B, Lee YT, Turcotte S, *et al.* Hypoxia promotes murine bone-marrow-derived stromal cell migration and tube formation. *Stem Cells* 2003;21(3):337–347.
98. Mangi AA, Noiseux N, Kong D, *et al.* Mesenchymal stem cells modified with Akt prevent remodeling and restore performance of infarcted hearts. *Nat Med* 2003;9(9):1195–1201. Epub 2003 Aug 1110.

99. Peister A, Mellad JA, Larson BL, *et al.* Adult stem cells from bone marrow (MSCs) isolated from different strains of inbred mice vary in surface epitopes, rates of proliferation, and differentiation potential. *Blood* 2004; 103(5):1662–1668.
100. Minguell JJ, Erices A, Conget P. Mesenchymal stem cells. *Exp Biol Med (Maywood)* 2001;226(6):507–520.
101. Pittenger MF, Martin BJ. Mesenchymal stem cells and their potential as cardiac therapeutics. *Circ Res* 2004;95(1):9–20.
102. Verfaillie CM, Pera MF, Lansdorp PM. Stem cells: hype and reality. *Hematology (Am Soc Hematol Educ Program)* 2002:369–391.
103. Grove JE, Bruscia E, Krause DS. Plasticity of bone marrow-derived stem cells. *Stem Cells* 2004;22(4):487–500.
104. Pittenger MF, Mackay AM, Beck SC, *et al.* Multilineage potential of adult human mesenchymal stem cells. *Science* 1999;284(5411):143–147.
105. Krause DS. Plasticity of marrow-derived stem cells. *Gene Ther* 2002; 9(11):754–758.
106. Mackay AM, Beck SC, Murphy JM, *et al.* Chondrogenic differentiation of cultured human mesenchymal stem cells from marrow. *Tissue Eng* 1998;4(4):415–428.
107. Song L, Tuan RS. Transdifferentiation potential of human mesenchymal stem cells derived from bone marrow. *Faseb J* 2004;18(9):980–982.
108. Liu P, Kalajzic I, Stover ML, *et al.* Human bone marrow stromal cells are efficiently transduced by vesicular stomatitis virus-pseudotyped retrovectors without affecting subsequent osteoblastic differentiation. *Bone* 2001;29(4):331–335.
109. Rangappa S, Fen C, Lee EH, *et al.* Transformation of adult mesenchymal stem cells isolated from the fatty tissue into cardiomyocytes. *Ann Thorac Surg* 2003;75(3):775–779.
110. Makino S, Fukuda K, Miyoshi S, *et al.* Cardiomyocytes can be generated from marrow stromal cells *in vitro*. *J Clin Invest* 1999;103(5):697–705.
111. Wang JS, Shum-Tim D, Galipeau J, *et al.* Marrow stromal cells for cellular cardiomyoplasty: feasibility and potential clinical advantages. *J Thorac Cardiovasc Surg* 2000;120(5):999–1005.
112. Dai W, Hale SL, Martin BJ, *et al.* Allogeneic mesenchymal stem cell transplantation in postinfarcted rat myocardium: short- and long-term effects. *Circulation* 2005;112(2):214–223.

113. Kamihata H, Matsubara H, Nishiue T, *et al.* Implantation of bone marrow mononuclear cells into ischemic myocardium enhances collateral perfusion and regional function via side supply of angioblasts, angiogenic ligands, and cytokines. *Circulation* 2001;104(9):1046–1052.
114. Kinnaird T, Stabile E, Burnett MS, *et al.* Marrow-derived stromal cells express genes encoding a broad spectrum of arteriogenic cytokines and promote *in vitro* and *in vivo* arteriogenesis through paracrine mechanisms. *Circ Res* 2004;94(5):678–685.
115. Kinnaird T, Stabile E, Burnett MS, *et al.* Local delivery of marrow-derived stromal cells augments collateral perfusion through paracrine mechanisms. *Circulation* 2004;109(12):1543–1549.
116. Heil M, Ziegelhoeffer T, Mees B, Schaper W. A different outlook on the role of bone marrow stem cells in vascular growth: bone marrow delivers software not hardware. *Circ Res* 2004;94(5):573–574.
117. Kinnaird T, Stabile E, Burnett MS, Epstein SE. Bone marrow-derived cells for enhancing collateral development: mechanisms, animal data, and initial clinical experiences. *Circ Res* 2004;95(4):354–363.
118. Noiseux N GM, Mirotsou M, Pratt R Dzau VJ. Adult mesenchymal stem cells genetically engineered to overexpress Akt exhibit improved resistance to apoptosis, glucose metabolism, and angiogenic potential. *Can J Cardiol* 2004;20:(Suppl D):97D.
119. Gnecchi M, He H, Liang OD, *et al.* Paracrine action accounts for marked protection of ischemic heart by Akt-modified mesenchymal stem cells. *Nat Med* 2005;11(4):367–368.
120. Gnecchi M, He H, Noiseux N, *et al.* Evidence supporting paracrine hypothesis for Akt-modified mesenchymal stem cell-mediated cardiac protection and functional improvement. *FASEB J* 2006;20(6):661–669.
121. Noiseux N L-IM, Gnecchi M, Zang L, *et al.* Transplantation of bone marrow-derived mesenchymal stem cells expressing Akt into infracted murine heart produces dramatic improvement in cardiac function despite infrequent cellular fusion. *Circulation* 2004;110(17):(supplement III):III–68.
122. Vulliet PR, Greeley M, Halloran SM, *et al.* Intra-coronary arterial injection of mesenchymal stromal cells and microinfarction in dogs. *Lancet* 2004; 363(9411):783–784.
123. Laflamme MA, Murry CE. Regenerating the heart. *Nat Biotechnol* 2005;23(7):845–856.

124. Menasche P. Skeletal myoblasts and cardiac repair. *J Mol Cell Cardiol* 2008;45(4):545–553.
125. Hierlihy AM, Seale P, Lobe CG, *et al.* The post-natal heart contains a myocardial stem cell population. *FEBS Lett* 2002;530(1–3):239–243.
126. Bearzi C, Rota M, Hosoda T, *et al.* Human cardiac stem cells. *Proc Natl Acad Sci USA* 2007;104(35):14068–14073.
127. Braun T, Martire A. Cardiac stem cells: paradigm shift or broken promise? A view from developmental biology. *Trends Biotechnol* 2007;25(10): 441–447.
128. Lyngbaek S, Schneider M, Hansen JL, Sheikh SP. Cardiac regeneration by resident stem and progenitor cells in the adult heart. *Basic Res Cardiol* 2007;102(2):101–114.
129. Davani S, Marandin A, Mersin N, *et al.* Mesenchymal progenitor cells differentiate into an endothelial phenotype, enhance vascular density, and improve heart function in a rat cellular cardiomyoplasty model. *Circulation* 2003;108 Suppl 1:II253–258.
130. Min JY, Sullivan MF, Yang Y, *et al.* Significant improvement of heart function by cotransplantation of human mesenchymal stem cells and fetal cardiomyocytes in postinfarcted pigs. *Ann Thorac Surg* 2002;74(5): 1568–1575.
131. Wang JS, Shum-Tim D, Chedrawy E, Chiu RC. The coronary delivery of marrow stromal cells for myocardial regeneration: pathophysiologic and therapeutic implications. *J Thorac Cardiovasc Surg* 2001;122(4):699–705.
132. Noiseux N, Gnecchi M, Lopez-Ilasaca M, *et al.* Mesenchymal stem cells overexpressing Akt dramatically repair infarcted myocardium and improve cardiac function despite infrequent cellular fusion or differentiation. *Mol Ther* 2006;14(6):840–850.
133. Ying QL, Nichols J, Evans EP, Smith AG. Changing potency by spontaneous fusion. *Nature* 2002;416(6880):545–548.
134. Li RK, Jia ZQ, Weisel RD, *et al.* Cardiomyocyte transplantation improves heart function. *Ann Thorac Surg* 1996;62(3):654–660;discussion 660–651.
135. Sakai T, Li RK, Weisel RD, *et al.* Fetal cell transplantation: a comparison of three cell types. *J Thorac Cardiovasc Surg* 1999;118(4):715–724.
136. Scorsin M, Hagege A, Vilquin JT, *et al.* Comparison of the effects of fetal cardiomyocyte and skeletal myoblast transplantation on postinfarction left ventricular function. *J Thorac Cardiovasc Surg* 2000;119(6):1169–1175.

137. Jia ZQ, Mickle DA, Weisel RD, *et al.* Transplanted cardiomyocytes survive in scar tissue and improve heart function. *Transplant Proc* 1997;29(4): 2093–2094.
138. Laflamme MA, Chen KY, Naumova AV, *et al.* Cardiomyocytes derived from human embryonic stem cells in prosurvival factors enhance function of infarcted rat hearts. *Nat Biotechnol* 2007;25(9):1015–1024.
139. Leobon B, Garcin I, Menasche P, *et al.* Myoblasts transplanted into rat infarcted myocardium are functionally isolated from their host. *Proc Natl Acad Sci USA* 2003;100(13):7808–7811.
140. He JQ, Ma Y, Lee Y, *et al.* Human embryonic stem cells develop into multiple types of cardiac myocytes: action potential characterization. *Circ Res* 2003;93(1):32–39.
141. Kehat I, Kenyagin-Karsenti D, Snir M, *et al.* Human embryonic stem cells can differentiate into myocytes with structural and functional properties of cardiomyocytes. *J Clin Invest* 2001;108(3):407–414.
142. Hodgson DM, Behfar A, Zingman LV, *et al.* Stable benefit of embryonic stem cell therapy in myocardial infarction. *Am J Physiol Heart Circ Physiol* 2004;287(2):H471–479.
143. Singla DK, Hacker TA, Ma L, *et al.* Transplantation of embryonic stem cells into the infarcted mouse heart: formation of multiple cell types. *J Mol Cell Cardiol* 2006;40(1):195–200.
144. Strauer BE, Kornowski R. Stem cell therapy in perspective. *Circulation* 2003;107(7):929–934.
145. Badorff C, Brandes RP, Popp R, *et al.* Transdifferentiation of blood-derived human adult endothelial progenitor cells into functionally active cardiomyocytes. *Circulation* 2003;107(7):1024–1032.
146. Condorelli G, Borello U, De Angelis L, *et al.* Cardiomyocytes induce endothelial cells to trans-differentiate into cardiac muscle: implications for myocardium regeneration. *Proc Natl Acad Sci USA* 2001;98(19): 10733–10738.
147. Kajstura J, Rota M, Whang B, *et al.* Bone marrow cells differentiate in cardiac cell lineages after infarction independently of cell fusion. *Circ Res* 2005;96(1):127–137. Epub 2004 Nov 2029.
148. Yoon J, Choi SC, Park CY, *et al.* Bone marrow-derived side population cells are capable of functional cardiomyogenic differentiation. *Mol Cells* 2008;25(2):216–223.

149. Balsam LB, Wagers AJ, Christensen JL, *et al.* Haematopoietic stem cells adopt mature haematopoietic fates in ischaemic myocardium. *Nature* 2004;428(6983):668–673.
150. Murry CE, Soonpaa MH, Reinecke H, *et al.* Haematopoietic stem cells do not transdifferentiate into cardiac myocytes in myocardial infarcts. *Nature* 2004;428(6983):664–668.
151. Anversa P, Leri A, Rota M, *et al.* Concise review: stem cells, myocardial regeneration, and methodological artifacts. *Stem Cells* 2007;25(3):589–601.
152. Alvarez-Dolado M, Pardal R, Garcia-Verdugo JM, *et al.* Fusion of bone-marrow-derived cells with Purkinje neurons, cardiomyocytes and hepatocytes. *Nature* 2003;425(6961):968–973. Epub 2003 Oct 2012.
153. Terada N, Hamazaki T, Oka M, *et al.* Bone marrow cells adopt the phenotype of other cells by spontaneous cell fusion. *Nature* 2002;416(6880): 542–545.
154. Zhang S, Wang D, Estrov Z, *et al.* Both cell fusion and transdifferentiation account for the transformation of human peripheral blood CD34-positive cells into cardiomyocytes *in vivo*. *Circulation* 2004;110(25):3803–3807.
155. Murry CE, Soonpaa MH, Reinecke H, *et al.* Haematopoietic stem cells do not transdifferentiate into cardiac myocytes in myocardial infarcts — Myogenic fusion of human bone marrow stromal cells, but not hematopoietic cells — Evidence for fusion between cardiac and skeletal muscle cells. *Nature* 2004;428(6983):664–668. Epub 2004 Mar 2021.
156. Reinecke H, Minami E, Poppa V, Murry CE. Evidence for fusion between cardiac and skeletal muscle cells. *Circ Res* 2004;94(6):e56–60. Epub 2004 Mar 2004.
157. Vassilopoulos G, Russell DW. Cell fusion: an alternative to stem cell plasticity and its therapeutic implications. *Curr Opin Genet Dev* 2003;13(5): 480–485.
158. Soriano P. Generalized lacZ expression with the ROSA26 Cre reporter strain. *Nat Genet* 1999;21(1):70–71.
159. Nguyen BK, Maltais S, Perrault LP, *et al.* Improved function and myocardial repair of infarcted heart by intracoronary injection of mesenchymal stem cell-derived growth factors. *J Cardiovasc Transl Res* 2010 Feb 26; [Epub ahead of print] PubMed PMID: 20559784.
160. Nian M, Lee P, Khaper N, Liu P. Inflammatory cytokines and postmyocardial infarction remodeling. *Circ Res* 2004;94(12):1543–1553.

161. Luttun A, Carmeliet P. De novo vasculogenesis in the heart. *Cardiovasc Res* 2003;58(2):378–389.
162. Buschmann I, Schaper W. Arteriogenesis Versus Angiogenesis: Two Mechanisms of Vessel Growth. *News Physiol Sci* 1999;14:121–125.
163. Buschmann I, Heil M, Jost M, Schaper W. Influence of inflammatory cytokines on arteriogenesis. *Microcirculation* 2003;10(3–4):371–379.
164. Kinnaird T, Stabile E, Epstein SE, Fuchs S. Current perspectives in therapeutic myocardial angiogenesis. *J Interv Cardiol* 2003;16(4):289–297.
165. Carmeliet P. Mechanisms of angiogenesis and arteriogenesis. *Nat Med* 2000;6(4):389–395.
166. Risau W. Mechanisms of angiogenesis. *Nature* 1997;386(6626):671–674.
167. Buschmann I, Schaper W. The pathophysiology of the collateral circulation (arteriogenesis). *J Pathol* 2000;190(3):338–342.
168. Epstein SE, Fuchs S, Zhou YF, *et al.* Therapeutic interventions for enhancing collateral development by administration of growth factors: basic principles, early results and potential hazards. *Cardiovasc Res* 2001;49(3):532–542.
169. Carmeliet P. Manipulating angiogenesis in medicine. *J Intern Med* 2004;255(5):538–561.
170. Kobayashi T, Hamano K, Li TS, *et al.* Enhancement of angiogenesis by the implantation of self bone marrow cells in a rat ischemic heart model. *J Surg Res* 2000;89(2):189–195.
171. Hirata K, Li TS, Nishida M, *et al.* Autologous bone marrow cell implantation as therapeutic angiogenesis for ischemic hindlimb in diabetic rat model. *Am J Physiol Heart Circ Physiol* 2003;284(1):H66–70.
172. Li TS, Hamano K, Suzuki K, *et al.* Improved angiogenic potency by implantation of *ex vivo* hypoxia prestimulated bone marrow cells in rats. *Am J Physiol Heart Circ Physiol* 2002;283(2):H468–473.
173. Fuchs S, Baffour R, Zhou YF, *et al.* Transendocardial delivery of autologous bone marrow enhances collateral perfusion and regional function in pigs with chronic experimental myocardial ischemia. *J Am Coll Cardiol* 2001;37(6):1726–1732.
174. Ziegelhoeffer T, Fernandez B, Kostin S, *et al.* Bone marrow-derived cells do not incorporate into the adult growing vasculature. *Circ Res* 2004;94(2): 230–238.
175. Ince H, Petzsch M, Kleine HD, *et al.* Prevention of left ventricular remodeling with granulocyte colony-stimulating factor after acute myocardial

infarction: final 1-year results of the Front-Integrated Revascularization and Stem Cell Liberation in Evolving Acute Myocardial Infarction by Granulocyte Colony-Stimulating Factor (FIRSTLINE-AMI) Trial. *Circulation* 2005;112(9 Suppl):I73–80.

176. Heldman AW, Hare JM. Cell therapy for myocardial infarction: special delivery. *J Mol Cell Cardiol* 2008;44(3):473–476.

177. Perin EC, Silva GV, Assad JA, *et al.* Comparison of intracoronary and transendocardial delivery of allogeneic mesenchymal cells in a canine model of acute myocardial infarction. *J Mol Cell Cardiol* 2008;44(3): 486–495.

178. Freyman T, Polin G, Osman H. A quantitative, randomized study evaluating three methods of mesenchymal stem cell delivery following myocardial infarction. *Eur Heart J* 2006;27(9):1114–1122.

179. Teng CJ, Luo J, Chiu RC, Shum-Tim D. Massive mechanical loss of microspheres with direct intramyocardial injection in the beating heart: implications for cellular cardiomyoplasty. *J Thorac Cardiovasc Surg* 2006;132(3):628–632.

180. Nesselmann C, Ma N, Bieback K, *et al.* Mesenchymal stem cells and cardiac repair. *J Cell Mol Med* 2008;12(5B):1795–1810.

181. Koc ON, Gerson SL. Akt helps stem cells heal the heart. *Nat Med* 2003;9(9):1109–1110.

182. Franke TF, Hornik CP, Segev L, *et al.* PI3K/Akt and apoptosis: size matters. *Oncogene* 2003;22(56):8983–8998.

183. Franke TF, Kaplan DR, Cantley LC. PI3K: downstream AKTion blocks apoptosis. *Cell* 1997;88(4):435–437.

184. Datta SR, Brunet A, Greenberg ME. Cellular survival: a play in three Akts. *Genes Dev* 1999;13(22):2905–2927.

185. Mirotsou M, Zhang Z, Deb A, *et al.* Secreted frizzled related protein 2 (Sfrp2) is the key Akt-mesenchymal stem cell-released paracrine factor mediating myocardial survival and repair. *Proc Natl Acad Sci USA* 2007.

186. Assmus B, Schachinger V, Teupe C, *et al.* Transplantation of Progenitor Cells and Regeneration Enhancement in Acute Myocardial Infarction (TOP-CARE-AMI). *Circulation* 2002;106(24):3009–3017.

187. Britten MB, Abolmaali ND, Assmus B, *et al.* Infarct remodeling after intracoronary progenitor cell treatment in patients with acute myocardial infarction

(TOPCARE-AMI):mechanistic insights from serial contrast-enhanced magnetic resonance imaging. *Circulation* 2003;108(18):2212–2218.

188. Schachinger V, Assmus B, Britten MB, *et al.*Transplantation of progenitor cells and regeneration enhancement in acute myocardial infarction: final one-year results of the TOPCARE-AMI Trial. *J Am Coll Cardiol* 2004; 44(8):1690–1699.
189. Schachinger V, Erbs S, Elsasser A, *et al.* Intracoronary bone marrow-derived progenitor cells in acute myocardial infarction. *N Engl J Med* 2006;355(12):1210–1221.
190. Wollert KC, Meyer GP, Lotz J, *et al.* Intracoronary autologous bone-marrow cell transfer after myocardial infarction: the BOOST randomised controlled clinical trial. *Lancet* 2004;364(9429):141–148.
191. Schaefer A, Meyer GP, Fuchs M, *et al.* Impact of intracoronary bone marrow cell transfer on diastolic function in patients after acute myocardial infarction: results from the BOOST trial. *Eur Heart J* 2006;27(8):929–935.
192. Meyer GP, Wollert KC, Lotz J, *et al.* Intracoronary bone marrow cell transfer after myocardial infarction: eighteen months' follow-up data from the randomized, controlled BOOST (BOne marrOw transfer to enhance ST-elevation infarct regeneration) trial. *Circulation* 2006;113(10):1287–1294.
193. Janssens S, Dubois C, Bogaert J, *et al.* Autologous bone marrow-derived stem-cell transfer in patients with ST-segment elevation myocardial infarction: double-blind, randomised controlled trial. *Lancet* 2006;367(9505):113–121.
194. Lunde K, Solheim S, Aakhus S, *et al.* Intracoronary injection of mononuclear bone marrow cells in acute myocardial infarction. *N Engl J Med* 2006;355(12):1199–1209.
195. Rosenzweig A. Cardiac cell therapy — mixed results from mixed cells. *N Engl J Med* 2006;355(12):1274–1277.
196. Abdel-Latif A, Bolli R, Tleyjeh IM, *et al.* Adult bone marrow-derived cells for cardiac repair: a systematic review and meta-analysis. *Arch Intern Med* 2007;167(10):989–997.
197. Kawamoto A, Asahara T. Role of progenitor endothelial cells in cardiovascular disease and upcoming therapies. *Catheter Cardiovasc Interv* 2007;70(4): 477–484.
198. Hofmann M, Wollert KC, Meyer GP, *et al.* Monitoring of bone marrow cell homing into the infarcted human myocardium. *Circulation* 2005;111(17): 2198–2202.

199. Stamm C, Westphal B, Kleine HD, *et al.* Autologous bone-marrow stem-cell transplantation for myocardial regeneration. *Lancet* 2003;361(9351): 45–46.
200. Bhatia M. AC133 expression in human stem cells. *Leukemia* 2001;15(11):1685–1688.
201. de Wynter EA, Buck D, Hart C, *et al.* CD34+AC133+ cells isolated from cord blood are highly enriched in long-term culture-initiating cells, NOD/SCID-repopulating cells and dendritic cell progenitors. *Stem Cells* 1998;16(6):387–396.
202. Kuci S, Wessels JT, Buhring HJ, *et al.* Identification of a novel class of human adherent CD34- stem cells that give rise to SCID-repopulating cells. *Blood* 2003;101(3):869–876.
203. Quirici N, Soligo D, Caneva L, *et al.* Differentiation and expansion of endothelial cells from human bone marrow CD133(+) cells. *Br J Haematol* 2001;115(1):186–194.
204. Agbulut O, Vandervelde S, Al Attar N, *et al.* Comparison of human skeletal myoblasts and bone marrow-derived $CD133^+$ progenitors for the repair of infarcted myocardium. *J Am Coll Cardiol* 2004;44(2):458–463.
205. Bartunek J, Vanderheyden M, Vandekerckhove B, *et al.* Intracoronary injection of CD133-positive enriched bone marrow progenitor cells promotes cardiac recovery after recent myocardial infarction: feasibility and safety. *Circulation* 2005;112(9 Suppl.):I178–183.
206. Mansour S, Roy DC, Lemieux B, *et al.* Stem cell therapy for the broken heart: mini-organ transplantation. *Transplant Proc* 2009;41(8):3353–3357. *Pub Med PMID*: 19857748.
207. Mansour S, Roy DC, Bouchard V, *et al.* COMPARE-AMI trial: comparison of intracoronary injection of $CD133^+$ bone marrow stem cells to placebo in patients after acute myocardial infarction and left ventricular dysfunction: study rationale and design. *J Cardiovasc Transl Res* 2010;3(2):153–159. Epub 2009 Nov. 12. PubMed PMID: 20560029.

# CHAPTER 3

# THE ROLE OF MECHANICAL FORCES IN THE CARDIOMYOGENIC DIFFERENTIATION OF STEM CELLS

*Daniel Pelaez, Joshua M. Hare and Herman S. Cheung*

## Abstract

It is well understood that complex biochemical interactions are, ultimately, the events that drive the processes through which living organisms interact, develop and sustain life. However, the role of the steady influx of physical stimuli into the system cannot be overlooked in this respect. Due to their potential to modify, initiate or guide underlying biochemical mechanisms, a physical stimulus' mode of action on biological systems must be extensively understood in order to be able to comprehend the onset and progression of some currently misunderstood pathologies. This knowledge might also afford future researchers a tool to exploit the effect of physical stimuli in the development of more effective regenerative therapies. This chapter will explore the current state of cellular-based therapies for the treatment of myocardial infarction, as well as advancements made towards a functional tissue engineering application of these technologies. It will specifically focus on the role of biomechanical forces on the cardiomyogenic differentiation of several progenitor and stem cell constituents being considered for such a purpose.

media used and the physical cues relevant to the functionality of obtained tissues in such a dynamic system.

### 1.3 *Tissue engineering considerations in myocardial regeneration*

Functionality is the ultimate goal when it comes to the pragmatic application of any regenerative therapy in medicine. When it comes to myocardial regeneration, the expression of genes and synthesis of proteins specific to muscle action are not enough to ensure the functional integration of the generated cells *in vivo*. As discussed above, obtained cardiac muscle cells must be able to engraft, migrate and proliferate within the host tissue. Furthermore, they must be capable of electrically coupling with host muscle cells, which calls for the development of highly specialized structures in the cells.[29,30] This brings the origin and state of the cells at the moment of implantation into consideration. While pure stem cells might be able to proliferate abundantly and differentiate into the desired tissue, they may lack or be unable to timely synthesize the necessary anchorage molecules to ensure their continuance in the injured area leading them to exert their effect on other, non-critical, areas in the body. On the other hand, if the implanted cells have achieved a fully differentiated state at the time of implantation, they would be unable, or at least highly limited in their capacity to proliferate. So while these cells would theoretically be able to remain in the desired area for the lifespan of the recipient, a vast amount of them would need to be generated and implanted in order to cover the volumetric extent of the infarcted region. Similarly, there would be no guarantee that these fully differentiated cells would be able to adequately integrate with the host tissue (adequately meaning in regional density and orientation). The ideal cell for regenerative implantation would then be one committed enough to ensure a correct interaction with the host tissue, yet primitive enough to proliferate into the entire affected area while still being able to respond to the *in vivo* environmental cues to guide its correct integration and maturation.

The selection of an adequate cell source is, thus, the initial crucial step to true functional tissue engineering, but by no means the only consideration. As in embryological development,[9–11] successful cellular-based regenerative therapies require a delicate balance between the clonogenic potential, rate of differentiation, and the timely introduction of biochemical and physical stimuli in the cells. Traditionally, control of these factors in cardiomyogenic differentiation has been accomplished by the *in vitro* treatment of cells solely with soluble factors. While several researchers have achieved maintenance of a partially correct cardiac phenotypic expression, no optimal *in vitro* conditions have been established for the full differentiation of any cell population into mature functional cardiomyocytes.

Recently, observations that cyclic tensile strain is capable of eliciting cardiovascular differentiation in stem cells[1,13,18,31–35] have led investigators to evaluate the introduction of mechanical strain as part of the differentiating protocol. Other forms of mechanical stress have already been proven effective in guiding the differentiation of stem and progenitor cells into several tissue lineages.[36–38] It is to be noticed that, in these studies, the cells differentiate into tissues that would normally be exposed to the same mechanical force that is guiding their differentiation. It would seem reasonable then, that the generation of functional muscular tissues, which are the only tissues in the body capable of generating mechanical force on their own, benefit from exposure to tensile stresses during their development. In fact, even in fully developed heart muscle, constant mechanical loading helps maintain the functionality of the cells in it. Soppa *et al.*[39] recently showed that prolonged mechanical unloading of the left ventricle led to unloading-induced atrophy and depressed contractility in rat hearts due to reduced sarcoplasmic reticulum $Ca^{2+}$ uptake and reduced myofilament sensitivity to $Ca^{2+}$.

Finally, we must consider that the application of exogenous force in the laboratory is not the only source of mechanical stress that the cells will experience during development. As a result of manipulation and, more importantly, as an inherent feature of adherent cell cultures, cells will be mechanically influenced by their attachment, migration and proliferation on the material chosen for their growth.[40,41] The microenvironment surrounding the cells is known to be one of the key epigenetic factors that will ultimately determine their fate. Growth substrate chemistry will also condition the cells to express specific anchorage and junction molecules to ensure their adaptation to and growth on the material. For example, myofibroblast communication can be controlled through inter-cellular mechanical coupling *via* specific membrane bound structures.[30] Equally as important, exploiting growth material chemistry to guide the cells towards the *in vitro* expression of cardiac specific anchorage molecules (such as connexin 43) can go a long way when it comes to their successful integration *in vivo*.[21] Finally, several studies have shown that the mechanical properties of the growth material itself can modulate and, in some cases, inhibit the differentiation of cells towards given lineages.[7,42–45] Growth substrate chemistry and mechanical properties are thus the final factor to be considered for the development of functional myocardial tissues.

## 2. Cell-Based Therapies for Myocardial Regeneration

Most of the cell-based therapies for myocardial regeneration developed during the past couple of decades have focused mainly on the selection and characterization of an ideal cell source for such an application. Hence, a large number of cell types have been, thus far, evaluated for their cardiomyogenic potential, beneficial effects on heart function and overall viability for use in regenerative therapies with varying degrees of success. This section will briefly present several of the most widely employed cell types for myocardial regeneration as well as briefly discuss some of the advantages and drawbacks associated with each.[16,22,23,26,29,46–53]

### 2.1 *Skeletal muscle-derived cells*

#### 2.1.1 *Skeletal myoblasts (SMBs)*

SMBs are a naturally attractive cell source for cardiomyogenesis due to their inherent myogenic potential as well as for their relatively straightforward accessibility. SMBs can be isolated from small tissue biopsies and expanded *in vitro* to abundant numbers.[53] Under appropriate conditions, SMBs have been shown to be capable of differentiating into nascent skeletal myotubes and form stable grafts following intra-cardiac delivery.[54] Similarly, transplantation of SMBs into injured hearts appears to limit adverse remodeling and result in a limited improvement of left ventricular (LV) function.[53–55] In 2003, Rubart *et al.*[56] isolated enhanced green fluorescent protein (EGFP)-expressing SMBs from transgenic mice for intra-cardiac transplantation into non-transgenic animals. By means of two-photon molecular excitation (TPME) laser scanning microscopy, spontaneous and induced intracellular calcium concentration transients in host and transplanted cells were then imaged in order to evaluate the degree functional integration of EGFP-SMBs within the host heart. Their results showed that even though mostly absent, intra-cellular calcium transients were detectable in a small fraction of the donor-derived myocytes around the graft/host border. While synchronous with neighboring cardiomyocyte, the observed donor-derived myocyte calcium concentration transients were heterogeneous in duration when compared to host cardiomyocytes. However, in a subsequent experiment performed by the same group[55] in which EGFP-expressing SMBs were transplanted into the hearts of transgenic mice expressing a cardiomyocyte-restricted, nuclear-localized β-gal, they demonstrated that a small population of cells in the transplanted heart expressed both donor- and host-derived reporter genes, indicating a fusion of these two cells types. The regional distribution of the fused cells was observed to be very similar to the distribution of donor-derived calcium concentration transient presenting cells in the previous project.

Rubart *et al.* presented the absence of a skeletal myocyte-cardiomyocyte gap junction complex and the voltage-dependent initiation of contractile activity in donor-derived myocytes, observed in similar studies, as suggestive of a non-functional coupling of skeletal myoblast-derived myocytes transplanted into the injured heart. They go on to discuss the beneficial effects seen in left ventricular function following SMB transplantation as likely due to other secondary, donor cell-mediated events.[55]

### 2.1.2 *Skeletal muscle stem cells (SkmSC)*

Alessandri *et al.*[57] recently identified and isolated a multipotent population of cells within human skeletal muscle capable of myogenic and neurogenic differentiation. Invernici *et al.*[21] confirmed the capability of SkmSC to undergo *in vitro* cardiomyogenic differentiation by treatment with retinoic acid. Their results showed that treatment with 1 nM 9-cis-retinoic acid significantly increased the expression of cardiac specific proteins α-cardiac actinin, atrial natriuretic peptide, cardiotin and cardiac troponin I after seven days. Invernici *et al.* then proceeded to evaluate the *in vivo* effect of RA-treated SkmSCs in an immunodeficient mouse model of myocardial infarction. Myocardial infarctions were surgically induced in the animals by permanent occlusion of the left anterior descending (LAD) coronary artery followed by peri-infarct injection of control (untreated) or RA-treated SkmSCs. The results of the animal study revealed that a small population of human nucleated cells was still present in the mice hearts receiving the RA-treated cells five weeks post-transplantation. However, any significant beneficial effect of the RA-treated cells *vs* untreated SkmSCs on left ventricular function was limited to an increase in the maximum rate of LV pressure rise and a decrease in the heart rate of the animals. Furthermore, omitting a group of animals receiving no treatment (vehicle) does not allow for a conclusive evaluation of the effect, if any, of these cells (treated or untreated) on LV function after myocardial infarction from this study.

## 2.2 *Resident cardiac progenitor cells*

### 2.2.1 *c-Kit$^+$ cells*

In order to determine the existence of a putative cardiac stem cell, Beltrami *et al.*[58] identified a population of cells in adult rat hearts positive for stem cell markers c-Kit, Sca-1 and MDR1 while negative for blood lineage markers (lin$^-$) including CD34 and CD45. They justified the focus on c-Kit$^+$ cells due to observations made by Orlic *et al.*[59] that a marrow-derived population of c-Kit$^+$ cells migrated to the injured heart and were involved in myocardial regeneration. C-Kit, or CD 117 encodes for a receptor tyrosine kinase that binds to stem cell factor (SCF). While very scarce (Beltrami *et al.* report ~1 c-Kit$^+$ cell per every 10,000 cardiomyocytes in the heart), these cells have been shown to have the capacity, under controlled conditions, to differentiate into cardiomyocytes, smooth muscle cells and vascular endothelial cells *in vitro*.[58] Similarly, investigations into other species have successfully indentified populations of c-Kit$^+$ within mouse[60] and human hearts.[61] Bearzi *et al.*[61] reported that human cardiac c-Kit$^+$ cells have a high clonogenic capacity and are multipotent and capable of restoring heart function following implantation into immunodeficient mice and rat models for myocardial infarction. Theyed accomplish this reportedly without undergoing cell fusion with host cardiomyocytes as evaluated by Bearzi *et al.* using a Cre-loxP flanked EGFP reporter system.

There is, however, an existing controversy as to the origin of these c-Kit$^+$ cells found in mammalian hearts. In fact, Fazel *et al.*[62] reported that c-Kit$^+$ cells were recruited by and migrated to the heart following myocardial infarction. There, these cells executed their effect through pro-angiogenic effects such as the secretion of VEGF and the reversal of the cardiac ratio of angiopoietin-1 to angiopoietin-2 in the infarct border zone. The group was also able to genetically trace the origin of these c-Kit$^+$ cells back to the bone marrow, strongly suggesting that they are not true cardiac resident stem cells.

### 2.2.2 *Isl-1$^+$ cells*

Yet, another sub-population of cells within the heart being postulated as resident cardiac stem cells are those positive for Islet-1, an LIM homeodomain transcription factor. During development, Isl-1$^+$ cells are the major constituent of the embryonic heart and give rise to several types of cardiac cells, leading researchers to the speculation that most cardiac tissues arise from a common progenitor cell population. Currently, Isl-1$^+$ cells have been successfully isolated from the embryonic and postnatal rat, mouse and human heart.[63,64] Laugwitz *et al.*[64] reported that, under the right culture conditions, these cells are capable of limited self-renewal and cardiomyogenic differentiation. Co-culture with cardiomyocytes in these studies led to the development of a fully differentiated cardiomyocyte phenotype amongst the Isl-1$^+$ cell population. However, due to their limited capacity for self-renewal, accompanied by the fact that it has proven difficult for researchers to identify any Isl-1$^+$ cell constituent in the adult heart, has led to the identification of these cells as embryonic cardiac progenitors, rather than cardiac resident stem cells. Moretti *et al.*[65] isolated embryonic Isl-1$^+$ cells and proved the cells were multipotent, with the capacity to differentiate into cardiac, smooth muscle and endothelial cells.

A couple of other different attempts have been made to identify and isolate resident cardiac stem cells. These generally rely on the expression of other stem cell-associated markers, such as multi drug resistance (MDR) genes which help identify side-population (SP) cells *via* flow cytometry[66] or different culture conditions that help renew and maintain clonogenic and multipotency characteristics of cells within them, as is the case with the use of cardioshpere-derived cells.[67,68] Yet despite the well-defined identification and isolation protocols for these cardiac progenitor cell populations, the scarcity of these cell populations within the adult heart as well as the associated donor site morbidity issues raised with their acquisition, limits the viability of their use for regenerative therapies.

## 2.3 *Stem cells*

Stem cells comprise a more abundant and, in some case, a more readily accessible source for multipotent cells capable of giving rise to any and all tissues within the cardiovascular system. Traditional stem cell populations investigated for myocardial regeneration include bone marrow-derived mesenchymal and hematopoietic stem cells, embryonic stem cells and adipose-derived stem cells. Additionally, other stem cell sources have also been explored for their capacity to regenerate the myocardium, which include genetically modified or induced-pluripotent stem cells and stem cells isolated from dental pulp tissues.

### 2.3.1 *Embryonic stem cells (ESC)*

The use of pluripotent embryonic stem cells in regenerative therapies is an obviously attractive option due to their capability for giving rise to tissues from the three germ layers. This includes potential for differentiation into mesodermal lineages and, hence, into cardiomyocytes. In fact, *in vitro* techniques have been developed in which a population of embryonic stem cells spontaneously differentiates into cardiomyocytes and present contractile activity. Yet, the identification of homogeneous ECS sub-populations, such as the Isl-1$^+$ sub-population described above that will exclusively commit to a cardiomyogenic lineage, is only the initial obstacle to a pragmatic use of this cell source. Optimization of culturing and differentiation conditions leading to the rise of cardiovascular tissues from these cells has proven to be a major challenge as well.[50] This includes the understanding of the molecular signaling pathways employed by ESCs undergoing cardiomyogenic differentiation as well as the ensuing genetic profiles that lead to cardiomyocyte formation from undifferentiated ESCs. Recently, both Synnergen *et al.*[69] and Faustino *et al.*[70] have taken on the task of elucidating the genetic expression profile of embryonic stem cells undergoing cardiomyogenic differentiation with highly promising results. Faustino *et al.* revealed that 3,656 quality-filtered genes, some increasing, some decreasing, and some constant throughout, were involved in the guided cardiopoietic lineage specification of embryonic stem cells cultured in a cocktail containing some 9 known cardio-inductive moieties. On the other hand, Synnergen *et al.* noted that a larger variation in gene expression was observed within a single cell line across two separate cardio-inductive protocols than amongst different cells lines cultured according to the same protocol, thus augmenting the importance for more clearly defined cardiomyogenic differentiation strategies.

Regardless of the molecular signaling pathway elicited, several researchers have successfully achieved mature cardiomyogenic phenotype expression from ESCs through various culturing techniques. One of the most common procedures used in this respect is the formation of embryoid bodies (EB) and subsequent culturing of these EBs on gelatin-coated culture surfaces. Apart from other parameters such as cell seeding densities and growth factor addition, this culture system generally gives rise to spontaneously contracting clusters of cells, which develop a fully differentiated cardiomyocyte phenotype.[27,28,71] Further proof-of-principle studies into the *in vivo* functional grafting of these cells in MI animal models have shown stable engraftment, alignment and coupling of transplanted cells within the host myocardium. Caspi *et al.*[27] were able to show that these cells form functional gap junctions with resident cardiomyocytes in immunodeficient rats without an apparent fusion of donor and host cells, although conclusive evidence to this effect was not provided.

However, despite the potential and encouraging results obtained, the use of these cells raises several concerns that go beyond the ethical issue of their acquisition. Both Caspi *et al.* and Huber *et al.*[28] demonstrated that these cells have the potential for teratoma formation when delivered *in vivo* in an undifferentiated state. Similarly, ESCs generally elicit adverse immunogenic reactions in the host as the cells differentiate and express their unique immunological complexes.

### 2.3.2 *Mesenchymal stem cells (MSC's)*

Mesenchymal stem cells are bone marrow-derived non-hematopoietic cells that have been proven capable of differentiating into cells from several different lineages. Their inclination to form tissues of the mesodermal lineage (cartilage, bone, tendon, muscle, etc.), and the ease with which they can be isolated and expanded to abundant number *in vitro*, makes them especially appealing for the regeneration of myocardial tissue. In 1999, Bittner *et al.*[72] demonstrated that dystrophic muscle was able to signal and recruit a circulating constituent of the bone marrow for its regeneration. The group transplanted healthy male mouse bone marrow into dystrophic (mdx) female mice recipients, and performed a subsequent histological analysis of both skeletal and cardiac muscle specimens. Their results showed the presence of Y chromosome positive cells in both the skeletal and cardiac muscle of the dystrophic female mice, leading them to the conclusion that a myogenic progenitor cell population resides within the bone marrow. This observation is similar to that later made by Orlic *et al.*[19] and Fazel *et al.*,[62] in which the number of marrow-derived c-Kit$^+$ cell numbers increased within the heart muscle after a myocardial infarction.

Similarly, Jackson *et al.*[12] transplanted a highly enriched side population (SP) constituent of bone marrow (CD34, c-Kit$^+$, Sca-1$^+$) into lethally irradiated mice subsequently rendered ischemic by a 60-minute coronary artery occlusion followed by reperfusion. The group was then able to locate these cells in the injured heart where a small number had engrafted and regenerated myocardial and endothelial tissues. However, the prevalence of the cells in the heart muscle and endothelial tissues was only determined to be 0.02% and 3.3% respectively.

In order to improve MSC engraftment in the host myocardium, researchers have thus attempted direct injection of these cells into the ischemic lesion and have shown an almost complete recovery of left ventricular function.[73] The mechanisms of repair, however, remain a highly contested issue. As with the coupling of skeletal myoblasts, researchers have shown that these cells do not acquire the functional attributes of cardiomyocytes when transplanted into the infarct region, and lack the spontaneous generation of intra-cellular calcium transients typical of mature cardiomyocytes.[74] Yet another set of investigators attributed the localization of donor-derived cells within the heart to cellular fusion of host and donor cells.[75] Nevertheless, these cells unequivocally help restore cardiac function and limit the adverse remodeling seen following a myocardial infarction. Whether this is a result from the release of anti-apoptotic, pro-angiogenic and mitogenic soluble factors or the functional engraftment and differentiation of a small number of these cells in the infarct region still remains to be confirmed. The development of protocols to improve the engraftment of these cells once transplanted can help shed some light into the mechanisms of repair engaged in these studies.

### 2.3.3 *Other stem cells*

Several other stem cell populations exist that can potentially give rise to cardiomyogenic tissue. These cells include human placenta-derived mesodermal cells,[20] umbilical cord blood-derived stem cells,[76] adipose tissue-derived progenitor cells,[67,77] dental pulp-derived stem cells,[67,78] and induced pluripotent stem cells,[79–83] among others. Yet the application of these cell sources towards a regenerative therapy for myocardial infarction remains in the early stages of development.

## 3. Mechanical Forces and Cardiovascular Differentiation

As discussed previously, mechanical forces play a crucial and integral part in tissue morphogenesis and, later in adulthood, as maintainers of structure and function. During cardiac development, Taber *et al.*[9] and Voronov *et al.*[11] independently showed that exogenous mechanical forces drive the formation of the cardiac tube as well as the initiation of cardiac looping. Furthermore, in their study, Voronov *et al.* were able to show that any perturbance in the delicate balance of forces driving the dextral rotation of the embryonic chick heart led to incorrect looping phenomena. Even more recently, Reckova *et al.*[10] determined that the hemodynamic environment in the developing heart, as well as the temporal patterns of mechanical

mechanical stimulation, both scaffolds were implanted into the heart of rats that had undergone surgical MI induction for six weeks and evaluated by gross histology and immunohistochemistry. Cells in the mechanically loaded PLCL scaffolds showed a significant upregulation in cardiomyogenic markers cardiac α-MHC, cardiac α-actin, GATA-4 and Nkx2.5 over static controls. PLCL scaffolds implanted into the MI-induced rats also presented less fibrotic tissue infiltration when compared to static PLGA scaffolds and stained positively for cardiac troponin I and α-sarcomeric actinin. Yet other researchers have gone a step further and have combined genetic manipulation and mechanical stimuli to induce ESC differentiation into cardiovascular phenotypes. Shimko *et al.*[18] transfected mouse ESCs with a 4.5 kb α-MHC promoter, seeded these cells in ring-shaped collagen/fibronectin scaffolds and subjected the cells to cyclic strain for 3 consecutive days. This stimulation resulted in a frequency-dependant regulation of myogenic markers α-cardiac actin, α-skeletal actin, α and β MHC and GATA-4. Finally, other embryonic-derived cell sources have also been subjected to mechanical loading and evaluated for their cardiovascular differentiation with an equal variation in outcomes.[13]

Conversely, less resrearch has been focused on the effect of mechanical loading on adult stem cell populations. However, some studies can provide insights into this effect. Park *et al.*,[33,84] Kurpinski *et al.*,[35] and Hamilton *et al.*[34] have all evaluated the effect of mechanical strain on the orientation of MSC cultures and *vice versa*. Park *et al.* demonstrated that human MSCs seeded on collagen type I-coated silicone membranes and subjected to cyclic strain respond differently depending on the direction of the applied stress (their study focuses on equi-axial *versus* uni-axial cyclic loading). Their results showed that MSCs subjected to equi-axial strain for one and three days undergo a downregulation of smooth muscle markers when compared to their static controls, while MSCs subjected to uni-axial stretching transiently upregulate their expression of α-actin and SM-22α after one day, but return to basal levels of expression after two days of mechanical stimulation. On the other hand, Kurpinski *et al.* used a micropatterning technique to guide MSC orientation on poly (dimethyl siloxane) (PDMS) membranes, and then subjected the cells to mechanical tensile loading in a manner parallel or perpendicular to their forced cellular alignment. Their results showed that when cells are aligned parallel to the direction of tensile loading, cellular proliferation and calponin I expression increase significantly over static controls. Similarly, their results showed a significant upregulation in lysyl oxidase (LOX) and aggrecanase expression, and a significant decrease in matrix metalloproteinase 1 (MMP1), biglycan (BGN), collagen type X α1 (ColXα1) and collagen type XI α1 (ColXIα1) expression. They discussed this observation as suggestive of cell induction towards a tension-bearing phenotype and away from a compression-bearing phenotype.[35] When cells are aligned perpendicular to the direction of mechanical strain, however, the expression of LOX as well as the proliferative capacity of the cells remains unaffected, while the other effects seen with parallel loading pattern are all observed to a lesser extent.

Finally, Hamilton *et al.* obtained seemingly contradicting results when employing the same mechanical loading system utilized by Park *et al.* in their equi-axial strain studies. Namely, Hamilton *et al.* seeded rat bone marrow-derived mesenchymal stem cells on collagen type I-coated silicone membranes and stimulated them with cyclic mechanical strain for a period of seven days. Their results showed a decrease in the proliferative capacity of the cells, but a significant increase in the level of α-actin and h1-calponin expression following the seven day stimulation, indicating active differentiation of the cells. Even though their study differs from the study by Park *et al.* in the species of cells utilized (human *versus* rat MSCs), their results are totally contrary to one another, which suggests the need to analyze the nature of the mechanical stimulus and the manner in which it is introduced into the differentiation protocols as well.

As we have learned from developmental studies, a fine balance of parameters and temporal mechanical force presentation is needed to achieve the accurate cellular phenotype. So, in the differentiation of stem and progenitors cells, a balance of parameters must be found that optimizes the effect of mechanical cyclical strain in the cardiovascular differentiation of the cells. Variables such as frequency, magnitude of strain, duration of stimuli application, strain rate and strain curve profile can all have an effect in the outcome of the differentiation protocol. Here, we will evaluate the effect of the first three above-mentioned parameters as permissible in the studies already presented.

### 3.1 *Frequency*

Under normal physiological conditions, cells of the cardiovascular system would be exposed to mechanical stimuli guided by the rate at which the heart contracts (the heart rate). Normally, this ranges from 60 to 100 beats per minute or 1 to 1.67 beats per second (also known as Hertz [Hz]). So naturally, in keeping with the biomimetic presentation of stimuli in differentiation protocols, we expect that most studies investigating the effect of mechanical stresses will apply loads within this range of frequencies. In fact, out of the 8 presented studies above in which mechanical strain is used to differentiate ESCs and MSCs[1,13,18,31–35] into cardiovascular structures, 7 utilize a 1 Hz frequency exclusively in their protocols. However, Shimko *et al.* explored the effect of a 1, 2 and 3 Hz frequency mechanical strain stimulus on their ring-shaped, ESC-seeded, collagen/fibronectin scaffolds. Surprisingly enough, they demonstrated that in such a system, the 3 Hz frequency stimulation significantly upregulates the expression of cardiomyogenic markers, such as α-cardiac actin, α-MHC and β-MHC, while the 1 Hz stimulus frequency actually downregulates the expression of these markers as well as downregulating the expression of GATA-4.

### 3.2 *Magnitude of strain*

While there is no established and unique degree of strain experienced by cells of the cardiovascular system, we do know that there is an optimal elongation at which muscles can maximize the amount of force generated, the point at which the most number of actin and myosin binding sites are available to each other. Hence, it wouldn't be outrageous to think that there is an optimal degree of elongation that could maximize the effect of mechanical strain upon the cells that make up this muscle. The degrees of elongation explored in the reviewed literature range from 2 to 20% of the original length of the constructs with only two studies performing strain-dependent studies.[1,31] In their study, Shimizu *et al.* studied the effect of a 2, 4, 6, 8 and 12% mechanical strain on Flk-1$^+$ mouse ES cells and were able to demonstrate a magnitude-dependent mechanical-induction of differentiation. Namely, the group demonstrated that while all levels of strain significantly increased the expression of SMC markers when compared to static controls, the 8 and 12% strain groups expressed the highest levels of differentiation markers at the gene and protein levels respectively. Furthermore, the 8% strain magnitude group was the only one that showed a statistically significant decrease in the expression of Flk-1$^+$ cells over the controls, demonstrating that this strain magnitude was the most effective, under their culturing conditions, for terminally differentiating the mouse-derived embryonic stem cells

Similarly, Schmelter *et al.* investigated the effect of 5, 10 and 20% cyclic mechanical strain on mouse ES cells. Their results showed a very interesting dichotomy in the strain magnitude-dependent cardiovascular differentiation in that, a 5 and 10% magnitude of strain showed a significant increase in the expression and immunohistochemistry staining of PECAM-1$^+$ regions, while a 20% strain magnitude showed no statistical difference to the controls in this respect. On the other hand, the 20% magnitude strain had the highest effect on the number of spontaneously beating foci observed in the study. This observation would seem to suggest that while all levels of strain might have a differentiation effect, a lower level of strain may be needed for angiogenic and smooth muscle lineage commitment, and a higher level of strain may induce the cells more towards the cardiomyogenic differentiation program.

### 3.3 *Duration of stimuli application*

Out of all the possible variables introduced through mechanical stimulation, the amount of time the cells need to be exposed to the stimulus to elicit their maximal response may be the most widely varied of all. In adulthood, cells are continuously exposed to mechanical stimuli, which unfortunately, might not constitute the best conditions for the recruitment, engraftment, and differentiation of more primitive progenitor cell populations. Unfortunately, little is known on the temporal presentation patterns of mechanical cues during embryogenesis in order to be able to model these patterns *in vitro* and harness them for cellular differentiation. Hence, most researchers have elaborated mechanical force-induced differentiation protocols that vary greatly in the duration of strain application. In the studies we have reviewed here, the application of mechanical tensile strain to the cells ranges from a two hour exposure to a two week continuous treatment of the cells, which constitutes an over 160-times difference. If considering mechanical strain as a differentiation-inducing moiety, this would be the equivalent of stimulating the cells with media constituent X at 10 mM or 1.6 M concentrations and expecting to observe similar results.

Hence, the optimization of mechanical strain-induced differentiation must account for the duration and intervals at which this stimulus is introduced in culture. Both Kurpinski *et al.*[35] and Park *et al.*[33] performed dose-dependent studies as part of their investigations. Kurpinski *et al.* demonstrated that at 1 Hz and 5% strain, a two and four day course of stimulation were needed in order to see statistically significant increases at the mRNA and protein levels respectively. On the other hand, Park *et al.* showed a statistically significant increase in smooth muscle markers for cells under uni-axial strain at 10% and 1 Hz after just one day of stimulation. This increase, however, was not significant and returned to control levels when the cells were left under mechanical stimulation for another consecutive day. Similarly, their study determined that the equi-axial strain applied at 10% strain and 1 Hz actually downregulated the expression of smooth muscle markers in a dose-dependent manner over the course of three days of stimulation (one day: down to ~50% & three days: down to ~25% of control level of expression). Nevertheless, when the same system was utilized by Hamilton *et al.*[34] to stimulate rat MSCs at a 1 Hz, 10% strain for 7 consecutive days, the resulting gene expression for smooth muscle cell markers was actually significantly increased over control level expression.

Finally, the study by Schmelter *et al.*[1] requires a special mention in this section as the group subjected their cells to a 10 or 20% mechanical strain at 1 Hz for only two hours, yet this resulted in a significant increase in smooth muscle cell and cardiomyogenic marker expression. This study is worth mentioning due to the fact that their observations on cellular marker expression was only performed four days after the application of tensile stress had ended. While the cells had time to recover and re-establish their own metabolic and differentiating rates, the cells stimulated with mechanical strain showed significant differences to those under static conditions four days after the fact. The results of this study strongly advocate for the quantized delivery of mechanical stimuli interrupted by recovery periods. Who is to say what their results might have looked like if the cells had been subjected to the two hour stimulus again after two days of recovery?

Here we have discussed just three of the main variables that can be introduced through the application of mechanical strain into any differentiation protocol, and hopefully made the case for the importance that these variables can have on the outcome of specific studies. It is, hence, necessary to conduct more parameter-related studies in order to attain the desired responses from the cells employed and, furthermore, maximize the effect the mechanical stimulation has on differentiation in hopes of producing more accurate and functionally active tissue regenerative therapies. Table 1 summarizes the discussed variables in the presented studies

**Table 1.** Comparison of the three parameters of mechanical strain discussed and their effect on the results obtained in different studies for Smooth Muscle Cell (SMC) and Cardiomyocyte (CM) differentiation. Data is sorted by strain magnitude first and stimulus duration second.

| Study | Cell type (species) | Time (hr) | Strain (%) | Freq. (Hz) | SMC | CM | NOTES |
|---|---|---|---|---|---|---|---|
| Shimizu *et al.* | ESC (mouse) | 24 | 2 | 1 | ✓ | - | |
| Shimizu *et al.* | ESC (mouse) | 24 | 4 | 1 | ✓ | - | |
| Schmelter *et al.* | ESC (mouse) | 2 | 5 | 1 | ✓ | × | |
| Kurpinski *et al.* | MSC (human) | 48 | 5 | 1 | × | ✓ | Parallel |
| Kurpinski *et al.* | MSC (human) | 96 | 5 | 1 | - | ✓✓ | Parallel |
| Shimizu *et al.* | ESC (mouse) | 24 | 6 | 1 | - | - | |
| Shimizu *et al.* | ESC (mouse) | 24 | 8 | 1 | ✓✓ | - | |
| Schmelter *et al.* | ESC (mouse) | 2 | 10 | 1 | ✓✓✓ | ✓✓ | |
| Park *et al.* | MSC (human) | 24 | 10 | 1 | ✓✓✓ | - | Uniaxial |
| Park *et al.* | MSC (human) | 48 | 10 | 1 | ✓✓ | - | Uniaxial |
| Park *et al.* | MSC (human) | 72 | 10 | 1 | ✓ | - | Uniaxial |
| Shimko *et al.* | ESC (mouse) | 72 | 10 | 1 | - | × | |
| Shimko *et al.* | ESC (mouse) | 72 | 10 | 2 | - | ✓ | |
| Shimko *et al.* | ESC (mouse) | 72 | 10 | 3 | - | ✓✓ | |
| Riha *et al.* | EMP (mouse) | 96 | 10 | 1 | ✓ | - | |
| Riha *et al.* | EMP (mouse) | 144 | 10 | 1 | ✓✓ | - | |
| Hamilton *et al.* | MSC (rat) | 168 | 10 | 1 | - | ✓✓ | |
| Gwak *et al.* | ESC (mouse) | 236 | 10 | 1 | ✓✓ | ✓✓✓ | |
| Shimizu *et al.* | ESC (mouse) | 24 | 12 | 1 | ✓✓ | - | |
| Schmelter *et al.* | ESC (mouse) | 2 | 20 | 1 | × | ✓✓✓ | |

**Legend:** ✓ = some data shown (up to gene expression); ✓✓ = strong data shown (including protein expression); ✓✓✓ = functional data shown (improvement in animal model or *in vitro* contraction); × = Data at or below static control levels; – = No data offered to this effect.

be quenched using broad-spectrum protease inhibitors. This study also showed that the method of freezing (–80°C *vs* liquid nitrogen) did not show any differences, but that the thawing methods did.[63]

Oxidative stress has been shown to cause aging of cells *in vivo* and *in vitro* and is an important factor when it comes to cell culture. This is especially true for cultures, which lack serum, or protein such as anti-oxidants. The accumulation of oxidative damage is thought to lead to the senescence of cell lines.[64] It has been shown that cell cultures grown in low oxygen environments have longer life spans when compared to cell lines grown in oxygen rich environments.[65,66] Harman was the first to suggest that the rate of oxygen consumption in relation to mitochondrial activity is the aging mechanism of cells.[67] There are two main sources of reactive oxygen species (ROS), endogenous (i.e., mitochondrial oxygen consumption and free radical production),[68] and exogenous (i.e., UV light damage). On the other hand, there are numerous enzymatic and non-enzymatic (i.e. vitamins) products, which counteract and regulate the level of ROS in the body and within cells.[64] The damage caused by ROS can take the form of single- and double-DNA strand breaks, deletions, base changes and chromosomal aberrations.[69] This type of damage to a cell's integrity leads to cellular senescence and ultimately apoptosis. Thus, it is important to factor in oxidative stress when undertaking cell culture and to keep in mind its effect on cellular aging and the effects of these changes in a possible human host.

These studies simply show that laboratory methods ought to be considered as having substantial effects on the viability and fitness of stem cells.

Finally, the scientific community ought to decide if it would prefer stem cells to be differentiated *in vitro*, or if the MSCs ought to be placed in a microenvironment *in vivo* within which they will differentiate. Studies where hematopoietic cells were injected into hearts that had suffered a myocardial infarct showed that transdifferentiation did not occur to a substantial degree.[70] Other studies showed that pre-manipulation of these cells with growth factors introduced to help pre-differentiate/enhance survival of the cells increased the viability of these cells in ischemic hearts.[71,72] Whereas, other studies showed that bone marrow stem cells which were injected directly into ischemic region of the heart were capable of regenerating myocardium *de novo*.[73–75]

If the consensus becomes that stem cell therapy is more efficacious once the cells have been manipulated into the cell line desired than the process of *in vitro* manipulation and its effect on the host body needs to be elucidated.

## 6. Effects of the Aged Microenvironment

A study by Carlson and Conboy tested the effects of young and aged serum on the *in vitro* proliferative and self-renewal potential of human ESCs. They found that adding aged serum to typical human ESC medium culture dramatically inhibited the replicative capacity, while ESCs cultured in medium with young serum added high levels of replication, similar to that of typical culture medium. Interestingly, they showed that a mixture of young and aged serum inhibited replication suggesting that the inhibitory factors of the aged milieu dominate over the young serum.[76]

In addition to mesenchymal stem cells, a distinct subpopulation of bone marrow cells is capable of differentiating into cardiomyocytes. Platelet-derived growth factor (PDGF) has been identified as a trophic factor, which increases this differentiation process and PDGF deficiency results in the pre-disposition to increased cardiac injury. To see whether PDGF played a role in the observed age-related decline in cardiomyogenic capacity of bone marrow cells, bone marrow cells from young and aged mice were cultured under conditions to direct differentiation into cardiac myocytes and PDGF induction was evaluated. This experiment showed that the PDGF-B induction pathways were impaired in the older cultures suggesting that the age-related decline in cardiomyogenic capacity was partly due to a lack of PDGF in the external milieu. Addition of PDGF restored cardiomyogenic differentiation capabilities in the aging cultures demonstrating that intrinsic changes within the bone marrow cells were unlikely to have had a role.[77]

Aging is associated with increased oxidative stress on cells due to a decline in anti-oxidant defenses and an increased production of oxidants. As mentioned above, this oxidation state in the aging cell leads to functional alterations, pathological conditions, and even death.[78] By artificially inducing oxidative stress on human hMSCs, it has been recently demonstrated that oxidative stress inhibits their proliferation,[79] differentiation[15] and induces apoptosis.[15]

HSC proliferation and differentiation are also influenced by the microenvironment. It was recently reported that pteridine neopterin (NP) produced from monocytes stimulates proliferation and differentiation of HSCs by activating bone marrow stromal cell function.[80] NP was injected into mice and at two weeks following treatment resulting in an increase in the number of leukocytes and CFU-GM in the bone marrow and spleen of young senescence accelerated mice (SAMs) but not in old SAMs. Additionally, the production of hematopoietic stimulating factors in response to NP increased in young SAMs, while aged SAMs showed no response.[81] Differentiation of HSCs to T cells and NK cells has also been analyzed and it was shown that young donor murine HSCs transplanted into aged mice exhibited a reduced differentiation compared to transplantation into young mice.[50] Furthermore, a separate study found that following transplantation of bone marrow from young mice B cell production was decreased in aged mice compared to young mice.[82]

## 7. From Bench to Bedside: Clinical Implications

While the results of many studies on age-related changes in stem cells are often contradictory, a great deal of inconsistency is due to varying definitions of age, as has been demonstrated earlier in this chapter. Another source of conflicting data is due to a lack of universally accepted markers to identify the various sub-populations of these cells. Furthermore, studies often use different sources of cells and extraction methods. However, even when the source of cells is isolated to the bone marrow, the site of extraction can have an effect on cellular function, as has been demonstrated with MSCs.[83] It has also been shown that culture conditions can influence cell behaviour. Considering these variations, researchers need to be sensitive when interpreting the results of their studies and contrasting them with others to avoid comparing two distinct cell lines.

Although it is difficult to draw specific conclusions on the effects of aging on stem cells, there is certainly a trend showing a decreased functional ability of these cells including decreased proliferation, mobilization, and differentiation. Considering the excitement over stem cells and their various regenerative capabilities, it would therefore seem likely that a therapeutic treatment involving autologous cell transplants in elderly patients would not be optimal. Rather, a better strategy for cellular therapy would be to isolate stem cell populations from young donors and transplant them into aged recipients. Unlike many other cells of the body, this transplant is feasible since these cells possess a unique immune tolerance.[84]

This concept of transplanting cells from young to aged recipients was tested by Edelberg *et al.* who used bone marrow-derived EPCs to treat the aging-associated decline in cardiac angiogenesis.[85] They found that transplantation of bone marrow from young mice maintained and restored the angiogenic function of exogenous cardiac tissue, but aged marrow failed to do so. Allogenic stem cell transplantations were also evaluated in the ability of HSCs to reconstitute the immune cells of irradiated mice and it was shown that transplants from young donors significantly affected lymphocyte reconstitution compared to aged donors.[86] A quicker lymphocyte recovery is important to help reduce the incidence of mortality due to infections that are often associated with transplants. Similarly, the efficacy of treating atherosclerosis with hematopoietic and stromal-enriched cells derived from young and aged marrow of mice has been tested in a murine model. It was shown that the atherosclerotic burden was significantly greater in mice that received treatment from old donor marrow compared with the results of the young marrow.[87]

It is quite evident that although this area of research comparing *in vivo* effects of young and aged donors has received little attention, it has significant clinical implications and will certainly be of great interest in the near future.

However, not all cellular therapies are affected by aging, but rather the effect of donor age has been reported to be cell-type dependant. A study using ischemic cardiomyopathic hearts reported that using aged smooth muscle cells resulted in significantly improved cardiac function while aged MSCs had very little benefit.[88] Recipient age has also been shown to be an important indicator of the beneficial outcome experienced in cellular therapy. This was demonstrated by an experiment with a myocardial infarction model of young and aged rats that received skeletal myoblasts isolated from young donor rats. Although cardiac function improved in all the recipients of myoblasts compared to the control, the improvement in the young rats was significantly greater than that of the old rats when using donors of the same age.[89]

Based on these findings, it seems that rather than being isolated to the characteristics of donor cells, there appears to be a relationship between the host and the donor in determining the efficacy of cell therapy. Furthermore, it is plausible that optimizing cell therapy is likely to involve allogenous transplants from younger healthy donors to elderly diseased patients. However, these findings represent the tip of the iceberg and a great deal of further research is required to elucidate possible risks and consequences associated with such allogenous transplants and to determine what the chronic effect will be.

## 8. Conclusion

As the field of stem cell research broadens and the scientific understanding of the role that age plays in cellular and clinical research heightens, stem cell therapy may become the forefront of medical intervention. With such great expectations of a relatively new field, the obvious need for proper exploration into the multiple facets of the effects of age on the therapeutic benefits of stem cell research cannot be more stressed.

The first step to properly characterizing the effect of any factor that alters the functionality of a clinical therapy is to appropriately define that factor. Although usually a very simple and straightforward case, the definition of age differs in being multi-faceted once appropriately analyzed.

Donor age is the definition most used and most widely known for age. There is an obvious decline in functionality of all organ systems and cellular processes in the aging human. However, the age at which stem cell function declines past a level of being therapeutic to a particular person is yet unknown. A review of the literature puts this timeline somewhere between 50–65 years of age, with more work needed for the community to understand the cellular cascades and microenvironment changes that allow for a decline in one's stem cell fitness

Laboratory age is the number of doublings a cell line has undergone *in vitro*. A thorough look into the effects of this doubling time on stem cell proliferation shows a clear decline over time as was first described by Hayflick. Since a large number of cells will likely be needed to treat each patient, a decrease in the proliferative capacity of a cell line diminishes its therapeutic potential.

Since age is known to impact many aspects of the human body, experiments deemed at quantifying the effects of age are required to be properly planned, executed and to appropriately measure a set number of endpoints relative to cellular function. As such, the community has used proliferation, differentiation and changes in morphology to define cellular aging. Proliferation widely varies among different cell lines and genetic alterations over multiple passages dictates how cell lines will behave (i.e., cell lineages into which they will differentiate). The differentiation of cell lines depends on the age of the donor from which the cell line was extracted, the laboratory age of the cell line, and the microenvironment in which it will be placed. Lastly, morphological changes that occur due to cellular aging may help indicate the process of senescence and may negatively impact the cells potential at integrating into a microenvironment.

Laboratory manipulations with stem cells can also alter their activity. As such, the level of oxidation and freeze thaw methods ought to be appropriately analyzed to confer the least amount of stress to stem cell lines. Furthermore, prior to implanting these cell lines into humans, the benefits and pitfalls of *in vivo* versus *in vitro* differentiation ought to be completely elucidated in order to confer the most amount of therapeutic benefit.

The aging population within which the North American society lives in will likely represent most of the patient population in the coming years. Thus, the role of the microenvironments within the human body where stem cells will likely be implemented have to be analyzed. As the literature review showed, the microenvironment also ages and may direct the aging of the surrounding cells/organs, and thus impact any therapy intended for the site.

As one reviews all the studies from laboratories directed at improving the understanding of cellular functions, it is clear that a lot is unknown, yet it is evident that a lot has been learnt. With a continuous outlook of elucidating and clarifying all the aspects of the impact of age on cellular fitness, the scientific community comes closer to implementing effective and efficient stem cell therapies into a population that, with the efforts already made in the field, now enjoys longer lives.

## References

1. Hayflick L, Moorhead PS. The serial cultivation of human diploid cell strains. *Exp Cell Res* 1961;25:585–621.
2. Zhou S, Greenberger JS, Epperly MW, *et al.* Age-related intrinsic changes in human bone-marrow-derived mesenchymal stem cells and their differentiation to osteoblasts. *Aging Cell* 2008;7:335–343.
3. Stenderup K, Justesen J, Clausen C, Kassem M. Aging is associated with decreased maximal life span and accelerated senescence of bone marrow stromal cells. *Bone* 2003;33:919–926.
4. Baxter MA, Wynn RF, Jowitt SN, *et al.* Study of telomere length reveals rapid aging of human marrow stromal cells following *in vitro* expansion. *Stem Cells* 2004;22:675–682.
5. Mueller SM, Glowacki J. Age-related decline in the osteogenic potential of human bone marrow cells cultured in three-dimensional collagen sponges. *J Cell Biochem* 2001;82:583–590.
6. Bonab MM, Alimoghaddam K, Talebian F, *et al.* Aging of mesenchymal stem cell *in vitro*. *BMC Cell Biol* 2006;7:14.
7. Stenderup K, Justesen J, Eriksen EF, *et al.* Number and proliferative capacity of osteogenic stem cells are maintained during aging and in patients with osteoporosis. *J Bone Miner Res* 2001;16:1120–1129.
8. Jiang Y, Mishima H, Sakai S, *et al.* Gene expression analysis of major lineage-defining factors in human bone marrow cells: effect of aging, gender, and age-related disorders. *J Orthop Res* 2008;26:910–917.
9. Banfi A, Muraglia A, Dozin B, *et al.* Proliferation kinetics and differentiation potential of *ex vivo* expanded human bone marrow stromal cells: Implications for their use in cell therapy. *Exp Hematol* 2000;28:707–715.
10. Oreffo RO, Bord S, Triffitt JT. Skeletal progenitor cells and ageing human populations. *Clin Sci (Lond)* 1998;94:549–555.
11. Jaiswal N, Haynesworth SE, Caplan AI, Bruder SP. Osteogenic differentiation of purified, culture-expanded human mesenchymal stem cells *in vitro*. *J Cell Biochem* 1997;64:295–312.
12. Pittenger MF, Mackay AM, Beck SC, *et al.* Multilineage potential of adult human mesenchymal stem cells. *Science* 1999;284:143–147.
13. Khoo ML, Shen B, Tao H, Ma DD. Long-term serial passage and neuronal differentiation capability of human bone marrow mesenchymal stem cells. *Stem Cells Dev* 2008;17:883–896.

14. Sawada R, Ito T, Tsuchiya T. Changes in expression of genes related to cell proliferation in human mesenchymal stem cells during *in vitro* culture in comparison with cancer cells. *J Artif Organs* 2006;9:179–184.
15. Stolzing A, Jones E, McGonagle D, Scutt A. Age-related changes in human bone marrow-derived mesenchymal stem cells: consequences for cell therapies. *Mech Ageing Dev* 2008;129:163–173.
16. Wagner W, Horn P, Castoldi M, *et al.* Replicative senescence of mesenchymal stem cells: a continuous and organized process. *PLoS ONE* 2008;3:e2213.
17. DiGirolamo CM, Stokes D, Colter D, *et al.* Propagation and senescence of human marrow stromal cells in culture: a simple colony-forming assay identifies samples with the greatest potential to propagate and differentiate. *Br J Haematol* 1999;107:275–281.
18. Oreffo RO, Bennett A, Carr AJ, Triffitt JT. Patients with primary osteoarthritis show no change with ageing in the number of osteogenic precursors. *Scand J Rheumatol* 1998;27:415–424.
19. Mendes SC, Tibbe JM, Veenhof M *et al.* Bone tissue-engineered implants using human bone marrow stromal cells: effect of culture conditions and donor age. *Tissue Eng* 2002;8:911–920.
20. Gotherstrom C, West A, Liden J, *et al.* Difference in gene expression between human fetal liver and adult bone marrow mesenchymal stem cells. *Haematologica* 2005;90:1017–1026.
21. Hacia JG, Lee CC, Jimenez DF *et al.* Age-related gene expression profiles of rhesus monkey bone marrow-derived mesenchymal stem cells. *J Cell Biochem* 2008;103:1198–1210.
22. Mets T, Verdonk G. Variations in the stromal cell population of human bone marrow during aging. *Mech Ageing Dev* 1981;15:41–49.
23. Nishida S, Endo N, Yamagiwa H, *et al.* Number of osteoprogenitor cells in human bone marrow markedly decreases after skeletal maturation. *J Bone Miner Metab* 1999;17:171–177.
24. D'Ippolito G, Schiller PC, Ricordi C, *et al.* Age-related osteogenic potential of mesenchymal stromal stem cells from human vertebral bone marrow. *J Bone Miner Res* 1999;14:1115–1122.
25. Majors AK, Boehm CA, Nitto H, *et al.* Characterization of human bone marrow stromal cells with respect to osteoblastic differentiation. *J Orthop Res* 1997;15:546–557.

Based on these clinical and experimental data discussed previously, the FDA recently approved an Osiris Inc. sponsored Phase I multi-center clinical trial in which allogeneic human MSCs were given intravenously, without immunosuppression, to patients following an acute myocardial infarction. The preliminary results were recently presented and are highly encouraging.[82]

The potential importance of these findings for the treatment of ischemic heart disease is apparent. In addition to their powerful replicative capacity, MSCs can easily be harvested from bone marrows, expanded *ex vivo*, and differentiated into many cell type lineages, if desired. Due to their immunotolerance property, the establishment of MSCs as effective "universal donor cells"[65] could then dramatically expand the therapeutic potential for cellular cardiomyoplasty. From a clinical perspective, these cells could be isolated and expanded from donors irrespective of their MHC haplotype, tested for their functional capabilities well in advance, and stored as an "off-the-shelf" cell population for immediate use when needed on any patient after an acute myocardial infarction. Such logistic advantages are not available with the use of autologous MSCs which is currently the cell source of choice. Perhaps more importantly, since such allogeneic MSCs can be obtained from young healthy donors, they could be of great value in patients with genetic cardiomyopathies and in elderly patients with multiple medical co-morbidities whose own MSCs could be dysfunctional. Thus, although some controversies persist, further investigations, both experimental and clinical, are warranted.

## Acknowledgments

We thank Marc Kandalaft for his help with the figure illustration. This work was supported in part by the Heart and Stroke Foundation of Quebec (HSFQ) and Fonds de la Recherche en Santé du Québec (FRSQ).

## References

1. Orlic D, Kajstura T, Chimenti S, *et al.* Bone marrow cells regenerate infarcted myocardium. *Nature* 2001;401:701–705.
2. Davani S, Marandin A, Mersin N, *et al.* Mesenchymal progenitor cells differentiate into an endothelial phenotype, enhance vascular density, and

improve heart function in a rat cellular cardiomyoplasty model. *Circulation* 2003;108II:253–258.

3. Dai W, Hale S, Martin B, *et al.* Allogeneic mesenchymal stem cell transplantation in postinfarcted rat myocardium: short and long-term effects. *Circulation* 2005;112:214–223.
4. Tang Y, Zhao Q, Qin X, *et al.* Paracrine action enhances the effects of autologous mesenchymal stem cell transplantation on vascular regeneration in rat model of myocardial infarction. *Ann Thorac Surg* 2005;80:229–237.
5. Marelli D, Desrosiers C, El-Alfy M, *et al.* Cell transplantation for myocardial repair: an experimental approach. *Cell Transplant* 1992;1:383–390.
6. Chiu RCJ, Zibaitis A, Kao RL. Cellular cardiomyoplasty: myocardial regeneration with satellite cell implantation. *Ann. Thorac Surg* 1995;60:12–18.
7. Hodgson DM, Behfar A, Zingman LV, *et al.* Stable benefit of embryonic stem cell therapy in myocardial infarction. *Am J Physiol* 2004;287: H471–479.
8. Wang JS, Shum-Tim D, Galipeau J, *et al.* Marrow stromal cells for cellular cardiomyoplasty: feasibility and clinical advantages *J Thorac Cardiovasc Surg* 2000;120:999–1006.
9. Zuk P, Zhu M, Ashjian P, *et al.* Human adipose tissue is a source of multipotent stem cells. *Mol Biol Cell* 2002;13(12):4279–4295.
10. Lee OK, Kuo TK, Chen WM, *et al.* Isolation of multipotent mesenchymal stem cells from umbilical cord blood. *Blood* 2004;103(5):1669–1675.
11. Schachinger V, Erbs S, Elsasser A, *et al.* Intracoronary bone-marrow derived progenitor cells in acute myocardial infarction. *N. Engl J Med* 2006; 355:1210–1221.
12. Heeschen C, Lehmann R, Honold J, *et al.* Profoundly reduced neovascularization capacity of bone marrow mononuclear cells derived from patients with chronic ischemic heart disease. *Circulation* 2004; 109:1615–1622.
13. Stolzing A, Scutt A. Age-related impairment of mesenchymal progenitor cell function. *Aging Cell* 2006;1:1–12.
14. Nauta AJ, Fibbe WE. Immunomodulatory properties of mesenchymal stromal cells. *Blood* 2007;110(10):3499–3506.
15. Faulkner J, Keirstead HS. Human embryonic stem cell-derived oligodendrocyte progenitors for the treatment of spinal cord injury. *Tranpl Immunol* 2005;15(2):131–142.

16. Yen BLJ, Yen ML, Liu KJ, Chiu RCJ. Recent advances on immune tolerance in stem cells. In: *Immune Tolerance Research Development* (ed.) Columbus F. Nova Science Publishers, Inc., Hauppauge, N.Y., 2008, Chap. 7, pp. 151–166.
17. Cohnheim J. Über Entzündung und Eiterung. *Arch Pathol Anat Physiol Klin Med* 1867;40:1.
18. Friedenstein AJ, Petrakova KV, Kurolesova AI, Frolova GP. Heterotopic of bone marrow. Analysis of precursor cells for osteogenic and hematopoietic tissues. *Transplantation* 1968;6:230–247.
19. Caplan AI. Mesenchymal stem cells. *J Orthop Res* 1991;9:641–650.
20. De Coppi P, Bartasch G, Siddiqui MM, *et al.* Isolation of amniotic stem cell lines with potential for therapy. *Nat Biotechnol* 2007;25(1):100–106.
21. In't Anker PS, Noort WA, Scherjon SA, *et al.* Mesenchymal stem cells in human second-trimester bone marrow, liver, lung and spleen exhibit a similar immunophenotype but a heterogeneous multilineage differentiation potential. *Haematologica* 2003;88(8):845–852.
22. Pittenger MF, MacKay AM, Beck SC, *et al.* Multilineage potential of adult human mesenchymal stem cells. *Science* 1999;284:143–147.
23. Dezawa M, Ishikawa H, Itokazu Y, *et al.* Bone marrow stromal cells generate muscle cells and repair muscle degeneration. *Science* 2005;309(5732): 314–317.
24. Brazelton TR, Rossi FM, Keshet GI, *et al.* From marrow to brain: expression of neuronal phenotypes in adult mice. *Science* 2000;290:1775–1779.
25. Menasche P, Hagege AA, Vilquin JT, *et al.* Autologous skeletal myoblast transplantation for severe postinfarction left ventricular dysfunction. *J Am Coll Cardiol* 2003;41:1078–1083.
26. Yen BL, Huang HI, Chien CC, *et al.* Isolation of multipotent cells from human term placenta. *Stem Cells* 2005;23(1):3–9.
27. Zhao Y, Wang H, Mazzone T. Identification of stem cells from human umbilical cord blood with embryonic and hematopoietic characteristics. *Exp Cell Res* 2006;312(13):2454–2464.
28. Billingham RE, Medawar PB. The technique of free skin grafting in mammals. *J Exp Biol* 1951;28:385–402.
29. Saito T, Kuang JQ, Bittira B, *et al.* Xenotransplant cardiac chimera: immune tolerance of adult stem cells. *Ann Thorac Surg* 2002;74:19–24.
30. Le Blanc K, Tammik C, Rosendahl K, *et al.* HLA expression and immunologic properties of differentiated and undifferentiated mesenchymal stem cells. *Exp Hematol* 2003;31:890–896.

31. Ryan J, Barry F, Murphy J, Mahon B. Mesenchymal stem cells avoid allogeneic rejection. *J Inflamm* 2005;2(3):1–11.
32. Aggarwal S, Pittenger M. Human mesenchymal stem cells modulate allogeneic immune cell responses. *Blood* 2005;105:1815–1822.
33. Rasmusson I. Immune modulation by mesenchymal stem cells. *Exp Cell Res* 2006;312(12):2169–2179.
34. Meisel R, Zibert A, Laryea M, *et al.* Human bone marrow stromal cells inhibit allogeneic T-cell responses by indoleamine 2,3-deoxygenase-mediated tryptophan degradation. *Blood* 2004;103:4465–4472.
35. Di Nicola M, Carlo-Stella C, Magni M, *et al.* Human bone marrow stromal cells suppress T lymphocyte proliferation induced by cellular or non-specific mitogenic stimuli. *Blood* 2002;99:3838–3843.
36. LeBlanc K, Tammik L, Sundberg B, *et al.* Mesenchymal stem cells inhibit and stimulate mixed lymphocyte cultures and mitogenic responses independently of the major histocompatibility complex. *Scand J Immunol* 2003;57:11–20.
37. Zhang W, Ge W, Li C, *et al.* Effects of mesenchymal stem cells on differentiation, maturation, and function of human monocyte-derived dendritic cells. *Stem Cell Dev* 2004;13:263–271.
38. Beyth S, Borovsky Z, Mevorach D, *et al.* Human mesenchymal stem cells alter antigen-presenting cell maturation and induce T-cell unresponsiveness. *Blood* 2005;105:2214–2219.
39. Rasmusson I, Ringden O, Sundberg B, LeBlanc K. Mesenchymal stem cells inhibit lymphocyte proliferation by mitogens and alloantigens by different mechanisms. *Exp Cell Res* 2005;305:33–41.
40. Anguera I, Miranda-Guardiola F, Bosch X, *et al.* Elevation of serum levels of anti-inflammatory cytokine interleukin-10 and decreased risks of coronary events in patients with unstable angina. *Am Heart J* 2002;144:811–817.
41. Bartholomew A, Sturgeon C, Satskas M, *et al.* Mesenchymal stem cells suppress lymphocyte proliferation *in vitro* and prolong skin graft survival *in vivo*. *Exp Hematol* 2002;30:42–48.
42. Le Blanc K, Tammik C, Rosendahl K, *et al.* HLA expression and immunologic properties of differentiated and undifferentiated mesenchymal stem cells. *Exp Hematol* 2003;31:890–896.
43. Krampera M, Glennie S, Dyson J, *et al.* Bone marrow mesenchymal stem cells inhibit the response of naïve and memory antigen-specific T-cells to their cognate peptide. *Blood* 2003;101:3722–3729.

44. Rasmusson I, Ringden O, Sundberg B, LeBlanc K. Mesenchymal stem cells inhibit the formation of cytotoxic T lymphocytes, but not activated cytotoxic T lymphocytes or natural killer cells. *Transplantation* 2003;76:1208–1213.
45. Tse WT, Pendleton JD, Beyer WM, *et al.* Suppression of allogeneic T-cell proliferation by human marrow stromal cells: implications in transplantation. *Transplantation* 2003;75:389–397.
46. Liu CT, Yang YJ, Yin F, *et al.* The immunobiological development of human bone marrow mesenchymal stem cells in the course of neuronal differentiation. *Cell Immunol* 2006;244:19–32.
47. Prevosto C, Zancolli M, Canevali P, *et al.* Generation of $CD4^+$ or $CD8^+$ regulatory T-cells upon mesenchymal stem cell-lymphocyte interaction. *Haematologica* 2007;92(7):881–888.
48. Maccario R, Podesta M, Moretta A, *et al.* Interaction of human mesenchymal stem cells with cells involved in alloantigen-specific immune response favors the differentiation of $CD4^+$ T-cell subsets expressing a regulatory/suppressive phenotype. *Haematologica* 2005;90:516–525.
49. Djouad F, Plence P, Bony C, *et al.* Immunosuppressive effect of mesenchymal stem cells favors tumor growth in allogeneic animals. *Blood* 2003;102:837–3844.
50. Glennie S, Soeiro I, Dyson PJ, *et al.* Bone marrow mesenchymal stem cells induce division arrest anergy of activated T-cells. *Blood* 2005;105(7):2821–2827.
51. Spaggiari GM, Capobianco A, Becchetti S, *et al.* Mesenchymal stem cell-natural killer cell interactions: evidence that activated NK cells are capable of killing MSCs, whereas MSCs can inhibit IL-2 induced NK-cell proliferation. *Blood* 2006;107(4):1484–1490.
52. Koc ON, Day J, Nieder M, *et al.* Allogeneic mesenchymal stem cell infusion for treatment of metachromatic leukodystrophy and Hurler syndrome. *Bone Marrow Transplant* 2002;30:215–222.
53. Horwitz EM, Gordon PL, Koo WK, *et al.* Isolated allogeneic bone marrow-derived mesenchymal cells engraft and stimulate growth in children with osteogenesis imperfecta: implications for cell therapy of bone. *Proc Natl Acad Sci USA* 2002;99:8932–8937.
54. Azizi SA, Stokes D, Augelli BJ, *et al.* Engraftment and migration of human bone marrow stromal cells implanted in the brains of albino rats: similarities to astrocyte grafts. *Proc Natl Acad Sci USA* 1998;95:3908–3913.

55. Zappia E, Casazza S, Pedemonte E, *et al.* Mesenchymal stem cells ameliorate experimental autoimmune encephalomyelitis inducing T-cell anergy. *Blood* 2005;106:1755–1761.
56. LeBlanc K, Rasmusson J, Sundberg B, *et al.* Treatment of severe acute graft-versus-host disease with third party haploidentical mesenchymal stem cells. *Lancet* 2004;363:1439–1441.
57. Ringden O, Uzunel M, Rasmusson I, *et al.* Mesenchymal stem cells for treatment of therapy-resistant graft-versus-host disease. *Transplantation* 2006;81(10):1390–1397.
58. Caparelli DJ, Cattaneo SM, Shake JG, *et al.* Cellular cardiomyoplasty with allogeneic mesenchymal stem cells results in improved cardiac performance in a swine model of myocardial infarction. *Circulation* 2001;104:II–59.
59. Makkar RR, Price M, Lill M, *et al.* Intramyocardial injection of allogeneic bone marrow-derived mesenchymal stem cells without immunosuppression preserves cardiac function in a porcine model of myocardial infarction. *J Cardiovasc Pharmacol Ther* 2005;10(4):225–233.
60. Amado LC, Saliaris AP, Schuleri KH, *et al.* Cardiac repair with intramyocardial injection of allogeneic mesenchymal stem cells after myocardial infarction. *PNAS* 2005;102:11474–11479.
61. Chiu R. "Stealth immune tolerance" in stem cell transplantation: potential for "universal donors" in myocardial regenerative therapy. *J Heart Lung Transplant* 2005;24(5):511–516.
62. Liechty KW, Mackenzie TC, Shaaban AF, *et al.* Human mesenchymal stem cells engraft and demonstrate site-specific differentiation after *in utero* transplantation in sheep. *Nat Med* 2000;11:1282–1286.
63. MacDonald D, Saito T, Shum-Tim D, Bernier PL and Chiu RCJ. Persistence of marrow stromal cells implanted into acutely infarcted myocardium: observations in a xenotransplant model. *J Thorac Cardiovasc Surg* 2005;130:1114–1121.
64. Luo J, Shum-Tim D, Chiu RCJ. Marrow stromal cells as universal donor cells for cardiac regenerative therapy: fact or fancy? In: *Stem Cell Therapy in Ischemic Heart Disease* (eds.) Dimarakis I, *et al.* Imperial College Press, London, UK, 2009, Chap. 8, pp. 117–137.
65. Atoui R, Asenjo JF, Duong M, *et al.* Marrow stomal cells as "universal donor cells" for myocardial regenerative therapy: their unique immune tolerance. *Ann Thorac Surg* 2008;85:571–580.

in patients with cardiomyopathy due to ischemia or possibly other etiologies. Restoration of ventricular function by cell transplantation is attained by attenuating scar expansion and ventricular dilation, and also by increasing regional and global contractility.[2–16] Initial studies of cell transplantation in animal models have demonstrated improvements in ventricular function after implantation of different types of myocytes, such as cardiomyocytes,[2,6,7,11,14,16] skeletal myoblasts,[3–5,9–11,14,15] and smooth muscle cells.[8,16] Other cell types, however, failed to show functional improvements; fibroblast transplantation led to increased fibroblast proliferation and collagen deposition,[16] whereas endothelial cells induced angiogenesis in the area of the infarct without significant functional recovery.[13]

Results from subsequent studies[17–22] utilizing bone marrow stem cells and bone marrow-derived mesenchymal stem cells (MSCs) as donor cells also demonstrated similar improvements in functional outcomes. There have been multiple subpopulations of circulating and bone marrow-derived stem cells identified and characterized to date which have resulted in improvements in cardiac function after implantation into infarcted myocardium. However, the magnitude of their efficacy in restoring cardiac function varies between different stem cell populations.[23,24]

Initially, the mechanism underlying the beneficial effects of cell transplantation was hypothesized to be the transdifferentiation of the donor cells into functional cardiomyocytes, replacing the necrotic cells in the penumbra of the infarct. It is now clear that other mechanisms are dominant. Early studies demonstrated that the transplanted cells respond to their new microenvironment by secreting cytokines and growth factors, influencing the host tissue and cells in a paracrine fashion, as well as the donor cells in an autocrine fashion.[25–29] Results from studies using donor stem cells engineered to produce angiogenic growth factors support the notion that the gene products exert proangiogenic effects on the host myocardium.[30,31] Further evidence of a paracrine effect of cell therapy was provided by a series of experiments documenting the cardioprotective effect of injecting cell-free medium conditioned by MSC (MSC-CM).[26,32–36] With this shift in paradigm, the underlying mechanisms of cell transplantation have become clearer. Augmentation and improvement of these mechanisms may increase the efficacy of cell therapy, and when applied clinically, may ultimately lead to a reduction in the morbidity and mortality associated with adverse cardiac remodeling after a myocardial infarction.

## 2. Paracrine Mechanisms

While the full extent of paracrine-mediated donor cell effects are yet to be elucidated, a number of potential effector pathways have been described in multiple studies.

### 2.1 *Angiogenesis*

Cell therapy generally involves the introduction of *ex vivo* cultured donor cells directly into an ischemic milieu, with varying degrees of inflammation depending on the time since infarction. The implanted cells may express and secrete angiogenic factors as a prosurvival response to ischemia. Notably, MSCs exposed to hypoxic conditions express vascular endothelial growth factor (VEGF), which may enhance their survival and subsequent engraftment into the host myocardium.[32,37,38] VEGF in donor cells also promotes angiogenesis and improves regional blood flow in the surrounding ischemic host myocardium.[37,39,40] Hepatocyte growth factor (HGF) is another known angiogenic and cardioprotective growth factor that has been shown to induce neovascularization and reduce apoptotic cell death.[41] Basic fibroblast growth factor (bFGF) also shows proangiogenic effects,[42] and demonstrated synergistic effects when combined with VEGF in cell therapy. MSC implantation experiments have shown an increase in both bFGF and VEGF expression, which was associated with increased perfusion and cardiac function.[27] These studies have generally indicated that greater angiogenic effect is associated with greater donor cell survival and functional improvement.

### 2.2 *Mobilization of circulating and bone marrow-derived stem cells*

Stem cells of both endogenous and exogenous origin may preferentially migrate to the site of myocardial infarction (MI) from the original source or site of injection. Endothelial progenitor cells (EPC) in the peripheral circulation, and MSCs from the bone marrow may be activated and mobilized towards the injured myocardium with appropriate signals.[25,43] Recent studies have suggested that the SDF-1a/chemokine receptor (CXCR4) signaling axis plays an important role in stem cell recruitment to the heart. CXCR4, a cell surface receptor for its ligand, SDF-1, is expressed on EPCs and hematopoetic stem cells (HSCs).[44–46] EPCs play an important role in maintaining the endothelium, participating in both reendothelialization and neovascularization.[47] Early after a myocardial infarction, however, endogenous expression of SDF-1 is depressed, and this level recovers to normal only after four to seven days.[48,49] MSCs that successfully engraft into the ischemic myocardium express and secrete SDF-1,[25] which may assist signaling to other stem cells migrating from the circulation or the bone marrow.

Another signaling axis known to be essential to stem cell signaling involves the ligand Sca-1 and its receptor c-kit. Mutant mice with depressed c-kit function showed greater cardiac decompensation than wildtype control mice after a myocardial infarction.[50] Smooth muscle cells (SMC) transplanted into murine hearts express c-kit,[51] and may enhance stem cell migration to the ischemic region through this mechanism as well.

### 2.3 *Activation and mobilization of cardiac-resident stem cells*

The traditional dogma that the heart is a terminally differentiated organ has been challenged and it is now believed that the heart contains a population of pluripotent cells, potentially capable of regenerating functional cardiomyocytes.[52,53] The role and prevalence of these cardiac-resident stem cells (CRSCs) is not fully understood, but they are able to differentiate into cardiomyocytes, endothelial cells and smooth muscle cells. These CRSCs express receptors for both HGF and insulin-like growth factor 1 (IGF-1), and upon activation, preferentially home to a zone of injury and proliferate, leading to some restoration of cardiac function in ischemic hearts.[54] As MSCs are able to secrete both HGF and IGF-1 in response to injury,[55] these cells may be able to activate CRSCs after transplantation, and enhance these endogenous mechanisms of post-infarction repair.

### 2.4 *Stabilization of the extracellular matrix*

Cell transplantation may influence extracellular matrix (ECM) homeostasis, preventing post-infarction left ventricular chamber dilatation through a paracrine-mediated mechanism. This may result in more favorable tissue remodeling, strengthening the scar formed by the infarct and limiting the decline in heart function.[29] Normal extracellular matrix homeostasis involves a balance between matrix degradation by matrix metalloproteinases (MMPs) and inhibition of MMP activity by the tissue inhibitors of matrix metalloproteinases (TIMPs). Disruption of homeostasis is seen in failing hearts, with increased MMP activity and decreased TIMP expression.[29]

Vascular smooth muscle cells (VSMCs) are capable of secreting TIMPs and different components of the ECM in response to external stresses and environmental stimuli to maintain local ECM homeostasis. Transplantation of VSMCs enhances the expression of TIMPs and attenuates the activity of MMPs, restoring the balance between matrix degradation and preservation.[29] Transplantation of MSCs also led to a marked decrease in fibrosis, cardiac dilation, apoptosis in the ischemic heart and maintained ventricular function, albeit without inducing actual regeneration of the myocardium.[56] In addition, MSCs may attenuate fibroblast proliferation[35] and downregulate the production of collagen type I and III in the ECM to improve ventricular remodeling and ultimately, cardiac function.[35,57]

## 3. Enhancing the Paracrine Effects of Cell Transplantation

Although the paracrine effects of cell transplantation therapy may be responsible for many of the beneficial effects on angiogenesis and restoration of function, limited cytokine expression and secretion even under the stimulus of the ischemic post-infarct milieu, as well as the massive donor cell death in the early days and weeks after implantation, may significantly limit the extent of the functional recovery potentially achievable by means of unmodified cell transplantation. For instance, although MSC transplantation in models of myocardial infarction improved global left ventricular function initially, the beneficial effect diminished after six months.[58] Enhancing the paracrine effects of cell transplantation may be accomplished by modifying the donor cells, altering the host myocardium, or through the use of biomaterials. These techniques, alone or in combination, may enhance donor cell engraftment and help overcome the limitations of unmodified cell transplantation.

### 3.1 *Altering the microenvironment by modification of donor cells*

Donor cells may be modified *ex vivo*, prior to implantation, to express therapeutically useful transgenes (cell-based gene therapy), or by preconditioning by exposure to hypoxia, hyperthermia or pharmacological compounds.

#### 3.1.1 *Cell-based gene therapy*

Cell-based gene therapy, first described as a technique to assist in donor cell tracking, has subsequently been used therapeutically to augment multiple effects of cell transplantation, including angiogenesis, donor cell survival, modulation of the extracellular matrix, and augmentation of endogenous myocardial repair mechanisms.

##### 3.1.1a Angiogenesis

*Ex vivo* modification of donor cells to express therapeutically useful transgenes for myocardial repair was first reported in 2001.[30,31] Cell therapy using skeletal myoblasts[30] and cardiomyocytes,[31] modified to overexpress VEGF, resulted in a significantly greater level of angiogenesis than that achievable with unmodified cells. Although the expression of the VEGF transgene was transient, the effect was seen to last for at least six months.[59] Transfection of donor cells with multiple transgenes, such as VEGF and bFGF, resulted in a further enhancement of regional perfusion.[60] Overexpression of VEGF by the donor cells induces sequential upregulation of the VEGF receptors, fetal liver kinase-1 (flk-1) and fms-like tyrosine kinase-1 (flt-1), in the host tissue via an enhanced paracrine mechanism.[61]

### 3.1.1b Enhanced cell survival

Transduction of VEGF in transplanted cells has been shown to enhance donor cell survival and myocardial recovery. This improvement has been attributed to the decrease in apoptosis[62] in different cell types, including cardiomyocytes,[62] skeletal myoblasts,[62] and MSCs,[63,64] subsequently leading to greater vascular densities and functional recovery. Another therapeutically useful gene is insulin-like growth factor-1 (IGF-1), which has a well-described antiapoptotic effect and which also upregulates VEGF.[65] Co-expression of VEGF and IGF-1 also acts synergistically to enhance donor cell survival and left ventricular function to a greater extent than VEGF or IGF-1 transgenes alone.[65]

Akt has also been shown to enhance cell transplantation by inhibiting apoptosis. It is associated with the activation of cell cycling, cellular proliferation and survival by targeting proapoptotic caspases. MSC survival and cardioprotection has been linked to Akt activity.[66,67] Conditioned medium derived from Akt-expressing MSC was able to induce greater myocardial functional recovery by the upregulation of angiogenic factors such as VEGF, bFGF, HGF, and IGF-1 through paracrine actions.[32] Akt-MSC also upregulated the expression of secreted frizzled-related protein-2 (Sfrp2), which alters the infarct zone milieu to favor cardiomyocyte cell survival by upregulation of beta-catenin, and Birc1b, another antiapoptotic gene.[33]

Improvements in MSC survival were also demonstrated by the use of MSC transfected with a plasmid encoding hypoxia-regulated heme oxygenase-1 (HO-1).[68] HO-1 was shown to have antiapoptotic and antioxidant properties, and has a cytoprotective effect in an ischemic environment. This gene would normally be expressed under hypoxic conditions and confer cellular protection to the MSCs. It was also seen to decrease inflammatory cytokine levels, as well as MSC apoptosis after implantation.[68]

MSCs have also been engineered to express another antiapoptotic gene, Bcl-2, which protects the injected cells against ischemia and increases cell survival after transplantation.[69] Increased Bcl-2 expression delayed cell death, increased VEGF expression, and augmented cell growth in the first 48 hours,[69] albeit modestly. The antiapoptotic effects of these molecules have all been shown to improve donor cell survival, and may also have a prosurvival effect on the host cells remaining in the penumbra of the infarct.

#### 3.1.1c Augmentation of endogenous repair mechanisms

Cell-based gene therapy can also be applied to enhance the endogenous repair mechanisms normally activated after myocardial injury, possibly by improving the recruitment and transmigration of multipotent stem cells. MSC engineered to overexpress SDF-1 enhanced myocardial function via trophic support without any evidence of cardiomyocyte regeneration.[70] MSCs may self-renew at the site of implantation, and may serve as a continuous source of SDF-1 in the ischemic myocardium. Smooth muscle cells overexpressing stem cell factor also increased EPC recruitment and homing after implantation into post-infarct murine hearts.[51]

#### 3.1.1d ECM remodeling

Skeletal muscle cells (SkM) expressing relaxin promoted collagen turnover and reduced fibrosis via paracrine actions on ECM remodeling and neovascularization.[71] This modulation in ECM turnover was also associated with improved angiogenesis and contractility in post-infarct myocardium.

### 3.1.2 *Cellular preconditioning*

#### 3.1.2a Hypoxic and hyperthermic preconditioning

Ischemic preconditioning has been demonstrated to have a marked protective effect against subsequent ischemic insults. In cultured cells, hypoxia can be used to simulate ischemia and mimic its preconditioning effects. This hypoxic preconditioning upregulates multiple antiapoptotic and angiogenic factors.[32–34,66,67,69,72] Preconditioning of MSCs enhanced their survival and angiogenic effect after transplantation into ischemic myocardium. Hypoxic preconditioning increased expression of VEGF[32,34,69] and activation of Akt[66,67] and endothelial nitric oxide synthase (eNOS).[66] Chronic hypoxia increases eNOS expression and confers resistance to ischemia in cardiomyocytes.[73] BMSCs also responded to hypoxic preconditioning by becoming more tolerant to lethal ischemia.[66]

Physiologically relevant levels of hyperthermia have also been used to achieve preconditioning. Hyperthermia induces overexpression of heat shock protein-70 (HSP 70) in cardiac myoblasts, conferring protection against oxidative stress.[74] HSP 27, a molecular chaperone, has also been noted to have a protective effect against ischemic injury.[75] Currie and colleagues described the link between heat shock proteins and myocardial protection.[76] Exposure to moderate hyperthermia for 15 minutes led to upregulation of HSP and catalase activity after 24 hours[76] with improved resistance to subsequent ischemic and reperfusion injury. Suzuki and colleagues also employed this mechanism to enhance survival of skeletal myoblasts delivered into a subsequently heterotopically transplanted rat heart.[77] Subsequently, Nakamura demonstrated that hyperthermic preconditioning of smooth muscle cells prior to transplantation into an infarcted heart also reduced donor cell apoptosis and enhanced ventricular function.[78]

### 3.1.2b Pharmacological preconditioning

While pharmacological pretreatment of the host myocardium elicits cardioprotective effects, enhancing donor cell survival and their effects, similar effects have been obtained by exposing donor cells to statins prior to implantation into the myocardium. MSCs pretreated with lovastatin had reduced apoptosis and greater cell survival when stressed by hypoxia or serum deprivation.[79] Other pleiotropic effects of statins include an increase in endothelial nitric oxide synthase (eNOS) expression and activity. eNOS contributes to mobilization and functional activity of EPCs. As a consequence, the effect of statins on mobilization of EPCs and improvement in cardiac function was attenuated in eNOS-deficient mice.[80]

Diazoxide (DZ) pretreatment increases donor cell survival and also upregulates various cardioprotective genes. Niagara and colleagues reported reduced skeletal muscle cell injury and apoptosis after preconditioning the cells with DZ for 30 minutes.[81] Improved cell survival and heart function was noted in rats after implantation of DZ-preconditioned SkM cells.[81] The improved survival of the SkM and enhanced myocardial repair was linked to the release of bFGF and HGF and activation of the phosphatidyinositol 3-kinase/Akt (PI3K/Akt) pathway.[81]

Pretreatment of MSC with SDF-1, a member of the chemokine CXC subfamily, has also been reported to reduce apoptosis.[82] In addition to its role in cell death, SDF-1 has been implicated in stem cell recruitment, and may activate other signaling pathways that play a crucial role in cell trafficking and interaction with the cellular environment. SDF-1 may also modulate the phosphatidyl-inositol triphosphate (PI3K)/Akt pathway, which is a common mechanism for prosurvival effects in many cell types.[83,84] Preconditioning by SDF-1 had a protective effect against $H_2O_2$ stress, with reduced apoptosis compared to controls[82] (Fig. 1). As expected, a CXCR4 antagonist (AMD) attenuated the beneficial effects of SDF-1.

Another potential avenue for pharmacological preconditioning may involve the angiopoietin-1/Tie-2 signaling axis, which is recognized as an important mediator of vessel growth, remodeling and maturation.[85] It also modulates a potent antiapoptotic effect in many different cell types, including endothelial cells[86] and cardiomyocytes.[87] Angiopoietin-1 also

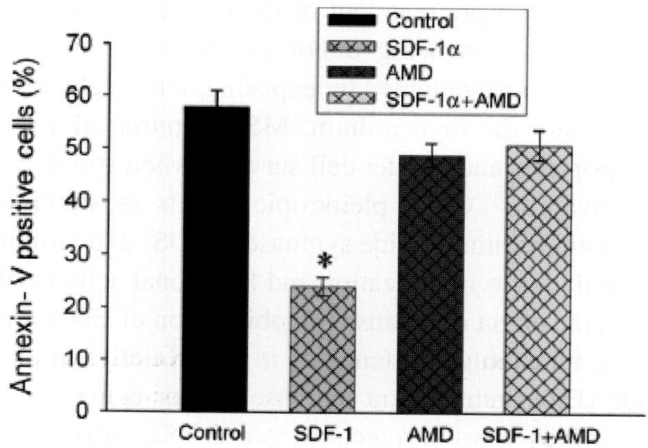


**Fig. 1.** Apoptosis was determined by flow cytometry after staining with annexin V-FITC. All values were expressed as mean ± SEM. *$P < 0.05$ vs. control. (Reproduced with permission from Pasha *et al.*[82])

protects MSCs from serum deprivation and hypoxia-induced apoptosis.[88] This protective effect may be mediated through the PI3K/Akt pathway, as it was attenuated by wortmannin, a PI3K inhibitor.

### 3.2 *Altering the microenvironment by pretreatment of the myocardium*

Prior to the transplantation of stem cells into the heart, the hostile myocardial microenvironment that ensues after an acute or chronic myocardial infarction may be directly modified to permit greater donor cell engraftment. As previously noted, donor cell survival after implantation into an infarct zone is suboptimal, with some studies reporting as low as a 1% survival rate,[46] and generally leading to low engraftment — as few as 0.1% of the transplanted cells have been reported to survive to ten weeks[89] — into the myocardium. One may anticipate that pretreatment of the scar to render it more hospitable to the transplanted cells will enhance their long-term survival and engraftment. This pretreatment may be accomplished by pharmacological means, gene or protein therapy, or more recently, by transmyocardial revascularization.

#### 3.2.1 *Pharmacological pretreatment*

Statins, 3-hydroxy-3-methylglutaryl coenzyme A (HMG-CoA) reductase inhibitors, are an established class of highly effective cholesterol-lowering drugs,[90] and have also been used for their pleiotropic effects to enhance the results of cell transplantation. These pleiotropic effects, such as inhibition of proinflammatory cytokine activity, reduced cardiomyocyte apoptosis, improved endothelial function and increased immune tolerance after transplantation, may also augment the effects of cell therapy.[91,92] There is increasing evidence that statins may inhibit apoptosis in a variety of cell types. Atorvastatin, administered from three days prior to, and up to four days after myocardial ischemia and reperfusion in swine, increased perfusion, decreased apoptosis, oxidative and inflammatory stress, ultimately facilitating survival and differentiation of donor MSC (Fig. 2).[93] However, an earlier study had demonstrated that oral pravastatin had no synergistic effect with bone marrow mononuclear cell transplantation in

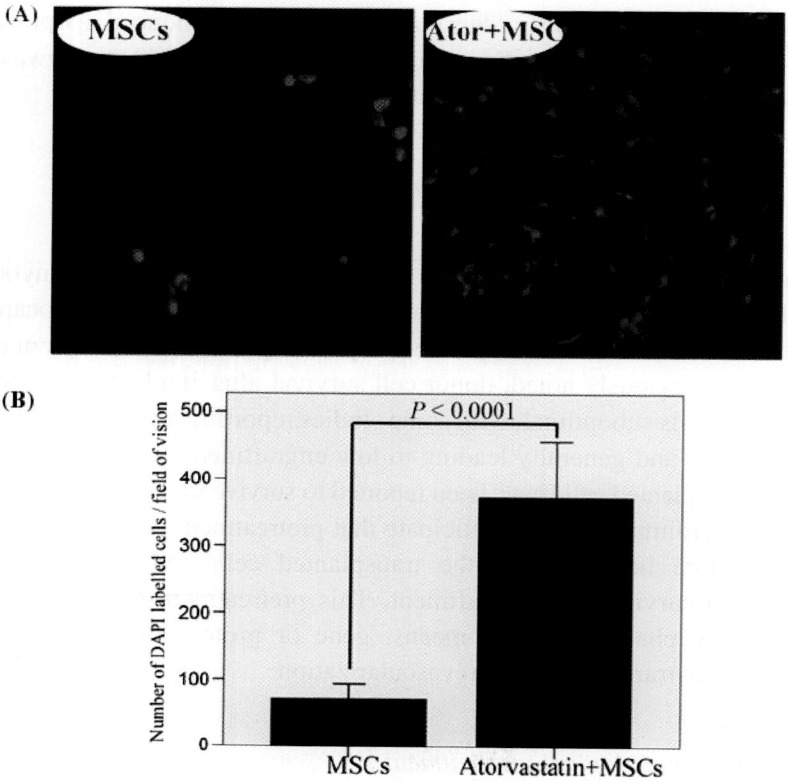


**Fig. 2.** Survival potential of implanted mesenchymal stem cells *in vivo*. **(A)** DAPI-labeled cells could be observed in group mesenchymal stem cells only and group Ator+mesenchymal stem cells. **(B)** Significant difference in survival potential between group mesenchymal stem cells only and group Ator+mesenchymal stem cells ($P < 0.0001$). The final magnification for (A) is 400×. (Reproduced with permission from Yang *et al.*[93])

promoting angiogenesis, although it did improve ventricular function by an anti-inflammatory mechanism.[94]

Phosphodiesterase-5 inhibitors, pharmacological agents used to treat both pulmonary hypertension and erectile dysfunction, are now recognized to play a vital role in vascular disease. For instance, sildenafil has been shown to have preconditioning-like cardioprotective effects in an animal model of I/R injury[95] via NO generated from endothelial and/or inducible nitric oxide synthases (eNOS/iNOS) and opening of mitochondrial

ATP-sensitive potassium channels.[96] Since many of the phosphodiesterase-5 inhibitors are FDA-approved, clinical use of pharmacological ischemic preconditioning may well be realized in the near future.

Another pharmacological agent, anakinra, a recombinant human interleukin-1 (IL-1) receptor antagonist, has also been studied recently with promising results in an infarct model. IL-1 receptor antagonist (IL-1Ra) is a member of the IL-1 family and is a naturally occurring anti-inflammatory protein that behaves as an acute phase reactant.[97,98] The utility of IL-1Ra levels after an acute myocardial infarction as a marker of myocardial injury and inflammation remains to be fully elucidated.[99,100] While the precise role of endogenous IL-1Ra is unclear, forced IL-Ra expression confers a cytoprotective effect, with a modest but statistically significant reduction in infarct size and apoptosis[101] (Fig. 3). While these agents have not yet been

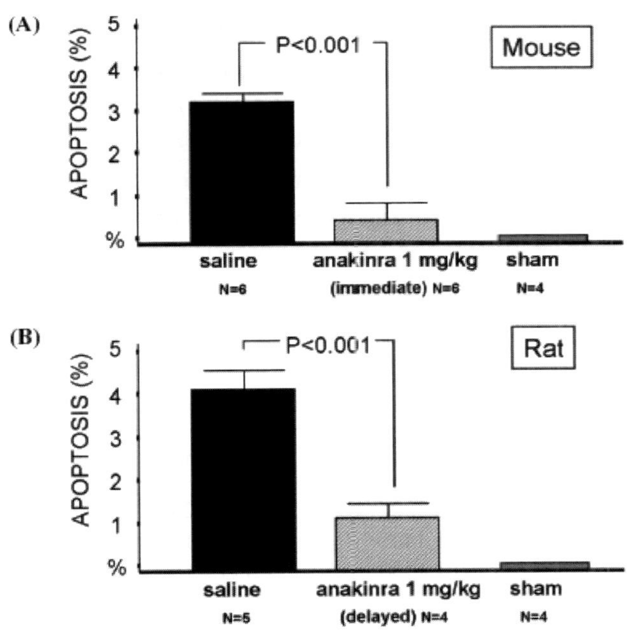


**Fig. 3.** Apoptosis. Apototic rates in saline-treated, anakinra-treated, and sham-operated animals are shown. A significantly higher apoptotic rate in saline- vs. anakinra-treated AMI animals was found with both immediate anakinra (in the mouse; **A**) and delayed anakinra group (in the rat; **B**). (Reproduced with permission from Abbate *et al.*[101])

Recent studies suggest that TMR upregulates proangiogenic factors such as NFkB, increases vascular maturation and upregulates angiopoietin-1.[115]

More recently, TMR treatment shortly followed by cell transplantation was shown to improve post-transplantation cell survival. Improved survival of the donor mesenchymal stem cells was also associated with greater angiogenesis and functional recovery.[116] An additive effect with proangiogenic cell-based gene therapy was also noted.

### 3.3 *Tissue engineering and biomaterials/biocomposites*

Another approach to the problem of suboptimal cell retention and survival[117–119] has been to utilize natural or synthetic biomaterials as cell delivery matrices, with the hypothesis that these structural frameworks may be more favorable matrices for cell delivery than a cell suspension in culture medium. Varying groups have used alginate hydrogels and fibrin matrices, as well as scaffolds composed of gelatin, collagen, hyaluronic acid and chitosan, which have all demonstrated success in promoting angiogenesis through the delivery of growth factors. Synthetic expanded polytetrafluoroethylene (ePTFE) patches have also been evaluated, but developed calcification and a foreign-body response.[120] However, synthetic and biologically-derived materials may be combined to obtain both structural stability and cellularization responses.[121]

Christman and colleagues have demonstrated that skeletal myoblasts suspended within a fibrin glue mixture were able to improve cardiac function,[122] likely due to improved donor cell retention and survival, as well as vasculogenesis within the infarct.[123] Interestingly, an injection of cell-free fibrin alone was also able to sustain wall thickness and attenuated the deterioration of LV function,[122] presumably by providing physical support to the infarcted ventricular wall.

A recent study[124] reported that use of an injectable polyethylene glycolated (PEGylated) fibrin biomatrix may enhance the results of bone marrow-derived mononuclear cell transplantation in infarcted myocardium. Fibrin itself has been used extensively due to its advantageous traits, such as biocompatibility and biodegradability, but it is rapidly cleared from the interstitium and thus has a limited potential for depot drug delivery. In contrast, this PEGylated fibrin biomaterial binds covalently to growth

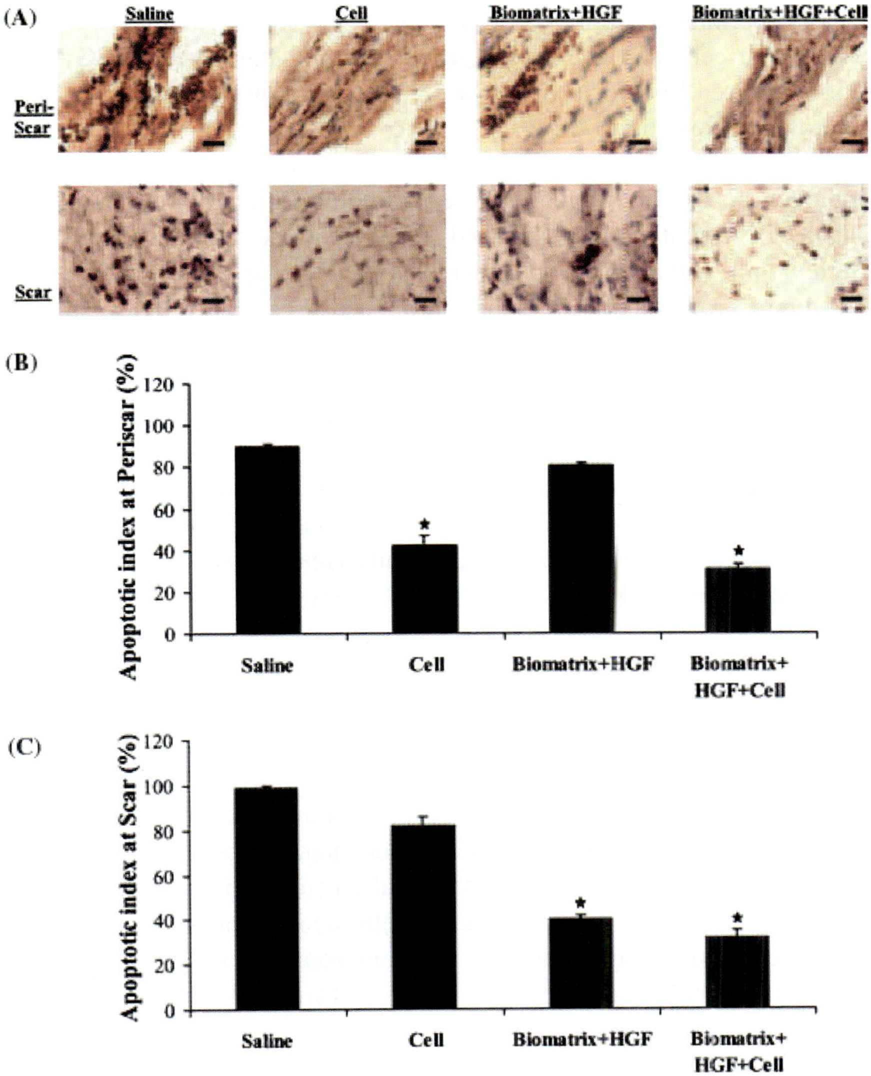


**Fig. 6.** The effect on apoptosis by different treatments was measured by TUNEL staining. **(A)** The distribution of apoptotic cells (brown) in the scar (top) and periscar (bottom) areas (20× magnification, scale bar: 200 μm). **(B)** Bar graph compares the apoptotic indices among the groups in the periscar area. **(C)** Bar graph compares the apoptotic indices among the groups in the scar area. Error bars represent mean ± SEM, $^*P < 0.05$ versus saline group. (Reproduced with permission from Zhang *et al.*[124])

factors, permitting prolonged release into the myocardium. Combined delivery of cells and hepatocyte growth factor (HGF) in the PEGylated fibrin reduced apoptosis in the scar and peri-scar areas (Fig. 6), and improved LV ejection.[124]

Collagen scaffolds have also been used to similar effect, promoting angiogenesis and arteriogenesis in cryo-injured myocardium.[125] Collagen sponge is currently FDA approved for clinical use as a hemostatic aid. Both *in vitro* and *in vivo* studies demonstrated the capacity of the scaffold to support growth and differentiation of seeded cardiomyocytes, smooth muscle cells and endothelial cells. The collagen sponge attached to the epicardial surface of both cryo-injured and non-injured hearts, and the scaffold volume decreased to about 60% of its original volume after 60 days, demonstrating its ability to be absorbed *in vivo*.[125] Increases in blood vessel density were seen in both the scar and the border zone, and the newly formed vessels were stable for at least 60 days. Anversa and colleagues have also reported that a similar scaffold was able to recruit cardiogenic stem cells.[126]

## 4. Conclusion

Despite the dramatic improvements in myocardial perfusion and function noted in animal studies of cell transplantation, human clinical trials have demonstrated much more modest effects, with increases in LVEF of only approximately 3%–6%.[127,128] Greater understanding of the mechanisms by which cell therapies work has highlighted the importance of the microenvironment into which the donor cells are implanted. The implanted cells themselves may alter the microenvironment through paracrine effects to augment angiogenesis, enhance cell survival, augment endogenous repair mechanisms and stem cell recruitment, and stabilize the extracellular matrix. However, these effects are relatively subtle when unmodified cells are used for implantation therapy. Augmentation of these paracrine effects through cell-based gene therapy, pretreatment of both the cells and the myocardium, and the use of biomaterials to ameliorate the injurious environment may enhance the benefits of cell therapy. These combined therapies may represent the most promising future applications of cell transplantation. Further studies elucidating the other mediators and mechanisms of paracrine effects and the interaction between donor cell types, specific effects and durability of these effects are required to help cell therapies achieve their full potential.

## References


1. Rosamond W, Flegal K, Friday G, *et al.* Heart disease and stroke statistics — 2007 update: a report from the American Heart Association Statistics Committee and Stroke Statistics Subcommittee. *Circulation* 2007;115: e69–e171.
2. Roell W, Lu ZJ, Bloch W, *et al.* Cellular cardiomyoplasty improves survival after myocardial injury. *Circulation* 2002;105:2435–2441.
3. Pouzet B, Vilquin JT, Hagège AA, *et al.* Factors affecting functional outcome after autologous skeletal myoblast transplantation. *Ann Thorac Surg* 2001;71:844–851.
4. Jain M, DerSimonian H, Brenner DA, *et al.* Cell therapy attenuates deleterious ventricular remodeling and improves cardiac performance after myocardial infarction. *Circulation* 2001;103:1920–1927.
5. Pouzet B, Vilquin JT, Hagège AA, *et al.* Intramyocardial transplantation of autologous myoblasts. Can tissue processing be optimized? *Circulation* 2000;102:III-210–III-215.
6. Li RK, Weisel RD, Mickle DAG, *et al.* Autologous porcine heart cell transplantation improved heart function after a myocardial infarction. *J Thorac Cardiovasc Surg* 2000;119:62–68.
7. Sakai T, Li RK, Weisel RD, *et al.* Autologous heart cell transplantation improves cardiac function after myocardial injury. *Ann Thorac Surg* 1999;68:2074–2080.
8. Li RK, Jia ZQ, Weisel RD, *et al.* Smooth muscle cell transplantation into myocardial scar tissue improves heart function. *J Mol Cell Cardiol* 1999;31: 513–522.
9. Atkins BZ, Hueman MT, Meuchel J, *et al.* Cellular cardiomyoplasty improves diastolic properties of injured heart. *J Surg Res* 1999;85:234–242.
10. Taylor DA, Atkins BZ, Hungspreugs P, *et al.* Regenerating functional myocardium: improved performance after skeletal myoblast transplantation. *Nat Med* 1998;4:929–933.

11. Scorsin M, Hagège A, Marotte F, *et al.* Does transplantation of cardiomyocytes improve function of infarcted myocardium? *Circulation* 1997; 96(suppl 2):188–193.
12. Li RK, Jia ZQ, Weisel RD, *et al.* Cardiomyocyte transplantation improves heart function. *Ann Thorac Surg* 1996;62:654–660.
13. Kim EJ, Li RK, Weisel RD, *et al.* Angiogenesis by endothelial cell transplantation. *J Thorac Cardiovasc Surg* 2001;122:963–971.
14. Scorsin M, Hagège A, Vilquin J, *et al.* Comparison of the effects of fetal cardiomyocyte and skeletal myoblast transplantation on postinfarction left ventricular function. *J Thorac Cardiovasc Surg* 2000;119:1169–1175.
15. Hutcheson KA, Atkins BZ, Hueman MT, *et al.* Comparison of benefits on myocardial performance of cellular cardiomyoplasty with skeletal myoblasts and fibroblasts. *Cell Transplant* 2000;9:359–368.
16. Sakai T, Li RK, Weisel RD, *et al.* Fetal cell transplantation: a comparison of three cell types. *J Thorac Cardiovasc Surg* 1999;118:715–725.
17. Tomita S, Li RK, Weisel RD, *et al.* Autologous transplantation of bone marrow cells improves damaged heart function. *Circulation* 1999;100(suppl 2): 247–256.
18. Kocher AA, Schuster MD, Szabolcs MJ, *et al.* Neovascularization of ischemic myocardium by human bone-marrow-derived angioblasts prevents cardiomyocyte apoptosis, reduces remodeling and improves cardiac function. *Nat Med* 2001;7:430–436.
19. Orlic D, Kajstura J, Chimenti S, *et al.* Bone marrow cells regenerate infarcted myocardium. *Nature* 2001;410:701–705.
20. Fuchs S, Baffour R, Zhou YF, *et al.* Transendocardial delivery of autologous bone marrow enhances collateral perfusion and regional function in pigs with chronic experimental myocardial ischemia. *J Am Coll Cardiol* 2001;37:1726–1732.
21. Kamihata H, Matsubara H, Nishiue T, *et al.* Implantation of bone marrow mononuclear cells into ischemic myocardium enhances collateral perfusion and regional function via side supply of angioblasts, angiogenic ligands, and cytokines. *Circulation* 2001;104:1046–1052.
22. Tomita S, Mickle DAG, Weisel RD, *et al.* Improved heart function with myogenesis and angiogenesis following autologous porcine bone marrow stromal cell transplantation. *J Thorac Cardiovasc Surg* 2002;123: 1132–1140.

23. Galli D, Innocenzi A, Staszewsky L, *et al.* Mesoangioblasts, vessel associated multipotent stem cells, repair the infarcted heart by multiple cellular mechanisms: a comparison with bone marrow progenitors, fibroblasts, and endothelial cells. *Arterioscler Thromb Vasc Biol* 2005;25:692–697.
24. Yau TM, Tomita S, Weisel RD, *et al.* Beneficial effect of autologous cell transplantation on infarcted heart function: direct comparison between bone marrow stromal cells and heart cells. *Ann Thorac Surg* 2003;75:169–176.
25. Tang YL, Zhao Q, Qin X, *et al.* Paracrine action enhances the effects of autologous mesenchymal stem cell transplantation on vascular regeneration in rat model of myocardial infarction. *Ann Thorac Surg* 2005;80:229–236.
26. Gnecchi M, He H, Liang OD, *et al.* Paracrine action accounts for marked protection of ischemic heart by Akt-modified mesenchymal stem cells. *Nat Med* 2005;11:367–368.
27. Kinnaird T, Stabile E, Burnett MS, *et al.* Local delivery of marrow-derived stromal cells augments collateral perfusion through paracrine mechanisms. *Circulation* 2004;109:1543–1549.
28. Tang YL, Qian K, Zhang YC, *et al.* Mobilizing of hematopoietic stem cells to ischemic myocardium by plasmid mediated stromal-cell-derived factor-1alpha (SDF-1alpha) treatment. *Regul Pept* 2005;125:1–8.
29. Fedak PW, Szmitko PE, Weisel RD, *et al.* Cell transplantation preserves matrix homeostasis: a novel paracrine mechanism. *J Thorac Cardiovasc Surg* 2005;130:1430–1439.
30. Suzuki K, Murtuza B, Smolenski RT, *et al.* Cell transplantation for the treatment of acute myocardial infarction using vascular endothelial growth factor expressing skeletal myoblasts. *Circulation* 2001;104(suppl 1):207–212.
31. Yau TM, Fung K, Weisel RD, *et al.* Enhanced myocardial angiogenesis by gene transfer with transplanted cells. *Circulation* 2001;104:I218-I222.
32. Gnecchi M, He H, Noiseux N, *et al.* Evidence supporting paracrine hypothesis for Akt-modified mesenchymal stem cell-mediated cardiac protection and functional improvement. *FASEB J* 2006;20:661–669.
33. Mirotsou M, Zhang Z, Deb A, *et al.* Secreted frizzled related protein 2 (Sfrp2) is the key Akt-mesenchymal stem cell-released paracrine factor mediating myocardial survival and repair. *Proc Natl Acad Sci USA* 2007; 104:1643–1648.
34. Hung SC, Pochampally RR, Chen SC, *et al.* Angiogenic effects of human multipotent stromal cell conditioned medium activate the PI3K-Akt pathway

in hypoxic endothelial cells to inhibit apoptosis, increase survival, and stimulate angiogenesis. *Stem Cells* 2007;25:2363–2370.

35. Ohnishi S, Sumiyoshi H, Kitamura S, *et al.* Mesenchymal stem cells attenuate cardiac fibroblast proliferation and collagen synthesis through paracrine actions. *FEBS Lett* 2007;581:3961–3966.
36. Ohnishi S, Yanagawa B, Tanaka K, *et al.* Transplantation of mesenchymal stem cells attenuates myocardial injury and dysfunction in a rat model of acute myocarditis. *J Mol Cell Cardiol* 2007;42:88–97.
37. Xu M, Uemura R, Dai Y, *et al. In vitro* and *in vivo* effects of bone marrow stem cells on cardiac structure and function. *J Mol Cell Cardiol* 2007;42: 441–448.
38. Li W, Ma N, Ong LL, *et al.* Bcl-2 engineered MSCs inhibited apoptosis and improved heart function. *Stem Cells* 2007; 25:2118–2127.
39. Tse HF, Siu CW, Zhu SG, *et al.* Paracrine effects of direct intramyocardial implantation of bone marrow derived cells to enhance neovascularization in chronic ischemic myocardium. *Eur J Heart Fail* 2007;9:747–753.
40. Tang YL, Zhao Q, Zhang YC, *et al.* Autologous mesenchymal stem cell transplantation induce VEGF and neovascularization in ischemic myocardium. *Regul Pept* 2004;117:3–10.
41. Rehman J, Traktuev D, Li J, *et al.* Secretion of angiogenic and antiapoptotic factors by human adipose stromal cells. *Circulation* 2004;109:1292–1298.
42. Kano MR, Morishita Y, Iwata C, *et al.* VEGF-A and FGF-2 synergistically promote neoangiogenesis through enhancement of endogenous PDGF-B-PDGFRbeta signaling. *J Cell Sci* 2005;118:3759–3768.
43. Kawada H, Fujita J, Kinjo K, *et al.* Nonhematopoietic mesenchymal stem cells can be mobilized and differentiate into cardiomyocytes after myocardial infarction. *Blood* 2004;104:3581–3587.
44. Kahn J, Byk T, Jansson-Sjostrand L, *et al.* Overexpression of CXCR4 on human CD34_ progenitors increases their proliferation, migration, and NOD/SCID repopulation. *Blood* 2004;103:2942–2949.
45. Peled A, Petit I, Kollet O, *et al.* Dependence of human stem cell engraftment and repopulation of NOD/SCID mice on CXCR4. *Science* 283: 845–848, 1999.
46. Yamaguchi J, Kusano KF, Masuo O, *et al.* Stromal cell-derived factor-1 effects on *ex vivo* expanded endothelial progenitor cell recruitment for ischemic neovascularization. *Circulation* 2003;107:1322–1328.

47. Jo DY, Hwang JH, Kim JM, *et al.* Human bone marrow endothelial cells elaborate non-stromal-cell-derived factor-1 (SDF-1)-dependent chemoattraction and SDF-1-dependent transmigration of hematopoietic progenitors. *Br J Hematol* 2003;121:649–652.
48. Kucia M, Ratajczak J, Reca R, *et al.* Tissue-specific muscle, neural and liver stem/progenitor cells reside in the bone marrow, respond to an SDF-1 gradient and are mobilized into peripheral blood during stress and tissue injury. *Blood Cells Mol Dis* 2004;32:52–57.
49. Abbott JD, Huang Y, Liu D, *et al.* Stromal cell-derived factor-1 alpha plays a critical role in stem cell recruitment to the heart after myocardial infarction but is not sufficient to induce homing in the absence of injury. *Circulation* 2004;110:3300–3305.
50. Cimini M, Fazel S, Zhuo S, *et al.* c-kit dysfunction impairs myocardial healing after infarction. *Circulation* 2007;116:I77–I82.
51. Fazel S, Chen L, Weisel RD, *et al.* Cell transplantation preserves cardiac function after infarction by infarct stabilization: augmentation by stem cell factor. *J Thorac Cardiovasc Surg* 2005;130:1310–1318.
52. Beltrami AP, Barlucchi L, Torella D, *et al.* Adult cardiac stem cells are multipotent and support myocardial regeneration. *Cell* 2003;114:763–776.
53. Urbanek K, Quaini F, Tasca G, *et al.* Intense myocyte formation from cardiac stem cells in human cardiac hypertrophy. *Proc Natl Acad Sci USA* 2003;100:10440–10445.
54. Linke A, Muller P, Nurzynska D, *et al.* Stem cells in the dog heart are self-renewing, clonogenic, and multipotent and regenerate infarcted myocardium, improving cardiac function. *Proc Natl Acad Sci USA* 2005;102:8966–8971.
55. Wang M, Crisostomo PR, Herring C, *et al.* Human progenitor cells from bone marrow or adipose tissue produce VEGF, HGF, and IGF-I in response to TNF by a p38 MAPK-dependent mechanism. *Am J Physiol Regul Integr Comp Physiol* 2006;291:R880–R884.
56. Berry MF, Engler AJ, Woo YJ, *et al.* Mesenchymal stem cell injection after myocardial infarction improves myocardial compliance. *Am J Physiol Regul Integr Comp Physiol* 2006;290:H2196–H2203.
57. Xu X, Xu Z, Xu Y, *et al.* Selective down-regulation of extracellular matrix gene expression by bone marrow derived stem cell transplantation into infarcted myocardium. *Circ J* 2005;69:1275–1283.

58. Dai W, Hale SL, Martin BJ, *et al.* Allogeneic mesenchymal stem cell transplantation in postinfarcted rat myocardium: short- and long-term effects. *Circulation* 2005;112:214–223.
59. Kim C, Li RK, Li G, *et al.* Effects of cell-based angiogenic gene therapy at 6 months: persistent angiogenesis and absence of oncogenicity. *Ann Thorac Surg* 2007;83:640–646.
60. Yau TM, Kim C, Li G, *et al.* Enhanced angiogenesis with multimodal cell-based gene therapy. *Ann Thorac Surg* 2007;83:1110–1119.
61. Yau TM, Li G, Zhang Y, *et al.* Vascular endothelial growth factor receptor up-regulation in response to cell-based angiogenic gene therapy. *Ann Thorac Surg* 2005;79:2056–2064.
62. Yau TM, Kim C, Ng D, *et al.* Increasing transplanted cell survival with cell-based angiogenic gene therapy. *Ann Thorac Surg* 2005;80:1779–1786.
63. Matsumoto R, Omura T, Yoshiyama M, *et al.* Vascular endothelial growth factor-expressing mesenchymal stem cell transplantation for the treatment of acute myocardial infarction. *Arterioscler Thromb Vasc Biol* 2005;25: 1168–1173.
64. Yang J, Zhou W, Zheng W, *et al.* Effects of myocardial transplantation of marrow mesenchymal stem cells transfected with vascular endothelial growth factor for the improvement of heart function and angiogenesis after myocardial infarction. *Cardiology* 2007;107:17–29.
65. Yau TM, Kim C, Li G, *et al.* Maximizing ventricular function with multimodal cell-based gene therapy. *Circulation* 2005;112:I123–I128.
66. Uemura R, Xu M, Ahmad N, *et al.* Bone marrow stem cells prevent left ventricular remodeling of ischemic heart through paracrine signaling. *Circ Res* 2006;98:1414–1421.
67. Noiseux N, Gnecchi M, Lopez-Ilasaca M, *et al.* Mesenchymal stem cells overexpressing Akt dramatically repair infarcted myocardium and improve cardiac function despite infrequent cellular fusion or differentiation. *Mol Ther* 2006;14:840–850.
68. Tang YL, Tang Y, Zhang YC, *et al.* Improved graft mesenchymal stem cell survival in ischemic heart with a hypoxia-regulated heme oxygenase-1 vector. *J Am Col Cardiol* 2005;46:1339–1350.
69. Li W, Ma N, Ong LL, *et al.* Bcl-2 engineered MSCs inhibited apoptosis and improved heart function. *Stem Cells* 2007;25:2118–2127.

70. Zhang M, Mal N, Kiedrowski M, *et al.* SDF-1 expression by mesenchymal stem cells results in trophic support of cardiac myocytes after myocardial infarction. *FASEB J* 2007;21:3197–3207.
71. Formigli L, Perna AM, Meacci E, *et al.* Paracrine effects of transplanted myoblasts and relaxin on post-infarction heart remodeling. *J Cell Mol Med* 2007;11:1087–1100.
72. Jiang S, Haider H, Idris NM, *et al.* Supportive interaction between cell survival signaling and angiocompetent factors enhances donor cell survival and promotes angiomyogenesis for cardiac repair. *Circ Res* 2006;99: 776–784.
73. Shi Y, Baker JE, Zhang C, *et al.* Chronic hypoxia increases endothelial nitric oxide synthase generation of nitric oxide by increasing heart shock protein 90 association and serine phosphorylation. *Circ Res* 2002;91:300–306.
74. Su CY, Chong KY, Chen J, *et al.* A physiologically relevant hyperthermia selectively activates constitutive hsp70 in H9c2 cardiac myoblasts and confers oxidative protection. *J Mol Cell Cardiol* 1999;31:845–855.
75. Liu L, Zhang XJ, Jiang SR, *et al.* Heat shock protein 27 regulates oxidative stress-induced apoptosis in cardiomyocytes: mechanisms via reactive oxygen species generation and Akt activation. *Chin Med J* 2007;120: 2271–2277.
76. Currie RW, Karmazyn M, Kloc M, *et al.* Heat-shock response is associated with enhanced postischemic ventricular recovery. *Circ Res* 1998;63:543–549.
77. Suzuki K, Smolenski RT, Jayakumar J, *et al.* Heat shock treatment enhances graft cell survival in skeletal myoblast transplantation to the heart. *Circulation* 2000;102:III-216–III-221.
78. Nakamura Y, Yasuda T, Weisel R, *et al.* Enhanced cell transplantation: preventing apoptosis increases cell survival and ventricular function. *Am J Physiol Heart Circ Physiol* 2006;291:H939–H947.
79. Xu R, Chen J, Cong X, *et al.* Lovastatin protects mesenchymal stem cells against hypoxia- and serum deprivation-induced apoptosis by activation of PI3K/Akt and ERK1/2. *J Cell Biochem* 2008;103:256–269.
80. Landmesser U, Engberding N, Bahlmann FH, *et al.* Statin-induced improvement of endothelial progenitor cell mobilization, myocardial neovascularization, left ventricular function, and survival after experimental myocardial infarction requires endothelial nitric oxide synthase. *Circulation* 2004;110:1933–1939.

81. Niagara MI, Haider HK, Jiang S. Pharmacologically preconditioned skeletal myoblasts are resistant to oxidative stress and promote angiomyogenesis via release of paracrine factors in the infarcted heart. *Circ Res* 2007;100: 545–555.
82. Pasha Z, Wang Y, Sheikh R, *et al.* Preconditioning enhances cell survival and differentiation of stem cells during transplantation in infarcted myocardium. *Cardiovasc Res* 2008;77:134–142.
83. Derman MP, Chen JY, Spokes KC, *et al.* An 11-amino acid sequence from c-met initiates epithelial chemotaxis via phosphatidylinositol 3-kinase and phospholipase C. *J Biol Chem* 1996;271:4251–4255.
84. Kundra V, Escorbedo J, Kazlauskas A, *et al.* Regulation of chemotaxis by the platelet-derived growth factor receptor. *Nature* 1994;367:474–476.
85. Thurston G. Role of angiopoietins and Tie receptor tyrosine kinases in angiogenesis and lymphangiogenesis. *Cell Tissue Res* 2003;314:61–68.
86. Papapetropoulos A, Garcia-Cardena G, Dengler TJ, *et al.* Direct actions of angiopoietin-1 on human endothelium: evidence for network stabilization, cell survival, and interaction with other angiogenic growth factors. *Lab Invest* 1999;79:213–223.
87. Wang Z, Cui M, Sun L, *et al.* Angiopoietin-1 protects H9c2 cells from H2O2-induced apoptosis through AKT signaling. *Biochem Biophys Res Commun* 2007;359:685–690.
88. Liu X, Jiang J, Gui C, *et al.* Angiopoietin-1 protects mesenchymal stem cells against serum deprivation and hypoxia-induced apoptosis through the PI3K/Akt pathway. *Acta Pharmacol Sin* 2008;29:815–822.
89. Carr CA, Stuckey DJ, Tatton L, *et al.* Bone marrow-derived stromal cells home to and remain in the infarcted rat heart but fail to improve function: an *in vivo* cine-MRI study. *Am J Physiol Heart Circ Physiol* 2008;295: H533–H542.
90. Calabro P, Yeh ET. The pleiotropic effects of statins. *Curr Opin Cardiol* 2005;20:541–546.
91. Endres M. Statins: Potential new indications in inflammatory conditions. *Atheroscler Suppl* 2006;7(1):31–35.
92. Hong MK, Lee CW, Kim YH, *et al.* Usefulness of follow-up low-density lipoprotein cholesterol level as an independent predictor of changes of coronary atherosclerotic plaque size as determined by intravascular ultrasound analysis after statin therapy. *Am J Cardiol* 2006;98:866–870.

93. Yang YJ, Qian HY, Huang J, *et al.* Atorvastatin treatment improves survival and effects of implanted mesenchymal stem cells in post-infarct swine hearts. *Eur Heart J* 2008;29:1578–1590.
94. Li TS, Takahashi M, Suzuki R, *et al.* Pravastatin improves remodeling and cardiac function after myocardial infarction by an anti-inflammatory mechanism rather than by the induction of angiogenesis. *Ann Thorac Surg* 2006;81:2217–2226.
95. Salloum F, Yin C, Xi L, Kukreja RC. Sildenafil induces delayed preconditioning through inducible nitric oxide synthase-dependent pathway in mouse heart. *Circ Res* 2003;92:595–597.
96. Goyal SN, Arora S, Nandave M, *et al.* New therapeutic targets for myocardial infarction. *Curr Sci* 2008;95:332–339.
97. Dinarello CA. Interleukin-1. *Cytokine Growth Factor Rev* 1997;8:253–265.
98. Gabay C, Kushner I. Acute-phase proteins and other systemic responses to inflammation. *N Engl J Med* 1999;340:448–454.
99. Patti G, D'ambrosio A, Mega S, *et al.* Early interleukin-1 receptor antagonist elevation in patients with acute myocardial infarction. *J Am Coll Cardiol* 2004;43:35–38.
100. Suzuki K, Murtuza B, Smolenski RT, *et al.* Overexpression of interleukin-1 receptor antagonist provides cardioprotetion against ischemia-reperfusion injury associated with reduction of apoptosis. *Circulation* 2001;104:I308–I313.
101. Abbate A, Salloum F, Vecile E, *et al.* Anakinra, a recombinant human interleukin-1 receptor antagonist, inhibits apoptosis in experimental acute myocardial infarction. *Circulation* 2008;117:2670–2683.
102. Retuerto M, Schalch P, Patejunas G, *et al.* Angiogenic pretreatment improves the efficacy of cellular cardiomyoplasty performed with fetal cardiomyocyte implantation. *J Thorac Cardiovasc Surg* 2004;127 1041–1046.
103. Lin HH, Chen YH, Chang PF, *et al.* Heme oxygenase-1 promotes neovascularization in ischemic heart by coinduction of VEGF and SDF-1. *J Mol Cell Cardiol* 2008;45:44–45.
104. Bekeredjian R, Chen S, Grayburn P, *et al.* Augmentation of cardiac protein delivery using ultrasound targeted microbubble destruction. *Ultrasound Med Biol* 2004;31:687–691.
105. Bekeredjian R, Chen S, Frenkel PA, Grayburn PA, Shohet RV. Ultrasound-targeted microbubble destruction can repeatedly direct highly specific plasmid expression to the heart. *Circulation* 2003;108:1022–1026.

118. Aicher A, Brenner W, Zuhayra M, *et al.* Assessment of the tissue distribution of transplanted human endothelial progenitor cells by radioactive labeling. *Circulation* 2003;107:2134–2139.
119. Retuerto MA, Schalch P, Patejunas G, *et al.* Angiogenic pretreatment improves the efficacy of cellular cardiomyoplasty performed with fetal cardiomyocyte implantation. *J Thorac Cardiovasc Surg* 2004;127:1041–1049.
120. Robinson KA, Li J, Mathison M, *et al.* Extracellular matrix scaffold for cardiac repair. *Circulation* 2005;112:I135–I143.
121. Boublik J, Park H, Radisic M, *et al.* Mechanical properties and remodeling of hybrid cardiac constructs made from heart cells, fibrin, and biodegradable, elastomeric knitted fabric. *Tissue Eng* 2005;11:1122–1132.
122. Christman KL, Fok HH, Sievers RE, *et al.* Fibrin glue alone and skeletal myoblasts in a fibrin scaffold preserve cardiac function after myocardial infarction. *Tissue Eng* 2004;10:403–409.
123. Christman KL, Vardanian AJ, Fang Q, *et al.* Injectable fibrin scaffold improves cell transplant survival, reduces infarct expansion, and induces neovasculature formation in ischemic myocardium. *J Am Coll Cardiol* 2004;44:654–660.
124. Zhang G, Hu Q, Braunlin EA, *et al.* Enhancing efficacy of stem cell transplantation to the heart with a PEGylated fibrin biomatrix. *Tissue Eng* 2008;14(6):1025–1036.
125. Callegari A, Bollini S, Iop L, *et al.* Neovascularization induced by porous collagen scaffold implanted on intact and cryoinjured rat hearts. *Biomaterials* 2007;28:5449–5461.
126. Anversa P, Leri A, Kajstura J. Cardiac regeneration. *J Am Coll Cardiol* 2006;47:1769–1776.
127. Janssens S, Dubois C, Bogaert J, *et al.* Autologous bone marrow-derived stem-cell transfer in patients with ST-segment elevation myocardial infarction: double-blind, randomized controlled trial. *Lancet* 2006;367:113–121.
128. Lunde K, Solheim S, Aakhus S, *et al.* Intracoronary injection of mononuclear bone marrow cells in acute myocardial infarction. *N Engl J Med* 2006;355:1199–1209.

# CHAPTER 7

# EFFECT OF NANOFIBROUS SCAFFOLDING ON STEM CELL DIFFERENTIATION AND TISSUE FORMATION

*Laura A. Smith and Peter X. Ma*

## Abstract

Through mimicking aspects of the native extracellular matrix, nanofibrous scaffolding attempts to induce a favorable cellular response. Three methods currently exist capable of producing nanofibrous scaffolds with fibers of a diameter similar to the extracellular matrix. They are electrospinning, self assembly and thermally induced phase separation. Using these types of scaffolds, preliminary work with stem cells indicates that they can increase cellular attachment, proliferation and differentiation compared to traditional scaffolds. The nanofibrous scaffolds most likely produce this enhanced cellular response compared to traditional scaffolds through several mechanisms including differences in protein adsorption, integrin signaling, cytoskeletal organization, and direct interactions with the nanofibers themselves. The data reviewed here indicate that nanofibrous scaffolding for tissue engineering is an important advancement for tissue engineering with stem cells.

## 1. Introduction

The number of human tissue transplants doubled over ten years from 1994 to 2004 and reached 1.5 million in 2004.[1,2] As the need for human the cells cultured on them.[50] These results along with the integrin data indicate that the cells may also directly bind to the nanofibers. The differences in morphology have been associated with differences in Rac expression in mouse embryonic stem cells cultured on nanofibers and smooth films.[44] While with pre-osteoblasts, differences in RhoA expression in cells cultured on the nanofiber and smooth films have been associated with both the differences in morphology and differentiation.[50] Both Rac and RhoA regulate cytoskeletal organization and other cellular functions.

## 4. Conclusion

Emulating the nanofibrous structure of the ECM using advanced scaffolding fabrication technologies, alters the microenvironment from that of traditional tissue engineering scaffolds with smooth pore walls. This change enhances the attachment, proliferation and differentiation of stem cells on the nanofibers compared to the smooth materials. Therefore, nanofibrous scaffolds represent an important advancement in tissue engineering biomaterials and stem cell-based regenerative medicine.

## References

1. Wang S, *et al.* Infections and human tissue transplants: review of FDA MedWath reports 2001–2004. *Cell Tissue Bank* 2007;8:211–219.
2. Statistical Abstract of the United States: 2004–2005 Section 3 Health and Nutrition, No. 161 Organ Transplants and Grafts: 1990 to 2001. 2004, U.S. Census Bureau, Washington DC, p. 114.
3. Langer R, Vacanti J. Tissue engineering. *Science* 1993;260:920–926.
4. Ma PX. Biomimetic materials for tissue engineering. *Adv Drug Deliv Rev* 2008;60(2):184–198.
5. Abbott A. Cell culture: biology's new dimension. *Nature* 2003;424: 870–872.
6. Cukierman E, *et al.* Taking cell-matrix adhesions to the third dimensions. *Science* 2001;294:1708–1712.
7. Kadler K. Matrix loading: assembly of extracellular matrix collagen fibrils during embryogenesis. *Birth Defects Res C Embryo Today* 2004;72:1–11.

8. Wei G, Ma P. Nanostructured biomaterials for regeneration. *Adv Funct Mater* 2008;18:3568–3582.
9. Matthews JA, *et al.* Electrospinning of collagen nanofibers. *Biomacromolecules* 2002;3(2):232–238.
10. Yang F, *et al.* Electrospinning of nano/micro scale poly(L-lactic acid) aligned fibers and their potential in neural tissue engineering. *Biomaterials* 2005;26:2603–2610.
11. Li WJ, *et al.* Electrospun nanofibrous structure: A novel scaffold for tissue engineering. *J Biomed Mater Res* 2002;60(4):613–621.
12. Li MY, *et al.* Electrospun protein fibers as matrices for tissue engineering. *Biomaterials* 2005;26(30):5999–6008.
13. Jin HJ, *et al.* Human bone marrow stromal cell responses on electrospun silk fibroin mats. *Biomaterials* 2004;25(6):1039–1047.
14. Li CM, *et al.* Electrospun silk-BMP-2 scaffolds for bone tissue engineering. *Biomaterials* 2006;27:3115–3124.
15. Luu YK, *et al.* Development of a nanostructured DNA delivery scaffold *via* electrospinning of PLGA and PLA-PEG block copolymers. *J Control Release* 2003;89(2):341–353.
16. Decher G. Fuzzy nanoassemblies: Toward layered polymeric multicomposites. *Science* 1997;277(5330):1232–1237.
17. Philp D, Stoddart JF. *Self-Assembly in Natural and Unnatural Systems.* Angewandte Chemie-International Edition in English, 1996, Vol. 35, No. 11, pp. 1155–1196.
18. Whitesides GM, Mathias, JP, Seto CT. Molecular self-assembly and nanochemistry — a chemical strategy for the synthesis of nanostructures. *Science* 1991;254(5036):1312–1319.
19. Hartgerink JD, Beniash E, Stupp SI. Self-assembly and mineralization of peptide-amphiphile nanofibers. *Science* 2001;294(5547):1684–1688.
20. Zhang SG. Fabrication of novel biomaterials through molecular self-assembly. *Nat Biotechnol* 2003;21(10):1171–1178.
21. Yu YC, Tirrell M, Fields GB. Minimal lipidation stabilizes protein-like molecular architecture. *J Am Chem Soc* 1998;120(39):9979–9987.
22. Liu GJ, Qiao LJ, A. GuoA. Diblock copolymer nanofibers *Macromolecules* 1996;29:5508–5510.
23. Liu DJ, *et al.* Fluorescent self-assembled polyphenylene dendrimer nanofibers. *Macromolecules* 2003;36:8489–8498.

40. [illegible] Enhancing the osteogenic [illegible] by nanofibers. *Tissue Eng* 2005 [illegible]
41. [illegible] of mesenchymal stem cells [illegible] nanofibers. *Stem Cells* 2006;24:2391–2397.
42. [illegible] of neural stem cells [illegible] nanofibrous scaffolds. *J Biomater* [illegible] 2004 [illegible]
43. [illegible] A, Beck L, Ma PX. Fabrication and tissue [illegible] nanofibrous scaffolds. In: *Nanotechnologies for Tissue* [illegible] Kumar C. Wiley-VCH, Weinheim, Germany, [illegible]
44. [illegible] A, *et al.* Three-dimensional nanofibrous scaffolds [illegible] embryonic stem cells. *Stem Cells* [illegible]
45. [illegible] Selective differentiation of neural progenitor [illegible] nanofibers. *Science* 2004;303:1352–1355.
46. [illegible] The influence of three-dimensional [illegible] scaffolds [illegible] differentiation of embryonic stem cells. *Biomaterials* [illegible]
47. [illegible] Multilineage differentiation of human mesenchymal stem cells in a three-dimensional nanofibrous scaffold. *Biomaterials* [illegible]
48. Woo KM, Chen VJ, Ma PX. Nano-fibrous scaffolding architecture selectively enhances protein adsorption contributing to cell attachment. *J Biomed Mater Res A* 2003;67(2):531–537.
49. Woo KM, *et al.* Nano-fibrous scaffolding promotes osteoblast differentiation and biomineralization. *Biomaterials* 2007;28:335–343.
50. [illegible] X, Ma PX. Induction of osteoblast differentiation [illegible] nanofibrous matrix. *Biomaterials* [illegible]

# PART II

# TISSUE ENGINEERING AND BIOENGINEERING OF STEM CELLS

widely used tools in biomedical research since the late 1980s. Mutations engineered in mouse ES cells are introduced back into the mouse by injecting the modified ES cells into blastocyst stage embryos, giving rise to chimeric mice, which are then bred to achieve germline transmission of the mutated genes. The power of gene targeting in mouse ES cells lies at least partly in the possibility to pre-screen ES cell clones in culture for relatively rare events — such as homologous recombination at a predetermined locus — before establishing a mouse line that carries the targeted mutation. Developing mouse ES cells and establishing gene targeting in mouse ES cells were the two key technological advancements that made knockout mice possible, which were recognized by the 2007 Nobel Prize in Physiology or Medicine.

Today, gene targeting techniques in mouse ES cells have been refined to such a degree that we can make genetic modifications ranging from point mutations, defined large chromosomal re-arrangements (deletions, duplications, inversions and translocations)[6] to inducible and/or tissue/cell-type specific genetic modifications with a high degree of temporal and spatial control.[7] These reagents have been instrumental in 1) assessing gene function; 2) modeling human diseases; 3) tracking gene expression through a reporter gene introduced into an endogenous locus; and 4) serving as functional genomic tools for genetic studies.[8]

The isolation of human ES cells in the late 1990s provided exciting new possibilities for both basic research of human biology and for development of novel therapies for human diseases through transplantation strategies.[9] On the one hand, just as mouse ES cells, human ES cells can serve as a tool for basic research. Much of what we know about human gene function has come from one of several ways: 1) identifying mutations in genes that cause human genetic disorders or predisposition to a disease; 2) extrapolating data from model organisms such as the laboratory mouse; 3) investigating the *in vitro* function of human gene products either by studying their structure or biochemical function in a test tube or by studying their role in a cell culture system. It is often difficult, if not impossible, to experimentally manipulate endogenous human genes and to study their role *in vitro* in a highly relevant cell type that can be isolated in sufficient quantity. It is even more challenging to do so to study their role *in vivo*. Since human ES cells can potentially turn into virtually any type of cell *in vitro* or *in vivo* (other than cells of the extra-embryonic origin) under appropriate conditions, the effect of any induced genetic changes in human ES cells can then be assessed in many different cell types. For example, gain or loss of function mutations can be introduced into a human ES cell line, and any effect of such genetic alterations can be assessed after transplanting the cells or their differentiated derivatives into an experimental animal.

On the other hand, unlike mouse ES cells, human ES cells can be directly used as a tool to develop cell transplantation-based therapies for a variety of human conditions. The excitement generated by human ES cells is in large part due to the potential of such cells for therapeutic development. A spectrum of human diseases or conditions where cells have been lost, damaged or degenerating, may benefit from cellular transplant with derivatives of human ES cells: type I diabetes, Parkinson's disease, and spinal cord injury, to name a few. Current challenges to this approach include the knowledge and ability to differentiate human ES cells into the desired cell types *in vitro* and/or *in vivo*, ways to deliver these cells or their derivatives into the body, the functional integration and long-term survival of differentiated derivatives *in vivo*, and the problem of immune rejection and tumorigenicity associated, respectively, with allograft transplant of cells in general and that of ES cells in particular. The development of patient-specific induced pluripotent stem (iPS) cells may bypass the issue of immune rejection in future.[10–12] However, whether iPS cells are identical to their human ES cell counterparts, especially in terms of their full differentiation potential, remains to be investigated systematically.

To achieve the full potential of human ES cells or iPS cells, both as a research tool and as a tool for therapeutic development, one critical element lies in our ability to genetically modify these cells.[13] Genetic engineering has several important applications in human ES and iPS cells. First, loss or gain of function mutations can be engineered to assess gene function, as in mouse ES cells. Second, the cells can be engineered to express a reporter gene to track transplanted cells; similarly, genetic epitope tagging can be used to track an endogenous protein. Third, the cells can be engineered to express any gene of interest that may enhance therapeutic efficacy, or alleviate any deleterious effect of transplanted frequency. This is expressed as the ratio (or percentage) of the number of targeted clones over the total number of stable transfectants successfully screened:

$$\text{Relative targeting frequency} = \frac{\text{Number of targeted clones}}{\text{Number of total clones screened}} \times 100\%$$

In contrast, the absolute targeting frequency refers to the ratio of the number of targeted clones over the total number of cells transfected. In general, it is the relative targeting frequency, rather than the absolute targeting frequency, that is the most relevant measure to the robustness of gene targeting in ES cells for two reasons: 1) the total number of stable transfectants is usually not rate-limiting; 2) the most labor-intensive step of a gene targeting experiment is the initial molecular screen for targeted clones among the stable transfectants. Unless noted otherwise, we will refer to relative gene targeting frequency as gene targeting frequency or, simply, targeting frequency below.

As discussed below, the targeting frequency can be enhanced in several ways, including: 1) the use of longer homology arms, 2) the use of isogenic DNA for the homology arms, 3) applying negative selection, and 4) applying a promoterless gene trap targeting strategy. The first two methods increase the number of targeted clones, thus increasing both the absolute and the relative targeting frequencies. In contrast, the last two methods reduce the number of random integrants, thus increasing the relative targeting frequency without significantly affecting the absolute targeting frequency.

### 2.2.1 *The length of homology arms*

A typical replacement gene targeting vector consists of 5′ and 3′ homology arms flanking a drug resistance gene (Fig. 1). The two homology arms should be co-linear along the targeted chromosomal locus. In other words, they have to be in the same orientation and order as they appear on the chromosome. Correct gene targeting requires a cross-over (marked as "×" in Fig. 1) event within each of the two homology arms. If the two homology arms reside next to each other on the chromosome (i.e., there is

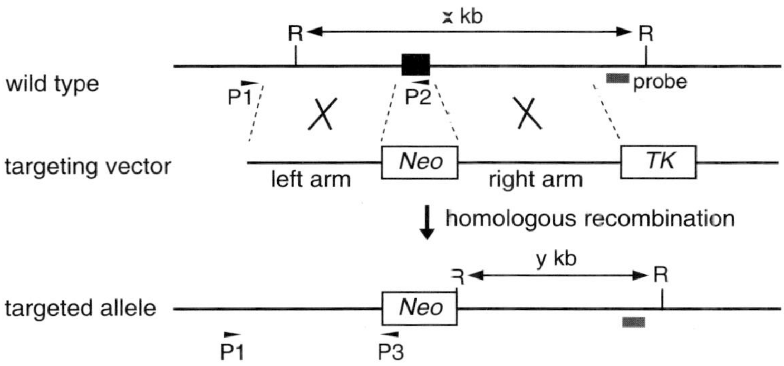


**Fig. 1.** Basic gene targeting scheme with a replacement vector. Black box indicates an exon. *Neo*, positive selection marker; *TK*, negative selection marker; R, restriction enzyme used to digest genomic DNA for Southern blot; kb, kilobase; P1, P2 and P3, PCR primers used to detect targeted clones among the stable transfectants. Either PCR or Southern blot can be used in an initial screen to detect targeted clones. PCR: P1 and P2 amplify the wild type band; P1 and P3 amplify the targeted band of a different size. Southern blot: the external probe detects an *x* kb wild type band and a *y* kb targeted band.

no gap in between), the recombination product is a net insertion of the (positive) selection cassette. If there is a gap (usually of several kilobases, or kbs) between the two homology arms on the chromosome, the recombination product is a replacement of the gap sequence with the selection cassette, hence the name "replacement targeting vector". This is the most common configuration for a targeting vector that is intended to create a simple loss of function allele. In such cases, the gap would span the critical exon(s) of the endogenous gene by design in order to be deleted (i.e., replaced by the selection cassette) in the targeted clones. In Fig. 1, the genomic region surrounding the exon (black box) is replaced with a Neo selection cassette.

In contrast, a much less commonly used type of targeting vector is the insertion vector. An insertion targeting vector contains only one region of homology. The vector is linearized within the single region of homology. When introduced into ES cells, a single cross-over within the region of homology leads to an insertion of the entire vector into the homologous locus. The end result is a duplication of the homology region at the targeted locus, with the duplicated regions flanking the selection cassette plus any vector backbone. Although the simplicity of insertion vectors renders it readily adaptable for large scale applications,[18,19] this advantage is usually outweighed by the versatility of replacement targeting vectors. For this reason, we focus our discussion on replacement targeting vectors only.

As the total length of homology increases, the probability of achieving a correctly targeted event also increases, up to a certain extent.[20–22] In practice, a targeting construct ideally contains eight to ten kb total length of homology, preferably divided more or less equally between the 5′ and 3′ homology arms. In cases where PCR is the desired method for the initial screen for targeted clones, one arm is usually designed to be much shorter than the other, because any PCR product that can distinguish targeted clones from random integrants has to span one of the homology arms (see Section 2.3) — a short arm will make this task less challenging. In contrast, if a Southern blot is used as the initial screen, there would be no advantage for a short arm.

### 2.2.2 *The use of isogenic DNA to generate the homology arms*

Isogenic DNA is often used to generate the homology arms. It has been well documented that the use of isogenic DNA may enhance the targeting frequency by 4–20 fold in mouse ES cells.[20,23] The concept of isogenic DNA concerns sequence polymorphisms between different inbred mouse strains. Most mouse ES cells are derived from an inbred strain, often a substrain of strain 129. There is significant sequence polymorphism among different inbred strains and to a certain extent even among 129 substrains, such that homology arms derived from one strain of mouse may contain enough mismatches compared with chromosomal DNA from a different strain to substantially reduce the targeting frequency. Ideally, genomic libraries in phage or BAC (bacterial artificial chromosome) vectors are used to derive homology arms. Long range genomic PCR, even with commercial high fidelity PCR systems, may introduce enough sequence errors to affect targeting frequencies. Thus, careful sequencing analysis needs to be conducted to minimize, if not eliminate, the errors introduced by PCR when constructing the homology arms.

### 2.2.3 *Negative selection*

There are two methods that are commonly used to enrich targeted clones among the stable transfectants: negative selection and promoterless gene trap targeting strategy. Both methods reduce the number of random integrants, thereby reducing the total number of stable transfectants that need to be screened in order to obtain a set number of targeted clones. In other words, these methods work by increasing the relative targeting frequency without any significant change to the absolute targeting frequency.

ES cell clones, containing a randomly inserted construct, can be selected against by including a negative selection marker, such as the herpes simplex virus thymidine kinase (HSV-TK, or TK) gene, outside the homology arms in the targeting vector (Fig. 1). When homologous recombination occurs via two cross-overs with a replacement targeting vector, only the elements between the homology arms are swapped into the chromosomal locus, leaving behind HSV-TK. HSV-TK can only be integrated into the genome when the entire targeting construct randomly integrates somewhere in the genome. Cells expressing HSV-TK can be selected against with either ganciclovir or FIAU ([1-(2′-deoxy-2′-fluoro-ß-D-arabinofuranosyl)-5-iodouracil]), which is metabolized by HSV-TK into a toxic product that kills the cells. While negative selection does increase targeting frequency (typically by 3 to 8 fold), selection with HSV-TK is not 100%. In other words, not all random integrants are killed by negative selection. Failure to obtain a higher enrichment is not due to a failure in selection, but due to either loss or mutation of the HSV-TK gene during integration into the genome.[24]

### 2.2.4 *Promoterless gene trap targeting strategy*

Another way to enrich targeted clones is the promoterless gene trap targeting strategy.[25,26] This strategy only works for genes that are expressed in ES cells. In this approach, the selection marker does not carry its own promoter. In order for the selection marker to be expressed, the gene must be integrated into the genome in such a way that it is placed downstream of an active promoter.

Upon homologous recombination, the selection marker is placed, by design, under the promoter control of the targeted gene and consequently expressed. When the vector is randomly inserted into the genome, more often than not, it is inserted into a locus at an orientation that does not lead to the functional expression of the selection marker. In a small portion of random integrants, however, the selection marker is placed, by chance, downstream of an active promoter of a gene at the insertion site. Thus, this strategy, like negative selection, reduces but does not eliminate random integrants. If an exogenous splice acceptor precedes the coding sequence for the promoterless selection marker, the selection marker can be expressed when it lands in an intron of a gene in the right orientation. If no splice acceptor is provided, the coding sequence for the selection marker needs to be placed downstream of an endogenous splice acceptor, potentially providing a greater level of enrichment for targeted clones. In addition, the knockin marker can have its own translation start site, or be in frame with an upstream, endogenous translation start site, which may also lead to a greater level of enrichment.

## 2.3 *Molecular screens*

Either Southern blot or PCR can be used to screen for targeted clones. A typical scheme for the choice of primers (for PCR) or the probe and the restriction enzyme (for Southern blot) is depicted in Fig. 1. Regardless of the method, it has to distinguish targeted clones from random integrants. In practice, this is achieved by 1) detecting a wild type band and a targeted band that are of sufficiently different size; and 2) NOT detecting a band corresponding to any random integration of the targeting vector.

In the case of PCR, three primers are usually used, with one common primer for both the wild type and targeted alleles that reside outside of the homology arm (P1 in Fig. 1). The second and third primers (P2 and P3 in Fig. 1), in combination with the common primer, allow for the amplification of the wild type and targeted allele respectively. The product from P1 and P2 differs in size from that from P1 and P3. Because random integration does not generally bring vector sequence in close proximity to the genomic sequence for P1, it is not amplified by any two of the three primers. The end result is that all random integrants show the wild type band only (one knows that these are random integrants because the colonies have survived drug selection, so must carry the positive selection marker). Only targeted clones show both a wild type band and a targeted band. Note that in Fig. 1, both the P1/P2 and the P1/P3 primer pairs have to amplify across one homology arm in order to distinguish among the wild type allele, the targeted allele and any random integration, which is not amplified.

In the case of Southern blot, a probe that resides out of the homology arm, termed an external probe, is used in the initial screen. A restriction enzyme is chosen to digest the genomic DNA such that the probe will detect a wild type band (x kb in Fig. 1), and a targeted band (y kb in Fig. 1) of different sizes. An external probe is used because it is not part of the targeting vector sequence, and therefore will not hybridize with any random integration site. In a fashion analogous to PCR, the restriction enzyme fragments detected by the probe, either from the wild type or the targeted allele, have to span across at least one homology arm (plus the probe sequence) in order to distinguish between the wild type allele and the targeted allele (any random integration is not detected).

Southern blot is more labor-intensive and less time-efficient than PCR. However, it is a more reliable method than PCR for two reasons: 1) the wild type band in Southern blot serves as an internal control for the probe, while there is no internal control for the targeted allele-specific primer (P3 in Fig. 1) in PCR; and 2) the intensity of the wild type band and the targeted band in Southern blot is indicative of the relative amount of the two alleles and consequently the purity of the targeted clones can be estimated with Southern blot, which is not the case with PCR. While the Southern blot analysis is being conducted, it is preferable to freeze down the picked colonies in a 96-well format to avoid excessive passage of the individual clones. This requires that the cells can be frozen down and thawed without significant loss of cell viability.

### 2.4 *Reporter genes*

A reporter gene, introduced into the targeted locus, functions as a read-out of gene expression for the targeted gene. Because most of the proximal and distal regulatory elements are presumably retained following gene targeting, a reporter gene introduced by homologous recombination is more likely to faithfully recapitulate the expression pattern of the targeted gene when compared with other experimental approaches such as conventional transgenesis or even BAC transgenesis. One of the first reporter genes, and still extensively used, is β-galactosidase, encoded by the bacterial gene LacZ.[27] β-galactosidase has a high turn-over rate, allowing for very low detection levels. Recently, fluorescent proteins have become more widely used as reporter proteins.[28] Among the most commonly used fluorescent reporter is green fluorescent protein (GFP) or its derivatives, originally isolated from the jellyfish.[29] There have been many different mutations made to GFP that have allowed for many different colored fluorescent proteins, including blue, cyan and yellow, to name a few. Other sources of fluorescent proteins have also been explored. A major advantage of fluorescent proteins over more traditional reporter proteins, such as β-galactosidase, is the ability to track these proteins in live cell cultures or even in live animals without addition of any exogenous factors. The open reading frame of the reporter can be in frame with the endogenous protein, have its own translation initiation site, such as a Kozak sequence, or an IRES (internal ribosome entry site) element.

## 2.5 *Site-specific recombination*

Site-specific recombination has been extensively used in combination with homologous recombination in mouse ES cells to expand the capabilty of genetic modifications.[30] Two site-specific recombination systems are in widespread use: the Cre-lox*P* recombination system derived from bacteriophage P1, and the FLP-Frt recombination system derived from yeast. Cre is the site-specific recombinase that recognizes the lox*P* site; FLPase recognizes the Frt site. Each of the recombination sites, lox*P* or Frt, is a specific, directional 34 base pair sequence. When two recombination sites (e.g., two lox*P* sites) are in the same orientation on the chromosome, site-specific recombination (e.g., by Cre) leads to the deletion of the sequence between the two sites. When they are in opposite orientations, the sequence between the two sites is inverted following recombination.

Therefore, depending on the orientations of the two recombination sites, different recombination products can be obtained.

There are a number of applications for site-specific recombination systems in the context of gene targeting: removal of a selection cassette following gene targeting, recombinase-mediated cassette exchange (RMCE), chromosome engineering (large deletions, duplications, inversions, translocations), gene activation, or inactivation through conditional gene targeting.

## 2.6 *Conditional gene targeting*

The constitutive inactivation of genes in the mouse leads to mice that are always deficient for the product of the deleted gene. This can cause complications in the analysis of the gene of interest. First, if the gene product is crucial for development, absence of the gene product can result in embryonic lethality, in which case there is no mouse to study for a phenotype that appears later in embryonic development or after birth. Second, the mouse can compensate for the loss of the gene product, by compensatory expression (e.g., upregulation) of other genes. Third, many gene products serve multiple different roles in different cell types. Deleting the gene from all cell types may significantly complicate analysis of the gene in a particular cell type or signaling pathway. These complications can be avoided by applying conditional gene targeting strategies. Conditional gene targeting allows for inactivation or activation of genes in a specific group of cells and/or during a defined period of time.[7]

The first element of a conditional knock-out using Cre-mediated recombination is the generation of a targeted mouse line in which all, or an essential part, of a gene of interest is flanked by two lox*P* sites in the same orientation. This is called a floxed (flanked by lox*P*) allele or conditional allele. This is accomplished using traditional homologous recombination strategies. Because selection marker expression can interfere with endogenous gene expression, it is usually removed with a second site-specific recombination system (i.e. FLP-Frt).

The second element is the generation of a Cre transgene or knock-in line that expresses Cre at the appropriate time, in the desired tissue(s) or

### 3.1 *Targeting HPRT — a test locus in male human ES cells*

The gene encoding HPRT (also known as HPRT1, or hypoxanthine phosphoribosyltransferase 1) resides on the X chromosome in both mice and humans. Loss of HPRT activity leads to drug resistance to 6-Thioguinine (6-TG). Because male (XY) ES cells carry only one copy of HPRT, HPRT targeted XY ES cell clones can be readily selected with 6-TG rather than through the more labor-intensive molecular screens (e.g., PCR or Southern blot). For this reason, the HPRT locus has been traditionally used to study the variables that affect targeting frequencies in mouse ES cells.[4,5] It has also been used as a proof of principle locus for establishing and testing gene targeting strategies in human ES cells.

Three groups have reported gene targeting at HPRT in different human ES cells with a plasmid-based method.[38,43,44] Zwaka and Thomson were the first to report successful gene targeting in human ES cells.[44] HPRT was one of the two loci they targeted in H1.1 cells. The authors electroporated cells in clumps instead of in single cell suspension because H1.1 cells exhibit an intrinsically low clonal expansion efficiency (~1%). They found that, with a modified set of electroporation parameters (320V, 200 μF in regular culture medium instead of PBS), several hundred colonies could be obtained from $1.5 \times 10^7$ electroporated cells. With a replacement targeting vector containing 11.9 kb total length of homology (1.9 kb + 10 kb), isogenic DNA and HSV-TK-based negative selection, a ~14% targeting frequency was observed. Without negative selection, it is about ~2%. Thus, HSV-TK negative selection provided a ~7 fold enrichment for targeted clones. Consistent with published literature on CHO (Chinese Hamster Ovary) cells,[17] the authors reported that a lipofection or cationic reagent-based transfection method did not lead to any detected gene targeting events in the limited number of colonies screened, suggesting that electroporation is associated with a higher targeting frequency and may be the delivery method of choice for gene targeting in human ES cells.

Urbach *et al.* targeted HPRT in H13 cells.[43] Instead of electroporation, they used ExGen 500, a cationic re-agent-based vector delivery. With 8.5 kb total length of homology, non-isogenic DNA and without negative selection, the authors observed a targeting frequency of ~1%. This study remains the only reported case where a cationic reagent delivery method was successfully used for gene targeting in human ES cells. It should be noted that the efficiency of stable transfection with ExGen 500 is rather low in this study, at < 10 drug resistant colonies per $1 \times 10^7$ transfected cells. Consequently, a much higher number of cells need to be transfected — a total of 2 targeted clones were obtained from $>10^8$ transfected cells.

More recently, Di Domenico et al reported gene targeting at the HPRT locus in H1 cells.[38] Using 6.9 kb total length of homology (4.8 kb + 2.1 kb), non-isogenic DNA and without negative selection, the authors observed a ~0.2% targeting frequency under standard culture conditions. Interestingly, when the authors repeated the same gene targeting protocol in physiological oxygen (2%), the targeting frequency was increased to ~2.3%, an impressive ~10× increase. It was not clear why culturing human ES cells at a lower oxygen concentration would lead to an increased gene targeting frequency. It remains to be seen whether this observation is generally applicable to other cell lines or loci. In addition, the authors demonstrated a second round of gene targeting to correct the mutation introduced in the first step of targeting. Finally, using recombinase-mediated cassette exchange (RMCE)[45] utilizing two incompatible lox*P* sites (one wild type lox*P* and one variant), the authors achieved highly efficient cassette exchange when a positive selection scheme is applied for the donor cassette. A GFP reporter introduced into the HPRT locus lost expression after a number of passages, providing a cautionary note that a knock-in reporter may be silenced at certain loci.

### 3.2 *Promoterless gene trap targeting*

The HPRT locus is rather unique since inactivating HPRT in male ES cells leads to immediate resistance to the drug 6-TG, which can be selected for in culture. A similar selection scheme is not available for most genes in the human genome. Therefore, labor-intensive molecular screens, either by PCR or Southern blot, are typically required for the initial detection of targeted clones. One way to increase the (relative) gene targeting frequency is the promoterless gene trap approach.[25,26] In this strategy, the positive selection marker lacks a promoter; the expression of the selection marker relies on expression of the endogenous promoter (see Section 2.2.4).

If random integration of the targeting construct occurs, expression of the selectable marker usually does not occur. Therefore, targeted clones are drug-resistant, while many random integrants are drug-sensitive and eliminated during drug selection. For this strategy to work, the targeted gene must be expressed in ES cells.

Two groups have reported gene targeting using the promoterless gene trap targeting strategy in human ES cells.[39,44] Zwaka and Thomson targeted POU5F1 (also known as Oct4), which encodes a pluripotency marker.[44] The targeting vector contains an insertion of IRES-GFP-IRES-Neo into the 3′ UTR of the POU5F1 gene. With 7.9 kb (6.3 + 1.6) total length of homology, isogenic DNA but without negative selection, a ~27% targeting frequency was obtained in H1.1 cells. This frequency was further improved to ~40% when the total length of homology was increased to 12.8 kb. In addition to the general promoterless gene trap targeting strategy, the configuration of the trapping selection marker may be partly responsible for the high targeting frequency. The Neo coding sequence follows IRES-GFP-IRES in the 3′ UTR of the endogenous POU5F1 gene, and consequently the translation of Neo is likely to be less efficient than if the Neo is put towards the 5′ of the gene and without the two extra IRES elements. It is possible that random integrants that even express some amount of the transcript failed to survive drug selection, leading to a higher level of enrichment for the targeted clones. This strategy presumably relies on a relatively high level of expression for the gene to be targeted, and it remains to be seen whether this strategy can be readily applied to other genes. Importantly, a GFP knock-in reporter at the POU5F1 locus is expressed in undifferentiated H1.1 cells, but is turned off following differentiation, as would be expected as a reporter for a pluripotency marker.

A second example of promoterless gene trap targeting was reported by Irion *et al.*[39] The authors targeted the ROSA26 locus in HES2 cells. The murine ROSA26 locus has served as a universal promoter for several widely used reporter lines where ubiquitous expression is desired.[46,47] Irion *et al.* identified a homologous locus in humans based on sequence similarity and synteny. With 5.1 kb total length of homology, isogenic DNA and without negative selection, a ~2.3% gene targeting frequency was observed with a promoterless gene trap targeting strategy. The authors employed a FLEx switch system[48] where two wild type loxP sites and two mutant loxP sites were configured in such a way that the expression is irreversibly switched from one reporter to another in a Cre-dependent manner. FACS sorting was used to detect Cre recombination products where a red fluorescent marker (tdRFP) is switched on. The Cre recombination efficiency was estimated to be at ~5%, sufficient for most applications. Finally, using RMCE discussed above, the authors demonstrated efficient swapping of the tdRFP with another reporter. A positive selection scheme for RMCE greatly enhanced the efficiency to detect the swapped product, but is not required. Importantly, a reporter gene introduced into the human ROSA26 locus such as tdRFP, EGFP or puromycin is broadly expressed by cells of a variety of lineages without any significant gene silencing. Thus, the human ROSA26 targeted lines would be very useful when expressing any gene of interest in a broad expression pattern through RMCE.

### 3.3 *Targeting a gene not expressed in human ES cells*

The promoterless gene trap targeting strategy is a very robust method, but can only be used if the gene of interest is expressed in the cell line at high enough levels. Therefore, if the desired gene is not expressed in the cell line or is expressed only at very low levels, an alternative method must be used. This is particularly relevant when constructing knock-in reporter lines to track lineage-restricted human ES cell derivatives.

To accomplish gene targeting at a locus that is not expressed in ES cells, the drug selection cassette has to carry its own promoter. Because the expression of the selection marker is not dependent on the site of integration as in the promoterless gene trap strategy, it is important to have a sufficient amount of homology to increase the probability of achieving a targeted event. Since the positive selection marker can be expressed at many integration loci across the genome, drug-resistant clones can have the targeting construct integrated anywhere into the genome. As a result, this strategy is generally less robust and more laborious, requiring analysis of a larger number of clones to identify the rare targeted clone. Together, the following two studies illustrate the possibility to construct knock-in reporter lines by targeting genes not expressed in human ES cells to track the differentiation of these cells along specific lineages.

Davis *et al.* provided the first detailed report on targeting a gene not expressed in human ES cells with a targeting strategy applicable to all genes.[37] The authors targeted MIXL1, a transient marker for the primitive streak during embyrogenesis, in HES3 cells. They showed that knocking in a GFP reporter into the MLXL1 locus facilitated the isolation of primitive streak-derived primitive hematopoietic precursors. This study illustrated the general utility of a knock-in line in studying an otherwise inaccessible developmental stage or event. By comparing the protein expression of GFP and MLXL1, the authors noted that GFP has a longer half life than MLXL1. This observation serves as an important reminder that a knock-in reporter may not exactly mimic the expression of an endogenous protein temporally. Such discrepancy may also occur at a spatial level due to differential subcellular localization or post-translational modifications. In this case, however, the higher stability of GFP renders it a useful, albeit transient tracer for the cell lineage of interest.

We tested gene targeting at the Fezf2 locus (also known as Fezl) in the HUES9 cell line.[41] This is a neuronal gene, the expression of which marks the identity of corticospinal neurons and other related subcortical projection neurons during development.[49,50] With 8.3 kb total length of homology and negative selection, a ~1.5% targeting frequency was observed. Negative selection significantly increased the targeting frequency by ~5 fold. Interestingly, Cre mediated excision of the Neo cassette is highly efficient, at ~30%. The intrinsically high clonal expansion efficiency is critical to manipulations where single cells are plated at a low density to allow for clonal expansion without any drug selection. In this regard, we observed a ~24% clonal expansion efficiency with HUES9 cells, as compared with ~1% of H1.1 cells previously reported.[44] This intrinsically high clonal expansion efficiency is rather remarkable considering that an inhibitor of Rho-associated Kinase (ROCK), Y-27632, or a neurotrophin cocktail is required to obtain a similar clonal expansion efficiency for the KhES cell lines or the H1 and H9 cell lines respectively.[51,52] The long-term effects of the ROCK inhibitor or neurotrophin cocktail on the full differentiation potential and other characteristics of various human ES cells remain to be assessed comprehensively. Thus, the choice of human ES cell lines that can undergo efficient clonal expansion may be an important consideration in genetic manipulations that require single cell dissociation. Out of three initially targeted clones karyotyped, one exhibited trisomies 12 and 17 in a subset of the cells (~15%). This is consistent with previous reports that trisomies 12 and 17 occur frequently in human ES cell culture.[53,54] However, following transient Cre expression and clonal expansion, 100% cells exhibited normal karyotype in three out of three subclones analyzed. Thus, trisomies 12 and 17 may occur in HUES9 culture, but homogenous, karyotypically normal subclones can be readily obtained following one round of clonal expansion. Therefore, clonal expansion is an effective method to purify karyotypically normal cells from karyotypically abnormal cells that arise spontaneously in culture. Again, ES cell lines that can undergo efficient clonal expansion may have an advantage in this regard. Importantly, upon neural differentiation, the knock-in reporter EYFP is expressed in a subset of the cells, indicating proper functionality of the reporter gene.

Of all the plasmid-based gene targeting studies reported, some used isogenic DNA,[39,41,44] while others did not.[37,38,43] Most of these studies did not provide detailed information on sequence discrepancy between the targeting vector and the genomic alleles. Although it is clear that isogenic DNA is not required to target genes in human cells, including human ES cells,[37,38,43,55] the impact of any sequence discrepancy between the targeting vector and the genomic allele to be targeted, including any errors introduced into the homology arms by long range genomic PCR, remains to be investigated systematically.[41] A careful study on this topic requires the construction of multiple targeting vectors with varying degrees of sequence polymorphisms to be tested in several different human ES cell lines. Depending on the level of sequence polymorphism that can be tolerated when targeting genes in human ES cells, the hybrid nature of human ES cells may be a consideration when targeting the second allele of the same gene.

### 3.4 *Viral vector-based gene targeting*

Suzuki *et al.* reported gene targeting at HPRT with a helper-dependent adenoviral vector (HDAdV)-based delivery system.[42] One advantage of the adenovirus-based vector is the large size of insert it can carry so longer homology regions can be accommodated. In this case, the authors packed in ~23 kb of total length of homology in the HDAdV-based targeting vector. A ~45% targeting frequency was observed at HPRT in KhES1 cells. A limited test in a second KhES line, KhES3, which exhibits a significantly lower replating efficiency, confirmed a comparable targeting frequency. One would hypothesize that the impressive targeting frequency in this experiment, as compared with those from other experiments at HPRT (Table 1), is at least partly due to the longer homology regions used. However, in a control experiment where the same plasmid vector that was used to make the virus was introduced instead by electroporation into KhES1 cells, only a ~0.58% targeting frequency was observed. This result indicates that there are additional factors in the packaged viral particles that either enhance homologous recombination or suppress random integration.

In addition to adenovirus-based targeting vector delivery, the adeno-associated virus (AAV), a single stranded DNA virus, has also been used to perform gene targeting in other human cell types.[56] The advantage of AAV-based gene targeting is that only short regions of homology are required. It remains to be seen if this strategy can be adapted to human ES cells. Overall, viral-based targeting vector delivery presents an advantage for cells that have not been adapted for efficient clonal expansion following enzymatic dissociation.

### 3.5 *Zinc finger nuclease to enhance gene targeting frequency*

Zinc finger nucleases have been explored to enhance gene targeting frequency, taking advantage of homology-directed repair of double-strand breaks.[40] To target a gene of interest, a pair of zinc finger nucleases was engineered to bind a particular sequence in the targeted locus. The genes encoding the two zinc finger nucleases and a donor sequence that serves as a targeting vector were introduced into human ES cells via integrase-defective lentiviral vectors.[40] Upon expression of the zinc finger nucleases, the targeting vector serves as the donor sequence to repair the double-strand break cut by the nucleases, leading to homologous recombination. With 1.9 kb total homology, Lombardo et al observed up to ~5%

estimated absolute targeting frequency at the CCR5 locus in HUES3 cells, as indicated by the expression of the knock-in marker GFP. PCR analysis confirmed the presence of the expected targeted band in a population of virally infected cells. This study did not derive clonal targeted lines, and consequently no detailed confirmation with Southern blot, PCR or sequencing analysis on the targeted clones was provided. The remarkable part of this method is that targeted events were detected without any positive selection, due to the unusually high absolute targeting frequency achieved with zinc finger nucleases and the lentiviral vectors used. Thus, this method has great potential as an *in vivo* gene targeting system. Its general applicability in human ES cells may be limited by the technical complexity and the high level of expertise required to engineer sequence-specific zinc finger nucleases. In addition, whether the nucleases only induce the desired targeted modification without any off-target effects in human ES cells remains to be validated.

## 4. Concluding Remarks

Targeted modification allows for pre-designed genetic alterations at pre-determined loci, leading to the highest precision possible in the genetic modifications. Although limited in number, the successful examples in the literature have already illustrated great potential for this approach in human ES cells. Human ES cells can be genetically engineered without significant loss of karyotypic stability or pluripotency, just as their mouse counterparts. We anticipate that gene targeting will also be extended to human iPS cells in the near future, with important applications in both basic research and therapeutic development.

There are several unique challenges for targeted manipulations in human ES or iPS cells. First, with human pluripotent cells, it is not possible (or ethical) to check pluripotency *via* chimera formation followed by germline transmission, which represent the most stringent test for the developmental potential of mouse ES cells. Thus, it is important to check in various ways for the pluripotency of human ES cells, especially after multiple steps of genetic manipulations. Current methods include pluripotency marker expression, *in vitro* differentiation, and *in vivo* teratoma formation. Second, many human ES cell lines have not been adapted to enzymatic dissociation into single cells, and consequently these cell lines have an intrinsically low clonal expansion efficiency. This presents a challenge when electroporation is used for vector delivery, especially when the cells need to be plated at low density, such as in Cre-mediated excision. Treatment with exogenous factors, such as a ROCK inhibitor or a neurotrophin cocktail, may overcome this problem.[51,52] However, cell lines that have an intrinsically high clonal expansion efficiency[41] or have been adapted to clonal expansion by enzymatic dissociation[57–59] may offer an advantage here since any potential complication with an exogenous factor(s) can be avoided. Finally, it is not yet known to what degree sequence polymorphisms between the targeting vector and the targeted allele affect gene targeting frequency in human ES cells. Hence, the degree of polymorphisms between the two alleles of any given gene may be a consideration in gene targeting, especially when it is desirable to target both alleles of the same gene.

Several other methods have been explored to genetically modify human ES cells, each with their own advantages and disadvantages. These include plasmid-based random integration[60,61] viral vector-based integration,[62] integrase-mediated site selective integration,[63] bacterial artificial chromosome (BAC) transgenesis,[64] shRNA based gene knock-down,[65] and inducible gene expression systems.[66] Together with targeted modifications, these methods comprise the repertoire of genetic tools that will be instrumental in interrogating gene function, studying self renewal and differentiation, repairing genetic lesions and enhancing therapeutic efficacy of human pluripotent stem cells and their derivatives.

## Notes added in proof

While this chapter is in press, a number of new reports have been published on successful homologous recombination in human pluripotent stem cells using bacterial artificial chromosome-based strategy, Zinc finger nuclease-based strategy or adeno-associated virus-based strategy, in addition to the traditional plasmid-based targeting strategy. We apologize for not being able to include these new exciting studies in our discussion.

## Acknowledgments

Supported by a grant from the California Institute for Regenerative Medicine (CIRM) to B.Z. (RS1-00333-1). K.M.R. was a predoctoral trainee of the CIRM Interdisciplinary Stem Cell Training Program at UCSD.

## Nomenclature:

**ES cells:** Embryonic stem cells. Derived from blastocyst stage embryos, ES cells can re-populate all three germ layers when introduced back into early stage embryos, including contribution to the germline. ES cells are pluripotent, but not totipotent, because they cannot contribute to extra-embryonic tissues and cannot develop into an embryo on their own.

**iPS cells**: Induced pluripotent stem cells. iPS cells are ES-like cells that are derived by re-programming somatic cells with one or more transcriptional factors. They mimic ES cells in their pluripotency, but differ in their origin. Whether iPS cells can functionally replace ES cells under various conditions remains to be investigated.

**Neo:** Neomycin phosphotransferase gene, also known as neomycin resistance gene or aminoglycoside phosphotransferase gene. Neo confers resistance to G418 (also known as Geneticin), a drug related to neomycin. It is by far the most commonly used positive selection marker for gene targeting.

**HPRT**: Hypoxanthine phosphoribosyltransferase 1 gene, also known as HPRT1. HPRT resides on the X chromosome and confers resistance to HAT medium in mammalian culture. Loss of HPRT activity in mammalian cells leads to 6-TG (6-thioguinine) resistance.

**Gene targeting frequency (or targeting frequency):** Most frequently refers to the relative (or effective) gene targeting frequency, expressed as the ratio (or percentage) of the number of targeted clones over that of the total stable transfectants screened successfully. This is an important measure for the robustness of gene targeting.

24. Bradley A, Zheng B, Liu P. Thirteen years of manipulating the mouse genome: a personal history. *Int J Dev Biol* 1998;42:943–950.
25. Doetschman T, Maeda N, Smithies O. Targeted mutation of the Hprt gene in mouse embryonic stem cells. *Proc Natl Acad Sci USA* 1988;85: 8583–8587.
26. Dorin JR, Inglis JD, Porteous DJ. Selection for precise chromosomal targeting of a dominant marker by homologous recombination. *Science* 1989;243:1357–1360.
27. Goring DR, Rossant J, Clapoff S, *et al.* *In situ* detection of beta-galactosidase in lenses of transgenic mice with a gamma-crystallin/lacZ gene. *Science* 1987;235:456–458.
28. Service RF. Nobel Prize in chemistry. Three scientists bask in prize's fluorescent glow. *Science* 2008;322:361.
29. Giepmans BN, Adams SR, Ellisman MH, Tsien RY. The fluorescent toolbox for assessing protein location and function. *Science* 2006;312:217–224.
30. Branda CS, Dymecki SM. Talking about a revolution: The impact of site-specific recombinases on genetic analyses in mice. *Dev Cell* 2004;6:7–28.
31. Feil R, Brocard J, Mascrez B, *et al.* Ligand-activated site-specific recombination in mice. *Proc Natl Acad Sci USA* 1996;93:10887–10890.
32. Feil R, Wagner J, Metzger D, Chambon P. Regulation of Cre recombinase activity by mutated estrogen receptor ligand-binding domains. *Biochem Biophys Res Commun* 1997;237:752–757.
33. Hunter NL, Awatramani RB, Farley FW, Dymecki SM. Ligand-activated Flpe for temporally regulated gene modifications. *Genesis* 2005;41:99–109.
34. Stec DE, Davisson RL, Haskell RE, *et al.* Efficient liver-specific deletion of a floxed human angiotensinogen transgene by adenoviral delivery of Cre recombinase *in vivo*. *J Biol Chem* 1999;274:21285–21290.
35. Chang BH, Liao W, Li L, *et al.* Liver-specific inactivation of the abetalipoproteinemia gene completely abrogates very low density lipoprotein/low density lipoprotein production in a viable conditional knockout mouse. *J Biol Chem* 1999;274:6051–6055.
36. Rinaldi A, Marshall KR, Preston CM. A non-cytotoxic herpes simplex virus vector which expresses Cre recombinase directs efficient site specific recombination. *Virus Res* 1999;65:11–20.
37. Davis RP, Ng ES, Costa M, *et al.* Targeting a GFP reporter gene to the MIXL1 locus of human embryonic stem cells identifies human primitive

streak-like cells and enables isolation of primitive hematopoietic precursors. *Blood* 2008;111:1876–1884.

38. Di Domenico AI, Christodoulou I, Pells SC, *et al.* Sequential genetic modification of the HPRT locus in human ESCs combining gene targeting and recombinase-mediated cassette exchange. *Cloning Stem Cells* 2008;10:217–230.
39. Irion S, Luche H, Gadue P, *et al.* Identification and targeting of the ROSA26 locus in human embryonic stem cells. *Nat Biotechnol* 2007;25: 1477–1482.
40. Lombardo A, Genovese P, Beausejour CM, *et al.* Gene editing in human stem cells using zinc finger nucleases and integrase-defective lentiviral vector delivery. *Nat Biotechnol* 2007;25:1298–1306.
41. Ruby KM, Zheng B. Gene targeting in a HUES line of human embryonic stem cells via electroporation. *Stem Cells* 2009; 27(7):1496–1506.
42. Suzuki K, Mitsui K, Aizawa E, *et al.* Highly efficient transient gene expression and gene targeting in primate embryonic stem cells with helper-dependent adenoviral vectors. *Proc Natl Acad Sci USA* 2008;105: 13781–13786.
43. Urbach A, Schuldiner M, Benvenisty N. Modeling for Lesch-Nyhan disease by gene targeting in human embryonic stem cells. *Stem Cells* 2004;22:635–641.
44. Zwaka TP, Thomson JA. Homologous recombination in human embryonic stem cells. *Nat Biotechnol* 2003;21:319–321.
45. Bouhassira EE, Westerman K, Leboulch P. Transcriptional behavior of LCR enhancer elements integrated at the same chromosomal locus by recombinase-mediated cassette exchange. *Blood* 1997;90:3332–3344.
46. Awatramani R, Soriano P, Mai JJ, Dymecki S. An FLP indicator mouse expressing alkaline phosphatase from the ROSA26 locus. *Nat Genet* 2001;29:257–259.
47. Soriano P. Generalized lacZ expression with the ROSA26 Cre reporter strain. *Nat Genet* 1999;21:70–71.
48. Schnutgen F, Doerflinger N, Calleja C, *et al.* A directional strategy for monitoring Cre-mediated recombination at the cellular level in the mouse. *Nat Biotechnol* 2003;21:562–565.
49. Molyneaux BJ, Arlotta P, Hirata T, *et al.* Fezl is required for the birth and specification of corticospinal motor neurons. *Neuron* 2005;47:817–831.

50. Chen B, Schaevitz LR, McConnell SK. Fezl regulates the differentiation and axon targeting of layer 5 subcortical projection neurons in cerebral cortex. *Proc Natl Acad Sci USA* 2005;102:17184–17189.
51. Pyle AD, Lock LF, Donovan PJ. Neurotrophins mediate human embryonic stem cell survival. *Nat Biotechnol* 2006;24:344–350.
52. Watanabe K, Ueno M, Kamiya D, *et al.* A ROCK inhibitor permits survival of dissociated human embryonic stem cells. *Nat Biotechnol* 2007;25: 681–686.
53. Cowan CA, Klimanskaya I, McMahon J, *et al.* Derivation of embryonic stem-cell lines from human blastocysts. *N Engl J Med* 2004;350: 1353–1356.
54. Draper JS, Smith K, Gokhale P, *et al.* Recurrent gain of chromosomes 17q and 12 in cultured human embryonic stem cells. *Nat Biotechnol* 2004; 22:53–54.
55. Sedivy JM, Vogelstein B, Liber HL, *et al.* Gene targeting in human cells without isogenic DNA. *Science* 1999;283:9a.
56. Vasileva A, Jessberger R. Precise hit: adeno-associated virus in gene targeting. *Nat Rev Microbiol* 2005;3:837–847.
57. Costa M, Dottori M, Sourris K, *et al.* A method for genetic modification of human embryonic stem cells using electroporation. *Nat Protoc* 2007;2: 792–796.
58. Ellerstrom C, Strehl R, Noaksson K, *et al.* Facilitated expansion of human embryonic stem cells by single-cell enzymatic dissociation. *Stem Cells* 2007;25:1690–1696.
59. Hasegawa K, Fujioka T, Nakamura Y, *et al.* A method for the selection of human embryonic stem cell sublines with high replating efficiency after single-cell dissociation. *Stem Cells* 2006;24:2649–2660.
60. Costa M, Dottori M, Ng E, *et al.* The hESC line Envy expresses high levels of GFP in all differentiated progeny. *Nat Methods* 2005;2:259–260.
61. Gerrard L, Zhao D, Clark AJ Cui W. Stably transfected human embryonic stem cell clones express OCT4-specific green fluorescent protein and maintain self-renewal and pluripotency. *Stem Cells* 2005;23:124–133.
62. Ma Y, Ramezani A, Lewis R, *et al.* High-level sustained transgene expression in human embryonic stem cells using lentiviral vectors. *Stem Cells* 2003;21:111–117.

63. Thyagarajan B, Liu Y, Shin S, *et al.* Creation of engineered human embryonic stem cell lines using phiC31 integrase. *Stem Cells* 2008;26:119–126.
64. Placantonakis DG, Tomishima MJ, Lafaille F, *et al.* Bac transgenesis in human ES cells as a novel tool to define the human neural lineage. *Stem Cells* 2009;27:521–532.
65. Hohenstein KA, Pyle AD, Chern JY, *et al.* Nucleofection mediates high-efficiency stable gene knockdown and transgene expression in human embryonic stem cells. *Stem Cells* 2008;26:1436–1443.
66. Zhou BY, Ye Z, Chen G, *et al.* Inducible and reversible transgene expression in human stem cells after efficient and stable gene transfer. *Stem Cells* 2007;25:779–789.

# CHAPTER 9

# BIO-ARTIFICIAL MYOCARDIUM FOR THE TREATMENT OF ISCHEMIC HEART DISEASE: FIRST CLINICAL EXPERIENCE

*Juan C. Chachques*

## Abstract

The stem cell niche, a specialized environment surrounding stem cells, provides crucial support needed for stem cell maintenance. Compromised niche function may lead to the selection of stem cells that no longer depend on self-renewal factors produced by its environment. If the stem cell niche has aged, it might not be capable of supporting the transplanted stem cells. The objective of stem cell transplantation associated with tissue engineered approaches in cardiology is to create a myocardial repair procedure as a new modality in the treatment of heart failure. The use of efficient scaffolds will lead to re-establishment of a beneficial atmosphere for cell survival, multiplication, differentiation and function. The development of bio-engineered platforms consists in obtaining newly designed biodegradable scaffolds (constructs) that will support cell survival and early extracellular instruction. The stem cells to be implanted could be pre-differentiated *in-vitro* into myogenic and/or cardiomyogenic cells, and pre-adapted to resist their implantation into a highly stressed tissue. Afterwards, the construct may induce rapid vascularization to ensure tissue remodeling and regeneration into a newly functional myocardium. From the clinical point of view, cardiac tissue engineering may allow the replacement of the pathologic myocardium by a bioartificial functional tissue. A "bio-active implant" on the myocardial surface might reinforce the ventricular wall, hence limiting in optimal functioning of the skeletal muscle. CMP provides an autologous source of circulatory assistance, presents low intra- and mid- long-term mortality and has reduced costs.[8–10]

Concerning the mechanisms of action, a reduction in mechanical stress seems to contribute to a reduced level of myocardial apoptosis after CMP. Subsequent recurrence of LV dilatation due to the detrimental evolution of the underlying myocardial disease observed in some cases could, in turn, instigate a return to pathologic levels of wall stress, and to the vicious cycle of apoptotic cell loss and further progressive LV enlargement. In addition, long-term results of dynamic cardiomyoplasty are limited by the patient's pre-operative condition, and by a high incidence of sudden cardiac death. These results could be improved using modified skeletal muscle stimulation protocols and cardioverter-defibrillator implantation.

The scientific advances achieved in the past years concerning the potential of skeletal muscles should allow exploring in a more physiological basis the concept of "cardiac bio-assist." Present knowledge of the vascular anatomy of the latissimus dorsi muscle and the adaptive response of muscle to electrical stimulation are related with viable and powerful skeletal muscle grafts. Some clinical series strongly suggest that CMP offers a relatively secure mid- to long-term bridge to heart transplantation, allowing critically ill patients to improve their quality of life while waiting for a heart donor. CMP represents in many cases a definitive surgical treatment for LV failure and principally for severe RV cardiomyopathy.[11–13]

## 4. Cell-Based Regenerative Therapy

Grafting of healthy cells into the diseased myocardium holds enormous potential as an approach to cardiovascular pathology. The goal of cell transplantation is to grow new muscle fibers (myogenesis) and/or to develop new blood vessels (angiogenesis) in the damaged myocardium.[14] The encouraging results of experimental studies have opened the way to the clinical application of cellular cardiomyoplasty in patients with akinetic and non-viable post-infarction scar, low ejection fraction, and in patients with idiopathic and Chagas' disease cardiopathy.

Chagas' disease is the infection with the protozoan parasite trypanosoma cruzi, a form of trypanosomiasis endemic in Central and South America. It is named after the Brazilian physician Carlos Chagas who discovered the parasite. Four main pathogenetic mechanisms explain the development of chronic Chagas heart disease: autonomic nervous system derangements, microvascular disturbances, parasite-dependent myocardial aggression, and immune-mediated myocardial injury. In the last decades, millions of people from this part of America have migrated to the United States and Europe (mainly to Spain and Portugal), changing the scenario of acute Chagas' disease associated with blood transfusion in the USA and Europe. France is affected by the chagasic infections detected in the French Guiana territory, this population being part of the European Union. Long-term patients developed severe cardiac arrhythmias, dilated cardiomyopathy, and heart failure. In chagasic patients, who undergo heart transplantation and immunosuppression, the risk of late re-activation of Chagas disease by means of an isolated organ lesion is important.

Adult autologous stem cells do not raise ethical, tumorogenesis, donor availability and immunological problems, especially when cells are cultivated with autologous human serum.[15] The exact evolution of implanted cells into the host pathological myocardium has not been completely elucidated. Potentially, this process may include transdifferentiation of transplanted stem cells (cellular plasticity), fusion of implanted cells with resident cells (chimerization), reactive angiogenesis or paracrine secretion of angiogenic growth factors, and modulation of inflammation at the level of the extracellular matrix.

### 4.1 *Limitations of cell therapy*

Cell transplantation for cardiac support and regeneration may repair the injured heart, but is limited by a poor effect in systolic function.[16–18] This can be due to the lack of gap junctions between the native myocardium and the grafted cells. Also, cell transplantation seems to be limited by the relocation of transplanted cells to remote organs and non-infarcted myocardium, and by the death of transplanted cells. Most cell death occurs in the first few days post-transplantation, likely from a combination of ischemia, apoptosis, and inflammation. Apoptosis can be induced by anchorage-dependent cells detaching from the surrounding extracellular matrix. Interventions known to enhance transplanted cell survival include heat shock, overexpressing antiapoptotic proteins, free radical scavengers, anti-inflammatory therapy and co-delivery of extracellular matrix molecules. Combinatorial use of such interventions could enhance graft cell survival. In spite of these possibilities, until now cell transplantation constitutes a passive therapeutic approach, the only effects which seem to be related to the reduction of the myocardial fibrosis and the limitation of adverse ventricular remodeling. Development of strategies for improving cell survival and differentiation should be encouraged, e.g., by using tissue engineering, pre-vascularization, pre-conditioning procedures like *in vitro* cell electrostimulation, cell cultures under hypoxia conditions, combination of angiogenic and myogenic stem cells.[19–23]

## 5. Stem Cells: New Developments

Resident stem cells have been identified in the heart as in many other organs, some of them with recognized proliferative activity, such as skin and blood or others more static as central nervous system components. Cardiac stem cells have been isolated from human and murine hearts and characterized. Even in human hearts with the presence of native stem cells, myocardial renewal is an insufficient mechanism to restore heart damage.

Cellular cardiomyoplasty's goal is to provide exogenous stem cells that can improve the natural insufficient reparative cardiac activity after a myocardial injury. It is highly possible that the recruitment of stems cells, which circulate and mostly originated in the bone marrow, help create structures other than cardiac muscle to restore the regional architecture and generate the adequate niche for native and migrating stem cells. An adequate level of inflammation with reparative characteristic is critical, not only to limit the local necrosis, but to reach an adequate support of regulatory cytokines. These cytokines could be secreted by the injected or recruited cells in a paracrine action, as have been demonstrated after bone marrow-mesenchymal-derived stem cell injection, with a direct effect on resident cells. Also, it was demonstrated that the paracrine effects of human skeletal myoblasts transplanted in infarcted myocardium.[24,25]

Stem cell therapy can help repair damaged heart tissue.[26] Yet many of the suitable cells currently identified for human use are difficult to obtain and involve invasive procedures (e.g., skeletal myoblasts, bone marrow cells, adipose-derived stromal cells). For these reasons, there is a big interest in searching for novel stem cells with a higher cardiomyogenic potential than those available (Table 1).[18,27,28]

A new approach consists in the characterization of stem cells from the endometrium isolated during menstrual bleeding. By their main surface markers, differentiation potential, and morphological signs, these cells belong to mesenchymal stem cells. Specific features of this cell type are high clonogenic activity and low capacity to adipocyte differentiation. Potent cardiac precursor-like cells can be harvested from human menstrual blood. This represents a new, non-invasive, and potent source of cardiac

**Table 1.** Properties of cells useful for myocardial regeneration.

| |
|---|
| **Myogenesis or Cardiomyogenesis** |
| Skeletal Myoblasts |
| Smooth Muscle Cells |
| Bone Marrow- Mesenchymal Stem Cells |
| Umbilical Cord Mesenchymal Stem Cells |
| Endometrial Mesenchymal Stem Cells (isolated from the menstrual blood) |
| Pluripotent Stem Cells from Adult Testis |
| Embryonic Stem Cells |
| Fetal and Neonatal Cardiomyocytes |
| Induced Pluripotent Stem Cells (iPSC) |
| Atrial Cardiomyocytes as Biological Pacemakers |
| Adult Ventricular Cardiomyocytes |
| Epicardial Stem Cells |
| Cardiospheres |
| **Angiogenesis and Arteriogenesis Induction** |
| Bone Marrow Mononuclear Fraction |
| Peripheral Blood Mononuclear Fraction |
| Bone Marrow and Peripheral Blood Endothelial Progenitor Cells |
| Umbilical Cord Blood Cells |
| Endothelial Cells |
| Mesothelial Cells from Omentum |
| Adipocyte Derived Stem Cells |
| Menstrual Blood Cells |

stem cell therapeutic material.[29,30] A recent publication[31] showed that menstrual blood-derived mesenchymal cells (MMCs) began beating spontaneously after induction, exhibiting cardiomyocyte-specific action potentials. Cardiac troponin-I-positive cardiomyocytes accounted for 27%–32% of the MMCs *in vitro*. The MMCs proliferated, on average, 28 generations without affecting cardiomyogenic transdifferentiation ability, and expressed mRNA of GATA-4 before cardiomyogenic induction. Transplanted MMCs significantly restored impaired cardiac function, decreasing the myocardial infarction (MI) area in the nude rat model, with tissue of MMC-derived cardiomyocytes observed in the MI area *in vivo*. Thus, MMCs appear to be a potential novel, easily accessible source of material for cardiac stem cell-based therapy. Furthermore, these cells can be used to induce angiogenesis for critical limb ischemia.[32]

In another published study,[33] it was demonstrated that human primordial germ cells and mouse neonatal and adult germline stem cells are pluripotent and show similar properties to embryonic stem cells. This study describes the successful establishment of human adult germline stem cells derived from spermatogonial cells of adult human testis. Cellular and molecular characterization of these cells revealed many similarities to human embryonic stem cells, and the germline stem cells produced teratomas after transplantation into immunodeficient mice. The human adult germline stem cells differentiated into various types of somatic cells of all three germ layers when grown under conditions used to induce the differentiation of human embryonic stem cells. Therefore, it seems that the generation of human adult germline stem cells from testicular biopsies may provide simple and non-controversial access to individual cell-based therapy without the ethical and immunological problems associated with human embryonic stem cells.

Injectable hydrogel biomaterials based on hydrophilic, biocompatible polymers are of interest as a delivery system for cardiac drug or cell therapy. The high water content of these polymers creates a tissue-like environment, and *in-situ* polymerization provides a means of injection and gelation of a cell suspension polymer mixture directly in the site of the infarct.[34–36]

## 6. Tissue Engineering: State of the Art

The stem cell niche, a specialized environment surrounding stem cells, provides crucial support needed for stem cell maintenance. Compromised niche function may lead to the selection of stem cells that no longer depend on self-renewal factors produced by its environment. The objective of stem cell transplantation associated with tissue engineered approaches in cardiology is to create a myocardial repair procedure as a new modality in the treatment of heart failure. If the stem cell niche has aged, it might not be capable of supporting the transplanted stem cells.[37,38]

Tissue engineering is an emerging field (starting in the 1970s), which is based in the use of a combination of cells, engineering materials, and suitable biochemical factors to improve or replace biological functions. Probably the first definition of tissue engineering was by Langer and Vacanti,[39] who stated it to be "an interdisciplinary field that applies the principles of engineering and life sciences toward the development of biological substitutes that restore, maintain, or improve tissue function or a whole organ". Engineering materials can be implanted or "seeded" into a natural or synthetic structure capable of supporting three-dimensional tissue formation (Table 2). These scaffolds are often critical, both *ex vivo* as well as *in vivo*, to recapitulating the *in vivo* milieu and allowing cells to influence their own microenvironments. Such scaffolds serve at least one

**Table 2.** Scaffold materials used in myocardium tissue engineering.

| |
|---|
| **Naturals** |
| Gelatin Meshes |
| Alginate |
| Polyglycolic Acid |
| Collagen I and IV Meshes |
| Fibrin |
| **Synthetics** |
| Polylactic Acid |
| Polyvinyl Alcohol |
| Polyhydroxibutyrate |
| Polyurethane Meshes |
| Elastomeric co-Polymers |
| Polyglactin (Vicryl mesh: Dermagraft) |
| Poly(N-isopropylacrylamide) |
| Poly-co-Caprolactone (PGCL) |
| Non-woven Poly(lactide)- and Poly(glycolide)-based (PLGA) |
| Electrospinning Based Materials (Electrospun Nanofibers) |

of the following purposes: allowing cell attachment and migration; delivering and retaining cells and biochemical factors; enabling diffusion of vital cell nutrients and expressed products; and exerting certain mechanical and biological influences to modify the behavior of the cell phase.[40–46] Specially designed bioreactors systems are used to manufacture tissue *in vitro* which will replace diseased one *in vivo*.[47–49]

To achieve the goal of tissue reconstruction, scaffolds must meet some specific requirements. A high porosity and an adequate pore size are necessary to facilitate cell seeding and diffusion throughout the whole structure of both cells and nutrients. Biodegradability is essential since scaffolds need to be absorbed by the surrounding tissues without the necessity of surgical removal. The rate at which degradation occurs has to coincide as much as possible with the rate of tissue formation. This means that while cells are fabricating their own natural matrix structure around themselves, the scaffold is able to provide structural integrity within the body, and eventually it will break down leaving the neo-tissue, newly formed tissue which will take over the mechanical load. Tissue engineering current clinical applications include specialties such as orthopedics, urology, dermatology, plastic surgery, neurosurgery, dentistry, tracheal replacement and cardiovascular surgery (heart valves and small-caliber vessels).[50–53]

More than a decade after the first reports on successful 3D cardiac cell culture for experimental and potential clinical application, the interest and scientific investigations in the field of myocardial tissue engineering continues to growth. Tissue engineering might contribute to improve the efficiency of cellular therapy for organ regeneration. The objective of cellular cardiomyoplasty is to regenerate the myocardium by the implantation of living cells. However, in ischemic disease the extracellular matrix is often disrupted or destroyed. Therefore it could be important to associate a procedure aiming at regenerating both myocardial cells and the extracellular matrix. Our work is currently focused on evaluating the potential of a biodegradable 3-dimensional matrix seeded with cells and grafted onto the infarcted ventricle.[54–56]

The cardiac connective tissue is mainly composed of collagen, with smaller amounts of elastin, laminin and fibronectin. There are two types of collagen fibers in the normal adult heart: Types I and III which are produced by fibroblasts and myofibroblasts. The fiber Type I represents 80% of collagen protein in the heart, and Type III is near 10%. These fibers provide structural support and give the heart properties that include stiffness and resistance to deformation. They have also shown to be an important role as a link between contractile elements of adjacent myocytes and carrying some information useful for cell function. In the infarcted zone the extracellular myocardial matrix is modified with collagen Type I decreasing from 80% to 40%.

## 7. Development of Bio-Artificial Myocardium

Extracellular matrix remodeling in heart failure (excessive matrix degradation and myocardial fibrosis) contributes to LV dilatation and progressive cardiac dysfunction. Research and development of bio-artificial myocardium is of great clinical interest. The rationale for the use of specific biomaterials is to allow the creation of a micro atmosphere, where the exogenous and endogenous cells find the microenvironmental optimal for repair with a low scar production. The cell microenvironment could be custom designed in order to obtain the release of determined factors or control cellular adhesion or mechanical function. We hypothesize also that an exogenous cellularized matrix would adjust the proportion of collagens Types I and III in the scar zone and in the adjacent and remote zones.

### 7.1 *Pre-clinical studies*

The objective of cellular cardiomyoplasty is to regenerate the myocardium using implantation of living cells. Because the extracellular myocardial matrix is deeply altered in ischemic cardiomyopathies, it seems important to create a procedure aiming at regenerating both myocardial cells and the extracellular matrix. We evaluated the potential of a collagen matrix seeded with cells and grafted onto infarcted ventricles.[54] A myocardial infarction was created in mice using coronary artery ligation. Animals were randomly assigned to 4 local myocardial treatment groups. Group I underwent sham treatment (injection of cell culture medium). Group II underwent injection of human umbilical cord

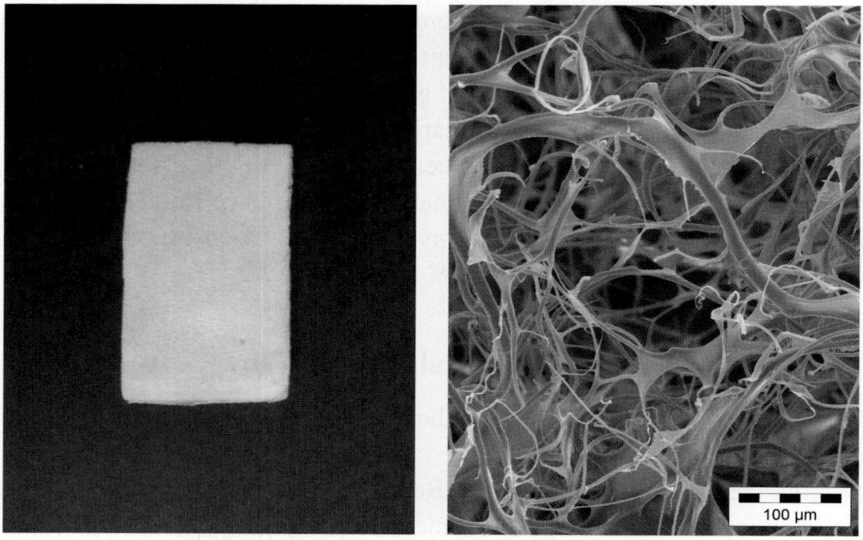


(A) (B)

**Fig. 1.** (**A**) Three-dimensional type 1 collagen matrix for myocardial support and regeneration. Dimensions 5 × 7 × 0.6 cm. (**B**) Electron microscopy of the collagen matrix.

blood mononuclear cells (HUCBCs). Group III underwent injection of HUCBCs and fixation onto the epicardium of a collagen matrix seeded with HUCBCs. Group IV underwent fixation of collagen matrix (without cells) onto the infarct.

### 7.1.1 *Collagen matrix preparation*

Scaffolds were composed of lyophilized, non-denatured, native type I collagen (bovine origin) obtained from a commercially available collagen kit (Pangen 2, Urgo Laboratory, Chenove, France) (Fig. 1). Circular samples of the collagen matrix were obtained using casting cutters; the dimension of each sample was 4 × 3 × 1.5 mm. The patch was then placed into enzyme-linked immunosorbent assay (ELISA) plaques, and 5 million HUCBCs suspended in medium (Medium 199) were seeded onto each matrix. ELISA plaques containing tissue patches were centrifuged for 10 minutes at 900 g to promote regular distribution of HUCBCs into the

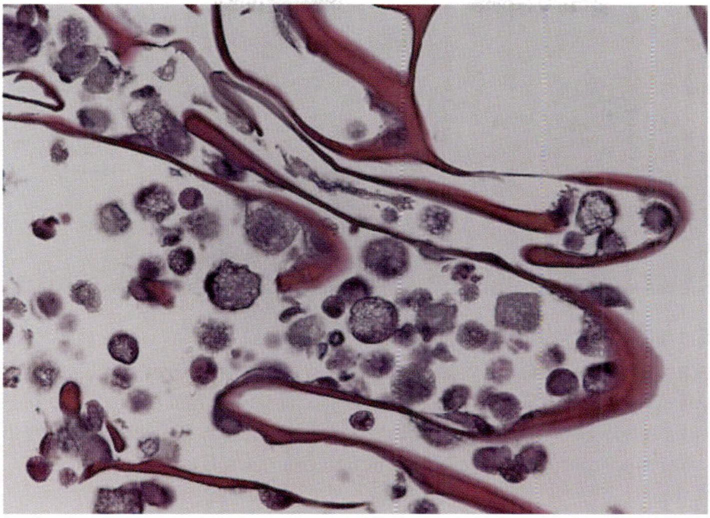

**Fig. 2.** Histological study showing the bone marrow cells (BMC) seeded into the matrix using centrifugation (10 min at 900 g). H.E. stain, magnification × 400.

matrix (Fig. 2). After intra-myocardial injections, the patch prepared immediately before (without cell cultivation) was applied to the surface of the epicardium of the ischemic area and fixed with 2 absorbable sutures (7–0 polyglactin, Vicryl). Echocardiography was performed on post-operative days seven and 45, followed by histological studies.

### 7.1.2 *Results*

Echocardiography showed that the association between the cell-loaded matrix and the intrainfarct cell implants was the most efficient approach to limiting post-ischemic ventricular dilation and remodeling (Fig. 3). Ejection fraction improved in both cell-treated groups. The collagen matrix alone did not improve left ventricular (LV) function and remodeling. Histology in Group III showed fragments of the collagen matrix thickening and protecting the infarct scars. Segments of the matrix were consistently aligned along the LV wall, and cells were assembled within the collagen fibers in large populations.

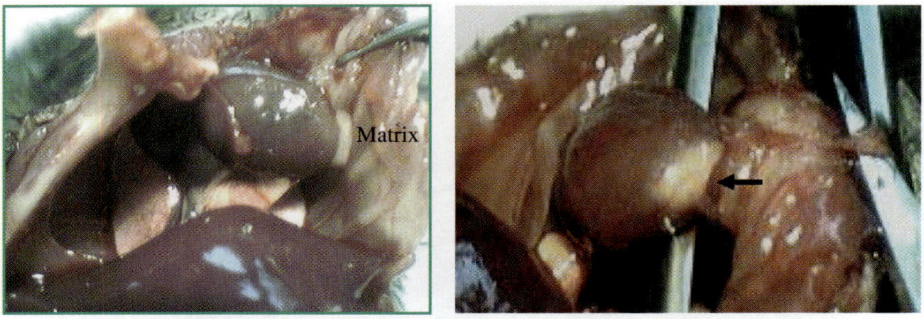


(A) (B)

**Fig. 3.** (**A**) Experimental study designed to assess the effects of a cell-seeded collagen matrix grafted onto the infarcted LV. The ischemic area was first treated with the injection of stem cells followed by the fixation of the collagen matrix. (**B**) After 45 days the matrix and cells were incorporated to the LV infarction zone (arrow).

In conclusion, intra-myocardial injection of HUCBCs preserves LV function following infarction. The use of a cell-seeded matrix combined with cell injections prevents ventricular wall thinning and limits post-ischemic remodeling. This tissue engineering approach seems to improve the efficiency of cellular cardiomyoplasty, and could emerge as a new therapeutic tool for the prevention of adverse remodeling and progressive heart failure.

## 7.2 *MAGNUM clinical trial*

We evaluated the clinical application of tissue engineering procedures using a biological matrix associated with intra-infarct cell therapy. The goal was to develop a bio-artificial myocardium. Thereby the MAGNUM Clinical Trial (**M**yocardial **A**ssistance by **G**rafting a **N**ew **U**pgraded bioartificial **M**yocardium) was conceived to evaluate intrainfarct cell therapy associated with a cell-seeded collagen scaffold grafted onto infarcted ventricles.[55]

In 15 patients (aged 54.2 ± 3.8 years) presenting LV post-ischemic myocardial scars and with indication for a single OP-CABG, autologous mononuclear bone marrow cells (BMC) were implanted during surgery in the scar. A collagen matrix seeded with BMC was added on top of the scarred area (Fig. 4).

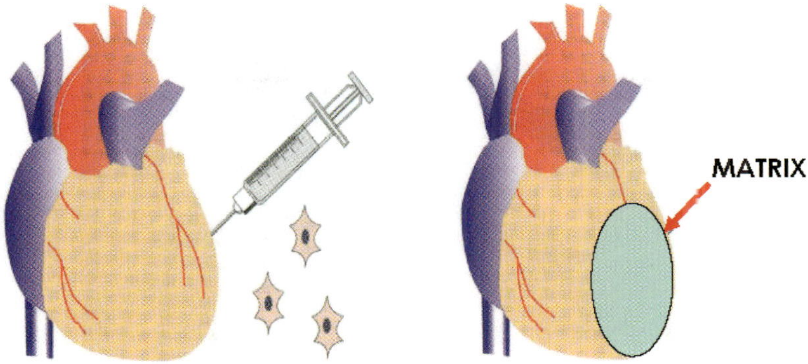


**Fig. 4.** MAGNUM Clinical Trial: surgical approach designed for myocardial support and regeneration. In the same procedure the myocardial infarction scar is treated by stem cells and by a cell-seeded collagen matrix covering the infarcted area.

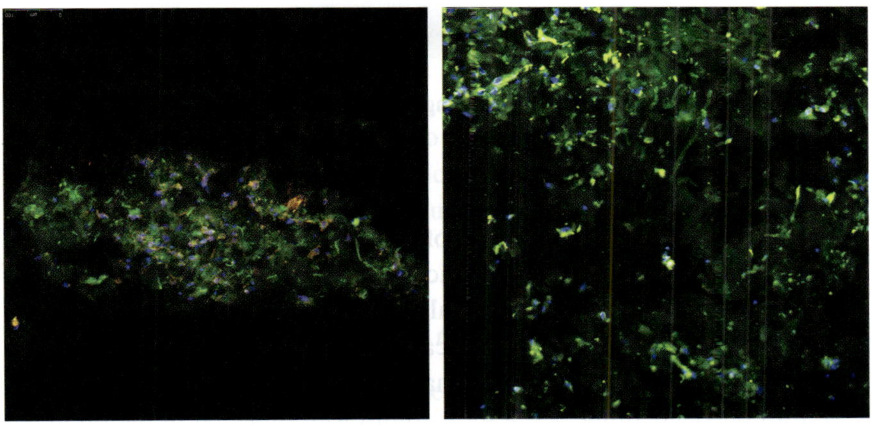

**Fig. 5.** Confocal microscopy showing the 3D collagen matrix (in green) and the seeded cells (blue).

Collagen matrix was prepared from a commercially available CE Mark collagen kit (Pangen 2; Urgo Laboratory, Chenove, France). This 3-dimensional biodegradable matrix (size: $5 \times 7 \times 0.6$ cm) was manufactured using a lyophilized non-denatured, native Type I collagen. The matrix pores measured 50 to 100 $\mu$m. In the operating room, matrices were placed into a petri dish. Afterward, the cell suspension ($250 \pm 28$ million BMC diluted in 10 ml medium) was seeded onto each matrix (Fig. 5).

bone marrow aspiration, bone marrow cell (BMC) injections or matrix seeding, and cellularized matrix surgical implantation onto the epicardium. The number of BMC obtained by crest iliac aspiration can be enough for both treatments. The cell matrix seeding procedures are easily carried out. During surgery, intramyocardial cell injections followed by the fixation of a cellularized matrix onto the infarted area can be performed without any technical problem. MAGNUM trial data suggests that this therapeutic approach is safe. Specifically, there was no evidence of an increased rate of pro-arrhythmic effects. It was found that the thickness of the infarcted wall was significantly greater in the cell-seeded matrix group than in the cell therapy group. A passive girdling effect of the cell-seeded collagen matrix generating a reduction of the ventricular wall stress and improving strain distribution and infarct scar elasticity could explain the functional benefits observed in the matrix group patients (Table 3).

Transplanted BMC and matrix seeded cells may release growth factors that may preserve extracellular matrix and promote the recruitment of cardiac stem cells that would provide a new endogenous pool of contractile cells. In addition, transdifferentiation of BMC-derived haemopoietic stem cells to cardiomyocytes and potential cardiomyogenic

**Table 3.** Benefits of associate cell transplantation with tissue engineering.

| |
|---|
| **Stem Cell Therapy** |
| Improves myocardial viability and reduce infarct scar fibrosis. |
| Recovers viability and function of perinfarct borderzone (hibernating and partially ischemic myocardium). |
| Paracrine antiapoptotic and angiogenic effects. |
| **Collagen Scaffold** |
| Increases the thickness of the infarct scar with viable tissues. |
| Helps to normalize cardiac wall stress in injured regions. |
| Improves diastolic function, ventricular compliance and limits adverse post-ischemic remodelling. |
| Improves engraftment of the transplanted cells |
| Promotes formation of new vessels (angiogenesis and arteriogenesis) |
| Induces regeneration of the extracellular collagen matrix. |

properties of mesenchymal BMC can account for the beneficial effects of this new therapeutic procedure.

Future matrix improvements would include the cross-linking of anti-apoptotic and angiogenic factors. It will be also important to decrease the inflammatory response and prolongation of the absorption delay by additional chemical and/or physical cross-linking treatments. Electrostimulation and shear stress could be incorporated to precondition matrices. Novel technologies such as nanofabrication, molecular bio-imaging, genetic reprogramming, and cell fusion techniques will contribute to the development of this field.[56]

## 8. New Developments

### 8.1 *Elastomeric scaffolds and membranes*

Polymeric networks can be tailored to match desired mechanical properties by the combination of suitably chosen co-monomers and also by controlling the crystallinity (in case the polymer can crystallize) and/or the macroscopic and microscopic porosity of the network.[58,59] The porous architecture of elastomeric networks can be engineered to combine not only host cells but also modulate solute diffusion and material degradation kinetics.

### 8.2 *Nanomaterials gels*

Recently, good progress in the design and fabrication of synthetic biomaterials with biomimetic characteristics has been accomplished in the field of nanotechnology for direct applications in biomedicine. The main purpose of these materials is to display structural and functional properties similar to extracellular matrices, containing truly three-dimensional nanonetworks and eventual control in the delivery and effective concentration of "therapeutic drugs." Nanomaterials are emerging as the main candidates to ensure the achievement of a proper instructive cellular niche with good drug release/administration properties. Synthetic nanomaterials are attractive platforms because of their pure composition, predictive toxicology, target specificity, low manufacturing costs, control in degradability, etc. Proteins, peptides and polysaccharides are top on the list for their versatility in nanomaterial design and fabrication. The 3-dimensional control of microenvironment is fundamental for cell differentiation, morphogenesis, and survival when is strictly accompanied by well-defined biophysical and geometrical properties.[60,61] For instance, angiogenesis control in the therapeutic context of myocardial regeneration will require the use of a highly innovative nanotechnological platform for proper cardiac tissue regeneration. It is important to remark that VEGF signaling is critical for angiogenesis as well as differentiation of a number of other cell types. Angiogenesis is a focus of not only developmental biologists, but also of cancer biologists. Angiogenic inhibitory molecules and pathways could potentially be used to "starve" tumors.

Until now, scaffolds used for myocardial repair have been structurally incompatible with recapitulating cardiac anisotropy. Tissue engineering microfabrication techniques have been used to create an accordion-like honeycomb microstructure in poly(glycerol sebacate), which yields porous, elastomeric three-dimensional (3D) scaffolds with controllable stiffness and anisotropy.[62] Accordion-like honeycomb scaffolds with cultured neonatal rat heart cells demonstrated utility through closely matched mechanical properties compared to native adult rat RV myocardium, with stiffness controlled by polymer curing time, heart cell contractility inducible by electric field stimulation with directionally-dependent electrical excitation thresholds and, greater heart cell alignment than isotropic control scaffolds. Prototype bilaminar scaffolds with 3D interconnected pore networks yielded electrically excitable grafts with multilayered neonatal rat heart cells. Accordion-like honeycombs can thus overcome principal structural-mechanical limitations of previous scaffolds, promoting the formation of grafts with aligned heart cells and mechanical properties more closely resembling native myocardium.

### 8.3 *Effect of mechanical stimuli on stem cells*

The positive influence of dynamic flow and fluid shear stress has been described for primary hepatocytes, chondrocytes, and osteoblasts.[63] Progress has been slower in the area of large-scale expansion of stem cells and their progeny-technology that would be necessary to meet clinical demands with regard to cardiac tissue engineering. Since a supportive influence of shear stress on active mesodermal differentiation was observed,[64] this approach could favour cardiac differentiation in other types of stem cells, such as bone marrow-derived stem cells.

## 8.4 *Cardiac pacing and myogenic cell transplantation: the dynamic duo*

### 8.4.1 *In-vitro cell electrostimulation*

*Ex-vivo* cell electrostimulation was applied by our group in the driving process of conditioning bone marrow stem cells towards cardiac-type myogenic cells. *In vitro* electrostimulation of human bone marrow cell cultures for myogenic preconditioning have been performed using a bipolar system, including an external pacemaker and specific electrodes, submerged into the culture medium. We induced AC current using balanced charge capacitive coupled biphasic pulses. After three weeks, we observed an increase of cell multiplication, improved cell organization, and cardiomyogenic pre-differentiation. Since stem cells can differentiate into fibroblasts after implantation in myocardial scars, this method could be proposed to precondition cells or a matrix (grafted with cells) before implantation.[21,65,66]

### 8.4.2 *In-vivo cell electrostimulation*

Atrial synchronized biventricular pacing is indicated in many heart failure patients to correct conduction disorders associated with chronic systolic and diastolic dysfunction. Electrostimulation associated with cellular cardiomyoplasty was proposed by our group to transform passive cell therapy into "dynamic cellular support". The principles of electrophysiological conditioning of muscle fibers (e.g., dynamic cardiomyoplasty) was applied by our group in cellular cardiomyoplasty since skeletal myofibers express predominantly fatigue sensitive fast myosin, which is not suitable for cardiac work. Electrostimulation of the ventricles following skeletal myoblasts implantation induced the contraction of the transplanted cells and a higher expression of slow myosin, the renal artery.[7] Some examples of the different modes of stem cell delivery targeting different organs are shown in Table 1.

## 3. Traditional Cell Immobilization Techniques: Potential in Stem Cell Delivery

Immobilization of cells are being defined as the physical confinement or localization of intact cells to a defined region of space without appreciable loss of catalytic activity.[21] While stem cells show significant therapeutic potential, there are limitations precluding their use in clinical or supplemental therapy. To provide functional properties, a minimum level of viable cells is required. However, the stability of stem cell cultures is often significantly diminished prior to administration. Like other cell lines, stem cells are also sensitive to its microenvironmental parameters, such as oxygen and pH.

There are currently a myriad of techniques available for immobilization of stem cells on a variety of natural and synthetic polymer supports. The selection of the supports is very much dependant on the type of application. The search for matrices which provide facile, secure immobilization with good interaction with substrates, and which conform in shape, size, density to the use for which they are intended, still continues. A variety of techniques and supports investigated for immobilization have been reviewed.[22–25]

Hydrogels, which chemically or physically hold the cells to provide stability, structural support, or immuno-isolation, have been investigated for cell immobilization in biomedical applications. For this, it must have proper permeability to allow sufficient diffusion and transport of oxygen and essential nutrients, metabolic waste, and secretory products across the hydrogel network.[26] This, along with adequate chemical and mechanical stability of the hydrogel, determines the success of the immobilization process. Biocompatibility is another important parameter for successful cultivation of cells within the polymer. The hydrogel must be non-toxic, and it should be relatively inert and not interfere with cell function.[27] For *in vivo* applications, host tissue must accept the cell-hydrogel transplant with only minor inflammatory response.[28]

**Table 1.** Modes of stem cell administration targeting liver, heart and kidney.

| Target organs | Stem cell delivery route | Effects: Strengths | Effects: Limitations | Reference |
|---|---|---|---|---|
| LIVER | Intravenous | Convenient; less invasive | Immunoreaction; entrapment of cells in lungs | 8,9,10,11 |
| | Intrahepatic | Conducive to the cells repopulating in the liver | Invasive method | 5 |
| | Intraperitoneal | Higher amount of cells can be delivered; direct delivery at the site without much loss | Probability of mechanical damage to the cells | 12 |
| | Portal vein | Accelerates hepatic regeneration | Portal hypertension; embolism of lung; invasive method | 13 |
| | Intrasplenic | Blood from spleen drains directly into liver. Thus this method can maintain high conc. of the released cytokines and factors needed for the diseased liver regeneration. | Portal vein embolism; impairment of hepatic microcirculation and function; organ embolisation | 14,15 |
| HEART | Transepicardial | Large number of cells can be delivered | Highly invasive | 16 |
| | Intravenous | Widely used in clinical settings; convenient way | Lack of specific targeting; very few cells reach the affected area; less useful for treating chronic myocardial ischemia | 17,18 |

*(Continued)*

**Table 1.** *(Continued)*

| Target organs | Stem cell delivery route | Effects: Strengths | Effects: Limitations | Reference |
|---|---|---|---|---|
| | Transendocardial | Good for therapies that do not need any target; imaging technologies associated with the method makes it a convenient way | Meticulous method; lack of accuracy with fluoroscopy in two dimensional orientation | 19 |
| | Trans-coronary-venous | Greater cell retention potential; good safety profile | Lack of site-specificity; technically difficult; entrapment of cells in the microvasculature of the lungs, liver and other tissues | 20 |
| KIDNEY | Intra-arterial | Efficient engraftment into glomerular and tubular structures during the early phase of ischemia reperfusion injury | The optimal time frame for acute renal failure stem cell therapy is unknown | 7 |

Three main methods for immobilizing cells in hydrogels are available: adhesion, matrix entrapment, and microencapsulation.[29] Adhesion is based on the attachment of cells to the polymer substrate. This method is effective for surface binding, either on top of gel films or within hydrogel foams. Immobilization by adhesion is generally used to stabilize cells for culture or analytical procedures, provide a structural template directing cell growth and differentiation, or both.

Matrix entrapment is sometimes called macroencapsulation when the hydrogel isolates the entrapped cells and provides immunoprotection. Hydrogels are ideal for matrix entrapment because the crosslinks of both synthetic and naturally derived hydrogels provide the essential 3-dimensional mesh, and porous network to prevent the cells from diffusing into surrounding medium while allowing the transport of substrates, wastes, and other essential molecules *via* the bulk fluid. In addition to *in vitro* applications shared with the adhesion technique, matrix entrapment can be used with *in vivo* studies to protect transplanted cell-hydrogel complexes from mechanical and immunological damage.

Microencapsulation involves utilizing a spherical, semi-permeable, thin and strong membrane to surround a liquid or solid matrix containing biological material, including living cells. Its primary purpose is to protect the encapsulated cells from the host's immune system, allowing cell survival and function.[29] Of these, the most widely used and studied immobilization technique is the entrapment of cells within a polymeric matrix. Entrapment techniques based on the formation of thermal and ionotropic gels have proven useful for live cell applications. An array of polymers, such as agarose, alginate, chitosan has been chosen as the support material for the gel matrix. Recognizing the complexities inherent to the process, a variety of materials have been investigated for use in matrix entrapment of cells. The major polymers currently under investigation for the encapsulation of live cells include alginate, HEMA-MMA and other hydrogels. However, this technology also has its backlogs. The support materials for matrix entrapment are insufficiently immunoprotective and have shown in certain cases to instigate an inflammatory response.[30] In addition, diffusional properties and inadequate mechanical strength limit the proliferation of the entrapped cells. Furthermore, diffusional limitations of both substrates and metabolic by-products can lead to the development of steep gradients regarding pH and inhibitory products that can hinder the viability and metabolic activity of the entrapped stem cells. Therefore, despite reported advantages, the associated drawbacks of immobilizing live cells by entrapment in gel matrices have limited the influence of this technology in commercial and experimental products.

## 4. Introduction to Artificial Cell: A Promising Stem Cell Delivery System

It has been reported that cell immobilization can lead to modification of cell wall and cell membrane compositions.[31] The physiological alteration may also have a profound impact on cell stress resistance. Although not much is known about the physiological effects of microencapsulation technique on the cells, the data on cellular physiological alteration of other immobilization methods provide us a way on how to study the microencapsulated cells. There are reports that microencapsulated hybridoma cells presented a better growth pattern, and improved their viability and antibody production.[32] Microencapsulation of cells is being studied extensively to confront limitations with traditional immobilization technologies. The concept of microencapsulation in "artificial cells", which are ultrathin polymeric or biological membranes, were first prepared in the laboratory of T.M.S. Chang at McGill University in Canada in the 1960's.[4] Artificial cell microencapsulation is used to encapsulate biologically active materials in specialized ultrathin semi-permeable polymer membranes.[33] The principle of mammalian cell microencapsulation is that the permeability of the membrane is engineered to allow the passage of oxygen, important nutrients, and cellular products, but it stops the ingress of immunoglobulins or immune cells responsible for transplant rejection.[34] The primary application of encapsulation is immunoprotection of healthy xenogeneic or allogeneic cells for transplantation into a recipient in need of functional replacement of a metabolic tissue. The protected cells then function and secrete an effective supply of the needed hormone, protein, or other bioactive secretory product for the host. Perhaps the well investigated clinical application of microencapsulation and subsequent transplantation of cells is in the treatment of diabetes. The semi-permeable membrane allows the passage of oxygen, nutrients, and cell products, including insulin as needed, but it protects the transplanted cells from the patient's immune system. In addition to diabetes, microencapsulation of cells has the potential as a treatment for several other diseases and disorders such as Parkinson's disease or liver failure.[35,36] The artificial cell concept has a lot of applications for microencapsulation-based oral therapy in renal and liver failure, physiologically responsive gene therapy, as well as somatic gene therapy.[37] Few applications of artificial cells based on encapsulation mammalian cells are summarized in Table 2, while Table 3 mentions some biotechnologically important micro-encapsulated recombinant micro-organisms, and describes their mode of action by overexpressing certain therapeutically important proteins. Fig. 1 shows how an encapsulation membrane serves as an immunobarrier, allows the bidirectional exchange of small molecules, including nutrients, wastes, selected substrates and products, and prevents the passage of large substances such as cells, immunocytes and antibodies.[60,61] Thus, cell encapsulation promises immuno-isolation, which has initiated a flurry of research into bio-artificial organs and tissue engineering. Recent advances in molecular biology, cell biology, biotechnology, nanotechnology and other areas have resulted in rapid developments in this area for basic research and for gene therapy, enzyme therapy, cell therapy, blood substitutes, liver support systems and other areas. Significant advances have made the translation of this concept to clinical use, for example, in the treatment of Type 1 diabetes using encapsulated islets, increasingly practicable. Accompanying these myriad avenues of research has been the development of a multitude of polymers from which to choose when encapsulating a given cell species. In order to successfully encapsulate a cell while maintaining its function, a polymer with appropriate mechanical strength, pore size, capsule uniformity, degradation characteristics, biocompatibility and low immunogenicity must be chosen.

### 4.1 *Designing of artificial cells for use in stem cell therapy*

Designing microcapsules for use in transplantation or for oral administration requires a subtle balance which optimizes capsule robustness, while maintaining cell viability and biocompatibility. The use of different membranes allows for variations in permeability, mass transfer,

**Table 2.** Examples of artificial cell usage for other cell therapeutic applications.

| Targeted disease | Microcapsule membrane polymer | Encapsulated/ coencapsulated cells | Mode of action | Ref. |
|---|---|---|---|---|
| Testosterone deficiency | APA | Leydig cells | Secretion of testosterone | 38 |
| Cancer | APA | CHO cells | Metalloproteinase 2 secretion stops angiogenesis | 39 |
| Bioartificial pancreas, diabetes | Alg-polylysine-polyethyl-eneimine/APA | Rat and hamster islets | Secretion of insulin | 40–46 |
| Myocardial infarction | APA | CHO cells | VEGF expression helps in angiogenesis | 47 |
| Diabetes | Alginate-poly-l-ornithine | Rat Sertoli's cells with islet cell | Higher insulin release | 48 |
| Hyper-bilirubinemia | APA | Hepatocytes | Lower blood total bilirubin level and remove ammonia | 49,50 |
| Treatment of hypopara-thyroidism | Alginate hydrogel | Parathyroid cells | Secretion of intact parathyroid hormone | 51,52 |
| Suppression of ovarian and colon cancer | APA | Inducible nitric oxide synthase expressing cells | Overexpression of inducible nitric oxide synthase prevents cancer | 53 |
| Pancreatic carcinoma | Cellulose sulphate | HEK cells expressing CYP 2B1 | Secretion of CYP2B1 activates ifosfamide needed for treating pancreatic cancer | 54,55 |
| Dermal diseases | Alginate + $CaCl_2$ | Skin fibroblasts | Various volatile organic compounds released from skin fibroblasts determines the physiological state of skin | 56 |

**Table 3.** Examples of artificial cell usage using microorganisms.

| Targeted therapy | Encapsulated bacterial cells | Proposed mode of action | References |
|---|---|---|---|
| Kidney dialysis | *E. coli* DH5 | Recombinant *E. coli* DH5 cells overexpress *Klebsiella aerogenes* urease enzymes that lower elevated blood levels of urea and ammonia. | 57,58 |
| High blood cholesterol levels | Lactobacillus Plantarum LP80 | Overproduction of bile salt hydrolase (BSH) enzyme from the genetically modified cells deconjugates intraluminal bile acids making them less likely to be reabsorbed into the enterohepatic circulation, causing *de novo* synthesis of bile acids in the liver from blood serum cholesterol. | 59 |
| Colon cancer | *Lactobacillus Plantarum* LP80 and *L. reuteri* | The BSH enzyme is overproduced by LP80 (pCBH1) cells and hydrolyzes available conjugated bile acids in the intestinal lumen. *L. reuteri*, shown to precipitate and bind bile acids, then binds the deconjugated bile acids making them incapable of leaving the microcapsule and thus less bioavailable for exfoliation of the gastrointestinal tract and any potential carcinogenic damage. | 59 |

mechanical stability, biocompatibility, and buffering capability that can be exploited to fit a desired application. The mass transport properties of a membrane are critical, since the influx rate of molecules, essential for cell survival and proliferation, and the outflow rate of metabolic waste ultimately determine the viability of encapsulated cells. For example, while a certain minimum pore size and maximum wall thickness are

## 5. Potential and Current Progress of Artificial Cells in Stem Cell Therapy

Stem cell transplantation has emerged as a potential therapeutic tool for treating myocardial infarction, renal failure, as well as in liver diseases. However, the donors (if allogeneic or xenogeneic) stem cells in general behave with strong immunogenicity when transplanted in a mismatched histocompatibility recipient. So, it is always considered safer and more desirable to use autologous stem cells for this purpose. Then there comes another hurdle of culturing the autologous stem cells *ex vivo*, which proved to be very time consuming, economically unfavorable, and logistically impossible. Stolzing *et al.* has shown that adult stem cells obtained from elderly donors or those with diabetes, renal failure and severe ischemic heart disease differentiates very slowly and shows early signs of apoptosis.[63] Thus, these drawbacks of autologous stem cells inhibit its successful implementations as a potential therapeutic tool. Hence, innovation of a device that will be able to shield the donor allogeneic or xenogeneic stem cells from the host immune system, and at the same time will be able to perform its function, will be of immense importance at this stage.

Thus, artificial cells emerge as an ideal delivery system in stem cell transplantation. The artificial stem cells can efficiently micro-encapsulate the donor stem cells and protect them from the host immune system. Moreover, its proven improved mass transfer of the substrate and product between the external environment and the inside stem cell containing phase (due to the smaller size of the microcapsules and higher surface-to-volume ratio), will make the cell microenvironment less hostile and more hospitable for a long time inside the donor body. Artificial cells have high chemical and mechanical stability in a wide range of solvents under various adverse conditions,[64] which increases its range of application in delivering stem cells to different parts of the body. The possibility of incorporating water-soluble nutrients, substrates, and differentiation inducing factors inside the artificial cells to enhance stem cell viability and functionality, is an added advantage. Fig. 4 shows some probable applicable areas of artificial stem therapy. Table 5 represents some recent applications of artificial cells in stem cell research.

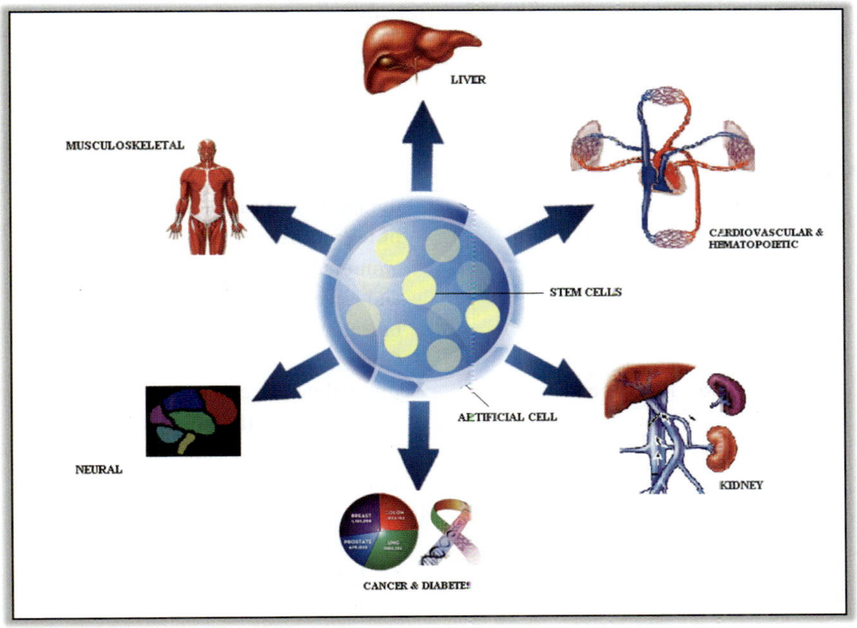


**Fig. 4.** Probable organs and diseases for application of microencapsulated stem cells.

**Table 5.** Examples of current artificial cells for stem cell therapy.

| Microcapsule membrane polymer | Encapsulated cells | Mode of action | Reference |
|---|---|---|---|
| Agarose | Mouse embryonic stem cells | Formation of embryoid body-like spherical tissues | 65 |
| Alginate poly-L-lysine | Embryonic stem cell line D3 | Differentiation into hepatocytes | 66, 67 |
| Alginate hydrogel | Murine embryonic stem cells | Osteogenic differentiation | 68 |
| Alginate poly-L-lysine | Human foetal myoblast stem cells | Secretion of growth factors | 69 |

(*Continued*)

**Table 5.** (*Continued*)

| Microcapsule membrane polymer | Encapsulated cells | Mode of action | Reference |
|---|---|---|---|
| Alginate poly-L-lysine | Coencapsulation of bone marrow stem cells with hepatocytes | Stem cells increase the durability and functioning of hepatocytes; it helps in ammonia removal *in vitro* and lowers blood total bilirubin level in treated Gunn rats | 70,71 |
| Calcium alginate hydrogel | Human embryonic stem cells | Better maintenance of stem cells in an undifferentiated form without exposure to animal feeder layer | 72 |
| Ultrahigh-viscosity alginate | Murine mesenchymal progenitor cell transfected with cDNA encoding bone morphogenetic protein 4 | Helps in cartilage repair by enhancing the production of chondrogenic components; suppresses chondrogenic hypertrophy | 73 |

In a study by Maguire *et al*,[66] embryonic stem cells were encapsulated in alginate-poly-l-lysine microcapsule, and their viability, differentiation potential and differentiated cellular function was analyzed. The report showed that when cultured in Iscove's modified Dulbecco's medium in encapsulated form, the stem cells can be almost fully viable for at least 20 days post-encapsulation. The Iscove's modified Dulbecco's medium is used to induce differentiation of the embryonic stem cells into hepatocytes. Hepatocyte function was evaluated by measuring urea secretion and albumin synthesis. By varying the cell densities for encapsulation, they found that at five million cells per ml the cells have maximum functional activity as shown on the 20th day post-encapsulation (Fig. 5A). To further confirm the functional activity of the differentiated embryonic stem cells, the stem cells (at five million cells per ml seeding density) were also cultured in knock-out DMEM containing ESGRO to prevent differentiation.

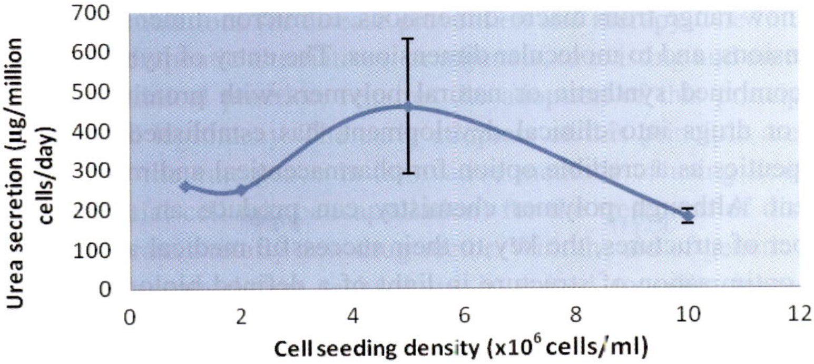


**(A)**

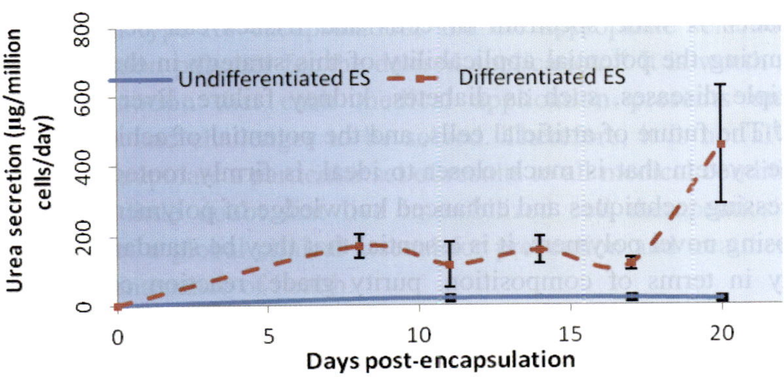


**(B)**

**Fig. 5** (**A**) Relation between initial encapsulated embryonic stem cell seeding density (cells/ml) and urea secretion (µg/million cells/day) at day 20 post-encapsulation.[66] (**B**) Urea secretion profile from encapsulated differentiated embryonic stem cells and undifferentiated stem cells with respect to time (days). Graphs designed from data.[66]

Comparison of the differentiated and non-differentiated encapsulated cells confirms that it is the differentiation of the stem cells into hepatocyte that causes the secretion of the urea, which was not detected in the undifferentiated one (Fig. 5B).

## 6. Conclusion and Future Works

At the start of the 21st century, research is poised at the interphase of material chemistry, polymer science and nanomaterial science. Artificial

32. Orive G, Hernandez RM, Gascon AR, *et al.* Survival of different cell lines in alginate-agarose microcapsules. *Eur J Pharm Sci* 2003;18:23–30.
33. Prakash S, Chang TMS. Preparation and *in vitro* analysis of microencapsulated genetically-engineered *Escherichia coli* dh5 cells for urea and ammonia removal. *Biotechnol Bioeng* 1995;46(6):621–626.
34. Christenson L, Dionne K, Lysaught M. Biomedical application of immobilized cells. In: *Fundamentals of Animal Cell Encapsulation and Immobilization* (ed.) Goosen MFA. CRC Press, Boca Raton, FL, 1993, pp. 7–41.
35. Chang TM. Hybrid artificial cells: Microencapsulation of living cells. *ASAIO J* 1992;38:128–130.
36. Sefton MV, Stevenson WTK. Microencapsulation of live animal-cells using polyacrylates. *Adv Polymer Sci* 1993;107:143–197.
37. Prakash S, Jones ML. Artificial cell therapy: New strategies for the therapeutic delivery of live bacteria. *J Biomed Biotechnol* 2005;14:44–56.
38. Machluf M, Orsola A, Boorjian S, *et al.* Microencapsulation of Leydig cells: a system for testosterone supplementation. *Endocrinology* 2003;144:4975–4979.
39. Jiang Q, Zhang S-Z, Peng J-P, Wang X-L. Preparation and *in vitro* studies of microencapsulated cells releasing human tissue inhibitor of metalloproteinase-2. *J Zhejiang Univ Sci B* 2005;6(9):859–864.
40. Sun AM, O'Shea GM, Goosen MF. Injectable microencapsulated islet cells as a bioartificial pancreas. *Appl Biochem Biotechnol* 1984;10:87–99.
41. Hamaguchi K, Tatsumoto N, Fujii S, *et al.* Microencapsulation of pancreatic islets. A technique and its application to culture and transplantation. *Diabetes Res Clin Pract* 1986;2(6):337–345.
42. Sun AM. Microencapsulation of pancreatic islet cells: a bioartificial endocrine pancreas. *Methods Enzymol* 1988;137:575–580.
43. Soon-Shiong P, *et al.* Insulin independence in a type 1 diabetic patient after encapsulated islet transplantation. *Lancet* 1994;343:950–951.
44. Duvivier-Kali VF, Omer A, Parent RJ, *et al.* Complete protection of islets against allorejection and autoimmunity by a simple barium–alginate membrane. *Diabetes* 2001;50:1698–1705.
45. Sakai S, Ono T, Ijima H, Kawakami K. Synthesis and transport characterization of alginate/aminopropyl–silicate/alginate microcapsule: application to bioartificial pancreas. *Biomaterials* 2001;22:2827–2834.
46. De Vos P, Hamel AF, Tatarkiewicz K. Considerations for successful transplantation of encapsulated pancreatic islets. *Diabetologia* 2002;45:159–173.

47. Zhang H, Zhu S-J, Wang W, *et al.* Transplantation of microencapsulated genetically modified xenogeneic cells augments angiogenesis and improves heart function. *Gene Therapy* 2008;15:40–48.
48. Luca G, Calafiore R, Basta G, *et al.* Improved function of rat islets upon co-microencapsulation with Sertoli's cells in alginate/poly-L-ornithine. *AAPS PharmSciTech* 2001;2(3):E15.
49. Bruni S, Chang TMS. Encapsulated hepatocytes for controlling hyper-bilirubinemia in Gunn Rats. *Int J Artif Organs* 1991;14:239–241.
50. Bruni S, Chang TMS. Kinetics of UDP glucuronosyl–transferase in bilirubin conjugation by encapsulated hepatocytes for transplantation into Gunn rats. *J Artif Organs* 1995;19:449–457.
51. Hasse C, Schrezenmeir J, Stinner B, *et al.* Successful allotransplantation of microencapsulated parathyroids in rats. *World J Surg* 1994;18:630–34.
52. Decker GA, Stark JH, Botha JR, *et al.* Allotransplantation of parathyroid cells. *Lancet* 1995;345:124.
53. Xu W, Liu L, Charles IG. Microencapsulated iNOS expressing cells cause tumor suppression in mice. *FASEB J* 2002;16:213–215.
54. Löhr M, Hoffmeyer A, Kröger J *et al.* Microencapsulated cell-mediated treatment of inoperable pancreatic carcinoma. *Lancet* 2001;357:1591–1592.
55. M. Löhr, Bago ZT, Bergmeister H. Cell therapy using microencapsulated 293 cells transfected with a gene construct expressing CYP2B1, an ifosfamide converting enzyme, instilled intra-arterially in patients with advanced-stage pancreatic carcinoma: a phase I/II study. *J Mol Med* 1999;77:393–398.
56. Acevedo C, Sánchez E, Reyes J, Young M. Volatile organic compounds produced by human skin. *Cells Biol Res* 2007;40:347–355.
57. Prakash S, Chang TMS. Microencapsulated genetically engineered live *E-coli* DH5 cells administered orally to maintain normal plasma urea level in uremic rats. *Nature Med* 1996;2:883–887.
58. Chang TMS, Prakash S. Microencapsulated genetically engineered microorganisms for clinical application. *[6,217,859]* 4-17-2001. U.S. 7-31-1997.
59. Jones M, Chen HM, Ouyang W, Metz T, Prakash S. Deconjugation of bile acids with immobilized genetically engineered *Lactobacillus plantarum* 80 (pCBH1) cells and their potential for live cell therapy. *Cell Transplant* 2003;12:196–197.
60. Chang TMS, Prakash S. Therapeutic uses of microencapsulated genetically engineered cells. *Mol Med Today* 1998;4(5):221–227.

61. Orive G, Hernández RM, Rodríguez Gascón A, *et al.* History, challenges and perspectives of cell microencapsulation. *Trends Biotechnol* 2004;22(2): 87–92.
62. Babensee JE, Cornelius RM, Brash JL, Sefton MV. Immunoblot analysis of proteins associated with HEMA-MMA microcapsules: Human serum proteins *in vitro* and rat proteins following implantation. *Biomaterials* 1998; 19(7–9):839–849.
63. Stolzing A, Scutt A. Age-related impairment of mesenchymal progenitor cell function. *Aging Cell* 2006;1:1–12.
64. Green KD, Gill IS, Khan JA, Vulfson EN. Microencapsulation of yeast cells and their use as a biocatalyst in organic solvents. *Biotechnol Bioeng* 1996;49:535–543.
65. Sakai S, Hashimoto I, Kawakami K. Production of cell-enclosing hollow-core agarose microcapsules *via* jetting in water-immiscible liquid paraffin and formation of embryoid body-like spherical tissues from mouse ES cells enclosed within these microcapsules. *Biotechnol Bioeng* 2008;99:235–243.
66. Maguire T, Novik E, Schloss R, Yarmush M. Alginate-PLL microencapsulation: effect on the differentiation of embryonic stem cells into hepatocytes. *Biotechnol Bioeng* 2005;93(3):581–591.
67. Maguire TJ, Novik EI, Schloss R, Yarmush ML. Alginate encapsulation and hepatic differentiation of embryonic stem cells bioengineering conference, 2005. *Proc IEEE 31st Annual Northeast.*
68. Hwang Y, Cho J, Tay F *et al.* The use of murine embryonic stem cells, alginate encapsulation, and rotary microgravity bioreactor in bone tissue engineering. *Biomaterials* 2009;30:499–507.
69. Li AA, Bourgeois J, Potter M, Chang PL. Isolation of human foetal myoblasts and its application for microencapsulation. *J Cell Mol Med* 2008; 12(1):271–280.
70. Liu Z, Chang TMS. Effects of bone marrow cells on hepatocytes: when co-cultured or co-encapsulated together. *Artif Cells Blood Substit Immobil Biotechnol* 2000;28:365–374.
71. Liu ZC, Chang TMS. Coencapsulation hepatocytes and bone marrow stem cells: *In vitro* conversion of ammonia and *in vivo* studies on the lowering of bilirubin in Gunn rats after transplantation. *Int J Artif Organs* 2003;26: 491–497.

72. Siti-Ismail N, Bishop AE, Polak JM, Mantalaris A. The benefit of human embryonic stem cell encapsulation for prolonged feeder-free maintenance. *Biomaterials* 2008;29:3946–3952.
73. Steinert A, Weber M, Dimmler A, *et al.* Chondrogenic differentiation of mesenchymal progenitor cells encapsulated in ultrahighviscosity alginate. *J Orthop Res* 2003;21(6):1090–1097.
74. Prakash S, Bhathena J. Live bacterial cells as orally delivered therapeutics. *Expert Opin Biol Ther* 2005;5(10):1281–1301.
75. Chen HM, Wei OY, Bisi LY, *et al.* Reaction of chitosan with genipin and its fluorogenic attributes for potential microcapsule membrane characterization. *J Biomed Mater Res Part A* 2005;75A(4):917–927.
76. Paul A, Ge Y, Prakash S, Shum-Tim D. Microencapsulated stem cells for tissue repairing: implications in cell-based myocardial therapy. *Regen Med* 2009;4(5):733–745.

# PART III

## APPLICATIONS OF CELL THERAPY — FROM BENCH TO BEDSIDE

applicability, have fueled much interest in these versatile cells.[1] The "gold-standard" of stem cells are the embryonic-source stem cells, of which embryonic stem cells (ESC) are the best studied type. Possessing near totipotent differentiation ability, ESCs are derived from the inner cell mass of pre-implantation embryos and are able to differentiate into all cells of different germ layers as well as germ cells. The derivation of mouse ESCs in the 1980's was a landmark achievement,[2,3] ushering in the new field of transgenic mice research. Isolation of the human counterpart was successfully achieved in 1998 and hailed as a major breakthrough.[4] However, while the pluripotency of human ESCs is likely similar to mouse ESCs, the human cells are much more difficult to culture *in vitro* and have been shackled by ethical problems given the need to destroy an embryo in the isolation process. In addition, the tumorigenicity of ESCs has yet to be resolved. A very similar population of stem cells coined the "inducible pluripotent stem" (iPS) cells have recently been isolated and gained much interest of late. Terminally differentiated cells can be 'reprogrammed' back to pluripotency by the addition of a handful of genes.[5–7] These cells have been touted as the "new stem cell of choice," since theoretically it would be possible to establish donor-specific stem cells with ESC-like pluripotency without ethical or immunological concern by using this technology. However, several problems still preclude iPS from clinical use in the near future, including the use of viral vectors for introduction of genes, the inclusion of oncogenes in the genetic "cocktail," and *in vivo* teratoma formation. Thus, despite the pluripotency of ESCs and iPS, clinical application still awaits solutions to these significant matters.

Adult stem cells (ASCs), also known as somatic stem cells, are another broad category of stem cells. ASCs are able to self renew, but in a much more limited matter than ESCs, and are also lineage-restricted in their differentiation capacity, differentiating into cells of the organ of origin of the ASC. The first ASCs to be identified were the hematopoeitic stem cells (HSCs) of the bone marrow (BM), and most of our knowledge regarding ASC biology has been derived from studies of this population of post-natal stem cells.[8] To date, ASCs from a number of other organ systems have been isolated, including the brain, liver, pancreas, and gastrointestinal tract.[9–11] Moreover, a second population of progenitor/stem cells have been identified in the BM: the mesenchymal stromal or stem cells (MSCs) with multipotent potential. Recent *in vitro* and *in vivo* data show that in addition to differentiation into mesodermal lineages of osteoblast, adipocytes, chondrocytes, and myocytes,[12,13] MSCs are able to differentiate into phenotypes of another germ layer, including neural cells and hepatocytes.[14–17] These reports overturning the long-held dogma of lineage-restricted differentiation have generated much excitement, since it now appears that autologous ASCs from one organ system can be used for repair in a completely different system. Moreover, even if allogeneic sources are required, isolation of ASCs — unlike ESCs — poses no ethical concern. However, despite recent findings of increased plasticity, ASCs still have a more limited repetoire of differentiation capacity and proliferative potential when compared with ESCs. Moreover, cell numbers can be limited or difficult to obtain, requiring invasive procedures. Nevertheless, clinical research in a wide range of diseases is being conducted using ASCs in the hopes of seeing therapeutic effect.[18]

## 2. Progenitor/Stem Cells from Fetal Sources

Despite the excitement generated from ASC plasticity, the fact remains that these cells are rare and numbers decrease with age.[19] Moreover, invasive procedures are often required to obtain ASCs, i.e., whether of BM-, brain-, or adipose tissue-origin. Recently, a number of laboratories have isolated progenitor/stem cells from fetal tissue, including umbilical cord blood (UCB), umbilical cord, amniotic fluid, amnion, and placenta (discussed in detail below). These fetal tissues are derived from the embryo, develop along with the growing embryo/fetus, and are discarded after the birth of the neonate. Arguably the most critical of these components is the placenta, since successful formation is critical to fetal development and growth. The placenta is actually a fetomaternal organ, with the *decidua basalis* derived from the maternal decidualized endometrium, with the remaining layers fetal in origin. While the functional cell of the placenta is the trophoblast, this complex organ also contains a wide variety of other fetal cells, including endothelial, stromal, and hematopoietic cells. This remarkable organ is discarded post-partum after having performed its many decades. In recent years, this tissue has been widely used for ophthalmological indications and wound healing.[45–47] More recently, the amniotic membrane has been used in ocular surface reconstruction, promoting the development of corneal or conjunctival epithelium with the absence of acute rejection.[46] The attention has turned recently to using the cellular portion of the amnion for isolation of stem cells. A number of laboratories have successfully reported the isolation of a variety of stem cells from this source. Amnion-derived (AD) MSCs can be isolated by mechanical peeling of the amniotic membrane with subsequent digestion with collagenase.[48,49] These cells are able to adhere and proliferate on tissue culture plates for up to 10 passages. However, reports have shown that the proliferation rate eventually slows down, and that cells isolated from first- and second-trimester specimens proliferate better than third-trimester cells.[50] Characterization of AD MSCs by surface marker show that these cells display a profile similar to BM MSCs, being positive for CD73, CD90, CD105, and HLA-ABC as well as CD44, CD29, CD10, CD13, CD54, and CD166. Hematopoietic markers HLA-DR, CD34, CD45, and the monocyte marker CD14 are negative. Detection of ESC markers in AD MSCs has been reported, including the surface markers SSEA-3 and SSEA-4 (at the RNA level) as well as Oct4.[51–54] AD MSCs have been reported to be able to differentiate into adipocytes, chondrocytes, osteoblasts, cardiac and skeletal muscle cells of the mesoderm lineage.[30,49,51] Moreover, a few studies have also demonstrated differentiation into an ectodermal, neural phenotype.[48,50]

### 3.3 *Amniotic epithelial cells (AECs)*

Besides isolation of MSCs, several groups have reported isolation of another type of multipotent cells from the amnion: amniotic epithelial cells (AECs). The isolation methods of AECs are different than that for MSCs, and isolated cells display a cuboidal epithelial morphology, rather than fibroblastic.[55,56] The data show that AECs are pluripotent cells which possess differentiation capacity encompassing all three germ cell layers; thus, as with AD MSCs, AECs can differentiate into mesodermal and ectodermal/neural lineages, but additionally can also differentiate into endodermal cell types such as hepatocytes.[55,56] Interestingly, AECs share many of the MSC surface marker profile that AD MSCs express.

However, AECs have been shown to also express a number of ESC markers on the cell surface, including SSEA-3, SSEA-4, TRA-1–60, and TRA-1–81.[57] Furthermore, AECs also express three ESC pluripotency markers: Oct4, Sox2, and Nanog.[55] In addition to differences in morphology and pluripotency, AECs can be distinguished from AD MSCs by the lack of expression of α4 intergrin or CD49d.[53]

A number of studies using either AD MSCs or AECs show potential for cell transplantation. *In vitro* studies showed that amniotic membrane-isolated cells did not induce allogenic or xenogeneic immune response, with these cells effectively suppressing lymphocyte proliferation.[53,58]

### 3.4 *MSCs from Wharton's jelly (WJ MSCs)*

Another popular fetal source of MSCs is Wharton's jelly which comprises the main structure of umbilical cord.[59] As mentioned previously, UCB is a rich source for HSCs, and Wharton's jelly is thought to play a role in providing stromal support for the HSCs in the umbilical cord.[59,60] Thus, the Wharton's jelly presumably would present MSC-like cells to create an environment similar to the BM, where the majority of hematopoiesis occurs. Wharton's jelly (WJ) MSCs can be isolated from the umbilical cord after removal of amniotic membrane and blood vessels, with subsequent enzymatic digestion by collagenase. After digestion, the remaining connective tissue are removed and discarded, and the suspended cells seeded to tissue culture plates for incubation.[60,61] Fibroblast-like adherent cells are the population of cells outgrowing, and these cells have been characterized as MSCs based on the expression of the markers CD29, CD44, CD73, CD90, CD105, CD166, and HLA-ABC. Similar to MSCs from other sources, WJ MSCs are also negative for CD34, CD45, and HLA-DR. Expression of ESC pluripotent markers, Oct4, Sox2, and Nanog, were also found in Wharton's jelly-derived cells in a porcine model.[62] WJ MSCs show typical mesodermal differentiation potential, capable of forming adipocytes, osteoblast, cartilage, and cardiac muscle,[61] as well as further being able to differentiate into neural-like cells *in vitro*[63] and *in vivo*.[61,64,65] Coconi *et al.* had reported that Wharton's jelly contains CD105$^+$, MSC like cells showing *in vitro* and *in vivo* myogenic differentiation potential, supporting its application on muscle regeneration.[66]

Furthermore, WJ MSCs can undergo cardiomyocytic differentiation, with formation of myotube structures and spontaneous beating, showing its potential for cardiac repair.[67] Animal studies showed that transplantation of WJ MSCs improved neurological function and increased cortical neuronal activity by the regulation of β1-integrin expression in a rat brain-ischemia model.[68] In SCID mice, WJ MSCs can improve hematopoietic engraftment,[69] and it has recently been described that WJ MSCs produce cytokines and other factors that may support hematopoiesis.[70] Moreover, Weiss *et al.* showed that human WJ MSCs cells were tolerated in xenotransplantation into rodents,[71] supported by *in vitro* characterization of the immunomodulation properties of WJ MSCs.[70]

Both UCB and WJ MSCs appear to have potential for therapeutic application. Similar to other fetal-derived MSCs, UCB and WJ MSCs grow rapidly and have doubling times shorter than adult BM MSCs.[72–74] However, although derived from the same developmental period, these two sources of fetal MSCs are not identical. First, cells derived from WJ have been reported to have higher frequencies of colony forming units (CFUs).[73,75] Second, WJ MSCs express osteopontin, a regulator of hematopoietic cells,[76] and hyaluronan, both considered as important components of the HSC niche.[71,77]

### 3.5 *Placenta-derived MSCs and multipotent cells*

Human term placenta is considered a stem cell niche which contains various types of stem cells — including some of the cell populations mentioned above — and thus have attracted attention as an alternative stem cell source.[78,79] In our laboratory, we have isolated a population of multipotent cells, the placenta-derived multipotent cells (PDMCs), from the placenta proper.[25] The amnion and UCB were removed from the placenta prior to isolation of cells. The organ is then mechanically, enzymatically treated, and cultured in BM MSC medium. After two to three weeks, cells with fibroblast-like morphology can be seen in culture dishes. PDMCs display MSC markers such as SH-2/CD105, CD29, CD44, CD73, CD90/Thy-1, and CD166, but are negative for the hematopoietic markers CD14, CD34, CD45, CD117/c-kit; the endothelial markers AC133, von Willebrand factor, Flk-1; and trophoblast markers HLA-G and cytokeratin 7.[25,80] Furthermore, PDMCs also express ESC markers such as SSEA-4, TRA-1–60, and TRA-1–81,[25] showing their more primitive developmental stage. These cells are multipotent as they possess the ability to differentiate into the phenotypes of osteoblasts, adipocytes, neural cells,[25,81] endothelial cells,[82] and hepatocytes.[83]

Isolation of MSCs from the placenta has also been reported by a number of other laboratories.[84,85] Fetal membranes and maternal parts were removed from the placenta, and cells were isolated by mincing the specimens with further enzyme digestion or flushed directly through nylon filters. These cells also show a surface marker profile similar to BM MSCs, and can differentiate into mesodermal phenotypes readily.

In addition to the common advantage that FSCs have in terms of better growth potential, placenta-derived progenitor/stem cells may have an additional advantage in that a large number of cells can be obtained at one time. This is particularly important for clinical applications since *in vitro* passaging to expand cell numbers is known to be associated with causing chromosomal aberrations which precludes clinical use for fear of carcinogenic transformation of the cells.[86,87] Thus, the ability to obtain large cell numbers immediately or very soon after isolation is a distinct advantage for clinical use, and placenta-derived cells may thus be particularly suited for therapy.[88]

## 4. Pre-term FSCs: Amniotic Fluid MSCs

The cavity enclosed by amnion is filled with fluid surrounding and protecting the fetus. The liquid, known as amniotic fluid (AF), contains proteins, carbohydrates, lipids, phospholipids, urea, and electrolytes, all which aid in the growth of the fetus. In the late stages of gestation much of the AF consists of fetal urine. Furthermore, AF contains multiple cell types derived from the fetus.[89,90] Several reports using samples from amniocentesis have found AF as a source of multipotent non-ESCs.[91 92] Cells isolated from AF showed positivity for surface expression of CD73, CD44, CD90, CD105 and HLA-ABC, but negative expression of CD10, CD11b, CD14, CD34, CD117, and HLA-DR, presenting a profile similar to BM MSCs. Furthermore, two ESC markers — SSEA-4[91] and Oct4[92] — have been reported in these cells. AF MSCs can differentiate into adipocytes, osteocytes of the mesodermal lineage or ectodermal neural cells under appropriate conditions. In addition, AF MSCs have also been reported to be capable of endothelial, renal, and hepatic differentiation.[91,93,94] The number of cells that can be obtained during amniocentesis is a concern, since there is a limitation on the amount of AF (usually about 10–20 ml) that can be obtained as to not risk injury to the fetus; *ex vivo* expansion is invariably needed. One recent report showed that AF MSCs can be manufactured in large numbers from diagnostic amniocentesis, thus supporting the viability of clinical trials of amniotic fluid MSC-based therapies.[94] Further data is required to verify whether *ex vivo* expansion affects the chromosomal stability of these cells.

Among the various fetal sources of progenitor/stem cells, AF-derived cells would be the only source that can be ethically obtained during pregnancy, i.e., in the second-trimester as part of amniocentesis. This has been touted as the reason that AF cells possess enhanced differentiation and proliferative capacity, since developmentally they are closer to ESCs than other FSCs, which are isolated from a later stage of development. However, the fact remains that amniocentesis is an invasive procedure and associated with complications, including infection to the fetus and/or mother and a 0.1% risk of miscarriage. Moreover, this procedure is not necessary for all pregnancies; indications to perform amniocentesis are generally for pregnancies at risk for genetic abnormalities. So the accessibility of AF is not universal, and the procurement of AF progenitor/stem cells needs always to be weighed against the very real risks of amniocentesis.

## 5. Immunomodulatory Properties of FSCs

It is the hope that, as with HSCs, other newly isolated types of stem cells can also have therapeutic applications. Indeed, clinical studies using autologous MSCs or same-donor MSCs from previously HLA-matched HSC transplantation have proven successful, although patient numbers remain small.[95–99] While such results are promising, autologous and same-donor use limits prevalent application of such versatile cells. Allogeneic use of non-HSC populations would strongly increase the range of use of such cells, but immunological rejection is a major concern. Even with HSC transplantation, an established clinical treatment, immune complications still occur, resulting in such lethal complications as graft-versus-host disease. However, UCB HSC transplantation is associated with less immune complications than adult BM HSC therapy.[26] This had led many to hypothesize that ESCs and FSCs may show less immune reaction than ASCs. Moreover, the paradoxical survival of the fetal allograft during pregnancy is living proof of the "immune-privileged" status of embryonic and fetal cells. A multitude of theories have been put forth to explain this phenomenon, which has long fascinated immunologists. More recently, research has begun to shed light on some of these mechanisms. These include the expression of non-classical MHC molecules by trophoblast cells,[100] tryptophan catabolism by the enzyme indoleamine 2, 3-dioxygenase (IDO),[101] and alterations to the complement system,[102] a part of the innate immune system. Studies have also documented a role for regulatory T cells (Tregs),[103] a sub-population of T cells which are $CD4^{+}CD25^{bright}$ and have immune-tolerant properties. More recent data also showed that the T lymphocyte inhibitory costimulatory molecule, programmed death ligand 1 (PD-L1), also plays a role in maintenance of fetomaternal tolerance.[104] Interestingly, a few of these fetomaternal tolerance mechanisms actually have been implicated in the immunosuppressive effects of BM MSCs, including the expression of IDO[105] and the generation of Tregs.[106,107]

While the immune characteristics of BM MSCs are increasingly being studied [reviewed in[108]], there are only a few reports regarding the immune properties of the more developmentally primitive stem cells , the ESCs and FSCs. The few studies using ESCs — both human and mouse — have documented that these stem cells are also immunosuppressive towards T lymphocyte s *in vitro*, and may be tolerated *in vivo* after transplantation in immunocompetent mice. Regardless of the source of stem cells — whether adult BM MSCs, FSCs, or ESCs — the immunosuppressive results using *in vitro* mixed lymphocyte cultures and against T cell s have been qualitatively similar.[88,109–112] However, there are some important specific differences in the immunobiology of ESCs and FSCs versus BM MSCs. In our comparative study using PDMCs and BM MSCs, we found that PDMCs suppress both mitogen — and alloantigen-stimulated PBMC proliferation to a greater extent than BM MSCs.[110] Human ESCs and most FSCs are positive for MHC I molecules but express little or no MHC II or costimulatory molecules, similar to BM MSCs.[113,114] However, BM MSCs upregulate HLA -DR expression strongly after 48 hours of stimulation with interferon-γ (IFN-γ) but hESCs do not,[111,114] even after up to seven days of stimulation.[115] A similar trend is seen with FSCs. We found that PDMCs do not express HLA-DR even after two days of IFN-γ stimulation,[110] while others have found that fetal liver MSCs require seven days of stimulation before expression of surface HLA-DR.[116] FSCs derived from the placenta also show some placenta-specific tolerance mechanisms not found in BM MSCs. The expression of HLA-G, a placenta-specific MHC-I antigen critical to the immune tolerant state of pregnancy, shows a developmentally-specific pattern of expression in MSCs isolated from different embryonic and fetal stages. In ESC-derived MSCs, there is surface expression HLA-G which is increased after IFN-γ stimulation, while PDMCs express surface HLA-G only after IFN-γ stimulation but not before; BM MSCs do not express HLA-G regardless of IFN-γ stimulation.[110,117] Thus, the developmental stage in which the stem cells are isolated from may influence not only the more often considered parameters of proliferation and differentiation capacity, but also immune interactions. This aspect of stem cell biology clearly warrants further research, especially since encouraging data in this field can immediately impact and advance therapeutic application of stem cells.

## 6. Conclusion

FSCs are a novel source for cell therapy. Further research on these stem/progenitor cells is still required since many of these FSC populations have only very recently been reported on. As a whole, FSCs isolated from various fetal tissue have biological and non-biological (i.e., ethical and accessibility) advantages over both ESCs and ASCs. Morevoer, these cells may possess immunomodulatory effects which have therapeutic value. Current data on FSCs show that these are very promising cell sources for clinical applications.

## Acknowledgments

This work was supported by funding from the National Science Council of Taiwan (grants NSC97-2320-B-400-005-MY3 to B.L.Y. and NSC97-3111-B-002-009 to M.L. Yen).

## References


1. Hipp J, Atala A. Sources of stem cells for regenerative medicine. *Stem Cell Rev* 2008;4:3–11.
2. Evans MJ, Kaufman MH. Establishment in culture of pluripotential cells from mouse embryos. *Nature* 1981;292:154–156.
3. Martin GR. Isolation of a pluripotent cell line from early mouse embryos cultured in medium conditioned by teratocarcinoma stem cells. *Proc Natl Acad Sci USA* 1981;78:7634–7638.
4. Thomson JA, Itskovitz-Eldor J, Shapiro SS, *et al.* Embryonic stem cell lines derived from human blastocysts. *Science* 1998;282:1145–1147.
5. Takahashi K, Tanabe K, Ohnuki M, *et al.* Induction of pluripotent stem cells from adult human fibroblasts by defined factors. *Cell* 2007;131:861–872.
6. Takahashi K, Yamanaka S. Induction of pluripotent stem cells from mouse embryonic and adult fibroblast cultures by defined factors. *Cell* 2006;126:663–676.
7. Yamanaka S. Induction of pluripotent stem cells from mouse fibroblasts by four transcription factors. *Cell Prolif* 2008;41 Suppl 1:51–56.
8. Orkin SH. Diversification of haematopoietic stem cells to specific lineages. *Nat Rev Genet* 2000;1:57–64.
9. Elabd C, Chiellini C, Massoudi A, *et al.* Human adipose tissue-derived multipotent stem cells differentiate *in vitro* and *in vivo* into osteocyte-like cells. *Biochem Biophys Res Commun* 2007;361:342–348.
10. Herrera MB, Bruno S, Buttiglieri S, *et al.* Isolation and characterization of a stem cell population from adult human liver. *Stem Cells* 2006;24:2840–2850.
11. Vescovi AL, Parati EA, Gritti A, *et al.* Isolation and cloning of multipotential stem cells from the embryonic human CNS and establishment of transplantable human neural stem cell lines by epigenetic stimulation. *Exp Neurol* 1999;156:71–83.
12. Pittenger MF, Mackay AM, Beck SC, *et al.* Multilineage potential of adult human mesenchymal stem cells. *Science* 1999;284:143–147.
13. Prockop DJ. Marrow stromal cells as stem cells for nonhematopoietic tissues. *Science* 1997;276:71–74.
14. Lee KD, Kuo TK, Whang-Peng J, *et al.* *In vitro* hepatic differentiation of human mesenchymal stem cells. *Hepatology* 2004;40:1275–1284.
15. Sanchez-Ramos J, Song S, Cardozo-Pelaez F, *et al.* Adult bone marrow stromal cells differentiate into neural cells *in vitro*. *Exp Neurol* 2000;164:247–256.

43. Mareschi K, Biasin E, Piacibello W, *et al.* Isolation of human mesenchymal stem cells: bone marrow versus umbilical cord blood. *Haematologica* 2001;86:1099–1100.
44. Wexler SA, Donaldson C, Denning-Kendall P, *et al.* Adult bone marrow is a rich source of human mesenchymal 'stem' cells but umbilical cord and mobilized adult blood are not. *Br J Haematol* 2003;121:368–374.
45. Faulk WP, Matthews R, Stevens PJ, *et al.* Human amnion as an adjunct in wound healing. *Lancet* 1980;1:1156–1158.
46. Gomes JA, Romano A, Santos MS, Dua HS. Amniotic membrane use in ophthalmology. *Curr Opin Ophthalmol* 2005;16:233–240.
47. Tosi GM, Massaro-Giordano M, Caporossi A, Toti P. Amniotic membrane transplantation in ocular surface disorders. *J Cell Physiol* 2005;202:849–851.
48. Sakuragawa N, Kakinuma K, Kikuchi A, *et al.* Human amnion mesenchyme cells express phenotypes of neuroglial progenitor cells. *J Neurosci Res* 2004;78:208–214.
49. Soncini M, Vertua E, Gibelli L, *et al.* Isolation and characterization of mesenchymal cells from human fetal membranes. *J Tissue Eng Regen Med* 2007;1:296–305.
50. Portmann-Lanz CB, Schoeberlein A, Huber A, *et al.* Placental mesenchymal stem cells as potential autologous graft for pre- and perinatal neuroregeneration. *Am J Obstet Gynecol* 2006;194:664–673.
51. Alviano F, Fossati V, Marchionni C, *et al.* Term amniotic membrane is a high throughput source for multipotent mesenchymal stem cells with the ability to differentiate into endothelial cells *in vitro*. *BMC Dev Biol* 2007;7:11.
52. Wei JP, Zhang TS, Kawa S, *et al.* Human amnion-isolated cells normalize blood glucose in streptozotocin-induced diabetic mice. *Cell Transplant* 2003;12:545–552.
53. Wolbank S, Peterbauer A, Fahrner M, *et al.* Dose-dependent immunomodulatory effect of human stem cells from amniotic membrane: a comparison with human mesenchymal stem cells from adipose tissue. *Tissue Eng* 2007;13:1173–1183.
54. Zhao P, Ise H, Hongo M, *et al.* Human amniotic mesenchymal cells have some characteristics of cardiomyocytes. *Transplantation* 2005;79:528–535.
55. Miki T, Lehmann T, Cai H, *et al.* Stem cell characteristics of amniotic epithelial cells. *Stem Cells* 2005;23:1549–1559.

56. Takashima S, Ise H, Zhao P, *et al.* Human amniotic epithelial cells possess hepatocyte-like characteristics and functions. *Cell Struct Funct* 2004;29:73–84.
57. Ilancheran S, Michalska A, Peh G, *et al.* Stem cells derived from human fetal membranes display multilineage differentiation potential. *Biol Reprod* 2007;77:577–588.
58. Bailo M, Soncini M, Vertua E, *et al.* Engraftment potential of human amnion and chorion cells derived from term placenta. *Transplantation* 2004;78:1439–1448.
59. Troyer DL, Weiss ML. Wharton's jelly-derived cells are a primitive stromal cell population. *Stem Cells* 2008;26:591–599.
60. Bakhshi T, Zabriskie RC, Bodie S, *et al.* Mesenchymal stem cells from the Wharton's jelly of umbilical cord segments provide stromal support for the maintenance of cord blood hematopoietic stem cells during long-term *ex vivo* culture. *Transfusion* 2008;48:2638–2644.
61. Wang HS, Hung SC, Peng ST, *et al.* Mesenchymal stem cells in the Wharton's jelly of the human umbilical cord. *Stem Cells* 2004;22: 1330–1337.
62. Carlin R, Davis D, Weiss M, *et al.* Expression of early transcription factors Oct-4, Sox-2 and Nanog by porcine umbilical cord (PUC) matrix cells. *Reprod Biol Endocrinol* 2006;4:8.
63. Mitchell KE, Weiss ML, Mitchell BM, *et al.* Matrix cells from Wharton's jelly form neurons and glia. *Stem Cells* 2003;21:50–60.
64. Fu YS, Shih YT, Cheng YC, Min MY. Transformation of human umbilical mesenchymal cells into neurons *in vitro*. *J Biomed Sci* 2004;11:652–660.
65. Ma L, Feng XY, Cui BL, *et al.* Human umbilical cord Wharton's Jelly-derived mesenchymal stem cells differentiation into nerve-like cells. *Chin Med J (Engl)* 2005;118:1987–1993.
66. Conconi MT, Burra P, Di Liddo R, *et al.* CD105(+) cells from Wharton's jelly show *in vitro* and *in vivo* myogenic differentiative potential. *Int J Mol Med* 2006;18:1089–1096.
67. Pereira WC, Khushnooma I, Madkaikar M, Ghosh K. Reproducible methodology for the isolation of mesenchymal stem cells from human umbilical cord and its potential for cardiomyocyte generation. *J Tissue Eng Regen Med* 2008;2:394–399.

68. Ding DC, Shyu WC, Chiang MF, *et al*. Enhancement of neuroplasticity through upregulation of beta1-integrin in human umbilical cord-derived stromal cell implanted stroke model. *Neurobiol Dis* 2007;27:339–353.
69. Friedman R, Betancur M, Boissel L, *et al*. Umbilical cord mesenchymal stem cells: adjuvants for human cell transplantation. *Biol Blood Marrow Transplant* 2007;13:1477–1486.
70. Weiss ML, Anderson C, Medicetty S, *et al*. Immune properties of human umbilical cord Wharton's jelly-derived cells. *Stem Cells* 2008;26:2865–2874.
71. Weiss ML, Medicetty S, Bledsoe AR, *et al*. Human umbilical cord matrix stem cells: preliminary characterization and effect of transplantation in a rodent model of Parkinson's disease. *Stem Cells* 2006;24:781–792.
72. Baksh D, Yao R, Tuan RS. Comparison of proliferative and multilineage differentiation potential of human mesenchymal stem cells derived from umbilical cord and bone marrow. *Stem Cells* 2007;25:1384–1392.
73. Karahuseyinoglu S, Cinar O, Kilic E, *et al*. Biology of stem cells in human umbilical cord stroma: *in situ* and *in vitro* surveys. *Stem Cells* 2007;25:319–331.
74. Lund RD, Wang S, Lu B, *et al*. Cells isolated from umbilical cord tissue rescue photoreceptors and visual functions in a rodent model of retinal disease. *Stem Cells* 2007;25:602–611.
75. Sarugaser R, Lickorish D, Baksh D, *et al*. Human umbilical cord perivascular (HUCPV) cells: a source of mesenchymal progenitors. *Stem Cells* 2005;23:220–229.
76. Nilsson SK, Johnston HM, Whitty GA, *et al*. Osteopontin, a key component of the hematopoietic stem cell niche and regulator of primitive hematopoietic progenitor cells. *Blood* 2005;106:1232–1239.
77. Raio L, Cromi A, Ghezzi F, *et al*. Hyaluronan content of Wharton's jelly in healthy and Down syndrome fetuses. *Matrix Biol* 2005;24:166–174.
78. Fauza D. Amniotic fluid and placental stem cells. *Best Pract Res Clin Obstet Gynaecol* 2004;18:877–891.
79. Matikainen T, Laine J. Placenta — an alternative source of stem cells. *Toxicol Appl Pharmacol* 2005;207:544–549.
80. Li C, Zhang W, Jiang X, Mao N. Human-placenta-derived mesenchymal stem cells inhibit proliferation and function of allogeneic immune cells. *Cell Tissue Res* 2007;330:437–446.

81. Yen BL, Chien CC, Chen YC, *et al.* Placenta-derived multipotent cells differentiate into neuronal and glial cells *in vitro*. *Tissue Eng Part A* 2008;14:9–17.
82. Wu CC, Chao YC, Chen CN, *et al.* Synergism of biochemical and mechanical stimuli in the differentiation of human placenta-derived multipotent cells into endothelial cells. *J Biomech* 2008;41:813–821.
83. Chien CC, Yen BL, Lee FK, *et al. In vitro* differentiation of human placenta-derived multipotent cells into hepatocyte-like cells. *Stem Cells* 2006;24:1759–1768.
84. Fukuchi Y, Nakajima H, Sugiyama D, *et al.* Human placenta-derived cells have mesenchymal stem/progenitor cell potential. *Stem Cells* 2004; 22:649–658.
85. In 't Anker PS, Scherjon SA, Kleijburg-van der Keur C, *et al.* Isolation of mesenchymal stem cells of fetal or maternal origin from human placenta. *Stem Cells* 2004;22:1338–1345.
86. Burns JS, Abdallah BM, Guldberg P, *et al.* Tumorigenic heterogeneity inÿ-cancer stem cells evolved from long-term cultures of telomerase-immortalized human mesenchymal stem cells. *Cancer Res* 2005;65:3126–3135.
87. Rubio D, Garcia-Castro J, Martin MC, *et al.* Spontaneous human adult stem cell transformation. *Cancer Res* 2005;65:3035–3039.
88. Brooke G, Cook M, Blair C, *et al.* Therapeutic applications of mesenchymal stromal cells. *Semin Cell Dev Biol* 2007;18:846–858.
89. Polgar K, Adany R, Abel G, *et al.* Characterization of rapidly adhering amniotic fluid cells by combined immunofluorescence and phagocytosis assays. *Am J Hum Genet* 1989;45:786–792.
90. Priest RE, Marimuthu KM, Priest JH. Origin of cells in human amniotic fluid cultures: ultrastructural features. *Lab Invest* 1978;39:106–109.
91. De Coppi P, Bartsch G, Jr., Siddiqui MM, *et al.* Isolation of amniotic stem cell lines with potential for therapy *Nat Biotechnol* 2007;25:100–106.
92. Tsai MS, Lee JL, Chang YJ, Hwang SM. Isolation of human multipotent mesenchymal stem cells from second-trimester amniotic fluid using a novel two-stage culture protocol. *Hum Reprod* 2004;19:1450–1456.
93. Perin L, Giuliani S, Jin D, *et al.* Renal differentiation of amniotic fluid stem cells. *Cell Prolif* 2007;40:936–948.
94. Zheng YB, Gao ZL, Xie C, *et al.* Characterization and hepatogenic differentiation of mesenchymal stem cells from human amniotic fluid and human bone marrow: a comparative study. *Cell Biol Int* 2008;32:1439–1448.

95. Bang OY, Lee JS, Lee PH, Lee G. Autologous mesenchymal stem cell transplantation in stroke patients. *Ann Neurol* 2005;57:874–882.
96. Chen SL, Fang WW, Qian J, *et al.* Improvement of cardiac function after transplantation of autologous bone marrow mesenchymal stem cells in patients with acute myocardial infarction. *Chin Med J (Engl)* 2004;117:1443–1448.
97. Koc ON, Day J, Nieder M, *et al.* Allogeneic mesenchymal stem cell infusion for treatment of metachromatic leukodystrophy (MLD) and Hurler syndrome (MPS-IH). *Bone Marrow Transplant* 2002;30:215–222.
98. Koc ON, Gerson SL, Cooper BW, *et al.* Rapid hematopoietic recovery after coinfusion of autologous-blood stem cells and culture-expanded marrow mesenchymal stem cells in advanced breast cancer patients receiving high-dose chemotherapy. *J Clin Oncol* 2000;18:307–316.
99. Mazzini L, Fagioli F, Boccaletti R, *et al.* Stem cell therapy in amyotrophic lateral sclerosis: a methodological approach in humans. *Amyotroph Lateral Scler Other Motor Neuron Disord* 2003;4:158–161.
100. Ishitani A, Sageshima N, Lee N, *et al.* Protein expression and peptide binding suggest unique and interacting functional roles for HLA-E, F, and G in maternal-placental immune recognition. *J Immunol* 2003;171:1376–1384.
101. Munn DH, Zhou M, Attwood JT, *et al.* Prevention of allogeneic fetal rejection by tryptophan catabolism. *Science* 1998;281:1191–1193.
102. Hsi BL, Hunt JS, Atkinson JP. Differential expression of complement regulatory proteins on subpopulations of human trophoblast cells. *J Reprod Immunol* 1991;19:209–223.
103. Aluvihare VR, Kallikourdis M, Betz AG. Regulatory T cells mediate maternal tolerance to the fetus. *Nat Immunol* 2004;5:266–271.
104. Guleria I, Khosroshahi A, Ansari MJ, *et al.* A critical role for the programmed death ligand 1 in fetomaternal tolerance. *J Exp Med* 2005; 202:231–237.
105. Meisel R, Zibert A, Laryea M, *et al.* Human bone marrow stromal cells inhibit allogeneic T-cell responses by indoleamine 2,3-dioxygenase-mediated tryptophan degradation. *Blood* 2004;103:4619–4621.
106. Maccario R, Podesta M, Moretta A, *et al.* Interaction of human mesenchymal stem cells with cells involved in alloantigen-specific immune response favors the differentiation of CD4+ T-cell subsets expressing a regulatory/suppressive phenotype. *Haematologica* 2005;90:516–525.

107. Prevosto C, Zancolli M, Canevali P, *et al.* Generation of CD4+ or CD8+ regulatory T cells upon mesenchymal stem cell-lymphocyte interaction. *Haematologica* 2007;92:881–888.
108. Rasmusson I. Immune modulation by mesenchymal stem cells. *Exp Cell Res* 2006;312:2169–2179.
109. Bonde S, Zavazava N. Immunogenicity and engraftment of mouse embryonic stem cells in allogeneic recipients. *Stem Cells* 2006;24:2192–2201.
110. Chang CJ, Yen ML, Chen YC, *et al.* Placenta-derived multipotent cells exhibit immunosuppressive properties that are enhanced in the presence of interferon-gamma. *Stem Cells* 2006;24:2466–2477.
111. Drukker M, Katchman H, Katz G, *et al.* Human embryonic stem cells and their differentiated derivatives are less susceptible to immune rejection than adult cells. *Stem Cells* 2006;24:221–229.
112. Li L, Baroja ML, Majumdar A, *et al.* Human embryonic stem cells possess immune-privileged properties. *Stem Cells* 2004;22:448–456.
113. Aggarwal S, Pittenger MF. Human mesenchymal stem cells modulate allogeneic immune cell responses. *Blood* 2005;105:1815–1822.
114. Drukker M, Katz G, Urbach A, *et al.* Characterization of the expression of MHC proteins in human embryonic stem cells. *Proc Natl Acad Sci USA* 2002;99:9864–9869.
115. Grinnemo KH, Kumagai-Braesch M, Mansson-Broberg A, *et al.* Human embryonic stem cells are immunogenic in allogeneic and xenogeneic settings. *Reprod Biomed Online* 2006;13:712–724.
116. Gotherstrom C, Ringden O, Tammik C, *et al.* Immunologic properties of human fetal mesenchymal stem cells. *Am J Obstet Gynecol* 2004;190:239–245.
117. Yen BL, Chang CJ, Liu KJ, *et al.* Human embryonic stem cell-derived mesenchymal progenitors possess strong immunosuppressive effects toward natural killer cells as well as T lymphocytes. *Stem Cells* 2009;27:451–456.

# CHAPTER 12

# CARTILAGE REGENERATION WITH AND WITHOUT CELL TRANSPLANTATION

*Avital Mendelson, Chang Hun Lee and Jeremy J. Mao*

## Abstract

The majority of cartilage regeneration approaches in experimental testing to date involve cell delivery. Cells that have been delivered for cartilage regeneration include, but are not limited to, chondrocytes, mesenchymal stem cells, and adipose stem cells. Despite its scientific merit, cell delivery faces critical drawbacks including scarce cell availability, donor site trauma, possible immune rejection, pathogen transmission, tumorigenesis, and long-term storage difficulties. Chondrocytes only account for approximately 5% of articular cartilage volume. Microfracture is a clinical procedure to remove degenerated articular cartilage by arthroscopy and to induce marrow bleeding into cartilage defect. However, microfracture leads to fibrous tissue or fibrocartilage at best. Is it possible to regenerate articular cartilage by recruiting innate cells that are capable of differentiating into articular (hyaline) chondrocytes? This review explores sources of cells that may be recruited or homed for the regeneration of hyaline cartilage, including synovial cells, adipose stem cells, bone marrow mesenchymal stem cells, hematopoietic stem cells, and circulating fibrocytes. Some of these cell sources have not been fully explored for their recruitment potential to regenerate articular cartilage. Tissue regeneration by chemotactically targeted cell homing may offer advantages of lower cost, enhanced marketability, and ease of clinical implementation potentially as novel reparative strategies.

## 1. Introduction

Since the inception of the field of tissue engineering, cartilage regeneration strategies have been largely based on cell transplantation. Langer and Vacanti published one of the first papers showing that cartilage could be regenerated by seeding an anatomically shaped scaffold with cells and culturing it subcutaneously.[1] This sparked a sudden interest in cell-based tissue engineering approaches and product development. Although Langer and Vacanti initially proposed the use of fully differentiated cells such as chondrocytes, the scientific community soon realized that fully differentiated cells are not only scarce as an autologous cell source, but are also difficult to expand *ex vivo*. Furthermore, they carry the risk of immunorejection, limiting their widespread use. Subsequently, an interest arose in using bone marrow stem/stromal cells (originally discovered in 1976)[2] as well as human embryonic stem cells (discovered in 1998)[3] as cell sources for cartilage repair. Additionally, one of the stated motivations for the recent discovery of induced pluripotent stem cells (iPS) is to transplant them for regenerative therapies.[4,5] However, despite its scientific merit, cell delivery encounters potential issues in clinical application. Because articular cartilage naturally contains a very low cell density, perhaps it would be possible to regenerate cartilage by cell homing. This chapter will explore both cell delivery and cell homing approaches for cartilage regeneration.

## 2. Cell-Based Cartilage Tissue Engineering Approaches

Since cartilage has an ordered structure, a scaffold is frequently used to define the shape of the tissue, provide an attachment site for cells, and guide tissue formation.[6] The conventional approach behind cell-based cartilage tissue engineering strategies is to fabricate a biodegradable scaffold, seed it with progenitor cells or differentiated cells, and culture it *in vitro* or *in vivo*, either alone or in combination with cytokines, a bioreactor, mechanical stimulation or oxygen tension (Fig. 1). The most common growth factors used in cartilage regeneration include transforming growth factor β1 and β3 (TGF-β1 and TGF-β3), bone morphogenic protein (BMP), basic fibroblast growth factor (bFGF), and insulin–like growth factor (IGF).[7]

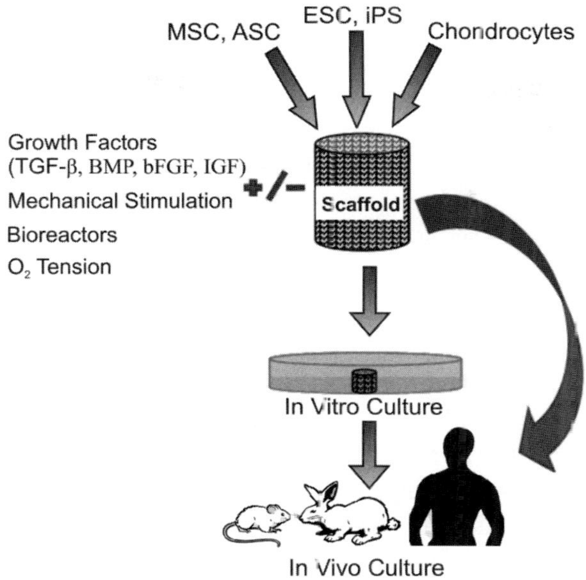


**Fig. 1.** General approach for cell based tissue engineered cartilage.

Several elegant approaches have been described for the delivery of cells in cartilage regeneration. For example, an osteochondral construct was fabricated by press–coating a high density pellet of chondrogenically induced human mesenchymal progenitor cells (hMPCs) onto one face of the construct, and osteogenically induced hMPCs onto the opposing face of the construct. After 10 weeks in culture, the construct formed cartilage–like and bone–like layers.[8] In addition to *in vitro* culture, many researchers have investigated the possibility of regenerating cartilage *in vivo*. In one such study, a bioceramic scaffold was fabricated from β-tricalcium phosphate (β-TCP) powder, seeded with autologous chondrocytes or left unseeded as a control and implanted in sheep for up to 24 weeks. Following explantation, the cell seeded constructs were fully covered with tissue, whereas the acellular constructs were not filled with tissue.[9] A different approach used swine chondrocyte seeded fibrin glue infused polytetrafluoroethylene (ePTFE) membrane to support engineered cartilage. Constructs were implanted subcutaneously in nude mice for

12 weeks. New cartilage tissue was formed with lacunae structures similar to native tissue and tightly bonded to the ePTFE scaffold material.[10] Another osteochondral construct was fabricated from medical grade polycaprolactone (mPCL) to serve as the bone region and fibrin glue for the cartilage portion. The entire construct was seeded with bone marrow derived mesenchymal stem cells (bMSCs) and implanted in adult white rabbits. However, at six months post–operation, only two of the six implanted constructs showed mature cartilage formation.[11]

Additionally, gene therapy has been combined with cell delivery approaches for cartilage regeneration. Periosteal derived rabbit MSCs were modified to overexpress the BMP 7, seeded onto polyglycolic acid scaffolds and implanted *in situ* into a rabbit osteochondral defect model. Constructs harvested after eight and 12 weeks had an enhanced cartilage regenerative ability as compared to the empty defect and empty vector transduced, cell–seeded control groups.[12] Recently, high density chondrocyte culture has been attempted to eliminate the need for a scaffold in cartilage regeneration, since highly confluent chondrocytes generate chondral tissue without the presence of synthetic scaffolds.[13]

Many of these aforementioned studies used adult stem cells. However, when cultured *in vitro*, adult stem cells have a reduced ability to expand and differentiate into numerous cell types as compared to *in vivo* culture. Embryonic stem cells (ESCs), on the other hand, are more capable of multipotency *in vitro*, but are limited in use because of their controversial nature. Recently, it was discovered that mouse embryonic or adult fibroblast cells can be reprogrammed to become ESC–like pluripotent stem cells by inducing the following genes: Oct3/4, Sox 2, c-Myc, and Klf4. However, the process of somatic cell nuclear transfer (SCNT), used to create IPS cells, has been linked to premature aging, respiratory conditions as well as organ abnormalities. Furthermore, SCNT could potentially form tumors *in vivo,* thus hindering its clinical use.[14]

Most of the previous work in cartilage regeneration has focused on the repair of small, localized cartilage or osteochondral defects by bioengineered plugs.[15,16] A number of studies have shown that composite cartilage–bone tissue can be regenerated in surgically created focal defects.[6,17–20] However, commercial approaches to replace focal cartilage defects with processed tissues or cells in patients are only marginally successful. Current clinical treatment methods for focal osteoarthritis, such as abrasion arthroplasty or autologous chondrocyte implantation, have limitations including the loss of chondrocyte phenotype, poor integration and guarded functional outcome.[6,21] Clinically, focal cartilage defects deteriorate into more severe arthritis that warrant total joint arthroplasty.[22–24] Accordingly, biological replacement of the entire synovial joint has been advocated.[15,24–26] We and others have previously reported that stratified layers of cartilage and bone can be regenerated in dimensions of an entire human synovial joint ectopically *in vivo* from several cell sources, such as a single population of bone marrow–derived mesenchymal stem cells (MSCs)[26–28] or differentiated chondrocytes and osteoblasts.[29,30]

In summary, cell seeding is a meritorious scientific approach for cartilage regeneration. The seeded stem cells or chondrocytes are capable of generating cartilage tissue. However, cell delivery approaches encounter critical barriers including scarce cell availability, donor site morbidity, potential pathogen transmission or immune rejection, risk for tumor formation, long-term storage and regulatory approval. The next section below will explore approaches for cartilage regeneration without cell seeding.

## 3. Acellular Cartilage Tissue Engineering Approaches

To date, there have been few attempts to regenerate cartilage without cell transplantation. Of these efforts, the general approach is to implant acellular, biomaterial based scaffolds into the defect site alone or in combination with growth factors or chemoattractants. In one study, a two–layered osteochondral scaffold was fabricated from basal porous β-tricalcium phosphate (β-TCP) to serve as the bone layer and a collagen type I/II fibrous layer to act as the cartilage layer. Scaffolds were implanted in Göttinger minipigs alone or in combination with a mixture of growth factors containing BMP 2, 3, 4, 6, 7, TGF β1, β2, β3, FGF-1, osteocalcin and osteonectin. After 12 weeks, the group with the growth factors was able to regenerate a thicker layer of cartilage. However, after 56 weeks, there was no difference in the cartilage formed between the growth factor group and the scaffold alone group, which could be attributed to a complete resorption of growth factors by 52 weeks.[31]

## References


1. Langer R, Vacanti JP. Tissue engineering. *Science* 1993;260:920–926.
2. Friedenstein AJ, *et al.* Fibroblast precursors in normal and irradiated mouse hematopoietic organs. *Exp Hematol* 1976;4:267–274.
3. Thomson JA, *et al.* Embryonic stem cell lines derived from human blastocysts. *Science* 1998;282:1145–1147.
4. Takahashi K, *et al.* Induction of pluripotent stem cells from adult fibroblasts by defined factors. *Cell* 2007;131:861–872.
5. Yu J, *et al.* Induced pluripotent stem cell lines derived from human somatic cells. *Science* 2007;318:1917–1920.
6. Mano JF, *et al.* Osteochondral defects: Present situation and tissue engineering approaches. *J Tissue Eng Regen Med* 2007;1:261–273.
7. Kinner B, *et al.* Regeneration of articular cartilage. *Adv Biochem Engin/Biotechnol* 2005;94:91–123.
8. Tuli R, *et al.* Human mesenchymal progenitor cell-based tissue engineering of a single unit osteochondral construct. *Tissue Eng* 2004;10:1169–1179.
9. Guo X, *et al.* Repair of osteochondral defects with autologous chondrocytes seeded on bioceramic scaffold in sheep. *Tissue Eng* 2004;10(11/12): 1830–1840.
10. Xu JW, *et al.* Tissue engineered cartilage composite with expanded polytetrafluoroethylene membrane. *Ann Plast Surg* 2001;46(5):527–532.
11. Shao XX, *et al.* Evaluation of a hybrid scaffold/cell construct in repair of high-load-bearing osteochondral defects in rabbits. *Biomaterials* 2006;27:1071–1080.
12. Mason JE, *et al.* Cartilage and bone regeneration using gene-enhanced tissue engineering. *Clin Orthop Relat Res* 2000;379:171–178.
13. Park K, *et al.* Scaffold-free engineered porcine cartilage construct for cartilage defect repair — *in vitro* and *in vivo* study. *Artif Organs* 2006;30(8):586–596.
14. Choumerianou D, *et al.* Stem cells: promises versus limitations. *Tissue Eng Part B* 2008;14(1):53–60.
15. Mao JJ. Stem-cell-driven regeneration of synovial joints. *Biol Cell* 2005;97:289–301.
16. Darling EM. Athanasiou KA. Biomechanical strategies for articular cartilage regeneration. *Ann Biomed Eng* 2004;31:1114–1124.

17. Gao J, *et al.* Repair of osteochondral defect with tissue-engineered two-phase composite material of injectable calcium phosphate and hyaluronan sponge. *Tissue Eng* 2002;8:827–837.
18. Jiang CC, *et al.* Repair of porcine articular cartilage defect with a biphasic osteochondral composite. *J Orthop Res* 2007;25:1277–1290.
19. Lee CR, *et al.* Effects of a cultured autologous chondrocyte-seeded type II collagen scaffold on the healing of a chondral defect in a canine model. *J Orthop Res* 2003;21:272–281.
20. Schaefer D, *et al.* Tissue-engineered composites for the repair of large osteochondral defects. *Arthritis Rheum* 2002;46:2524–2534.
21. Wood JJ, *et al.* Autologous cultured chondrocytes: adverse events reported to the United States food and drug administration. *J Bone Joint Surg Am* 2006;88,503–507.
22. Scanzello CR, Plaas A, Crow MK. Innate immune system activation in osteoarthritis: is osteoarthritis a chronic wound? *Curr Opin Rheumatol* 2008;20:565–572.
23. Buckwalter JA, Martin JA. Osteoarthritis. *Adv Drug Deliv Rev* 2006;58:150–167.
24. Caplan AI, Goldberg VM. Principles of tissue engineered regeneration of skeletal tissues. *Clin Orthop Relat Res* 1999;S12–S16.
25. Karp JM, *et al.* Mesenchymal stem cell homing: the devil is in the details. *Cell Stem Cell* 2009;4:206–216.
26. Sackstein R, *et al.* *Ex vivo* glycan engineering of CD44 programs human multipotent mesenchymal stromal cell trafficking to bone. *Nat Med* 2008;14:181–187.
27. Rochefort GY, *et al.* Multipotential mesenchymal stem cells are mobilized into peripheral blood by hypoxia. *Stem Cells* 2006;24:2202–2208.
28. Wang CH, *et al.* Late-outgrowth endothelial cells attenuate intimal hyperplasia contributed by mesenchymal stem cells after vascular injury. *Arterioscler Thromb Vasc Biol* 2008;28(1):54–60.
29. Wynn RF, *et al.* A small proportion of mesenchymal stem cells strongly expresses functionally active CXCR4 receptor capable of promoting migration to bone marrow. *Blood* 2004;104:2643–2645.
30. Weng Y, *et al.* Tissue-engineered composites of bone and cartilage for mandible condylar reconstruction. *J Oral Maxillofac Surg* 2001;59:185–190.

44. Christopher MJ, et al. Suppression of CXCL12 production by bone marrow osteoblasts is a common and critical pathway for cytokine-induced mobilization. *Blood* 2009;114(7):1331–1339.
45. Yong KL, et al. Cord blood progenitor cells have greater transendothelial migratory activity and increased responses to SDF-1 and MIP-3β compared with mobilized adult progenitor cells. *Br J Haematol* 1999;107:441–449.
46. Wang CH, et al. Late-outgrowth endothelial cells attenuate intimal hyperplasia contributed by mesenchymal stem cells after vascular injury. *Arterioscler Thromb Vasc Biol* 2008;28(1):54–60.
47. Wynn RF, et al. A small proportion of mesenchymal stem cells strongly expresses functionally active CXCR4 receptor capable of promoting migration to bone marrow. *Blood* 104:2643–2645.
48. Sackstein R, et al. Ex vivo glycan engineering of CD44 programs human multipotent mesenchymal stromal cell trafficking to bone. *Nat Med* 2008;14:181–187.
49. Shi M, et al. Regulation of CXCR4 expression in human mesenchymal stem cells by cytokine treatment: role in homing efficiency in NOD/SCID mice. *Haematologica* 2007;92(7):897–904.
50. Cristino S, et al. Expression of CXC chemokines and their receptors is modulated during chondrogenic differentiation of human mesenchymal stem cells grown in three-dimensional scaffold: Evidence in native cartilage. *Tissue Eng Part A* 2008;14(1):97–105.
51. Chiu YC, et al. Stromal cell-derived factor-1 induces matrix metalloprotease-13 expression in human chondrocytes. *Mol Pharmacol* 2007;72(3):695–703.
52. Wu Q, et al. Extracellular calcium increases CXCR4 expression on bone marrow-derived cells and enhances pro-angiogenesis therapy. *J Cell Mol Med* 2009.
53. Schantz JT, et al. Cell guidance in tissue engineering: SDF-1 mediates site-directed homing of mesenchymal stem cells within three-dimensional polycaprolactone scaffolds. *Tissue Eng* 2007;13(11):2615–2624.
54. Thieme S, et al. Stromal cell-derived factor-1α directed chemoattraction of transiently CXCR4 overexpressing bone marrow stromal cells into functionalized three-dimensional biomimetic scaffolds. *Tissue Eng Part C Methods* 2009;15(4):687–696.
55. Patterns in Nature. http://jolnluca.blogspot.com/2008_08_01_archive.html. Accessed 5/5/10.

# CHAPTER 13

# TRANSCRIPTIONAL REGULATION AND CLINICAL APPLICATIONS OF NEURAL STEM CELLS

*Yi-Chao Hsu and Ing-Ming Chiu*

## Abstract

Stem cells self-renew and generate various cell types in their respective lineages. They can be derived from blastocysts or reprogrammed from developing and adult tissue sources. Neural stem cells (NSCs), with the characteristics of self-renewal and multipotency, can be isolated from embryonic stem cells, embryonic ectoderm, and developing or adult brain tissues. Adult neurogenesis occurs in two neurogenic regions in the brain: the subventricular zone (SVZ) of the lateral ventricle and the subgranular zone in the dentate gyrus of the hippocampus. These two regions contain neural stem or progenitor cells that can self-renew and differentiate into neurons, astroglial cells and oligodendrocytes. Here, we will review the isolation and characterization of NSCs from ES cells, developing and adult brains. The transcriptional regulation and molecular markers that are used to identify NSCs will also be reviewed. NSCs have been proposed as a promising cellular source for the treatment of diseases in nervous systems. For clinical application of NSCs in neurodegenerative disorders and damaged neurons, we discuss several critical problems that remain to be resolved, such as the reliable sources of neural stem/progenitor cells for autologous transplantation.

## 1. Introduction

Neurons, astrocytes and oligodendrocytes are the major cell types present in the adult mammalian brain. Neurons are the functional units of the nervous system and are responsible for learning, memory, information processing and transmission. Glia cells, including astrocytes and oligodendrocytes, support the neurons for proper functions in the nervous system. Before 1990s, neurogenesis in the mammalian central nervous system (CNS) was not determined because there were no new neurons found in the mouse striatum after the first few days post-partum. Reynolds and Weiss are the first to demonstrate that cells isolated from the striatum of the adult mouse brain can proliferate *in vitro* when cultured in the presence of epidermal growth factor (EGF).[1] The cultured cells initially expressed Nestin, and subsequently presented the morphology and marker proteins of neurons and astrocytes. The terms "self-renewal" and "multipotency" of NSCs have been defined, based on the characterization of *in vitro*-cultured NSCs.[1] Gage *et al.* identified another subset of neural stem/progenitor cells that can proliferate in response to fibroblast growth factor 2 (FGF2) from the adult rat hippocampus.[2] Gage *et al.* further found a subset of neural stem/progenitor cells present in the dentate gyrus of the hippocampus.[3] It is now believed that adult neurogenesis occurs in two neurogenic regions in the brain: the SVZ of the lateral ventricle and the subgranular zone in the dentate gyrus of the hippocampus.[4] These two regions contain neural stem and progenitor cells that can proliferate and differentiate into neurons and glial cells. Increasing experiments have focused on obtaining sufficient NSCs from reliable sources for autologous transplantation as well as the control of NSC differentiation in adult nervous systems.

Here, we first introduce the current knowledge of NSC biology, including the definition and sources of NSCs, the methods and protocols for the isolation and characterization of NSCs from ES cells, developing or adult brains. The transcriptional regulation of NSCs, neurogenic niches and molecular markers that are used to identify NSCs will be described. We will also discuss the critical problems involved in the clinical application of NSCs.

## 2. Definition and Sources of Neural Stem Cells (NSCs)

NSCs arise from embryonic ectoderm that forms neuroepithelial cells. These neuroepithelial cells will generate radial glia that give rise to NSCs and neural progenitors in adult neurogenic regions.[5] The differences between NSCs and neural progenitor cells depend on the sustaining ability to self-renew and differentiate. NSCs are multipotent stem cells with unlimited self-renewal whereas progenitor cells are lineage-restricted cells with limited self-renewal and proliferation capacity.[6] Bartlett *et al.* demonstrated that the resident hippocampal precursor is a neurogenic progenitor capable of proliferation and multipotential differentiation, but is unable to self-renew.[7] Adult NSCs are therefore defined as cells in the adult nervous system that can self-renew and differentiate into all types of neural cells, including neurons, astrocytes and oligodendrocytes.[8] The CNS develops from a small number of highly plastic cells that proliferate, acquire regional identities and produce different cell types. These cells have been defined as NSCs on the basis of their potential to generate neurons and glia cells, and their ability to self-renew *in vitro*. However, this definition does not necessarily reflect the behavior of these cells *in vivo*.[9] In the brain, it appears that NSCs are specified in neurogenic regions and developmental time-points, whereas ES-derived NSCs *in vitro* are not in the same situation. Although the sources of NSCs could be ES, embryonic, developing and adult brains, the differences among them remain to be clarified.

During mammalian development, ES cells arise from the inner cell mass of blastocyst in the dividing embryo. They are capable of forming cells of various tissues, which expand by cell division until terminal differentiation.[10] Using ES neural differentiation as a platform therefore may facilitate the isolation of NSCs. ES cells could then acquire NSC identity with a default mechanism.[10,11] Recent data, using mouse ES cells[10,11] and human ES cells,[12,13] support the default mechanism model (Fig. 1). Primitive NSCs can be derived from ES cells. ES cells are found to directly develop into primitive NSCs with a default process, which is independent of instructive factors, such as EGF and FGFs. The primitive NSCs exhibit characteristics, including gene expression profile and

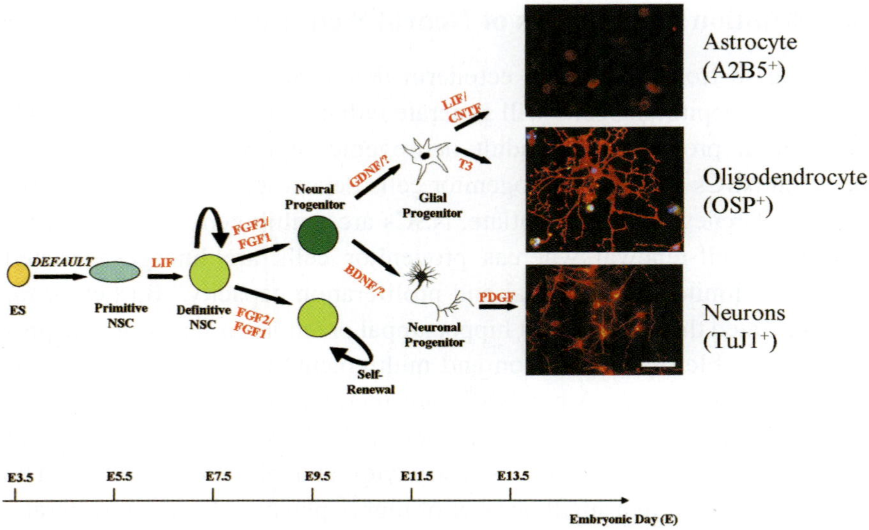


**Fig. 1.** The ontogeny and regulation of neural stem cells (NSCs) from embryonic stem (ES) cells. ES cells will become primitive NSCs (pNSCs) by a default mechanism. In the presence of leukemia inhibitory factor (LIF), the pNSCs are maintained in undifferentiated and proliferative state and give rise to FGF2/FGF1-dependent definitive NSCs (dNSCs). In the presence of FGF2 and FGF1, the dNSCs can self-renew repeatedly and generate neural progenitors, which are responsive to differentiation factors. The dNSCs is presented as a hierarchy beginning with the multipotent stem cells and progressing to the terminally differentiated neuronal and glial cell lineages. Differentiation along the glial lineage may be a default state of development reflected in the progression of NSCs along the neuronal progenitor → glial progenitor → astrocyte lineage. The restrictions of fate at several steps require the signaling of FGF2/FGF1, followed by withdrawal of FGF and the presence of other growth factors, including brain-derived neurotrophic factor (BDNF), glial cell-derived neurotrophic factor (GDNF) or platelet-derived growth factor (PDGF). The question mark (?) means other undefined factors. Glial progenitors can be further differentiated into astrocytes and oligodendrocytes by LIF, ciliary neurotrophic factor (CNTF) and triiodothyronine (T3). Neuronal progenitors can be further differentiated into neurons by platelet-derived growth factor (PDGF) or other factors. Scale bar = 50 μm.

differentiation potential, that are analogous to forebrain-derived NSCs. Therefore, *in vivo* there are two distinct sphere-forming NSC populations that are present at different stages of development from embryonic day (E) 5.5–7.5 to adulthood.[10,11] Pluripotent ES cells derived from the E3.5 inner cell mass will commence a direct default transition in the absence of inhibitory influences (e.g., TGFβ-related signaling) to yield leukemia inhibitory factor (LIF)-dependent primitive NSCs, similar to those that can be isolated from the E5.5–E7.5 epiblast. LIF-dependent (but not FGF2-dependent) sphere-forming cells are present in the earlier mouse embryo.[14] The primitive NSCs can be passaged to give rise to definitive, FGF2-dependent NSCs, analogous to the FGF2-dependent NSCs that can be isolated from the E8.5 neural plate.[15] FGF2-responsive definitive NSCs first appear in E8.5 mouse embryos. The sequential expression of FGF2 and FGF1 within the developing forebrain neuroepithelium fits with the different functions played in NSCs regulation.[16] In addition, recent studies revealed that definitive NSCs are derived from later stages and depend on Notch signaling while primitive NSCs are derived from earlier stages and depend on LIF signaling, but not on Notch signaling.[14]

Heparan sulphate proteoglycan (HSPG) represents low affinity, high capacity binging sites and are necessary for both FGF2 and FGF1 to activate the cognate tyrosine kinase receptors.[17] For instance, FGF1, which binds FGFR4 with high affinity, is more potent than FGF2, which does not bind FGFR4, to induce NGF synthesis and secretion by astrocytes.[18] Neurons, which bear all FGFRs, have been shown to be influenced by both FGF1 and FGF2.[19] Modifications of the composition of cell surface HSPG can regulate the specificity of neuronal cells to FGF1 and FGF2.[17,20] Interestingly, when developing neurons were switching from FGF2-dependent to FGF1-dependent around E11.5, the synthesis of HSPG was simultaneously switching from the type that binds FGF2 to FGF1.[17] During embryonic brain development, the definitive NSCs will generate neurons through asymmetric and symmetric divisions in an FGF2/FGF1-dependent manner. In the presence of FGF2/FGF1, this self-renewal can be performed by symmetric cell divisions, which generate two daughter cells (FGF2/FGF1 dependent NSCs) with the same fate. The FGF2/FGF1 responsive definitive NSCs can further differentiate to produce neuronal and glial progenitors through asymmetric divisions (Figs. 1 and 2). Using FGFR antagonist SU5402 and FGFR1$^{-/-}$ ES cells, van der Kooy *et al.* demonstrated that FGF signaling is not required for default neuralization of ES cells, but is crucial for the ES-derived primitive NSCs proliferation.[11]

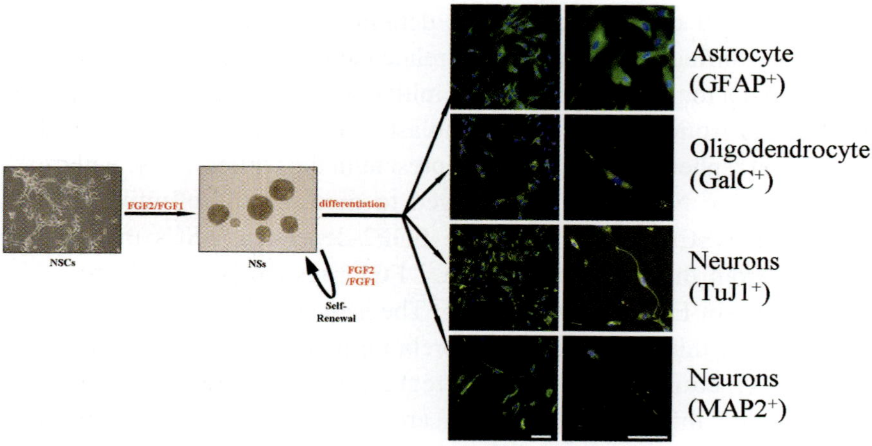


**Fig. 2.** Neural stem cell-derived neurospheres give rise to neurons, astrocytes and oligodendrocytes cell lineages under differentiation conditions. The definitive NSCs will proliferate in an FGF2/FGF1-dependent manner to generate neurospheres. The neurospheres are a cluster of NSCs and neural progenitor cells. In the presence of FGF2 and FGF1, this self-renewal can be passaged indefinitely. Under differentiation conditions, the NSCs can be differentiated to produce neurons, astrocytes and oligodendrocytes. When induced to differentiate, neurospheres generate glial fibrillary acidic protein (GFAP)-positive astrocytes, galactosylceramidase (GalC)-positive oligodendrocytes, and neurons that are positive for ßIII-tubulin and microtubule-associated protein 2 (MAP2). In the immunostaining, primary antibodies used included anti-GFAP, anti-GalC, anti-ßIII-tubulin (TuJ1) and anti-MAP2 antibodies. Cell nuclei were counterstained with the nuclear dye 4′,6-diamidino-2-phenylindole (DAPI). Scale bar = 100 μM.

## 3. Isolation and Characterization of NSCs

Recently, flow cytometry and fluorescence-activated cell sorting (FACS) have been applied extensively in neural stem cell biology, such as isolation of different precursor and progenitor populations from the CNS and peripheral nervous system (PNS). The FACS technology has been used successfully to resolve the complexity of lineage progress in the hematopoietic and other systems. NSCs that had been isolated from brain tissues by cell-surface markers, such as CD133,[21–23] or CD24,[24,25] or GFP expression are driven by NSC-specific promoters. These promoters include *Sox1*,[26–29] *Sox2*,[30,31] *Nestin*[32,33] and *FGF1*.[34] These NSCs thus isolated were cultured in the presence of growth factors and examined to determine whether they could expand to form neurospheres.[34–37] The capacity to form neurospheres was defined as self-renewal. The potential for neural differentiation of these isolated cells upon withdrawal of growth factors or administration of inducing factors was used to determine multipotency.[30,38]

NSCs or progenitors isolated from the adult CNS were shown to proliferate in the presence of the mitogen EGF[1] or FGF2[2] to form neurospheres of proliferating and undifferentiated neural cells. These neurospheres could be serially passaged to form more neurospheres, or differentiated neuronal and glial cell types when the EGF or FGF2 was removed from the medium. Isolation of NSCs from developing or adult brain tissues therefore rely on the presence of EGF and FGF2. NSCs can be maintained in Dulbecco's Modified Eagle's medium (DMEM) plus F12 medium supplemented with 10% fetal bovine serum, and then shifted to serum-free medium, containing EGF and FGF2.[39,40] This provides a stringent culture system, which culls differentiated cells in primary CNS cultures and allows NSCs to proliferate and expand exponentially.[1,39] In addition, it is further demonstrated that NSCs can respond to FGF1, and is regulated by heparan sulphate proteoglycans that bind to FGF1 specifically and are expressed within the same time frame in the developing neuroepithelium.[17,41] Progenitors restricted to the astrocyte cell lineage can be stimulated by EGF or FGF2.[41]

FGF1 plays an important role in cellular transformation and in the proliferation of ES cells and NSCs. We tested the morphological changes of human fetal glial CHII cells by culturing in the presence of keratinocyte growth factor (KGF), nerve growth factor (NGF), FGF1, and FGF1 plus heparin, The CHII glial cells did not show morphological changes when cultured with either KGF or NGF (Figs. 3A-C). By contrast, the CHII cells showed remarkable morphological changes when cultured with FGF1 (Fig. 3D). This morphological transformation was further enhanced when both FGF1 and heparin were added (Fig. 3E). The results suggest that fetal glial cells respond to FGF1, but do not respond to EGF or KGF.

The prototypic FGFs, FGF1 and FGF2, were first purified from brain extracts thirty years ago and were cloned in the mid-1980s.[42] FGF1 is important in sustaining NSC growth and self-renewal capacity.[43,44]

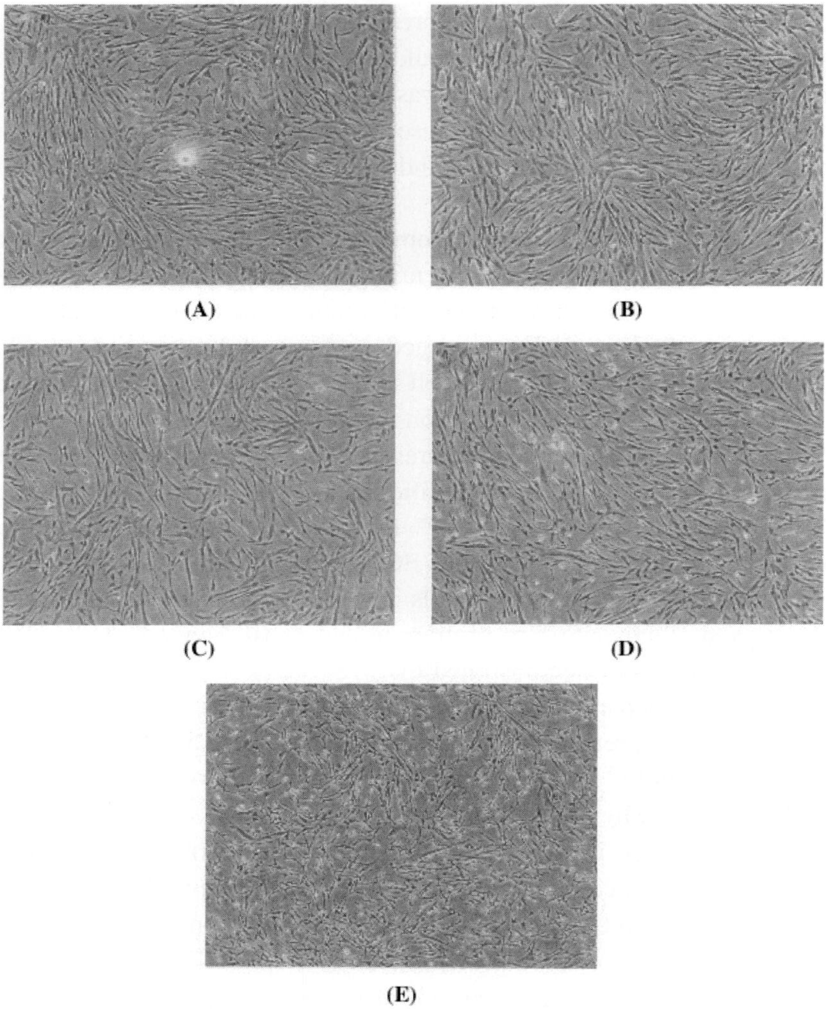

Fig. 3. FGF1 induces morphological changes of human fetal glial CHII cells, but KGF and NGF do not. Human fetal glial CHII cells were cultured in Dulbecco's modified Eagle medium with 10% calf serum (**A**), or in the presence of 40 ng/ml KGF (**B**), 40 ng/ml NGF (**C**), 40 ng/ml FGF1 (**D**), or 40 ng/ml FGF1 plus 10 μg/ml heparin (**E**).

The trophic effects of FGF1 also have been demonstrated in primary neuronal cultures and in neuronal cell lines.[45,46] The human *FGF1* gene is over 120 kbp long and contains three protein-coding exons and a long 3′-untranslated region. It also contains at least four upstream untranslated exons, designated 1A, 1B, 1C, and 1D, which are alternatively spliced to the first protein-coding exon.[47,48] This tissue-specific expression of the four *FGF1* mRNA generated by alternative splicing relies on the use of different promoters. Thus, *FGF1A* transcript predominates in the human kidney,[48] and *FGF1C* and *1D* transcripts predominate in vascular smooth muscle cells and fibroblasts.[49,50] *FGF1B* is the major transcript within the human brain[48] and retina.[51] Moreover, the expression of *FGF1B* mRNA is restricted to sensory and motor nuclei in the brain stem, spinal cord and other areas that are known to be abundant for neural stem/progenitor cells.[52,53]

By using transgenic mouse in which SV40 T antigen (Tag) reporter gene was placed under the control of F1B, activation of F1B promoter was shown in neural stem/progenitor cells of the SVZ near the segmental region.[4,6,43,54] The F1B-driven SV40 T antigen were shown to be expressed in FGF1B-positive human U-1240 MG cells, but not in FGF1B-negative U-1242 MG cells by Western blotting analysis (Fig. 4)

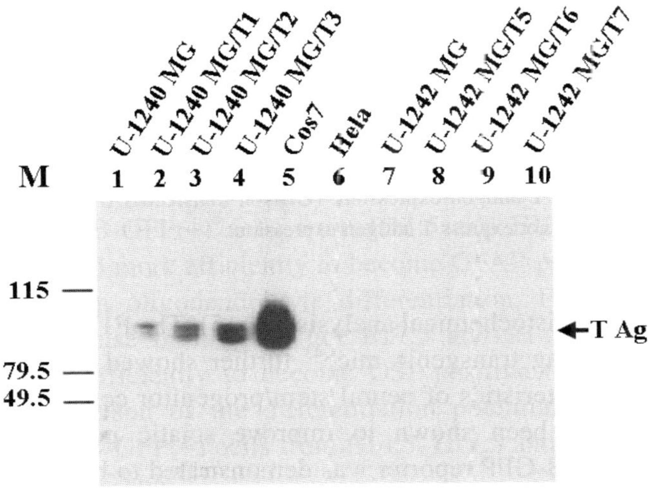


**Fig. 4.** Western blotting analysis of F1B-Tag transfected glioblastoma cell lines. U-1240 MG and U-1242 MG cells were transfected with F1B-Tag and pSV2neo. Cell lysates (100 µg) from stably transfected cells of each indicated cell line were electrophoresed, blotted onto a nitrocellulose filter, and reacted with anti-T antigen antibody. Cos7 (*lane 5*) is the positive control, and HeLa (*lane 6*) is the negative control.

**Table 2.** Quantitation of sciatic nerve repair using cell therapy.

| | Success rate | Sciatic functional index (SFI) | Area of myelinated axons ($\mu m^2$) | No. of myelinated axons | No. of blood vessels |
|---|---|---|---|---|---|
| Silicon tube | 1/3 | $-77 \pm 9$ | N/A | N/A | N/A |
| Autograft | 3/3 | $-79 \pm 7$ | $10.3 \pm 2.5$ | $1905 \pm 371$ | $58 \pm 13$ |
| PLA conduits | 3/4 | $-69 \pm 10$ | $6.5 \pm 1.3$** | $829 \pm 165$** | $40 \pm 9$ |
| PLA conduits with NSCs | 4/4 | $-47 \pm 10$** | $9.4 \pm 1.8$ | $1856 \pm 315$ | $48 \pm 11$ |

**$p < 0.05$, deviated from other groups.
N/A (not available); PLA (poly lactic acid); NSCs (neural stem cells).

that were made of either polylactide[56] or chitosan-gold.[55] The sciatic functional index as well as the histological comparisons of sciatic nerve injury repair using NSCs is shown in Table 2. Functional characteristics of NSCs correlate with the expression of several molecular markers that appear to define neural stem or progenitor cells. These molecular markers specific for NSCs include members of the *Pax* and *Hes* gene families, members of the Notch and Wnt signaling pathways, RNA binding proteins (Musashi-1, Musashi-2), and transcription factors (Sox1, Sox2),[26–31,57] cell surface markers (CD24, CD133),[21–25] and intermediate filament (Nestin).[32,33] Expression of the majority of these markers is activated during the initial phases of neural induction and is then maintained in NSCs or progenitor populations throughout ontogeny. The factors involved in the molecular mechanisms that control these molecular markers are key regulatory components that could help define the state of NSCs, including the ability to self-renew, maintenance of NSC or progenitor morphological identity, symmetric or asymmetric cellular division, and differentiation into various cell types.

The neurosphere culture system now has been widely accepted as a NSC assay that applied in the study of neural development, NSC self-renewal, plasticity and therapeutic application. Nevertheless, use of the neurosphere assay has some limitations.[58] First of all, the formation of neurospheres is argued for the possibility of aggregation. Secondly, the generation of neurospheres from certain regions of the CNS does not unambiguously refer to the same NSC population. Thirdly, different neurosphere culture protocols make it difficult to compare the results from different laboratories. Several research groups have focused on these problems and clarified the shortcomings of neurosphere assay. As such, van der Kooy *et al.* demonstrated that single NSCs, when encapsulated in agarose, proliferated as clonal, free-floating spheres. They observed the formation of neurospheres from single cells and found that clonal neurospheres can be grown by avoiding movement-induced aggregation, by single-cell tracking, and by encapsulation of single cells.[59] Merkle *et al.* specifically traced the NSCs and followed their progeny *in vivo*. They showed that post-natal NSCs in different regions produce different types of neurons, even when grafted or grown in culture. These results suggest that NSCs are a restricted and diverse population of progenitors rather than being plastic and homogeneous.[9,60,61] Therefore, a reliable protocol for neurosphere culture system is needed to compare the capacity of self-renewal. Of note, Chojnacki and Weiss described a detailed protocol for the neurosphere assay, and recommend that low-density embryonic neurosphere cultures be used to practice the skills required for successful generation of neurospheres, before proceeding to adult NSC cultures.[58]

## 4. Transcriptional Regulation of NSCs

### 4.1 *Sox transcription factors and NSCs*

The Sox family proteins contain a group of transcription factors characterized by the presence of an SRY box, a 79 amino acid motif that encodes a high mobility group (HMG-type) DNA binding domain. The Sox genes encoding proteins that are highly conserved throughout evolution were originally identified through sequence homology.[26,62,63] All Sox genes contain an HMG box closely related to that of the mammalian testes-determining gene SRY. The Sox family belongs to a subclass of HMG box proteins, the members of which show greatly restricted tissue distribution and bind to specific DNA sequences. To date, 26 vertebrate Sox genes have been identified and are classified into 7 subgroups (SoxA to SoxG) based on sequence homology. At least 12 members of the Sox gene family

Stat3 is present and active in the developing mouse CNS as early as E7.5, several days prior to gliogenesis. Recently, Foshay *et al.* induced the Stat3 dominant negative ES cells for neural differentiation and demonstrated that Stat3 is functioning very early in neural development to regulate NSC differentiation. The loss of Stat3 resulted in production of significantly fewer NSCs along with decreased expression of the NSC marker Nestin.[81] Interestingly, the T cell leukemia 3 (*Tlx3*) gene has been implicated in specification of glutamatergic sensory neurons in the spinal cord. In cranial sensory ganglia, Tlx3 is highly expressed in differentiating neurons during early embryogenesis. Kondo *et al.* demonstrated that Tlx3 can promote neuronal differentiation from mouse ES cells.[82] Interestingly, Kim *et al.* recently reported a method and demonstrated that hypoxia inducible factor-1$\alpha$ protein can mediate the increase in dopaminergic neurons from mouse ES cell-derived neural progenitor/stem cells.[83]

### 4.4 *Transcription factors for adult neurogenesis*

Adult neurogenesis occurs in two neurogenic regions in the brain: the SVZ of the lateral ventricle and the subgranular zone in the dentate gyrus of the hippocampus.[4] Transcriptional regulation is important for the maintenance of the self-renewal and multipotency of adult NSC. Bmi-1 belongs to the chromatic remodeling factors that repress the expression of arrays of genes; Bmi-1 is required for the post-natal maintenance of stem cells in multiple tissues, including the CNS and PNS.[84] The reduced self-renewal of NSCs from Bmi-1-deficient mice leads to their post-natal depletion. In the absence of Bmi-1, the cyclin-dependent kinase inhibitor gene p16Ink4a is upregulated in NSCs, reducing the rate of proliferation. p16Ink4a deficiency partially reverses the self-renewal defect in Bmi-1$^{-/-}$ NSCs.[85]

Tlx is another transcription factor that has been shown to regulate adult neurogenesis. Tlx was initially identified as an orphan nuclear receptor expressed in vertebrate forebrains and is highly expressed in the adult brain. The brains of Tlx-null mice have no obvious defects during embryogenesis; however, mature mice suffer from retinopathies, severe limbic defects, aggressiveness, reduced copulation and progressively violent behavior.[86] Tlx-expressing cells isolated by FACS from adult brains can proliferate, self-renew and differentiate into all neural cell types *in vitro*. By contrast, Tlx-null cells isolated from adult mutant brains fail to proliferate. *In vivo*, NSCs from Tlx mutant mice lose the ability to proliferate; and the number of Nestin-positive NSCs is reduced in neurogenic areas in the adult brain of Tlx-null mice. Recently, Tlx is shown to regulate cell cycle progression in NSCs of the developing brain. Increased expression of a cyclin-dependent kinase inhibitor p21 and decreased expression of cyclin D1 provide a molecular basis for the deficiency of cell cycle progression in embryonic brains of Tlx-null mice.[87] In addition, Tlx is reported as a transcriptional repressor to inhibit NSC differentiation into astrocytes.[86] Tlx can silence glia-specific expression of the astrocyte marker GFAP in NSCs, suggesting that transcriptional repression may be crucial in maintaining the undifferentiated state of these cells.[86]

Paired box (Pax) proteins are defined by the presence of a 128-amino acid DNA-binding domain, the paired domain (PD), which makes sequence-specific contacts with DNA. In mammals, nine *Pax* genes have been identified and implicated in CNS development. Of note, Pax6 has been demonstrated to promote the neurogenesis in SVZ and direct the generation of dopaminergic periglomerular cells. Inhibition of Pax6 by heterochronic transplantation of embryonic Pax6-null progenitors into the post-natal SVZ or dominant-negative construct results in a severe reduction of dopaminergic periglomerular cells.[88] Embryonic Pax6-null progenitors also fail to generate superficial granule cells, suggesting that Pax6 has a role in determining phenotypes of both granule cells and periglomerular cells.[89] In addition, Pax6 becomes downregulated in a subpopulation of neuroblasts that reach the olfactory bulb.[89]

## 5. Therapeutic Potential and Clinical Application of NSCs

NSC biology holds tremendous potential for neurological therapy. This approach is not limited to the use of NSCs for transplantation, but includes the stimulation of endogenous stem cells and the multiple bioactive molecules that they express during reciprocal interactions with the diseased CNS and PNS. Several critical problems remain to be resolved: (i) the isolation methods and protocols of human NSCs should be standardized; (ii) the clinical efficacy of NSC transplants must be evaluated in more adequate animal models; (iii) the mechanism of intrinsic brain repair need to be better characterized; and (iv) the long-term survival of the transplanted NSCs is very important in the diseased brain and dependent on the stem cell niche. In addition, there is no validated method available for tracking NSCs in human patients after transplantation. The ideal imaging technique for tracking NSCs would be safe and yield high temporal and spatial resolution, good sensitivity and specificity.

The ideal sources of NSCs for clinical application should be easy to obtain and to amplify, effective in cellular or molecular replacement, tolerant to immune rejection, and resistant to tumorigenesis. Primary human NSCs may be obtained through the following routes: primary neurosphere cultures, immortalized NSCs or ES-cell derived NSCs.

Human ES cells may provide an unlimited supply of rapidly dividing cells that can differentiate along any lineage. *In vitro,* an enriched population of midbrain NSCs can be derived from mouse or human ES cells. The dopamine neurons generated by these stem cells show electrophysiological and behavioral properties expected of neurons from the midbrain.[90–93] Of note, Cho *et al.* reported a highly efficient and large-scale generation of functional dopamine neurons from human ES cells.[94] They obtained a large number of dopaminergic neurons within a short time period and minimized potential contamination of unwanted cells or pathogens coming from the feeder layer. The unique feature of their method is the generation of homogeneous spherical neural masses from the human ES-derived neural precursors. These spherical neural masses provide several advantages: (i) long time passages without losing their differentiation capability into dopaminergic neurons; (ii) differentiation into dopaminergic neurons at much higher efficiency than that from previous reports; (iii) the induction of dopaminergic neurons from masses only takes 14 days; and (iv) no feeder cells are required during differentiation. In addition, Kang *et al.* also reported an efficient method to induce oligodendrocyte from human ES cells.[95]

Successful engraftment of transplanted NSCs, including survival, acquisition of specific phenotypes and integration into the recipient tissue, depends on the interplay between intrinsic potentialities of donor elements and specific properties of the recipient environment. Fetal primary cells are usually committed at their site of origin after implantation; they will complete their maturation process through cell-autonomous mechanisms. By contrast, multipotent NSCs necessarily require extrinsic information to direct their differentiation. Despite the multipotentiality of NSCs, the phenotypes that they actually generate in the adult brain are determined by the repertoire of inductive signals that is provided by the host environment. The molecular interactions between NSCs and the diseased microenvironment are important for the paracrine and immunomodulatory function of NSCs, even if the transplanted NSCs are not integrated in the CNS.

Transplanting multipotent NSCs into injured brain regions indicate that the host environment might exert a powerful gliogenic, rather than neurogenic activity. Many pathological conditions, either traumatic or degenerative, are associated with a prominent glial reaction and inflammatory response. So, the possibility that the environment of the injured brain contains strong gliogenic signals has to be taken into consideration when planning strategy for NSC therapy. Interleukin-6, a pro-inflammatory cytokine that is expressed in injured nervous tissue, triggers glial differentiation of NSCs *in vitro*,[96] and interferes with endogenous neurogenesis when overexpressed in the intact adult hippocampus.[97] The pro-inflammatory cytokines TNF$\alpha$ and IFN$\gamma$ participate in the mobilization of neural precursors *in vitro*[98] in association with increasing the expression of matrix metalloproteinases in the cells.[99] Other cytokines also play a role in attracting stem and precursor cell migration, including PDGF,[100] SDF-1,[101] MCP-1[102] and HGF.[103]

Efficient neurogenic activity requires the presence of endogenous neurons and an appropriate microenvironment. It remains to be determined the specific NSC therapy that is suitable for different kinds of CNS diseases. Theoretically, diseases in which clinical efficacy could be determined by a single biological mechanism, such as Parkinson's or Huntington's disease, might have increased chances of success. Multiple sclerosis and Alzheimer's diseases are still challenging for NSC therapy because their pathology is widespread in multiple sites of the CNS and impairing neuronal, as well as glial functions.[104] While targeting localized lesions that cause great disability can be contemplated, addressing multiple lesions that extend throughout the CNS remains a great challenge, even with migratory NSCs. In addition, the inflammatory and neurodegenerative microenvironment might also promote or hinder NSC function. The number of neurons that are generated by transplanted NSCs is lower in the lesion than in the intact host striatum, and most of them are localized in partially injured or intact regions and do not repopulate neuron-depleted areas.

When transplanting NSCs in spinal cord injury, NSCs integrated along axons surrounding the lesion site. These cells differentiated only along astrocytic and oligodendroglial lineages, supporting the notion that the adult injured spinal cord provides molecular cues for glial differentiation, but not for neuronal differentiation.[105] Transplantation of NSCs in Parkinson's disease models led to increased tyrosine hydroxylase in the brains of animals.[106] Neuronal progenitor cells derived from neonatal rat SVZ was transplanted into the striatum of adult rats after unilateral 6-hydroxydopamine lesions.[107] These NSCs survived and migrated, and many differentiated into neurons. Therefore, the lesioned brain contains intrinsic cues sufficient to direct the specific expression of dopaminergic traits in immature multi-potent NSCs.

## 6. Patient-Specific NSCs from Induced Pluripotent Stem Cells

Generation of patient-specific NSCs has been expected as a promising cell source to avoid immunosuppression. Yamanaka factors (Oct4, Sox2, Klf4 and c-myc) have been shown to generate induced pluripotent stem cells (iPS) from mouse[108–111] or human[112–114] fibroblasts. These iPS cells are similar to ESCs in terms of their capacity for self-renewal and their differentiation potential. Recently, Yamanaka's group further described a modified protocol for the generation of iPS cells that does not require c-myc.[115]

Human ES-derived NSCs showed their therapeutic potentials in the animal models of neurodegenerative diseases.[92,116–118] Daddi *et al.* reported the isolation of an expandable and homogenous population of NSCs from human ES cells using a defined media supplemented with EGF, FGF2 and LIF.[119] The human ES-derived NSC cell line exhibited no chromosome abnormalities and did not form tumors after implantation into rat ischemic brains and into nude rat brains and flanks. Furthermore, the human ES-derived NSC migrated toward the ischemia-injured adult brain parenchyma and improved the independent use of the stroke-impaired forelimb two months post-transplantation.[119]

Wernig *et al.* demonstrated that human iPS cells can be efficiently differentiated into neural precursor cells, giving rise to neuronal and glial cell types in culture.[120] Upon transplantation into the fetal mouse brain, the cells migrate into various brain regions and differentiate into glia and neurons, including glutamatergic, GABAergic, and catecholaminergic subtypes. Electrophysiological recordings and morphological analysis demonstrated that the grafted neurons had mature neuronal activity and were functionally integrated in the host brain. Furthermore, iPS cells were induced to differentiate into dopamine neurons of midbrain character and were able to improve behavior in a rat model of Parkinson's disease upon transplantation into the adult brain. These results suggest the therapeutic potential of directly reprogrammed fibroblasts for neuronal cell replacement in the animal model.[120]

Direct reprogramming of somatic cells to iPS provides a promising cell source for regenerative medicine, enabling the generation of patient-specific cells of any lineage without the use of embryonic material. Future works investigating the biology of iPS cells will help apply the iPS cells in the treatments of neurodegenerative diseases. Development of iPS cells from patients with amyotrophic lateral sclerosis further attests the possibility of future cell-based therapy.[121]

## References

1. Reynolds BA, Weiss S. A multipotent EGF-responsive striatal embryonic progenitor cell produces neurons and astrocytes. *Science* 1992;255:1707–1710.
2. Gage FH, Ray J, Fisher LJ. Isolation, characterization, and use of stem cells from the CNS. *Annu Rev Neurosci* 1995;18:159–192.
3. Gage FH, Kempermann G, Palmer TD, *et al.* Multipotent progenitor cells in the adult dentate gyrus. *J Neurobiol* 1998;36:249–266.
4. Zhao C, Deng W, Gage FH. Mechanisms and functional implications of adult neurogenesis. *Cell* 2008;132:645–660.
5. Weiner LP. Definitions and criteria for stem cells. *Methods Mol Biol* 2008;438:3–8.

6. Taupin P. Neural progenitor and stem cells in the adult central nervous system. *Ann Acad Med Singapore* 2006;35:814–820.
7. Bull ND, Bartlett PF. The adult mouse hippocampal progenitor is neurogenic but not a stem cell. *J Neurosci* 2005;25:10815–10821.
8. Gage FH. Mammalian neural stem cells. *Science* 2000;287:1433–1438.
9. Merkle FT, varez-Buylla A. Mosaic organization of neural stem cells in the adult brain. *Curr Opin Cell Biol* 2006;18:704–709.
10. Tropepe V, Hitoshi S, Sirard C, *et al.* Direct neural fate specification from embryonic stem cells: a primitive mammalian neural stem cell stage acquired through a default mechanism. *Neuron* 2001;30:65–78.
11. Smukler SR, Runciman SB, Xu S, van der Kooy KD. Embryonic stem cells assume a primitive neural stem cell fate in the absence of extrinsic influences. *J Cell Biol* 2006;172:79–90.
12. Brons IG, Smithers LE, Trotter MW, *et al.* Derivation of pluripotent epiblast stem cells from mammalian embryos. *Nature* 2007;448:191–195.
13. Vallier L, Reynolds D, Pedersen RA. Nodal inhibits differentiation of human embryonic stem cells along the neuroectodermal default pathway. *Dev Biol* 2004;275:403–421.
14. Hitoshi S, Seaberg RM, Koscik C, *et al.* Primitive neural stem cells from the mammalian epiblast differentiate to definitive neural stem cells under the control of Notch signaling. *Genes Dev* 2004;18:1806–1811.
15. Uchida N, Buck DW, He D, *et al.* Direct isolation of human central nervous system stem cells. *Proc Natl Acad Sci USA* 2000;97:14720–14725.
16. Bartlett PF, Richards LR, Kilpatrick TJ, *et al.* Regulation of neural precursor differentiation in the embryonic and adult forebrain. *Clin Exp Pharmacol Physiol* 1995;22:559–562.
17. Nurcombe V, Ford MD, Wildschut JA, Bartlett PF. Developmental regulation of neural response to FGF-1 and FGF-2 by heparan sulfate proteoglycan. *Science* 1993;260:103–106.
18. Yoshida K, Gage FH. Cooperative regulation of nerve growth factor synthesis and secretion in fibroblasts and astrocytes by fibroblast growth factor and other cytokines. *Brain Res* 1992;569:14–25.
19. Plotnikov AN, Hubbard SR, Schlessinger J, Mohammadi M. Crystal structures of two FGF-FGFR complexes reveal the determinants of ligand-receptor specificity. *Cell* 2000;101:413–424.

20. Brickman YG, Ford MD, Small DH, *et al.* Heparan sulfates mediate the binding of basic fibroblast growth factor to a specific receptor on neural precursor cells. *J Biol Chem* 1995;270:24941–24948.
21. Pruszak J, Sonntag KC, Aung MH, *et al.* Markers and methods for cell sorting of human embryonic stem cell-derived neural cell populations. *Stem Cells* 2007;25:2257–2268.
22. Panchision DM, Chen HL, Pistollato F, *et al.* Optimized flow cytometric analysis of central nervous system tissue reveals novel functional relationships among cells expressing CD133, CD15, and CD24. *Stem Cells* 2007;25:1560–1570.
23. Barraud P, Stott S, Mollgard K, *et al.* *In vitro* characterization of a human neural progenitor cell coexpressing SSEA4 and CD133. *J Neurosci Res* 2007;85:250–259.
24. Huhn SL, Yung Y, Cheshier S, *et al.* Identification of phenotypic neural stem cells in a pediatric astroblastoma. *J Neurosurg* 2005;103:446–450.
25. Murayama A, Matsuzaki Y, Kawaguchi A, *et al.* Flow cytometric analysis of neural stem cells in the developing and adult mouse brain. *J Neurosci Res* 2002;69:837–847.
26. Wegner M, Stolt CC. From stem cells to neurons and glia: a Soxist's view of neural development. *Trends Neurosci* 2005;28:583–588.
27. Aubert J, Stavridis MP, Tweedie S, *et al.* Screening for mammalian neural genes via fluorescence-activated cell sorter purification of neural precursors from Sox1-gfp knock-in mice. *Proc Natl Acad Sci USA* 2003;100 Suppl 1:11836–11841.
28. Johnson CE, Crawford BE, Stavridis M, *et al.* Essential alterations of heparan sulfate during the differentiation of embryonic stem cells to Sox1-enhanced green fluorescent protein-expressing neural progenitor cells. *Stem Cells* 2007;25:1913–1923.
29. Lang RJ, Haynes JM, Kelly J, *et al.* Electrical and neurotransmitter activity of mature neurons derived from mouse embryonic stem cells by Sox-1 lineage selection and directed differentiation. *Eur J Neurosci* 2004;20:3209–3221.
30. Suh H, Consiglio A, Ray J, *et al.* *In vivo* fate analysis reveals the multipotent and self-renewal capacities of $Sox2^+$ neural stem cells in the adult hippocampus. *Cell Stem Cell* 2007;1:515–528.

31. D'Amour KA, Gage FH. Genetic and functional differences between multipotent neural and pluripotent embryonic stem cells. *Proc Natl Acad Sci USA* 2003;100 Suppl 1:11866–11872.
32. Park JH, Ahn JI, Kim SY, *et al.* Genetic modification does not affect the stemness of neural stem cells in nestin promoter-GFP transgenic mice. *Neurosci Lett* 2007;421:185–190.
33. Ma BF, Liu XM, Xie XM, *et al.* Slower cycling of nestin-positive cells in neurosphere culture. *Neuroreport* 2006;17:377–381.
34. Hsu YC, Lee DC, Chen SL, *et al.* Brain-specific 1B promoter of FGF1 gene facilitates the isolation of neural stem/progenitor cells with self-renewal and multipotent capacities. *Dev Dyn* 2008;238:302–314.
35. Heo C, Chang KA, Choi HS, *et al.* Effects of the monomeric, oligomeric, and fibrillar Abeta42 peptides on the proliferation and differentiation of adult neural stem cells from subventricular zone. *J Neurochem* 2007;102:493–500.
36. Pollard SM, Benchoua A, Lowell S. Neural stem cells, neurons, and glia. *Methods Enzymol* 2006;418:151–169.
37. Pollard SM, Wallbank R, Tomlinson S, *et al.* Fibroblast growth factor induces a neural stem cell phenotype in foetal forebrain progenitors and during embryonic stem cell differentiation. *Mol Cell Neurosci* 2008;38:393–403.
38. Johe KK, Hazel TG, Muller T, *et al.* Single factors direct the differentiation of stem cells from the fetal and adult central nervous system. *Genes Dev* 1996;10:3129–3140.
39. Vescovi AL, Parati EA, Gritti A, *et al.* Clonal analyses and cryopreservation of neural stem cell cultures. *Exp Neurol* 2002;156:71–83.
40. Gritti A, Parati EA, Cova L, *et al.* Multipotential stem cells from the adult mouse brain proliferate and self-renew in response to basic fibroblast growth factor. *J Neurosci* 1996;16:1091–1100.
41. Bartlett PF, Richards LR, Kilpatrick TJ, *et al.* Regulation of neural precursor differentiation in the embryonic and adult forebrain. *Ciba Found Symp* 1995;193:85–99.
42. Mason I. Initiation to end point: the multiple roles of fibroblast growth factors in neural development. *Nat Rev Neurosci* 2007;8:583–596.
43. Chiu IM, Touhalisky K, Liu Y, *et al.* Tumorigenesis in transgenic mice in which the SV40 T antigen is driven by the brain-specific FGF1 promoter. *Oncogene* 2000;19:6229–6239.

44. Kalyani AJ, Mujtaba T, Rao MS. Neuroepithelial stem cells from the embryonic spinal cord: isolation, characterization, and clonal analysis. *J Neurobiol* 1999;38:207–224.
45. Klein S, Roghani M, Rifkin DB. Fibroblast growth factors as angiogenesis factors: new insights into their mechanism of action. *EXS* 7 1997;9:159–192.
46. Gospodarowicz D. Fibroblast growth factors: from genes to clinical applications. *Cell Biol Rev* 1991;25:307–309.
47. Payson RA, Canatan H, Chotani MA, *et al.* Cloning of two novel forms of human acidic fibroblast growth factor (aFGF) mRNA. *Nucleic Acids Res* 1993;21:489–495.
48. Myers RL, Payson RA, Chotani MA, *et al.* Gene structure and differential expression of acidic fibroblast growth factor mRNA: identification and distribution of four different transcripts. *Oncogene* 1993;8:341–349.
49. Chotani MA, Payson RA, Winkles JA, Chiu IM. Human fibroblast growth factor 1 gene expression in vascular smooth muscle cells is modulated via an alternate promoter in response to serum and phorbol ester. *Nucleic Acids Res* 1995;23:434–441.
50. Chotani MA, Touhalisky K, Chiu IM. The small GTPases Ras, Rac, and Cdc42 transcriptionally regulate expression of human fibroblast growth factor 1. *J Biol Chem* 2000;275:30432–30438.
51. Myers RL, Chedid M, Tronick SR, Chiu IM. Different fibroblast growth factor 1 (FGF-1) transcripts in neural tissues, glioblastomas and kidney carcinoma cell lines. *Oncogene* 1995;11:785–789.
52. Alam KY, Frostholm A, Hackshaw KV, *et al.* Characterization of the 1B promoter of fibroblast growth factor 1 and its expression in the adult and developing mouse brain. *J Biol Chem* 1996;271:30263–30271.
53. Chiu IM, Touhalisky K, Baran C. Multiple controlling mechanisms of FGF1 gene expression through multiple tissue-specific promoters. *Prog Nucleic Acid Res Mol Biol* 2001;70:155–174.
54. Weiss WA, Israel M, Cobbs C, *et al.* Neuropathology of genetically engineered mice: consensus report and recommendations from an international forum. *Oncogene* 2002;21:7453–7463.
55. Lin YL, Jen JC, Hsu SH, Chiu IM. Sciatic nerve repair by microgrooved nerve conduits made of chitosan-gold nanocomposites. *Surg Neurol* 2008;70:S1–S18.

83. Kim TS, Misumi S, Jung CG, *et al.* Increase in dopaminergic neurons from mouse embryonic stem cell-derived neural progenitor/stem cells is mediated by hypoxia inducible factor-1alpha. *J Neurosci Res* 2008;86:2353–2362.
84. Molofsky AV, He S, Bydon M, *et al.* Bmi-1 promotes neural stem cell self-renewal and neural development but not mouse growth and survival by repressing the p16Ink4a and p19Arf senescence pathways. *Genes Dev* 2005;19:1432–1437.
85. Molofsky AV, Pardal R, Iwashita T, *et al.* Bmi-1 dependence distinguishes neural stem cell self-renewal from progenitor proliferation. *Nature* 2003;425:962–967.
86. Shi Y, Chichung LD, Taupin P, *et al.* Expression and function of orphan nuclear receptor TLX in adult neural stem cells. *Nature* 2004;427:78–83.
87. Li W, Sun G, Yang S, *et al.* Nuclear receptor TLX regulates cell cycle progression in neural stem cells of the developing brain. *Mol Endocrinol* 2008;22:56–64.
88. Hack MA, Saghatelyan A, de Chevigny A, *et al.* Neuronal fate determinants of adult olfactory bulb neurogenesis. *Nat. Neurosci* 2005;8:865–872.
89. Kohwi M, Osumi N, Rubenstein JL, varez-Buylla A. Pax6 is required for making specific subpopulations of granule and periglomerular neurons in the olfactory bulb. *J Neurosci* 2005;25:6997–7003.
90. Kim JH, Auerbach JM, Rodriguez-Gomez JA, *et al.* Dopamine neurons derived from embryonic stem cells function in an animal model of Parkinson's disease. *Nature* 2002;418:50–56.
91. Kim DS, Kim JY, Kang M, *et al.* Derivation of functional dopamine neurons from embryonic stem cells. *Cell Transplant* 2007;16:117–123.
92. Cho YH, Kim DS, Kim PG, *et al.* Dopamine neurons derived from embryonic stem cells efficiently induce behavioral recovery in a Parkinsonian rat model. *Biochem Biophys Res Commun* 2006;341:6–12.
93. Kim DW, Chung S, Hwang M, *et al.* Stromal cell-derived inducing activity, Nurr1, and signaling molecules synergistically induce dopaminergic neurons from mouse embryonic stem cells. *Stem Cells* 2006;24:557–567.
94. Cho MS, Lee YE, Kim JY, *et al.* Highly efficient and large-scale generation of functional dopamine neurons from human embryonic stem cells. *Proc Natl Acad Sci USA* 2008;105:3392–3397.
95. Kang SM, Cho MS, Seo H, *et al.* Efficient induction of oligodendrocytes from human embryonic stem cells. *Stem Cells* 2007;25:419–424.

44. Kalyani AJ, Mujtaba T, Rao MS. Neuroepithelial stem cells from the embryonic spinal cord: isolation, characterization, and clonal analysis. *J Neurobiol* 1999;38:207–224.
45. Klein S, Roghani M, Rifkin DB. Fibroblast growth factors as angiogenesis factors: new insights into their mechanism of action. *EXS* 7 1997;9:159–192.
46. Gospodarowicz D. Fibroblast growth factors: from genes to clinical applications. *Cell Biol Rev* 1991;25:307–309.
47. Payson RA, Canatan H, Chotani MA, *et al.* Cloning of two novel forms of human acidic fibroblast growth factor (aFGF) mRNA. *Nucleic Acids Res* 1993;21:489–495.
48. Myers RL, Payson RA, Chotani MA, *et al.* Gene structure and differential expression of acidic fibroblast growth factor mRNA: identification and distribution of four different transcripts. *Oncogene* 1993;8:341–349.
49. Chotani MA, Payson RA, Winkles JA, Chiu IM. Human fibroblast growth factor 1 gene expression in vascular smooth muscle cells is modulated via an alternate promoter in response to serum and phorbol ester. *Nucleic Acids Res* 1995;23:434–441.
50. Chotani MA, Touhalisky K, Chiu IM. The small GTPases Ras, Rac, and Cdc42 transcriptionally regulate expression of human fibroblast growth factor 1. *J Biol Chem* 2000;275:30432–30438.
51. Myers RL, Chedid M, Tronick SR, Chiu IM. Different fibroblast growth factor 1 (FGF-1) transcripts in neural tissues, glioblastomas and kidney carcinoma cell lines. *Oncogene* 1995;11:785–789.
52. Alam KY, Frostholm A, Hackshaw KV, *et al.* Characterization of the 1B promoter of fibroblast growth factor 1 and its expression in the adult and developing mouse brain. *J Biol Chem* 1996;271:30263–30271.
53. Chiu IM, Touhalisky K, Baran C. Multiple controlling mechanisms of FGF1 gene expression through multiple tissue-specific promoters. *Prog Nucleic Acid Res Mol Biol* 2001;70:155–174.
54. Weiss WA, Israel M, Cobbs C, *et al.* Neuropathology of genetically engineered mice: consensus report and recommendations from an international forum. *Oncogene* 2002;21:7453–7463.
55. Lin YL, Jen JC, Hsu SH, Chiu IM. Sciatic nerve repair by microgrooved nerve conduits made of chitosan-gold nanocomposites. *Surg Neurol* 2008;70:S1–S18.

56. Hsu SH, Su CH, Chiu IM. A novel approach to align adult neural stem cells on micropatterned conduits for peripheral nerve regeneration: a feasibility study. *Artif Organs* 2009;33:26–35.
57. Ellis P, Fagan BM, Magness ST, *et al.* SOX2, a persistent marker for multipotential neural stem cells derived from embryonic stem cells, the embryo or the adult. *Dev Neurosci* 2004;26:148–165.
58. Chojnacki A, Weiss S. Production of neurons, astrocytes and oligodendrocytes from mammalian CNS stem cells. *Nat Protoc* 2008;3:935–940.
59. Coles-Takabe BL, Brain I, Purpura KA, *et al.* Don't look: growing clonal versus nonclonal neural stem cell colonies. *Stem Cells* 2008;26:2938–2944.
60. Merkle FT, Mirzadeh Z, varez-Buylla A. Mosaic organization of neural stem cells in the adult brain. *Science* 2007;317:381–384.
61. Mirzadeh Z, Merkle FT, Soriano-Navarro M, *et al.* Neural stem cells confer unique pinwheel architecture to the ventricular surface in neurogenic regions of the adult brain. *Cell Stem Cell* 2008;3:265–278.
62. Bowles J, Schepers G, Koopman P. Phylogeny of the SOX family of developmental transcription factors based on sequence and structural indicators. *Dev Biol* 2000;227:239–255.
63. Pevny L, Placzek M. SOX genes and neural progenitor identity. *Curr Opin Neurobiol* 2005;15:7–13.
64. Wood HB, Episkopou V. Comparative expression of the mouse Sox1, Sox2 and Sox3 genes from pre-gastrulation to early somite stages. *Mech Dev* 1999;86:197–201.
65. Malas S, Postlethwaite M, Ekonomou A, *et al.* Sox1-deficient mice suffer from epilepsy associated with abnormal ventral forebrain development and olfactory cortex hyperexcitability. *Neuroscience* 2003;119:421–432.
66. Rizzoti K, Brunelli S, Carmignac D, *et al.* SOX3 is required during the formation of the hypothalamo-pituitary axis. *Nat Gene* 2004;36:247–255.
67. Ferri AL, Cavallaro M, Braida D, *et al.* Sox2 deficiency causes neurodegeneration and impaired neurogenesis in the adult mouse brain. *Development* 2004;131:3805–3819.
68. Bylund M, Andersson E, Novitch BG, Muhr J. Vertebrate neurogenesis is counteracted by Sox1-3 activity. *Nat Neurosci* 2003;6:1162–1168.
69. Pevny LH, Sockanathan S, Placzek M, Lovell-Badge R. A role for SOX1 in neural determination. *Development* 1998;125:1967–1978.

70. Uchikawa M, Ishida Y, Takemoto T, *et al.* Functional analysis of chicken Sox2 enhancers highlights an array of diverse regulatory elements that are conserved in mammals. *Dev Cell* 2003;4:509–519.
71. Sandberg M, Kallstrom M, Muhr J. Sox21 promotes the progression of vertebrate neurogenesis. *Nat Neurosci* 2005;8:995–1001.
72. Kageyama R, Ohtsuka T, Kobayashi T. Roles of Hes genes in neural development. *Dev Growth Differ* 2008;50 Suppl 1:S97–103.
73. Kageyama R, Ohtsuka T, Hatakeyama J, Ohsawa R. Roles of bHLH genes in neural stem cell differentiation. *Exp Cell Res* 2005;306:343–348.
74. Ishibashi M, Moriyoshi K, Sasai Y, *et al.* Persistent expression of helix-loop-helix factor HES-1 prevents mammalian neural differentiation in the central nervous system. *EMBO J* 1994;13:1799–1805.
75. Kageyama R. Regulation of neuronal differentiation by bHLH factors. *Tanpakushitsu Kakusan Koso* 2000;45:1605–1611.
76. Allen T, Lobe CG. A comparison of Notch, Hes and Grg expression during murine embryonic and post-natal development. *Cell Mol Biol (Noisy-le-grand)* 1999;45:687–708.
77. Sasai Y, Kageyama R, Tagawa Y, *et al.* Two mammalian helix-loop-helix factors structurally related to Drosophila hairy and enhancer of split. *Genes Dev* 1992;6:2620–2634.
78. Chen H, Thiagalingam A, Chopra H, *et al.* Conservation of the Drosophila lateral inhibition pathway in human lung cancer: a hairy-related protein (HES-1) directly represses achaete-scute homolog-1 expression. *Proc Natl Acad Sci USA* 1997;94:5355–5360.
79. Wang J, Rao S, Chu J, *et al.* A protein interaction network for pluripotency of embryonic stem cells. *Nature* 2006;444:364–368.
80. Suter DM, Tirefort D, Julien S, Krause KH. A Sox1 to Pax6 switch drives neuroectoderm to radial glia progression during differentiation of mouse embryonic stem cells. *Stem Cells* 2009;27:49–58.
81. Foshay KM, Gallicano GI. Regulation of Sox2 by STAT3 initiates commitment to the neural precursor cell fate. *Stem Cells Dev* 2008;17:269–278.
82. Kondo T, Sheets PL, Zopf DA, *et al.* Tlx3 exerts context-dependent transcriptional regulation and promotes neuronal differentiation from embryonic stem cells. *Proc Natl Acad Sci USA* 2008;105:5780–5785.

83. Kim TS, Misumi S, Jung CG, *et al.* Increase in dopaminergic neurons from mouse embryonic stem cell-derived neural progenitor/stem cells is mediated by hypoxia inducible factor-1alpha. *J Neurosci Res* 2008;86:2353–2362.
84. Molofsky AV, He S, Bydon M, *et al.* Bmi-1 promotes neural stem cell self-renewal and neural development but not mouse growth and survival by repressing the p16Ink4a and p19Arf senescence pathways. *Genes Dev* 2005;19:1432–1437.
85. Molofsky AV, Pardal R, Iwashita T, *et al.* Bmi-1 dependence distinguishes neural stem cell self-renewal from progenitor proliferation. *Nature* 2003;425:962–967.
86. Shi Y, Chichung LD, Taupin P, *et al.* Expression and function of orphan nuclear receptor TLX in adult neural stem cells. *Nature* 2004;427:78–83.
87. Li W, Sun G, Yang S, *et al.* Nuclear receptor TLX regulates cell cycle progression in neural stem cells of the developing brain. *Mol Endocrinol* 2008;22:56–64.
88. Hack MA, Saghatelyan A, de Chevigny A, *et al.* Neuronal fate determinants of adult olfactory bulb neurogenesis. *Nat. Neurosci* 2005;8:865–872.
89. Kohwi M, Osumi N, Rubenstein JL, varez-Buylla A. Pax6 is required for making specific subpopulations of granule and periglomerular neurons in the olfactory bulb. *J Neurosci* 2005;25:6997–7003.
90. Kim JH, Auerbach JM, Rodriguez-Gomez JA, *et al.* Dopamine neurons derived from embryonic stem cells function in an animal model of Parkinson's disease. *Nature* 2002;418:50–56.
91. Kim DS, Kim JY, Kang M, *et al.* Derivation of functional dopamine neurons from embryonic stem cells. *Cell Transplant* 2007;16:117–123.
92. Cho YH, Kim DS, Kim PG, *et al.* Dopamine neurons derived from embryonic stem cells efficiently induce behavioral recovery in a Parkinsonian rat model. *Biochem Biophys Res Commun* 2006;341:6–12.
93. Kim DW, Chung S, Hwang M, *et al.* Stromal cell-derived inducing activity, Nurr1, and signaling molecules synergistically induce dopaminergic neurons from mouse embryonic stem cells. *Stem Cells* 2006;24:557–567.
94. Cho MS, Lee YE, Kim JY, *et al.* Highly efficient and large-scale generation of functional dopamine neurons from human embryonic stem cells. *Proc Natl Acad Sci USA* 2008;105:3392–3397.
95. Kang SM, Cho MS, Seo H, *et al.* Efficient induction of oligodendrocytes from human embryonic stem cells. *Stem Cells* 2007;25:419–424.

96. Bonni A, Sun Y, Nadal-Vicens M, *et al.* Regulation of gliogenesis in the central nervous system by the JAK-STAT signaling pathway. *Science* 1997;278:477–483.
97. Vallieres L, Campbell IL, Gage FH, Sawchenko PE. Reduced hippocampal neurogenesis in adult transgenic mice with chronic astrocytic production of interleukin-6. *J Neurosci* 2002;22:486–492.
98. Ben-Hur T, Ben-Menachem O, Furer V, *et al.* Effects of proinflammatory cytokines on the growth, fate, and motility of multipotential neural precursor cells. *Mol Cell Neurosci* 2003;24:623–631.
99. Ben-Hur T, Ben-Yosef Y, Mizrachi-Kol R, *et al.* Cytokine-mediated modulation of MMPs and TIMPs in multipotential neural precursor cells. *J Neuroimmunol* 2006;175:12–18.
100. Armstrong RC, Harvath L, Dubois-Dalcq ME. Type 1 astrocytes and oligodendrocyte-type 2 astrocyte glial progenitors migrate toward distinct molecules. *J Neurosci Res* 1990;27:400–407.
101. Imitola J, Raddassi K, Park KI, *et al.* Directed migration of neural stem cells to sites of CNS injury by the stromal cell-derived factor 1alpha/CXC chemokine receptor 4 pathway. *Proc Natl Acad Sci USA* 2004;101:18117–18122.
102. Belmadani A, Tran PB, Ren D, Miller RJ. Chemokines regulate the migration of neural progenitors to sites of neuroinflammation. *J Neurosci* 2006;26:3182–3191.
103. Lalive PH, Paglinawan R, Biollaz G, *et al.* TGF-beta-treated microglia induce oligodendrocyte precursor cell chemotaxis through the HGF-c-Met pathway. *Eur J Immunol* 2005;35:727–737.
104. Imitola J. Prospects for neural stem cell-based therapies for neurological diseases. *Neurotherapeutics* 2007;4:701–714.
105. Vroemen M, Aigner L, Winkler J, Weidner N. Adult neural progenitor cell grafts survive after acute spinal cord injury and integrate along axonal pathways. *Eur J Neurosci* 2003;18:743–751.
106. Anton R, Kordower JH, Maidment NT, *et al.* Neural-targeted gene therapy for rodent and primate hemiparkinsonism. *Exp Neurol* 1994;127:207–218.
107. Lundberg C, Field PM, Ajayi YO, *et al.* Conditionally immortalized neural progenitor cell lines integrate and differentiate after grafting to the adult rat striatum. A combined autoradiographic and electron microscopic study. *Brain Res* 1996;737:295–300.

108. Takahashi K, Yamanaka S. Induction of pluripotent stem cells from mouse embryonic and adult fibroblast cultures by defined factors. *Cell* 2006;126: 663–676.
109. Okita K, Ichisaka T, Yamanaka S. Generation of germline-competent induced pluripotent stem cells. *Nature* 2007;448:313–317.
110. Meissner A, Wernig M, Jaenisch R. Direct reprogramming of genetically unmodified fibroblasts into pluripotent stem cells. *Nat Biotechnol* 2007;25:1177–1181.
111. Wernig M, Meissner A, Foreman R, *et al. In vitro* reprogramming of fibroblasts into a pluripotent ES-cell-like state. *Nature* 2007;448:318–324.
112. Takahashi K, Tanabe K, Ohnuki M, *et al.* Induction of pluripotent stem cells from adult human fibroblasts by defined factors. *Cell* 2007;131:861–872.
113. Yu J, Vodyanik MA, Smuga-Otto K, *et al.* Induced pluripotent stem cell lines derived from human somatic cells. *Science* 2007;318:1917–1920.
114. Park IH, Zhao R, West JA, *et al.* Reprogramming of human somatic cells to pluripotency with defined factors. *Nature* 2008;451:141–146.
115. Nakagawa M, Koyanagi M, Tanabe K, *et al.* Generation of induced pluripotent stem cells without Myc from mouse and human fibroblasts. *Nat Biotechnol* 2008;26:101–106.
116. Hsu YC, Lee DC, Chiu IM. Neural stem cells, neural progenitors, and neurotrophic factors. *Cell Transplant* 2007;16:133–150.
117. Colombo E, Giannelli SG, Galli R, *et al.* Embryonic stem-derived versus somatic neural stem cells: a comparative analysis of their developmental potential and molecular phenotype. *Stem Cells* 2006;24:825–834.
118. Sanberg PR. Neural stem cells for Parkinson's disease: to protect and repair. *Proc Natl Acad Sci USA* 2007;104:11869–11870.
119. Daadi MM, Maag AL, Steinberg GK. Adherent self-renewable human embryonic stem cell-derived neural stem cell line: functional engraftment in experimental stroke model. *PLoS ONE* 2008;3:e1644.
120. Wernig M, Zhao JP, Pruszak J, *et al.* Neurons derived from reprogrammed fibroblasts functionally integrate into the fetal brain and improve symptoms of rats with Parkinson's disease. *Proc Natl Acad Sci USA* 2008;105: 5856–5861.
121. Dimos JT, Rodolfa KT, Niakan KK, *et al.* Induced pluripotent stem cells generated from patients with ALS can be differentiated into motor neurons. *Science* 2008;321:1218–1221.

# CHAPTER 14

## CELLULAR CARDIOMYOPLASTY: EVIDENCE OF CELLULAR THERAPY, MECHANISMS AND CONTROVERSIES

*Adil Al-Kindi, Yin Ge and Dominique Shum-Tim*

### Abstract

Cardiomyocytes are terminally differentiated cells that the heart cannot replace when they are damaged. A couple of decades ago, attempts were made to exogenously replace lost cardiac cells in hope of ultimately avoiding heart failure. However, despite promising initial results, the progress has been humble. One of the main limiting factors has been lack of clear understanding of the mechanism behind the functional improvement observed. Three main hypotheses emerged; the oldest is "trans-differentiation" which assumes that transplanted primitive cells need to differentiate to cardiac cells before contributing to the function. Evidence also supported "fusion", in which transplanted cells fuse with primitive cardiac cells to improve cardiac function. However, due to the paucity of trans-differentiated or fused cells, it was thought that it was unlikely that these mechanisms are the sole contributors. Evidence has thus emerged that transplanted stem cells actually exert a paracrine effect on the surrounding cells and extracellular matrix with angiogenic, prosurvival and anti-inflammatory effects.

In this chapter, we review the evidence behind the mechanisms of functional improvement in "cellular cardiomyoplasty" and carefully investigate the evidence and controversies behind transdifferentiation, fusion and paracrine hypotheses. Evidence from both *in-vivo* and *in-vitro* studies is explored.

## 1. Introduction

With advances in medical and surgical therapies, patients with cardiovascular diseases currently have their best survival rates ever. However, this in turn has led to an epidemic of congestive heart failure (CHF) in the world and especially in North America. CHF is currently the most prevalent chronic disease in North America with approximately five million cases in the USA alone. It remains the most common cause of hospitalization in patients more than 65 years, with an incidence that has increased by 155% in the last 20 years.[1] The current estimate is that over 550,000 new cases are diagnosed annually in the USA. These patients have frequent hospitalization with high morbidity and mortality reaching as high as 40% annually.[2]

Efforts in dealing with this problem have resulted in advances being made in different treatment modalities. Currently, patients receive a range of highly sophisticated medical,[3] cardiac resynchronization therapy (CRT),[4,5] surgical ventricular remodeling (SVR),[6,7] ventricular assist devices (VADs),[8] and heart transplantation.[9,10] These current therapies have improved the prognosis of this disease over the years. However, they have proven to be associated with inherent limited success, complications, and significant cost as they do not address the fundamental pathophysiological problem related to the loss of functional contractile cardiomyocytes in patients with CHF.

Cardiomyocytes are terminally differentiated cells. In other words, these cells have exited the cell cycle, and are not able to re-enter and divide in certain circumstances. On the other hand, cells with stem cell properties have been identified in the heart that may be able to divide and multiply, giving rise to new cardiomyocytes of similar properties to the native cardiac cells.[11] However, it seems that their natural contribution is physiologically insignificant, as such cells have not been able to notably repair damaged mammalian hearts. Therefore, to address this issue, scientists have attempted the transplant of various cell types to replace the lost cardiac cells.[12–18] Reports of different cells used include skeletal myoblasts,[12,13] embryonic stem cells (ESC),[14,15] resident cardiac stem cells,[16,18] and bone marrow cells (BMCs).[19–23] These cells have demonstrated multipotency with their ability to regenerate not only the heart, but other tissue organs including bone,[24] cartilage,[25] tendon,[26] fat,[27] and muscle.[28]

In addition to their tremendous differentiation plasticity, MSCs have gained popularity because of their readily availability, relative ease to harvest, ability to be cultured, expanded *in vitro*, and stored to be used as needed.[29] Adding to this, mounting evidence has emerged recently, from our lab that has shown that MSCs have unique immune tolerance, and can act as "universal donors" not only in autologous, but also extending to xenotransplantation.[30–32] These studies have demonstrated that MSCs transplanted across species not only demonstrated no immune rejection in the recipient, but also contributed to the functional improvement of the ischemic heart.

Since its discovery over two decades ago, "cellular cardiomyoplasty" has achieved important milestones. Our understanding of the cellular repair has gone beyond the microscopic appearance to studying the gene regulation involved and the chemical signaling. It has also progressed from the bench to the bedside. A number of clinical trials, including randomized ones, have been conducted to test for the safety and feasibility of cellular therapy on the ischemic and failing heart.[33–38]

However, despite all this, the results in our view have been humble. A number of logistical problems exist, ranging from the best ways of cell delivery,[39–41] to optimizing cellular retention and minimizing causes of cellular loss.[42–45] The therapeutic benefit, if any, has been sub-optimal whether in animal studies[46,47] or in the clinical trials.[37,48]

One of the major problems regarding our current approach is lack of clear understanding of the mechanism of functional improvement. Different schools have emerged, advocating the role of transdifferentiation,[19,49,50] cellular fusion,[51,52] or paracrine effects.[53] However, none of these schools have taken us beyond reasonable doubt regarding each theory. Animal studies are still being conducted in order to understand the possible mechanism.

In this chapter, the objective is to review evidence regarding each of the three main mechanisms of functional improvement: transdifferentiation, fusion, and paracrine effect. A better understanding of the current evidence will certainly direct future research towards a better therapeutic approach.

## 1.1 *The zebrafish model*

Unlike humans, where the ability to regenerate is very restricted and limited to the liver and finger tips, the zebrafish has the ability to regenerate not only lost parts of its fins, spinal cord and retina,[54,55] but also parts of the heart. This has been called epimorphic regeneration. Keating *et al.* described the process of fin regeneration.[56] The first step is formation of wound epithelium that involves migration of existing epithelial cells to cover the wound. This is then followed by creation of the primary blastema. The third step involves maturation of the blastema. The fourth stage is differentiation of the blastema forming new bones, nerves and blood vessels. The authors did not find evidence that the cells derived from slow cycling cells of primitive origin. Rather, they came from existing mature cells that were able to re-enter the cell cycle.

Classical regeneration consists of three main steps:[57]

(1) Dedifferentiation of cells neighboring the site of injury
(2) Proliferation of the dedifferentiated cells localized in an area called the blastema
(3) Redifferentiation of the multipotent cells into the terminally differentiated cell types which were lost

This regenerative potential was first described on the heart of the zebrafish by Poss *et al.*[58] Following resection of 20% of ventricular myocardium, a large clot formed on the resected area. Beginning at two to four days post-amputation (dpa), the clot was replaced by fibrin reaching a maximum thickness by 9 dpa. The fish at 7 dpa were indistinguishable in activity from the control. From 9 to 30 dpa, cardiac myofibers surrounded, penetrated, and replaced the clot. By 60 days, the fibrin clot had completely disappeared, and the size and shape of the ventricles appeared grossly normal. In addition, the contractile properties were indistinguishable from the control. The restoration of cardiac muscle was not the result of hypertrophy, but rather from cell proliferation as assayed by bromodeoxyuridine (BrdU), which is a marker of DNA synthesis. Injured hearts compared to controls had 17% *vs.* 3% of compact, and trabecular cardiomyocytes near the amputation plane incorporating BrdU at 7 dpa. The study also showed that mps1 mutant zebrafish lost the ability to regenerate the myocardium as seen by large connective tissue scar filling the defect.

As Poss demonstrated this chronological picture of the zebrafish heart regeneration, the question remained as to the origin of the new cells and whether cardiomyocytes had to undergo any form of dedifferentiation before replicating and differentiating.[59] In addition to this, the genetic regulation of the process and signaling mechanisms involved were still to be answered.

Using the same experimental model as his predecessor, Raya *et al.* were not able to detect Nkx2.5 and Tbx5[60] in the regenerating cells. Nkx2.5 and Tbx5 are part of the earliest known markers of cardiac lineage. The authors concluded that their inability to detect early cardiac markers during zebrafish heart regeneration indicates that *de novo* produced cardiomyocytes are unlikely to be derived from undifferentiated stem cells. They believed that mature cardiomyocytes are able to re-enter the cell cycle giving rise to new cardiomyocytes.

Lien *et al.* demonstrated some genes are upregulated and others are downregulated at different times.[61] Genes coding for wound response/inflammatory factors, secreted molecules, and matrix metalloproteinases are expressed in regenerating heart in sequential patterns. The authors found that both platelet-derived growth factor-a and -b (PDGF-A and PDGF-B) are upregulated in regenerating zebrafish hearts. PDGF-B homodimers induce DNA synthesis in adult zebrafish cardiomyocytes. Using a chemical inhibitor of PDGF receptor, DNA synthesis decreased in cardiomyocytes both *in vitro* and *in vivo* during regeneration. However, the block was incomplete, indicating that there are other parallel pathways. Comparisons of gene expression profiles between heart and fin regeneration revealed that of 662 transcripts that are differentially expressed during heart regeneration, 132 genes are also differentially expressed during fin regeneration. Thus, the results of Lien still suggested that it is the mature cardiomyocytes that are able to re-enter the cell cycle. Thus, the theory was that mature cardiomyocytes that have already exited the cell cycle are able to re-enter the cell cycle and multiply again giving rise to new cardiomyocytes.

However, contrary to the prevalent ideology at that time, Lepilina *et al.* provided the first evidence that new cardiomyocytes arise from a pool of undifferentiated progenitor cells.[62] They used the different folding properties and stability of a green fluorescent protein (EGFP) and a red fluorescent protein (RFP) that are expressed under the control of the cardiac myosin light chain 2 (cmlc2) promoter, that is turned on during myocardial differentiation. With EGFP folding faster and RFP being more stable, the origin of the new cardiomyocytes could be determined. If the new cardiomyocytes are $EGFP^+RFP^-$, then they arise from undifferentiated progenitor cells. However, if the new cardiomyocytes are $EGFP^-RFP^+$, then they arise from dedifferentiation of existing cardiomyocytes.

Using transgenic zebrafish for EGFP and RFP, the new cells formed at 7 dpa were $EGFP^+RFP^-$, indicating their origin from undifferentiated progenitor cells. Contrary to the study by Raya *et al.* early myocardial markers were expressed in these new cells, such as nkx2.5, hand2, and tbx20, suggesting that progenitor cells give rise to new cardiomyocytes. The fact that the authors were not able to detect any $EGFP^-RFP^+$ cells suggests that the progenitor cells were not derived from the dedifferentiation of the surrounding cardiomyocytes. They also discovered a role for epicardial cells. These cells invaded the surface of the newly formed cells and eventually invaded the regenerating myocardium. This invasion resulted in the formation of blood vessels. Blocking the signaling involved in this process resulted in the eventual formation of scar tissue.

The understanding of the zebrafish heart regeneration has evolved from re-entering of mature cardiomyocytes into cell cycle to the presence of primitive undifferentiated cells that give rise to the new cardiomyocytes. There is no evidence so far as to the nature of these primitive cells. Indirect evidence is only available to suggest their presence.

Nevertheless, the presence of these progenitor cells is equivalent to cardiac stem cells in mammalian hearts, such as mice, rats and human.[63] It is not clear as to why these cells are capable of giving rise to whole portions of lost ventricles in the zebrafish, while their contribution to myocardial regeneration in mammals has been very modest.

We chose to start the chapter with the zebrafish model to overcome the skepticism surrounding myocardial regeneration that there is an existing animal model that is naturally able to regenerate its damaged heart. Thus, in the context of the next sections in this chapter, we will review the evidence regarding different hypotheses for myocardial regeneration.

## 2. Transdifferentiation

Transdifferentiation was the first hypothesis to gain solid ground in the work towards solving the mystery of mechanism of cellular cardiomyoplasty. The logic behind it is that if transplanted cells are to have a therapeutic effect on the heart, they need to differentiate into contractile cardiomyocytes, and improve the function of the ischemic or failing heart. This concept gained great popularity from the initial positive results in its favor. Studies were conducted with different types of cells and can be traced back to the early days of cellular cardiomyoplasty, when skeletal myoblasts were tried as the transplant cells.

However, caution is needed when interpreting some of the results of these early studies, as some of them failed to test for therapeutic mechanism other than transdifferentiation. Thus, other mechanisms, such as fusion and paracrine effects that may have contributed to the therapeutic effect observed, may have been overlooked.

### 2.1 *If skeletal muscles can regenerate, why not use them to regenerate the heart?*

Although adult skeletal muscle fibers are terminally differentiated like cardiomyocytes, it has been observed that damaged skeletal muscle cells are able to regenerate. This has been attributed to the presence of undifferentiated myoblasts called satellite cells. These satellite cells were first described in 1961 by Mauro,[64] who then suggested that they may be the source of regenerating skeletal muscle nuclei, and might play a role in regenerative processes of the muscle. Satellite cells are primitive cells that are sequestered between the basement membrane and sarcolemma of individual muscle fibers. The defining characteristic of the satellite cell is that the basal lamina that surrounds the satellite cell and the associated myofiber is continuous.[65] These cells are normally quiescent, but are able to proliferate and differentiate when stimulated by skeletal muscle injury. Satellite cell numbers vary with the species, age, and muscle fiber type. Satellite cells constitute 30% of the muscle nuclei in the neonate, and decrease with age to 4% in the adult and 2% in the senile (29–30 months) mouse.[66] Attempts have been made to use these satellite cells to replace damaged or defective skeletal muscle cells. When transplanted *in vivo*, the majority of cells quickly die and only a minority undergo division and differentiation.[67]

Given the regenerative potential, attempts were made to transplant satellite cells into infarcted myocardium hoping that a "milieu-dependent differentiation" would occur, and that skeletal muscle satellite cells implanted will differentiate into cardiac muscle fibers. The theoretical advantage of using skeletal muscles is that skeletal muscle cells are among the most ischemia-tolerant in the body and, consequently, are capable of forming large grafts in the injured heart.[68] Chiu *et al.* demonstrated early that, at least from the morphologic point of view, satellite cells, when implanted into the injured myocardium, can survive and possibly differentiate into cardiac myocytes.[49] They introduced the concept of "milieu-influenced differentiation", in that transplanted myoblasts, in an environment surrounded by cardiomyocytes, will result in the skeletal myoblasts differentiating into cells of cardiac nature because of the influence of local environmental factors that have not yet been fully elucidated.

Following these initial studies, studies were conducted to further understand and optimize satellite cell transplantation. The differentiation observed was gradual and took several weeks. Many of the satellite cells fused into multinucleated myotubes after transplantation. This is a very active process in the first two weeks. With time, these myotubes grew in length and fused into long myofibers. In the stretched form, myotubes displayed regular cross-striations three weeks after transplantation. Myotubes (the new striated myofibers) also started to express the gap junction protein connexin 43 along their entire surfaces at apparent contacts with the surviving cardiomyocytes.[69] These cells were also positive for cardiac troponin T and myosin heavy chain. More evidence suggested that there was, in addition to forming these elongated structures closely resembling skeletal myotubes and being positive for myogen, at the periphery of the transplanted lesion, a smaller cluster of myogenin-negative cells visually similar to immature cardiomyocytes with a single centrally located nucleus.[70]

However, others have demonstrated that these primitive forms of cells maintain their skeletal muscle origin, and fail to differentiate into cardiac lineages. Murry *et al.* have shown that grafts expressed skeletal muscle myosin heavy chains and failed to express cardiac markers, such as $\alpha$-myosin, heavy chain, cardiac troponin-I, and atrial natriuretic peptide.[71] Cell culture experiments showed that proliferating skeletal myoblasts expressed abundant amounts of N-cadherin and connexin 43. When cells differentiated into myotubes, however, both proteins were markedly downregulated. Immunostaining revealed that skeletal muscle grafts in the heart had undetectable levels of N-cadherin and connexin 43, indicating that the grafts were not electromechanically coupled with one another or with host myocardium.[72] The authors believed that it is unlikely that transplanted skeletal muscles contract synchronously with the host myocardium, despite the fact that they did when co-cultured with cardiomyocytes.

Regardless of the controversy whether the transplanted myoblasts did differentiate into functional cardiomyocytes, some performed functional studies on the transplanted hearts to see whether there was any functional improvement. Pouzet *et al.* demonstrated that one-week after left coronary artery ligation, hearts receiving autologous skeletal myoblasts transplanted into the infarcted scar, demonstrated significant improvement in baseline ejection fraction in the groups with post-infarct ejection fraction of less than 40%, but not in the more than 40% stratum. This improvement was linearly associated with the number of injected myoblasts. The study, however, failed to demonstrate the histological features of this functional improvement.[73] When cells were transplanted one week after myocardial damage, Taylor *et al.* were also able to demonstrate some contractility in the transplanted hearts. Rather than using echocardiography as with Pouzet *et al.* they used sonomicrometry crystals implanted at the border of the injured and non-injured region. The authors demonstrated improvement in segmental stroke work in 5 of 12 myoblast transplanted hearts with two others showing a borderline improvement.[12]

An extensive study, in terms of assessing the functional improvement, was put forward by Jain *et al.*[74] One week after surgically induced MI, skeletal myoblasts were injected into the heart. *In vivo* cardiac function was assessed by maximum exercise capacity testing, and *ex vivo* function was determined by pressure-volume curves obtained from isolated, red cell–perfused, balloon–in–left ventricle (LV) hearts. At three and six weeks after cell therapy, 92% (13 of 14) of MI + cell hearts showed evidence of myoblast graft survival. MI + cell hearts exhibited attenuation of global ventricular dilation, and reduced septum–to–free wall diameter compared with MI hearts not receiving cell therapy. Furthermore, cell therapy improved both post-MI *in vivo* exercise capacity and *ex vivo* LV systolic pressures. This study demonstrated the survival of the transplanted myoblasts at the time of functional studies, but unfortunately did not look into the possibility of differentiation of these cells to cardiomyocytes.

With evidence that skeletal myoblasts improved function, phase I clinical trials were undertaken. A clinical trial from Paris, in which patients with severe left ventricular dysfunction, with akinetic and scar area on imaging, as well as undergoing coronary artery bypass for ischemic territories, was reported. The patients had autologous myoblasts obtained before surgery, and these were injected into the scar area at the time of the bypass surgery. The authors found that the patients had an improved ejection fraction post-op.[75] However, it is plausible that this observed improvement in function was secondary to the bypass and not to the transplanted cells, as the study did not include any control group. In addition, there was an increased incidence of ventricular arrhythmias that may be attributable to the transplanted cells.

## 2.2 *Primary progenitor cells and the evolution of the transdifferentiation theory*

Orlic *et al.* at the turn of the century, pioneered the concept of transdifferentiation in cellular cardiomyoplasty using bone marrow cells (BMC) in 3 different studies.[19,76,77] Using Lin$^-$c-kit$^{POS}$ in these studies, they demonstrated the potential to regenerate infarcted myocardium, and improve ventricular function compared to sham treated animals. When BMC were directly injected into the border zone of an infarcted heart,[19] 40% of the treated animals demonstrated evidence of infarct repair. Using the expression of enhanced green fluorescent protein (GFP), and the Y chromosome of the donor cell to detect their presence post-transplant, the authors were able to demonstrate differentiation along the myocytes, smooth muscle, and endothelial lineages. These cells positive for GFP and Y chromosome were positive for markers of differentiated cells such as connexin 43. To confirm that the newly formed myocytes represent cells that are functionally competent, the expression of myocytes enhancer factor 2 (MEF2), the cardiac specific transcription factor GATA-4, and the early marker of myocyte development Csx/Nkx2.5 were examined. The MEF2 proteins were recruited by GATA-4 to activate synergistically the promoters of several cardiac genes, such as myosin light chain, troponin T, troponin I, α-myosin heavy chain, desmin, atrial natriuretic factor, and α-actin. When the heart was reconstituted, all GFP$^+$/Y-chromosome cells expressed MEF2 and GATA-4, but only 40% expressed Csx/Nkx2.5. The majority of cells formed were myocytes, then endothelial cells, and smooth muscle cells. There was significant improvement in cardiac function in those animals treated with Lin$^-$c-kit$^{POS}$ compared to the sham group.

In his other study,[77] the methodology was changed to bone marrow stimulation with cytokines to mobilize Lin$^-$c-kit$^{POS}$ cells instead of directly injecting them into the myocardium. Similar results were obtained in this study in terms of cell differentiation, cell markers, and improvement in cardiac function. These results appeared only in those animals treated with stem cell factor (SCF), and granulocyte-colony-stimulating factor (G-CSF).

The potential of Lin$^-$c-kit$^{POS}$ cells in myocardial regeneration has been documented in subsequent studies.[16,78,79] When these cells, marked with EGFP and Y chromosome, were transplanted into infarcted myocardium, they showed evidence of differentiation into myocytes and coronary vessels.[78] The new myocytes generated expressed GATA-4, Nkx2.5, MEF2C, α-sarcomeric actin, cardiac myosin heavy chain, troponin I, desmin, connexin 43, and N-cadherin. The treated rats showed evidence of improved LV performance compared to no effect in untreated rats.

The studies proved that these new cardiomyocytes and blood vessels were produced by transdifferentiation and not cell fusion, as the newly formed cells had only one set of X and Y chromosomes, while 2 X-chromosomes are present in the native cardiomyocytes. The small number of cardiomyocytes that were binucleated also contained one set of X and Y chromosome in each nucleus. The regenerated myocardium was of male origin, whereas the native myocytes were of female origin.

When nuclear transfer techniques were used with Lin$^-$c-kit$^{POS}$ cells, there was regeneration of myocardium and reduction of scar area by 38% at one month.[79] The myocytes formed were functionally competent and expressed contractile proteins, desmin, connexin 43, and N-cadherin. There was improvement in ventricular hemodynamics and a reduction in diastolic wall stress. Formation of the new cells was the result of transdifferentiation and not fusion. These cells were mononucleated and had a smaller cell volume than the average native myocytes, that rules out the potential of fusion as the mechanism behind cellular differentiation. Fused cells should have volumes 20 folds larger than those observed in the study.

## 2.3 *Supporting in vivo and in vitro evidence*

*In vitro* studies with different types of progenitor cells, such as CD,[31–80] human umbilical cord blood-derived mesenchymal stem cells (UCBMSCs),[81] and MSCs[82,83] demonstrated differentiation to cardiomyocytes under certain controlled conditions. The pluripotency and potential to differentiate by MSCs without the presence of cardiac cells was demonstrated by Makino *et al.*[82] Isolated MSCs were treated with 5-azacytidine and the cells were observed to beat spontaneously. A week later, these cells connected with adjoining cells and went on to beat spontaneously after three weeks. When these cells were further analyzed, they exhibited some features of cardiomyocytes. They stained for myosin, desmin, and actinin. They also expressed atrial natriuretic peptide and brain natriuretic peptide. Electron microscopy confirmed that these markers correlate with a cardiomyocyte-like ultrastructure. Electrophysiological studies showed several types of action potentials generated by these cells. These cells also expressed cardiac specific genes, such as GATA4 and Nkx2.5. When adult rat ventricular cardiomyocytes were co-cultured with cardiac side population (CSP) cells *in vitro* for 14 to 21 days, 10% of CSP cells of CD31-type showed spontaneous contractions at low frequency (<1Hz).[80] These cells demonstrated intracellular calcium transients that are indistinguishable from those in co-cultured adult cardiomyocytes. The cells remained mononucleated as they were originally and did not resemble the binucleated native cardiomyocytes.

UCBMSCs have also demonstrated plasticity towards cardiac lineage *in vitro*.[81] Co-culturing these cells with fetal murine cardiomyocytes resulted in cells that exhibited rhythmic and synchronous contraction.

These cells showed evidence of cardiac differentiation, being positive for markers specific for cardiomyocytes, such as troponin-I and connexin 43. The cells also expressed cardiac specific markers such as Csx/Nkx-2.5, GATA4, hANP, hBNP, actin, troponin T and I. The cells were most likely the result of only transdifferentiation, as analysis of the nuclear content showed no cells having double nuclei.

Cells have also demonstrated *in vivo* evidence of the potential to transdifferentiate to cardiomyocytes and improve cardiac function. This was described earlier[19,23,76–79] with transplanted cells showing evidence of transdifferentiation as the main mechanism responsible for the new cardiomyocytes detected. Some of these studies assessed, in addition to cardiac markers, the functional parameters post-transplant. These parameters showed improvement in myocardial contractility,[77–79] and decrease in the scar area.[77,84] The importance of these studies is that they allowed us to understand the cellular transplant process beyond that of cell differentiation. In the clinical setting, improvement in measured parameters is of more significance.

## 2.4 *After they differentiate, do they help improve function?*

The main objective of cellular cardiomyoplasty is to improve heart function, and ameliorate the negative inotropic effects that damage the heart after ischemic events or myopathies. The theory of transdifferentiation assumes that cells differentiate to the cells normally available in the heart and improve the function to pre-damaged levels. Thus, transplanted cells in the transdifferentiation theory should differentiate into cardiomyocytes and blood vessels. The cardiomyocytes will thus contract, aiding the heart and improving ventricular function. This extra contractility is aided by the newly formed blood vessels. Objective measures are needed to prove the efficacy of cell therapy. Many studies *in vivo* and clinical trials have tried to acquire measures to prove the efficacy of cell therapy. $Lin^{-}c\text{-}kit^{POS}$ cells transplanted into mice showed evidence of wall movement as early as 15 days that becomes more progressive with time.[79] BMC treated animals had a 42% higher thickness to chamber radius ratio.[77] The ejection fraction was 48, 62 and 114% higher in treated *vs* in non-treated mice at 9, 16 and 26 days after

adipose tissue.[89] The separated MSCs, when exposed to specific doses of 5-azacytidine *in vitro*, show evidence of transformation to cardiomyocyte-like features.[89,90] After a couple of weeks in culture, the cells beat spontaneously when observed under phase contrast microscope. A few weeks later, these cells started showing evidence of organization and gap junction formation. To prove that these cells differentiated into cardiac cell lines, genetic content was tested. The cells exhibited cardiac specific mRNA, such as transcription factors, GATA-4 and Nkx2.5, the ventricular and atrial myosin light chain MLC-2v and MLC-2a, and atrial natriuretic peptide.[90] The cells also stained positive for various immune markers specific for cardiac cells such as $\alpha$-actinin, $\beta$-myosin heavy chain, and connexin 43.[89,90] The cells, on the other hand, did not stain for skeletal muscle specific markers, such as MyoD or smooth muscle actin. These cells generated various electrical activity specific for various areas in the heart.

CD29+ population progenitor cells in brown adipose tissue were found to be able to differentiate into cardiomyocytes with high efficiency.[91] These cells were transplanted into infarct border zone of an acute myocardial infarction model in rat. Results clearly indicated that implantation of $CD29^+$ brown adipose tissue-derived cells (BATDCs) led to the reduction of the infarction area, and improvement of left ventricular function by forming newly developed cardiomyocytes in comparison with the control. These cells were also able to differentiate into vascular cells, such as endothelial cells (ECs) and smooth muscle cells (SMCs). The authors did not observe the occurrence of cell fusion mechanism between donor and host-derived cells in the experiments.

The significance of the findings in these studies is numerous. The fact, that *in vitro* these cells are capable of differentiating to cardiac lines in the same manner that MSCs isolated form the bone marrow, is very promising. As cells of fat origin can easily be obtained from different parts of the body, adipose stem cells may be substituted for cellular cell therapy in regenerating the heart.

### 2.7 *Too low to be significant*

There is one common finding in all the *in vivo* studies discussed earlier, that is, the amount of differentiated cells remaining alive at the end is very low.[92–94] Different factors have been attributed as the cause behind this low retention rate.

Our lab was one of the first to adopt the concept of "cellular wash-out" to explain the cell loss following intra-myocardial cell delivery in cellular cardiomyoplasty. Teng *et al.*[44] studied the mechanical loss following direct intra-myocardial injection in the beating heart. The study, which used fluorescent microspheres, similar in size to MSCs but immune to biological losses, looked into the amount retained in the heart after 10 minutes following direct intra-myocardial injection. The amount of microspheres retained, which resemble cells, did not exceed 11% with a larger animal being used. Thus, the conclusion was that with the extensive blood supply and venous drainage of the heart, there is a massive initial mechanical loss.

The transplanted cells that survive the initial mechanical loss have to survive other factors that work against their differentiation. Various inflammatory factors that are related to post-infarction response reduce the amount of cells retained even further. The timing of transplant has been shown to be better one week after infarct, and not immediately as the inflammatory process subsides.[95] Those that survive the inflammatory response have to survive the relative ischemia until adequate angiogenesis occurs. Ultimately those that survive these entire events and do not undergo apoptosis can, as the hypothesis suggests, undergo transdifferentiation. Thus, it is not surprising that few weeks post-transplant, there are only few islands of transdifferentiated cells identified. Despite all this, studies demonstrated improvement in cardiac function in treated hearts. The question remains whether transdifferentiation is responsible for contributing significantly to the contractile improvement of the ventricle, or are there other mechanisms that are either co-contributing or solely responsible for the therapeutic seen effect.

## 3. Cellular Fusion

Fusion has emerged as a potential mechanism by which transplanted cells contribute to myocardial regeneration. Cell fusion is defined as the process in which non-destructive merging of the contents of two cells by artificial means, resulting in a heterokaryon that will reproduce genetically alike, multinucleated progeny for a few generations. This process is not a new discovery, but has been well described in other body systems including the hematopoetic system.

In this section, we will review the evidence behind fusion in different body systems before concentrating on evidence of fusion as the mechanism behind regenerative process in the heart. Evidence in support of fusion will be reviewed, while also reviewing counter evidence against this process.

### 3.1 *Giant cell formation*

Multinucleated giant cells (MGCs) have been shown to arise by a process of cellular fusion, as shown using morphological, immunocytochemical and chromosomal analysis.[96,97] Various receptors and cytokines have been described playing an important role in this process. P2Z/P2X7 receptor is a plasma membrane receptor that expresses response to extracellular ATP.[98] When this receptor is blocked with oxidized ATP, the generation of multinucleated giant cells is also blocked without decreasing monocyte migration or membrane adhesion molecule expression. Macrophages that are hyper-expressive for this P2Z/P2X7 receptor spontaneously fuse to form MGCs, compared to those that are hypo-expressive for this same receptor.[97]

The process of MGCs formation by fusion is stimulated and inhibited by certain environmental milieus that include various cytokines. Interferon-gamma (IFN-gamma), interleukin (IL)-3,[99] granulocyte/macrophage colony-stimulating factor (GM-CSF) 1,25-dihyoxycholecaliferol (1,25-(OH)2D3), retinoic acid (RA), and IL-6 have been shown to enhance the formation of MGCs.[100] Other factors, such as IL-4, had an inhibitory effect[100] or showed no effect,[101] although IL-4 had a stimulatory effect in murine macrophages.[102] The most striking enhancing effect was seen with the combination of IL-3 and IFN-gamma.[100] Various molecules are upregulated by these cytokines including intercellular cell adhesion molecule-1 (ICAM-1), HLA-DR,[99] and LFA-1.[101]

### 3.2 *More evidence of cell fusion*

Terada *et al.* have shown that BM cells adopt the phenotype of other cells by spontaneous cell fusion.[103] BM cells from female transgenic mice expressing green fluorescent protein (GFP) were mixed with mouse male embryonic stem cells in culture medium, containing leukemia inhibitory factor (LIF). IL-3 was added to the culture for the first seven days. The authors found three weeks later that GFP-positive clones morphologically similar to embryonic stem cells. The GFP expression demonstrated that these embryonic cells were derived from bone marrow cells. When LIF was removed, these bone marrow-derived, embryonic stem-like (BMESL) cells differentiated into various morphologies, including beating cardiac myocytes.

When the genetic composition of these BMESL was analyzed, the DNA content demonstrated over-diploid DNA content. About 85% of the cell clones demonstrated tetraploid (4n) DNA content, and about 15% had hexaploid (6n) DNA content. The karyotype demonstrated both X and Y chromosomes, of donor and recipient DNA matter. Using PCR amplification, the BMESL cells genotype was shown to be polymorphic between the BM cells (C57BL/6) and embryonic cell genome (129/Sv). These data strongly suggest that BMESL are generated by cell fusion. However, the frequency of this cell fusion was very low at only 2–11 clones per $10^6$ BM cells. This low frequency raises questions whether fusion accounts for the high levels of differentiation seen in other studies.[104] Fusion could be partly, but unlikely solely, responsible for the differentiation of cells seen.

With fusion, cells residing in one tissue organ have the capacity to produce cell types for other tissues and organs. Further attempts to prove the concept of fusion involved the use of various primitive cell types from other organs other than the bone marrow. Previous reports have demonstrated the potential of stem cells isolated from the central nervous system (CNS) tissue to produce cells of hematopoietic lineage[105] and skeletal myoblasts[106] when co-cultured with cells of these tissues. Thus, neural stem cells may have the same differentiation potential as BM stem cells. However, the mechanism of this differentiation is still not clear. Some evidence have pointed out that fusion might be responsible for this phenotypic change. Using distinct transgenic markers, embryonic stem cells (ESC) and CNS cells were isolated.[107] Neurospheres cultures were expanded for three days and then HT2 ES cells were added. Cells carrying the transgenic marker for CNS cells were selected. These cells expressed OCT4-GiP transgene that is only expressed in germline and pluripotent cells like ES, and not in CNS cells. These cultures also showed expression of the hygromycine resistance marker carried only by the HT2 ES cells. The nuclei of these cells were enlarged and contained multiple nucleoli. Chromosomal analysis also indicated fusion of both CNS and ES cells, producing karyotypes such as XXXY. This study showed that CNS cells have the potency to form cells with properties similar to those of inner cell mass that are capable of giving rise to differentiated cell types representing the 3 germ layers. However, the altered phenotypes observed were proven not to be the result of transdifferentiation, but rather through generation of hybrid cells by fusion.

As evidence emerges confirming the possibility of cell fusion, studies have shown the existence of co-mechanisms and variables that contribute to the final cellular outcome. Weimann *et al.* also shown that Purkinje neurons could result from cell fusion in two studies.[108,109] Purkinje neurons are mononucleate diploid cells that are generated only during gestation, and not replaced after loss through trauma or genetic disease. The authors showed in an earlier study[108] that bone marrow derived cells (BMDCs) contributed to Purkinje neurons in the brain of adult women, who received bone marrow from male donors for the treatment of hematological malignancies. However, they did not demonstrate the underlying mechanism behind it. In their subsequent study,[109] they transplanted $GFP^+$ BMDC into irradiated mice. The resultant Purkinje neurons expressed donor GFP, calbindin (a marker for Purkinje neurons), two nuclei, one of which expressed donor Y-chromosome, whereas the other did not. Further evidence points to fusion occurring spontaneously and physiologically to generate stable heterokaryons. Numerous GFP-positive cells were found to be binucleate Purkinje/BMDC heterokaryons in which the nuclei remained intact and distinct.

### 3.3 *The liver: transdifferentiation or fusion?*

The liver has been the center of many regenerative studies. In addition to transdifferentiation as the mechanism for observed phenotypic change, some studies have demonstrated findings that suggest fusion as partly or solely responsible for this observation. One of the major advantages of reviewing liver transplant studies is that these studies, in addition to assessing phenotypic and genetic changes, can also reliably assess the functional changes by measuring liver function. Using different model designs, analysis techniques and donor cells, evidence points to the potential of fusion as a mechanism in the observed differentiation of cells.

Lethally irradiated R26R mice were transplanted with bone marrow cells, expressing Cre recombinase and green fluorescent protein (GFP). The hepatocytes produced showed supportive evidence of cell fusion. R26R mice are conditional Cre reporter lines. When Cre expressing cells of bone marrow were transplanted in R26R mice, LacZ was expressed in the newly formed hepatocytes. This indicates that the newly formed cells are the result of fusion between donor and recipient cells.[52] The chromosomal composition was also supportive for the fusion concept. Most X-gal stained cells contained two or more nuclei. If the observed new cells in the liver were the result of transdifferentiation alone, cells would not have stained for X-gal that identifies the newly formed LacZ cells, neither would they have been multinucleated. In addition, GFP was only expressed in recipient cells, thus transdifferentiation would exclude their expression in new cells. However, new hepatocytes also expressed GFP. As the recipient mice had liver failure, there was normalization of LFTs and albumin after transplant, indicating differentiation and function of the transplanted cells.

Other studies performed in a similar manner, supported these findings.[110,111] Cytogenetic analysis of differentiated hepatocytes demonstrated diploid to tetraploid karyotypes (XXXY to XXXXYY).[110] The presence of the Y chromosome by itself is a confirmation that fusion has taken place, as donor and recipient cells are always mismatched.

These studies proved that fusion exists as a mechanism for new cell formation. Evidence also exists with the bone marrow cells fusing in solid tissue organs, producing cells specific to those organs and unlike those of hematopoietc cells. Advocates of the fusion concept argued that the presence of the recipient phenotype and donor chromosomes do not necessarily mean "transdifferentiation". They argued that studies that interpreted the demonstrated phenotype as solely the result of transdifferentiation have failed to use the proper analytic tests that can demonstrate cellular and nuclear fusion.

### 3.4 *Evidence of cell fusion in the heart*

Evidence for stem cell fusion also exists in the heart. In the Alvarez-Dolado *et al.* study described earlier, there was also evidence that transplanted HSCs fused with cardiomyocytes.[52] In the same study that used irradiated R26R mice transplanted with bone marrow cells expressing Cre recombinase and green fluorescent protein (GFP), there was evidence of generation of β-gal$^+$ cells in the heart. These can only be produced when Cre recombinase from the donor cells excised the floxed stop cassette of the reporter gene in the R26R nucleus. β-gal$^+$ cells were integrated in the myocardial wall, and had morphology and alignment that was indistinguishable from the surrounding cardiac muscle fibers. All GFP$^+$ cardiomyocytes expressed LacZ, indicating fusion and not transdifferentiation. The fused cells had the morphology of cardiomyocytes and expressed troponin I. These findings were supported by another study that used a similar detection method of Cre recombinase/GFP to detect LacZ positive cells.[112] This fusion was observed as early as three days at the infarct border zone. The fusion rate was significantly enhanced by the presence of Akt1 (MSC-Akt), which is a prosurvival gene in murine. However, the fusion events were not influenced by overexpression of Akt1. Despite the decrease in the number of LacZ positive cells at 28 days, hearts that had evidence of fused cells showed evidence of decrease in infarct size, and restoration of cardiac function compared to sham operated animals. Acquiring cardiomyocyte morphology in LacZ animals was very infrequent, suggesting that the mechanism of functional improvement may have also been contributed by other mechanisms.

When green fluorescent protein (GFP)-labeled BM Lin$^-$ Scal$^+$ hematopoietic progenitors were intravenously transplanted into neonatal mice continuously expressing cyan fluorescence protein (CFP), they formed cardiomyocytes that expressed GFP$^+$ that also co-expressed CFP$^+$ as detected by lambda image acquisition, and linear unmixing analysis using conofocal microscopy.[113] FISH analysis also supported this fusion by demonstrating the presence of both donor and recipient cells in the GFP$^+$/CFP$^+$ cardiomyocytes. This study demonstrated that BM cells delivered intravenously could migrate to the heart, and fuse with native cardiomyocytes. However, the model was not ischemia-based and it did not investigate the potential contribution of the cells to cardiac function.

Other types of cells have been studied other than BM derived for evidence of fusion with cardiomyocytes.[114] When GFP$^{+}$/LacZ neonatal cardiomyocytes were cultured with C2C12 skeletal myoblasts, multinucleated myotubes that carried both GFP and LacZ were formed, suggesting fusion of double-labeled myocytes with unlabelled C2C12. This was also confirmed again when Cre recombinase cardiomyocytes were cocultured with myoblasts from floxed-LacZ reporter mice. *In vivo*, C2C12 myo-blasts carrying floxed-LacZ gene were grafted into normal hearts of α-MHC-Cre$^{+}$ or into α-MHC-Cre$^{-}$ mice. LacZ cells were only detected in α-MHC-Cre$^{+}$ where they showed either punctate staining or abundant staining. α-MHC-Cre$^{-}$ mice did not show any LacZ cells, indicating that no fusion occurred. This study demonstrated the potential of cells other than BM cells to fuse with cardiomyocytes. It may suggest that the mechanism of earlier studies, where myoblasts were successfully used to improve cardiac function in the failing heart, may involve fusion. However, the evidence in the previous section on transdifferentiation proved that transdifferentiation does occur in skeletal myoblasts when they are transplanted into the heart. This study is limited by the fact that fusion occurred in normal hearts, and that it did not look into the effects of ischemia nor did it investigate the therapeutic potential of transplanted myoblasts.

## 3.5 *Factors regulating fusion and other mechanisms of acquiring combined characteristics*

Factors that regulate the fusion process have been reported. The presence of Akt1, a prosurvival gene in murine, enhances the fusion rate. However, overexpression of this same gene had no additive effect on the rate of fusion.[112] Physiological stress did not seem to be a factor that enhances the rate of cell fusion. Mice had pathological hypertrophy induced by pressure over-load and exercise program. Despite the visible differences in heart size, there was no significant increase in the number of eGFP-expressing cardiomyocytes compared to the sham operated groups. The eGFP is expressed as a result of replacing the recipient β-galactosidase by donor Cre recombinase.

From a different prospective, it has been shown that combined characteristics of two types of cells may be obtained by mechanisms other than complete fusion of cellular and nuclear content. Koyanagi *et al.* came up with findings that supported acquiring characteristics other than by classical cell fusion.[115] As described by Rustom *et al.*[116] nanotubular structures exist that connect neighboring mammalian cells. These nanotubes have a diameter of 50 to 200 nm and can stretch several cell diameters in length. They allow the transfer of multi-protein complexes and organelles between cells. Thus, the acquiring of the donor characteristics may be through this mechanism rather than the classical cellular or nuclear fusion.

Koyanagi *et al.* infected neonatal cardiomyocytes with GFP encoding adenovirus, while endothelial progenitor cells were labeled with Dil-ac-LDL. Six hours after co-culture of these 2 cells, ultrafine intercellular structures were observed between these cells. The nanotubular structures were only transiently established and their number decreased after 48 hours. The rate of cells forming these structures was very low at only 0.5% at six hours, and 2.6% at 24 hours. After six days, 2.1% of the cells stained positive for both GFP and Dil-ac-LD. To determine that nanotubular structures allowed for the transport of organelles, cardiomyocytes were labeled with cell permanent MitoTraker green probe. Then using time-lapse video microscopy, Mito Traker-green positive complexes were observed to move between cardiomyocytes and Dil-ac-LDL labeled EPC.

### 3.6 *Is it fusion or transdifferentiation or both?*

Studies have involved either transdifferentiation or fusion as the mechanism behind transplanted cells acquiring characteristics of native cardiomyocytes. However, some studies have demonstrated that fusion and transdifferentiation co-exist. Although the majority of cells demonstrated both X and Y chromosomes, Wang *et al.*[110] demonstrated that 6% of the cells did not exhibit both the X and Y chromosomes, indicating that some level of transdifferentiation does occur, although at a lower rate. However, this low level of donor type cells transdifferentiation to hepatocytes could be the result of contamination with recipient bone marrow cells that fuse with hepatocytes, and then undergo reduction division.[110]

When fumarylacetoacetate hydrolase deficient mice ($Fah^{-/-}$) had hematopoietic cells from $Fah^{+/+}$ mice transplanted to them,[111] the mice showed regenerating liver nodules with normal histology that expressed Fah. As the study reported by Wang *et al.*, when the cells in these nodules were analyzed, they also demonstrated polyploidy and contained the expected percentage of donor DNA. These cells contained only 12 to 48% of the donor DNA. If HSCs transdifferentiated, then the DNA content would be mostly from the donor origin. In addition, these cells showed transformation and loss of their hematopoietic markers, such as CD45.

### 3.7 *Evidence against fusion as the principle mechanism behind cellular cardiomyoplasty*

Despite the evidence that fusion in the heart does occur, there are findings that it may not be responsible for the improvement in cardiac function seen after cellular transplantation. The rate of fusion has been observed to be very low.[117] $GFP^+$ mature cardiomyocytes that also expressed donor markers, evidence of fusion and not only transdifferentiation, made a proportion of only 0.0001% to 0.0344% in the xenografts model that looked into the differentiation rate.[118] This study did not look into the functional improvement of the animals, but cells produced by fusion are at such a low rate that it is unlikely to be responsible for any therapeutic effect.

The rate of fusion varied among the different studies. However, the consensus in most of these studies is that it occurs at a very low rate. The problem with comparing these studies is that they use different types of cells, purification methods, detection methods, and methods to confirm the presence of fusion. Human umbilical endothelial vein cells (HUVECs) have been reported to exhibit differentiation potential when co-cultured with neonatal cardiomyocytes. When cardiomyocyte markers were detected (sarcomeric myosin) in HUVEC-rat neonatal cardiomyocytes co-culture system of cells containing nuclei, only 1.2% of the cells were immune-positive for human nuclear antigen (HNA). Of these 1.2% cells, 67% were multinucleated, compared to 13% when these HUVECs were cultured alone. To confirm that these cells are the result of fusion rather than transdifferentiation, a Cre/lox reporter system was used to detect this fusion process. At six days, cells were labeled with X-gal, with antibodies against HNA, sacromeric myosin, and β-galactosidase. Cells containing all cell makers were identified and were mostly multinucleated. These cells accounted for a small percentage of only 0.15% of the estimated total cells of about $5 \times 10^5$ cells in the culture.[119] In a similar designed study, the observation was that only 0.05% of cells showed evidence of fusion. In addition, the observed heterokaryons produced showed decreased expression of vWF over time indicating dominance of the cardiac phenotype post-fusion. However, the study fell short in that it did not test for the expression of human cardiac gene.[120]

Low rate of cell fusion was also an observation when cells of hematopoietic origin demonstrated the potential for fusion. There was low engraftment of transplanted $Lin^-c\text{-}kit^+$ hematopoietic cells into the infarcted myocardium after left coronary artery (LCA) ligation.[51] This engraftment was sustained at very low levels after 28 days. Most of these cells maintained their hematopoietic markers and were negative for cardiac markers, such as α-actin, troponin T, and connexin 43. However at very low frequency, and only in the border zone of the infarct, $GFP^+$ cells with characteristic cardiomyocytes morphology, including cross-striation, were observed. They also expressed α-actin, troponin T, and connexin 43. Although these cells showed absence of the CD 45 marker, they all stained positive for LacZ that demonstrated the occurrence of fusion. However, the rate of this was so low that the authors did not believe it to have any physiological significance. CD 34 cells that are also of hematopoietic origin demonstrated a low rate of fusion when co-cultured with cardiomyocytes. The rate was slightly higher than previously described, but still very low at only 0.2%. This fusion increased to 0.36% when the cultures were exposed to hypoxia.

Bone marrow cells have been the most studied. MSCs demonstrated transient engraftment within infarcted myocardium. The fusion, as demonstrated by LacZ staining, was at a low rate. However, unlike HSCs that demonstrated decline in differentiated cells, the number of fused cells remained relatively constant up to 28 days.[112] This fusion was not increased with over expression of Akt. BMCs, taken from the sternum of humans, were co-cultured with cardiomyocytes after being treated with 5-azacytidine and stained with Vybrant/Dio. Using two-color fluorescence labeling performed by laser scanning cytometry, of the 103 double fusion cells analyzed, only 6 showed donor as well as host mRNA. The other 88 cells analyzed showed only specific rat mRNA. A high degree of double fluorescence was observed in this study, but the low rate of double DNA marker could be explained by the acquiring of host cells of donor cells dye as the latter die. Thus, caution should be exercised not to interpret the presence of double fluorescent cells as indicative of fusion using the method described.[121]

As much as strong evidence was demonstrated regarding the occurrence of fusion, there was also evidence to the contrary. BMCs from male transgenic mice, expressing enhanced green fluorescent protein (EGFP), were transplanted in female mice with induced myocardial infarction, with resultant differentiated cells, but no evidence of fusion. Newly formed myocytes and vascular cells had only one set of X and Y chromosomes, whereas two X chromosomes were detected exclusively in the surviving myocytes. There were no cells in the area of cardiac repair that showed Y chromosome labeling in combination with more than X chromosome signal. Also, newly formed binucleated myocytes carried only one Y and one X chromosome in each nucleus. The regenerated myocytes were of male origin, while the spared myocytes were of female phenotype.[122] The use of cardiac stem cells (CSCs) reached similar conclusions.[123] CSCs delivered intra-coronary ischemia after 90 minutes in a rat model showed functional and structural improvement in the treated rats. A diploid DNA content was found in the new cardiomyocytes, indicating that cell fusion did not contribute to tissue reconstitution. Another study using cardiac side population (cardiac SP) cells demonstrated similar findings.[80] Transplanted cells that demonstrated cardiomyocytes differentiation did not demonstrate any evidence of cellular or nuclear fusion. Cardiac SP are mononuclear. After differentiation into cardiomyocytes, they remained mononuclear. The cells that demonstrated the greatest differentiation potential were those negative for CD 31 expression and positive for stem cell antigen 1 (Scal1).

Bearzi *et al.* successfully isolated c-kit-positive cells from the human heart. These human cardiac stem cells (hCSCs), when injected into infarcted myocardium of immunodeficient mice or rats, generated chimeric heart that contains human myocardium composed of myocytes and blood vessels. The newly generated myocardium contained only one set of human chromosomes. In addition, the injected hCSCs were initially infected with Cre recombinase, while the mice expressed loxP-flanked

EGFP. With any fusion occurring, EGFP expression will occur. None of the newly formed cardiomyocytes and blood vessels expressed EGFP, putting the possibility of fusion behind the differentiation observed. Since female human cells were used in male rat models, the lack of female human X chromosome with male rat Y chromosome within newly formed cells is significant.[124] In another study using C-kit-positive cells, these findings were echoed in the same way.[79] The newly formed myocytes were 93% mononucleated and 7% binucleated, showing that the majority of new cells formed were by mechanisms other than fusion.

The latter 3 studies demonstrated that fusion is absent even in ideal conditions. Nishiyama *et al.* on the other hand demonstrated the potential of human umbilical cord blood-derived mesenchymal stem cells (UCBMSCs) to differentiate to cardiomyocytes in the absence of conditions that will allow potential fusion, thus showing that fusion cannot be the sole mechanism responsible for cell formation.[81] In this experiment, UCBMSCs were co-cultured with murine fetal cardiomyocytes. However, these two types of cells were not in direct contact. The murine fetal cardiomyocytes were seeded on top of a floating collagen film, and the UCBMSCs were seeded on the bottom of the film. Successful differentiation of UCBMSCs into cardiomyocytes ruled out fusion as the possible mechanism in the setting of this experiment, as the two types of cells did not have a direct cell-to-cell contact that is a pre-requisite for fusion to take place. When further analysis of the differentiated cells was performed, the differentiated cells did not exhibit double nuclei, but were GFP-positive as the native UCBMSCs.

The last study leads the way for the potential role of the paracrine in the regenerative process in the heart. Even if there were observed differentiation, this seems to be solely dependent on a fine balance of various cytokines that may play a role in observed therapeutic effects.

## 4. Paracrine Mechanism

Observations related to the two previously mentioned mechanisms led invariably to a similar conclusion: whether the mechanism mentioned involved cellular transdifferentiation or fusion, the degree of remuscularization observed was extremely low, only showing on histology an occasional cluster of implanted cells.[51,92,94,118] These observations led to the consideration that the implanted cells perhaps led to an improvement of the ventricular function not through mechanical contribution, but through growth factors and cytokines. These, in turn, are hypothesized to work through various mechanisms, including improving angiogenesis, diminishing cellular death through antiapoptotic pathways, limiting ventricular remodeling through matrix modeling, or even recruiting and enhancing endogenous myocardial repair by stem cells.[32,34,85,86,125,126] We will review the evidence behind each factor thought to be involved in the paracrine mechanism, following which we will explore recent results concerning the immunomodulatory effects of marrow stromal cells on inflammation and ventricular remodeling. Finally, we will conclude with strong evidence supporting the paracrine mechanism, including improvement timeline and use of *in vivo* injection of factors without cells.

## 4.1 *Angiogenesis*

Of all the cytokines with angiogenic activity, vascular endothelial growth factor (VEGF) is certainly the most studied. Recently, clinical trials using VEGF to stimulate angiogenesis in patients with coronary artery disease have shown encouraging results, with improvement in left ventricular perfusion.[127] With these observations in mind, the effects of stem cell therapy on a peri-infarct or ischemic area expression of VEGF, as well as other angiogenic factors, have been investigated. In an early series of experiments by Kamihata *et al.*, bone marrow-derived mononuclear cells (BM-MNCs) were injected into a peri-ischemic zone created by coronary ligation in a swine model. Whereas the control groups (coronary microvascular endothelial cells and medium) did not show improvement, the BM-MNC group showed a 48% EF increase at three weeks, compared to baseline (60 minutes post-op). Similarly, infarct size was lessened only in the BM-MNC group. Quantitative immunohistochemistry demonstrated increased capillary density. mRNA expression analysis, compared to control, revealed increased expression not only of VEGF, but also basic fibroblast growth factor (bFGF) and angiopoeitin-1 (ang-1), known to be potent angiogenic ligands. Similarly, increases in interleukin-1 b (IL-1b) and tumor necrosis factor alpha (TNF-$\alpha$) expression were noted.[128] Both were previously shown to induce angiogenesis, IL-1b through stimulation of the VEGF pathway,[129] and TNF-$\alpha$ through stimulatory effects (IL-1 production, MHC-I expression) on endothelial cells.[130]

In humans, recent results from the REPAIR-AMI trial lend weight to the angiogenesis argument. Infusion of bone marrow-derived progenitor cells (BMCs) was shown to be associated with functional cardiac repair.[131] At the same time, there was an associated improvement in coronary flow reserve (CRF), and maximal vascular conductance in the infarct related artery. These results support the idea that angiogenic activity of the BMCs promoted neovascularization.[132] There exists a caveat to the interpretation of these studies. As mentioned by Kamihata *et al.* BM-MNCs represent a heterogeneous mix of different cell lineages including hematopoietic cells, fibroblasts, osteoblasts, and myogenic cells.[128] Similarly, the BMCs provided in the REPAIR-AMI trial were composed of a variety of hematopoietic, mesenchymal, and other progenitor cells, as well as mononuclear cells.[131] The question becomes which lineage(s) more specifically is/are responsible for the observed angiogenic effect.

A study by Tang *et al.* provides insight into the role played by bone marrow-derived mesenchymal stem cells (MSCs) in angiogenesis. Using a rat model, the authors showed that the treated MSC group showed a significant improvement in LVEF. Quantitative immunohistochemistry demonstrated increased capillary density mostly in the center of the scar, with the peri-infarct area showing moderate, non-statistically significant improvement. This data was correlated with ventricular blood flow, also showing similar improvement. Finally, immune-stain for VEGF demonstrated increased expression in scar, border, and normal zone of the treatment group.[133] An *in vitro* study by Kinnaird *et al.* validated the ability of MSCs to secrete angiogenic factors. ELISA analysis of the cultured MSC *vs* aortic endothelial cells control (MAECs) media revealed a significantly increased amount of VEGF, bFGF, placental growth factor (PlGF), and monocyte chemo-attractant protein-1 (MCP-1). Subsequent proliferation assays of endothelial and smooth muscle cells showed that the MSC culture medium enhanced cell proliferation.[134]

Hypoxic media has also been shown to further increase MSCs secretion of angiogenic factors. MSCs that were cultured in a hypoxic medium for over 24 hours showed a 50% increase in VEGF production. TNF stimulation of the cell demonstrated comparable results.[135] Similarly, work by Gnecchi *et al.* have shown that not only do MSCs express various angiogenic factors, such as VEGF, fibroblast growth factor-2 (FGF-2), hepatocyte growth factor (HGF), insulin-like growth factor-1 (IGF-I), and thymosin 4 (TB4), all known to have angiogenic properties, they also upregulate expression under hypoxic environment.[136] Because post-infarction cardiac muscle is often under significant ischemia, these results take on additional significance when considering the role played by angiogenesis in cellular therapy.

Other cell lineages used for cellular therapy, such as hematopoietic stem cells (HSCs) or endothelial progenitor cells (EPCs), both also derived from the bone marrow, have also been shown to exert potential paracrine effects favoring angiogenesis. HSCs, for example, are known to both secrete and respond to the effects of VEGF and ang-1.[137,138] EPCs, known for their potential to directly differentiate into endothelial cells, have also been shown to secrete various angiogenic factors: VEGF, HGF, granulocyte colony–stimulating factor (G-CSF), and granulocyte-macrophage colony–stimulating factor (GM-CSF).[139] Interestingly, EPCs recruitment and activation is modulated by ischemia through the same aforementioned angiogenic factors in addition to stromal-derived factor-1 (SDF-1), PlGF, and bFGF.[140,141]

### 4.2 *Prosurvival*

The role of paracrine factors secreted by stem cells such as MSCs potentially extends beyond that of angiogenesis. An early report by Gnecchi *et al.* suggested that co-culturing of MSCs with cardiomyocytes protected the latter from an ischemic environment. Similar results *in vivo* were reported by the authors, noting a decrease in the treatment group of TUNEL-positive (apoptotic) cardiomyocytes.[53] The question became which factors were responsible for this prosurvival effect. The previously mentioned work by Tang *et al.* suggested a possible role for VEGF, as the authors noted a decrease in apoptotic cardiomyocytes in the MSC treated groups, along with an increased expression of VEGF. The evidence, however, is ambiguous. Is VEGF's antiapoptotic role due to its angiogenic capacities, involved in protecting native cardiomyocytes through better perfusion, is there involvement of a prosurvival pathway, or is there a combination of both features?

A study by Uemura *et al.* showed that co-culturing of cardiomyocytes with bone marrow stem cells (BMSCs) reduced the quantitative amount of apoptotic cardiomyocytes under a hypoxic environment. The authors demonstrated significant secretion of VEGF, bFGF, SDF-1, and IGF-1by the BMSCs especially under hypoxic medium. Furthermore, the authors demonstrated the *in vivo* effects of the cells, showing an increased LV function as well as improved wall thickness. At the same time, TUNEL stain showed a decreased amount of apoptotic cardiomyocytes in the treated groups.[142] Similar results were obtained by Xu *et al.*, who also noted that *in vitro* hypoxic culture of BMSCs with cardiomyocytes resulted in increased cardiomyocyte expression (2.9 times) of antiapoptotic protein bcl-2.[143] Later work from the same group strengthens the causality link. An *in vitro* experiment by Dai *et al.* examined the effects of BMSC (free of HSCs) on cardiomyocyte co-cultures under hypoxic environment and oxidative stress, as mimicked by $H_2O_2$. The authors examined the role of HIF-1a, part of the signaling cascade leading to VEGF expression in BMSCs. Their results provided evidence as to the role played by VEGF in limiting cardiomyocyte apoptosis in the following ways: (1) Levels of HIF-1a were elevated by hypoxic environment. (2) These levels were correlated with VEGF expression. (3) VEGF expressed through this pathway or added in the culture medium provided protection against the ischemic environment and oxidative stress. (4) Blockage of the HIF-1a pathway led to a loss in stem cell efficiency.[144] Recent work by Markel *et al.* examined the con-sequence of silencing VEGF through RNA interference. Again, VEGF knock-out virtually eliminated the therapeutic potential of MSC.[145] Other *in vivo* work by Tang *et al.* confirmed that MSC implantation, in addition to functional LVEF improvement and increased expression of VEGF, was also associated with decreased cardiomyocytes expression of Bax, a proapoptotic protein, by nearly 60%.[146]

A study from Takahashi *et al.* using a population of BM-MNCs, further identified IL-1b, PDGF, and TGF-b, in addition to VEGF, bFGF, and IGF-1, as potential modulators of this antiapoptotic effect. These factors were also upregulated by a hypoxic environment. Supernatant extracts with the cytokines were shown to reduce cardiomyocyte death *in vitro*.

factor of 3, whereas levels of IL-6 were increased by a factor of 2.[172] Pasqui *et al.* confirmed a similar trend, with increased TNF-α and IFN-γ, and decreased IL-10.[173]

Work by Kilic *et al.* demonstrated that pro-inflammatory to anti-inflammatory ratio, especially IL-6:IL-10 had strong prognostic value for subsequent cardiac events (OR 2.2, 95% CI 1.2 to 3.9, both at six months and one year) in a patient population composed of unstable angina and NSTEMI.[174] Similar findings were reported in an earlier study by Anguera *et al.*[175] Further work by Tziakas *et al.* suggested that between pro-inflammatory and anti-inflammatory markers, the latter had stronger predictive values for long-term cardiac prognosis.[176]

Biologically, inflammatory cytokines have been shown to accelerate symptoms of congestive heart failure, affecting ventricular remodeling by inducing cardiomyocyte hypertrophy and eventually apoptosis. Furthermore, TNF has been shown to affect the ECM through activation of MMPs, therefore increasing early MMP/TIMP ratio.[177] Therapies with ACE inhibitors or beta-blockers, known to improve the course of heart failure, were hypothesized to be partially attributable to their inhibitory effects on inflammatory cytokines.[178,179] Although initial animal models have been promising, therapy aimed at directly suppressing inflammatory factors has so far been proven disappointing in clinical trials. One potential explanation is the blocking of biological roles of low levels of TNF such as cytoprotection in early ischemia,[177] and tissue repair (angiogenesis). Increased IL-10, on the other hand, has been shown to decrease levels of inflammatory cytokines in the myocardium.[180,181]

Our own work with transplanted xenogenic MSC therapy suggests that these cells may possess a unique immunomodulatory effect. Transplantation of human MSCs, as opposed to human fibroblast into a rat infarct model, did not produce an inflammatory reaction and graft rejection. Moreover, ventricular function improved compared to control.[30] Previous *in vitro* experimentation supported these findings.[182] Because MSCs are known to alter the immune system by inhibiting inflammatory cytokine (TNF-α and IFN-γ) and increasing anti-inflammatory cytokines (IL-10),[183] this may explain both of our experimental findings.

Increase levels of IL-10 and decreased levels of inflammatory cytokines have also been hypothesized as the mechanism behind MSC therapy in treatment of acute renal failure.[184] Recently, work by Burchfield *et al.* directly examined the role of IL-10 in BM-MNC therapy for the heart. Using both wild-type and IL-10 knock-out MNCs, the authors demonstrated that at 14 days post-infarct, IL-10 wild-type (WT) was associated with, compared to knock-out: (1) a significant decrease in LV end-diastolic pressure (LVEDP) and LV end-systolic volume (LVESV); (2) a significant decrease in fibrosis; and (3) a significant decrease in number of infiltrating T lymphocytes. Other MNC-mediated healing processes, such as the release of VEGF or IGF-1, were not affected.[149] Our own recent results confirm the previous findings. We tested the hypothesis that changes in pro-inflammatory to anti-inflammatory cytokines in the microenvironment may reflect the effect of stem cell therapy on the acutely ischemic environment. Rats which underwent experimental infarct by coronary ligation received either culture media or $3 \times 10^6$ MSCs. Echocardiography was measured at baseline, 12 and 24 hours post-op. Similarly, myocardial tissues were harvested at 12 and 24 hours for quantitative PCR of cytokine expressions. Early results suggested that the treatment group showed significant reduction in pro- to anti-inflammatory cytokine ratio. These observations correlated with improved ventricular EF at both 12 and 24 hours.[185]

## 4.6 *The paracrine hypothesis*

We have described various mechanisms through which stem cells are believed to exert their paracrine effects in the context of cellular therapy. Whether the beneficial effects involve angiogenesis, antiapoptosis, ECM modulation, endogenous stem cell recruitment, or anti-inflammatory effects, there is good evidence to link MSC in these pathways. Further evidence is provided by the experimental design of many studies, in which stem cell cultured environment was able to replicate, at least in part, the *in vivo* effects of stem cell therapy. The works from Gnecchi *et al.*, for example, showed that injection of MSC conditioned medium, containing significant quantities of VEGF, FGF-2, IGF-I, and TB4, significantly improved ventricular function relative to control.[53,13] Similar results were subsequently replicated by other groups.[186]

Another often cited argument for the paracrine hypothesis is the time-line of ventricular improvement. Work by Gnecchi *et al.* showed that MSC therapy may have a functional effect within 72 hours. Similarly, the early infarct area was reduced.[53,136] Our recent preliminary data shows significant LV improvement as early as 12 or 24 hours.[185] Because these changes occur so early, improvement through paracrine effects becomes the most likely mechanism, as these occur before a time-line delay required for transdifferentiation or even fusion to occur.

The totality of the paracrine effect, however, is unlikely to occur all within such a limited time-frame. Because MSCs have been showed to exert significant antiapoptotic effect on cardiomyocytes *in vitro* under a hypoxic condition, it may be hypothesized that this effect would occur almost immediately. Similarly, anti-inflammatory cytokines may have early effects in reducing cardiomyocyte casualties. However, they would also play a role in term-term prognosis through modulation of MMP expression, affecting ECM homeostasis and the ventricular remodeling process. Lastly, angiogenesis and stem cell recruitment, activation, and differentiation may be best viewed as slow, continuous processes occurring in the context of many weeks.

Therefore, although paracrine effects are the most likely hypotheses underlying the working of cellular therapy for myocardial ischemia, many of the mechanisms occur within different timeframes and conditions. Culture medium injection, for example, is likely to simulate the benefits of early antiapoptotic and anti-inflammatory effects of MSCs. However, angiogenic benefits, as well as the long-term effect on remodeling would be unlikely to be present. Further clarification of the relative contribution of different protective mechanisms is therefore necessary, as future direction may lead to enhancement of the effects of a particular pathway through genetic manipulation to achieve maximum therapeutic benefits.

## 5. Closing Remarks

The search for an answer for the mechanism behind cellular cardiomyoplasty is not easy, and it may be a while before we can reach a convincing answer. Currently, the three main streams of thought are transdifferentiation, fusion, and paracrine effect. The birth of these three mechanisms came as knowledge and technology allowing us to probe the details behind them.

In the early days, transdifferentiation was the only hypothesis in the search towards a mechanism. It was believed that functional improvement implied more contracting cells. Thus, transplanted cells were thought to differentiate to achieve functional benefit. In addition, staining techniques that were most commonly available supported this. There is good evidence that there is a degree of transdifferentiation of pluri-potent cells to cardiomyocytes. However, the paucity of these differentiated cells seems unlikely to account for the improved function and remodeling of the heart.

As studies were performed to further understand transdifferentiation, fusion emerged as an alternate explanation. Some studies totally refuted the concept that transdifferentiation occurred, and that the observed differentiation is the result of cellular fusion. However, paucity of the fused cells, led researchers to consider other mechanisms that are either solely or partially responsible for the therapeutic effect.

The paracrine effect has recently gained popularity. With the discovery of the potential role of the various cytokines like VEGF, bFGF, HIF-1a, HGF, IL-10 and many more, it seems plausible, at least with the current evidence, that cytokines may be the mechanism behind the benefits of cellular cardiomyoplasty. In support of this theory is the observation that the effects of cellular therapy occur far earlier than the time required for transdifferentiation or fusion to occur.

It is possible that the three described mechanisms actually co-exist and all contribute to the observed therapeutic effect. However, it is difficult with the current available evidence to make a conclusive opinion. The studies we have reviewed are very heterogeneous, using different types of cells, different culture methods, different delivery methods, and different analysis techniques, preventing us from analyzing the relative contribution of each mechanism. To gain better understanding, further studies designed to investigate and detect different mechanisms at the same time are required.

## References


1. Roger VL, Weston SA, Redfield MM, *et al.* Trends in heart failure incidence and survival in a community-based population. *JAMA* 2004 Jul 21;292(3):344–350.
2. Kostuk WJ. Congestive heart failure: what can we offer our patients? *CMAJ* 2001 Oct 16;165(8):1053–1055.
3. Viganego F, Le Jemtel TH. Progression and management of chronic heart failure. *Panminerva Med* 2007 Sep;49(3):109–118.
4. Kass DA. An epidemic of dyssynchrony: but what does it mean? *J Am Coll Cardiol* 2008 Jan 1;51(1):12–17.
5. Miske G, Acevedo C, Goodlive TW, *et al.* Cardiac resynchronization therapy and tools to identify responders. *Congest Heart Fail* 2005 Jul-Aug;11(4):199–206.
6. De Bonis M, Alfieri O. Surgical methods to reverse left ventricular remodeling. *Curr Heart Fail Rep* 2007 Dec;4(4):214–220.
7. Blom AS, Acker MA. The surgical treatment of end-stage heart failure. *Curr Probl Cardiol* 2007 Oct;32(10):553–599.
8. Stahovich M, Chillcott S, Dembitsky WP. The next treatment option: using ventricular assist devices for heart failure. *Crit Care Nurs Q* 2007 Oct-Dec;30(4):337–346.
9. Kirklin JK, McGiffin DC, Pinderski LJ, Tallaj J. Selection of patients and techniques of heart transplantation. *Surg Clin North Am* 2004 Feb; 84(1):257–287, xi–xii.
10. Kirklin JK, Pambukian SV, McGiffin DC, Benza RL. Current outcomes following heart transplantation. *Semin Thorac Cardiovasc Surg* 2004 Winter;16(4):395–403.
11. Smits AM, van Vliet P, Metz CH, *et al.* Human cardiomyocyte progenitor cells differentiate into functional mature cardiomyocytes: an *in vitro* model for studying human cardiac physiology and pathophysiology. *Nat Protoc* 2009;4(2):232–243.
12. Taylor DA, Atkins BZ, Hungspreugs P, *et al.* Regenerating functional myocardium: improved performance after skeletal myoblast transplantation. *Nat Med* 1998 Aug;4(8):929–933.
13. Ghostine S, Carrion C, Souza LC, *et al.* Long-term efficacy of myoblast transplantation on regional structure and function after myocardial infarction. *Circulation* 2002 Sept 24;106(12 Suppl 1):I131–I136.

14. Kolossov E, Bostani T, Roell W, *et al*. Engraftment of engineered ES cell-derived cardiomyocytes but not BM cells restores contractile function to the infarcted myocardium. *J Exp Med* 2006 Oct 2;203(10):2315–2327.
15. Kofidis T, Lebl DR, Swijnenburg RJ, *et al*. Allopurinol/uricase and ibuprofen enhance engraftment of cardiomyocyte-enriched human embryonic stem cells and improve cardiac function following myocardial injury. *Eur J Cardiothorac Surg* 2006 Jan;29(1):50–55.
16. Beltrami AP, Barlucchi L, Torella D, *et al*. Adult cardiac stem cells are multipotent and support myocardial regeneration. *Cell* 2003 Sep 19; 114(6):763–776.
17. Chandy T, Mooradian DL, Rao GH. Evaluation of modified alginate-chitosan-polyethylene glycol microcapsules for cell encapsulation. *Artif Organs* 1999 Oct;23(10):894–903.
18. Laugwitz KL, Moretti A, Lam J, *et al*. Postnatal isl1+ cardioblasts enter fully differentiated cardiomyocyte lineages. *Nature* 2005 Feb 10;433(7026):647–653.
19. Orlic D, Kajstura J, Chimenti S, *et al*. Bone marrow cells regenerate infarcted myocardium. *Nature* 2001 Apr 5;410(6829):701–705.
20. Laflamme MA, Murry CE. Regenerating the heart. *Nat Biotechnol* 2005 Jul;23(7):845–856.
21. Xu M, Wani M, Dai YS, *et al*. Differentiation of bone marrow stromal cells into the cardiac phenotype requires intercellular communication with myocytes. *Circulation* 2004 Oct 26;110(17):2658–2665.
22. Li X, Yu X, Lin Q, *et al*. Bone marrow mesenchymal stem cells differentiate into functional cardiac phenotypes by cardiac microenvironment. *J Mol Cell Cardiol* 2007 Feb;42(2):295–303.
23. Toma C, Pittenger MF, Cahill KS, *et al*. Human mesenchymal stem cells differentiate to a cardiomyocyte phenotype in the adult murine heart. *Circulation* 2002 Jan 1;105(1):93–98.
24. Granero-Molto F, Weis JA, Longobardi L, Spagnoli A. Role of mesenchymal stem cells in regenerative medicine: application to bone and cartilage repair. *Expert Opin Biol Ther* 2008 Mar;8(3):255–268.
25. Vilquin JT, Rosset P. Mesenchymal stem cells in bone and cartilage repair: current status. *Regen Med* 2006 Jul;1(4):589–604.
26. Petite H, Viateau V, Bensaid W, *et al*. Tissue-engineered bone regeneration. *Nat Biotechnol* 2000 Sep;18(9):959–963.

27. Krause DS. Plasticity of marrow-derived stem cells. *Gene Ther* 2002 Jun;9(11):754–758.
28. Ferrari G, Cusella-De Angelis G, Coletta M, *et al.* Muscle regeneration by bone marrow-derived myogenic progenitors. *Science* 1998 Mar 6; 279(5356):1528–1530.
29. Pittenger MF, Martin BJ. Mesenchymal stem cells and their potential as cardiac therapeutics. *Circ Res* 2004 Jul 9;95(1):9–20.
30. Atoui R, Asenjo JF, Duong M, *et al.* Marrow stromal cells as universal donor cells for myocardial regenerative therapy: their unique immune tolerance. *Ann Thorac Surg* 2008 Feb;85(2):571–579.
31. MacDonald DJ, Luo J, Saito T, *et al.* Persistence of marrow stromal cells implanted into acutely infarcted myocardium: observations in a xenotransplant model. *J Thorac Cardiovasc Surg* 2005 Oct; 130(4):1114–1121.
32. Saito T, Kuang JQ, Bittira B, *et al.* Xenotransplant cardiac chimera: immune tolerance of adult stem cells. *Ann Thorac Surg* 2002 Jul;74(1):19–24; discussion.
33. Fuchs S, Satler LF, Kornowski R, *et al.* Catheter-based autologous bone marrow myocardial injection in no-option patients with advanced coronary artery disease: a feasibility study. *J Am Coll Cardiol* 2003 May 21; 41(10):1721–1724.
34. Hamano K, Nishida M, Hirata K, *et al.* Local implantation of autologous bone marrow cells for therapeutic angiogenesis in patients with ischemic heart disease: clinical trial and preliminary results. *Jpn Circ J* 2001 Sep; 65(9):845–847.
35. Hendrikx M, Hensen K, Clijsters C, *et al.* Recovery of regional but not global contractile function by the direct intramyocardial autologous bone marrow transplantation: results from a randomized controlled clinical trial. *Circulation* 2006 Jul 4;114(1 Suppl):I101–107.
36. Stamm C, Kleine HD, Choi YH, *et al.* Intramyocardial delivery of CD133+ bone marrow cells and coronary artery bypass grafting for chronic ischemic heart disease: safety and efficacy studies. *J Thorac Cardiovasc Surg* 2007 Mar;133(3):717–725.
37. Wollert KC, Meyer GP, Lotz J, *et al.* Intracoronary autologous bone-marrow cell transfer after myocardial infarction: the BOOST randomised controlled clinical trial. *Lancet* 2004 Jul 10–16;364(9429):141–148.

38. Bartunek J, Vanderheyden M, Vandekerckhove B, *et al.* Intracoronary injection of CD133-positive enriched bone marrow progenitor cells promotes cardiac recovery after recent myocardial infarction: feasibility and safety. *Circulation* 2005 Aug 30;112(9 Suppl):I178–183.
39. Amado LC, Saliaris AP, Schuleri KH, *et al.* Cardiac repair with intramyocardial injection of allogeneic mesenchymal stem cells after myocardial infarction. *Proc Natl Acad Sci USA* 2005 Aug 9;102(32):11474–11479.
40. Hou D, Youssef EA, Brinton TJ, *et al.* Radiolabeled cell distribution after intramyocardial, intracoronary, and interstitial retrograde coronary venous delivery: implications for current clinical trials. *Circulation* 2005 Aug 30;112(9 Suppl):I150–156.
41. Perin EC, Lopez J. Methods of stem cell delivery in cardiac diseases. *Nat Clin Pract Cardiovasc Med* 2006 Mar;3(Suppl 1):S110–113.
42. Ishida M, Tomita S, Nakatani T, *et al.* Acute effects of direct cell implantation into the heart: a pressure-volume study to analyze cardiac function. *J Heart Lung Transplant* 2004 Jul;23(7):881–888.
43. Grossman PM, Han Z, Palasis M, *et al.* Incomplete retention after direct myocardial injection. *Cathet Cardiovasc Interv* 2002 Mar;55(3):392–397.
44. Teng CJ, Luo J, Chiu RC, Shum-Tim D. Massive mechanical loss of microspheres with direct intramyocardial injection in the beating heart: implications for cellular cardiomyoplasty. *J Thorac Cardiovasc Surg* 2006 Sep;132(3):628–632.
45. Qu Z, Balkir L, van Deutekom JC, *et al.* Development of approaches to improve cell survival in myoblast transfer therapy. *J Cell Biol* 1998 Sep 7;142(5):1257–1267.
46. Moelker AD, Baks T, Wever KM, *et al.* Intracoronary delivery of umbilical cord blood derived unrestricted somatic stem cells is not suitable to improve LV function after myocardial infarction in swine. *J Mol Cell Cardiol* 2007 Apr;42(4):735–745.
47. Chavakis E. IL-8: a new player in the homing of endothelial progenitor cells to ischemic myocardium. *J Mol Cell Cardiol* 2006 Apr;40(4):442–445.
48. Kang HJ, Kim HS, Zhang SY, *et al.* Effects of intracoronary infusion of peripheral blood stem-cells mobilised with granulocyte-colony stimulating factor on left ventricular systolic function and restenosis after coronary stenting in myocardial infarction: the MAGIC cell randomised clinical trial. *Lancet* 2004 Mar 6;363(9411):751–756.

74. Jain M, DerSimonian H, Brenner DA, *et al.* Cell therapy attenuates deleterious ventricular remodeling and improves cardiac performance after myocardial infarction. *Circulation* 2001 Apr 10;103(14):1920–1927.
75. Menasche P, Hagege A, Scorsin M, *et al.* [Autologous skeletal myoblast transplantation for cardiac insufficiency. First clinical case]. *Arch Mal Coeur Vaiss* 2001 Mar;94(3):180–182.
76. Orlic D, Kajstura J, Chimenti S, *et al.* Transplanted adult bone marrow cells repair myocardial infarcts in mice. *Ann NY Acad Sci* 2001 Jun;938: 221–229; discussion 9–30.
77. Orlic D, Kajstura J, Chimenti S, *et al.* Mobilized bone marrow cells repair the infarcted heart, improving function and survival. *Proc Natl Acad Sci USA* 2001 Aug 28;98(18):10344–10349.
78. Kajstura J, Rota M, Whang B, *et al.* Bone marrow cells differentiate in cardiac cell lineages after infarction independently of cell fusion. *Circ Res* 2005 Jan 7;96(1):127–137.
79. Lanza R, Moore MA, Wakayama T, *et al.* Regeneration of the infarcted heart with stem cells derived by nuclear transplantation. *Circ Res* 2004 Apr 2;94(6):820–827.
80. Pfister O, Mouquet F, Jain M, *et al.* CD31- but Not CD31+ cardiac side population cells exhibit functional cardio-myogenic differentiation. *Circ Res* 2005 Jul 8;97(1):52–61.
81. Nishiyama N, Miyoshi S, Hida N, *et al.* The significant cardiomyogenic potential of human umbilical cord blood-derived mesenchymal stem cells *in vitro*. *Stem Cells* 2007 Aug;25(8):2017–2024.
82. Makino S, Fukuda K, Miyoshi S, *et al.* Cardiomyocytes can be generated from marrow stromal cells *in vitro*. *J Clin Invest* 1999 Mar;103(5):697–705.
83. Howlett CR, Cave J, Williamson M, *et al.* Mineralization in *in vitro* cultures of rabbit marrow stromal cells. *Clin Orthop Relat Res* 1986 Dec(213):251–263.
84. Balsam LB, Wagers AJ, Christensen JL, *et al.* Haematopoietic stem cells adopt mature haematopoietic fates in ischaemic myocardium. *Nature* 2004 Apr 8;428(6983):668–673.
85. Bittira B, Shum-Tim D, Al-Khaldi A, Chiu RC. Mobilization and homing of bone marrow stromal cells in myocardial infarction. *Eur J Cardiothorac Surg* 2003 Sep;24(3):393–398.

86. Jiang W, Ma A, Wang T, *et al.* Homing and differentiation of mesenchymal stem cells delivered intravenously to ischemic myocardium *in vivo*: a time-series study. *Pflugers Arch* 2006 Oct;453(1):43–52.
87. Zuk PA, Zhu M, Mizuno H, *et al.* Multi-lineage cells from human adipose tissue: implications for cell-based therapies. *Tissue Eng* 2001 Apr;7(2):211–228.
88. Erickson GR, Gimble JM, Franklin DM, *et al.* Chondrogenic potential of adipose tissue-derived stromal cells *in vitro* and *in vivo*. *Biochem Biophys Res Commun* 2002 Jan 18;290(2):763–769.
89. Rangappa S, Fen C, Lee EH, *et al.* Transformation of adult mesenchymal stem cells isolated from the fatty tissue into cardiomyocytes. *Ann Thorac Surg* 2003 Mar;75(3):775–779.
90. Planat-Benard V, Menard C, Andre M, *et al.* Spontaneous cardiomyocyte differentiation from adipose tissue stroma cells. *Circ Res* 2004 Feb 6; 94(2):223–229.
91. Yamada Y, Wang XD, Yokoyama S, *et al.* Cardiac progenitor cells in brown adipose tissue repaired damaged myocardium. *Biochem Biophys Res Commun* 2006 Apr 7;342(2):662–670.
92. Suzuki K, Murtuza B, Beauchamp JR, *et al.* Role of interleukin-1beta in acute inflammation and graft death after cell transplantation to the heart. *Circulation* 2004 Sep 14;110(11 Suppl 1):II219–II224.
93. Muller-Ehmsen J, Whittaker P, Kloner RA, *et al.* Survival and development of neonatal rat cardiomyocytes transplanted into adult myocardium. *J Mol Cell Cardiol* 2002 Feb;34(2):107–116.
94. Yasuda T, Weisel RD, Kiani C, *et al.* Quantitative analysis of survival of transplanted smooth muscle cells with real-time polymerase chain reaction. *J Thorac Cardiovasc Surg* 2005 Apr;129(4):904–911.
95. Hu X, Wang J, Chen J, *et al.* Optimal temporal delivery of bone marrow mesenchymal stem cells in rats with myocardial infarction. *Eur J Cardiothorac Surg* 2007 Mar;31(3):438–443.
96. Parwaresch MR, Kreipe H, Radzun HJ. Human macrophage hybrid forming spontaneous giant cells. *Virchows Arch B Cell Pathol Incl Mol Pathol* 1986;51(2):89–96.
97. Chiozzi P, Sanz JM, Ferrari D, *et al.* Spontaneous cell fusion in macrophage cultures expressing high levels of the P2Z/P2X7 receptor. *J Cell Biol* 1997 Aug 11;138(3):697–706.

98. Falzoni S, Munerati M, Ferrari D, *et al.* The purinergic P2Z receptor of human macrophage cells. Characterization and possible physiological role. *J Clin Invest* 1995 Mar;95(3):1207–1216.
99. Fais S, Burgio VL, Silvestri M, *et al.* Multinucleated giant cells generation induced by interferon-gamma. Changes in the expression and distribution of the intercellular adhesion molecule-1 during macrophages fusion and multinucleated giant cell formation. *Lab Invest* 1994 Nov;71(5):737–744.
100. Enelow RI, Sullivan GW, Carper HT, Mandell GL. Induction of multinucleated giant cell formation from *in vitro* culture of human monocytes with interleukin-3 and interferon-gamma: comparison with other stimulating factors. *Am J Respir Cell Mol Biol* 1992 Jan;6(1):57–62.
101. Most J, Neumayer HP, Dierich MP. Cytokine-induced generation of multinucleated giant cells *in vitro* requires interferon-gamma and expression of LFA-1. *Eur J Immunol* 1990 Aug;20(8):1661–1667.
102. McNally AK, DeFife KM, Anderson JM. Interleukin-4-induced macrophage fusion is prevented by inhibitors of mannose receptor activity. *Am J Pathol* 1996 Sep;149(3):975–985.
103. Terada N, Hamazaki T, Oka M, *et al.* Bone marrow cells adopt the phenotype of other cells by spontaneous cell fusion. *Nature* 2002 Apr 4;416(6880):542–545.
104. Lagasse E, Connors H, Al-Dhalimy M, *et al.* Purified hematopoietic stem cells can differentiate into hepatocytes *in vivo*. *Nat Med* 2000 Nov; 6(11):1229–1234.
105. Bjornson CR, Rietze RL, Reynolds BA, *et al.* Turning brain into blood: a hematopoietic fate adopted by adult neural stem cells *in vivo*. *Science* 1999 Jan 22;283(5401):534–537.
106. Galli R, Borello U, Gritti A, *et al.* Skeletal myogenic potential of human and mouse neural stem cells. *Nat Neurosci* 2000 Oct;3(10):986–991.
107. Ying QL, Nichols J, Evans EP, Smith AG. Changing potency by spontaneous fusion. *Nature* 2002 Apr 4;416(6880):545–548.
108. Weimann JM, Charlton CA, Brazelton TR, *et al.* Contribution of transplanted bone marrow cells to Purkinje neurons in human adult brains. *Proc Natl Acad Sci USA* 2003 Feb 18;100(4):2088–2093.
109. Weimann JM, Johansson CB, Trejo A, Blau HM. Stable reprogrammed heterokaryons form spontaneously in Purkinje neurons after bone marrow transplant. *Nat Cell Biol* 2003 Nov;5(11):959–966.

110. Wang X, Willenbring H, Akkari Y, *et al.* Cell fusion is the principal source of bone-marrow-derived hepatocytes. *Nature* 2003 Apr 24; 422(6934):897–901.
111. Vassilopoulos G, Wang PR, Russell DW. Transplanted bone marrow regenerates liver by cell fusion. *Nature* 2003 Apr 24;422(6934):901–904.
112. Noiseux N, Gnecchi M, Lopez-Ilasaca M, *et al.* Mesenchymal stem cells overexpressing *Akt* dramatically repair infarcted myocardium and improve cardiac function despite infrequent cellular fusion or differentiation. *Mol Ther* 2006 Dec;14(6):840–850.
113. Ishikawa F, Shimazu H, Shultz LD, *et al.* Purified human hematopoietic stem cells contribute to the generation of cardiomyocytes through cell fusion. *FASEB J* 2006 May;20(7):950–952.
114. Reinecke H, Minami E, Poppa V, Murry CE. Evidence for fusion between cardiac and skeletal muscle cells. *Circ Res* 2004 Apr 2;94(6):e56–e60.
115. Koyanagi M, Brandes RP, Haendeler J, *et al.* Cell-to-cell connection of endothelial progenitor cells with cardiac myocytes by nanotubes: a novel mechanism for cell fate changes? *Circ Res* 2005 May 27;96(10):1039–1041.
116. Rustom A, Saffrich R, Markovic I, *et al.* Nanotubular highways for intercellular organelle transport. *Science* 2004 Feb 13;303(5660):1007–1010.
117. Andrade J, Lam JT, Zamora M, *et al.* Predominant fusion of bone marrow-derived cardiomyocytes. *Cardiovasc Res* 2005 Dec 1;68(3):387–393.
118. Dedja A, Zaglia T, Dall'Olmo L, *et al.* Hybrid cardiomyocytes derived by cell fusion in heterotopic cardiac xenografts. *FASEB J* 2006 Dec; 20(14):2534–2536.
119. Welikson RE, Kaestner S, Reinecke H, Hauschka SD. Human umbilical vein endothelial cells fuse with cardiomyocytes but do not activate cardiac gene expression. *J Mol Cell Cardiol* 2006 Apr;40(4):520–528.
120. Matsuura K, Wada H, Nagai T, *et al.* Cardiomyocytes fuse with surrounding noncardiomyocytes and reenter the cell cycle. *J Cell Biol* 2004 Oct 25;167(2):351–363.
121. Garbade J, Schubert A, Rastan AJ, *et al.* Fusion of bone marrow-derived stem cells with cardiomyocytes in a hete-rologous *in vitro* model. *Eur J Cardiothorac Surg* 2005 Nov;28(5):685–691.
122. Kajstura J, Leri A, Finato N, *et al.* Myocyte proliferation in end-stage cardiac failure in humans. *Proc Natl Acad Sci USA* 1998 Jul 21;95(15):8801–8805.

123. Dawn B, Stein AB, Urbanek K, *et al.* Cardiac stem cells delivered intravascularly traverse the vessel barrier, regenerate infarcted myocardium, and improve cardiac function. *Proc Natl Acad Sci USA* 2005 Mar 8;102(10):3766–3771.
124. Bearzi C, Rota M, Hosoda T, *et al.* Human cardiac stem cells. *Proc Natl Acad Sci USA* 2007 Aug 28;104(35):14068–14073.
125. Zhang M, Methot D, Poppa V, *et al.* Cardiomyocyte grafting for cardiac repair: graft cell death and anti-death strategies. *J Mol Cell Cardiol* 2001 May;33(5):907–921.
126. Ye L, Haider H, Guo C, Sim EK. Cell-based VEGF delivery prevents donor cell apoptosis after transplantation. *Ann Thorac Surg* 2007 Mar;83(3):1233–1234; author reply 4.
127. Yoon YS, Johnson IA, Park JS, *et al.* Therapeutic myo-cardial angiogenesis with vascular endothelial growth factors. *Mol Cell Biochem* 2004 Sep;264(1–2):63–74.
128. Kamihata H, Matsubara H, Nishiue T, *et al.* Implantation of bone marrow mononuclear cells into ischemic myocardium enhances collateral perfusion and regional function via side supply of angioblasts, angiogenic ligands, and cytokines. *Circulation* 2001 Aug 28;104(9):1046–1052.
129. Voronov E, Shouval DS, Krelin Y, *et al.* IL-1 is required for tumor invasiveness and angiogenesis. *Proc Natl Acad Sci USA* 2003 Mar 4;100(5):2645–2650.
130. Leibovich SJ, Polverini PJ, Shepard HM, *et al.* Macrophage-induced angiogenesis is mediated by tumour necrosis factor-alpha. *Nature* 1987 Oct 15–21;329(6140):630–632.
131. Schachinger V, Erbs S, Elsasser A, *et al.* Intracoronary bone marrow-derived progenitor cells in acute myocardial infarction. *New Engl J Med* 2006 Sep 21;355(12):1210–1221.
132. Erbs S, Linke A, Schachinger V, *et al.* Restoration of microvascular function in the infarct-related artery by intracoronary transplantation of bone marrow progenitor cells in patients with acute myocardial infarction: the Doppler Substudy of the Reinfusion of Enriched Progenitor Cells and Infarct Remodeling in Acute Myocardial Infarction (REPAIR-AMI) trial. *Circulation* 2007 Jul 24;116(4):366–374.
133. Tang YL, Zhao Q, Zhang YC, *et al.* Autologous mesenchymal stem cell transplantation induce VEGF and neovascularization in ischemic myocardium. *Regul Pept* 2004 Jan 15;117(1):3–10.

134. Kinnaird T, Stabile E, Burnett MS, *et al.* Local delivery of marrow-derived stromal cells augments collateral perfusion through paracrine mechanisms. *Circulation* 2004 Mar 30;109(12):1543–1549.
135. Wang M, Zhang W, Crisostomo P, *et al.* STAT3 mediates bone marrow mesenchymal stem cell VEGF production. *J Mol Cell Cardiol* 2007 Jun;42(6):1009–1015.
136. Gnecchi M, He H, Noiseux N, *et al.* Evidence supporting paracrine hypothesis for Akt-modified mesenchymal stem cell-mediated cardiac protection and functional improvement. *FASEB J* 2006 Apr;20(6):661–669.
137. Gerber HP, Malik AK, Solar GP, *et al.* VEGF regulates haematopoietic stem cell survival by an internal autocrine loop mechanism. *Nature* 2002 Jun 27;417(6892):954–958.
138. Takakura N, Watanabe T, Suenobu S, *et al.* A role for hematopoietic stem cells in promoting angiogenesis. *Cell* 2000 Jul 21;102(2):199–209.
139. Rehman J, Li J, Orschell CM, March KL. Peripheral blood "endothelial progenitor cells" are derived from monocyte/macrophages and secrete angiogenic growth factors. *Circulation* 2003 Mar 4;107(8):1164–1169.
140. Young PP, Vaughan DE, Hatzopoulos AK. Biologic properties of endothelial progenitor cells and their potential for cell therapy. *Prog Cardiovasc Dis* 2007 May–Jun;49(6):421–429.
141. Roncalli JG, Tongers J, Renault MA, Losordo DW. Endothelial progenitor cells in regenerative medicine and cancer: a decade of research. *Trends Biotechnol* 2008 May;26(5):276–283.
142. Uemura R, Xu M, Ahmad N, Ashraf M. Bone marrow stem cells prevent left ventricular remodeling of ischemic heart through paracrine signaling. *Circ Res* 2006 Jun 9;98(11):1414–1421.
143. Xu M, Uemura R, Dai Y, *et al.* *In vitro* and *in vivo* effects of bone marrow stem cells on cardiac structure and function. *J Mol Cell Cardiol* 2007 Feb;42(2):441–448.
144. Dai Y, Xu M, Wang Y, *et al.* HIF-1alpha induced-VEGF overexpression in bone marrow stem cells protects cardiomyocytes against ischemia. *J Mol Cell Cardiol* 2007 Jun;42(6):1036–1044.
145. Markel TA, Wang Y, Herrmann JL, *et al.* VEGF is critical for stem cell-mediated cardioprotection and a crucial paracrine factor for defining the age threshold in adult and neonatal stem cell function. *Am J Physiol* 2008 Dec;295(6):H2308–H2314.

146. Tang YL, Zhao Q, Qin X, *et al.* Paracrine action enhances the effects of autologous mesenchymal stem cell transplantation on vascular regeneration in rat model of myocardial infarction. *Ann Thorac Surg* 2005 Jul;80(1):229–236; discussion 36–37.

147. Takahashi M, Li TS, Suzuki R, *et al.* Cytokines produced by bone marrow cells can contribute to functional improvement of the infarcted heart by protecting cardiomyocytes from ischemic injury. *Am J Physiol* 2006 Aug;291(2):H886–H893.

148. Imberti B, Morigi M, Tomasoni S, *et al.* Insulin-like growth factor-1 sustains stem cell mediated renal repair. *J Am Soc Nephrol* 2007 Nov;18(11):2921–2928.

149. Burchfield JS, Iwasaki M, Koyanagi M, *et al.* Interleukin-10 from transplanted bone marrow mononuclear cells contributes to cardiac protection after myocardial infarction. *Circ Res* 2008 Jul 18;103(2):203–211.

150. Korf-Klingebiel M, Kempf T, Sauer T, *et al.* Bone marrow cells are a rich source of growth factors and cytokines: implications for cell therapy trials after myocardial infarction. *Eur Heart J* 2008 Dec;29(23):2851–2858.

151. Gallagher GL, Jackson CJ, Hunyor SN. Myocardial extracellular matrix remodeling in ischemic heart failure. *Front Biosci* 2007;12 1410–1419.

152. Lindsey ML. MMP induction and inhibition in myocardial infarction. *Heart Fail Rev* 2004 Jan;9(1):7–19.

153. Xu X, Xu Z, Xu Y, Cui G. Effects of mesenchymal stem cell transplantation on extracellular matrix after myocardial infarction in rats. *Coron Art Dis* 2005 Jun;16(4):245–255.

154. Berry MF, Engler AJ, Woo YJ, *et al.* Mesenchymal stem cell injection after myocardial infarction improves myocardial compliance. *Am J Physiol* 2006 Jun;290(6):H2196–H2203.

155. Guo J, Lin GS, Bao CY, *et al.* Anti-inflammation role for mesenchymal stem cells transplantation in myocardial infarction. *Inflammation* 2007 Aug;30(3–4):97–104.

156. Ohnishi S, Sumiyoshi H, Kitamura S, Nagaya N. Mesenchymal stem cells attenuate cardiac fibroblast proliferation and collagen synthesis through paracrine actions. *FEBS Lett* 2007 Aug 21;581(21):3961–3966.

157. Nagaya N, Kangawa K, Itoh T, *et al.* Transplantation of mesenchymal stem cells improves cardiac function in a rat model of dilated cardiomyopathy. *Circulation* 2005 Aug 23;112(8):1128–1135.

158. Li L, Zhang Y, Li Y, *et al.* Mesenchymal stem cell transplantation attenuates cardiac fibrosis associated with isoproterenol-induced global heart failure. *Transplant Int* 2008 Dec;21(12):1181–1189.
159. Aupperle H, Garbade J, Schubert A, *et al.* Effects of autologous stem cells on immunohistochemical patterns and gene expression of metalloproteinases and their tissue inhibitors in doxorubicin cardiomyopathy in a rabbit model. *Vet Pathol* 2007 Jul;44(4):494–503.
160. Szmitko PE, Fedak PW, Weisel RD, *et al.* Endothelial progenitor cells: new hope for a broken heart. *Circulation* 2003 Jun 24;107(24):3093–3100.
161. Kucia M, Dawn B, Hunt G, *et al.* Cells expressing early cardiac markers reside in the bone marrow and are mobilized into the peripheral blood after myocardial infarction. *Circ Res* 2004 Dec 10;95(12):1191–1199.
162. Anversa P, Nadal-Ginard B. Myocyte renewal and ventricular remodelling. *Nature* 2002 Jan 10;415(6868):240–243.
163. Linke A, Muller P, Nurzynska D, *et al.* Stem cells in the dog heart are self-renewing, clonogenic, and multipotent and regenerate infarcted myocardium, improving cardiac function. *Proc Natl Acad Sci USA* 2005 Jun 21;102(25):8966–8971.
164. Urbanek K, Rota M, Cascapera S, *et al.* Cardiac stem cells possess growth factor-receptor systems that after activation regenerate the infarcted myocardium, improving ventricular function and long-term survival. *Circ Res* 2005 Sep 30;97(7):663–673.
165. Nakanishi C, Yamagishi M, Yamahara K, *et al.* Activation of cardiac progenitor cells through paracrine effects of mesenchymal stem cells. *Biochem Biophys Res Commun* 2008 Sep 12;374(1):11–16.
166. Urbich C, Aicher A, Heeschen C, *et al.* Soluble factors released by endothelial progenitor cells promote migration of endothelial cells and cardiac resident progenitor cells. *J Mol Cell Cardiol* 2005 Nov;39(5):733–742.
167. Abbott JD, Huang Y, Liu D, *et al.* Stromal cell-derived factor-1alpha plays a critical role in stem cell recruitment to the heart after myocardial infarction but is not sufficient to induce homing in the absence of injury. *Circulation* 2004 Nov 23;110(21):3300–3305.
168. Zhang M, Mal N, Kiedrowski M, *et al.* SDF-1 expression by mesenchymal stem cells results in trophic support of cardiac myocytes after myocardial infarction. *FASEB J* 2007 Oct;21(12):3197–3207.
169. Unzek S, Zhang M, Mal N, *et al.* SDF-1 recruits cardiac stem cell-like cells that depolarize *in vivo*. *Cell Transplant* 2007;16(9):879–886.

170. Haider H, Jiang S, Idris NM, Ashraf M. IGF-1-overexpressing mesenchymal stem cells accelerate bone marrow stem cell mobilization via paracrine activation of SDF-1alpha/CXCR4 signaling to promote myocardial repair. *Circ Res* 2008 Nov 21;103(11):1300–1308.
171. Fazel S, Chen L, Weisel RD, *et al.* Cell transplantation preserves cardiac function after infarction by infarct stabilization: augmentation by stem cell factor. *J Thorac Cardiovasc Surg* 2005 Nov;130(5):1310.
172. Smith DA, Irving SD, Sheldon J, *et al.* Serum levels of the antiinflammatory cytokine interleukin-10 are decreased in patients with unstable angina. *Circulation* 2001 Aug 14;104(7):746–749.
173. Pasqui AL, Di Renzo M, Auteri A, Puccetti L. Cytokines in acute coronary syndromes. *Int J Cardiol* 2005 Dec 7;105(3):355–356.
174. Kilic T, Ural D, Ural E, *et al.* Relation between proinflammatory to anti-inflammatory cytokine ratios and long-term prognosis in patients with non-ST elevation acute coronary syndrome. *Heart (Br Card Soc)* 2006 Aug;92(8):1041–1046.
175. Anguera I, Miranda-Guardiola F, Bosch X, *et al.* Elevation of serum levels of the anti-inflammatory cytokine interleukin-10 and decreased risk of coronary events in patients with unstable angina. *Am Heart J* 2002 Nov;144(5):811–817.
176. Tziakas DN, Chalikias GK, Kaski JC, *et al.* Inflammatory and anti-inflammatory variable clusters and risk prediction in acute coronary syndrome patients: a factor analysis approach. *Atherosclerosis* 2007 Jul;193(1):196–203.
177. Mann DL. Inflammatory mediators and the failing heart: past, present, and the foreseeable future. *Circ Res* 2002 Nov 29;91(11):988–998.
178. Gullestad L, Aukrust P, Ueland T, *et al.* Effect of high versus low-dose angiotensin converting enzyme inhibition on cytokine levels in chronic heart failure. *J Am Coll Cardiol* 1999 Dec;34(7):2061–2067.
179. Prabhu SD, Chandrasekar B, Murray DR, Freeman GL. Beta-adrenergic blockade in developing heart failure: effects on myocardial inflammatory cytokines, nitric oxide, and remodeling. *Circulation* 2000 May 2;101(17):2103–2109.
180. Damas JK, Aukrust P, Ueland T, *et al.* Monocyte chemoattractant protein-1 enhances and interleukin-10 suppresses the production of inflammatory cytokines in adult rat cardiomyocytes. *Basic Res Cardiol* 2001 Jul;96(4):345–352.

181. Matsumori A, Sasayama S. The role of inflammatory mediators in the failing heart: immunomodulation of cytokines in experimental models of heart failure. *Heart Fail Rev* 2001 Mar;6(2):129–136.
182. Grinnemo KH, Mansson A, Dellgren G, *et al.* Xenoreactivity and engraftment of human mesenchymal stem cells transplanted into infarcted rat myocardium. *J Thorac Cardiovasc Surg* 2004 May;127(5):1293–1300.
183. Aggarwal S, Pittenger MF. Human mesenchymal stem cells modulate allogeneic immune cell responses. *Blood* 2005 Feb 15;105(4):1815–1822.
184. Togel F, Hu Z, Weiss K, *et al.* Administered mesenchymal stem cells protect against ischemic acute renal failure through differentiation-independent mechanisms. *Am J Physiol Renal Physiol* 2005 Jul;289(1):F31–F42.
185. Chen G. Anti-inflammatory cytokines may play salutary paracrine effects in cellular cardiomyoplasty using mesenchymal stem cells. *Ann Thorac Surg* 2010 (in press).
186. Dai W, Hale SL, Kloner RA. Role of a paracrine action of mesenchymal stem cells in the improvement of left ventricular function after coronary artery occlusion in rats. *Reg Med* 2007 Jan;2(1):63–68.

# CHAPTER 15

# ENHANCED STEM CELL THERAPIES FOR CARDIO-PULMONARY DISEASES

*David W. Courtman*

## Abstract

Autologously derived stem and progenitor cells have been used in a number of pioneering human clinical trials to treat patients suffering from ischemic heart disease and idiopathic pulmonary hypertension. The limited success of these trials has stimulated the development of novel strategies to enhance the therapeutic index of cellular therapies. Culture optimization and transient genetic transfection may overcome some of the limitations of collecting cells from older and diseased patients, yet new cell-material based strategies will likely need to be developed to enhance cell survival, tissue specific engraftment, and ultimately therapeutic efficacy. Delivering cells with an associated coating of provisional matrix may produce a portable stem cell niche, providing a novel method of protecting stem cells during delivery to the patient.

## 1. Introduction

The tissue specific delivery of stem or progenitor cells holds the potential to regenerate damaged tissue and restore organ function. Indeed, the limited clinical successes that have been achieved with autologous stem or progenitor cell therapy in the treatment of both cardiac[1–3] and pulmonary diseases[4,5] point toward the ultimate potential of these approaches (for review see[6–8]). However, a successful and widely applicable clinical therapy will require substantive optimization in terms of cell isolation, processing, and delivery. Early phase cardiovascular trials have demonstrated that extensive organ specific therapeutic cell loss after delivery represents a critical limitation for cell therapy.[9–11] In animal models, direct cardiac injection can result in an immediate loss of up to 40% of the injected cells, presumably through leakage from the injection site or wash-out *via* the vasculature or lymphatic system.[11,12] This early loss is followed by a wave of apoptotic cell death persisting for up to four days.[13] The net result is a minimal retention of viable cells and a limited regeneration of functional tissue. Thus, it is believed that approaches to enhance organ specific (in this case cardiac) cell engraftment and survival will markedly increase the efficacy of regenerative cell therapies.

## 2. Cardiac Repair/Regeneration

Cardiovascular disease (CVD) represents the most significant health burden in North America with more then 71 million (43 million under the age 65) American adults suffering from one or more types of CVD. Congestive heart failure and myocardial infarction have incidences of 5 and 7.2 million respectively within the American population.[14] Thus, it is not surprising that considerable interest exists in the development of cell-based regenerative therapies to treat these diseases. A number of clinical trials have recently been completed using intra-coronary delivery of autologous cells for the treatment of myocardial dysfunction in the post-infarct setting. The Topcare AMI, Topcare CHD, Boost, and Magic trials all achieved modest, yet significant increases in myocardial function (left ventricular ejection fraction increases of approximately 5%) with infusion of bone marrow or peripheral blood-derived progenitor cells.[15–19] The positive results of these and similar trials, occurring in this complex disease setting, have been interpreted with cautious optimism, and even though the clinical improvement appears modest it is of note that it is of the same order of magnitude as other widely accepted therapies, such as thrombolysis and acute percutaneous interventions.[20] Although the exact mechanism of action, be it new blood vessel formation, reduced scarring, or muscle regeneration remains in debate, it is now widely believed that an effective therapy can be developed from adult autologous progenitor cells.[6,8] However, it is also believed that if these therapies are to be widely applied significant optimization of the therapeutic cells either through cell selection, genetic engineering or other modifications, will be required to increase their effectiveness.

Autologous progenitor cells hold many advantages over other cell types. They are readily available, often from bone marrow or peripheral blood, and extremely safe with little risk of immune rejection or the introduction of foreign genes or infectious agents. However, they do require patient-specific collection and processing, and there remains significant concern that cells from patients with chronic CVD may be less effective then those from young healthy donors.[21] In contrast, allogenic cells can be manufactured in batches from healthy donors, a process more amenable to off the shelf delivery. Many studies have demonstrated that allogenic progenitor cells, such as mesenchymal stromal cells (MSCs), are immunologically tolerated,[22] at least in the short-term, yet there remains concern that long term regeneration may be hampered by lack of histocompatability. In addition, the amplification of MSCs in culture increases the potential risk of introducing a highly proliferative transformed cell into the patient. Similarly, embryonic stem cells, although extremely attractive from a regenerative perspective, continue to generate concern over their potential for uncontrolled cell growth *in vivo*. Perhaps the most promising regenerative cell is the autologously-derived induced pluripotent stem (iPS) cell. Recently described transposon/transposase-based techniques to efficiently generate iPS cells have demonstrated the potential for this methodology to produce stem cells with profound regenerative potential.[23] However, much work is left to be done to generate a reproducible and clinically safe therapeutic cell. Although true pluripotent stem cells may be required for complete tissue regeneration, it is very likely that such therapies will always be accompanied by a degree of risk. In many cases, complete tissue regeneration may not be necessary, and an effective therapy may be induced with the use of low risk autologous progenitor cells. At least in the near term, these cells may be the most clinically viable option, particularly if there shortcomings can be ameliorated by manipulation in culture or co-delivery with biologically active materials.

## 2.1 *Routes of cell delivery*

In human trials, cells have been delivered to the myocardium *via* direct injection into the ventricular muscle or by delivery through an intra-coronary artery. In direct injection techniques, a specialized catheter is often used to target regions of the diseased ventricle that are most amenable to regeneration.[24] For example, myocardial infarction produces a central necrotic zone which may be beyond repair, yet a surrounding border zone often exists in which the myocytes are viable yet not contracting. It is believed that this hibernating myocardium is most amenable to restoration of contractile function. Mapping catheters can be used to detect hibernating regions and subsequently injection into these zones can be performed.[25,26] Direct injection involves the high pressure extrusion of a small volume of cells through a needle tip at the end of the catheter and typically involves multiple injection sites in the ventricle. As such, mapping and injection protocols are technically demanding and time consuming for medical personal and require expensive specialized equipment. To date, no studies have conclusively demonstrated a therapeutic benefit of direct injection over other modes of delivery, and as such, the added expense may not be warranted. Recent clinical trials have predominately used intra-coronary injection of cells to produce clinical benefit. In this method, a balloon catheter is advanced into the coronary artery of interest, and the balloon briefly inflated during the injection of cells through a distal port on the tip of the catheter. In this manner, reverse flow is limited and the cells are distributed throughout the distal vascular bed.

Each of these modes of delivery has benefits and drawbacks when developing novel cellular therapeutics. Direct injection will allow for the simultaneous delivery of solid or gel substrates, such as hydrogels or provisional matrix (for example, fibrinogen/fibrin) that may support cell attachment and survival. Yet such delivery will be limited to discrete sites and materials of low enough viscosity to be readily delivered through a cardiac catheter. In addition, direct myocardial injection will cause local tissue disruption, which may limit cell engraftment and stimulate lymphatic clearance of the therapeutic product. In contrast, intra-vascular delivery produces a much wider distribution of cells throughout the distal vascular tree, yet is limited by the potential for embolic occlusion of the microcirculation. To date, as many as 200 million bone marrow mononuclear cells have been delivered by the intra-coronary route in patients after myocardial infarction with no adverse consequences,[27] although the risk of occlusion will need to be assessed for each new cell type or combined therapy. Occlusion may result from physical blockage, in which the cell product unable to pass through or migrate out of the circulation, or adverse stimulation of a coagulation response. In addition, true tissue regeneration will require the delivered cells to migrate out of the microcirculation and engraft in the surrounding tissues. Thus intra-vascular delivery may be limited to specific cell products that meet these criteria.

## 3. Cell Therapy for Pulmonary Diseases

Pulmonary diseases are attractive targets for cell therapy, as the pulmonary circulation is easily accessible by intravenous injection. Indeed, the transient accumulation of cells in the lung is often observed as an unintended consequence of clinical stem cell therapies, such as bone marrow transplant. Chronic lung diseases, such as chronic obstructive pulmonary disease (COPD) are likely to require regeneration of the complete tissue architecture, and thus may be targets for true pluripotent stem cell therapy. However, diseases such as idiopathic pulmonary hypertension (iPH), which predominantly involve remodeling of the vasculature, may be amenable to targeted vascular repair with vascular progenitor cell therapy, or cells engineered to induce angiogenesis. In animal models, immune matched (syngeneic) adult smooth muscle cells or fibroblasts transiently transfected with either of the angiogenic genes endothelial nitric oxide synthase (eNOS) or vascular endothelial growth factor (VEGF), and subsequently delivered to the pulmonary vasculature, can prevent the onset of PPH and reverse established pulmonary hypertension by regenerating microcirculatory flow.[28–30] In more recent studies, endothelial progenitor cells (EPCs), derived in rodent models by adherent culture of bone marrow stroma, have demonstrated an innate ability to inhibit the onset of PPH, and when they are transfected with eNOS, they can potently reverse established disease.[31] On the basis of these results, combined with a series of large animal safety studies, a clinical trial of genetically engineered EPCs for the treatment of PPH has been initiated. In this trial, we validated protocols that were established to derive (by selective adherent culture) large numbers of human EPCs from peripheral blood (leukapheresis samples obtained from non-mobilized donors), and to transiently transfect these cells with eNOS by electroporation. Recently, two clinical studies from China have demonstrated the utility of autologous non-transformed EPCs in the treatment of established iPH in both children and adults.[4,5] In these studies, intravenous infusion of EPCs (0.4 to 22 million cells) was well tolerated, and patients displayed significant improvement in pulmonary arterial pressure and vascular resistance.

Acute lung injury (ALI) is another disease that may be amenable to cell therapy. In this case, cells may not be acting to regenerate tissue, but rather as regulators of immune responses. ALI is associated with a 39% mortality rate with 190,600 new cases in the US yearly, leading to 74,500 deaths and 3.6 million hospital days.[32] Sepsis and its complications, including acute lung injury (ALI) and multiple organ dysfunction syndrome (MODS), are important causes of morbidity and mortality in this patient population. Current effective treatment strategies for both ALI and sepsis are lacking. Over the past several years, the vascular delivery of marrow-derived stromal cells (MSCs) to the lung was evaluated for the treatment of ALI in rodent models. These studies showed a pronounced therapeutic role of both allogenic (strain mismatched) and syngeneic (matched inbred strain) MSCs in both mice and rats. A pronounced and significant reduction in endotoxin-induced pulmonary inflammation and vascular permeability was demonstrated in these models. MSCs are also effective in a clinically relevant murine model of sepsis and MODS, cecal-ligation-and-puncture (CLP), demonstrating a reduction in both systemic and pulmonary inflammation, renal and liver dysfunction, and a survival advantage in septic mice.[33]

In ALI and sepsis, the therapeutic mechanism of MSC action is likely immunomodulatory, which may, at least in part, be through a prostaglandinE2 stimulation of IL-10 by endogenous macrophages.[33] However, our understanding of MSC therapy is far from complete, and it is very likely that the spatial localization and direct release of chemokines by these cells both play important roles. The transfection of MSCs with the vasculoprotective factor, angiopoietin-1 (ANGPT1), can produce a synergistic effect, leading to nearly a complete reversal of endotoxin-induced ALI in mice.[34] In addition, ANGPT1 transfected fibroblasts protected rats from developing in response to LPS.[35] These results highlighted the potential benefit of localized cytokine secretion in the lungs. Taken together, these promising rodent studies demonstrated the pronounced immunomodulatory capacity of MSCs, and highlighted the potential for the development of novel cell-based therapeutic approaches to treat ALI in humans.

## 4. Enhancing Regenerative Potential

### 4.1 *Cell based gene therapy*

The use of autologous stem or progenitor cells is by far the safest mode of cell therapy. However, in many cases stem cells derived from the diseased patient may be sub-optimal. Thus, strategies to enhance the therapeutic potential of these cells are required. Physical and/or chemical treatment of cells in culture have had some limited successes in restoring cell function, and thus *in vitro* culture protocols should be developed with this in mind. The more direct approach of modifying cell function by gene therapy is also a viable option. Viral transduction holds the possibility of permanently modifying gene expression, yet introduces the risk of mutagenesis by inappropriate genomic incorporation. Non-viral transfection techniques that produce transient gene expression with little risk of genomic incorporation are the safest, and it is this technique that has been adopted for early stage clinical trials. The transient nature of gene expression, days to weeks, may be a drawback if the goal is to overcome a genetic abnormality in the patient, yet may have advantages in treating acute injuries or in stimulating therapeutic cell engraftment and repair programs. The use of transiently transfected cells for the treatment primary pulmonary hypertension (PPH) was demonstrated in animal models and a clinical trial was initiated.[28–31,36] In these studies, a number of angiogenic genes were shown to be therapeutic, and eNOS was chosen based both on its safety and efficacy. Unlike growth factors, eNOS remains intra-cellular and excessive production is likely to be self limiting, as this will lead to the death of the overexpressing cell. Cell-based gene therapy has a number of advantages over direct *in vivo* genetic manipulation. Cells *in vitro* can be subjected to a number of physical or chemical transfection strategies that are not applicable *in vivo*, and gene expression in the final clinical product can be regulated in a more reproducible fashion. However, careful selection of the appropriate transgene and optimization of the final cell product is always warranted.

### 4.2 *Enhancing therapeutic cell survival*

In many of the clinical studies, the therapeutic effect of the cells is very likely a consequence of their intra-vascular delivery, resulting in a wide distribution throughout the distal microvasculature, while allowing for a site specific (immediately pre-capillary) delivery of cytokines or a therapeutic transgene. This intra-vascular delivery and cellular distribution may be critical to the treatment of many cardiovascular diseases, particularly those in which angiogenesis is the key therapeutic modality (for example, peripheral vascular disease and ischemic heart disease). However, delivery of cells in suspension through the vasculature may induce cell death (anoikis) or the cells may not engraft in the target tissue. Strategies to enhance cell survival and engraftment will be required to optimize these therapies. Although genetically engineering the therapeutic cells with active intra-cellular mediators, such as Akt,[13] constitutively active integrin linked kinase (ILK),[37] or telemorase reverse transcriptase[7] showing increased cell survival, it is possible that these strategies will lead to unregulated cell growth, and markedly increase the risk of tumor formation. A better approach to promote survival and engraftment is to modify the microenvironment surrounding the cell. The absence of extracellular matrix interactions in these largely adherent cell populations can lead to anoikis (a cell type specific form of apoptotic cell death[38,39]) that involves a number of integrin mediated intra-cellular signalling molecules, such as focal adhesion kinase (FAK), integrin linked kinase (ILK), and extracellular signal regulated mitogen activated protein kinases (ERK/MAPK).[40–44] To promote appropriate intra-cellular signalling and cell survival, cell surface integrins need to be bound to immobilized ligands as these "solid state" receptors can respond in an opposite fashion to soluble ligands (antagonists).[42,43] Indeed, the precise morphological presentation of integrin binding partners within a matrix may be critical to activation and signalling, as integrin clustering may be required.[45,46]

To mimic these adhesive responses on cells in suspension, a strategy to immobilize provisional matrix molecules on individual cell surfaces was developed.[47] This degradable cellular encapsulation strategy is used to enhance the survival and engraftment of stem and progenitor cells, allowing for a suspension of individual encapsulated cells to be delivered to the tissue by simple upstream intra-vascular injection. With this approach, individual encapsulated cells lodge in the microvasculature, migrate from the capsule and engraft in the surrounding tissue. This is in contrast to previous cellular micro-encapsulation strategies that were developed to isolate allogeneic or xenogeneic cells from the host's immune system, while still allowing free passage of smaller molecules, including nutrients and cell products. The most commonly used micro-encapsulation platform of this type employs a calcium alginate encapsulation matrix stabilized by a polylysine coating, as developed by Sun *et al.*[48,49] A similar platform, developed by Sefton,[50,51] involves the micro-encapsulation of cells within a hydroxyethyl methacrylate-methyl methacrylate copolymer (HEMA-MMA) shell. Common between these and other immunoisolation-based micro-encapsulation strategies is the use of non-degradable polymers for prolonged encapsulation of the transplanted cells, as well as the encapsulation of hundreds to thousands of cells per microcapsule. Such strategies may be amenable to direct tissue injection, but are not applicable of cellular delivery through the vasculature.

In single cell encapsulation, the intention is to produce a temporary portable microenvironment capable of engaging membrane integrins, sustaining cell viability, and enhancing cellular engraftment into tissues of interest, in effect producing a cocoon around the cell. In its simplest form, it consists of surrounding an individual cell in an agarose gel supplemented with provisional matrix proteins. More complex iterations of cocooning involve supplementation with growth factors and cytokines, as well as more heterogeneous mixtures of matrix molecules and biological cross-linkers. It is envisioned that these cocoons could be developed into portable stem cell niches, allowing for the simultaneous tissue delivery of stem cells with a sustaining microenvironment. This novel, single cell approach is unlike traditional non-degradable multi-cellular micro-encapsulation strategies, and is principally designed to use the hydrogel simply to cluster and immobilize the provisional matrix molecules on the cell surface, while providing only a minimal impediment to cell migration from the cocoon and ultimate peri-vascular engraftment.

To date, single cell cocooning was tested on human and rat fibroblasts, as well as human and rat bone marrow stromal cells. In these adherent cell populations, apoptosis (anoikis) can be induced by holding the cells in suspension culture or by providing untethered ligands (such as RGD peptides). Our matrix supplemented cocooning strategy significantly enhanced survival of all of the tested cell types, likely the result of the provisional matrix proteins in the cocoon, fibrinogen and fibronectin, stimulating integrin mediated signalling, and clustering with the net result being an increase in intra-cellular ERK phosphorylation. Studies of ERK activity and inhibition combined with profound morphological changes in the cell surface, including membrane ruffling and surface invaginations in matrix supplemented cocoons, support this theory.[47] Integrin specific inhibition studies indicated a prominent role for $\beta_1$ containing integrins, and a more modest role for $\beta_3$ containing integrins in enhancing viability of cells in the matrix supplemented cocoons, indicating that $\beta_1$ integrins are the predominant binding partners for this matrix. Time-lapse video microscopy demonstrated that within 24 hours cocooned cells can easily escape from their capsule and establish strong contacts with the substratum. In fact, migration from the agarose cocoon is markedly enhanced by the addition of the provisional matrix molecules. Injection of cocooned bone marrow stromal cells into the rat pulmonary artery or femoral artery confirmed their ability to distribute throughout the downstream vasculature, escape from the capsules, and incorporate into the surrounding tissue, markedly enhancing stem cell engraftment above that seen for non-encapsulated cells.

## 5. Summary

True pluripotent stem cells have the capacity for complete tissue regeneration, and may in the future provide cures to many chronic and inherited diseases. However, much work remains to be done before these cells can be used to produce safe and efficacious clinical therapies. In contrast, adult stem and progenitor cells derived from the patient have shown promise as effective therapeutic agents in both ischemic heart and pulmonary diseases. Early clinical trials demonstrated that these cells are exceptionally safe, and it is widely believed that effective cell based clinical therapies can be developed with optimization of cell processing and the application of novel targeted delivery strategies.

## References


1. Singh S, *et al.* Stem cells improve left ventricular function in acute myocardial infarction. *Clin Cardiol* 2009;32(4):176–180.
2. Martin-Rendon E, *et al.* Autologous bone marrow stem cells to treat acute myocardial infarction: a systematic review. *Eur Heart J* 2008;29(15): 1807–1818.
3. Lipinski MJ, *et al.* Impact of intracoronary cell therapy on left ventricular function in the setting of acute myocardial infarction: a collaborative systematic review and meta-analysis of controlled clinical trials. *J Am Coll Cardiol* 2007;50(18):1761–1767.
4. Zhu JH, *et al.* Safety and efficacy of autologous endothelial progenitor cells transplantation in children with idiopathic pulmonary arterial hypertension: open-label pilot study. *Pediatr Transplant* 2008;12(6):650–655.
5. Wang XX, *et al.* Transplantation of autologous endothelial progenitor cells may be beneficial in patients with idiopathic pulmonary arterial hypertension: a pilot randomized controlled trial. *J Am Coll Cardiol* 2007;49(14):1566–1571.
6. Boyle AJ, *et al.* Controversies in cardiovascular medicine: ready for the next step. *Circulation* 2006;114(4):339–352.
7. Murasawa S, *et al.* Constitutive human telomerase reverse transcriptase expression enhances regenerative properties of endothelial progenitor cells. *Circulation* 2002;106(9):1133–1139.
8. Oettgen P, *et al.* Controversies in cardiovascular medicine. *Circulation* 2006;114(4):353–358.
9. Haider H, Ashraf M. Bone marrow stem cell transplantation for cardiac repair. *Am J Physiol Heart Circ Physiol* 2005;288(6):H2557–2567.
10. Menasche P. Stem cells for clinical use in cardiovascular medicine: current limitations and future perspectives. *Thromb Haemost* 2005;94(4): 697–701.

11. Reinecke H, Murry CE. Taking the death toll after cardiomyocyte grafting: a reminder of the importance of quantitative biology. *J Mol Cell Cardiol* 2002;34(3):251–253.
12. Muller-Ehmsen J, *et al.* Survival and development of neonatal rat cardiomyocytes transplanted into adult myocardium. *J Mol Cell Cardiol* 2002;34(2):107–116.
13. Zhang M, *et al.* Cardiomyocyte grafting for cardiac repair: graft cell death and anti-death strategies. *J Mol Cell Cardiol* 2001;33(5):907–921.
14. Thom T, *et al.* Heart disease and stroke statistics — 2006 update: a report from the American Heart Association Statistics Committee and Stroke Statistics Subcommittee. *Circulation* 2006;113(6):e85–151.
15. Assmus B, *et al.* Transcoronary transplantataion of progenitor cells in patients with persistent left ventricular dysfunction after myocardial infarction: a randomized controlled trial (TOPCARE-CHD). *Circulation* 2005;112(Suppl II):II-632.
16. Assmus B, *et al.* Transplantation of Progenitor Cells and Regeneration Enhancement in Acute Myocardial Infarction (TOPCARE-AMI). *Circulation* 2002;106(24):3009–3017.
17. Kang HJ, *et al.* Differential effect of intracoronary infusion of mobilized peripheral blood stem cells by granulocyte colony-stimulating factor on left ventricular function and remodeling in patients with acute myocardial infarction versus old myocardial infarction: the MAGIC Cell-3-DES randomized, controlled trial. *Circulation* 2006;114(1 Suppl):I145–151.
18. Schachinger V, *et al.* Transplantation of progenitor cells and regeneration enhancement in acute myocardial infarction: final one-year results of the TOPCARE-AMI Trial. *J Am Coll Cardiol* 2004;44(8):1690–1699.
19. Wollert KC, *et al.* Intracoronary autologous bone-marrow cell transfer after myocardial infarction: the BOOST randomised controlled clinical trial. *Lancet* 2004;364(9429):141–148.
20. Reffelmann T, Konemann S, Kloner, RA. Promise of blood- and bone marrow-derived stem cell transplantation for functional cardiac repair: putting it in perspective with existing therapy. *J Am Coll Cardiol* 2009;53(4):305–308.
21. Rupp S, *et al.* Statin therapy in patients with coronary artery disease improves the impaired endothelial progenitor cell differentiation into cardiomyogenic cells. *Basic Res Cardiol* 2004;99(1):61–68.

22. Chiu RC. MSC immune tolerance in cellular cardiomyoplasty. *Semin Thorac Cardiovasc Surg* 2008;20(2):115–118.
23. Woltjen K, *et al.* PiggyBac transposition reprograms fibroblasts to induced pluripotent stem cells. *Nature* 2009;458(7239):766–770.
24. Losordo DW, *et al.* Intramyocardial transplantation of autologous CD34+ stem cells for intractable angina: a phase I/IIa double-blind, randomized controlled trial. *Circulation* 2007;115(25):3165–3172.
25. Gyongyosi M, *et al.* Characterization of hibernating myocardium with NOGA electroanatomic endocardial mapping. *Am J Cardiol* 2005;95(6): 722–728.
26. Fallavollita JA, *et al.* Spatial heterogeneity of endocardial voltage amplitude in viable, chronically dysfunctional myocardium. *Basic Res Cardiol* 2004;99(3):212–222.
27. Assmus B, *et al.* Transcoronary transplantation of progenitor cells after myocardial infarction. *N Engl J Med* 2006;355(12):1222–1232.
28. Campbell AI, Kuliszewski MA, Stewart, DJ. Cell-based gene transfer to the pulmonary vasculature: endothelial nitric oxide synthase overexpression inhibits monocrotaline-induced pulmonary hypertension. *Am J Respir Cell Mol Biol* 1999;21(5):567–575.
29. Campbell AI, *et al.* Cell-based gene transfer of vascular endothelial growth factor attenuates monocrotaline-induced pulmonary hypertension. *Circulation* 2001;104(18):2242–2248.
30. Zhao YD, *et al.* Microvascular regeneration in established pulmonary hypertension by angiogenic gene transfer. *Am J Respir Cell Mol Biol* 2006; 35(2):182–189.
31. Zhao YD, *et al.* Rescue of monocrotaline-induced pulmonary arterial hypertension using bone marrow-derived endothelial-like progenitor cells: efficacy of combined cell and eNOS gene therapy in established disease. *Circ Res* 2005;96(4):442–450.
32. Rubenfeld GD, Caldwell E, Peabody E, *et al.* Incidence and outcomes of acute lung injury. *N Engl J Med* 2005;353:1685–1693.
33. Németh K, Leelahavanichkul A, Yuen PST, *et al.* Bone marrow stromal cells attenuate sepsis *via* prostaglandin E2–dependent reprogramming of host macrophages to increase their interleukin-10 production. *Nature Med* 2008;15:42–49.

34. Mei SHJ, McCarter SD, Deng Y, *et al.* Prevention of LPS-induced acute lung injury in mice by mesenchymal stem cells overexpressing angiopoietin 1. *PLos Med* 2007;4(9):e269.
35. McCarter SD, Mei SHJ, Lai PFH, *et al.* Cell-based angiopoietin-1 gene therapy for acute lung injury. *Am J Respir Crit Care Med* 2007;175(10): 1014–1026.
36. Zhao YD, *et al.* Protective role of angiopoietin-1 in experimental pulmonary hypertension. *Circ Res* 2003;92(9):984–991.
37. Cho HJ, *et al.* Regulation of endothelial cell and endothelial progenitor cell survival and vasculogenesis by integrin-linked kinase. *Arterioscler Thromb Vasc Biol* 2005;25(6):1154–1160.
38. Frisch SM, Ruoslahti, E. Integrins and anoikis. *Curr Opin Cell Biol* 1997; 9(5):701–706.
39. Valentijn AJ, Zouq N, Gilmore AP. Anoikis. *Biochem Soc Trans* 2004; 32(Pt 3):421–425.
40. Harnois C, *et al.* Human intestinal epithelial crypt cell survival and death: complex modulations of Bcl-2 homologs by Fak, PI3-K/Akt-1, MEK/Erk, and p38 signaling pathways. *J Cell Physiol* 2004;198(2):209–222.
41. Howe AK, Aplin AE, Juliano, RL. Anchorage-dependent ERK signaling — mechanisms and consequences. *Curr Opin Genet Dev* 2002;12(1):30–35.
42. Stupack DG, Cheresh, DA. Get a ligand, get a life: integrins, signaling and cell survival. *J Cell Sci* 2002;115(Pt 19):3729–3738.
43. Stupack DG, *et al.* Apoptosis of adherent cells by recruitment of caspase-8 to unligated integrins. *J Cell Biol* 2001;155(3):459–470.
44. Whitlock BB, *et al.* Differential roles for alpha(M)beta(2) integrin clustering or activation in the control of apoptosis *via* regulation of akt and ERK survival mechanisms. *J Cell Biol* 2000;151(6):1305–1320.
45. Calderwood DA. Integrin activation. *J Cell Sci* 2004;117(Pt 5):657–666.
46. Calderwood DA. Talin controls integrin activation. *Biochem Soc Trans* 2004;32(Pt 3):434–437.
47. Karoubi GK, *et al.* Single-cell hydrogel encapsulation for enhanced survival of human marrow stromal cells. *Biomaterials* 2009;30:5445–5455.
48. Lim F, Sun AM. Microencapsulated islets as bioartificial endocrine pancreas. *Science* 1980;210(4472):908–910.
49. O'Shea GM, Goosen MF, Sun AM. Prolonged survival of transplanted islets of Langerhans encapsulated in a biocompatible membrane. *Biochim Biophys Acta* 1984;804(1):133–136.

50. Sefton MV, Hwang JR, Babensee JE. Selected aspects of the microencapsulation of mammalian cells in HEMA-MMA. *Ann NY Acad Sci* 1997;831:260–270.
51. Uludag H, Sefton MV. Microencapsulated human hepatoma (HepG2) cells: *in vitro* growth and protein release. *J Biomed Mater Res* 1993;27(10): 1213–1224.

# CHAPTER 16

## STEM CELL THERAPY FOR MYOCARDIAL REGENERATION: THE CHINESE EXPERIENCE

*Race L. Kao, Tuanzhu Ha, Chuanfu Li, Xiang Gao, Fumin Zhang, Zhijian Yiang, Yijiang Chen and Wenzhu Ma*

## Abstract

In the last decade, stem cell research has gained significant attention in China with exponential increase in support during the last few years. Although both embryonic and adult stem cells can be used for cellular cardiomyoplasty, only clinical studies using adult stem cells are summarized in this chapter with our results described in detail. We harvested stem cells from skeletal muscle (satellite cells) or bone marrow from different patients and utilized for cellular cardiomyoplasty. Eighteen male patients suffering acute myocardial infarction were evenly assigned to coronary artery bypass graft and autologous satellite cell implantation or percutaneous coronary intervention and autologous bone marrow cell intra-coronary infusion. Cardiac functions were assessed before and at six month after the treatment. All patients survived the procedures without obvious arrhythmia, had an uneventful recovery, and were discharged from the hospital. Significant improvement in NYHA classification and left ventricular ejection fraction were observed to a similar degree for both treatments at six month later. Comparable improvements in local contractility, blood perfusion, tissue viability, and wall thickness at the infarct area for all patients receiving either type of autologous stem cells were also found. A longer follow-up time and large scale randomized controlled trail will be needed.

## 1. Introduction

Embryonic stem cells and adult stem cells are the two major types of stem cells that have been used for experimental and clinical studies. Embryonic stem cells are totipotent cells that have the capability to differentiate into any type of cell in the body. However, their application in regenerative medicine is limited due to ethical concerns, formation of teratoma, and possible rejection after utilization.[1] Recently, the induction of pluripotent stem cell lines from adult cells has been successfully achieved in different laboratories.[2–7] This accomplishment will clearly avoid the ethical concern, while induction of cancer from these cells and immune rejection after application remain uncertain. Using any type of stem cell or progenitor cell, one major limitation to overcome is directing the cells to differentiate into the desired type to repair, restore, or augment the function of an ailing organ. True cardiomyocytes derived from implanted stem cells are infrequent; therefore, directing differentiation of stem cells into heart muscle cells can be beneficial. Recently, human embryonic stem cells have been induced to form cardiomyocytes efficiently when cultured in defined media.[8,9] Activin and bone morphogenetic proteins induced differentiation of >30% of embryonic stem cells into cardiomyocytes, and they could be enriched to 80% – 90% by density-gradient centrifugation. If the embryonic-like cells derived from adult cells can also be induced to form cardiomyocytes, they could be excellent for cellular cardiomyoplasty.[3–7] This chapter will be confined to adult stem cells for myocardial regeneration.

Adult stem cells are undifferentiated cells residing in differentiated tissues capable of self-renewal and proliferation to produce differentiated cells. Adult stem cells can yield the specialized cell types of the tissue from which it originated and are capable of developing into cell types that are characteristic of other tissues (plasticity). Self renewal and plasticity of adult stem cells have been well established in recent years.[10–12] Cell therapy has emerged as a strategy for the treatment of many human diseases.[13–15] The aim of cellular cardiomyoplasty is to replace, repair, or enhance the biological function of damaged myocardium or failing heart.[16–18]

### 1.1 *Satellite cell for myocardial regeneration*

Since we initiated cellular cardiomyoplasty in 1989, our successful outcomes[19–22] have been confirmed by other investigators.[23] Clinical cellular cardiomyoplasty was first performed by Menasche's group in June of 2000.[24] Since then, a number of small scale uncontrolled clinical trials have been reported by different investigative groups. Skeletal muscle satellite cells (myoblasts) have the advantages of autologous availability, can be proliferated *in vitro* to a vast quantity, without tumorigenicity, more committed to myogenic differentiation, and are highly resistant to ischemia/hypoxia environment which allows good survival and engraftment after transplantation. Early clinical applications offered highly encouraging results from others and our observations were covered by recent reviews.[22,25,26] Although the survival, feasibility, safety, and encouraging outcomes have been observed in long-term follow-up studies;[24,27] the definitive long-term efficacy requires large scale, placebo-controlled, double-blind randomized trials such as the MAGIC study.[28]

## 1.2 *Bone marrow cells for cellular cardiomyoplasty*

Adult bone marrow contains multiple cell populations of differentiated cells and undifferentiated cells (stem cells) such as hematopoietic stem cells (HSC), mesenchymal stem cells (MSC) and endothelial progenitor cells. A mixed population of bone marrow cells rather than purified stem cells is commonly used for cellular cardiomyoplasty.[29–31] The safety and ease of obtaining the cells, the observation of new muscle tissue formation, the improvement of contractile function, the enhancement of local perfusion, and the prevention of remodeling and deterioration of the injured heart have been documented in studies using experimental animals and reviewed recently.[22,32–34]

Despite a lack of clear understanding for the beneficial mechanisms, Phase 1 clinical studies have shown the feasibility and safety of the procedure with encouraging functional improvements that are summarized in recent publications.[22,33,35–37] Treatment-controlled trials (TOPCARE-AMI, IACT, BOOST, MAGIC Cell-3-DES, ASTAMI) have been reported, but the number of patients involved are relatively small.[38–43] The randomized, placebo-controlled trials with small to medium size samples have also been reported recently.[44–48] So far, better improvement in left ventricular ejection fraction, less heart enlargement, significantly improved blood flow reserve, lower rate of mortality, heart attacks, and hospitalization due to heart failure all indicate the efficacy of cellular cardiomyoplasty using bone marrow cells. The beneficial mechanisms and the possible factors regulating the differentiation of bone marrow stem cells into heart muscle cells are under current investigation by many groups.

### 1.3 *The Chinese experience*

For the last decade, stem cell research has gained significant attention in China with exponential increase in support and publications during the last few years. Stem cell research[49] and stem cell-based clinical trial[50] in China were reviewed recently. We initiated cellular cardiomyoplasty using autologous satellite cells for patients with acute myocardial infarction in December of 2001. Our early clinical outcomes were reported in 2003.[51,52] Bone marrow mesenchymal stem cells,[53] bone marrow mononuclear cells,[54–56] and peripheral blood stem cells[57] have also been applied by different clinical centers for cellular cardiomyoplasty which started at a later date. This report summarized the pilot study using autologous stem cells harvested from skeletal muscle or bone marrow from different patients and compared their outcomes at 6 months after cellular cardiomyoplasty.

## 2. Patients and Methodology

### 2.1 *Patient selection*

The protocol and procedure of this clinical evaluation were approved by the Institutional Review Board for human study and Jiangsu Province Health Ministry, China. The procedures and methods were in compliance to the Helsinki Declaration of 1975. Written informed consent was obtained from all patients. Eighteen male patients with coronary heart diseases who suffered from acute myocardial infarction were recruited and evenly assigned to the two treatment groups. The average age of the patients was 64 years old (27–79 years) who had a history of left ventricular myocardial infarction and the majority of patients with a depressed left ventricular ejection fraction (LVEF). The heart function of the selected patients was classified as II-IV of New York Heart Association functional classification (NYHA). Two-D echocardiography, technetium-99 m methoxyisobutylisonitrile ($^{99m}$Tc-MIBI) and $^{18}$F-deoxyglucose were employed to examine the cardiac function, myocardial perfusion, and viable cardiomyocytes, respectively, before and at six month after cell transplantation as reported in our earlier publication.[51,52]

For the patients that received bone marrow derived stem cells, who suffered a recent myocardial infarction, percutaneous coronary intervention (PCI) was performed with balloon angioplasty and stent deployment for the selected vessels. Written informed consent was obtained from every patient with cardiac functional evaluations and cell administration scheduled three weeks after the PCI procedure. For the patients treated with satellite cells, all suffering from a recent myocardial infarction with coronary angiogram, cardiac functional evaluation was performed. After obtained written informed consent, muscle biopsy was procured from each patient and coronary artery bypass graft (CABG) procedure and satellite cell implantation were scheduled three weeks later.

## 2.2 *Isolation and culture of satellite cells*

Biopsy specimens (2–5 g) were taken from the *vastus lateralis* muscle under local anesthesia from each patient on an out-patient basis. The biopsy specimens were placed in Hanks' balanced salt solution without $Ca^{++}$ and $Mg^{++}$ but containing 1% antibiotics (5,000 IU/ml penicillin and 5,000 μg/ml streptomycin), and immediately transported to the laboratory for isolation of skeletal muscle satellite cells as previously described.[19–22] Briefly, the biopsy sample was minced (~1 mm$^3$) and dissociated using digestive enzymes (1% collagenase and 0.2% hyaluronidase; Sigma, St. Louis, MO) in Medium 199 at 37°C. The cell suspension was centrifuged at 650 × g for 10 min and washed with Medium 199 (Sigma) plus 10% fetal bovine serum (FBS) and 1% antibiotics. Skeletal muscle satellite cells were cultured in Medium 199 containing 20% FBS and 1% antibiotics at 37°C under humidified atmosphere of 95% air with 5% $CO_2$. The media was changed very three to four days and cell density was maintained below 75% ~ 80% confluences throughout the culture in order to avoid the formation of myotubes.

During the day for the CABG and cell implantation procedures, the cultured cells free of microbial contamination were recovered. The satellite cells were thoroughly washed before suspended in 4 ml of serum free medium 199 and injected (15 to 40 sites) into the peri-infarct and infracted areas. A small fraction of the cell suspension was used for cell counting, purity, viability, and myogenic capability determinations. The cell number was determined using an automated hemocytometer. The purity (>85%) of the satellite cells was documented with anti-CD56 monoclonal antibody using fluorescence-activated cell sorting (FACS) and the viability (>95%) using trypan blue exclusion. To examine the ability of satellite cells to form multinucleated myotubes *in vitro*, the cells were placed in 24 well tissue culture plates with $2 \times 10^4$ cells per well and the medium was changed to fusion medium containing reduced serum (2% FBS). Two weeks later, the cultures were observed for the formation of myotubes. All the satellite cell preparations from patients were observed to form multinucleated myotubes indicating the myogenic characteristic of cell preparations.

## 2.3 *Isolation and culture of BMSCs and BMMCs*

Twenty to forty ml of bone marrow was aspirated from the posterior iliac crest of each patient under local anesthesia into a syringe with heparin (5,000 IU). Venous blood of 200 ml was obtained with heparin to allow separation of plasma and cells by centrifugation. The cells were cultured in Iscove's modified Dulbecco medium (IMDM) containing 20% autologous plasma and 1% antibiotics. At 72 hours, the adherent cells were recovered, cultured in the same medium, and subcultured every three to four days to maintain cell density below 80% confluence as bone marrow mesenchymal stem cells (BMSCs). The non-adherent cells were subject to Ficoll density-gradient centrifugation [20] before extensively washed and cultured in IMDM culture medium with fresh medium added every three to four days as bone marrow mononuclear cells (BMMCs). A small fraction of the cell suspension was used for cell counting, purity, and viability determinations. Better than 90% of purity (with anti-CD133 monoclonal antibody for BMMCs using FACS) and >95% viability (trypan blue exclusion) without microbial contamination were observed for all cell preparations. The cells were washed with IMDM containing 20% autologous plasma and combined before finally suspended in 9 ml of the same medium for intra-coronary administration. The cell suspensions (3 ml) were infused slowly over three minutes into the culprit coronary artery through the central lumen of an over-the-wire balloon catheter with balloon inflated at low pressure to temporary stop the antegrade blood flow. Between each infusion, three minutes were allowed with the balloon deflated to restore normal blood perfusion.

### 2.4 *Statistical analysis*

All values were presented as means ± SEM. Two-sample *t*-tests were performed for comparisons between groups. Paired *t*-tests were used to compare the data before and after cellular cardiomyoplasty. SAS-PC was used for the analysis.

## 3. Results

Table 1 summarized the basic clinical characteristics of the patients that were not different between the two groups. There was one patient in each group (S4 and M5) who did not receive the concomitant vascular procedure. Patient S4 had respiratory and urethral infection that delayed his CABG procedure for three months. After opening the chest, his left anterior descending coronary artery (LAD) and right coronary artery (RCA) were completely occluded and coronary bypass procedure could not be performed. Patient M5 only had 50% stenosis of his LAD and balloon angioplasty or stent deployment was not required. All patients survived the procedures without obvious arrhythmia, had an uneventful recovery, and were discharged from the hospital.

At 6 month after cellular cardiomyoplasty, the NYHA was significantly improved ($P < 0.01$) in both groups and similar improvement was found either using satellite cells or bone marrow cells (Table 2). Patient S7 had uncorrected severe aortic regurgitation and was the only patient that did not show any improvement at follow-up examination. Although the total cell number given in the bone marrow cell group was higher than the satellite cell group, the difference was not statistically significant ($P = 0.056$).

Significant improvement in left ventricular ejection fraction (LVEF) was observed for both groups of patients at six months after cell therapy (Table 3). Improvement in LVEF was found in every patient with the

**Table 1.** Patients' clinical data and the results of coronary angiogram.

| Patients for satellite cell implantation | | | | Patients for bone marrow cell infusion | | | |
|---|---|---|---|---|---|---|---|
| Case | Age | Acute MI | Coronary angiogram | Case | Age | Acute MI | Coronary angiogram |
| S1 | 74 | Anterior wall | 100% stenosis at LAD and LCX; 30% stenosis at middle RCA | M1 | 38 | Anterior wall | Diffuse stenosis at middle and distal LAD |
| S2 | 67 | Anterior wall | 30% stenosis at LCM; LAD occluded; 95% stenosis at proximal LCX and RCA | M2 | 75 | Anterior wall | 90% stenosis at proximal LAD; 80% at middle LAD |
| S3 | 55 | Anterior wall | 90% stenosis at middle LCM; 90% stenosis at proximal LAD; 70% stenosis at distal LAD, proximal, middle LCX; diffuse stenosis at RCA | M3 | 71 | Anterior and inferior walls | 100% stenosis at proximal LAD; 100% at proximal RCA |
| S4# | 74 | Extensive anterior wall with aneurysm | 60% stenosis at LCM; 99% stenosis at LAD; diffuse stenosis at RCA | M4 | 78 | Inferior wall | 85% stenosis at proximal RCA; 100% at proximal LCX; 90% stenosis at diagonal; two stenoses at RCA |
| S5 | 62 | Inferior wall | 90% stenosis at proximal LAD; 85% stenosis at middle LAD; 80% stenosis at distal LCX; 80% stenosis at proximal RCA | M5# | 27 | Anterior wall | 50% stenosis at proximal LAD |

*(Continued)*

**Table 1.** *(Continued)*

| Patients for satellite cell implantation | | | | Patients for bone marrow cell infusion | | | |
|---|---|---|---|---|---|---|---|
| Case | Age | Acute MI | Coronary angiogram | Case | Age | Acute MI | Coronary angiogram |
| S6 | 73 | Lateral wall | 60–90% diffusion stenosis at LAD; occlusion at proximal LCX; 70% and 95% stenoses at proximal and middle RCA, respectively | M6 | 60 | Extensive anterior wall | 100% stenosis at proximal LAD; 70% stenosis at middle and distal LCX |
| S7 | 72 | Anterior wall | 100% stenosis at proximal LAD; 80% stenosis at proximal LCX; 50% stenosis at proximal RCA | M7 | 49 | Extensive anterior wall | 100% stenosis at proximal LAD |
| S8 | 68 | Anterior wall with aneurysm | 70% stenosis at proximal LAD; occlusion at distal LAD; 60% stenosis at proximal LCX; 85% stenosis at proximal RCA | M8 | 79 | Anterior wall | 100% stenosis at proximal LAD; 80% at middle LAD |
| S9 | 67 | Inferior wall | 90% stenosis at proximal LAD 95% stenosis at middle LCX 99% stenosis at middle RCA | M9 | 56 | Extensive anterior wall | 100% stenosis at proximal LAD |

[#] No coronary artery bypass graft (S4) or no percutaneous coronary intervention (M5). LAD = Left anterior descending coronary artery; LCM = left main coronary artery; LCX = left circumflex coronary artery; RCA = right coronary artery.

**Table 2.** Functional outcomes with type, number and site of cell administration.

| Patients for satellite cell | | | | | Patients for bone marrow cell | | | | | | |
|---|---|---|---|---|---|---|---|---|---|---|---|
| | | | | | | | | Cell number (in $10^6$) | | | |
| Case | NYHA before | NYHA after | Satellite cells (in $10^6$) | Site | Case | NYHA before | NYHA after | BMSC | BMMC | SUM | Site |
| S1 | II | I | 1.4 | LV apex | M1 | II | I | 1.1 | 0 | 1.1 | LAD |
| S2 | III | I | 3.0 | LV apex | M2 | II | I | 0.9 | 6.1 | 7.0 | LAD |
| S3 | III | I | 3.0 | LV apex | M3 | III–IV | II | 2.6 | 0 | 2.6 | LCX |
| S4 | III–IV | II | 7.0 | LV apex and peri-aneurysm | M4 | III | I | 1.3 | 3.4 | 4.7 | RCA |
| S5 | II | I | 1.2 | Inferior wall | M5 | II | I | 1.2 | 3.8 | 5.0 | LAD |
| S6 | II | I | 1.3 | Lateral wall | M6 | III | I | 1.1 | 2.4 | 3.5 | LAD |
| S7[#] | III | III | 1.7 | LV apex | M7 | III | I | 2.7 | 2.8 | 5.5 | LAD |
| S8 | II | I | 1.2 | LV apex and peri-aneurysm | M8 | II | I | 3.5 | 2.3 | 5.8 | LAD |
| S9 | II | I | 1.6 | Inferior wall | M9 | III | I | 1.0 | 1.6 | 2.6 | LAD |
| Mean ± SEM | 2.5 ± 0.2 | 1.3* ± 0.2 | 2.4 ± 0.3 | | Mean ± SEM | 2.6 ± 0.2 | 1.1* ± 0.1 | 1.7 ± 0.3 | 2.5 ± 0.6 | 4.2 ± 0.6 | |

NYHA = New York Heart Association Classification (for III–IV 3.5 was used for calculation); BMMC = bone marrow mononuclear cell; BMSC = bone marrow mesenchymal stem cell; SUM = BMMC + BMSC; LV = left ventricular; LAD = left anterior descending coronary artery; LCX = left circumflex coronary artery; RCA = right coronary artery. [#]Patient has uncorrected severe aortic regurgitation. *Significantly different from "Before" group with $P < 0.01$.

**Table 3.** Left ventricular diastolic diameter and left ventricular ejection fraction data before and after cellular cardiomyoplasty.

| Patients for satellite cell implanation | | | | | | | Pations for bone marrow cell infusion | | | | | | |
|---|---|---|---|---|---|---|---|---|---|---|---|---|---|
| | LVDD (mm) | | | LVEF (%) | | | | LVDD (mm) | | | LVEF (%) | | |
| Case | Before | After | Change | Before | After | Change | Case | Before | After | Change | Before | After | Change |
| S1 | 52 | 48 | −4 | 35 | 46 | +11.0 | M1 | 42 | 46 | +4 | 65.6 | 69.6 | +4.0 |
| S2 | 47 | 42 | −5 | 40 | 45.4 | +5.4 | M2 | 53 | 53 | 0 | 62.4 | 67.3 | +4.9 |
| S3 | 57 | 48 | −9 | 40 | 41 | +1.0 | M3 | 76 | 76 | 0 | 22.1 | 35.9 | +13.8 |
| S4 | 60 | 53 | −7 | 37 | 48 | +11.0 | M4 | 54 | 58 | +4 | 42.0 | 51.0 | +9.0 |
| S5 | 54 | 53 | −1 | 58 | 60 | +2.0 | M5 | 64 | 61 | −3 | 37.8 | 55.8 | +18.0 |
| S6 | 58 | 49 | −9 | 45 | 52 | +7.0 | M6 | 54 | 50 | −4 | 58.8 | 65.3 | +6.5 |
| S7# | 58 | 64 | +6 | 40 | 35 | −5.0 | M7 | 63 | 57 | −6 | 35.0 | 46.0 | +11.0 |
| S8 | 57 | 55 | −2 | 50 | 65 | +15.0 | M8 | 58 | 52 | −6 | 42.0 | 56.0 | +14.0 |
| S9 | 55 | 54 | −1 | 40 | 42 | +2.0 | M9 | 60 | 52 | −8 | 45.0 | 55.0 | +10.0 |
| Mean ± SEM | 55.3 ± 1.3 | 51.8 ± 2.0 | −3.6 ± 1.6 | 42.8 ± 2.4 | 48.3* ± 3.1 | +5.5 ± 2.1 | Mean ± SEM | 58.2 ± 3.1 | 56.1 ± 2.9 | −2.1 ± 1.3 | 45.6 ± 47 | 55.8* ± 3.6 | +10.1 ± 1.5 |

LVDD = Left ventricular diastolic diameter in mm; LVEF = left ventricular ejection fraction in %. #Patient has uncorrected severe aortic regurgitation.
*Significantly different from "Before" group with $P < 0.05$.

exception of patient S7 who suffered uncorrected severe aortic regurgitation. The increase in LVEF was higher in the bone marrow cell group but the difference between the different cell groups was not statistically different ($P = 0.09$). No significant changes were observed for left ventricular diastolic diameter (LVDD). The results from 2-D echo, $^{99m}$Tc-MIBI, $^{18}$F-deoxyglucose evaluations showed similar improvement (Fig. 1) in local contractility, blood perfusion, tissue viability, and wall thickness at the infarct area for all patients receiving either type of autologous stem cells by using the same methods reported by us in our earlier publication.[51,52]

## 4. Discussion

Cellular cardiomyoplasty is aimed at regenerating damaged myocardium, restoring lost perfusion and regaining ventricular function. After myocardial injury, the permanent loss of cardiomyocytes and subsequent remodeling often initiates the development of heart failure and unfavorable clinical manifestations. Since we initiated cellular cardiomyoplasty in 1989, promising results from experimental animals and clinical trials clearly support the safety, feasibility, and certain efficacy of this new therapy. However, the mechanisms of benefit, the type of progenitor cells, the time and route of cell administration, as well as the dose of cells given are unanswered questions. This is a pilot clinical trial performed at a single center to compare the skeletal muscle satellite cells versus bone marrow stem cells for the possibility of designing a randomized, controlled, double-blinded study.

Using experimental animals, skeletal muscle satellite cells are better than bone marrow derived cells[58,59] or have similar beneficial effect for both cells.[60] From a recent review,[61] after evaluating all experimental and clinical publications using skeletal myoblasts *versus* bone marrow stem cells, the authors concluded that further studies with longer-term basis will be needed to make any decision. Other than comparing bone marrow *versus* circulating progenitor cells in a controlled cross-over study,[48] a direct comparison of different stem cells in a single clinical center has not been reported. This study is unique in the following ways: (1) the study was performed in a single clinical center; (2) all the patients received standard clinical care after myocardial infarction (either CABG or PCI);

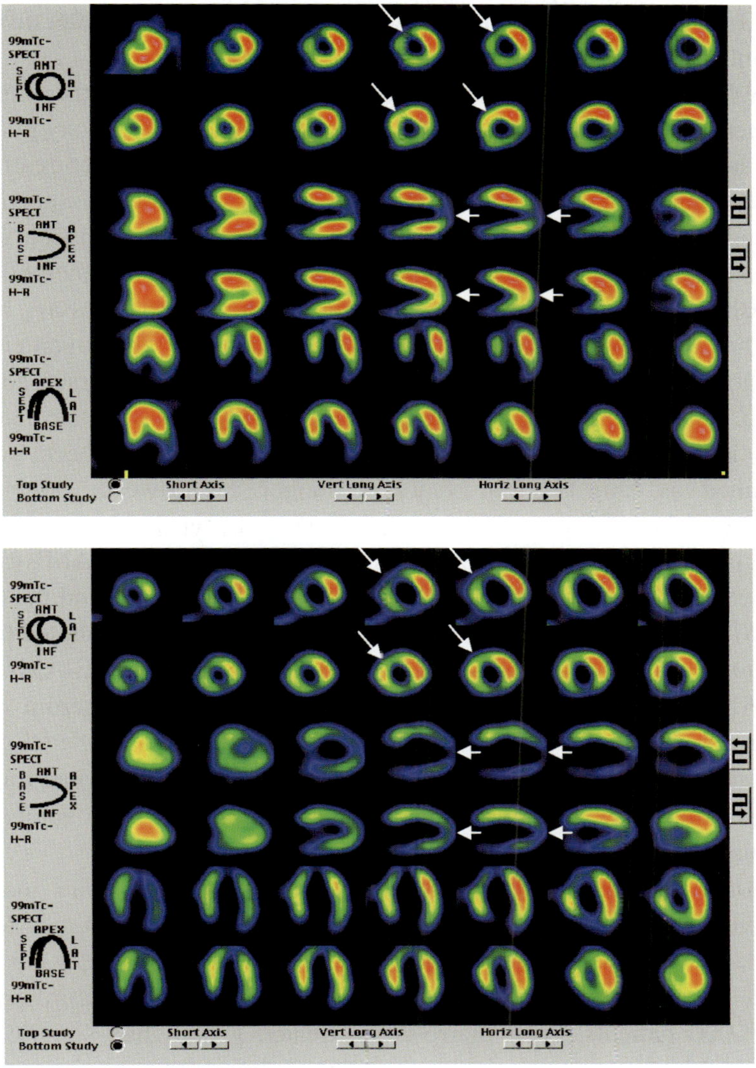


**Fig. 1. Perfusion images using technetium-99m methoxyisobutylisonitrile ($^{99m}$Tc-MIBI).** The $^{99m}$Tc-MIBI perfusion images of the short-axis (top), vertical long-axis (middle) and horizontal long-axis (bottom) from a representative patient of satellite cell implantation (upper panel) and a representative patient of bone marrow cell infusion (lower panel). The upper lines were obtained before cell therapy and the lower lines were results at 6 month after cell therapy. The arrows pointed to the sites where perfusion was significantly improved due to cell administration.

and (3) cellular cardiomyoplasty was performed at three weeks after myocardial infarction for both groups.

When a study was performed in a single clinical center, the care and evaluations to each patient (2-D echo, $^{99m}$Tc-MIBI, $^{18}$F-deoxyglucose) were be more uniform and directly comparable before and after treatment. Similar improvement in local contractility, blood perfusion, tissue viability, and wall thickness at the infarct area were observed in all patients who received either type of autologous stem cells by using the methods we published before.[51,52] A longer-term comparison will be necessary based on the BOOST trial[40] that observed significant improvement at six months, but no difference at 18 months for the cell versus control group. This may suggest the satellite cells should perform better than the bone marrow derived stem cells due to the beneficial effects which remained as long as four years or longer.[24,27] However, long-term (one year) beneficial outcomes using bone marrow derived stem cells were observed by the TOPCARE-AMI[38] and the REPAIR-AMI trials[47] that were different from the BOOST trial,[40] ASTAMI trial[44] and the other report.[46] One major difference between these studies was attributed to the solutions used with mononuclear cells.[62] The TOPCARE-AMI and REPAIR-AMI trials used culture medium with autologous serum while the other trials used saline or saline with serum or plasma.[40,44,46] Store mononuclear cells in saline plus plasma resulted with functional impairment of the cells.[62] For our study, culture medium with 20% autologous plasma was used to suspend the bone marrow cells.

Although bone marrow mesenchymal stem cells, bone marrow mononuclear cells, and circulating progenitor cells represent a different population of cells, recent meta-analyses combined them under the term adult or autologous bone marrow-derived cells.[63–65] Representing 500–1,000 patients, bone marrow cell-treated groups had significantly improved left ventricular ejection fraction, reduced infarct scar size, and decreased left ventricular end-systolic volume as compared to controls. Lower rates of recurrent myocardial infarction, death, re-hospitalization for coronary heart disease, and repeat revascularization are additional favorable outcomes of cell therapy. Greater cell numbers seem to be associated with more improvement, further supporting the notion that the delivered cells are producing the beneficial effects.

Although the optimal time after myocardial infarction for cellular cardiomyoplasty has not been established in any clinical study,[22,35,66,67] performing the treatment at a similar time after disease onset as in our study will allow more direct comparison between different stem cells employed. Cellular cardiomyoplasty procedures all suffer from very low cell retention and massive cell death after treatment irrespective of the type of stem cells studied.[68–71] Although the satellite cell (>85% purity) and bone marrow cell (>90% purity) preparations employed in our study still contain a mixed population of cells, the cell purity is significantly higher than most of the published reports. Higher purity of stem cells has the potential of higher retention and survival rates without the complications of non-stem cells for the treatment. Muscle samples of five to 10 g will be the recommended size for satellite cell isolation. Smaller samples make the isolation procedure difficult and require longer culture time to have sufficient satellite cells. This study only compared the six months follow-up results and longer time follow-up will be necessary especially judging from the lesson learned by the BOOST trial that observed significant improvement at six months, but no difference at 18 months for the cell versus control group.

After acute myocardial infraction (MI), the healing process can be divided into 4 phases: cardiomyocyte death, acute inflammation, tissue granulation, and remodeling or repair,[72] It is well known that MI is an inflammatory disease, and there is compelling evidence that the innate immune response plays an important role in myocardial ischemia-reperfusion injury and coronary heart disease.[72–76] Ischemia-reperfusion significantly increases tumor necrosis factor, interleukins-1, -6, and -8, interferon, and intercellular adhesion molecule-1 gene expression in myocardium.[76–78] These pro-inflammatory and immunoregulatory cytokines appear to be directly involved in the progression of myocardial ischemia-reperfusion injury, myocardial dysfunction, ventricular remodeling, coronary heart disease, and cardiac hypertrophy.[76–78]

Because innate immune and inflammatory responses are involved in myocardial ischemic injury, investigation of the innate immune modulation and anti-inflammatory activities of stem cells during cellular cardiomyoplasty may reveal the beneficial mechanisms. Adult tissues have been used to isolate stem cells that show plasticity, escape immune recognition, and inhibit immune responses. Adult stem cells can easily proliferate to vast numbers and be applied to inhibit immune responses by suppressing T and B cell proliferation, inducing T regulatory cells, modulating B cell and dendritic cell functions, and have been used to treat transplant rejection.[79,80] Stem cells do not induce lymphocyte proliferation and are not targets for cytotoxic lymphocytes or natural killer cells. No adverse events during or after adult stem cell transplantation have been observed, and no ectopic tissue formation has been noted.[79–81] Other than paracrine or endocrine effects, anti-proliferative, anti-inflammatory, and immunomodulatory effects of stem cells to prevent infarct expansion and ventricular remodeling may be the major benefits.[22,79–83]

If anti-inflammatory and immunosuppressive effects are the primary beneficial mechanisms of cellular cardiomyoplasty, this may partially explain why different kinds of stem cells and different times of cell treatment (after acute MI or an old infarct) resulted in similar favorable outcomes.[22,82] Stem cells can mediate immunosuppression and anti-inflammatory effects through secreted soluble factors and contact-dependent mechanisms.[80,84] More importantly, mesenchymal stem cells can exert anti-inflammatory effects even at the site of inflammation (similar to after MI).[84] Since a significant fraction of the stem cells are lost by apoptosis after cellular cardiomyoplasty, and apoptotic cells can have long-lasting effects, a major benefit of cell therapy may derive from immunomodulation and anti-inflammation effects. This is a pilot clinical trial performed at a single center to compare the skeletal muscle satellite cells versus mononuclear cells and mesenchymal stem cells derived from bone marrow for the possibility of designing a randomized, controlled, double-blinded study. The beneficial mechanisms of cellular cardiomyoplasty require additional studies.

## LIST OF ABBREVIATIONS

**ASTAMI:** Autologous Stem cell Transplantation in Acute Myocardial Infarction

**BOOST:** BOne marrOw transfer to enhance ST-elevation infarct regeneration

**BMMC:** Bone marrow mononuclear cells

**BMSC:** Bone marrow mesenchymal stem cells

**CABG:** Coronary artery bypass graft
**FACS:** Fluorescence-activated cell sorting
**FBS:** Fetal bovine serum
**HSC:** Hematopoietic stem cells
**IACT:** Intracoronary Autologous Bone Marrow Cell Transplantation in Chronic Coronary Artery Disease
**IMDM:** Iscove's modified Dulbecco medium
**LAD:** Left anterior descending coronary artery
**LVDD:** Left ventricular diastolic diameter
**LVEF:** Left ventricular ejection fraction
**MAGIC:** Myoblast Autologous Grafting in Ischemic Cardiomyopathy
**MAGIC Cell-3-DES:** Myocardial Regeneration and Angiogenesis in Myocardial Infarction with G-CSF and Intra-Coronary Stem Cell Infusion-3-Drug Eluting Stents
**MI:** Myocardial infarction
**MSC:** Mesenchymal stem cells
**NYHA:** New York Heart Association functional classification
**PCI:** Percutaneous coronary intervention
**RCA:** Right coronary artery
**REPAIR-AMI:** Reinfusion of Enriched Progenitor Cells and Infarct Remodeling in Acute Myocardial Infarction
**$^{99m}$Tc-MIBI:** Technetium-99m methoxyisobutylisonitrile
**TOPCARE-AMI:** Transplantation of Progenitor Cells and Regeneration Enhancement in Acute Myocardial Infarction

## References

1. Nussbaum J, Minami E, Laflamme MA, *et al*. Transplantation of undifferentiated murine embryonic stem cells in the heart: teratoma formation and immune response. *FASEB J* 2007;21:1345–1357.

79. Uccelli A, Pistoia V, Moretta L. Mesenchymal stem cells: a new strategy for immunosuppression? *Trends Immunol* 2007;28:219–226.
80. Stagg J. Immune regulation by mesenchymal stem cells: two sides to the coin. *Tissue Antigens* 2007;69:1–9.
81. Solheim S, Seljeflot I, Lunde K, *et al.* Inflammatory responses after intracoronary injection of autologous mononuclear bone marrow cells in patients with acute myocardial infarction. *Am Heart J* 2008;155:55.e1–55.e9.
82. Thum T, Bauersachs J, Poole-Wilson PA, *et al.* The dying stem cell hypothesis: immune modulation as a novel mechanism for progenitor cell therapy in cardiac muscle. *J Am Coll Cardiol* 2005;46:1799–802.
83. Tomchuck SL, Zwezdaryk KJ, Coffelt SB, *et al.* Toll-like receptors on human mesenchymal stem cells drive their migration and immunomodulating responses. *Stem Cells* 2008;26:99–107.
84. Rasmusson I. Immune modulation by mesenchymal stem cells. *Exp Cell Res* 2006;312:2169–79.

# CHAPTER 17

# SURGICAL AUTOLOGOUS PERIPHERAL BLOOD STEM CELL IMPLANTATION FOR CARDIOMYOPATHY: BANGKOK HEART HOSPITAL EXPERIENCE

*Kitipan V. Arom and Permyos Ruengsakulrach*

## Abstract

Heart failure caused by dilated cardiomyopathy (DCM) and ischemic cardiomyopathy (ICM) is a detrimental condition with few options for treatment. Between May 2005 and May 2009, 119 consecutive patients underwent intramyocardial autologous peripheral blood stem cell injection. Fifty were DCM and 69 were ICM. Mean age was 59.2 ± 12.1 years. The peripheral blood stem cells were isolated from the patient's own blood and cultured. The final product was named angiogenic cell precursors (ACPs). The number of cells prior to injection was 43.8 ± 35.3 million cells. Cells were injected into all areas of the left ventricle in DCM and were injected into non-viable myocardium and hypokinetic segments in ICM. Combined coronary artery surgery and ACP injection were performed in 34.8% of ICM.

There was no new ventricular arrhythmia. The New York Heart Association functional class and left ventricular ejection fraction (LVEF) was improved in both DCM and ICM. The 30-day mortality rate was 4% (2/50) and 4.3% (3/69) in DCM and ICM, respectively. The cardiac magnetic resonance imaging with gadolinium contrast showed reversed remodeling and decreased infarction volume in the left ventricle in the ICM after the ACP injection. A number of case-match studies were conducted to determine the efficacy of this treatment. There were trends of improvement in terms of LVEF in both DCM and ICM who had ACP injection compared with the control.

## 1. Introduction

Cardiomyopathy represents a heterogeneous group of myocardial diseases resulting in heart failure (HF). HF is a complex clinical syndrome that can result from any structural or functional cardiac disorder that impairs the ability of the ventricle to fill with or eject blood. The cardinal manifestations of HF are dyspnea and fatigue, which may limit exercise tolerance, and promote fluid retention, which may lead to pulmonary and peripheral edema. Both abnormalities can impair the functional capacity and quality of life of affected individuals, but they may not necessarily dominate the clinical picture at the same time. Ischemic cardiomyopathy (ICM) accounts for about half of these patients. Incidence of HF is increasing worldwide. Incidence increased generally with age and the survival rate has improved, however the survival rate was still approximately 30–40% at five years.[1–3] It is also the leading cause of hospitalization in patients older than 65 years of age. The incidence of HF in children without congenital heart disease was as low as 0.87/100,000 population, age less than 16 years.[4] The etiologies of heart failure in childhood include idiopathic/familial dilated cardiomyopathy, myocarditis, occult arrhythmia, cytotoxic drugs exposure, metabolic diseases, left ventricular noncompaction, etc. Overall one-year survival is 82% and event-free (death or transplantation) survival is 66%.

HF with preserved left ventricular ejection fraction (LVEF) is defined by the combination of clinical symptoms or signs of HF and LVEF equal or higher than 50%. HF with preserved LVEF accounts for nearly 50% of cases of HF. Prevalence is increasing with age. Most patients present with acute onset of pulmonary edema. Prognosis is similar to that of systolic heart failure and leads to frequent hospitalization for acute decompensation.

The American Heart Association (AHA)/American College of Cardiology (ACC) approach to the classification of chronic HF, published in 2001, was developed to emphasize both the evolution and the progression of chronic HF and to implement early therapeutic interventions to ultimately reduce morbidity and mortality.[5] Four stages of HF were identified (Table 1). However, only the latter two stages qualify for the

**Table 1.** ACC/AHA vs NYHA classification of heart failure.

| ACC/AHA stage | | NYHA functional class | |
|---|---|---|---|
| Stage | Description | Class | Description |
| A | People at high risk of developing HF but has no structural disorder of the heart. | No comparable functional class | |
| B | People who have developed structural heart disease but who have never had signs or symptoms of HF. | I (Mild) | No limitation of physical activity. Ordinary physical activity does not cause tiredness, palpitation, or dyspnea. |
| C | Patients who have current or prior symptoms of HF associated with underlying structural heart disease. | II (Mild) | Slight limitation of physical activity. Comfortable at rest, but ordinary physical activity results in tiredness, palpitation, or dyspnea. |
| | | III (Moderate) | Marked limitation of physical activity. Comfortable at rest, but less than ordinary activity causes tiredness, palpitation, or dyspnea. |
| D | Patients with advanced structural heart disease and marked symptoms of HF at rest despite maximal medical therapy and who require specialized treatment strategies such as mechanical circulatory support, continuous inotropic infusions, cardiac transplantation, or hospice care. | IV (Severe) | Severe limitation of physical activity. Unable to carry out any physical activity without discomfort. Symptoms at rest. If any physical activity is undertaken, discomfort increases. |

**Abbreviations:** AHA, American Heart Association; ACC, American College of Cardiology; NYHA, New York Heart Association.

traditional clinical diagnosis of HF. The AHA/ACC classification system is intended to complement rather than replace the New York Heart Association (NYHA) functional classification. The NYHA functional classification reflects a subjective assessment by a physician and changes frequently over short periods of time which primarily gauges the severity of symptoms in patients who are in stage C or D HF. The patients involved in our study were the patients with stage C or D or NYHA functional class III or IV, patients who had chronic myocardial infarction with myocardial scar from the cardiac magnetic resonance imaging or myocardial perfusion scan, and those who were diagnosed non-ischemic dilated cardiomyopathy (DCM).

The patient with stage D congestive heart failure tended to be younger males with dyslipidemia and with coronary artery disease. The prognostic value of these post-infarction scars is highlighted by the observation that heart failure develops when they involve approximately 25% of the left ventricle. The estimated one-year survival in chronic stage D congestive heart failure patient is around 70% with estimated one-year freedom from hospitalization or death is 33%.[6]

The treatments of heart failure include risk modifications, medical treatment, devices therapy, e.g., automatic implantable cardioverter defibrillator (AICD), cardiac resynchronization therapy, mechanical assisted left ventricular devices.

For ICM there is no specific management of post-infarction myocardial scars. Although coronary artery revascularization (by coronary artery bypass grafting or angioplasty) is effective in improving function of hibernating myocardium, it has little impact on infarcted areas. When these segments still harbor some viable cardiomyocytes, they can eventually benefit from an increased blood supply conveyed by the collaterals originating from the neighboring revascularized areas, but their overall recovery is likely to be limited. Surgical excision of the scars is another option, but the technique is aggressive. Surgical Treatment for Ischemic Heart Failure (STICH) trial was a trial to address the question of whether surgical ventricular reconstruction added to coronary artery bypass grafting (CABG) would decrease the rate of death or hospitalization for cardiac causes, as compared with CABG alone. A total of 1000 patients with a LVEF of 35% or less, coronary artery disease that was amenable to

CABG, and dominant anterior left ventricular dysfunction that was amenable to surgical ventricular reconstruction were randomly assigned to undergo either CABG alone or CABG with surgical ventricular reconstruction. The primary outcome was a composite of death from any cause and hospitalization for cardiac causes. Unfortunately, no significant difference was observed in the primary outcome, which occurred in 292 patients (59%) who were assigned to undergo CABG alone and in 289 patients (58%) who were assigned to undergo CABG with surgical ventricular reconstruction at the median follow-up of 48 months. Jones RH *et al.* in 2009 reported the results from this trial that surgical ventricular reconstruction reduced the end-systolic volume index by 19%, as compared with a reduction of 6% with CABG alone.[7] Cardiac symptoms and exercise tolerance improved from baseline to a similar degree in the two study groups. However, no significant difference was observed in the primary outcome, which occurred in 292 patients (59%) who were assigned to undergo CABG alone and in 289 patients (58%) who were assigned to undergo CABG with surgical ventricular reconstruction (hazard ratio for the combined approach, 0.99; 95% confidence interval, 0.84 to 1.17; $P = 0.90$). Addition of surgical ventricular reconstruction to CABG in patients with ischemic heart failure did not improve quality of life, but significantly increased health care costs.[8]

DCM is characterized by dilatation and impaired contractile function of the left ventricle or both ventricles. It may be idiopathic, familial/genetic, viral and/or immune, alcoholic/toxic, or associated with recognized cardiovascular disease in which the degree of myocardial dysfunction is not explained by the abnormal loading conditions or the extent of ischemic damage. Histology is nonspecific and presentation is usually with heart failure, which is often progressive. Arrhythmias, thromboembolism, and sudden death are common and may occur at any stage. Angiotensin-converting enzyme inhibitors and beta-blockers have improved myocardial gene expression, symptoms and the long-term survival in DCM especially in the early stage of disease. The implantation of an AICD significantly reduced the risk of sudden death from arrhythmia.

Surgical options are limited with heart transplantation being a definitive treatment. However, due to limitation of heart donors and limited improvement of long-term survival, this therapy is inadequate.

Transplantation of cells has undergone extensive investigations and promises to improve health and quality of life by repairing or regenerating cells, tissues or organs. Stem cells are undifferentiated cells generally characterized by their functional capacity to both self-renew and to generate a large number of differentiated progeny cells.

## 2. Types of Stem Cells

Stem cells can be obtained from many sources such as embryo, fetal, umbilical cord blood, bone marrow or peripheral blood. Conventionally, stem cells are either classified as those derived from embryo or adult tissues.

### 2.1 *Embryonic stem cell*

Embryonic stem cells, embryonal carcinomal cells, and embryonic germ cells are derived from the pre-implantation embryo (e.g., inner cell mass of blastocyst, morula, and single blastomeres), teratocarcinomas, and primordial germ cells, respectively. These cells are pluripotent; that is, they have the ability to form all embryonic germ layer derivatives except extracellular tissues (e.g., placenta). Stem cells found in adult organisms are present in most tissues and are referred to as adult stem cells, such as mesenchymal stem cells, hematopoietic stem cells, and neural stem cells. They are considered multipotent, since they can produce mature cell types of one or more lineages, but cannot reconstitute the organism as a whole. What determines stem cell potency largely depends on intrinsic properties of stem cells, as well as extrinsic cues provided by the niche (microenvironment where stem cells reside). Because of their exceptional properties, stem cells have the potential to be used for developmental biology, drug screening, functional genomics applications, and regenerative medicine. However, there are several problems for using embryonic stem cells clinically. The first is the ethical issue. Second, embryonic stem cells are allogeneic. Third, increased cell death resulting from ischemia has been observed when embryonic stem cell-derived cardiomyocytes were grafted into a normal myocardium. Finally, human embryonic stem cells have also been shown to have the potential to form teratomas.

## 2.2 *Adult stem cell*

The adult stem cells are the stem cells found in the mature tissue. Some scientists use the term "somatic stem cell" instead of adult stem cell. Most fetal and adult stem cells are considered to be multipotent and therefore capable of producing a small range of differentiated cell lineages appropriate to their location. Some adult stem cells or progenitor cells with the least differentiation potential such as skeletal myoblasts, circulating endothelial progenitor cells or epidermal stem cells in the basal layer of the skin are designated as unipotent. Adult stem cells that have been used for treatment of heart failure mainly were skeletal myoblast and hematopoietic stem cells.

### 2.2.1 *Skeletal myoblast*

Fetal cardiomyocytes have been the first to be used in proof-of-concept experiments designed to determine whether transplanted cells could engraft in post-infarction fibrotic scars and improve left ventricular function.[9,10] However, clinical applications was started with skeletal myoblasts, i.e., cells which lie in a quiescent state under the basal lamina of muscular fibers and, in case of injury, are rapidly mobilized, proliferate and fuse to effect muscle repair. Indeed, myoblasts feature several clinically relevant advantages, which explain why it looked sound to use them as the first generation of cells for the treatment of heart failure. These advantages include (1) an autologous origin which overcomes problems related to ethics, availability, and immunogenicity; (2) a high scalability potential, which allows growth of hundreds of millions of cells from a small muscular biopsy; (3) an advanced stage of differentiation along the myogenic pathway which should prevent tumor formation; and (4) a high resistance to ischemia, which is critical in view of the poor vascular environment intrinsic to post-infarction scars in which cells will be implanted. The decision to proceed with myoblasts to move the concept of cell therapy into the clinical arena was further based on a large experimental database,[11] and documenting, in both small and large animal models of myocardial infarction, the differentiation of myoblasts into myotubes, their sustained engraftment in post-infarction scars and an associated improvement in left ventricular function. Many investigators have successfully transplanted autologous skeletal myoblasts into post-infarcted hearts.

The accumulation of data documenting some efficacy of myoblast transplantation still contrasts with our ignorance of the mechanisms that underlie these effects. The lack of connection between engrafted myoblasts and the neighboring cardiomyocytes and the resulting inability of the graft to beat in synchrony with the host heart[12,13] make it unlikely that myoblasts can significantly contribute to increase systolic function, although they may contract in response to stretch activation of ion channels exerted by the surrounding myocardium. Indeed, a more likely mechanism of action is the mechanical buttressing of the infarcted segment by the transplanted cells, with a subsequent improvement in scar elasticity, which would translate into a limitation of ventricular remodeling. A reduction of wall stress placed on remote myocardium subsequent to this attenuation of ventricular dilation could, in turn, contribute to improve heart function.

The randomized, placebo-controlled, double-blind efficacy study named MAGIC trial started in June 2000 by Menasché P *et al.* They performed the first human transplantation of autologous myoblasts in a patient with severe ICM.[14] This case was the first of a series of 10, which included patients with a low LVEF (≤35%) in addition to providing some guidelines for the translation of cell therapy studies from bench to bedside. Overall, the patients have been symptomatically improved with a low incidence of hospitalizations for heart failure (0.13/patient-year). Ejection fraction, measured by echocardiography, initially increased from a baseline value of 24.3% ± 4% to 31% ± 4.1% ($P$ = .001) and has remained stable thereafter. An AICD was implanted in five patients for non-sustained (n = 1) or sustained (n = 4) ventricular tachycardia at 12.2 ± 18.6 (1–45) months and its readouts allowed to document subsequent arrhythmic storms in three of these patients at six, seven, and 18 months after implantation. One patient died 17.5 months after surgery, and autopsy showed clusters of myotubes in scar tissue.[15] This led to the multicenter MAGIC trial, which featured a randomized, double-blind, placebo-controlled dose-ranging design. All included patients have undergone a muscular biopsy, followed, three weeks later, by injection of cells (at 2 doses: 400 and 800 million) or a placebo solution in the core and at the margins of the akinetic nonviable scars. The consistency of the final cell therapy product has been ensured by a centralized production in 2 core manufacturing facilities working under similar procedural guidelines. As previously mentioned, all patients have been implanted with an AICD before hospital discharge. The primary end-points of the study are thus safety (occurrence of major adverse cardiac events and ventricular arrhythmias over the first six post-operative months), and efficacy (changes in regional wall motion and global ejection fraction analyzed by a centralized reading of the echocardiograms). Ninety-seven patients received myoblasts (400 or 800 million; n = 33 and n = 34, respectively) or the placebo (n = 30). Myoblast transfer did not improve regional or global LV function beyond that seen in control patients. The absolute change in ejection fraction (median [inter-quartile range]) between six months and baseline was 4.4% (0.2; 7.3), 3.4% (–0.3; 12.4), and 5.2% (–4.4; 11.0) in the placebo, low-dose, and high-dose groups, respectively ($P = 0.95$). However, the high-dose cell group demonstrated a significant decrease in LV volumes compared with the placebo group. Despite a higher number of arrhythmic events in the myoblast-treated patients, the six-month rates of major cardiac adverse events and of ventricular arrhythmias did not differ significantly between the pooled treatment and placebo groups.[16] These results lead to 3 main conclusions: (1) implanted myoblasts may exert some therapeutic benefits, possibly through paracrine signaling; (2) it remains uncertain whether these effects have an impact on patient outcomes; and (3) to move the field from proof of concept to active therapy requires the optimization of the best cells matching the target clinical setting (acute infarction or heart failure), their method of delivery, and strategies enabling the enhancement of graft survival and its functional integration.[16]

Bonaros N *et al.* in 2008 injected skeletal myoblast and human derived AC-133+ angiopoietic progenitor cells mobilized with recombinant granulocyte colony-stimulating factor (G-CSF) in peri-infarct area in nude rats with induced myocardial infarction by left anterior descending coronary artery ligation. Double cells injection led to increased cell engraftment, less apoptosis, higher cardiac troponin, increased secretion of chemoattractants and more angiogenesis was found compared with monotherapy.[17]

### 2.2.2 *Hematopoietic stem cell*

Blood contains multiple distinct cell types such as erythrocytes, granulocytes, lymphocytes, monocytes, and platelets. The finite life-time of these mature cells requires a well-organized system of replenishment and cell renewal. The concept of how hematopoietic stem cells (HSCs) and progenitors are organized has been under continuous re-appraisal since the 1960s. HSCs have been defined by two independent characteristics. First, they are multipotential, that is, individual stem cells can produce every different cell types found in the blood. Second, true stem cells are self-renewing, that is, during the proliferation of stem cells, differentiation ought to be balanced by the maintenance of the stem cell pool. By definition, stem cells are able to differentiate into multiple lineages and to self-renew, that is, maintain their own numbers. Stem cell self-renewal is tightly regulated, and the proper expression of stem cell genes is crucial to ensure self-renewal. It is not unlikely that competitive disadvantage is caused by de-regulated self-renewal. Self-renewal genes are believed to be highly expressed in HSCs, and constitutive overexpression of these genes may be involved in leukemia. Recently, several proteins have been identified that are believed to determine stem cell fate, including HoxB4, HoxA9, Bmi-1, FGF-1, Notch, and Wnt.[18–21] Expression of these genes is now considered necessary for maintaining stem cell characteristics. Mice deficient in STAT5, Bmi-1, or HOXA9 were shown to have impaired stem cell function, but overexpression of these genes has been implicated in leukemia.[19,20,22–25]

Hematopoietic stem cells or endothelial progenitor cells (EPCs) are normally found in very limited numbers in the peripheral circulation (less than 0.1% of all nucleated cells). EPCs were discovered in 1997 as circulating cells with the ability to differentiate into mature endothelium and take part in neo-angiogenesis. EPCs share markers of hematopoietic (CD34 and CD133) and endothelial (KDR, CD31, and vWf) lineages,[26] are derived from bone marrow and can be mobilized to the peripheral circulation in response to many stimuli. Tissue ischemia, through the release of growth factors and cytokines, mobilizes EPCs. EPCs could also be mobilized into peripheral blood by pharmacological mobilization induced by administration of granulocyte colony-stimulating factor

(G-CSF)[27] or CXCR4 receptor antagonists.[28] They are also mobilized after bone marrow damage as seen, for example, after partial bone marrow irradiation[29] or administration of cytostatic agents (e.g., cyclophosphamide).[30] EPCs in the peripheral circulation, specifically home on the ischemic sites to stimulate compensatory angiogenesis. Moreover, EPCs constitute a circulating pool of cells able to form a cellular patch at sites of endothelial injury, thus contributing directly to the homeostasis and repair of the endothelial layer. Taken together, these observations suggest that EPCs have a major role in cardiovascular biology; in fact, the extent of the circulating EPC pool is now considered a mirror of cardiovascular health. Virtually all risk factors for atherosclerosis have been associated with decrease and/or dysfunction of circulating EPCs, while an expanded EPC pool is associated with a decreased cardiovascular mortality. In patients, EPCs could be derived by administration of G-CSF, then EPCs are obtained by extra-corporeal continuous-flow apheresis machines, generally *via* peripheral venous access; occasionally central venous access may be required. Stem cells and granulocytes are separated from the red blood cell and plasma fractions of blood by centrifugation and the latter two components are returned to the donors during the apheresis procedure itself. The other technique is to separate the EPCs from the peripheral blood and then expand them in the laboratory as angiogenic cell precursors (ACPs) used in our study.

A sub-set of bone marrow-derived hematopoietic cells were the first adult stem cells or progenitor cells reported to differentiate into cardiomyocytes when transplanted into infarcted hearts of mice.[31] The first evidence that adult bone marrow-derived progenitor cells participate in the formation of cardiomyocytes in adult human hearts was based on reports of Y-chromosome-positive cardiomyocytes in female donor hearts transplanted in male recipients.[32] Animal studies of bone-marrow transplantation with labelled hematopoietic stem cells followed by myocardial infarction revealed cardiomyocytes derived from the transplanted cells, but at an exceptionally low rate.[33] However, other studies in animals have not demonstrated differentiation of hematopoietic progenitor cells into cardiomyocytes[31,34,35] or improvement in cardiac function.[36] Currently, no consensus exists on whether bone-marrow-derived progenitor cells differentiate into cardiomyocytes *in vivo*.

The clinical applications of the hematopoietic stem cell for heart failure emerged even before the underlying mechanisms of the cell were studied. Strauer B *et al.* reported the first clinical trial of intracoronary, autologous, mononuclear bone marrow cells transplantation for improving heart function and myocardial perfusion in patients after acute myocardial infarction in 2002.[37,38] The results demonstrated that transplanted autologous mononuclear bone marrow cells may lead to repair of infarcted tissue when applied during the immediate post-infarction period. "Transplantation of Progenitor Cells and Regeneration Enhancement in Acute Myocardial Infarction" (TOPCARE-AMI) trial was a clinical trial that started enrollment in October 2001 and reported their result in 2002. They used either bone marrow-derived or circulating blood-derived progenitor cells intracoronary infusion into the infarct coronary artery after acute myocardial infarction.[39] Transplantation of progenitor cells was associated with a significant increase in global LVEF from 51.6 ± 9.6% to 60.1 ± 8.6% ($P = 0.003$), improved regional wall motion in the infarct zone, and profoundly reduced end-systolic left ventricular volumes at four-month follow-up. In the BOOST (BOne marrOw transfer to enhance ST-elevation infarct regeneration) trial, the left ventricular ejection fraction had increased 6.7% after the intracoronary injection of autologous bone-marrow cells after successful percutaneous coronary intervention for acute ST-segment elevation myocardial infarction.[40] Schachinger V *et al.* designed a double-blind, placebo-controlled, randomized multicenter trial — the Reinfusion of Enriched Progenitor Cells and Infarct Remodeling in Acute Myocardial Infarction (REPAIR-AMI) trial. They found no difference in increasing of left ventricular ejection between the uses of circulating progenitor cells (endothelial progenitor cells) or bone marrow-derived progenitor cells. The LVEF had increased 5–8%.[41] The same results were also found in chronic myocardial ischemia. The LVEF increased by 9.2% and 10.5% at one week and three months after the intracoronary transplantation of autologous bone marrow-derived mononuclear cells.[42] The LVEF remained improved at six months and one year after the cells injection.[43] Several clinical trials and meta-analysis on bone-marrow and blood-derived stem cell were published.[44–49] Overall, hematopoietic stem cell transplantation is safe with modest improvements in LVEF, LV size and infarction areas in patients with both acute myocardial infarction and chronic ischemic heart disease, above and beyond conventional therapy.

The other potential adult stem cell for heart failure treatment is adult cardiac stem cells.[50] Beltrami A *et al.* in 2004 reported the existence in the adult rat heart of a population of $Lin^-$ $c\text{-}kit^{POS}$ cells that *in vitro* and *in vivo* exhibit all the properties expected for cardiac stem cells.[51] They are self-renewing, clonogenic, and multipotent, giving rise to a minimum of three differentiated cell types: myocytes, smooth muscle, and endothelial vascular cells. Moreover, when injected into an ischemic heart, a population of these cells or the clonal progeny of one of them reconstitute a well-differentiated myocardial wall that encompasses up to 70% of the LV. This regenerated ventricular wall is constituted by blood carrying new vessels and myocytes that, although smaller in size, have the anatomical, biochemical, and functional properties of young myocytes. There is also evidence that delivery of these cells in a myocardial infarction rat model resulted in limited myocardial infarct, attenuated myocardial remodeling, and ameliorated cardiac dysfunction at five weeks after myocardial infarction.[52] A subsequent preliminary report from the laboratory of Anversa *et al.* extended the isolation and expansion of $c\text{-}kit^{POS}$ cells to human heart tissue using surgical specimens of human myocardium, specifically, cultured slices of human atrium and ventricle.[53] When human $c\text{-}kit^{POS}$ cardiac progenitor cells were locally injected in the infarcted myocardium of immunodeficient rats and mice, they regenerated myocytes and coronary vessels of human origin. This repair process resulted in an improvement in cardiac function. Limited knowledge exists regarding the relationships of these cardiac stem cells to one another or the molecular networks that regulate their proliferation, self renewal, or lineage differentiation states. Why do the cardiac progenitors described by different groups display different characteristics, and what are the relationships between different multipotent cardiac progenitors? What dictates the decision of cardiovascular progenitors to adopt one fate versus another? How could we isolate and culture these cells enough for clinical use?

Several key issues still need to be addressed including (1) the optimal type of cells; (2) the mechanism by which cell engraftment improves cardiac function; (3) the most effective strategies for optimizing cell survival; and (4) the potential benefits of cell implantation in non-ischemic heart failure.

Angiogenic cell precursors (ACPs) used at the Bangkok Heart Hospital were generated from autologous peripheral blood. ACPs represent a heterogenic stem/progenitor cell population of hematopoietic cells that can potentially differentiate *in vivo* in response to tissue signals at the site of injection and lineage specific angiogenic precursors. The advantage over the bone-marrow stem cell is that their procurement does not require hospital admission or exposure to general anesthesia.

## 3. Delivery Methods

Four major types of cell deliveries currently applied, namely, (1) intravenous, (2) intracoronary artery, (3) intracoronary vein, and (4) intramyocardial injection. Advantages and disadvantages are summarized in Table 2.

**Table 2.** Advantages and disadvantages of different cardiac delivery methods for cell transplantation.

| Delivery methods | Advantage | Disadvantage |
|---|---|---|
| Intravenous | Simple and least invasive | Limited cell number to home into the infarction area<br>Homing to non-cardiac organs |
| Intracoronary vein | Useful for diffused/ completed occlusion of coronary arteries | Catheter and intravascular ultrasound technologies required<br>Limited cell number to home into the infarction area<br>Homing to non-cardiac organs |
| Intracoronary | Maximum concentration of cells at infarction area<br>Cell engraftment homogenously at infarct borders | In the case of a total occluded coronary artery, this may exclude the infracted area<br>Risk to induce myonecrosis<br>Optimal infusion intensity unknown |
| Intramyocardial (Endomyocardial) | Transcatheter<br>Less invasive compared with intramyocardial epicardial approach | Catheter and mapping technologies required |
| Intramyocardial (Epicardial) | Precise and accurate by direct visualization<br>Smaller number of cells required | Leads to "island" of cells and possible cause of arrhythmias |

In each method, different techniques are used to achieve maximal cell delivery. The direct intramyocardial cell transplantations are possible with epicardial (surgical) or endocardial (catheter) methods. The epicardial appoarch is superior to the endocardial appoarch in terms of simplicity, direct vision and maximal cell delivery. The drawbacks are invasiveness which required surgery. However, minimally invasive surgery, e.g., microthoracotomy, thoracoscopic surgery, robotic assisted surgery, may reduce this disadvantage.

Systemic intravenous delivery of cells to rats after myocardial infarctions, although feasible, is limited by entrapment of the donor cells in the lungs.[54] Freyman T *et al.* compared three delivery methods: intravenous, intracoronary and endocardial approaches in a porcine myocardial infarction model using mesenchymal stem cells from bone marrow.[55] The mean number of engrafted cells within the infarct zone was significantly greater following intracoronary infusion than either intravenous infusion or endocardial injection. Endocardial engraftment was greater than intravenous engraftment. However, the intracoronary approach was also associated with a higher incidence of decreased coronary blood flow. Perin EC *et al.* injected bone marrow mesenchymal cells in canine acute myocardial ischemia model.[56] They found that transendocardial cell injection showed higher cell retention with an increased vascularity and greater functional improvement than did the intracoronary artery injection. Hou D *et al.*[57] compared direct surgical intramyocardial injection, intracoronary artery and intracoronary vein in an ischemic swine model using peripheral blood mononuclear cells. There are significantly more cells retained in the heart after the intramyocardial injection compare with intracoronary artery infusion. The intracoronary vein injection had less cells retention than the intramyocardial injection.

## 4. Bangkok Heart Hospital Experiences

### 4.1 *Rationale*

The main rationale to employ cell-based therapies in heart failure is to replace damaged cardiac cells in an organotypic appropriate manner. Lost cardiac cells need to be replaced to allow the reestablishment of a functional heart. Cardiac cells such as myocardial cell, vascular cell and pacemaker cell have to be replaced to maintain ventricular contraction and to establish proper cardiac rhythm. In spite of the fact that there are presences of cardiac progenitor cells in the heart, resident stem cells cannot migrate from the viable tissue to the damaged area, home, grow, and differentiate to replace the dead cell lineages especially when the damage is caused by coronary artery disease.[58] Stem cells within the infarct die, as do all other cells deprived of oxygen supply. Furthermore, cell-based approaches could provide trophic support to tissue at risk in the surrounding infarct area or help promote survival, migration and differentiation of endogenous precursor cells.

In our study, we used peripheral blood-derived stem cells namely "angiogenic cell precursors". These cells formed a vascular tree in the experimental model and perhaps myocardial cells. The pacemaker cells were not studied. The delivery method chosen in our study was direct intramyocardial cell injection since this may give maximal cell retention in the heart muscle and therefore maximal benefit of the injection.

### 4.2 *Patients*

The patients who were diagnosed DCM or ICM were invited to this study. The study was approved by the Ethics Committee and Institutional Review Board. Informed consent was obtained before the procedure. Screening of severe contagious infections, HIV and hepatitis was done. Negative results were confirmed for inclusion of the patient in the study. Malignancy within the preceding three years was also an exclusion criteria. All patients had a recent coronary angiogram (within six months) confirming the coronary artery status before the procedure. Patients with coronary artery occlusion were informed and the coronary artery bypass grafting was suggested to be done at the same time as the cell injection. They all underwent pre-operative workups including routine chest x-ray, electrocardiography, and echocardiography without stressing, cardiac MRI (CMR) or Sestamibi myocardial perfusion scintigraphy. The patients were excluded from the CMR study if they had contra-indications such as metallic equipment implantation. They all undertook quality of life test (SF-36, multi-purpose, short-form health survey),[59] a six-minute walk test, New York Heart Association (NYHA) functional class evaluation, and routine laboratory tests required for general anesthesia and B-type natriuretic peptide (BNP). The left ventricular ejection fraction (LVEF), end-systolic volume and end-diastolic volume were determined using echocardiography or CMR. All patients, besides having end stage heart failure, had 2 or 3 accompanying co-morbidities such as renal failure, chronic obstructive lung disease, mild to moderate degrees of mitral/tricuspid regurgitation and pulmonary hypertension.

## 4.3 *Pre-operative investigations*

### 4.3.1 *Six-minute walk test*

Distance walked in the six-minute walk test is an important prognostic parameter used clinically to assess functional status in patients with HF. Exercise capacity in HF patients is typically assessed by means of objective performance testing such as cardiopulmonary exercise testing ($VO_2$peak) done either on a bicycle ergometer or treadmill.[60] Alternatively, the six-minute walk test is commonly used to assess functional exercise capacity in this patient population because it is less time consuming than a cardiopulmonary exercise test and does not require elaborate equipment or technically trained personnel.[61] By nature, being a constant load walking test during which patients choose their own walking intensity, the six-minute walk test is thought of by many to be a better reflection of the patient's true ability to function in routine daily activities.[62]

### 4.3.2 *Brain natriuretic peptide*

Brain natriuretic peptide (BNP), also called B-type natriuretic peptide, is a member of a family of structurally related hormones, the natriuretic peptides. This family also includes atrial natriuretic peptide (ANP) and C-type natriuretic peptide (CNP). BNP, a 32-amino acid protein, was first isolated from porcine brain.[63] As opposed to ANP and CNP, the BNP amino acid sequence varies greatly among species.[64] At physiologic concentrations, these neurohormones play a complex role on body fluid homeostasis and vascular tone.[65] It has recently gained a lot of popularity

confirmed negative results during the process. The multipotent progenitor cells are isolated from the blood, rich in CD45, $CD31^{Bright}$, $CD34^{+}CD45^{-/Dim}$ and $CD34^{Bright}$ cells. The cells at a concentration of 1.5–3.0 × $10^6$ cells/ml are then cultured under sterile conditions with vascular endothelial growth factor (VEGF, R&D Systems, Minneapolis, MN, USA) and 5 IU/ml heparin (Kamada, Beit-Kama, Israel). The process of cell expansion took five days. Number and viability of cells were checked and passed the following quality control before their use. The final product consisted of over 1.5 ± 0.5 million autologous endothelial progenitor cells was then suspended in 15 ml sterile cell culture medium. Acceptable culture parameters as assessed by microscopy and flow cytometry were in accordance with the following specifications: Cell viability ≥75% and Morphology — spindle-shaped, large cells forming long thread-like structures. Sterility tests were performed according to 21 Code Federal Regulation (CFR) 610.12. Assessment of cell culture sterility was performed on a sample of the cell fraction supernatant or phosphate buffered saline (PBS) following cell washing. Interim negative sterility results of all samples taken at different stages of the culture were compulsory for the release of the final product. The Bacterial Endotoxin test was performed according to United States Pharmacopeia (USP) 23. The Limulus Amebocyte Lysate (LAL) test was performed on a sample of supernatant taken from the cell culture. Endotoxin levels below the acceptable limits were compulsory for the release of the final product. Gram stain was used as a rapid and qualitative method for assessing bacterial contamination of tissue culture samples. Negative results of the Gram stain performed on samples taken from the washing medium of cells before vialing was compulsory for the release of the final product. Mycoplasma contamination was tested and a negative result of the test was also obtained. The product phenotype was assayed by immune staining, as well as for angiogenic potential (tube formation assay) and cytokine secretion. All cell preparations complied with pre-defined release criteria of safety and potency.

#### 4.4.1 *Immune staining*

Cell samples were washed in PBS and resuspended in 100 μl of PBS, stained with specific fluorochrome-conjugated anti-human antibodies or isotype-matched non-specific controls, and incubated in the dark for 30 minutes on ice. Cell suspension triplicates of five hundred thousand cells each were stained, assessed by FACS (FACSCalibur, Becton Dickinson), and analyzed by CellQuest Pro software (Becton Dickinson). The percentage of each marker was determined in each test tube and the mean and % Coefficient of Variance (% CV) was calculated for each one. The results were expressed as mean ± Standard Error (SE) of the percentage of stained cells. The number of stained cells was calculated by multiplying the number of harvested cells by the staining percentages obtained using the FACS. The total number and percentage of ACPs, as well as $CD34^+$ hematopoetic stem cell markers 31–33 were determined using flow cytometry. Harvested cells were tested for CD31, a molecule expressed by progenitor as well as mature angiogenic and endothelial cells and uptake of Acetilated Low Density Lipoprotein (AcLDL), a molecule rapidly uptaken and internalized by endothelial and angiogenic cells that is regularly used for their characterization. ACPs were defined as cells exhibiting high levels of CD31 (CD31Bright) concomitantly with uptake of AcLDL. Briefly, harvested cells were incubated in the dark, on ice, for 30 minutes with specific fluorochrome-conjugated CD34-APC (BD Biosciences, San Jose, CA, USA), CD31-PE (BD Biosciences), or with isotype-matched non-specific controls.

### 4.4.2 *Tube formation assay*

The angiogenesis potential of the cells was measured by their ability to form three-dimensional tube-like structures according to a widely-used scale using an *in vitro* angiogenesis assay kit (Chemicon) and scoring under an inverted light microscope (Nikon ECLIPSE TS-100).

### 4.4.3 *Analysis of cytokine secretion*

Samples of the harvested cells were washed in PBS and resuspended to one million in 1 ml X-vivo15 and grown for 24 hours in 24-well plates. Cytokine secretion in the supernatant was measured as compared to that of the medium only using flow cytometry and the BD™ CBA Human Angiogenesis Kit (Becton Dickinson).

## 4.5 *Surgical techniques*

### 4.5.1 *Thoracoscopic procedure*

Under general anesthesia with one-lung ventilation, the patient was placed in the right lateral decubitus position. A small one centimeter incision was made in the left chest at the 5th intercostal space on the posterior axillary line. The thoracoscope is placed through this incision. The chest cavity was examined and the other two instrumental access ports were introduced at the 3rd and 7th intercostal spaces on the posterior axillary line. The thoracoscope and appropriate instruments were used to allow the surgeon to open the pericardium longitudinally anterior and posterior to the phrenic nerve. This technique was accomplished with ease when the left pleural and pericardial cavity had never been invaded before. Time must be spent to free the pericardium from the heart without injury to the phrenic nerve. Damage to the phrenic nerve could be detrimental for this group of very seriously ill patients. The thoracoscopic instruments and pericardial traction stitches placed appropriately assist in reaching all regions of the left ventricular wall.

The cells injection was done with a 23-gauge butterfly needle with home-made guard. The thickness of the left ventricular wall, which is varied according to the severity and extent of the infarction, pre-determined by the CMR, helps in deciding the depth of the injection. The needle was brought to the heart and then the injections were done manually outside the chest with the extension line. There were 30 sites of injections, 0.5 cc/injection. The cells were injected into the hypokinetic or akinetic areas and the non-viable myocardium and surrounding area assessed previously by CMR or Sestamibi myocardial perfusion scintigraphy. The infarction in the interventricular septum area was also injected with the guide of trans-esophageal echocardiogram and a long 25-gauge needle through the free wall of the left ventricle. After adequate hemostasis, the small openings were closed with small chest drainage left in the 7th intercostal space opening.

### 4.5.2 *Combined off-pump coronary artery bypass grafting (OPCAB) and intramyocardial cells injection*

The off-pump coronary artery bypass grafting (OPCAB) operation was performed routinely at our institution.[68] OPCAB was carried out through a sternotomy incision, with or without take down of the left internal mammary artery, in the usual fashion. Three deep pericardial traction stitches were placed near the left upper and lower pulmonary veins and to the left of inferior vena cava, thereby achieving elevation of the apex of the heart. With perfectly placed stitches and aggressive traction, the apex of the heart should be elevated to about 90 degrees. To further assist in providing good presentation of the target arteries on the lateral and inferior aspect of the heart, patients were placed in a gentle right *decubitus* Trendelenburg position. Stabilization of the target arteries in the early phase of the study was accomplished with the Octopus III stabilizer (Medtronic Inc, Minneapolis, MN). With addition of suction capability of the Octopus device, the presentation and stabilization of the remote target arteries near the circumflex trunk were feasible. Heparin was given before the graft and coronary artery anastomoses. The intramyocardial cells injections were performed after Off-Pump coronary artery bypass surgery was completed and protamine given. The bypass surgery was performed on vessels where coronary arteries were occluded. The nonviable myocardial areas also were revascularized with cells injection. Since the incision in this situation was generous, the injection of cells was not difficult using the same injection devices and technique as described above. Most of the patients were extubated in the operating room. Usually they required a stay in the ICU at least overnight and four to five more days on the ward.

### 4.6 *Follow up*

All patients were followed in the same manner. Each patient was scheduled for a repeat of the pre-operative parameter measurements at one, three, six months, and one year.

### 4.7 *Statistical methods*

All results are expressed as mean ± standard deviation. Changes in left ventricular ejection fraction/NYHA functional class between pre-operative and the last follow-up left ventricular ejection fraction/NYHA functional class were compared by paired t-test. Relationships of the left ventricular ejection fraction between various time-points were compared using repeated-measures analysis of covariance.

## 4.8 *Results*

### 4.8.1 *Overall cases*

Between May 2005 and May 2009, 119 consecutive patients underwent intramyocardial autologous peripheral blood stem cell injection. Fifty were dilated cardiomyopathy (DCM) and 69 were ischemic cardiomyopathy (ICM). Mean age was 59.2 ± 12.1 years. The peripheral blood stem cells were isolated from the patient's own blood and cultured. The number of cells prior to injection was 43.8 ± 35.3 million cells. Cells were injected into all areas of the left ventricle in DCM and were injected into non-viable myocardium and hypokinetic segments in ICM. Combined coronary artery surgery and ACP injection were performed in 34.8% of ICM. Subsets of ICM and DCM were matched clinical characteristics with control groups to compare the efficacy of the cell injection as parts of the study.

There was no new ventricular arrhythmia. A 30-day mortality rate was 4% (2/50) and 4.3% (3/69) in DCM and ICM, respectively. Pre-operative and post-operative six-minute walk test at three months, B-type natriuretic peptide (BNP) at five days, NYHA/LVEF at six months were summarized in Table 3.

NYHA class improved from 3.0 ± 0.6 to 2.1 ± 0.9 at 411.2 ± 323.1 days ($P < 0.001$) in DCM and improved from 2.8 ± 0.6 to 1.9 ± 0.7 at 386.6 ± 309.5 days ($P < 0.001$) in ICM.

**Table 3.** Comparison of pre- and post-op evaluation in DCM and ICM.

| | DCM | | | ICM | | |
|---|---|---|---|---|---|---|
| | Pre | Post | *P* value | Pre | Post | *P* value |
| NYHA | 3 | 2.1 | < 0.001* | 2.8 | 1.9 | < 0.001* |
| Six-minute walk test (meters) | 375 | 418 | 0.3 | 355 | 421 | 0.1 |
| BNP (pg/ml) | 3692 | 3034 | 0.4 | 3947 | 2341 | 0.005* |
| LV ejection fraction (%) | 24 | 28 | 0.046* | 23 | 31 | < 0.001* |

*Statistically significant ($P < 0.05$).

LVEF increased from 23.8 ± 6.9% to 28.1 ± 11.6% at 299.6 ± 234.7 days ($P$ = 0.046) in DCM and increased from 23.1 ± 7.6% to 31.1 ± 9.9% at 340.7 ± 284.5 days ($P$ < 0.001) in ICM. There was no significant difference in changes of LVEF between combined coronary surgery plus ACP injection (improvement of 9.7 ± 11.1 points %) and ACPs injection alone (improvement of 6.9 ± 5.3 points %) in ICM ($P$ = 0.3). The serial measurements of the LVEF in ICM and DCM patients were shown in Figures 1 and 2. The comparisons were performed with repeated measured analysis of variance (ANOVA). There were significant increases in LVEF between pre-operative and post-operative treatments at three and six months in the ICM group. However, there was no significant increase in LVEF between the three and six months after the cell injection (Fig. 1). There was no significant increase in LVEF comparing between pre-operative and post-operative treatment

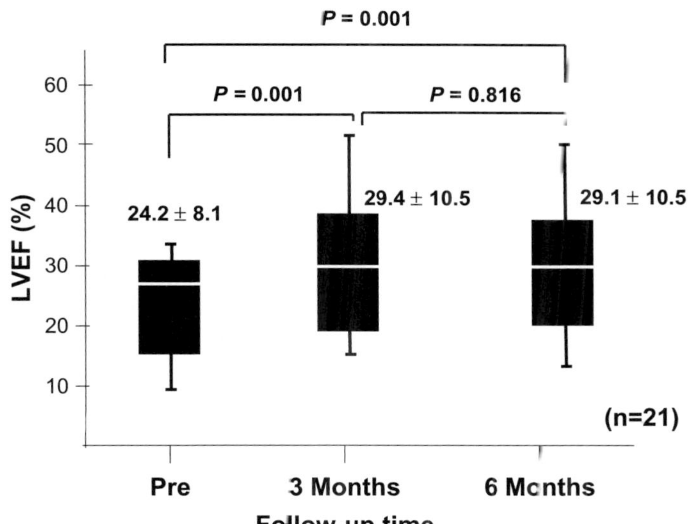


**Fig. 1.** Boxplot of the serial left ventricular ejection fraction of ICM patient: before and after the angiogenic cell precursors injection at the 3rd and 6th months. The lower and upper edges of the "box" are the first and third quartile of the data (50% of the data lie within the box). The "median" is shown as a line inside the box. The ends of the vertical lines or "whiskers" indicate the minimum and maximum values, unless outliers are present in which case the whiskers extend to a maximum of 1.5 times the inter-quartile range.

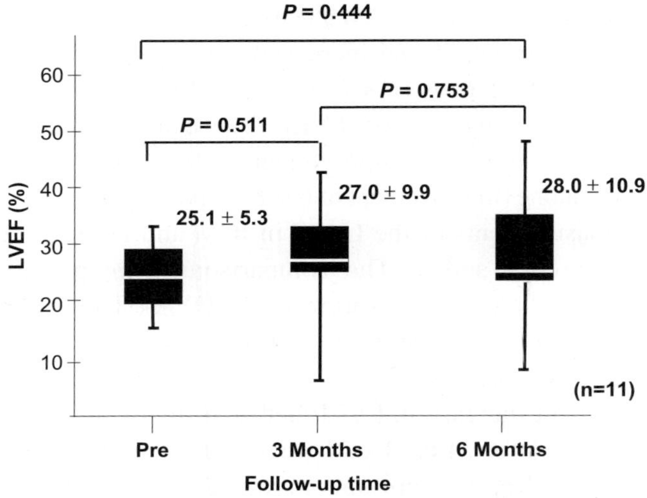


**Fig. 2.** Boxplot of the serial left ventricular ejection fraction of DCM patient: before and after the angiogenic cell precursors injection at the 3rd and 6th months.

in DCM both three and six months after the cell injection. However, the number of patients who had complete follow-up in both three and six months after the cell injection was low (n = 11).

In ICM patients, 25 consecutive patients with previous myocardial infarction had follow-up with cardiac MRI. Mean age was 59.0 ± 12.6 years, 24 were male and 17 were in the NYHA Class III and IV. Seventy-six percent had left ventricular ejection fraction (LVEF) less than 40%. Ten had ACP injection alone and 15 had combined CABG plus ACPs injection. The interval of follow-up was 11.6 ± 1.2 months.

There was a reversed remodeling of the left ventricle after the ACPs injection (Fig. 3). Decreases in LV end-diastolic and LV end-systolic volume were found (31.2 ± 62.5 ml, $P = 0.026$ and 31.0 ± 52.4 ml, $P = 0.01$, respectively), whereas infarction volume decreased (10.3 ± 22.7%, $P = 0.046$) (Table 4).

Quality of life post-operatively evaluated at three months had significantly improved for physical function, role physical, general health and vitality domains ($P$ = 0.001, < 0.001, 0.001 and 0.002, respectively) in

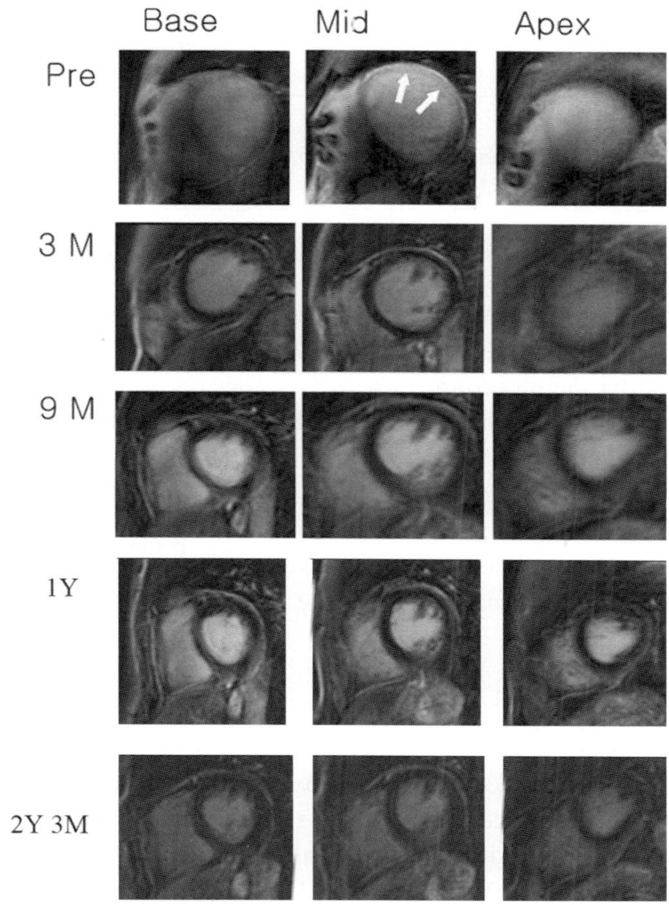


**Fig. 3.** Cardiac magnetic resonance imaging with gadolinium contrast. Myocardial infarction demonstrated as bright signal at the anterior and lateral walls of the left ventricle, extended from the base to apex on the first row, pre-operative. The left ventricular ejection fraction was 13.2% with left vertricular end diastolic volume (LVEDV) of 296 ml. The second row was obtained at three month after the ACPs injection alone. There was no myocardial scar and the LVEF was 20% with LVEDV of 268 ml. The third row was the result at nine months. There was no myocardial scar and LVEF increased to 36.5% with LVEDV of 175 ml. The LVEF increased to 48.5% and LVEDV decreased to 164 ml at one year on the fourth row. The fifth row shows a further reduction of LVEDV to 145.4 ml with stable of LVEF of 48.6% at two years and three months after the cell injection.

**Table 4.** Pre- and post-operative cardiac MRI parameters.

| CMR parameters | Pre-op | Post-op | *P* value |
|---|---|---|---|
| Infarction volume (%) | 35.6 ± 28.6 | 25.3 ± 21.1 | 0.046 |
| End-diastolic volume (ml) | 248.8 ± 76.6 | 217.6 ± 77.3 | 0.026 |
| End-systolic volume (ml) | 183.4 ± 84.3 | 152.5 ± 78.2 | 0.010 |

DCM. For ICM, physical function, role-physical, general heath and social function domains ($P = 0.048$, 0.011, 0.001 and 0.039, respectively) were improved after the procedure.

In conclusion, intramyocardial ACP injection is feasible and safe in both DCM and ICM. The NYHA, quality of life and ejection fraction had significantly improved in both DCM and ICM. In the next sections, the cell groups were compared with the control groups in which the patients' characteristics were matched between the two groups in order to make reasonable comparisons of the patients' outcomes.

### 4.8.2 *Case match studies*

Both control (medical treatment group) and cell injection group had medical treatment according to the standard heart failure guideline for the Joint Commission International (JCI) disease specific program and the ACC/AHA 2005 Guideline Update for diagnosis and management of chronic heart failure in the adult[69] by their own cardiologist. Pharmacological management is a poly-pharmacy approach. Medications that have the effect on the natural history of the disease, especially the neurohormonal antagonist (angiotensin converting enzyme inhibitors, beta blockers, aldosterone antagonist) were part of the treatment strategy. Each medication started at the appropriate level of NYHA class. Adverse reactions of medications were monitored and managed accordingly. The medications that potentially have deleterious effects in heart failure such as most of the calcium channel blockers, anti-arrhythmic class 1A, 1C, nonsteroidal anti-inflammatory drugs and Cox 2 inhibitors were avoided.

#### 4.8.2.1 Ischemic cardiomyopathy

##### 4.8.2.1.1 Medical treatments vs. intramyocardial cell injection[70]

The objective of this study was to assess the efficacy with short-term results of direct intramyocardial ACP injection directly into the myocardium in ICM compared with medical treatment alone.

(i) The Patients

Between July 11, 2005 and September 18, 2006, 25 patients (Cell group) underwent intramyocardial autologous stem cells injection. These 25 patients were composed of 14 patients with cell injection alone and 11 with combined cell injection and CABG. From our previous study, these two groups had no difference in pre-operative characteristics, intra-operative variables and post-operative outcomes. Therefore, these 25 patients were considered as a single homogenous group. The number of cells before injection was 27.4 ± 18.8 million cells. The cells were injected into the nonviable myocardium and hypokinetic segments in the cell group.

Seventeen case-matched patients from the heart failure database treated by medical means served as controls. Controls were matched by 10 pre-operative factors: age, sex, diabetes, hypertension, hypercholesterolemia, cerebrovascular accident, NYHA class, previous percutaneous coronary intervention, previous CABG, and LVEF. These groups, described in Table 5, showed no significant differences in the pre-operative characteristics.

(ii) Clinical Outcome

Many of the patients came to us terminally ill and had undergone conventional medical, surgical and device treatments previously. Close to half required inotrope support before surgery and all during ICU stay. Intra-aortic balloon support was utilized in 8% (2/25) of the cases pre-operatively. Their post-operative recovery was slower than that of routine coronary artery surgery patients. There was no major adverse cardiac event (MACE) such as neurological deficit, post-operative excessive bleeding, new renal insufficiency or new pulmonary failure, and there were no malignant arrhythmias noted.

All patients tolerated cardiac rehabilitation very well in the cell injection group. Six-minute walk tests showed an average improvement close

**Table 5.** Matching of 25 patients undergoing cell injection with 17 control patients.

| Pre-operative variables | Cell (n = 25) | Control (n = 17) | *P* value |
|---|---|---|---|
| Age (years) | 58.4 ± 13.7 | 65.9 ± 9.2 | 0.06 |
| Gender — male | 23 (92%) | 11 (64.7%) | 0.045 |
| Diabetes | 10 (40%) | 5 (29.4%) | 0.5 |
| Hypertension | 16 (64%) | 7 (41.2%) | 0.2 |
| Hypercholesterolemia | 20 (80%) | 9 (52.9%) | 0.1 |
| CVA | 3 (12%) | 1 (5.9%) | 0.6 |
| NYHA class | 2.9 ± 0.6 | 2.7 ± 0.6 | 0.2 |
| Previous PCI | 11 (44%) | 5 (29.4%) | 0.5 |
| Previous CABG | 7 (28%) | 7 (41.2%) | 0.5 |
| Pre-op LVEF | 26.1 ± 7.4 | 28.7 ± 9.6 | 0.3 |

**Abbreviations:** CVA, cerebrovascular accident; NYHA, New York Heart Association; PCI, percutaneous coronary intervention; CABG, coronary artery bypass grafting; LVEF, left ventricular ejection fraction.

to 154 meters in walking capacity (343.4 ± 123.0 meters before, to 497.5 ± 159.2 meters after, n = 9, $P = 0.03$ at 2.9 ± 2.6 months).

At an average of 229.9 ± 98.8 days after the injection, the NYHA functional class improved from pre-op of 2.9 ± 0.7 to post-op of 2.0 ± 0.9 (n = 25, $P < 0.001$). In contrast, the NYHA class was not improved in the control group (2.7 ± 0.5 pre-treatment vs. 2.3 ± 1 post-treatment, $P = 0.1$).

## • Left Ventricular Ejection Fraction

The LVEF was improved in 72% of patients (18/25). The LVEF improved by 6.4 ± 9.9 points % ($P = 0.003$) (from 26.1 ± 7.4% to 32.6 ± 11.4%) at 290.4 ± 210.3 days (Fig. 4). There was no statistical significance in changes of LVEF in the cell injection alone and combined OPCAB plus cell injection (7.4 ± 4.7 vs. 5.2 ± 14.2 point %, $P = 0.6$). The LVEF did not improve in the medically treated group. The LVEF was 31.3 ± 13.4% after medical treatment compared to 28.7 ± 9.9% during the pre-treatment period ($P > 0.05$).

## • Quality of Life

The quality of life assessed by the SF-36 at three months follow-up demonstrated a significant improvement of role physical ($P = 0.003$),

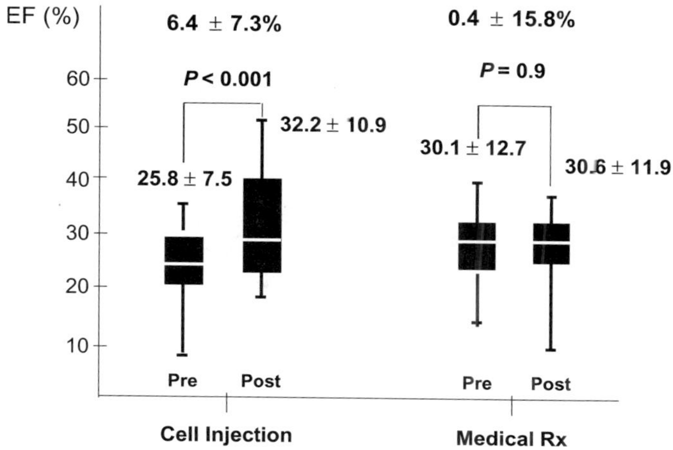


**Fig. 4.** Boxplot of the left ventricular ejection fraction of ICM patient: before and after the angiogenic cell precursors injection (left pair) and before and after medical treatment (right pair).

bodily pain ($P = 0.044$), general health ($P = 0.002$) and role-emotion ($P = 0.003$) domains in the cell group (Fig. 5).

For this comparison, we concluded that intramyocardial ACP injection in ICM significantly improved NYHA class and LVEF compared with the matching control (medical treatment alone). Six-minute walk test and quality of life also were improved after the ACP injection. In the next section, we compared the patients who had CABG surgery alone with patients who had CABG plus ACP injection.

### 4.8.2.1.2 CABG alone vs. cell injection or combined CABG plus cell injection

The objective was to determine efficacy of intramyocardial angiogenic cell precursors (ACP) injection for ICM compared with CABG surgery alone.

(i) The Patients

Twenty-five consecutive patients underwent ACP injection (cell group). Seventeen, previously revascularized, had ACP injection alone and 8 had

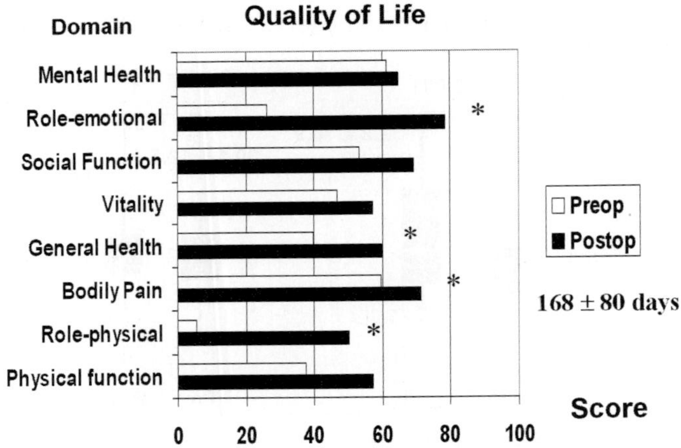


**Fig. 5.** The quality of life of ICM patient before and after the angiogenic cell precursors injection assessed by the SF-36 at three month follow up. * represents statistically significant ( $P < 0.05$).

combine OPCAB and ACP injection. These were the homogeneous group as shown in previous study. ACPs were isolated and cultured from the patient's own blood. The number of cells was 25.3 ± 19.3 million. Cells were injected into non-viable myocardium and hypokinetic segments.

Another 25 who underwent OPCAB alone were the control group. There was no significant difference in pre-operative co-morbidity and LVEF (Table 6). However, NYHA class was higher in the cell group. Mean age was 63 ± 9.7 years.

(ii) Clinical Outcome

In the cell group, there was no new ventricular arrhythmia. NYHA class improved from 2.6 ± 0.5 to 1.7 ± 0.9 at 352 ± 160.4 days ($P < 0.001$). LVEF increased from 27 ± 5% to 35.1 ± 9.6% at 273.6 ± 172.8 days ($P < 0.001$). There was no significant difference in changes of LVEF between combined OPCAB plus cell (+8.9 ± 10.8%) and cell alone (+7.8 ± 5.6%).

In the control group, NYHA class improved from 2.3 ± 0.6 to 1.6 ± 0.7 ($P < 0.001$). However, there was no significant improvement of LVEF (pre-op, 29.5 ± 6% *vs.* post-op, 32.8 ± 8%, $P = 0.08$). Improvement of LVEF was significantly higher in cell group ($P = 0.046$, Fig. 6).

**Table 6.** Matching of 25 patients undergoing cell injection with 25 control patients.

| Pre-operative variables | Cell ($n = 25$) | Control ($n = 25$) | $P$ value |
|---|---|---|---|
| Age (years) | 63 ± 9.7 | 63.2 ± 10.7 | 0.9 |
| Gender — male | 24 (96%) | 20 (80%) | 0.2 |
| Diabetes | 10 (40%) | 10 (40%) | 1 |
| Hypertension | 14 (56%) | 11 (44%) | 0.6 |
| Hypercholesterolemia | 21 (84%) | 13 (52%) | 0.03 |
| CVA | 3 (12.0%) | 0 | 0.2 |
| NYHA class | 2.6 ± 0.5 | 2.3 ± 0.6 | 0.03 |
| Previous PCI | 8 (32%) | 5 (20%) | 0.5 |
| Pre-op LVEF | 27 ± 5 | 29.5 ± 6 | 0.1 |

**Abbreviations:** CVA, cerebrovascular accident; NYHA, New York Heart Association; PCI, percutaneous coronary intervention; LVEF, left ventricular ejection fraction.

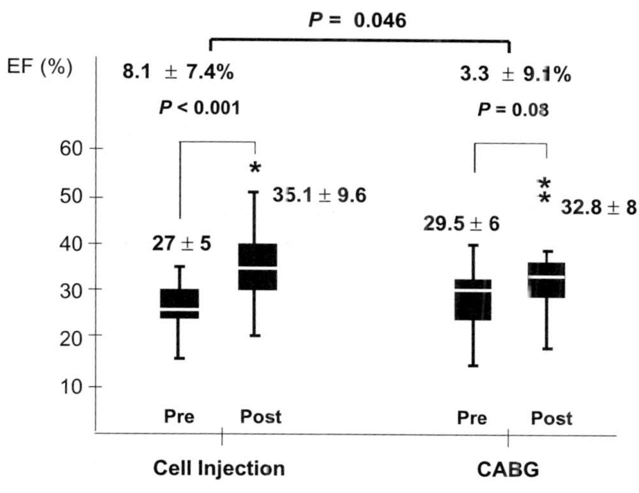


**Fig. 6.** Boxplot of the left ventricular ejection fraction of ICM patient: before and after the angiogenic cell precursors injection (left pair) and before and after CABG alone (right pair).* represents outlier.

For this comparison, we concluded that intramyocardial ACP injection in ICM significantly improved LVEF compared with CABG alone. NYHA functional class was improved in both groups.

#### 4.8.2.1.3 Multivariate analysis

The objectives were to determine the efficacy of intramyocardial ACP injection for ICM and the predictors of improvement in LVEF.

(i) The Patients

Ninety-four consecutive ischemic cardiomyopathy (ICM) patients with LVEF of less than 40% and completed follow up were studied. Mean age was 63.4 ± 11.6 years, 78 were male and 52 were in the NYHA Class III and IV. Twenty had medical treatment, 31 had CABG alone, 26 had ACP injection alone, and 17 had combined CABG plus ACP injection (Table 7). All patients in the medical treatment group, CABG alone group, cell injection or combined CABG plus cell injection groups received medical treatment according to the standard heart failure guideline for the Joint Commission International disease specific program and the ACC/AHA 2005 Guideline Update for Diagnosis and Management of Chronic Heart Failure in the Adult. The number of cells prior to injection was 36.6 ± 28.6 million. The ACPs were injected to the non-viable myocardium or hypokinetic areas of the left ventricle in the cell group.

**Table 7.** Patient characteristics.

| | Medical treatment (n = 20) | CABG alone (n = 31) | Cell injection alone (n = 26) | Combined CABG and cell injection (n = 17) |
|---|---|---|---|---|
| Age (mean ± SD, years) | 69.1 ± 9.2 | 64.1 ± 11.1 | 62.0 ± 10.5 | 57.5 ± 13.9 |
| NYHA class (mean ± SD) | 2.5 ± 0.8 | 2.4 ± 0.6 | 2.9 ± 0.6 | 2.6 ± 0.8 |
| Pre-op LVEF (mean ± SD, %) | 28.2 ± 7.9 | 29.3 ± 5.7 | 25.0 ± 7.0 | 21.1 ± 8.9 |
| Pulmonary hypertension | 1 (5%) | 1 (3.2%) | 5 (19.2%) | 3 (17.6%) |
| Diabetes mellitus | 5 (25%) | 15 (48.4%) | 14 (53.8%) | 5 (29.4%) |
| Hypertension | 6 (30%) | 15 (48.4%) | 16 (61.5%) | 10 (58.8%) |

**Abbreviations:** NYHA, New York Heart Association; LVEF, left ventricular ejection fraction.

(ii) Statistical Analysis

McNemar test was used for comparison of NYHA functional classes between pre- and post-treatments. Paired T-test was used to compare the mean difference of LVEF and NYHA Class between pre- and post-treatments.

Response to treatment was defined as an improvement in LVEF of more than or equal to 5 percentage points. Multivariate logistic regression was used to explore the association between response to treatment and pre-operative patients' characteristics using age, gender, diabetes, hypertension, NYHA class, pre-op LVEF, interval of follow-up and ACP injection.

(iii) Clinical Outcome

- ***New York Heart Association Functional Class***

For the medical treatment group (Table 8), the difference was 12.5% [95% confidence interval (CI), −14.83–22.94%, $P = 0.6$, McNemar Test]. For the coronary artery bypass grafting alone group (Table 9), the difference

**Table 8.** Comparisons of NYHA functional class: pre- and post-medical treatment.

| | | Post-treatment NYHA class | | |
|---|---|---|---|---|
| | | I–II | III–IV | |
| Pre-treatment NYHA class | I–II | 7 | 1 | 50% |
| | III–IV | 3 | 5 | 50% |
| | | 62.5% | 37.5% | |

**Table 9.** Comparisons of NYHA functional class: pre- and post-coronary artery bypass grafting.

| | | Post-operative NYHA class | | |
|---|---|---|---|---|
| | | I–II | III–IV | |
| Pre-operative NYHA class | I–II | 18 | 0 | 60% |
| | III–IV | 9 | 3 | 40% |
| | | 90% | 10% | |

was 30% (95% CI, 9.72–30%, $P = 0.004$, McNemar Test). For the cell injection group (cell injection alone and combined CABG plus cell injection, Table 10), the difference was 48.84% (95% CI, 27.82–56.73%, $P < 0.001$, McNemar Test).

- ***Left Ventricular Ejection Fraction***

There was no significant improvement of LVEF in the medical treatment and CABG group (2.6 ± 12.2, $P = 0.4$ and 3.5 ± 9.9, $P = 0.06$, respectively). LVEF increased by 6.9 ± 5.3 points % ($P < 0.001$) at 252 ± 179.1 days in ACP injection. LVEF increased by 6.8 ± 10.2 points % ($P = 0.014$) at 274 ± 218.1 days in CABG plus ACP injection (Fig. 7).

- ***Multivariate Logistic Regression Analysis***

The predictors for positive treatment response of more than 5% were ACP injection [$P = 0.036$, odds ratio (OR) 3.2, 95% confidence interval (CI): 1.1–9.4] and pre-op LVEF ($P = 0.02$, OR 1.1, 95% CI: 1.0–1.2).

For this multivariate analysis, we concluded that intramyocardial ACP injection is effective in the treatment of ICM. Pre-op LVEF and cell injection determined the improvement of post-operative LVEF in treated ICM patients. A large randomized trial is needed to confirm this results.

### 4.8.2.2 Dilated cardiomyopathy

The objective was to determine the efficacy of intramyocardial ACP injection in dilated cardiomyopathy.

**Table 10.** Comparisons of NYHA functional class: pre- and post-cell injection (cell injection alone and combined coronary artery bypass grafting plus cell injection).

| | | Post-operative NYHA class | | |
|---|---|---|---|---|
| | | I–II | III–IV | |
| Pre-operative | I–II | 11 | 2 | 30.2% |
| NYHA class | III–IV | 23 | 7 | 69.8% |
| | | 79.1% | 20.9% | |

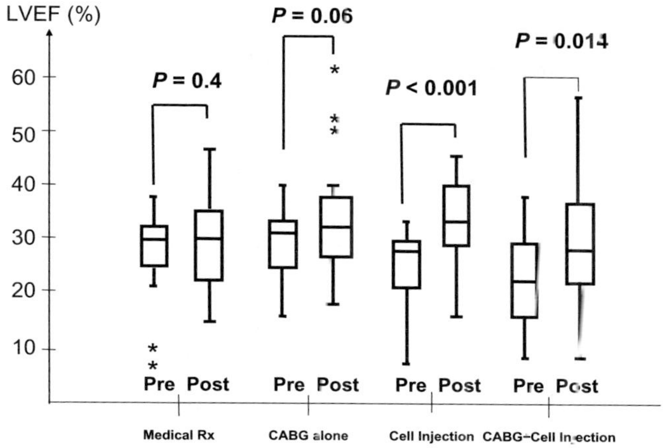


**Fig. 7.** Boxplot of the left ventricular ejection fraction of ICM patient: before (pre) and after (post) each treatment.* represents outlier.

**Table 11.** Patient characteristics.

| | Cell (n = 35) | Control (n = 17) | *P* value |
|---|---|---|---|
| Age (mean ± SD, years) | 56.7 ± 14.3 | 57.5 ± 14.3 | 0.8 |
| NYHA class (mean ± SD) | 3.0 ± 0.6 | 2.7 ± 1.0 | 0.2 |
| Pre-op LVEF (mean ± SD, %) | 23.9 ± 6.5 | 25.0 ± 8.9 | 0.6 |
| Pulmonary hypertension | 11 (31.4%) | 1 (5.9%) | 0.08 |
| Diabetes mellitus | 11 (31.4%) | 6 (35.3%) | 1 |
| Hypertension | 11 (31.4%) | 3 (17.6%) | 0.3 |
| ACEI used | 10 (28.6%) | 1 (5.9%) | 0.08 |
| Digitalis used | 11 (31.4%) | 5 (29.4%) | 1 |

**Abbreviations:** NYHA, New York Heart Association Class; LVEF, left ventricular ejection fraction; ACEI, angiotensin-converting enzyme inhibitor.

## (i) The Patients

Thirty-five dilated cardiomyopathy patients (cell group) underwent intramyocardial ACP injection. Seventeen dilated cardiomyopathy patients (control group) from heart failure database treated by medical means were matched with the cell group. The patient characteristics were summarized in Table 11.

(ii) Clinical Outcomes

In the cell group, there was no major adverse cardiac event (MACE) such as neurological deficit, post-operative excessive bleeding, new renal insufficiency or new pulmonary failure. There were no malignant arrhythmias, such as ventricular fibrillation, recurrent sustained ventricular tachycardia, and *torsades de pointes* ventricular tachycardia in the long QT syndrome or those with ventricular tachycardia associated with unstable hemodynamics noted in the peri-operative period.

There were 6 patients who died during the two-year follow-up. The two-year survival was approximately 72%. All patients had a sudden death with unknown cause and no autopsies were performed.

- ***New York Heart Association Functional Class***

At an average of 284.7 ± 136.2 days after the injection, the NYHA functional class improved by 1.1 ± 0.7 ($P < 0.001$). In contrast, the NYHA functional class was not significantly improved in the control group (2.45 ± 0.9 pre-treatment to 1.9 ± 0.5 post-treatment, $P = 0.052$).

All patients tolerated cardiac rehabilitation very well in the cell injection group. Six-minute walk tests at three months follow-up improved (pre-op 369.5 ± 122.4 *vs* post-op 425 ± 218.5 meters, $P = 0.2$).

- ***NT-ProB-type Natriuretic Peptide***

The NT-ProB-type natriuretic peptide (NT-ProBNP) decreased 1471.7 ± 2648.5 pg/ml at 5–7 days after the surgery (pre-op 3907.0 ± 3735.23 pg/ml *vs* post-op 2435.32 ± 2526.3 pg/ml, $P = 0.1$), and decreased 2100.4 ± 3382 pg/ml at three months post-operative (pre-op 3466.3 ± 3654 pg/ml *vs* post-op 1365.9 ± 1041.1 pg/ml, $P = 0.2$). The overall NT-ProBNP level decreased 1946.2 ± 3394.1 pg/ml at 84.4 ± 190.7 days ($P = 0.02$).

- ***Left Ventricular Ejection Fraction***

The LVEF was improved in 71.4% of patients (25/35) who underwent cells injection. The LVEF improved by 4.4 ± 10.6% ($P = 0.02$) (from 23.9 ± 6.5% to 28.3 ± 10.7%) at 192.7 ± 135.1 days (Fig. 8). There was a moderate positive correlation between the number of cells and the improvement of the LVEF ($P = 0.02$, $P = 0.47$). The LVEF did not improve in the medically treated group. The LVEF was 27.6 ± 7.6% after

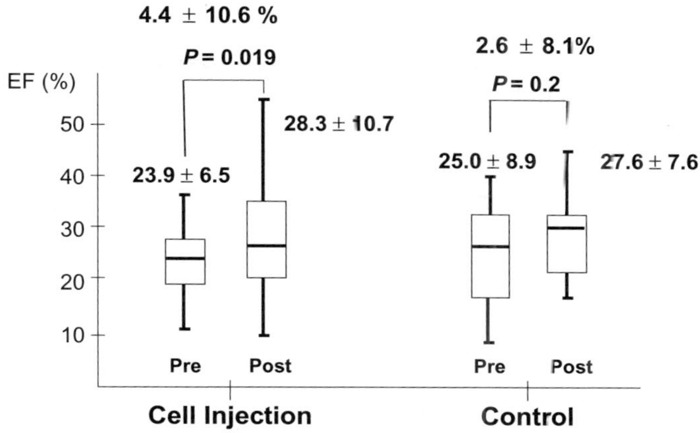


**Fig. 8.** Boxplot of the left ventricular ejection fraction of DCM patient: before and after the angiogenic cell precursors injection (left pair) and before and after medical treatment (right pair).

medical treatment compared to 25.0 ± 8.9% during pre treatment period ($P = 0.2$).

- Quality of Life

The quality of life assessed by the SF-36 at three month follow-up (Fig. 9) demonstrated a significant improvement of physical function ($P = 0.004$), role-physical ($P = 0.02$), general health ($P < 0.001$) and vitality domains ($P = 0.007$).

For this comparison, we concluded that ACP injection is safe for dilated cardiomyopathy, and has potential of improvement in heart function and functional class in patients more than medical treatment alone.

### 4.9 *Discussion*

This study was attempted to demonstrate the safety and efficacy of ACPs, derived and expanded from the autologous peripheral blood to treat end-stage heart failure patients in both ischemic and dilated cardiomyopathy. At this stage, it is impossible for us to conduct a randomized trial with the patients condition described above, since giving placebo injection could

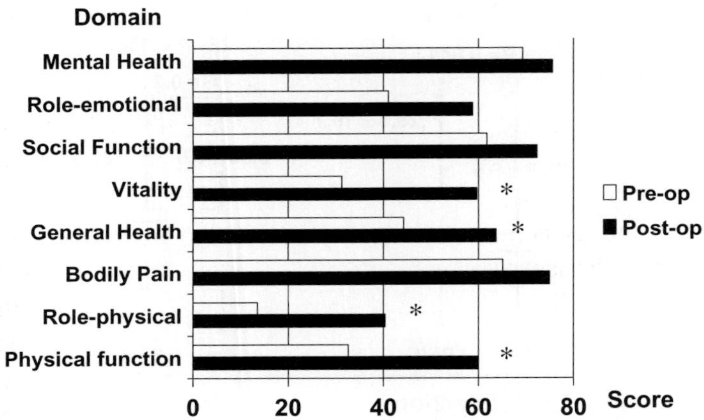


**Fig. 9.** The quality of life of DCM patient before and after the angiogenic cell precursors injection assessed by the SF-36 at 3 month follow-up.* represents statistically significant ($P < 0.05$).

be detrimental to their well being. Even though this is a non-randomized case-match study, the patients were not selected and did include all populations of dilated and ischemic cardiomyopathy: acute/chronic, post-coronary artery surgery, percutaneous coronary intervention, renal insufficiency and previous stroke. The computer matched groups were treated with optimal medical management by our heart failure cardiologist or patients who underwent coronary artery surgery at our institution during the same time period.

So far, bone marrow stem cells are the most commonly used stem cells for investigations clinically. Bone marrow is composed of multiple cell types, namely, hematopoietic, mesenchymal, and stromal stem cells, as well as other cell types yet to be characterized. The endothelial progenitor cell exists in the bone marrow as well as the systemic circulation. These cells have three surface markers in general (CD34, CD133, and the vascular endothelial growth factor-2) and have properties of embryonal angioblast and contribute to re-endotheliazation and neovascularization. The level of circulating endothelial progenitor cells positive for CD34 and kinase insert domain receptor predicts the occurrence of cardiovascular events and death from cardiovascular causes. The highly enriched $Lin^{-}c\text{-}kit^{+}$ adult bone marrow cells could regenerate functional myocardium within an infarcted region in mice. Bone marrow mesenchymal cell marker of CD29 showed contraction and exhibited ultrastructural features of sarcomere formation after coculturing with neonatal rat ventricular myocyte. The degree of bone marrow-dependent neovascularization induced in the ischemic myocardium is directly related to the numbers of $CD34^+$ angioblasts homing to the ischemic site. Increasing the numbers of mobilized angioblasts in the ischemic myocardium results in development of capillaries of intermediate and large lumen size and contributes to improved heart function by two complementary mechanisms: (1) protection of at-risk myocytes against apoptosis; and (2) induction of myocytes proliferation/regeneration. The adult peripheral blood $CD34^+$ cells can transdifferentiate into cardiomyocytes, mature endothelial cells and smooth muscle cell *in vivo* in animal models. Both cell fusion and transdifferentiation may account for the transformation of peripheral blood $CD34^+$ cells into cardiomyocytes *in vivo*. However, Gruh *et al.*[71] showed no convincing evidence of transdifferentiation of endothelial progenitor cells into cardiomyocytes when co-culturing neonatal rat cardiomyocytes. Koyanagi *et al.*[72] demonstrated an important role of E-cadherin for EPC differentiation into cardiomyocytes. The cadherins promote calcium-dependent cell-to-cell adhesion and regulate diverse signaling processes such as differentiation, proliferation, and migration.[73,74] The EPC can transiently form ultrafine intercellular connections with neonatal rat cardiomyocytes. This transient cell fusion resulting in the exchange of macromolecular complexes may contribute to the cell fate change of EPC during co-culture.

For the DCM, Roura *et al.* demonstrated defective vascularization and impaired vasculogenesis (the de novo vascular organization of mobilized endothelial progenitors) and angiogenesis in DCM patients. The defective vascularization was associated with reduced myocardial expression of vascular β-catenin, an important angiogenic regulator.[75] Werner *et al.* also showed that EPC transfer is effective in attenuating myocardial damage in a model of DCM.[76] Chu *et al.* demonstrated an angiogenesis effect of the mechanical puncture of myocardium. However, this was controversial.[77] These are the rationale used for intramyocardial ACPs injection in our study.

Its advantage also is cell retention compared with the transcoronary artery delivery method. Cell transplantation was investigated both in animal and clinical setting for the DCM. The transplanted ventricular heart cells or autologous smooth muscle cells in cardiomyopathic myocardium improved its contractile function in animals.[78] Clinical studies for the cell implantation in DCM are limited. Huang *et al.*[79] performed percutaneous coronary autologous bone marrow mononuclear cell transplantation in 10 patients. Cell injection improved six-minute-walk test, decreased re-hospitalization rate and elevated exercise ability; however the LVEF and LV size were not changed compared with control and the pre-treatment values. Wang *et al.* performed intracoronary injection of autologous mesenchymal stem cells in 12 DCM patients and found similar results.[80] Seth *et al.* performed intracoronary autologous bone marrow mononuclear cell transplantation in 24 DCM patients. The NYHA class improved and the LVEF improved by 5.4% (20 ± 7.4% to 25 ± 12%, $P < 0.05$) in the treatment group, but not in the control group.[81]

Intracoronary injection of bone marrow stem cell or EPC cell in patients after acute myocardial infarction improved the left ventricular function and viability of myocardium. However, there are a number of negative studies reported. Lunde *et al.*[82] studied the intracoronary injection of autologous bone marrow mononuclear cells in patients with acute ST-elevation myocardial infarction of the anterior wall at a median of six days after myocardial infarction treated with percutaneous coronary intervention in the acute phase. The median number of mononuclear cells injected was $68 \times 10^6$, the median percentage of viable cells was 95%, and the median number of $CD34^+$ cells was $0.7 \times 10^6$. LVEF had increased in both groups (mean change, 7.6 ± 10.4 percentage points). There were no significant differences between the groups with respect to the increase in LVEF, end-diastolic volume, or infarct size at six months, as compared with the control. Yoshioka *et al.*[83] did the direct transplantation of bone marrow $CD34^+$ cells into the peri-ischemic zone after one to two hours of left anterior descending coronary artery ligation in nonhuman primates, even without coronary bypass grafts or percutaneous coronary intervention, resulting in improved regional blood flow and cardiac function compared with the control (saline injection). They found that these cells secreted angiogenic cytokines which potentiate angiogenic activity of endogenous cells. They did not incorporate into the vascular structure or form cardiomyocytes by cell tracking using genetically marked green fluorescent protein. Hou *et al.*[57] compared the peripheral blood mononuclear cells distribution by three delivery methods, namely, intracoronary, intramyocardial and retrograde coronary venous injections after six days of myocardial infarction with 45 minutes balloon occlusion of the proximal left anterior descending coronary artery in Yorkshire domestic pigs. They found that the organs receiving the greatest fraction of cells for all delivery modalities were the lungs, with 26 ± 3% (intramyocardial), 47 ± 1% (intracoronary), and 43 ± 3% (retrograde coronary venous) of cells localized to the lungs. Significantly, more cells were retained in the heart after intramyocardial injection, 11.3 ± 3%, in comparison with intracoronary 2.6 ± 0.3% ($P < 0.05$). Retrograde coronary venous infusion efficiency was lower than the intramyocardial injection (3.2 ± 1%), but this difference did not reach statistical significance. We noted that both endoscopic and micro-invasive approaches allowed the surgeons to reach all the areas of left ventricular wall with minimal difficulty even in the redo cases. After all locations were approached, the injection could be done with ease.

Patel *et al.*[84] studied the efficacy of the intramyocardial $CD34^+$ bone marrow stem cell injection combined with OPCAB compared with OPCAB alone in patients with chronic myocardial infarction. They found that all the patients in the OPCAB plus stem cell therapy group had significantly improved LVEF over those in the OPCAB-only group. Stamm *et al.*[85] reported the result of intramyocardial purified $CD133^+$ bone marrow stem cells together with On-pump CABG surgery. Forty patients were stratified to undergo CABG with cell injection or CABG alone. They found that LVEF at six months was moderately, but significantly better in the cell-treated patients. These raise the questions: "Who will benefit from cell injection?" "What is the best cell preparation?" "What is the best delivery method?" "What are the effects of the number of cells and cell preparation?"

For overall cases, we evaluated the intramyocardial peripheral blood ACP injection in chronic myocardial infarction patients. The overall NYHA functional class improved as well as six-minute walk test. The quality of life assessed by SF36 improved in all 8 domains. However significant improvements were found on role physical function, role-physical, general health and social function domains. The LVEF was improved in 84.6% of patients (44/52). However, only 50.7% of patients had their LVEF increased more than 5% after the cell injection. The LVEF improved by 8.0 ± 8.1% ($P < 0.001$) (from 23.1 ± 7.6% to 31.1 ± 9.9%) at 340.7 ± 284.5 days. This is a cohort of patients who have ICM. These patients had already revascularized either by percutaneous intervention or CABG; therefore cell injection was only performed in this group of patients (n = 45). The other subset in the cell group was diagnosed with ICM, but did not have any revascularization before, therefore combined cell injection and CABG was carried out (n = 23). The other one had a redo CABG plus cell injection. This group should benefit from the combined procedure, if the areas bypassed were not completely scarred. From the cardiac MRI studies, intramyocardial ACPs injection could prevent remodeling effects on the LV in prior myocardial infraction patients. Infarction volume, end-diastolic and end-systolic LV volume were significantly reduced.

For the DCM, NYHA class improved from 3.0 ± 0.6 to 2.1 ± 0.9 at 411.2 ± 323.1 days ($P < 0.001$) and LVEF increased from 23.8 ± 6.9% to 28.1 ± 11.6% at 299.6 ± 234.7 days ($P = 0.046$). The LVEF was improved in 62.5% of patients (25/40). However only 40% of patients had their LVEF increased more than 5% after the cell injection. Quality of life post-operatively evaluated at three months has significantly improved for physical function, role physical, general health and vitality domains in DCM.

Our results were comparable to the results of intracoronary or transendocardial autologous bone marrow cells or intracoronary circulating progenitor cells injection in both acute and chronic myocardial ischemia models in previous reports. In the BOOST trial, the LVEF had increased 6.7% after six months of the intracoronary injection of autologous bone marrow cells after 4.8 days of successful percutaneous coronary intervention for acute ST-segment elevation myocardial infarction. The mean LVEF had increased by 0.7% in the control group. The LVEF at 18 months after the injection increased by 5.9% in the bone marrow group, and 3.1% in the control group.[86] This was not a statistically significant difference. Schachinger *et al.*[87] in 2004 and 2006 found no difference in increasing of LVEF between the uses of circulating progenitor cells or bone marrow-derived progenitor cells. The LVEF had increased 5–8%. The same results were also found in chronic myocardial ischemia. The LVEF increased by 9.2 and 10.5% at one week and three months after the intracoronary transplantation of autologous bone marrow-derived mononuclear cells. The LVEF remained improved at six months and one year after cell injection. Dobert *et al.*[88] in 2004 demonstrated the improvement of mean signal intensity in the infarct zone by means of $^{18}$F-fluorodeoxyglucose positron emission tomography at four months follow up after intracoronary infusion of bone marrow-/circulating blood-derived progenitor cells 4 ± 2 days after acute myocardial infarction. There were no significant differences in myocardial viability and perfusion between bone marrow cell and EPC infusion. Hendrikx *et al.*[89] in 2006 compared combined CABG and intramyocardial bone marrow $CD34^+$ cell injection (n = 10) with control (CABG alone and saline injection, n = 10) after 217 ± 162 days of infarction. The cells were injected into the peri-infarction zone. The number of cells was $60.25 \pm 31.35 \times 10^6$ nucleated cells and contained 1.42 ± 0.99% $CD34^+$ cells. They found that systolic thickening had improved significantly at four months in the cell implanted scars compared with the control. The proposed mechanism of action of these cells was angiogenesis, transdifferentiation, cytokine release/paracrine action and homing signal. The real mechanism explaining how these cells work is not quite clear at this point.

In our study, there was no major adverse cardiac event in spite of all patients being at very high risk. The few complications occurring in this study do not differ much from the trans-catheter approach in which death, acute myocardial infarction, or stent thrombosis were found in the intracoronary autologous bone marrow cells injection. For the intracoronary EPCs injection, the same complications were reported in the TOPCARE-AMI trial as 0%, 3.3% and 3.3%, respectively. During the 18 months of follow-up in the BOOST randomized controlled trial, there was 3.3% recurrent myocardial infarction and 17% required target-vessel revascularization. There was no documented ventricular tachycardia and syncope in either our study or previously reported series. Echocardiography did not reveal any evidence of intramyocardial tumor formation or calcifications. There was also no cancer diagnosed during the follow up. Perin *et al.*[90] in 2003 reported trans-myocardial injection of bone marrow mononuclear cells via the NOGA Myostar catheter in chronic myocardial ischemia patients. There was one death (7%) at 14 weeks, presumably from sudden cardiac death. There was no major peri-procedural complication otherwise. No sustained arrhythmias were associated with the injection procedures, nor did any significant arrhythmias occur while the patients were hospitalized. Tse *et al.*[91] in 2006 reported the long-term safety of electromechanical mapping-guided catheter-based intramyocardial autologous bone marrow cell injection for treatment of severe coronary artery disease. They demonstrated that direct intramyocardial injection of autologous bone marrow cells was not associated with any major long-term sequelae, including ventricular arrhythmia, myocardial damage, or development of intramyocardial tumor and calcification. The serial assessments with MRI at three and six months and computed tomography at 36 months was performed and did not find any evidence of intramyocardial tumor or calcification or worsening of LVEF after the procedure. No tumor mass or intramyocardial calcification was observed during the post-mortem examination in the patient who died at 20 months, or during surgery in another patient who underwent coronary artery bypass surgery at 12 months after bone marrow cell implantation. Two patients had died of stroke and coronary artery disease progression, respectively, at a mean of 44 months of follow-up. The incidence of ventricular arrhythmia after bone marrow cell injection was low compared with the skeletal myoblast implantation. Stamm *et al.*[85] in 2007 found no cell injection-related complications up to four years follow-up after intramyocardial delivery of $CD133^+$ bone marrow cells in chronically ischemic hearts of patients undergoing CABG. However, extensive intramyocardial calcification could be found after direct transplantation of unselected bone marrow cells into the acutely infarcted myocardium.

## 4.10 *Conclusions*

So far, we concluded that the intramyocardial ACPs injection is safe for both ICM and DCM. As far as the efficacy is concerned, our non-randomized studies of the case-matched studies comparing patients who underwent intramyocardial ACPs injection and patients who were treated by medical treatment alone and/or coronary surgery alone in our institution at the same time demonstrated efficacy of the type of cell and method used. However, the efficacy results were marginal especially in the DCM.

### 4.11 *Limitation of the study*

This is a non-randomized study. The LVEF has been followed up by either CMR or echocardiogram; therefore there is bias in the method of evaluation of the LVEF. The follow up was incomplete as these patients were mostly from overseas and cardiologists did not follow up on our schedule. However, the NHYA class and quality of life were able to be obtained directly from the patients.

## 5. Future Developments

A further development would be to identify the type of cells that have high efficacy and ease to harvest and expand. The adult stem cells still are the most common investigated stem cell in clinical trial since it is less concerned as an ethical issue. However, most clinical trials do not demonstrate substantial improvement in clinical outcomes in most cases, including us. There are a number of patients who had showed marked improvement to nearly normal heart. We are not absolutely sure or can predict the one that will have positive improvement in the cells that we currently used. More patients need to be studied to answer these questions and the development of more potent stem cells is needed.

The other possibility is to use a combination of adult stem cells that could give rise to different tissues such as endothelial progenitor cells and skeletal myoblasts. The cardiac progenitor cell is another potential for the adult stem cell to repair the heart since it is pre-programmed to be heart tissues.

The next generation of the induced pluripotent stem cell may provide more potent cells to alleviate heart failure.[92] One limitation is that the autologous stem cell may not be useful for treatment of genetic caused cardiomyopathy. The embryonic stem cell demonstrated the benefit in treatment of genetic cardiomyopathy. Directed differentiation needs to be studied further to be able to differentiate adult precursor cells in every organ that go on degeneration to replace them. Immunological barriers are also needed to be resolved to avoid the rejection, therefore the allogenic precursor cells could be used off the shelf.

The dose-response needs to be evaluated. The patient selection is also important. Basic sciences are required to explain the results and might help in the process of patient selection.

Another development would be a combined cell and other modality treatments such as growth factors, gene therapy and pharmacologic manipulations. Hsieh PC *et al.* injected platelet-derived growth factor (PDGF) with self-assembling peptide nanofibers to provide controlled release within the myocardium.[93] The serial echocardiogram from day one to three months showed significant improvement of ventricular function and reduced infarcted myocardium in the controlled delivery PDGF group without pulmonary toxicity. Stem cell homing could serve as a means of local drug delivery through the infusion of genetically engineering stem cells that secrete a gene product of interest, which could then be used to correct genetic deficiency states.

## References

1. Barker WH, Mullooly JP, Getchell W. Changing incidence and survival for heart failure in a well-defined older population, 1970–1974 and 1990–1994. *Circulation* 2006;113(6):799–805.
2. Roger VL, Weston SA, Redfield MM, *et al.* Trends in heart failure incidence and survival in a community-based population. *JAMA* 2004; 292(3):344–350.
3. de Giuli F, Khaw KT, Cowie MR, *et al.* Incidence and outcome of persons with a clinical diagnosis of heart failure in a general practice population of 696,884 in the United Kingdom. *Eur J Heart Fail* 2005;7(3):295–302.
4. Andrews RE, Fenton MJ, Ridout DA, Burch M. New-onset heart failure due to heart muscle disease in childhood: a prospective study in the United Kingdom and Ireland. *Circulation* 2008;117(1):79–84.
5. Hunt SA, Baker DW, Chin MH, *et al.* ACC/AHA Guidelines for the Evaluation and Management of Chronic Heart Failure in the Adult: Executive Summary a Report of the American College of Cardiology/American Heart

Association Task Force on Practice Guidelines (Committee to Revise the 1995 Guidelines for the Evaluation and Management of Heart Failure): Developed in Collaboration with the International Society for Heart and Lung Transplantation; Endorsed by the Heart Failure Society of America. *Circulation* 2001;104(24):2996–3007.

6. Costanzo MR, Mills RM, Wynne J. Characteristics of "Stage D" heart failure: insights from the Acute Decompensated Heart Failure National Registry Longitudinal Module (ADHERE LM). *Am Heart J* 2008;155(2):339–347.
7. Jones RH, Velazquez EJ, Michler RE. Coronary bypass surgery with or without surgical ventricular reconstruction. *N Engl J Med* 2009;360(17): 1705–1717.
8. Mark DB, Knight JD, Velazquez EJ, *et al.* Quality of life and economic outcomes with surgical ventricular reconstruction in ischemic heart failure: results from the Surgical Treatment for Ischemic Heart Failure trial. *Am Heart J* 2009;157(5):837–844, e831–833.
9. Leor J, Patterson M, Quinones MJ, *et al.* Transplantation of fetal myocardial tissue into the infarcted myocardium of rat. A potential method for repair of infarcted myocardium? *Circulation* 1996;94(9 Suppl):II332–336.
10. Scorsin M, Hagege AA, Marotte F, *et al.* Does transplantation of cardiomyocytes improve function of infarcted myocardium? *Circulation* 1997; 96(9 Suppl):II-188–193.
11. Dowell JD, Rubart M, Pasumarthi KB, *et al.* Myocyte and myogenic stem cell transplantation in the heart. *Cardiovasc Res* 2003;58(2):336–350.
12. Leobon B, Garcin I, Menasche P, *et al.* Myoblasts transplanted into rat infarcted myocardium are functionally isolated from their host. *Proc Natl Acad Sci USA* 2003;100(13):7808–7811.
13. Rubart M, Soonpaa MH, Nakajima H, Field LJ. Spontaneous and evoked intracellular calcium transients in donor-derived myocytes following intracardiac myoblast transplantation. *J Clin Invest* 2004;114(6):775–783.
14. Menasche P, Hagege AA, Scorsin M, *et al.* Myoblast transplantation for heart failure. *Lancet* 2001;357(9252):279–280.
15. Hagege AA, Carrion C, Menasche P, *et al.* Viability and differentiation of autologous skeletal myoblast grafts in ischaemic cardiomyopathy. *Lancet* 2003;361(9356):491–492.
16. Menasche P, Alfieri O, Janssens S, *et al.* The Myoblast Autologous Grafting in Ischemic Cardiomyopathy (MAGIC) trial: first randomized

placebo-controlled study of myoblast transplantation. *Circulation* 2008;117(9):1189–1200.

17. Bonaros N, Rauf R, Werner E, *et al.* Neoangiogenesis after combined transplantation of skeletal myoblasts and angiopoietic progenitors leads to increased cell engraftment and lower apoptosis rates in ischemic heart failure. *Interact Cardiovasc Thorac Surg* 2008;7(2):249–255.
18. Campbell C, Risueno RM, Salati S, *et al.* Signal control of hematopoietic stem cell fate: Wnt, Notch, and Hedgehog as the usual suspects. *Curr Opin Hematol* 2008;15(4):319–325.
19. Lawrence HJ, Christensen J, Fong S, *et al.* Loss of expression of the Hoxa-9 homeobox gene impairs the proliferation and repopulating ability of hematopoietic stem cells. *Blood* 2005;106(12):3988–3994.
20. Lessard J, Sauvageau G. Bmi-1 determines the proliferative capacity of normal and leukaemic stem cells. *Nature* 2003;423(6937):255–260.
21. Stier S, Cheng T, Dombkowski D, *et al.* Notch1 activation increases hematopoietic stem cell self-renewal in vivo and favors lymphoid over myeloid lineage outcome. *Blood* 2002;99(7):2369–2378.
22. Bunting KD, Bradley HL, Hawley TS, *et al.* Reduced lymphomyeloid repopulating activity from adult bone marrow and fetal liver of mice lacking expression of STAT5. *Blood* 2002;99(2):479–487.
23. Park IK, Qian D, Kiel M, Becker MW, Pihalja M, Weissman IL, Morrison SJ, Clarke MF. Bmi-1 is required for maintenance of adult self-renewing haematopoietic stem cells. *Nature* 2003;423(6937):302–305.
24. Kroon E, Thorsteinsdottir U, Mayotte N, Nakamura T, Sauvageau G. NUP98-HOXA9 expression in hemopoietic stem cells induces chronic and acute myeloid leukemias in mice. *Embo J* 2001;20(3):350–361.
25. Bromberg JF. Activation of STAT proteins and growth control. *Bioessays* 2001;23(2):161–169.
26. Fadini GP, Agostini C, Avogaro A. Characterization of endothelial progenitor cells. *Biochem Biophys Res Commun* 2005;336(1):1–2.
27. Petit I, Szyper-Kravitz M, Nagler A, *et al.* G-CSF induces stem cell mobilization by decreasing bone marrow SDF-1 and upregulating CXCR4. *Nat Immunol* 2002;3(7):687–694.
28. Broxmeyer HE, Orschell CM, Clapp DW, *et al.* Rapid mobilization of murine and human hematopoietic stem and progenitor cells with AMD3100, a CXCR4 antagonist. *J Exp Med* 2005;201(8):1307–1318.

29. Ponomaryov T, Peled A, Petit I, *et al.* Induction of the chemokine stromal-derived factor-1 following DNA damage improves human stem cell function. *J Clin Invest* 2000;106(11):1331–1339.
30. Levesque JP, Hendy J, Takamatsu Y, *et al.* Mobilization by either cyclophosphamide or granulocyte colony-stimulating factor transforms the bone marrow into a highly proteolytic environment. *Exp Hematol* 2002;30(5):440–449.
31. Leri A, Kajstura J, Anversa P. Cardiac stem cells and mechanisms of myocardial regeneration. *Physiol Rev* 2005;85(4):1373–1416.
32. Quaini F, Urbanek K, Beltrami AP, *et al.* Chimerism of the transplanted heart. *N Engl J Med* 2002;346(1):5–15.
33. Jackson KA, Majka SM, Wang H, *et al.* Regeneration of ischemic cardiac muscle and vascular endothelium by adult stem cells. *J Clin Invest* 2001;107(11):1395–1402.
34. Murry CE, Soonpaa MH, Reinecke H, *et al.* Haematopoietic stem cells do not transdifferentiate into cardiac myocytes in myocardial infarcts. *Nature* 2004;428(6983):664–668.
35. Balsam LB, Wagers AJ, Christensen JL, *et al.* Haematopoietic stem cells adopt mature haematopoietic fates in ischaemic myocardium. *Nature* 2004;428(6983):668–673.
36. Stuckey DJ, Carr CA, Martin-Rendon E, *et al.* Iron particles for noninvasive monitoring of bone marrow stromal cell engraftment into, and isolation of viable engrafted donor cells from, the heart. *Stem Cells* 2006;24(8): 1968–1975.
37. Strauer BE, Brehm M, Zeus T, *et al.* [Intracoronary, human autologous stem cell transplantation for myocardial regeneration following myocardial infarction]. *Dtsch Med Wochenschr* 2001;126(34–35):932–938.
38. Strauer BE, Brehm M, Zeus T, *et al.* Repair of infarcted myocardium by autologous intracoronary mononuclear bone marrow cell transplantation in humans. *Circulation* 2002;106(15):1913–1918.
39. Assmus B, Schachinger V, Teupe C, *et al.* Transplantation of Progenitor Cells and Regeneration Enhancement in Acute Myocardial Infarction (TOP-CARE-AMI). *Circulation* 2002;106(24):3009–3017.
40. Wollert KC, Meyer GP, Lotz J, *et al.* Intracoronary autologous bone-marrow cell transfer after myocardial infarction: the BOOST randomised controlled clinical trial. *Lancet* 2004;364(9429):141–148.

41. Schachinger V, Erbs S, Elsasser A, *et al.* Intracoronary bone marrow-derived progenitor cells in acute myocardial infarction. *N Engl J Med* 2006;355(12):1210–1221.
42. Gao LR, Wang ZG, Zhu ZM, *et al.* Effect of intracoronary transplantation of autologous bone marrow-derived mononuclear cells on outcomes of patients with refractory chronic heart failure secondary to ischemic cardiomyopathy. *Am J Cardiol* 2006;98(5):597–602.
43. Beeres SL, Bax JJ, Dibbets-Schneider P, *et al.* Sustained effect of autologous bone marrow mononuclear cell injection in patients with refractory angina pectoris and chronic myocardial ischemia: twelve-month follow-up results. *Am Heart J* 2006;152(4):684 e611–686.
44. Abdel-Latif A, Bolli R, Tleyjeh IM, *et al.* Adult bone marrow-derived cells for cardiac repair: a systematic review and meta-analysis. *Arch Intern Med* 2007;167(10):989–997.
45. Hristov M, Heussen N, Schober A, Weber C. Intracoronary infusion of autologous bone marrow cells and left ventricular function after acute myocardial infarction: a meta-analysis. *J Cell Mol Med* 2006;10(3):727–733.
46. Kang S, Yang YJ, Li CJ, Gao RL. Effects of intracoronary autologous bone marrow cells on left ventricular function in acute myocardial infarction: a systematic review and meta-analysis for randomized controlled trials. *Coron Artery Dis* 2008;19(5):327–335.
47. Lipinski MJ, Biondi-Zoccai GG, Abbate A, *et al.* Impact of intracoronary cell therapy on left ventricular function in the setting of acute myocardial infarction: a collaborative systematic review and meta-analysis of controlled clinical trials. *J Am Coll Cardiol* 2007;50(18):1761–1767.
48. Zhang SN, Sun AJ, Ge JB, *et al.* Intracoronary autologous bone marrow stem cells transfer for patients with acute myocardial infarction: a meta-analysis of randomised controlled trials. *Int J Cardiol* 2008.
49. Zohlnhofer D, Dibra A, Koppara T, *et al.* Stem cell mobilization by granulocyte colony-stimulating factor for myocardial recovery after acute myocardial infarction: a meta-analysis. *J Am Coll Cardiol* 2008;51(15): 1429–1437.
50. Hierlihy AM, Seale P, Lobe CG, *et al.* The post-natal heart contains a myocardial stem cell population. *FEBS Lett* 2002;530(1–3):239–243.
51. Beltrami AP, Barlucchi L, Torella D, *et al.* Adult cardiac stem cells are multipotent and support myocardial regeneration. *Cell* 2003;114(6):763–776.

52. Dawn B, Stein AB, Urbanek K, *et al*. Cardiac stem cells delivered intravascularly traverse the vessel barrier, regenerate infarcted myocardium, and improve cardiac function. *Proc Natl Acad Sci USA* 2005;102(10):3766–3771.
53. Bearzi C, Rota M, Hosoda T, *et al*. Human cardiac stem cells. *Proc Natl Acad Sci USA* 2007;104(35):14068–14073.
54. Barbash IM, Chouraqui P, Baron J, *et al*. Systemic delivery of bone marrow-derived mesenchymal stem cells to the infarcted myocardium: feasibility, cell migration, and body distribution. *Circulation* 2003;108(7):863–868.
55. Freyman T, Polin G, Osman H, *et al*. A quantitative, randomized study evaluating three methods of mesenchymal stem cell delivery following myocardial infarction. *Eur Heart J* 2006;27(9):1114–1122.
56. Perin EC, Silva GV, Assad JA, *et al*. Comparison of intracoronary and transendocardial delivery of allogeneic mesenchymal cells in a canine model of acute myocardial infarction. *J Mol Cell Cardiol* 2008, 44(3):486–495.
57. Hou D, Youssef EA, Brinton TJ, Zhang P, Rogers P, Price ET, Yeung AC, Johnstone BH, Yock PG, March KL. Radiolabeled cell distribution after intramyocardial, intracoronary, and interstitial retrograde coronary venous delivery: implications for current clinical trials. *Circulation* 2005;112(9 Suppl):I150–156.
58. Barile L, Chimenti I, Gaetani R, *et al*. Cardiac stem cells: isolation, expansion and experimental use for myocardial regeneration. *Nat Clin Pract Cardiovasc Med* 2007;4 Suppl 1:S9-S14.
59. Failde I, Ramos I. Validity and reliability of the SF-36 Health Survey Questionnaire in patients with coronary artery disease. *J Clin Epidemiol* 2000;53(4):359–365.
60. Clark AL, Rafferty D, Arbuthnott K. Exercise dynamics at submaximal workloads in patients with chronic heart failure. *J Card Fail* 1997;3(1):15–19.
61. Enright PL, McBurnie MA, Bittner V, *et al*. The six-min walk test: a quick measure of functional status in elderly adults. *Chest* 2003;123(2):387–398.
62. Guyatt GH, Sullivan MJ, Thompson PJ, *et al*. The six-minute walk: a new measure of exercise capacity in patients with chronic heart failure. *Can Med Assoc J* 1985;132(8):919–923.
63. Sudoh T, Kangawa K, Minamino N, Matsuo H. A new natriuretic peptide in porcine brain. *Nature* 1988;332(6159):78–81.

64. Porter JG, Arfsten A, Palisi T, *et al*. Cloning of a cDNA encoding porcine brain natriuretic peptide. *J Biol Chem* 1989;264(12):6689–6692.
65. Levin ER, Gardner DG, Samson WK. Natriuretic peptides. *N Engl J Med* 1998;339(5):321–328.
66. Ware JESK, Kosinski M, Gandek B. *Short Form 36 Health Survey Manual and Interpretation Guide*. New England Medical Health Centre, The Health Institute, Boston, 1993.
67. Porat Y, Porozov S, Belkin D, *et al*. Isolation of an adult blood-derived progenitor cell population capable of differentiation into angiogenic, myocardial and neural lineages. *Br J Haematol* 2006;135(5):703–714.
68. Arom KV, Flavin TF, Emery RW, *et al*. Safety and efficacy of off-pump coronary artery bypass grafting. *Ann Thorac Surg* 2000;69(3):704–710.
69. Hunt SA, Abraham WT, Chin MH, *et al*. ACC/AHA 2005 Guideline Update for the Diagnosis and Management of Chronic Heart Failure in the Adult: a report of the American College of Cardiology/American Heart Association Task Force on Practice Guidelines (Writing Committee to Update the 2001 Guidelines for the Evaluation and Management of Heart Failure): developed in collaboration with the American College of Chest Physicians and the International Society for Heart and Lung Transplantation: endorsed by the Heart Rhythm Society. *Circulation* 2005;112(12):e154–235.
70. Arom K, Ruengsakulrach P, Jotisakulratana V. Efficacy of intramyocardial injection of angiogenic cell precursors for ischemic cardiomyopathy: a case match study. *Innovations* 2008;3(1):38–45.
71. Gruh I, Beilner J, Blomer U, Schmiedl A, Schmidt-Richter I, Kruse ML, Haverich A, Martin U. No evidence of transdifferentiation of human endothelial progenitor cells into cardiomyocytes after coculture with neonatal rat cardiomyocytes. *Circulation* 2006;113(10):1326–1334.
72. Koyanagi M, Urbich C, Chavakis E, Hoffmann J, Rupp S, Badorff C, Zeiher AM, Starzinski-Powitz A, Haendeler J, Dimmeler S. Differentiation of circulating endothelial progenitor cells to a cardiomyogenic phenotype depends on E-cadherin. *FEBS Lett* 2005;579(27):6060–6066.
73. Rowlands TM, Symonds JM, Farookhi R, Blaschuk OW. Cadherins: crucial regulators of structure and function in reproductive tissues. *Rev Reprod* 2000;5(1):53–61.
74. Steinberg MS, McNutt PM. Cadherins and their connections: adhesion junctions have broader functions. *Curr Opin Cell Biol* 1999;11(5):554–560.

75. Roura S, Planas F, Prat-Vidal C, *et al.* Idiopathic dilated cardiomyopathy exhibits defective vascularization and vessel formation. *Eur J Heart Fail* 2007;9(10):995–1002.
76. Werner L, Deutsch V, Barshack I, *et al.* Transfer of endothelial progenitor cells improves myocardial performance in rats with dilated cardiomyopathy induced following experimental myocarditis. *J Mol Cell Cardiol* 2005;39(4):691–697.
77. Chu VF, Giaid A, Kuang JQ, *et al.* Thoracic Surgery Directors Association Award. Angiogenesis in transmyocardial revascularization: comparison of laser versus mechanical punctures. *Ann Thorac Surg* 1999;68(2):301–307; discussion 307–308.
78. Ohno N, Fedak PW, Weisel RD, *et al.* Transplantation of cryopreserved muscle cells in dilated cardiomyopathy: effects on left ventricular geometry and function. *J Thorac Cardiovasc Surg* 2003;126(5):1537–1548.
79. Huang RC, Yao K, Li YL, *et al.* Transplantation of autologous bone marrow mononuclear cells on patients with idiopathic dilated cardiomyopathy: early results on effect and security. *Zhonghua Xin Xue Guan Bing Za Zhi* 2006;34(2):111–113.
80. Wang JA, Xie XJ, He H, *et al.* A prospective, randomized, controlled trial of autologous mesenchymal stem cells transplantation for dilated cardiomyopathy. *Zhonghua Xin Xue Guan Bing Za Zhi* 2006;34(2):107–110.
81. Seth S, Narang R, Bhargava B, *et al.* Percutaneous intracoronary cellular cardiomyoplasty for nonischemic cardiomyopathy: clinical and histopathological results: the first-in-man ABCD (Autologous Bone Marrow Cells in Dilated Cardiomyopathy) trial. *J Am Coll Cardiol* 2006;48(11):2350–2351.
82. Lunde K, Solheim S, Aakhus S, Arnesen H, Abdelnoor M, Egeland T, Endresen K, Ilebekk A, Mangschau A, Fjeld JG, Smith HJ, Taraldsrud E, Grogaard HK, Bjornerheim R, Brekke M, Muller C, Hopp E, Ragnarsson A, Brinchmann JE, Forfang K. Intracoronary injection of mononuclear bone marrow cells in acute myocardial infarction. *N Engl J Med.* 2006;355(12): 1199–1209.
83. Yoshioka T, Ageyama N, Shibata H, Yasu T, Misawa Y, Takeuchi K, Matsui K, Yamamoto K, Terao K, Shimada K, Ikeda U, Ozawa K, Hanazono Y. Repair of infarcted myocardium mediated by transplanted bone marrow-derived CD34+ stem cells in a nonhuman primate model. *Stem Cells.* 2005;23(3):355–364.
84. Patel AN, Geffner L, Vina RF, Saslavsky J, Urschel HC, Jr., Kormos R, Benetti F. Surgical treatment for congestive heart failure with autologous

adult stem cell transplantation: a prospective randomized study. *J Thorac Cardiovasc Surg*. 2005;130(6):1631–1638.

85. Stamm C, Kleine HD, Choi YH, Dunkelmann S, Lauffs JA, Lorenzen B, David A, Liebold A, Nienaber C, Zurakowski D, Freund M, Steinhoff G. Intramyocardial delivery of CD133+ bone marrow cells and coronary artery bypass grafting for chronic ischemic heart disease: safety and efficacy studies. *J Thorac Cardiovasc Surg*. 2007;133(3):717–725.
86. Meyer GP, Wollert KC, Lotz J, *et al*. Intracoronary bone marrow cell transfer after myocardial infarction: eighteen months' follow-up data from the randomized, controlled BOOST (BOne marrOw transfer to enhance ST-elevation infarct regeneration) trial. *Circulation* 2006;113(10):1287–1294.
87. Schachinger V, Assmus B, Britten MB, Honold J, Lehmann R, Teupe C, Abolmaali ND, Vogl TJ, Hofmann WK, Martin H, Dimmeler S, Zeiher AM. Transplantation of progenitor cells and regeneration enhancement in acute myocardial infarction: final one-year results of the TOPCARE-AMI Trial. *J Am Coll Cardiol* 2004;44(8):1690–1699.
88. Dobert N, Britten M, Assmus B, Berner U, Menzel C, Lehmann R, Hamscho N, Schachinger V, Dimmeler S, Zeiher AM, Grunwald F. Transplantation of progenitor cells after reperfused acute myocardial infarction: evaluation of perfusion and myocardial viability with FDG-PET and thallium SPECT. *Eur J Nucl Med Mol Imaging* 2004;31(8):1146–1151.
89. Hendrikx M, Hensen K, Clijsters C, Jongen H, Koninckx R, Bijnens E, Ingels M, Jacobs A, Geukens R, Dendale P, Vijgen J, Dilling D, Steels P, Mees U, Rummens JL. Recovery of regional but not global contractile function by the direct intramyocardial autologous bone marrow transplantation: results from a randomized controlled clinical trial. *Circulation* 2006;114(1 Suppl):I101–107.
90. Perin EC, Dohmann HF, Borojevic R, Silva SA, Sousa AL, Mesquita CT, Rossi MI, Carvalho AC, Dutra HS, Dohmann HJ, Silva GV, Belem L, Vivacqua R, Rangel FO, Esporcatte R, Geng YJ, Vaughn WK, Assad JA, Mesquita ET, Willerson JT. Transendocardial, autologous bone marrow cell transplantation for severe, chronic ischemic heart failure. *Circulation* 2003;107(18):2294–2302.
91. Tse HF, Thambar S, Kwong YL, Rowlings P, Bellamy G, McCrohon J, Bastian B, Chan JK, Lo G, Ho CL, Lau CP. Safety of catheter-based intramyocardial autologous bone marrow cells implantation for therapeutic angiogenesis. *Am J Cardiol* 2006;98(1):60–62.

92. Yamanaka S. Strategies and new developments in the generation of patient-specific pluripotent stem cells. *Cell Stem Cell* 2007;1(1):39–49.
93. Hsieh PC, MacGillivray C, Gannon J, *et al*. Local controlled intramyocardial delivery of platelet-derived growth factor improves postinfarction ventricular function without pulmonary toxicity. *Circulation* 2006;114(7):637–644.

# INDEX